LISSA

ethnoGRAPHIC

University of Toronto Press is excited to announce a groundbreaking series that realizes ethnographic research in graphic novel form. The series speaks to a growing interest in comics as a powerful narrative medium and to a number of trends in anthropology, including a desire for a more imaginative and collaborative ethnography and for engaging with a broader public on contemporary issues. The goal is to create scholarly-informed narratives that are accessible, interpretively and aesthetically rich, and that foster greater cross-cultural understanding.

Books in the series combine the power of ethnographic research with the unique elements of comics as a sequential art—using page, panels, gutters, visuals, dialogue, captions, line, and lettering to tell the story. Beyond the graphic narrative, each book in the series will include:

→   A reading guide with discussion questions
→   Background information on the research behind the story
→   Methodological discussion of the challenges and benefits of transforming research into graphic novel form

Series Editors: Sherine Hamdy (University of California, Irvine) and Anne Brackenbury (University of Toronto Press)

Series Advisory Board: Juliet McMullin (University of California, Riverside), Stacy Leigh Pigg (Simon Fraser University), Nick Sousanis (San Francisco State University), Fiona Smyth (OCAD University)

FORTHCOMING TITLES

Gringo Love: Stories of Sex Tourism in Brazil by Marie-Eve Carrier-Moisan
Heshima: Islam and Friendship on the Swahili Coast by Sarah Hillewaert

A STORY ABOUT MEDICAL PROMISE, FRIENDSHIP, AND REVOLUTION

WRITTEN BY SHERINE HAMDY AND COLEMAN NYE
ILLUSTRATED BY SARULA BAO AND CAROLINE BREWER
LETTERING BY MARC PARENTEAU

UNIVERSITY OF TORONTO PRESS

Library and Archives Canada Cataloguing in Publication

Hamdy, Sherine, 1975–, author
    Lissa : a story about medical promise, friendship, and revolution / written by Sherine Hamdy and Coleman Nye ; art by Sarula Bao and Caroline Brewer.

(ethnoGRAPHIC)
Includes bibliographical references.
Issued in print and electronic formats.
ISBN 978-1-4875-9347-6 (softcover).—ISBN 978-1-4875-9349-0 (EPUB).—
ISBN 978-1-4875-9350-6 (PDF)

    1. Graphic novels. I. Brewer, Caroline, illustrator II. Nye, Coleman, author
III. Bao, Sarula, illustrator IV. Title.

PN6727.H33L57 2017   741.5'973   C2017-903597-5
                                               C2017-903598-3

We welcome comments and suggestions regarding any aspect of our publications—please feel free to contact us at news@utphighereducation.com or visit our Internet site at www.utppublishing.com.

North America
5201 Dufferin Street
North York, Ontario, Canada, M3H 5T8

2250 Military Road
Tonawanda, New York, USA, 14150
ORDERS PHONE: 1-800-565-9523
ORDERS FAX: 1-800-221-9985
ORDERS E-MAIL: utpbooks@utpress.utoronto.ca

UK, Ireland, and continental Europe
NBN International
Estover Road, Plymouth, PL6 7PY, UK
ORDERS PHONE: 44 (0) 1752 202301
ORDERS FAX: 44 (0) 1752 202333
ORDERS E-MAIL: enquiries@nbninternational.com

Every effort has been made to contact copyright holders; in the event of an error or omission, please notify the publisher.

The University of Toronto Press acknowledges the financial support for its publishing activities of the Government of Canada through the Canada Book Fund.

Printed in Canada

MIX
Paper from
responsible sources
FSC
www.fsc.org
FSC® C103567

li·ssa (li:sə) (colloquial Arabic, Egyptian):
1. There's still time, not yet; 2. It is still
the case

CONTENTS

ACKNOWLEDGMENTS

The authors would like to thank (in order of appearance in this project): Adia Benton, who took seriously the idea of anthropology in comics form and encouraged a RISD-Brown collaboration; Anne Brackenbury for her remarkable vision and editorial guidance; Richard Locke of the Watson Institute; Robert Brinkerhoff at RISD; and Paul Karasik, who brought the writers and illustrators together and guided the initial phases of visual translation. When the script was first drafted, we benefited from the thoughtful reviews of Megan Crowley-Matoka, Salih Can Aciksoz, Nick Sousanis, Juliet McMullin, and Pascal Menoret. At the illustration stage, we are indebted to Lina Ghaibeh and George Khoury (Jad), who insisted that the illustrators go to Egypt. The support of Toby Volkman of the Henry Luce Foundation enabled the Egypt trip, and Catherine Nellis and Laura Sadovnikoff helped with grant management. Francesco Dragone has shared his filmic vision, dedication, and enthusiasm through many stages of this project; and, while we were in Egypt, Alice Larotonda and Forrest Kolaski offered invaluable help in filming the "behind the scenes" documentary and in field logistics. We are grateful for the generous insights and support offered by many people in Cairo during and after our trip, including Ahmed El Guindi, who helped with logistics; Amina Elbendary, Hoda Elsadda, Reem Bashery, and Alia Mossallam of the Women and Memory Forum, who shared their experiences of the Egyptian Revolution; and Ms. Gigi Abdel Maaboud, from Cairo American College, who gave us a tour and information about what Anna's life in Maadi would have been like. Thanks also to Dr. Yasmin Moll for her help with archival footage. For sharing with us their expertise on comics and illustration, we are grateful to Mazen and Yamen El Gamal, Haitham and Mohamed Raafat

El-Seht (Twins Cartoon), and Professor Agnes Michalczyk and her students Alaa Darwish and Asmaa Moustafa. Dr. Dina Shokry from Kasr el Aini Forensic Medicine and her students, as well as Dr. Amr Shebaita from Tahrir Doctors, contributed much to the medical dimensions of our story and make appearances as themselves in the novel. Our respect and thanks go also to the Egyptian artists whose street art and graffiti we cite in the pages of this book. We are most deeply grateful to Ganzeer, who so generously designed the stunning graffiti composition on the final page of the novel. And we are indebted to Mohamed and Zainab for opening their home to us during our visit. Back at Brown, the Pembroke Center and Ed Steinfeld, John Mazza, and Alex La Ferriere from the Watson Institute continued to support us; Soha Bayoumi, Ahmed Ragab, and Mariz Kelada provided helpful feedback and input on the script; and Myra El Mir graciously helped with the art. We also thank Ian Straughn for helping us acquire key Egyptian comics and texts coming out of the revolution; Harriette Hemmasi from the Brown Digital Humanities Initiative; Khaled Al-Saai for hand-lettering the gorgeous calligraphy on page 219; and James Young, Krissy Pelley, and Emma Funk for their design ideas. Our final thanks is to Marc Parenteau, for his sustaining friendship and camaraderie, and for helping in the final essential stages with visual translation, pacing, lettering, and coaching. We all feel lucky to have been part of a remarkable team and are above all grateful to one another.

Note on Transliteration

As any scholar working in Egypt knows, using a consistent system for transliteration from Arabic sources is often a challenge. When making decisions about how to render proper names, we chose to use people's own spellings, in cases in which they have published or presented themselves publicly in English, rather than to follow standard academic transliteration. In the script and dialogue of the graphic ethnography itself, we use "ee" for the long vowel—ē as in "eagle"—even though guidelines from the *International Journal of Middle East Studies* suggest writing this vowel as ī. We also decided to go with popular spellings of common phrases. So the phrase "God willing," for example, is rendered "inshallah"—to reflect the sound of common speech.

LISSA AND THE TRANSDUCTION OF ETHNOGRAPHY

GEORGE E. MARCUS*
UNIVERSITY OF CALIFORNIA, IRVINE

"Transduction: the action or process of converting something,
and especially energy or a message, into another form."
Webster's Third New International Dictionary

The graphic novel *Lissa* forges a new path, instructing anthropologists and academics more broadly in remaking their work into new forms. Selecting the graphic novel form was inspired in itself, though many scholarly producers of long-form accounts—in sociology, philosophy, journalism, history, and biography especially—have experimented recently with the graphic novel. A shift to comics provides a move from ethnography to a popular narrative form that crosscuts high-low aesthetics and is present as a popular, affordable, and intellectually favored form in so many countries and regions, at a time when anthropologists are particularly eager for public and diverse receptions as a response to the continuous worldings of its once-contained field sites.

The question (and adventure) for Hamdy and Nye is how to achieve this shift. The parallel story of how they did—told in multiple media including comics, academic prose, a website, and a documentary film alongside the

---

* George Marcus is a Professor of Anthropology at UC Irvine who is widely celebrated for his writings on ethnographic methods and writing.

text—not only enhances the enjoyment of *Lissa* but is a methodological exemplar for other anthropologists whatever their experience with ethnography.

Ethnographies were originally established through the identity of the lone fieldworker amid made and found relationships among subjects—or, at least, this was an operating fiction of ethnographic writing. Here Hamdy and Nye transduce original "field" or spaces of fieldwork into a different genre or aesthetic of form altogether. This shift into a form in another medium requires, yes, perhaps personally learning other arts, but it most likely thrives in collaborations, in the cooperative reorganization of the field and of the standard habits of representation from which ethnography originally emerged. And such collaborations require skills of diplomacy, entrepreneurship, friendship, and a tolerance for the capacity of changing events along the way to transform the scales and qualities of what one as a scholar and as an author had established before.

Hamdy and Nye establish an intellectual affinity, and a desire to experiment, based on the comparative similarities they perceive in their differently located ethnographic research projects within medical anthropology. Their move to express their excitement by co-producing a different form and by exploring it beyond professional publications places them in new methodological terrain altogether. This is the terrain of alternative forms for the expression and development of ethnographic knowledge beyond longstanding, marginal experiments with alternative aesthetics. Collaboration between them first involves scripting a storyline that is both fictional and true to ethnography. Collaboration further becomes much more complex and challenging, requiring patience, organizational skills, and entrepreneurial talent. Such collaboration makes ethnography plural far beyond the earlier critiques of submerged or repressed polyphonic representation in classic ethnographic writing up to the present.

Crucially, there is the finding, recruiting, and incorporating of artistic talent. Fortuitously, Rhode Island School of Design (RISD) is close to Brown University, Hamdy's base. RISD's culture of comic artists and producers brings norms of collaborative openness (figuring out problems in studios) that the project needs. Grants are gotten (!), and the team goes to Cairo, the artists seeing places that the ethnographer (Hamdy mainly, but Nye as well in the comparative imaginary played out in the narrative) has seen with "new eyes," thus giving the ethnographer a new vision as well; the script becomes the new ethnographic reality. In the meantime, history itself has intervened, and events (in Tahrir Square and after) present a different Cairo to all (as vision itself becomes a key trope of Hamdy's concern with the blinding of revolutionaries as a distinctive form of repressive violence). From an anthropological perspective, this is a second act to earlier fieldwork with new dimensions, representational challenges, and events unfolding, but with the historical narrative of change not yet legible. The script and the visual narrative created for it—changing in word, sight, and narrative as events unfold—provide the foundation for new ethnography on site, in plural dimensions.

Prominent among the diverse new constituencies for this project in the making are Egyptian comic and graffiti artists sharing a transnational, embedded readership for the form that ethnographers Hamdy and Nye and their team are now developing. The world of anticipated anthropological reception is joined by a shift in form with other constituencies, notably local artists who trade in bridging vernacular and cosmopolitan tastes rooted in "local knowledge" (cf. Clifford Geertz) that become "nervous systems" (cf. Michael Taussig). The graphic novel, to have any impact at all, must have several constituencies across cultures. It imposes a higher standard for ethnography that is transduced into this popular (and proudly pulp) form.

Thus, for the many anthropologists today who have argued broadly for a public anthropology as the central purpose of their discipline, the collaborative entanglements in the production of *Lissa* offer the exemplar of a way forward. What is ethnographic becomes diffused in the collaborative making of another form, which has diverse readerships and a visceral temporality fashioned within the recent past and the near future. Ethnography within limits has refined many of these qualities in its own genre form in recent years, and in fact the graphic novel in its succession to first projects might be thought of as calling for the integration of forms of ethnographic production long considered marginal or perhaps eccentric, but now eliciting an opening of anthropological ideas to new and crossover receptions.

Beginning within the circle of common practices of anthropological scholarship and mutual excitement through sharing comparative ethnographic knowledge, *Lissa*'s creators establish a path to broader public receptions by transducing recognized ethnographic results to a form, in a sense, designed for circulating recursively in the worldly conditions that have defined the same original ethnographic projects. The craft of the graphic novel form is thus not supplementary or parallel to the original acts and genre writing of ethnography but a mature move into a second project in which the ethnographic becomes diffused in the making of other forms—and these other forms have diverse readerships and a temporality expressing both depth and emergence. Ethnography has many of these qualities, and in fact the graphic novel in its succession is a kinetic version of ethnography on the page.

The graphic novel, in succession, is yet another plateau in career scholarship. Where the latter then leads will truly depend on the broader and more diverse receptions that the graphic novel form offers, as well as on the stakes and the depth of the relationships in the collaborations (and the "second" fieldwork that they involve) for continued question-asking and problem-setting. Anthropological scholarship becomes driven by broader frames of reception than monographs and scholarly articles could hope for. Through this transduction, then, ethnography becomes a "public" good. This public anthropology is not a claim on the commitment of traditional ethnographic projects but a form for producing this anthropology today.

Lissa (meaning "not yet," "still," "there is time") is the unfolded essence of the human predicaments that the story tells, and it is also, in parallel, the essence of the collaborative process that has produced the novel. It is an exemplar of what's next, and doable, with clear lines to ethnography as a fulfillment of its narrative desire for diverse receptions (the latter day "can the subaltern speak?"—beyond the suspicion that she can't, at least in ethnographic writing). What comes after can be answered only by how a collaborative travels. This is more making, doing, than hoping for, in the longing for a public anthropology that tests its ideas, arguments, and findings as vernacular storytelling across cultures. The hope for this transduction of ethnography as public anthropology is expressed by the sentiment of *Lissa* itself—both within its story and among those who have made it: "still time, yet."

PART I

CAIRO

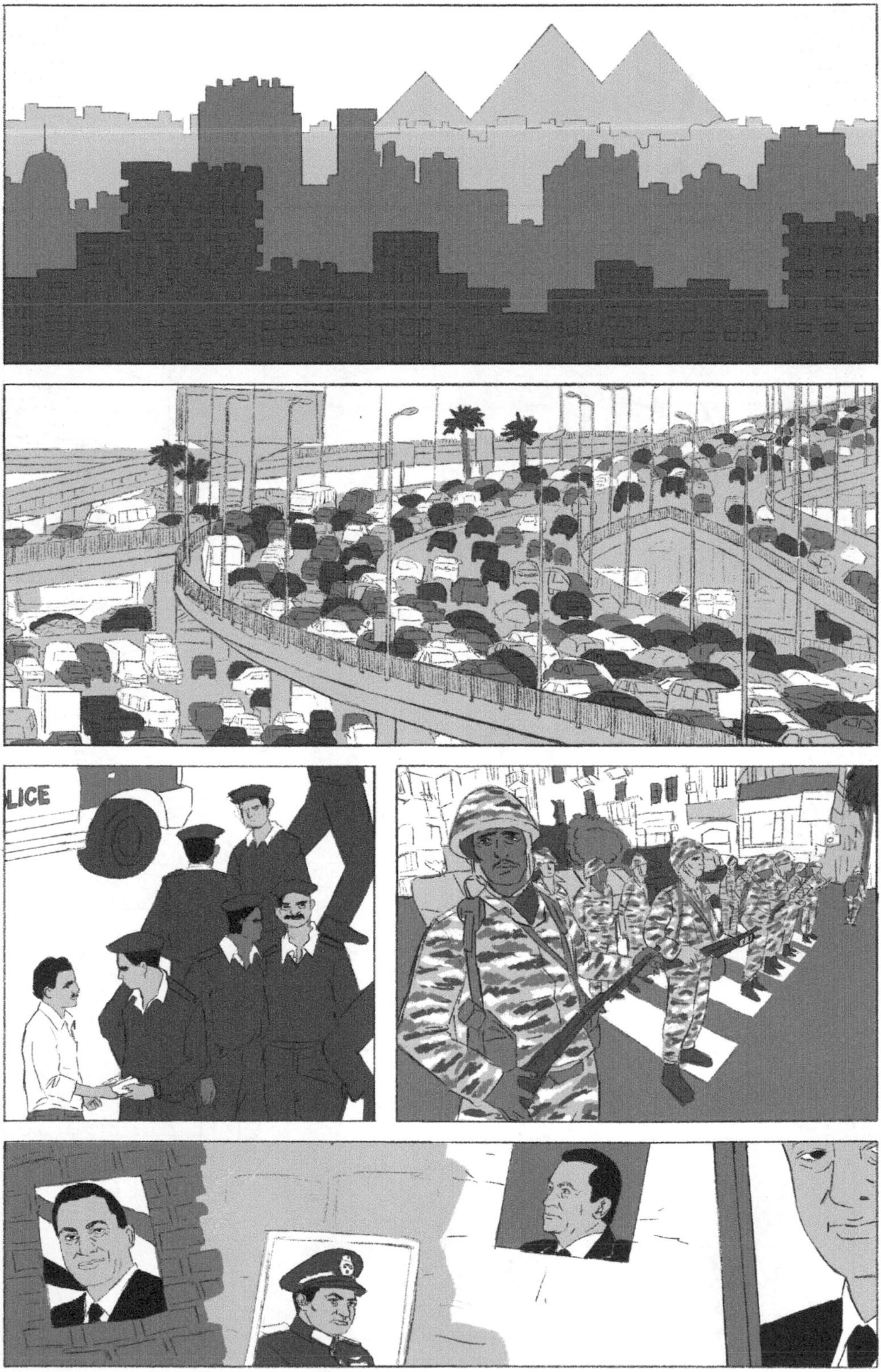
LICE

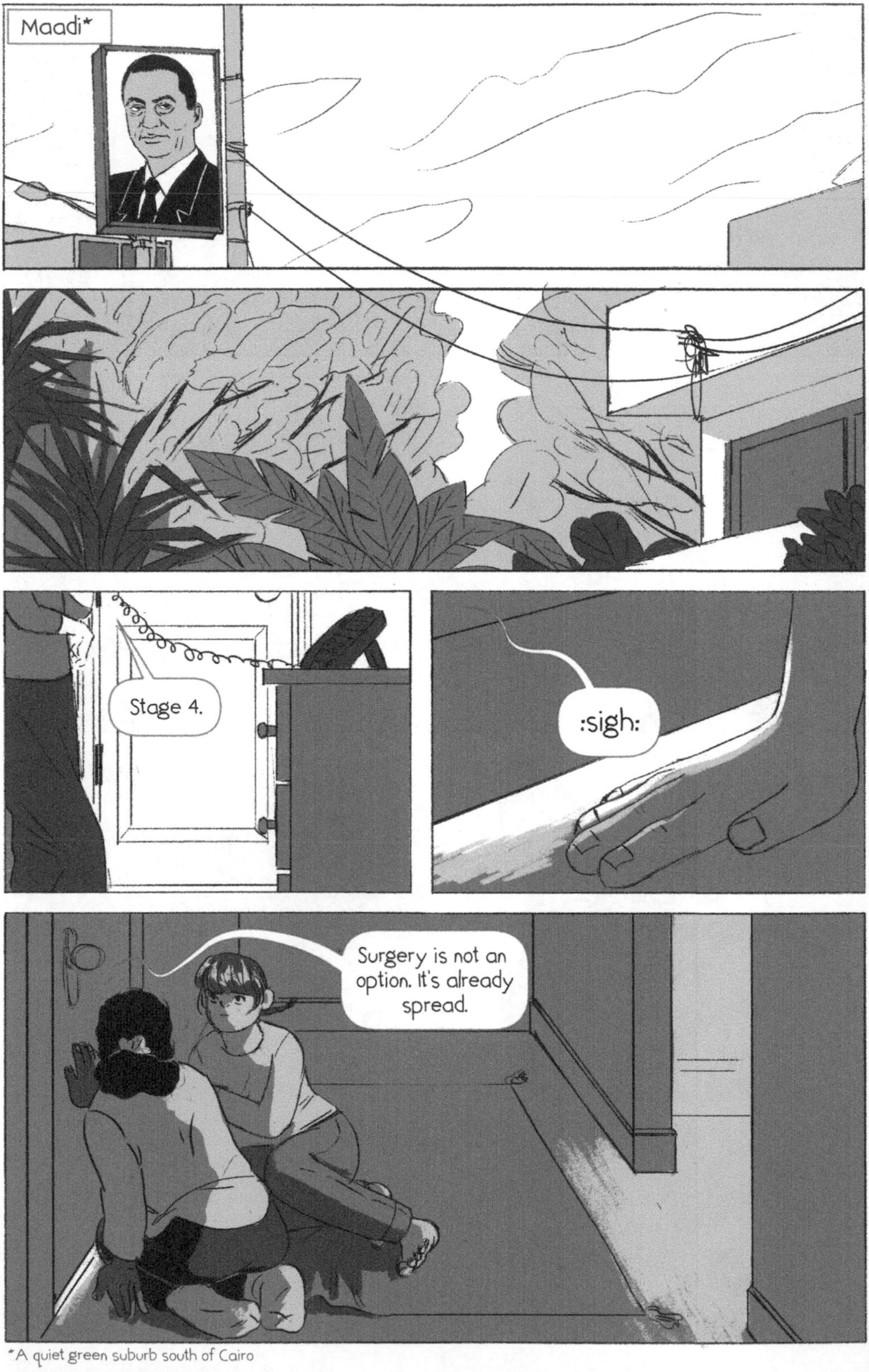
Maadi*
Stage 4.
:sigh:
Surgery is not an option. It's already spread.

*A quiet green suburb south of Cairo

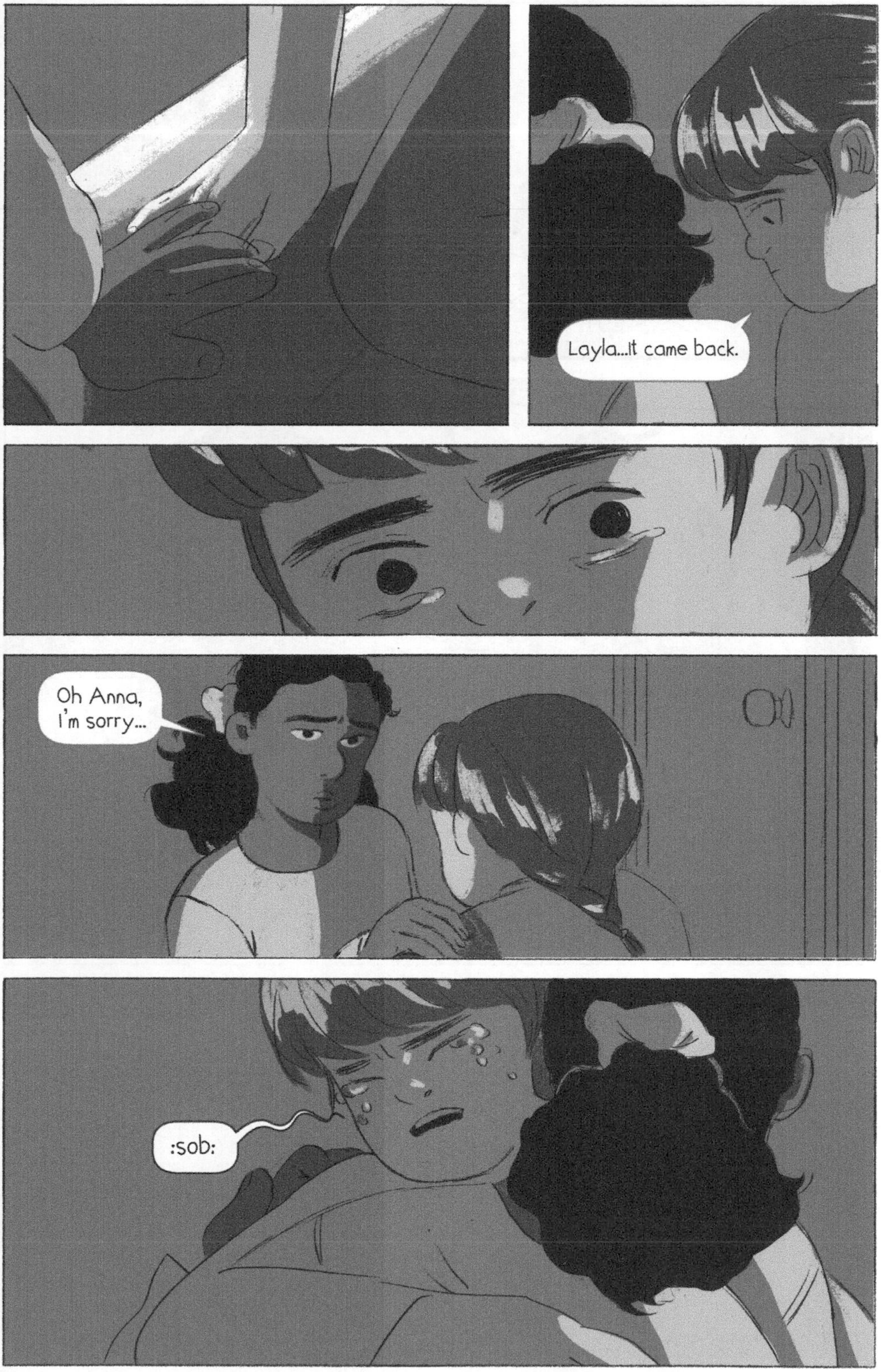
Layla...it came back.
Oh Anna, I'm sorry...
:sob:

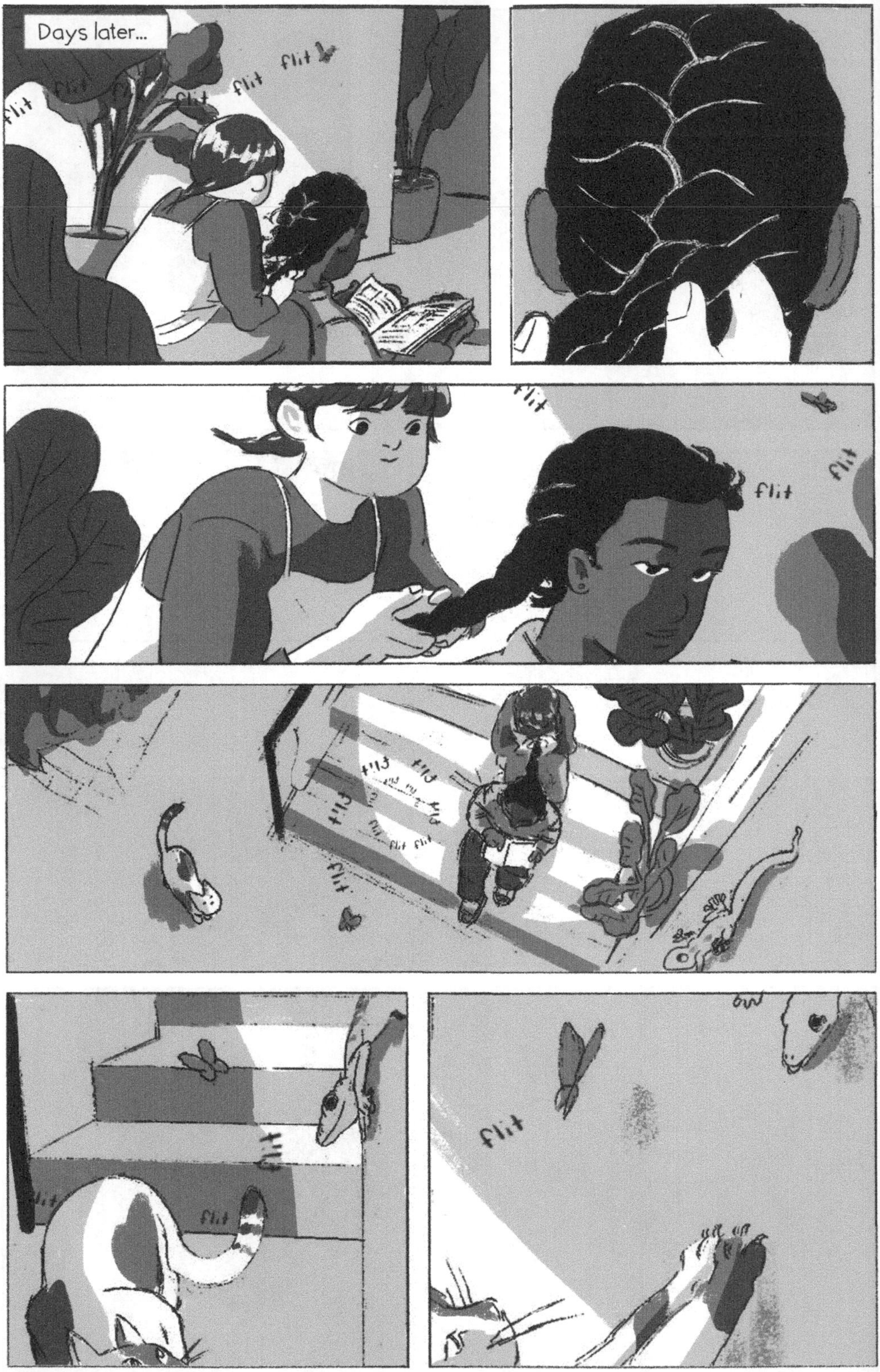
Days later...
flit
flit
flit
flit
flit
flit
flit
flit
flit
flit
flit
flit
flit
flit
flit
flit

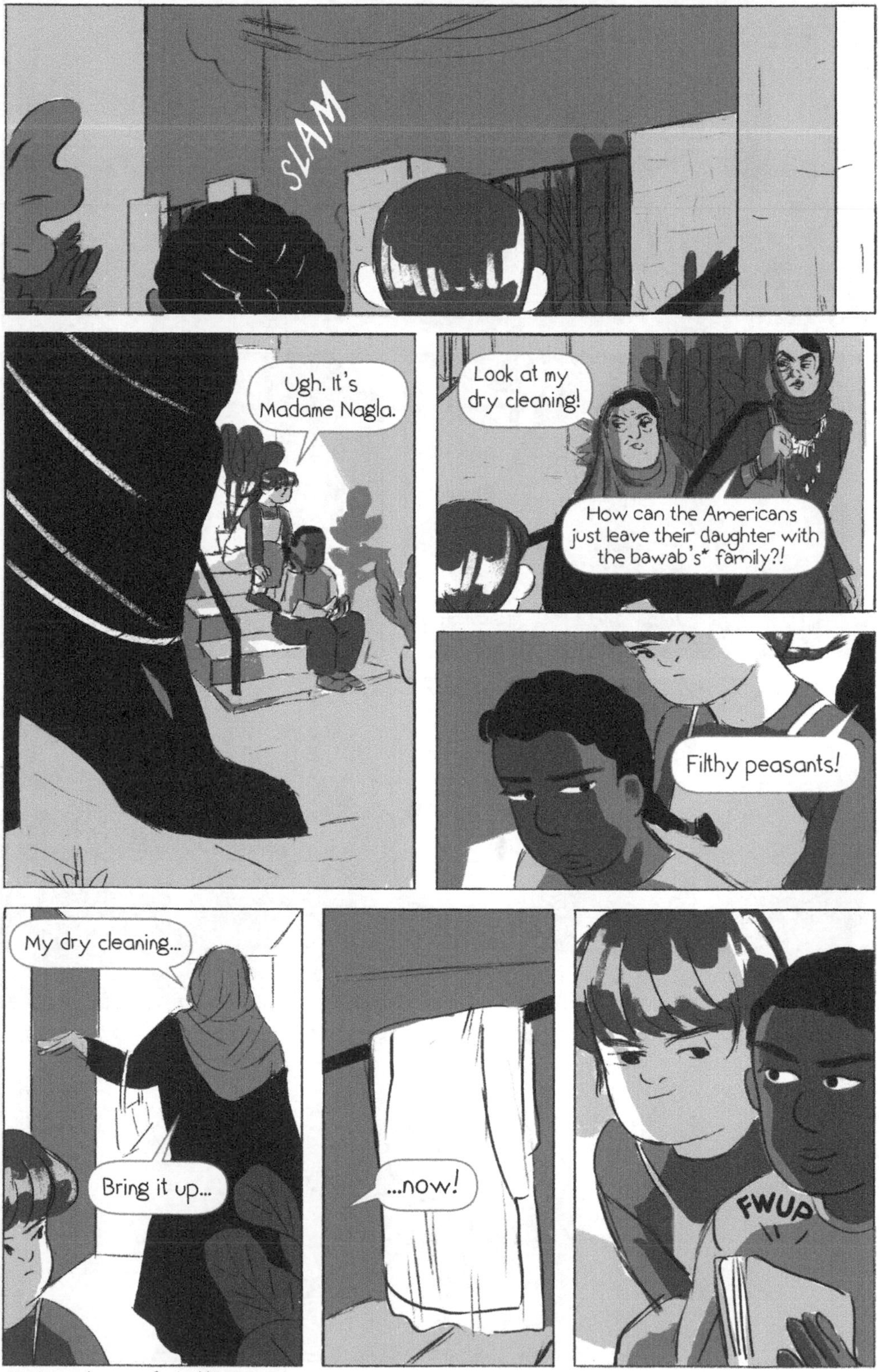
SLAM
Ugh. It's Madame Nagla.
Look at my dry cleaning!
How can the Americans just leave their daughter with the bawab's* family?!
Filthy peasants!
My dry cleaning...
Bring it up...
...now!
FWUP

*Porter or doorman of a building

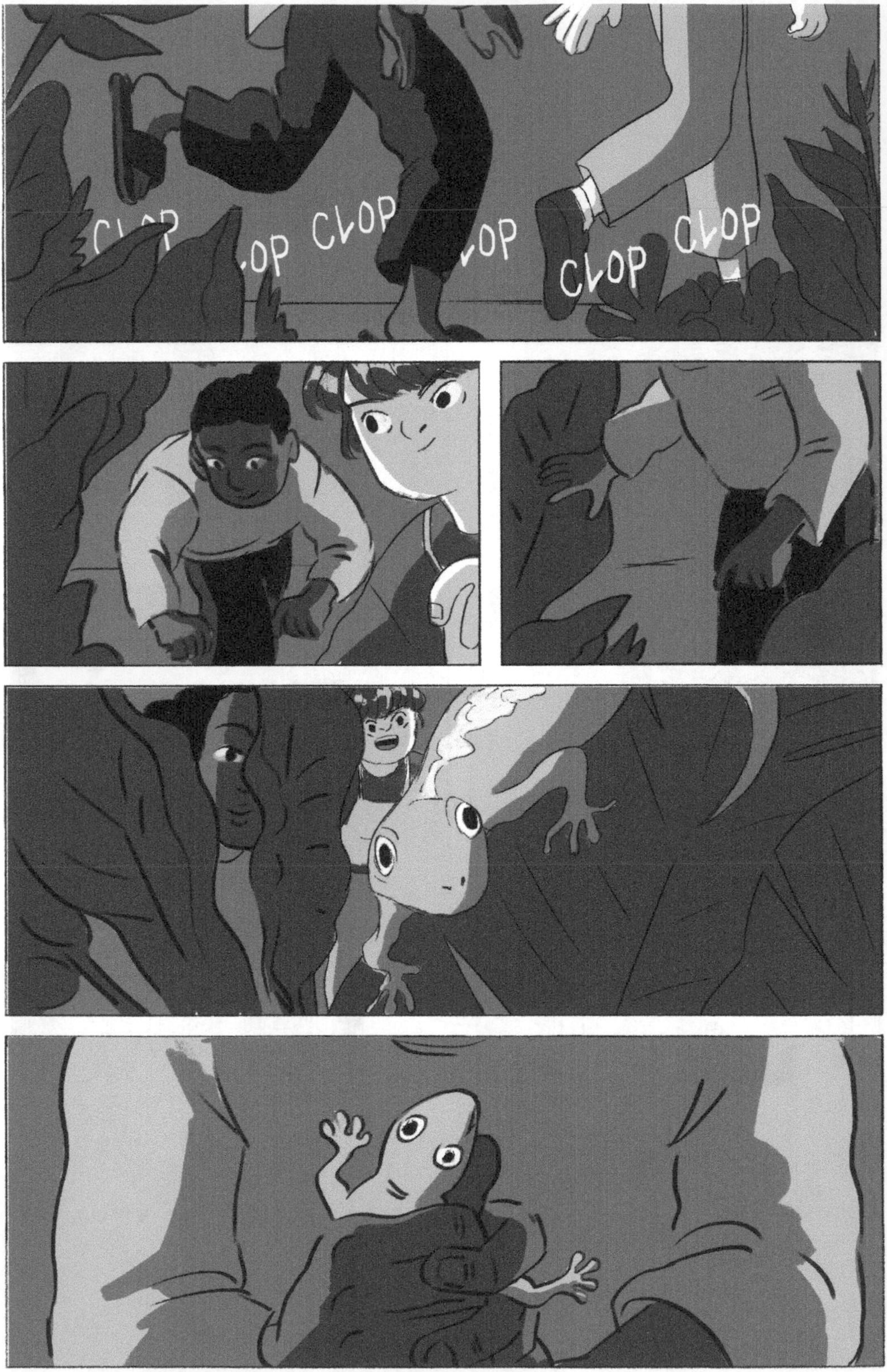
CLOP
CLOP
CLOP
CLOP
CLOP
CLOP

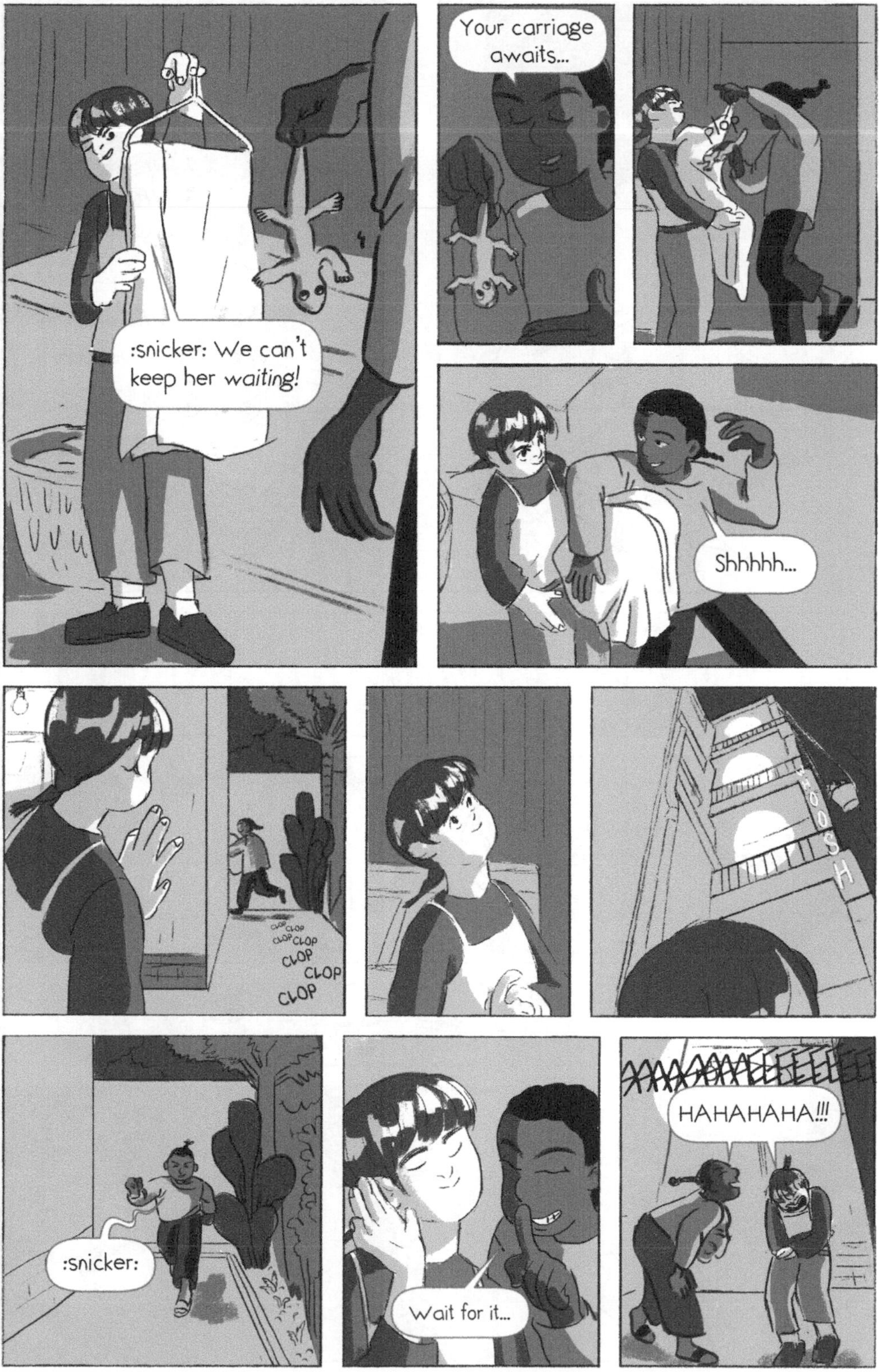
:snicker: We can't keep her *waiting!*
Your carriage awaits...
PLOP
Shhhhh...
CLOP CLOP CLOP CLOP CLOP CLOP CLOP
:snicker:
Wait for it...
HAHAHAHA!!!

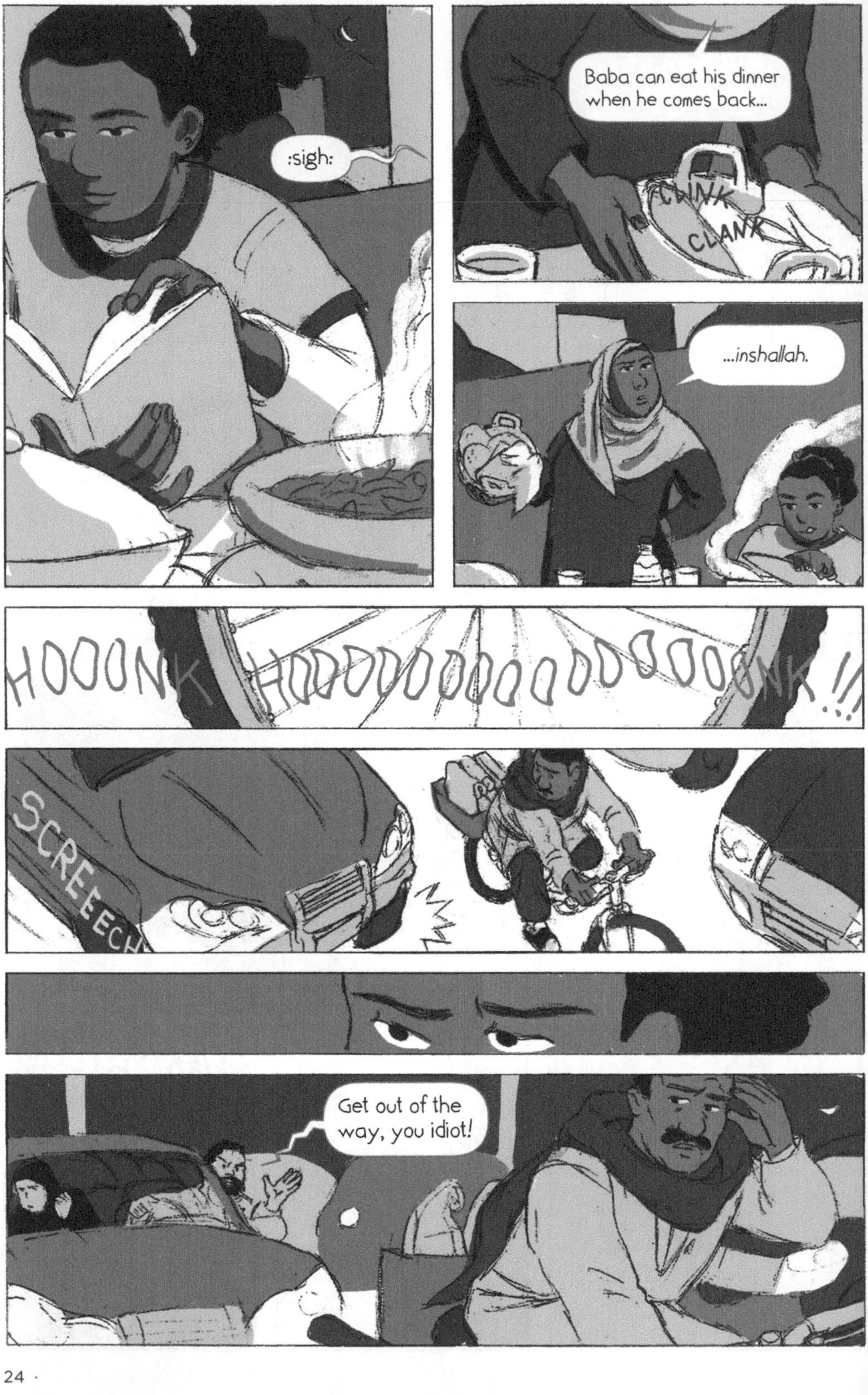
:sigh:
Baba can eat his dinner when he comes back...
CLINK
CLANK
...inshallah.
HOOONK HOOOOOOOOOOOOOOONK!!!
SCREEECH
Get out of the way, you idiot!

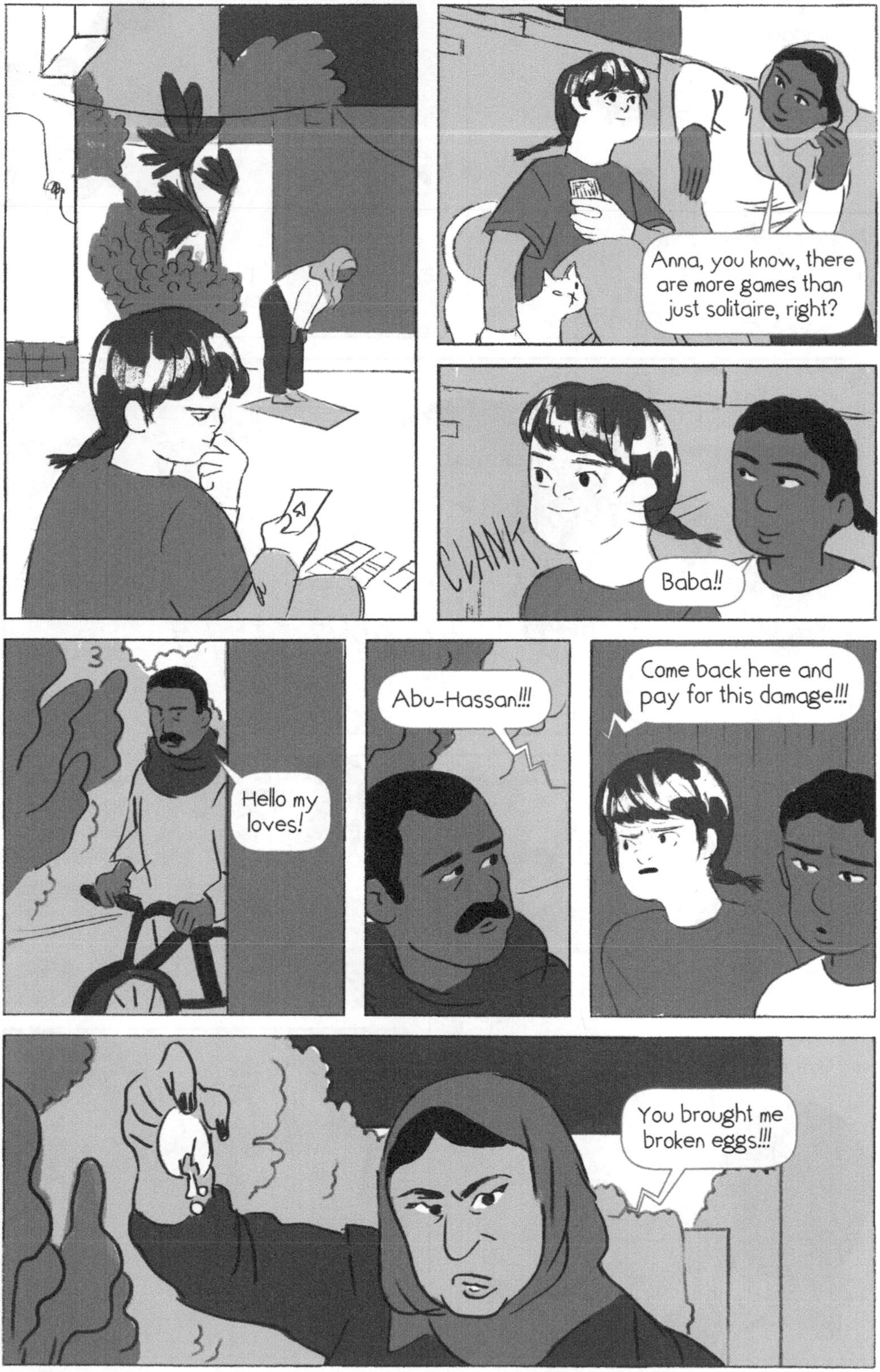
Anna, you know, there are more games than just solitaire, right?
CLANK
Baba!!
Hello my loves!
Abu-Hassan!!!
Come back here and pay for this damage!!!
You brought me broken eggs!!!

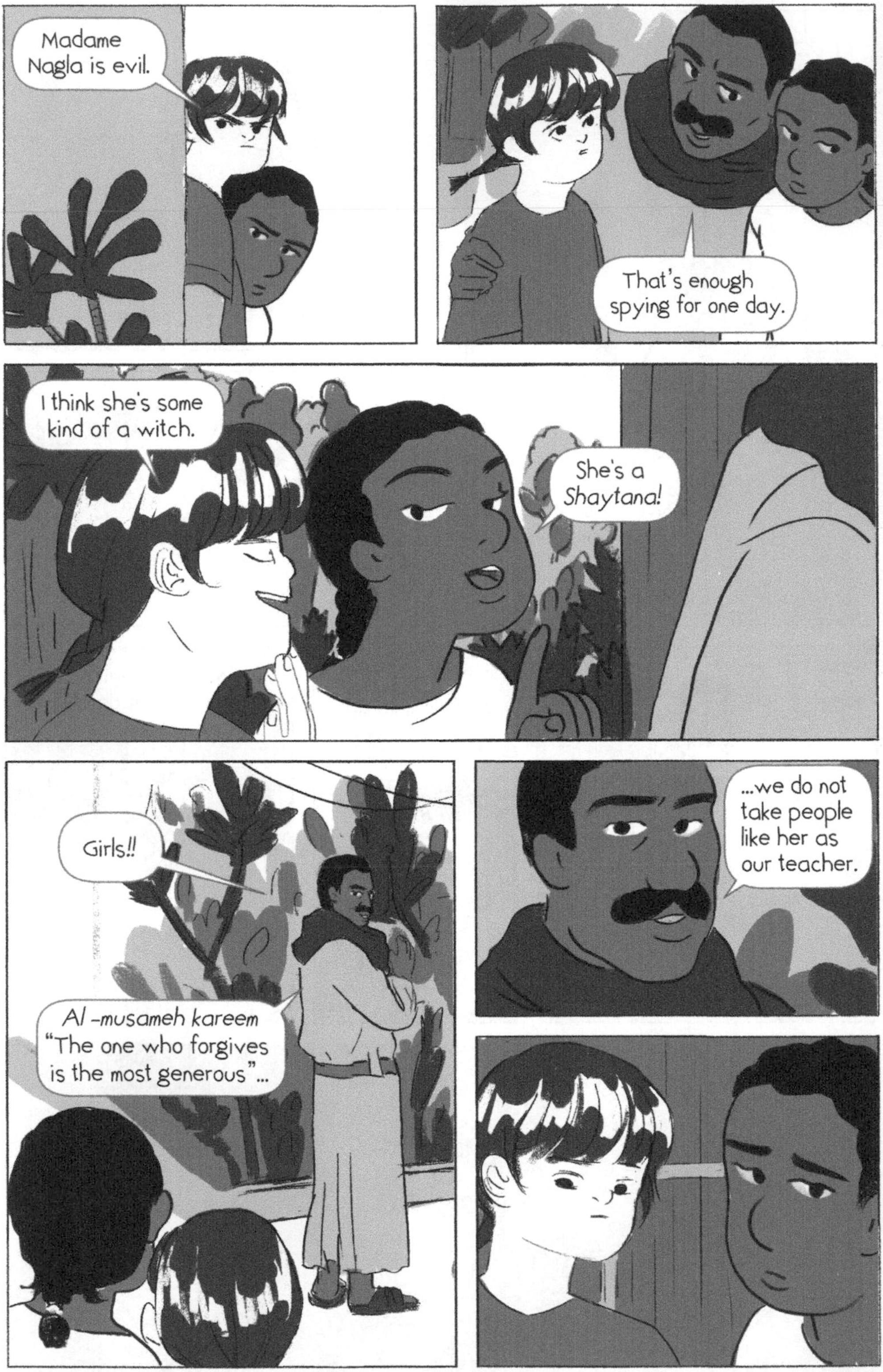
Madame Nagla is evil.
That's enough spying for one day.
I think she's some kind of a witch.
She's a *Shaytana*!
Girls!!
Al-musameh kareem "The one who forgives is the most generous"...
...we do not take people like her as our teacher.

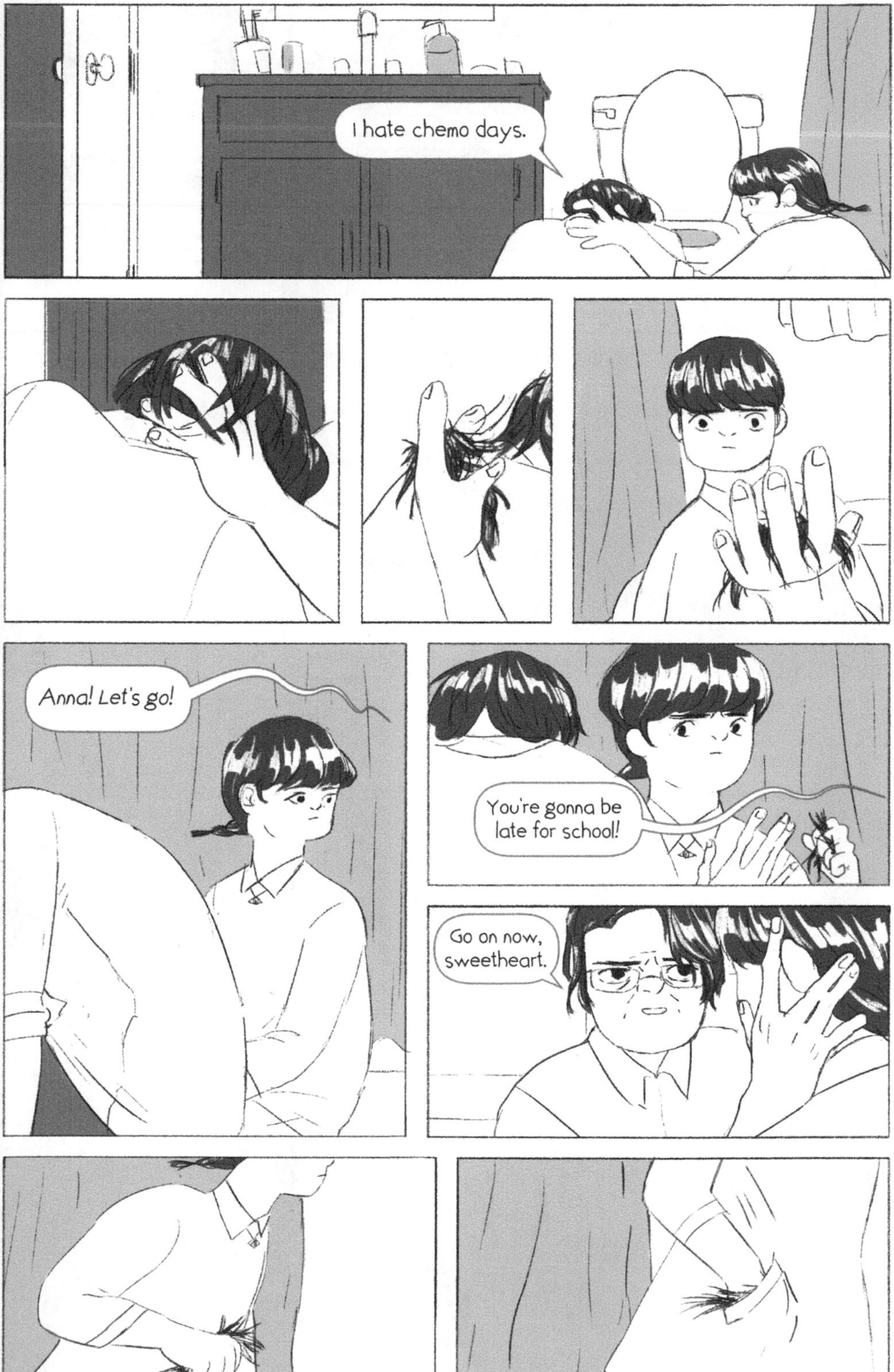
I hate chemo days.
Anna! Let's go!
You're gonna be late for school!
Go on now, sweetheart.

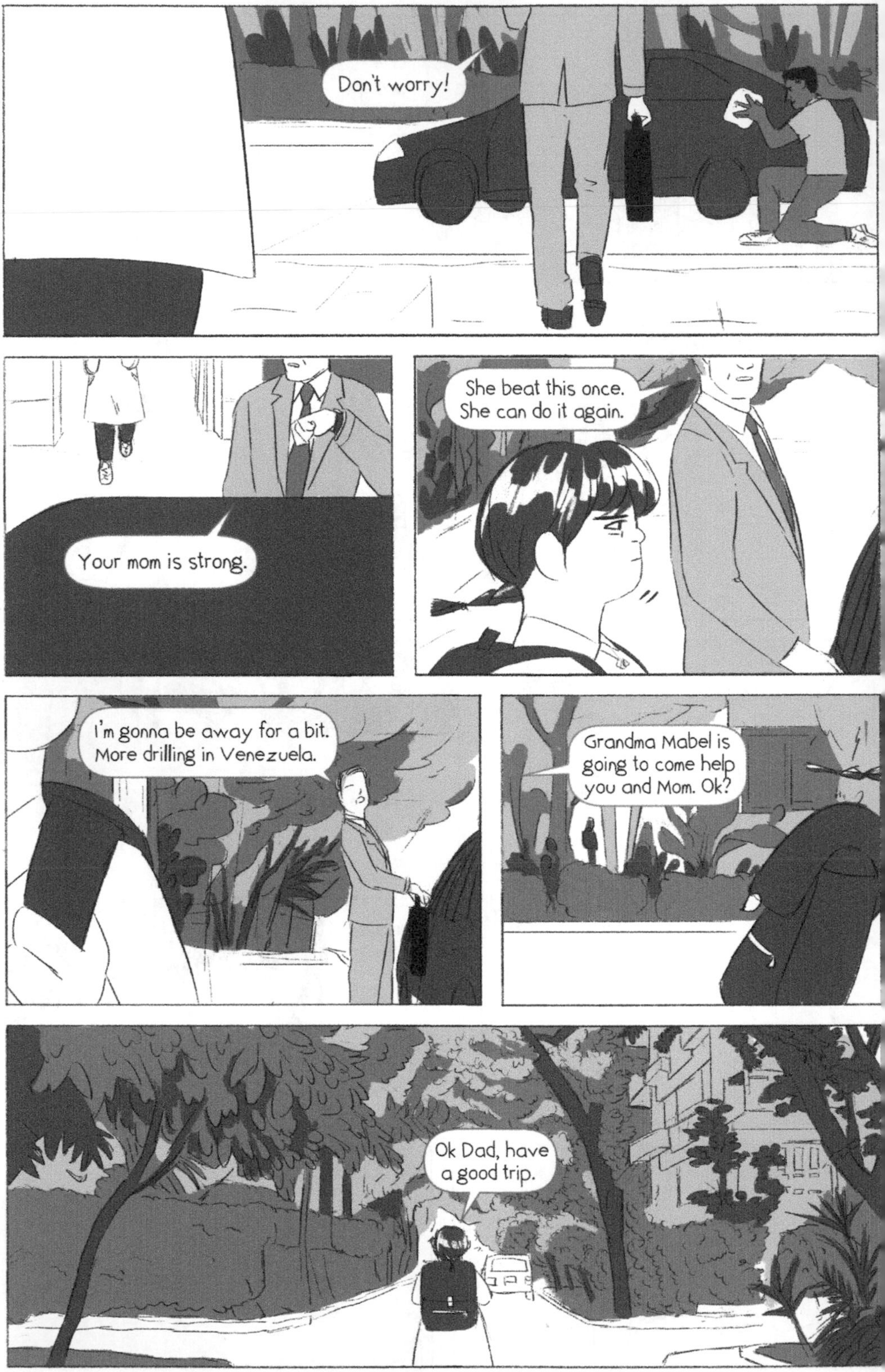
Don't worry!
Your mom is strong.
She beat this once. She can do it again.
I'm gonna be away for a bit. More drilling in Venezuela.
Grandma Mabel is going to come help you and Mom. Ok?
Ok Dad, have a good trip.

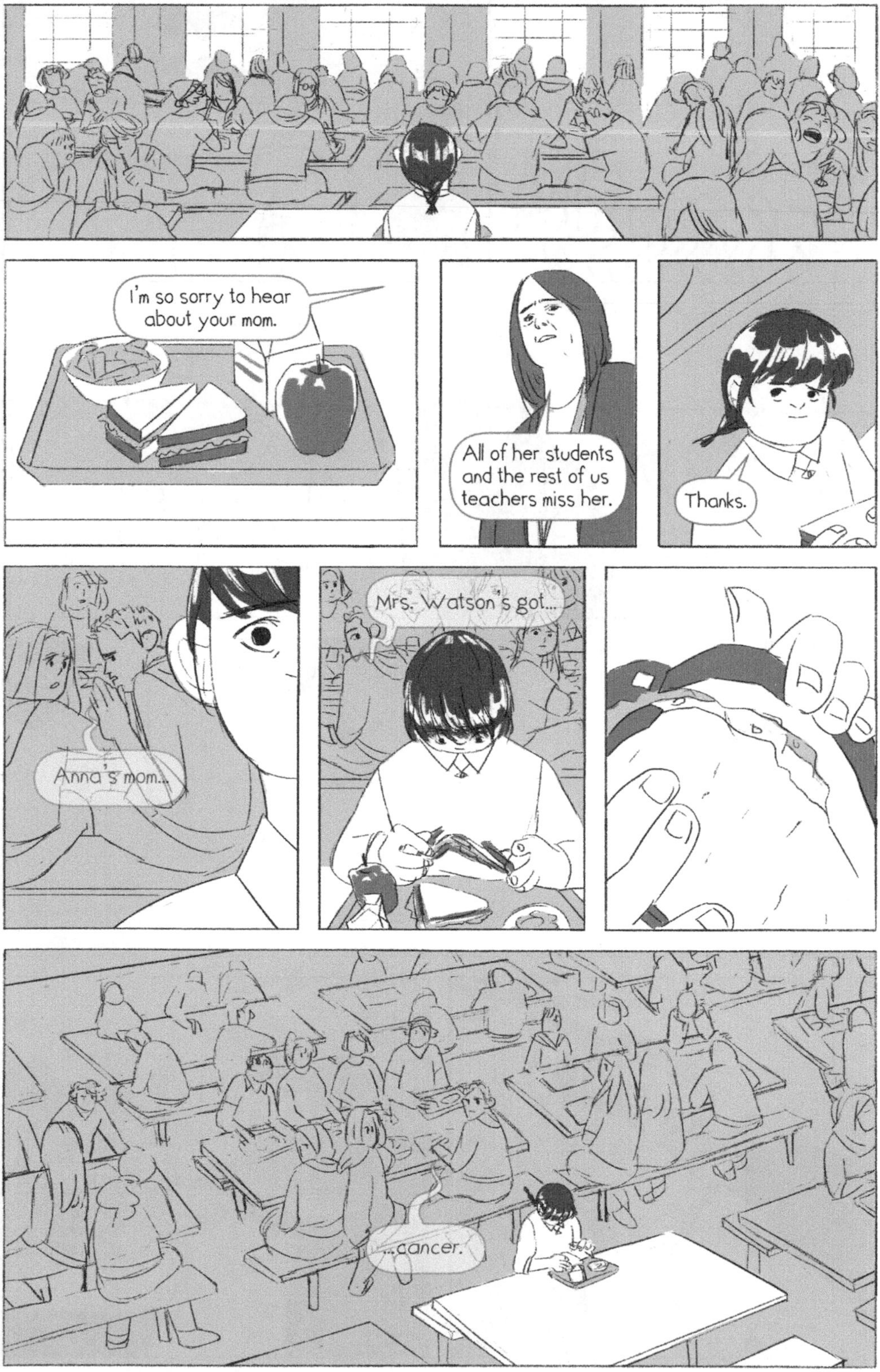
I'm so sorry to hear about your mom.
All of her students and the rest of us teachers miss her.
Thanks.
Anna's mom...
Mrs. Watson's got...
...cancer.

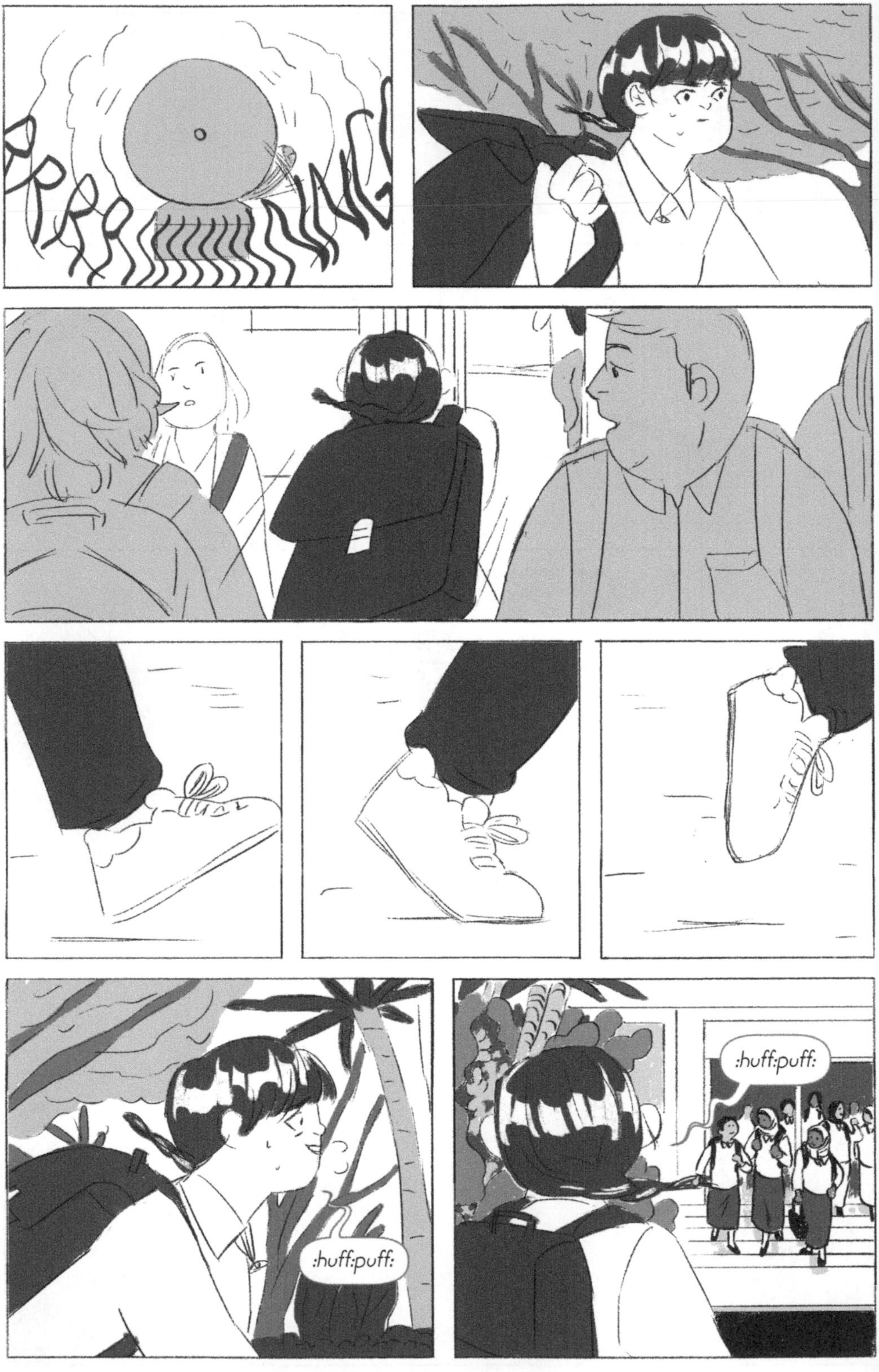
BRRRRING!
:huff:puff:
:huff:puff:

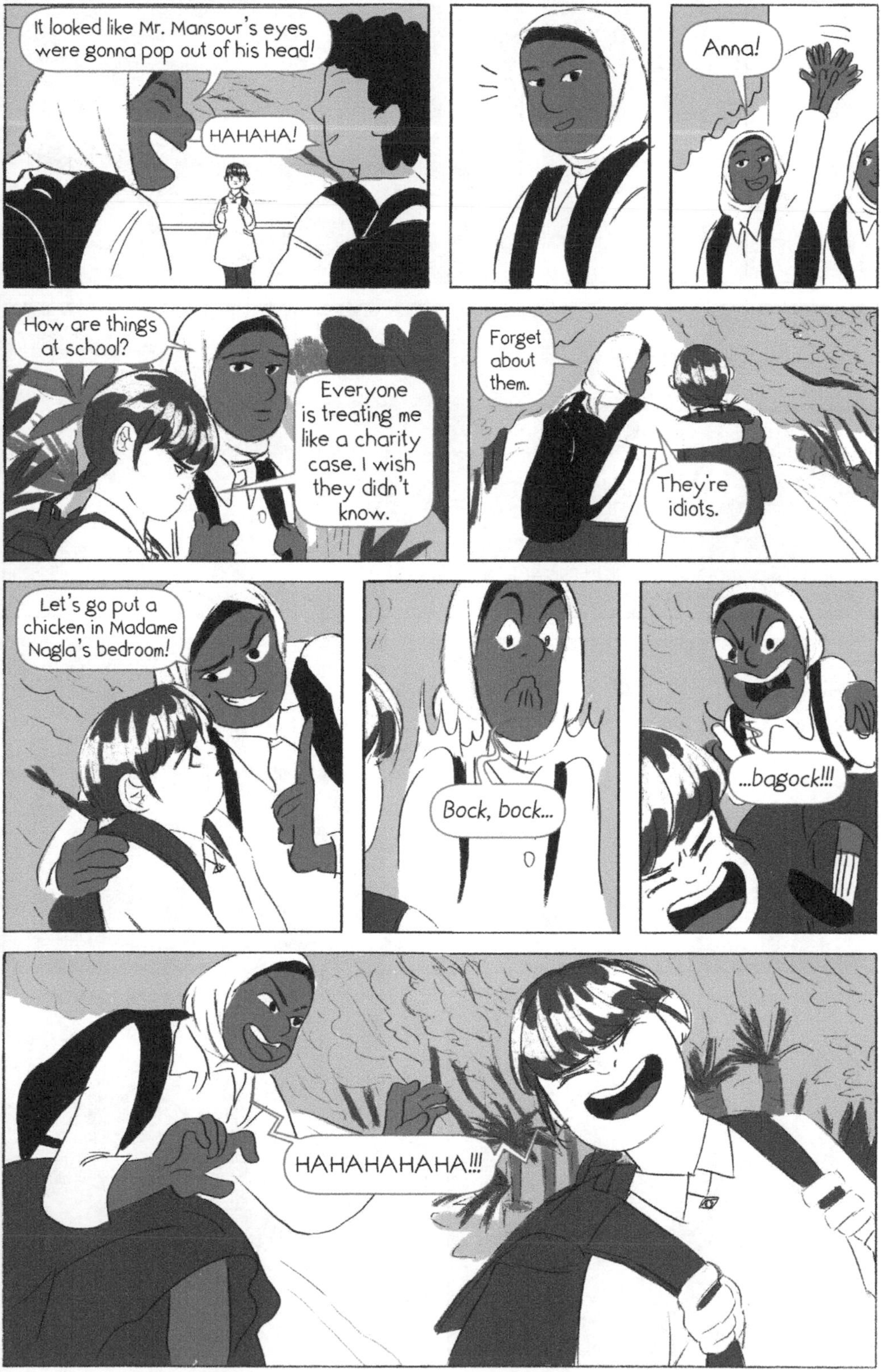

It looked like Mr. Mansour's eyes were gonna pop out of his head!
HAHAHA!
Anna!
How are things at school?
Everyone is treating me like a charity case. I wish they didn't know.
Forget about them.
They're idiots.
Let's go put a chicken in Madame Nagla's bedroom!
Bock, bock...
...bagock!!!
HAHAHAHAHA!!!

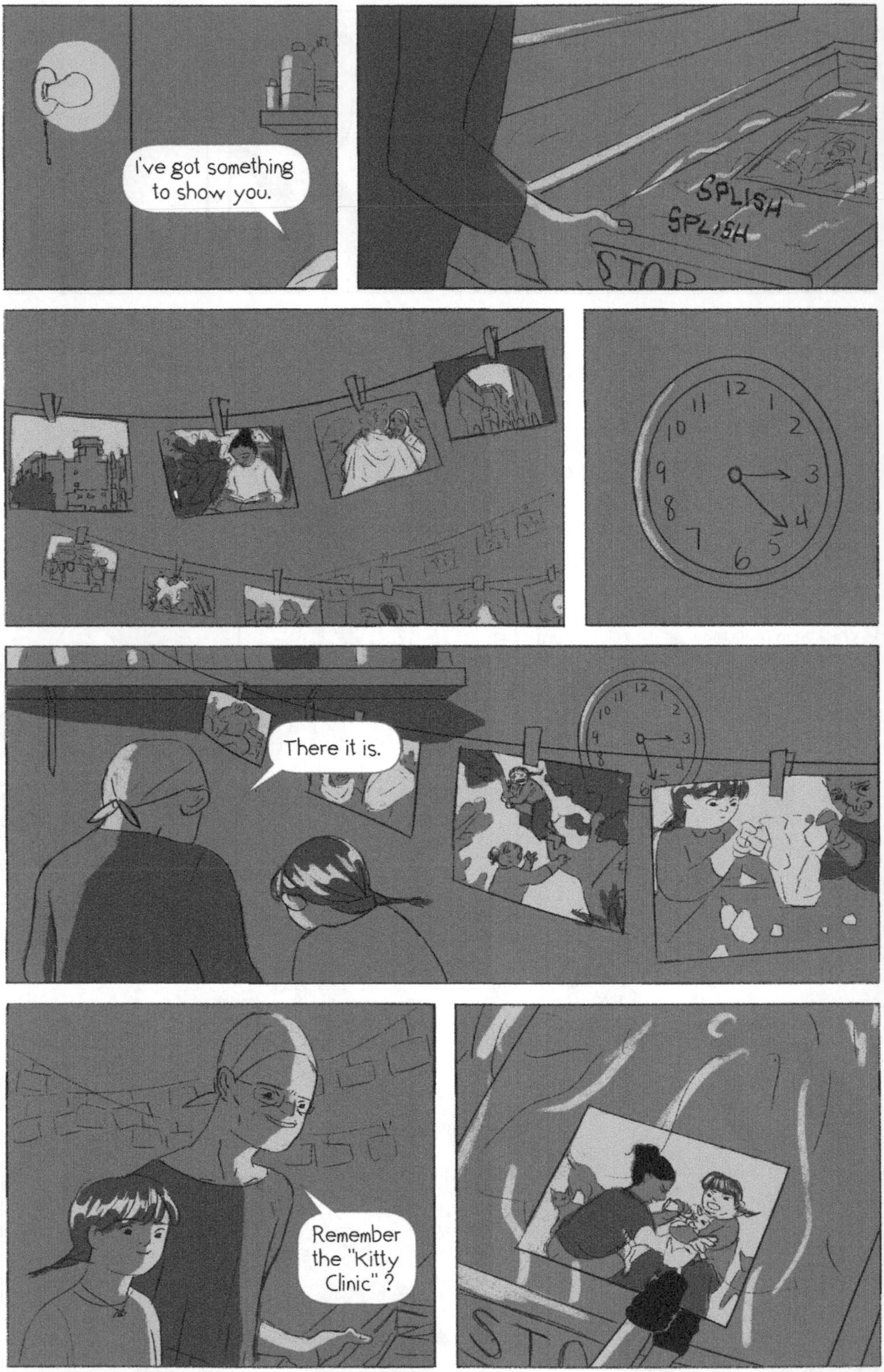
I've got something to show you.
SPLISH
SPLISH
STOP
There it is.
Remember the "Kitty Clinic"?
STO

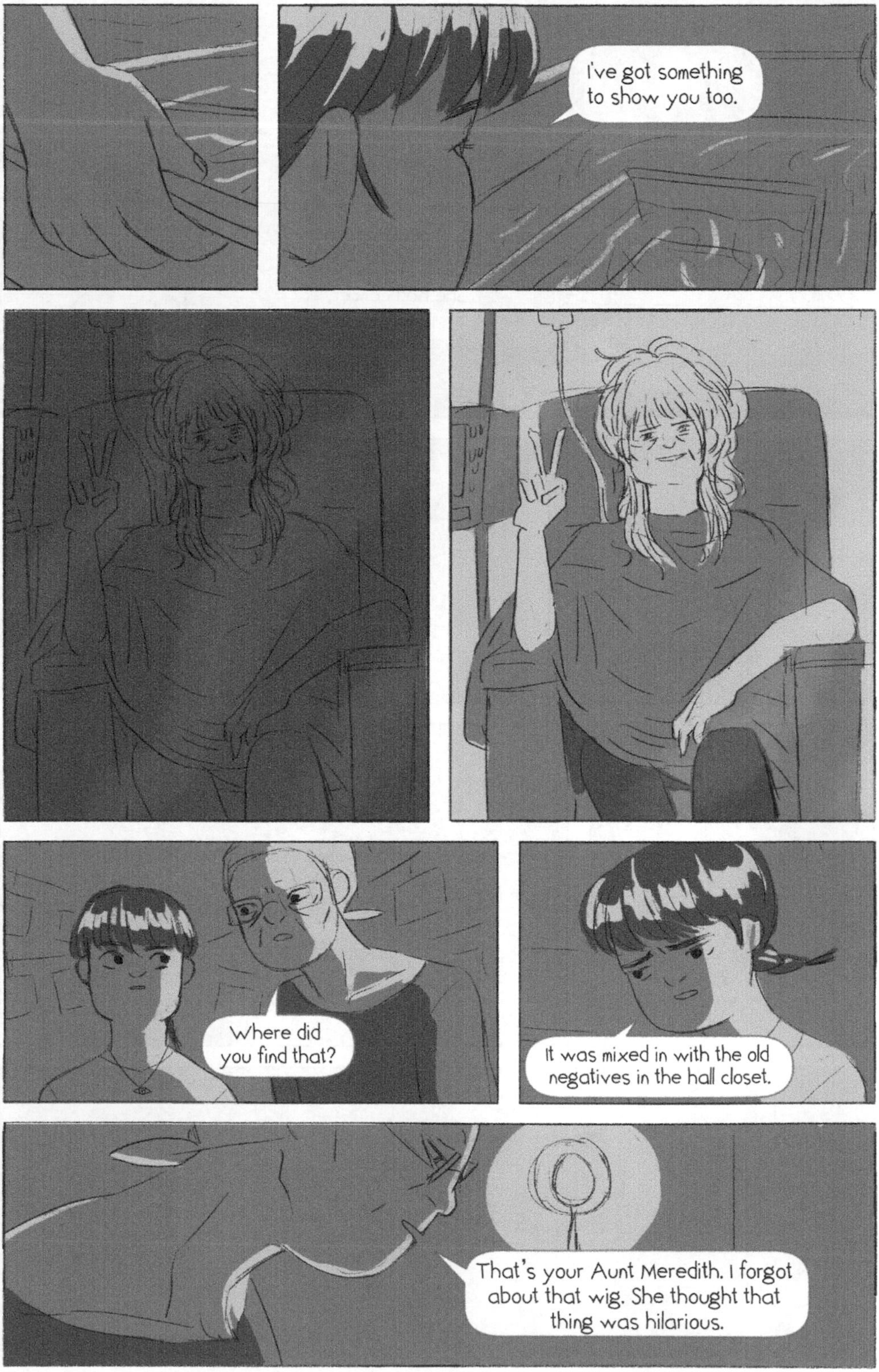
I've got something to show you too.
Where did you find that?
It was mixed in with the old negatives in the hall closet.
That's your Aunt Meredith. I forgot about that wig. She thought that thing was hilarious.

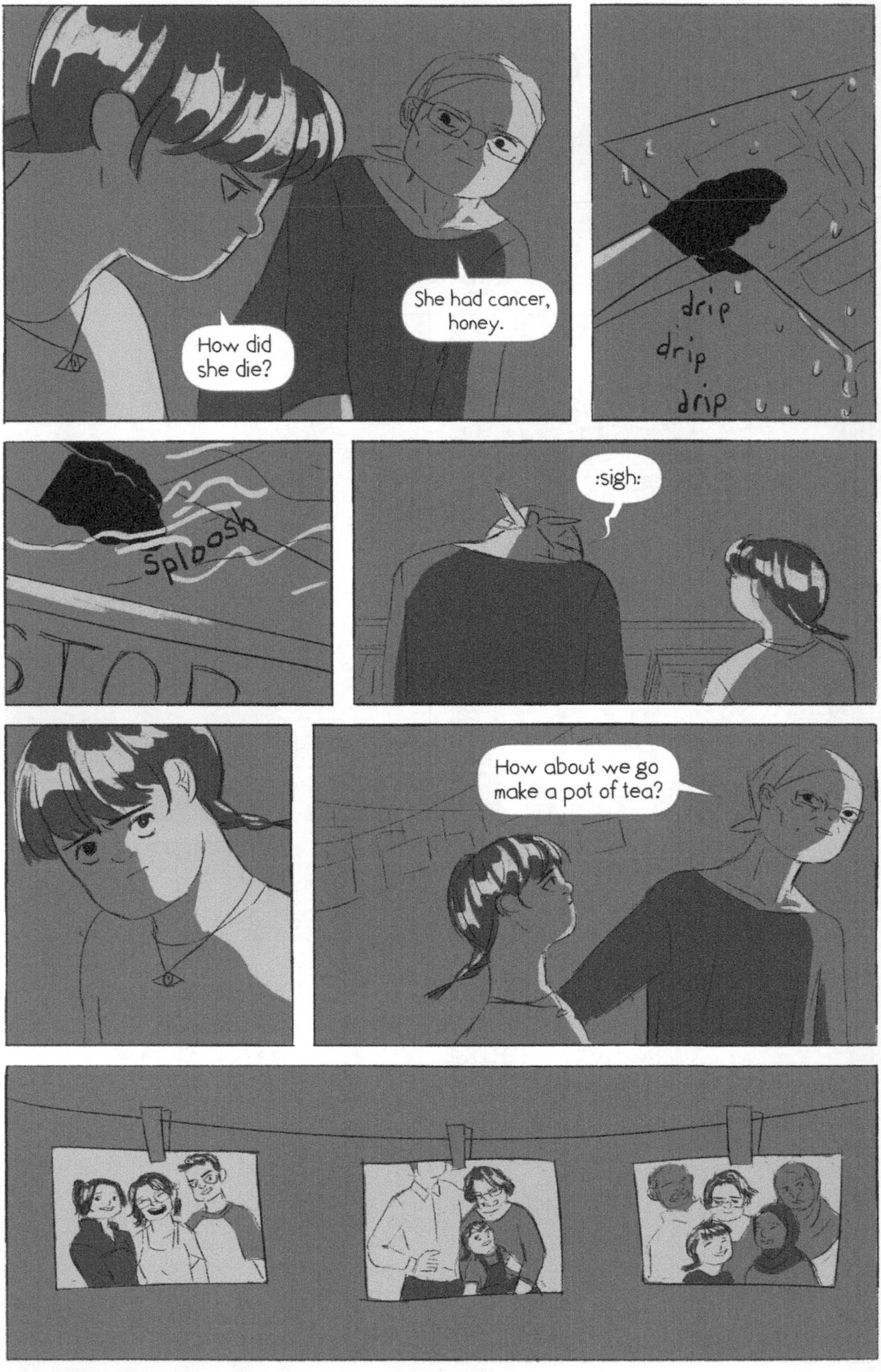
How did she die?
She had cancer, honey.
drip
drip
drip
Sploosh
:sigh:
How about we go make a pot of tea?

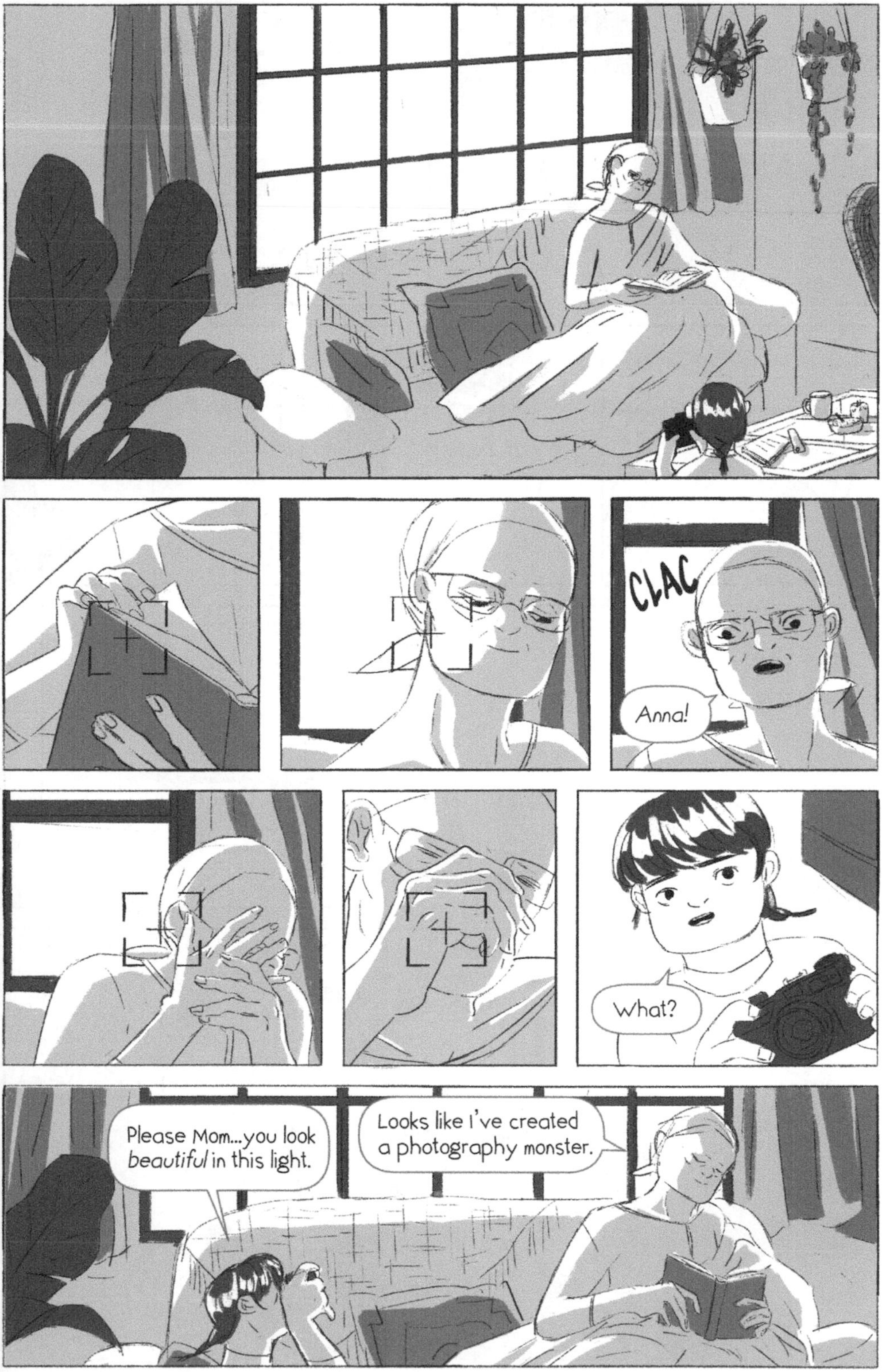
CLAC
Anna!
What?
Please Mom...you look *beautiful* in this light.
Looks like I've created a photography monster.

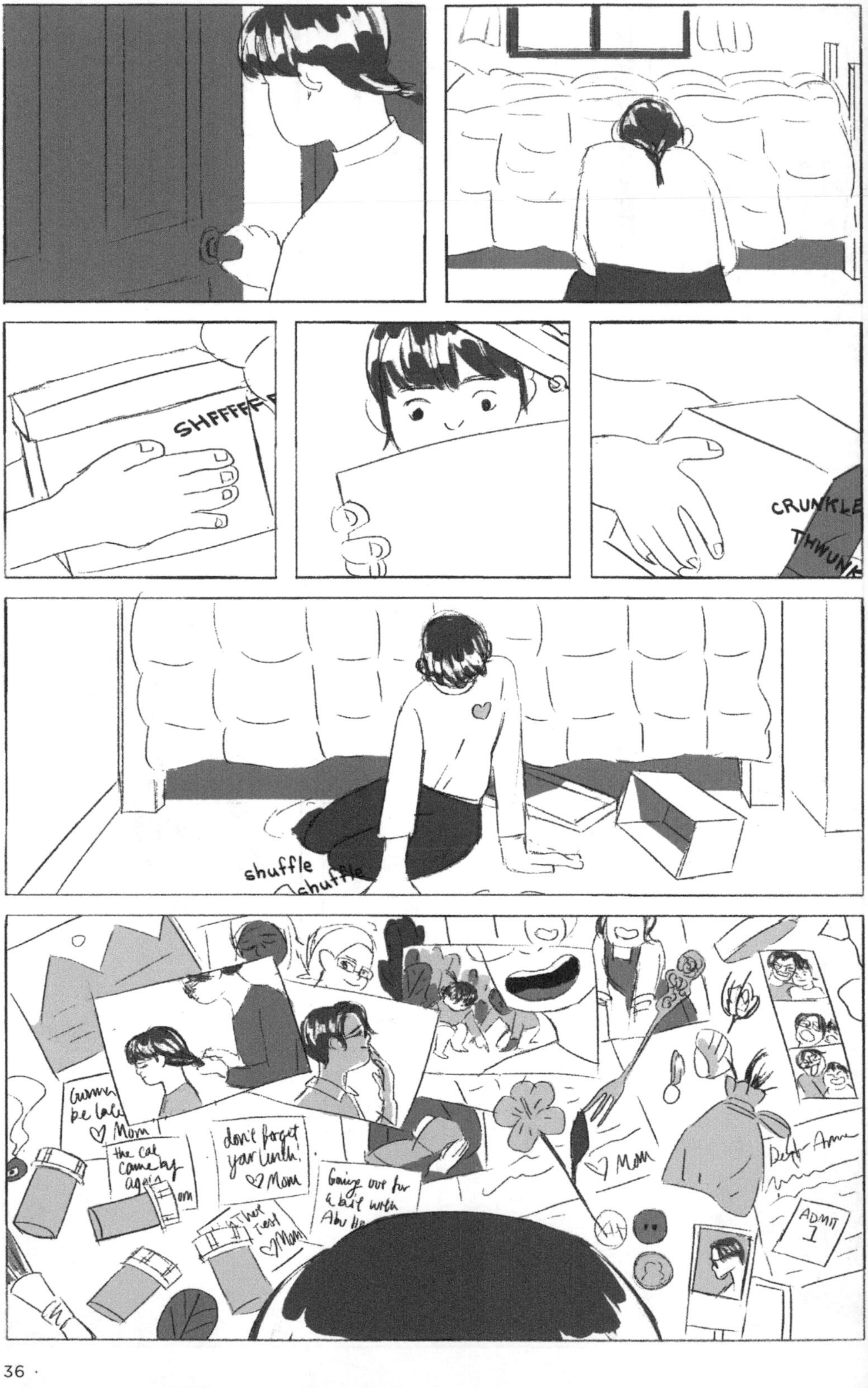
SHFFFFF
CRUNKLE
THWUNK
shuffle
shuffle
don't forget your lunch! ♡Mom
♡Mom
ADMIT 1

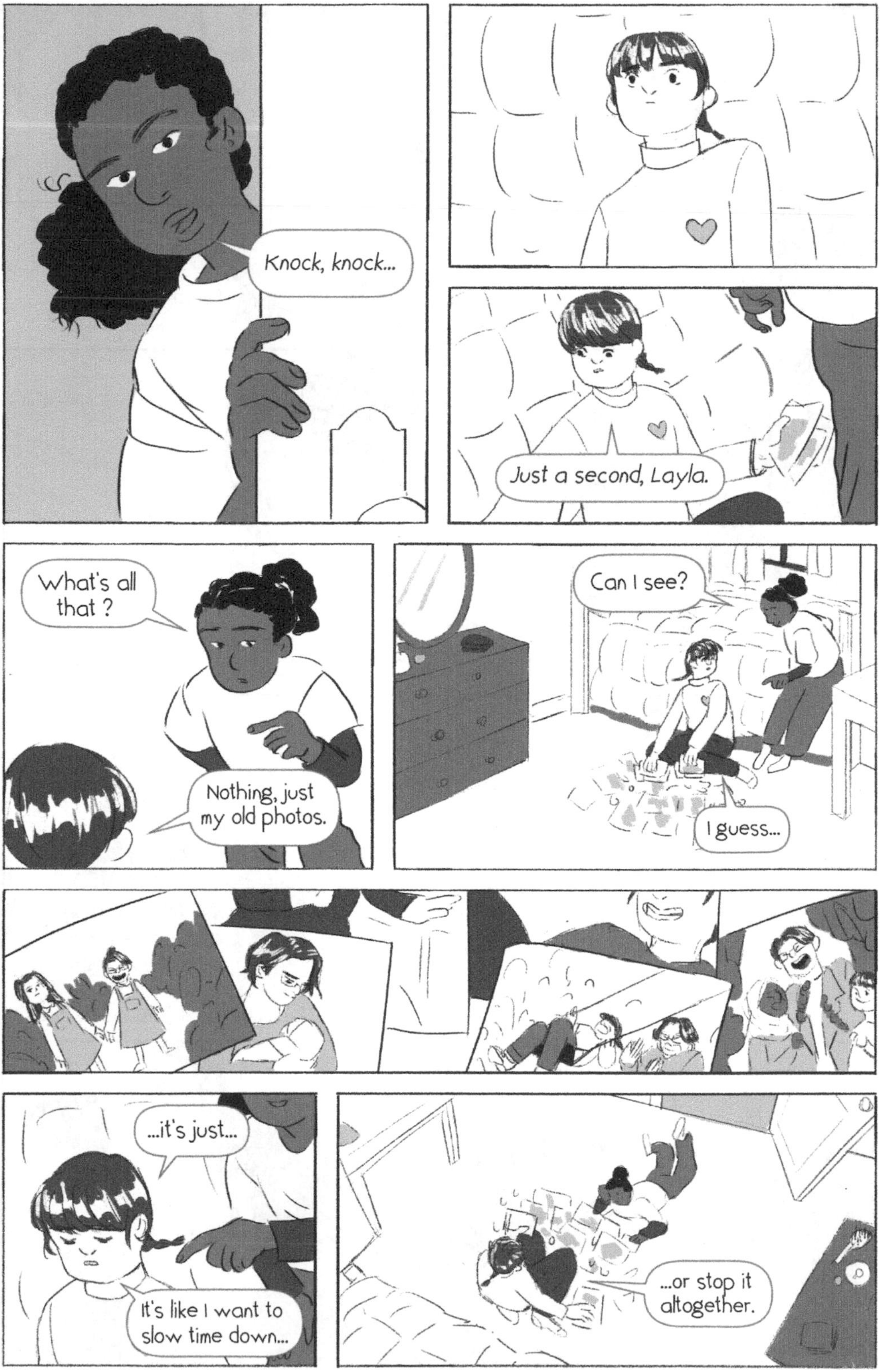
Knock, knock...
Just a second, Layla.
What's all that ?
Nothing, just my old photos.
Can I see?
I guess...
...it's just...
It's like I want to slow time down...
...or stop it altogether.

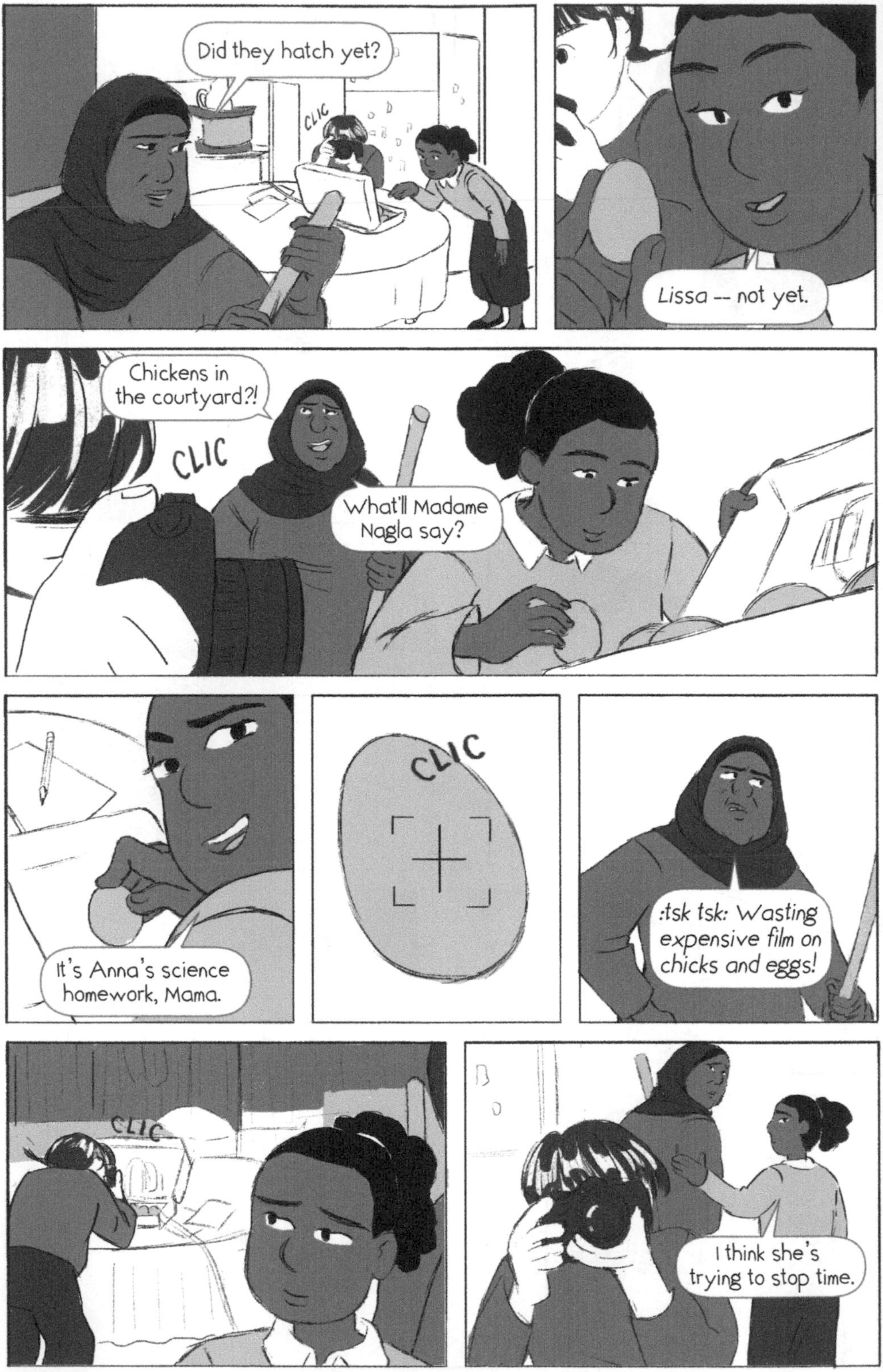
Did they hatch yet?
CLIC
Lissa -- not yet.
Chickens in the courtyard?!
CLIC
What'll Madame Nagla say?
It's Anna's science homework, Mama.
CLIC
:tsk tsk: Wasting expensive film on chicks and eggs!
CLIC
I think she's trying to stop time.

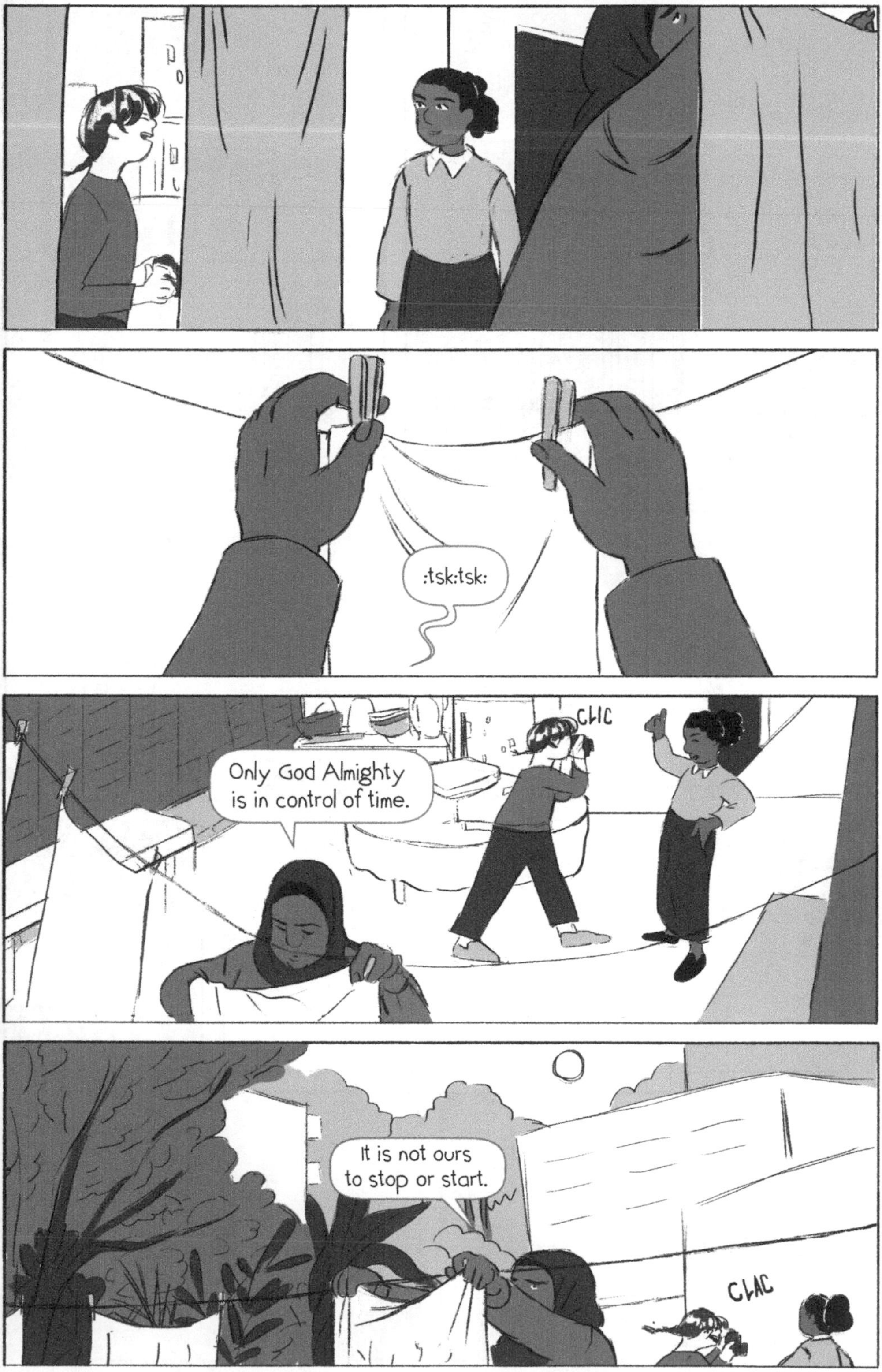
:tsk:tsk:
CLIC
Only God Almighty is in control of time.
It is not ours to stop or start.
CLAC

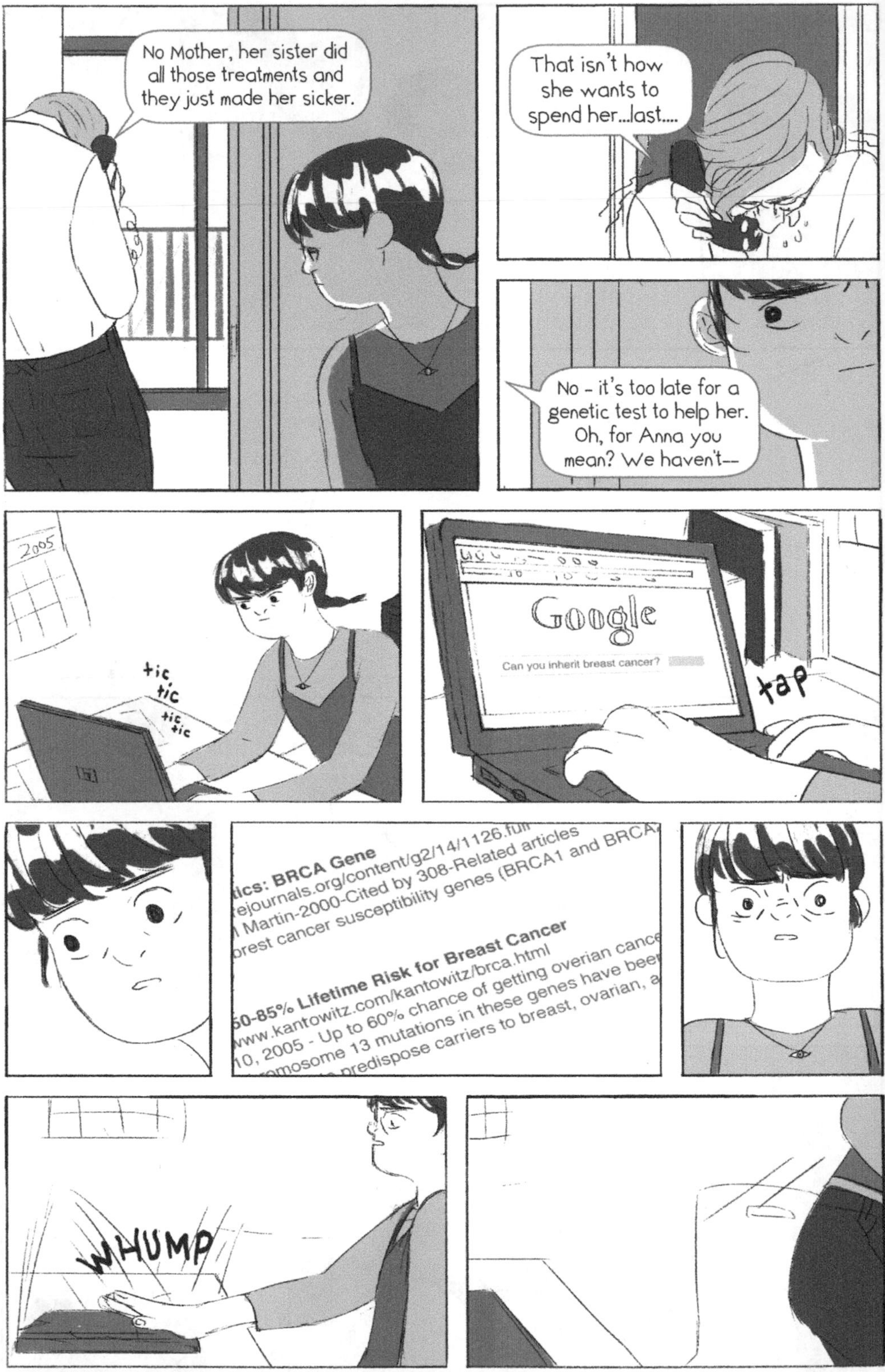
No Mother, her sister did all those treatments and they just made her sicker.
That isn't how she wants to spend her...last....
No - it's too late for a genetic test to help her. Oh, for Anna you mean? We haven't--
2005
tic tic tic tic
Google
Can you inherit breast cancer?
tap
tics: BRCA Gene
ejournals.org/content/g2/14/1126.full
Martin-2000-Cited by 308-Related articles
prest cancer susceptibility genes (BRCA1 and BRCA
50-85% Lifetime Risk for Breast Cancer
www.kantowitz.com/kantowitz/brca.html
10, 2005 - Up to 60% chance of getting overian cance
romosome 13 mutations in these genes have bee
predispose carriers to breast, ovarian, a
WHUMP

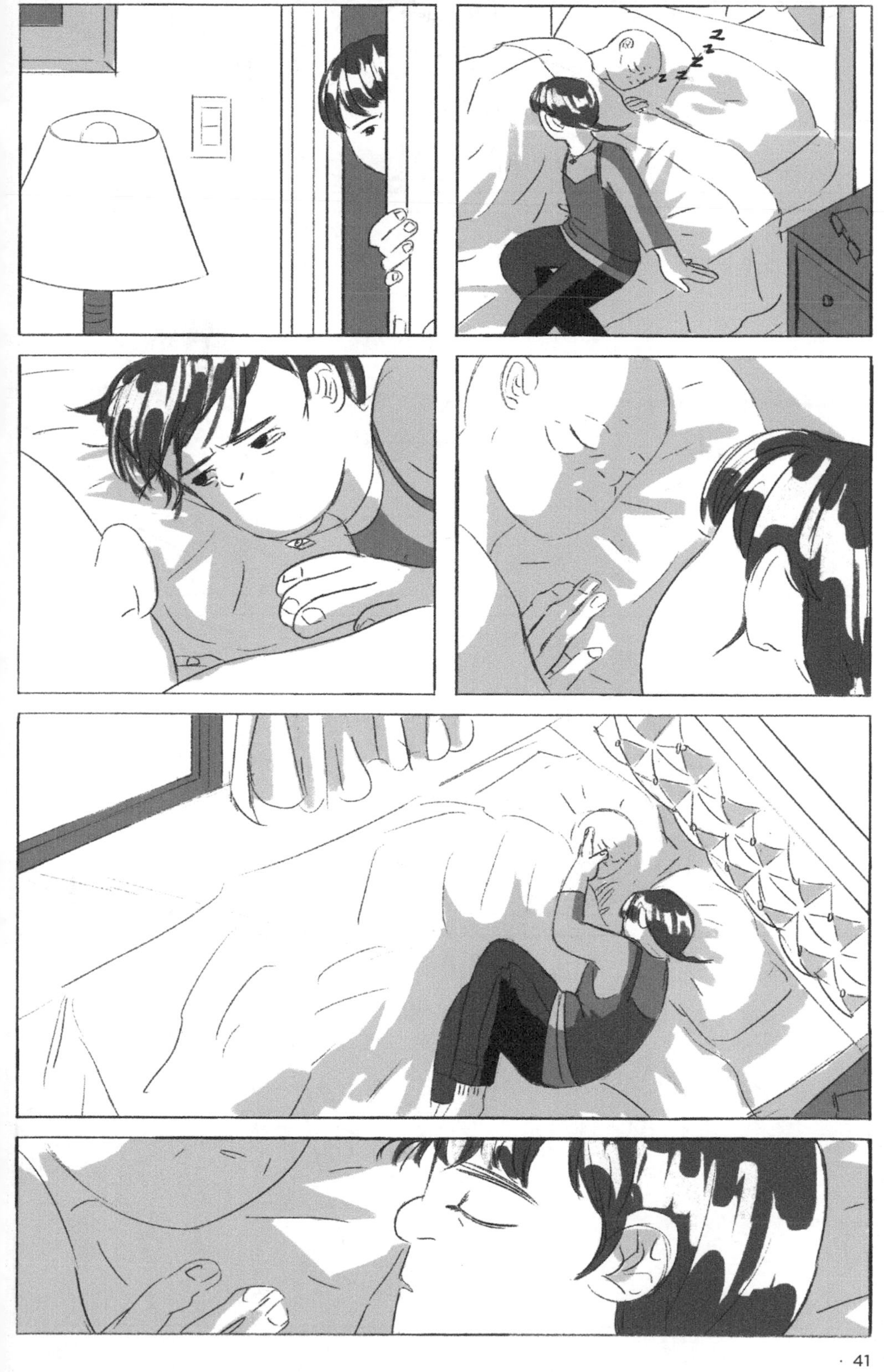

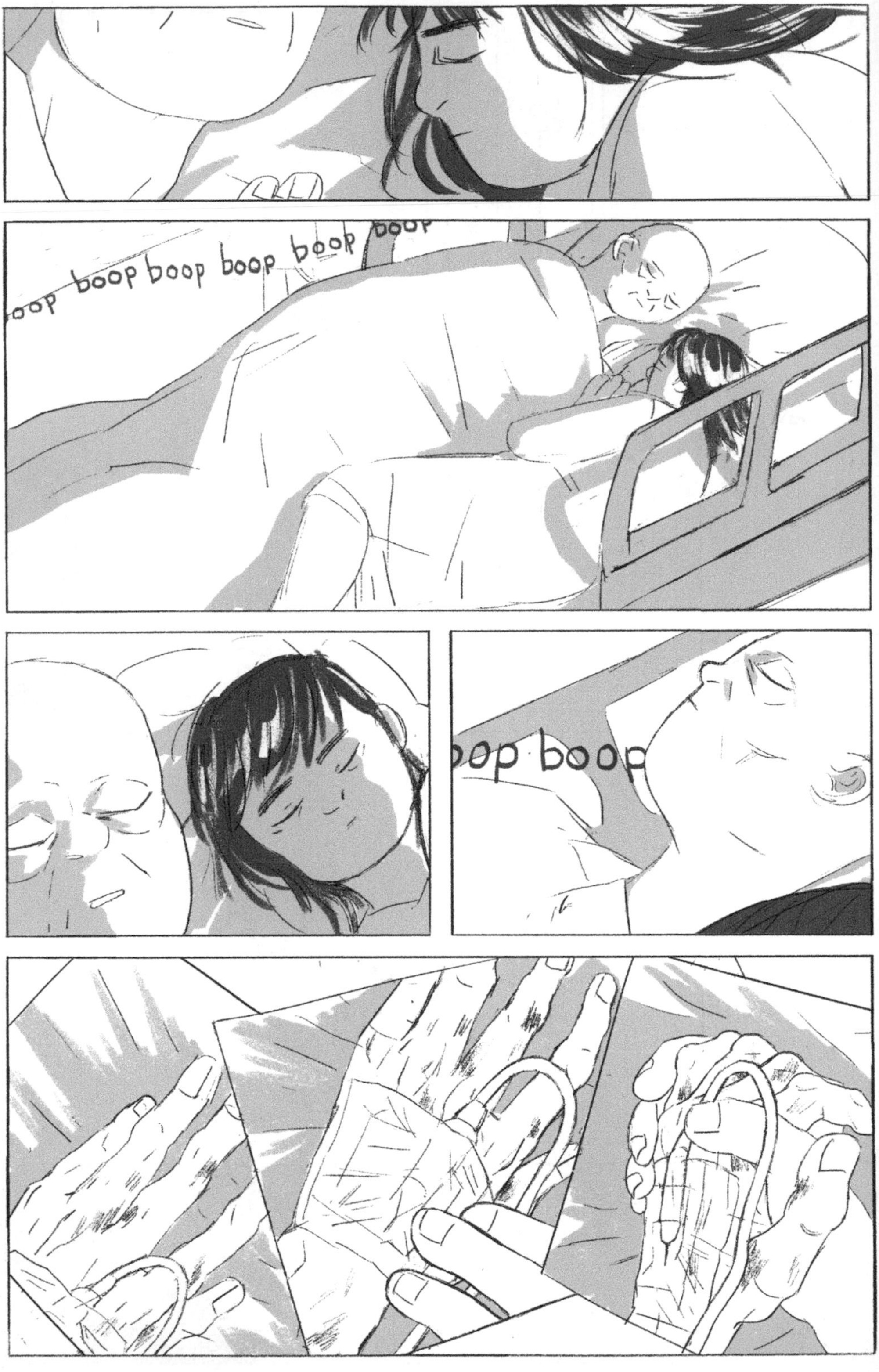
oop boop boop boop boop boop
oop boop

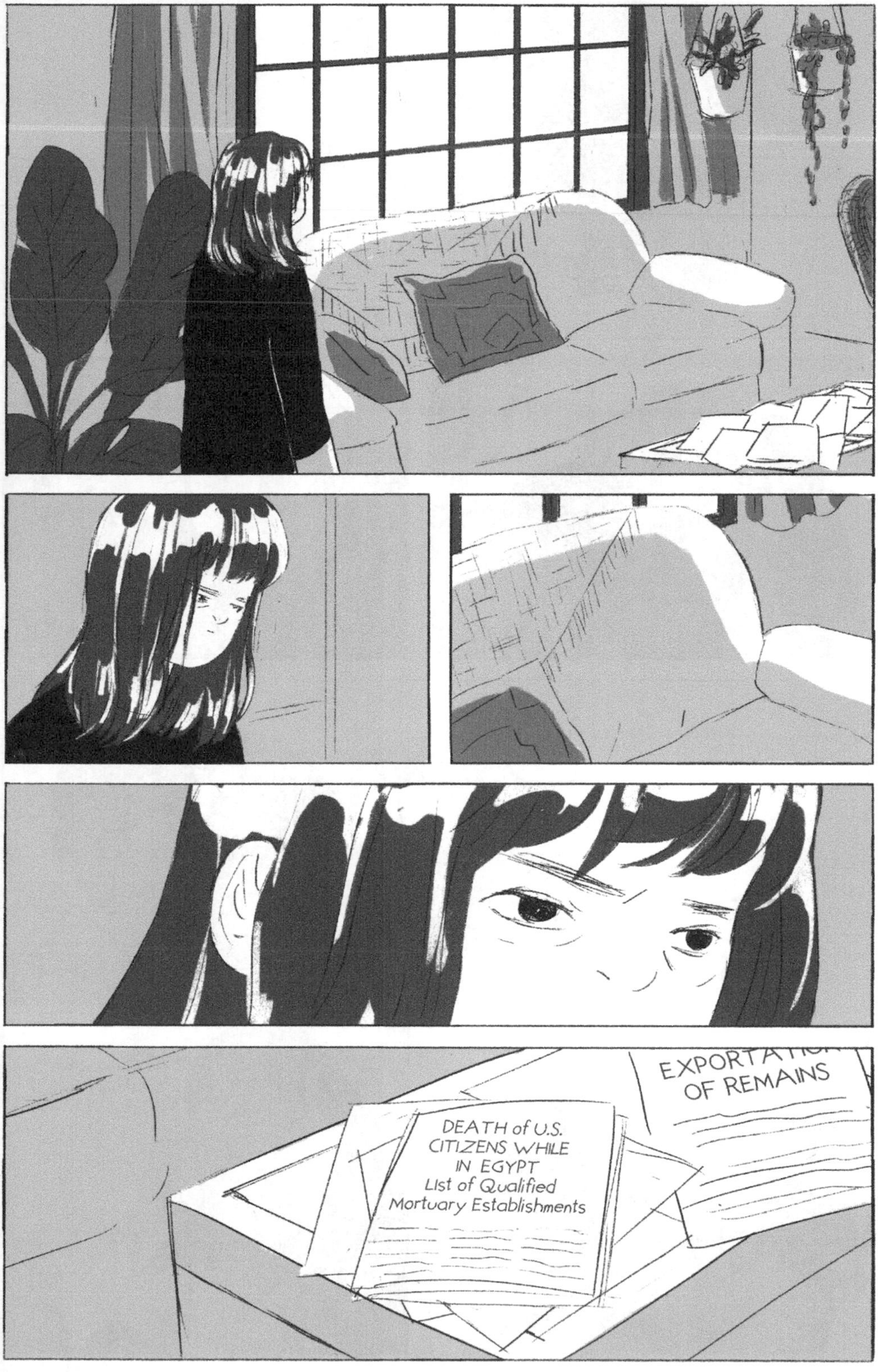
DEATH of U.S. CITIZENS WHILE IN EGYPT
List of Qualified Mortuary Establishments
EXPORTATION OF REMAINS

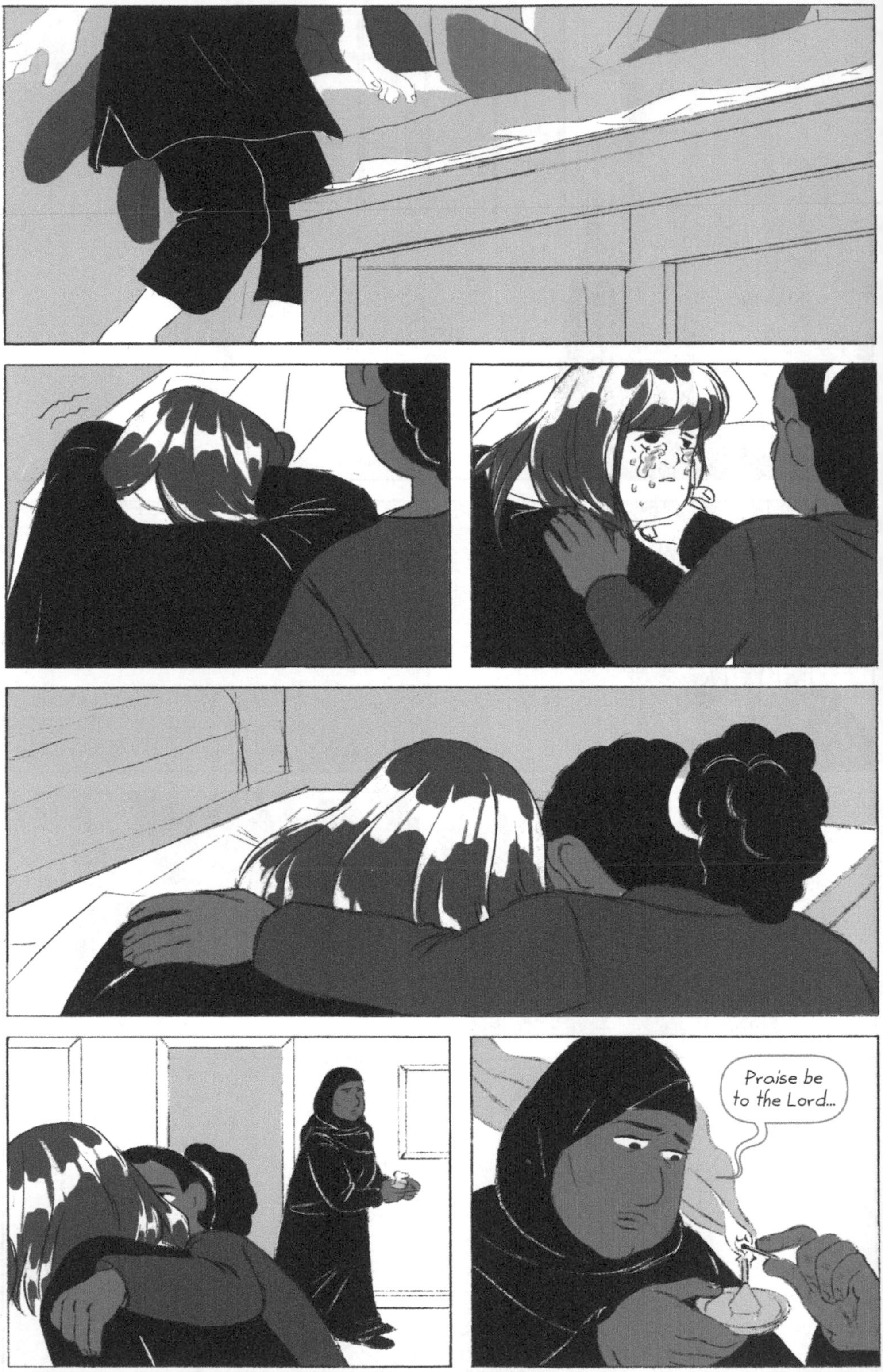
Praise be
to the Lord...

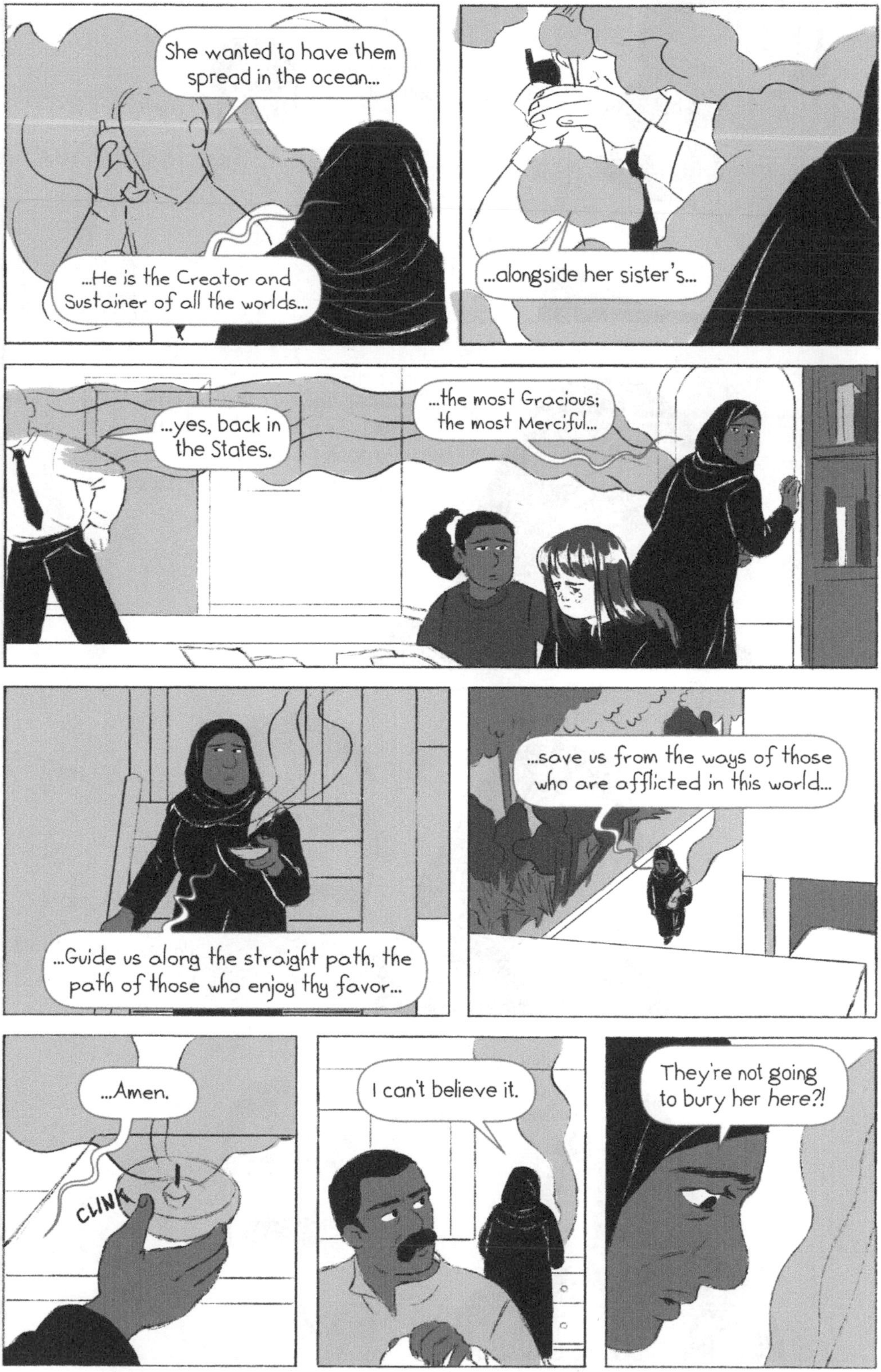
She wanted to have them spread in the ocean...
...He is the Creator and Sustainer of all the worlds...
...alongside her sister's...
...yes, back in the States.
...the most Gracious; the most Merciful...
...Guide us along the straight path, the path of those who enjoy thy favor...
...save us from the ways of those who are afflicted in this world...
...Amen.
CLINK
I can't believe it.
They're not going to bury her *here?!*

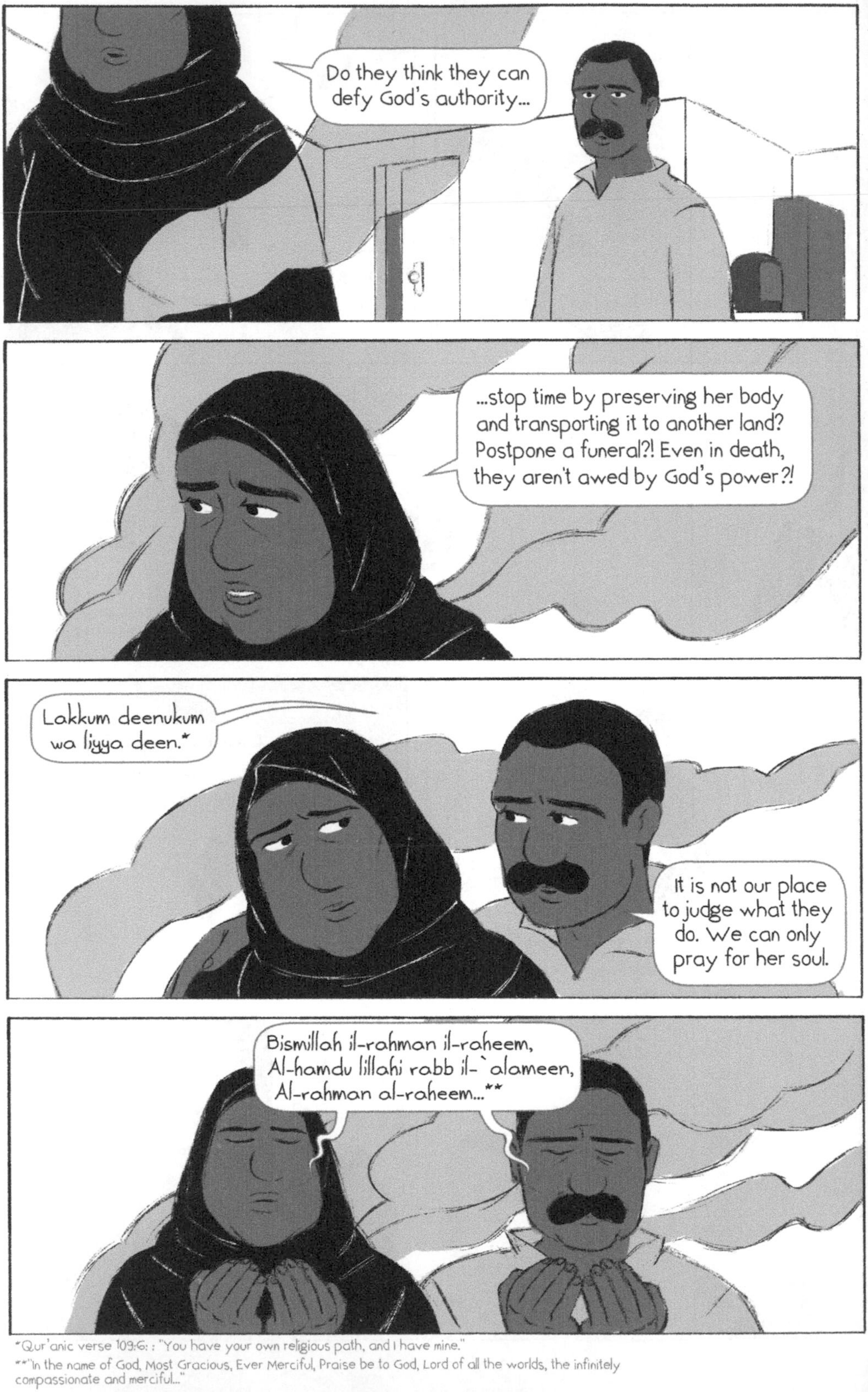
Do they think they can defy God's authority...
...stop time by preserving her body and transporting it to another land? Postpone a funeral?! Even in death, they aren't awed by God's power?!
Lakkum deenukum wa liyya deen.*
It is not our place to judge what they do. We can only pray for her soul.
Bismillah il-rahman il-raheem, Al-hamdu lillahi rabb il-`alameen, Al-rahman al-raheem...**

*Qur'anic verse 109:6: : "You have your own religious path, and I have mine."

**"In the name of God, Most Gracious, Ever Merciful, Praise be to God, Lord of all the worlds, the infinitely compassionate and merciful..."

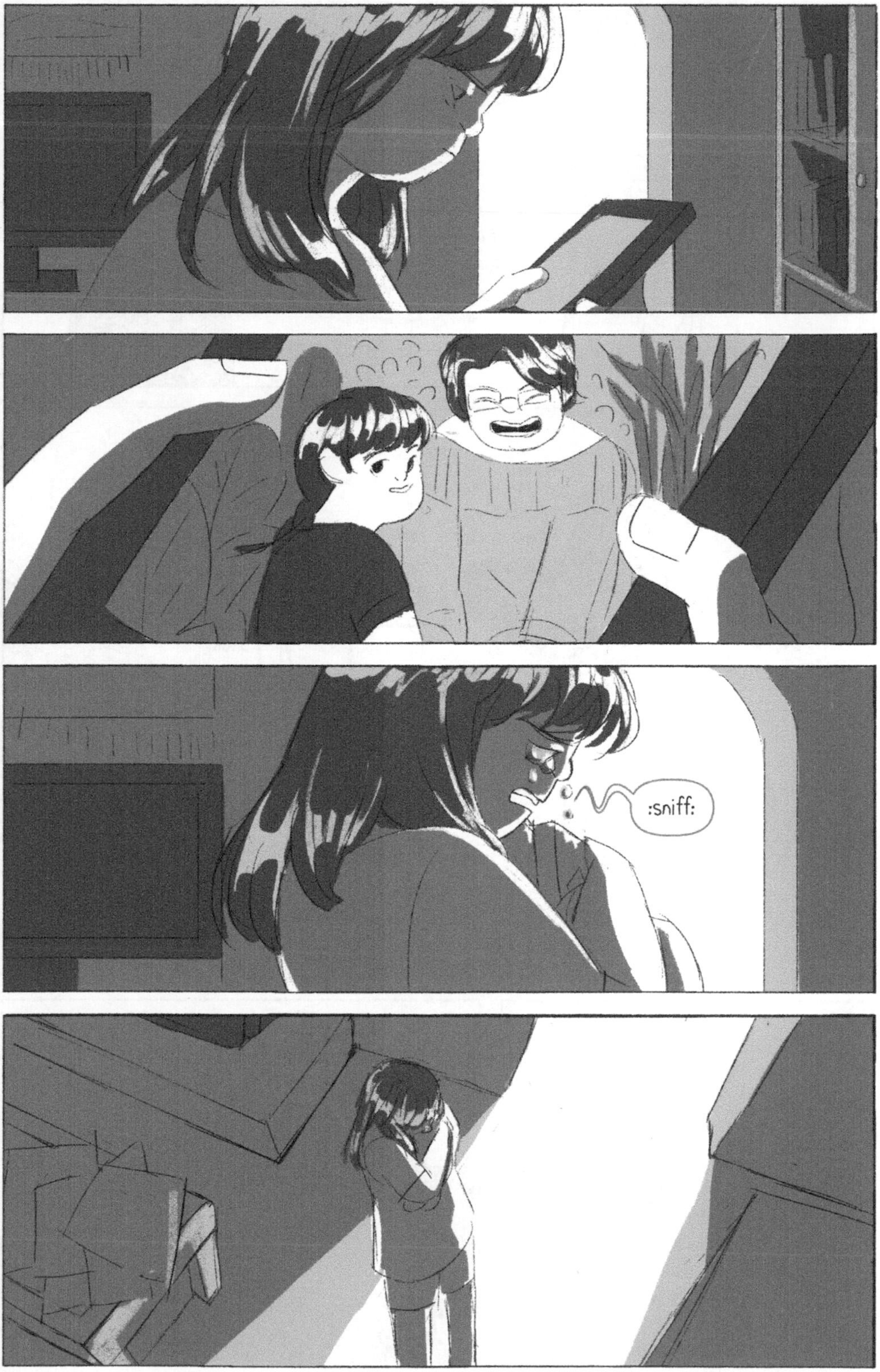
:sniff:

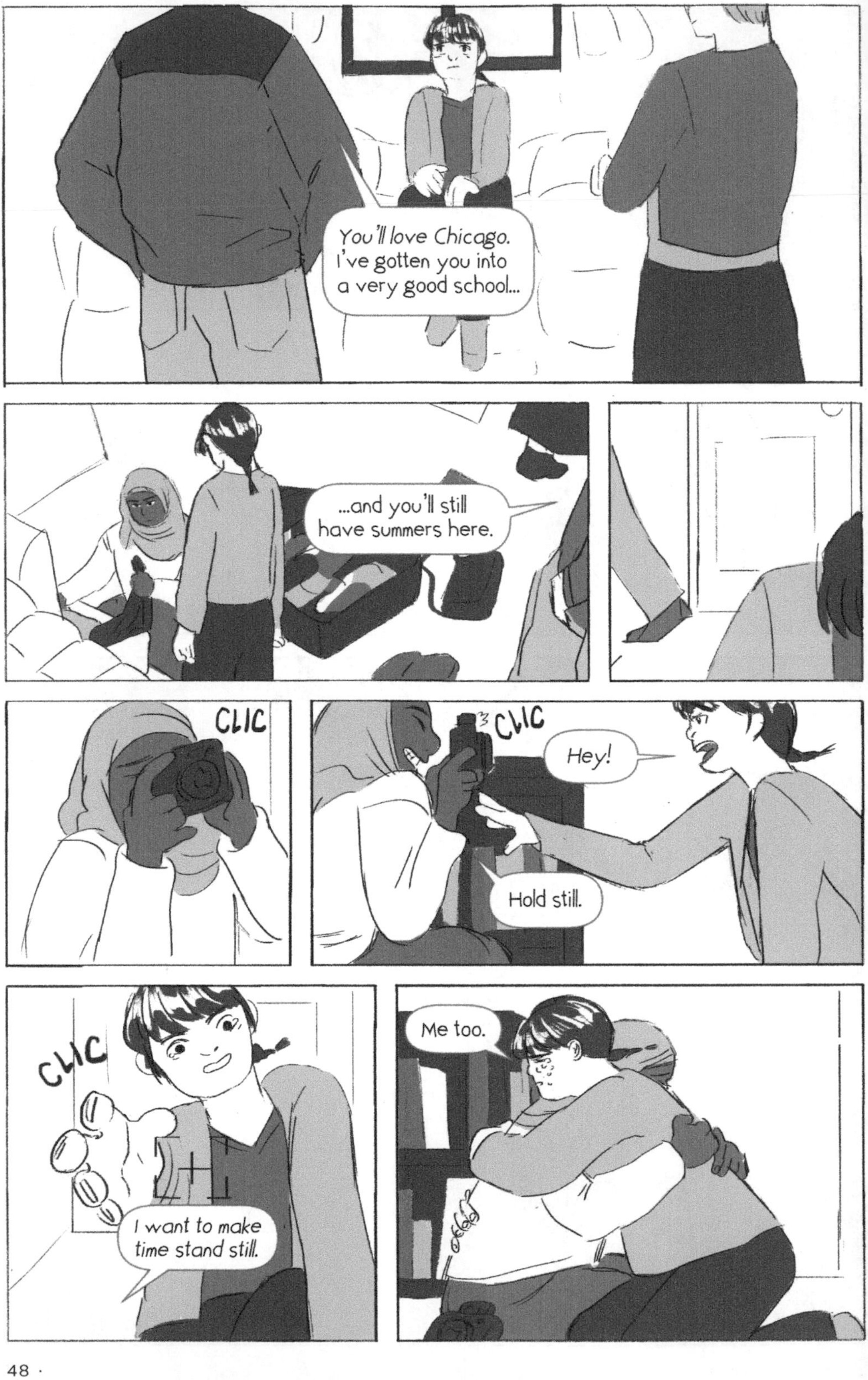
You'll love Chicago. I've gotten you into a very good school...
...and you'll still have summers here.
CLIC
CLIC
Hey!
Hold still.
CLIC
I want to make time stand still.
Me too.

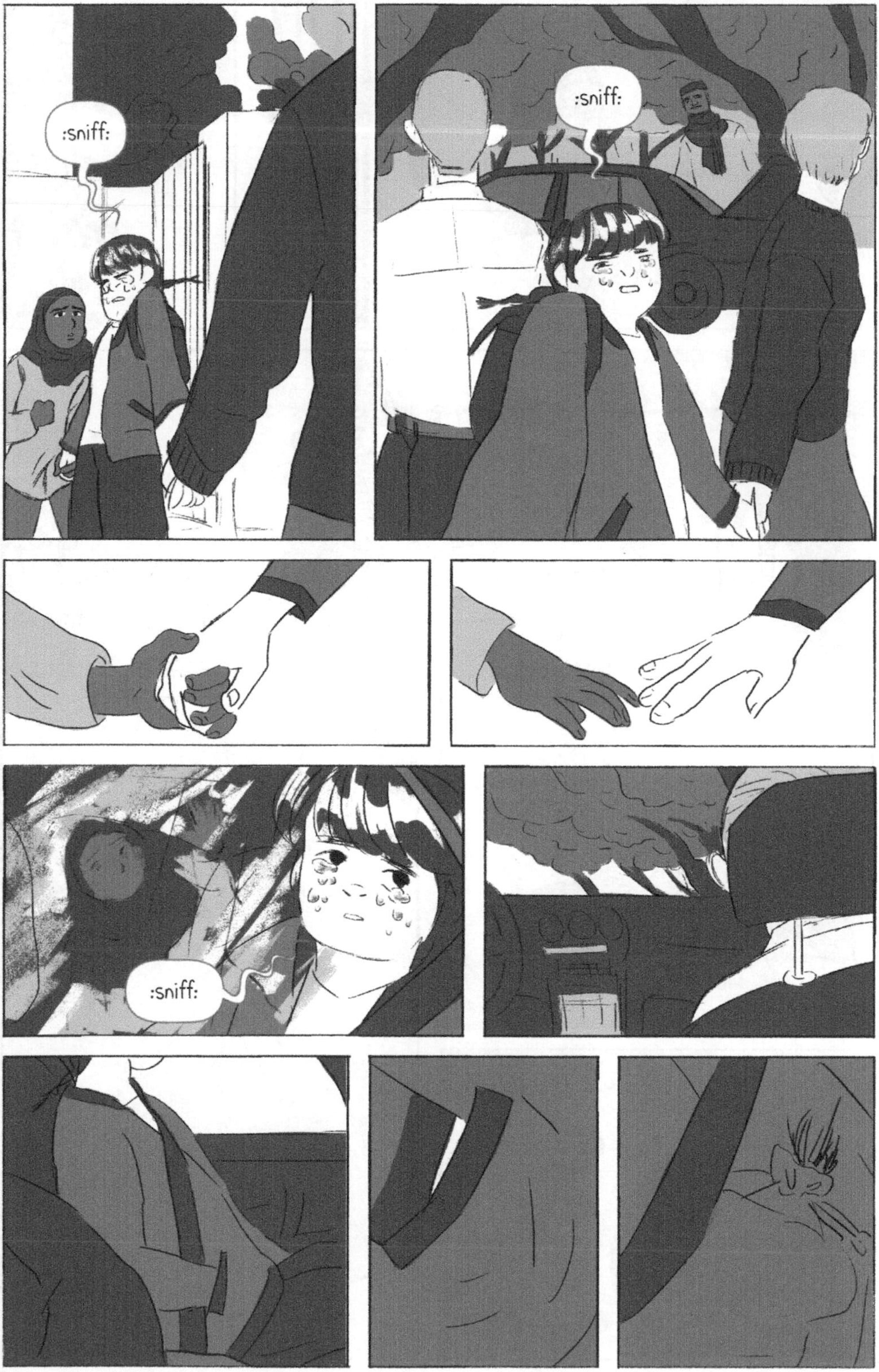
:sniff:
:sniff:
:sniff:

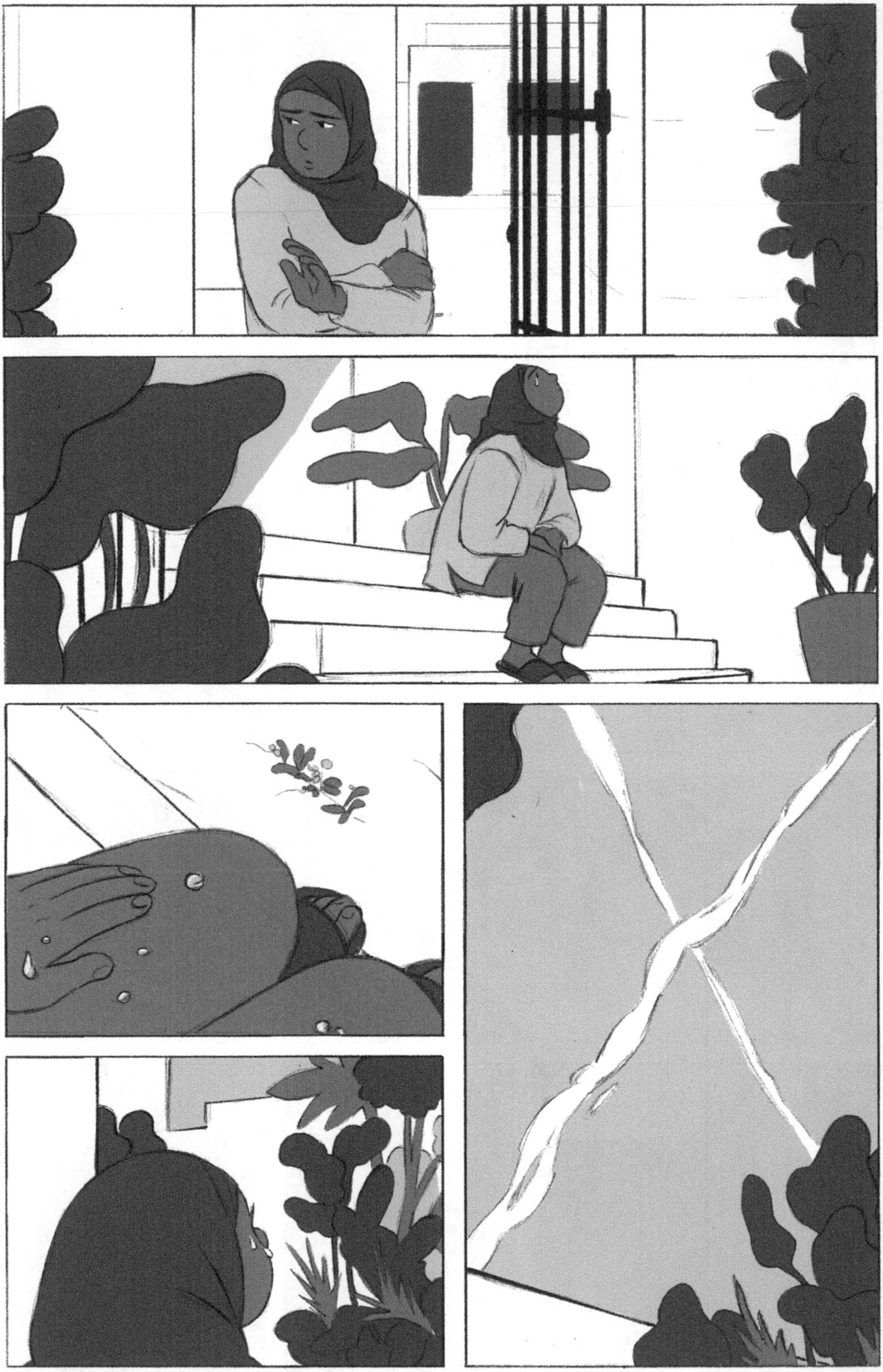

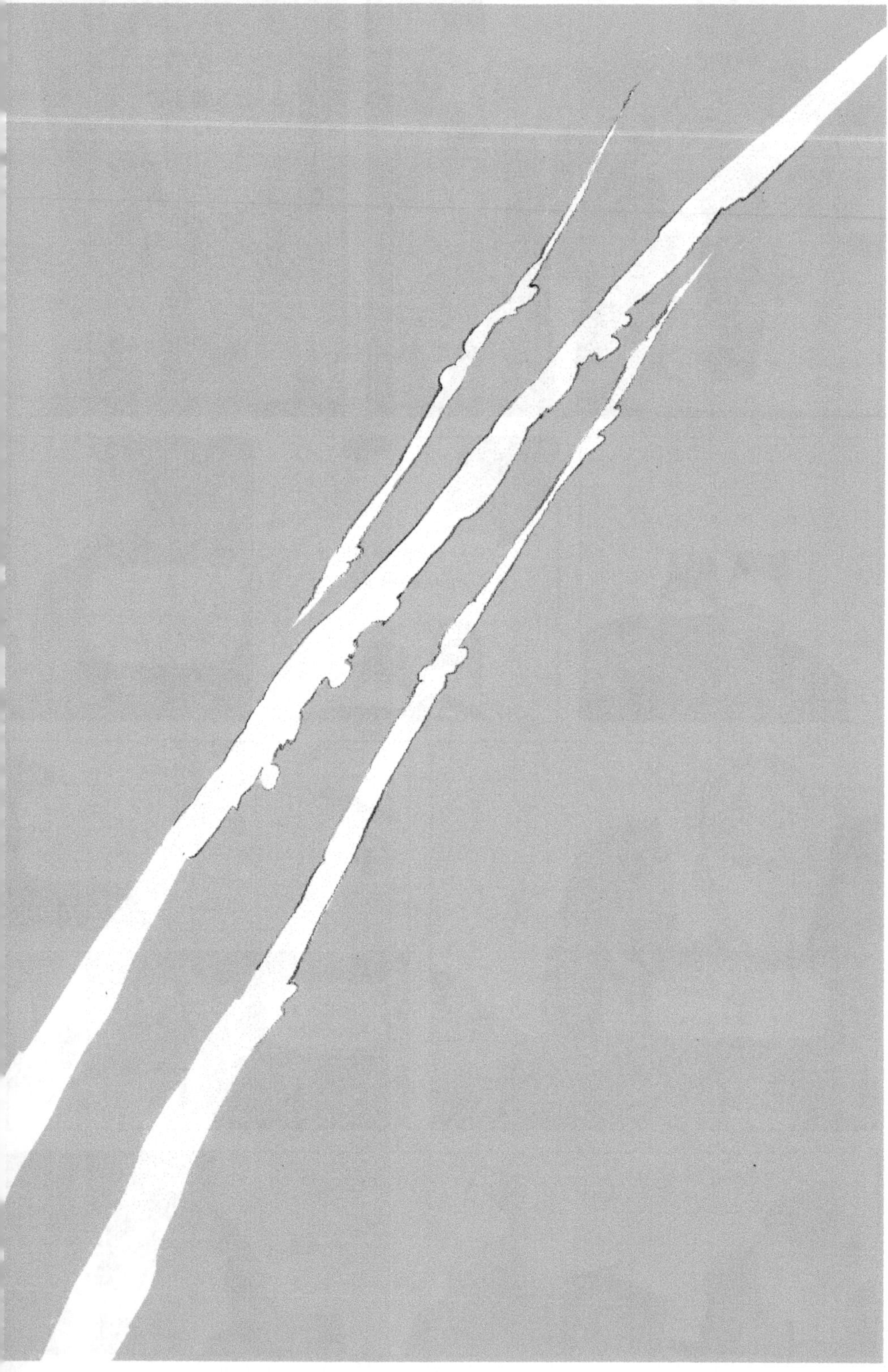

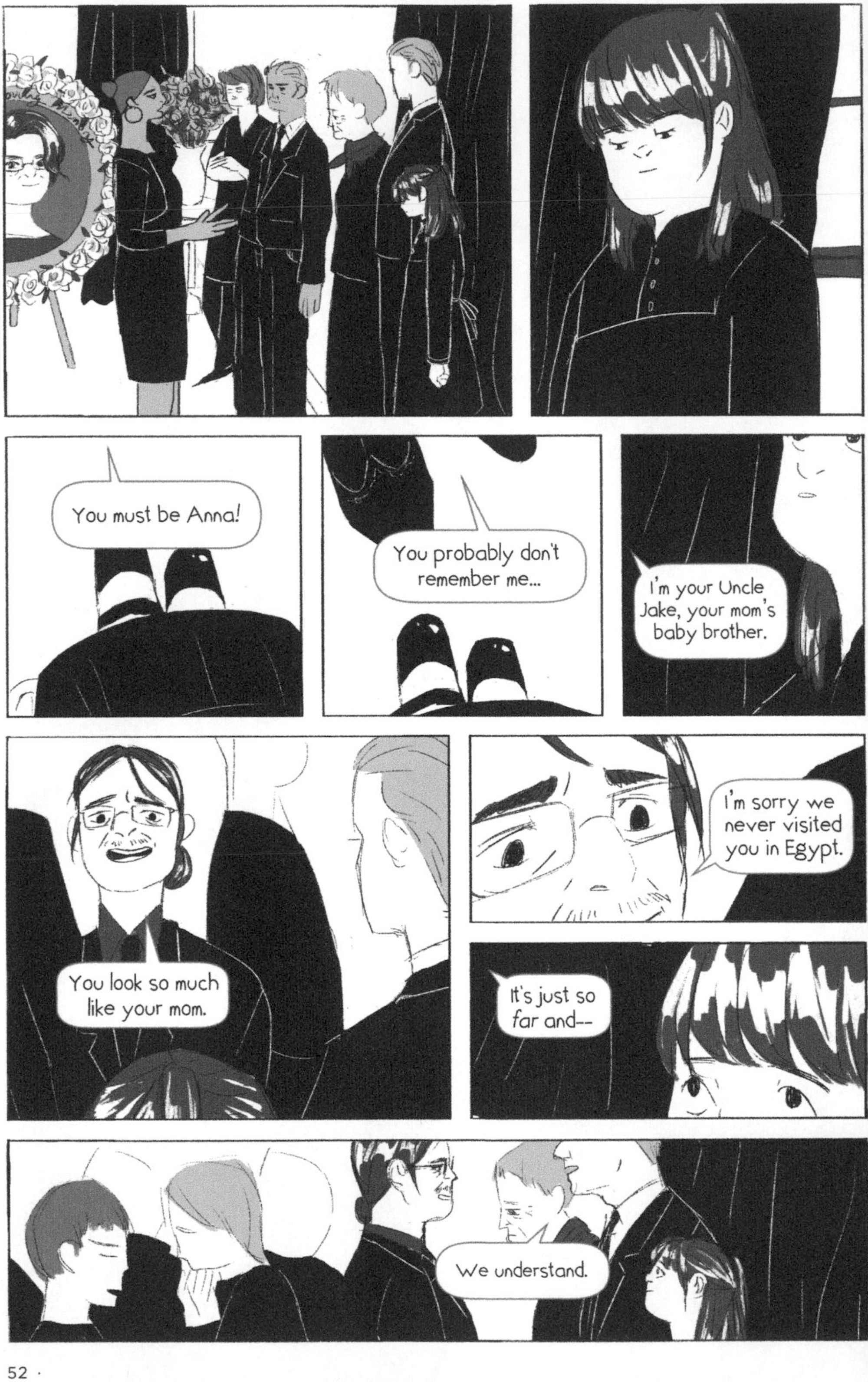
You must be Anna!
You probably don't remember me...
I'm your Uncle Jake, your mom's baby brother.
You look so much like your mom.
I'm sorry we never visited you in Egypt.
It's just so *far* and--
We understand.

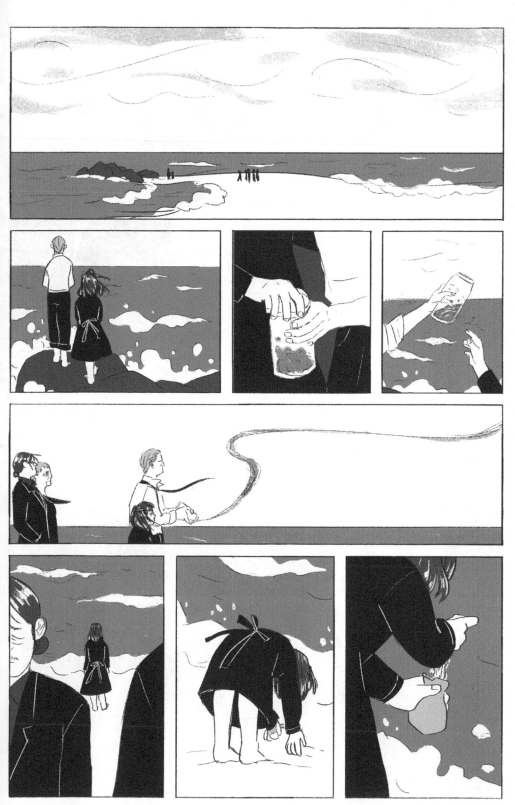

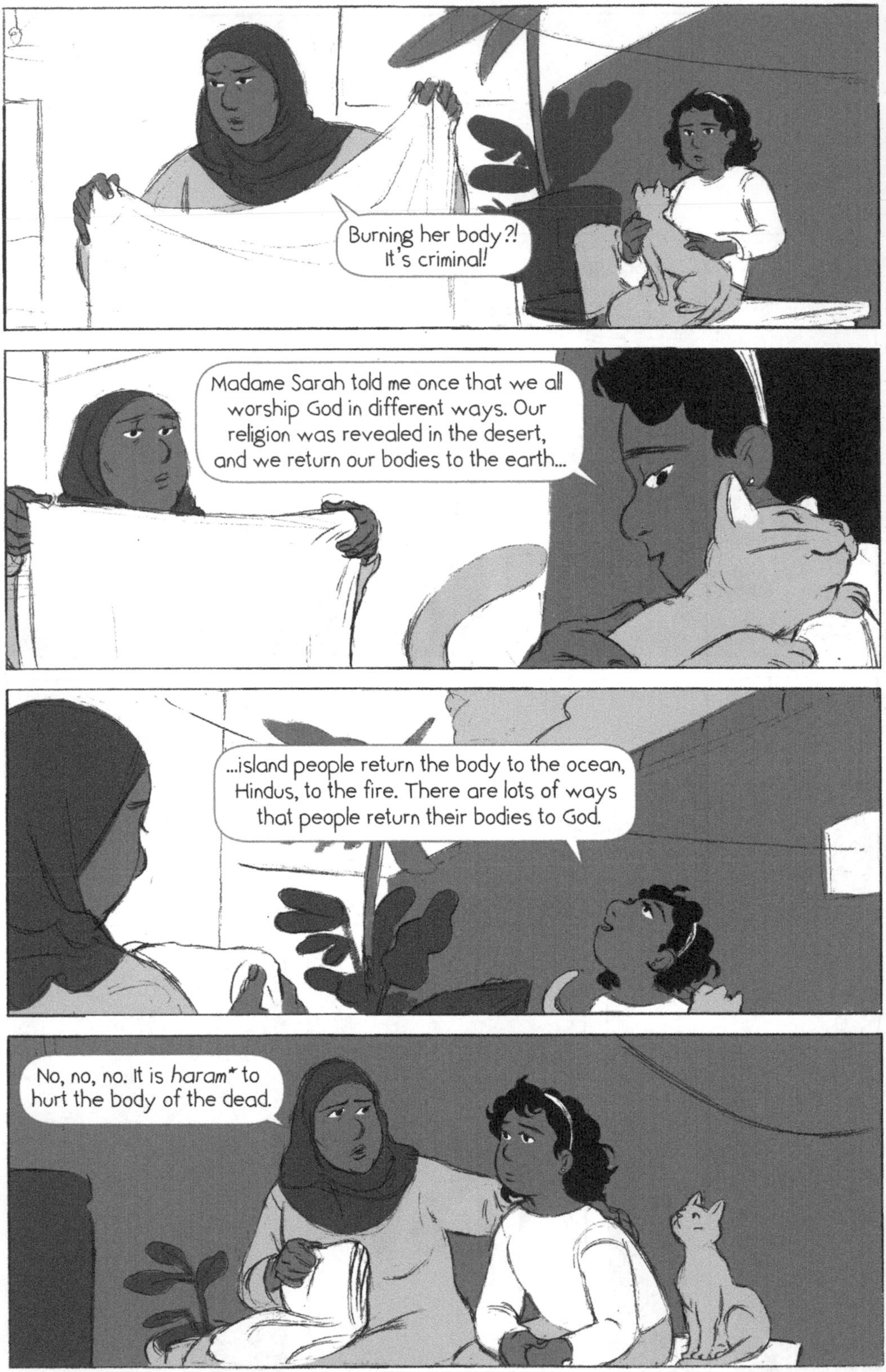

Burning her body?! It's criminal!
Madame Sarah told me once that we all worship God in different ways. Our religion was revealed in the desert, and we return our bodies to the earth...
...island people return the body to the ocean, Hindus, to the fire. There are lots of ways that people return their bodies to God.
No, no, no. It is *haram** to hurt the body of the dead.

*Forbidden or sinful

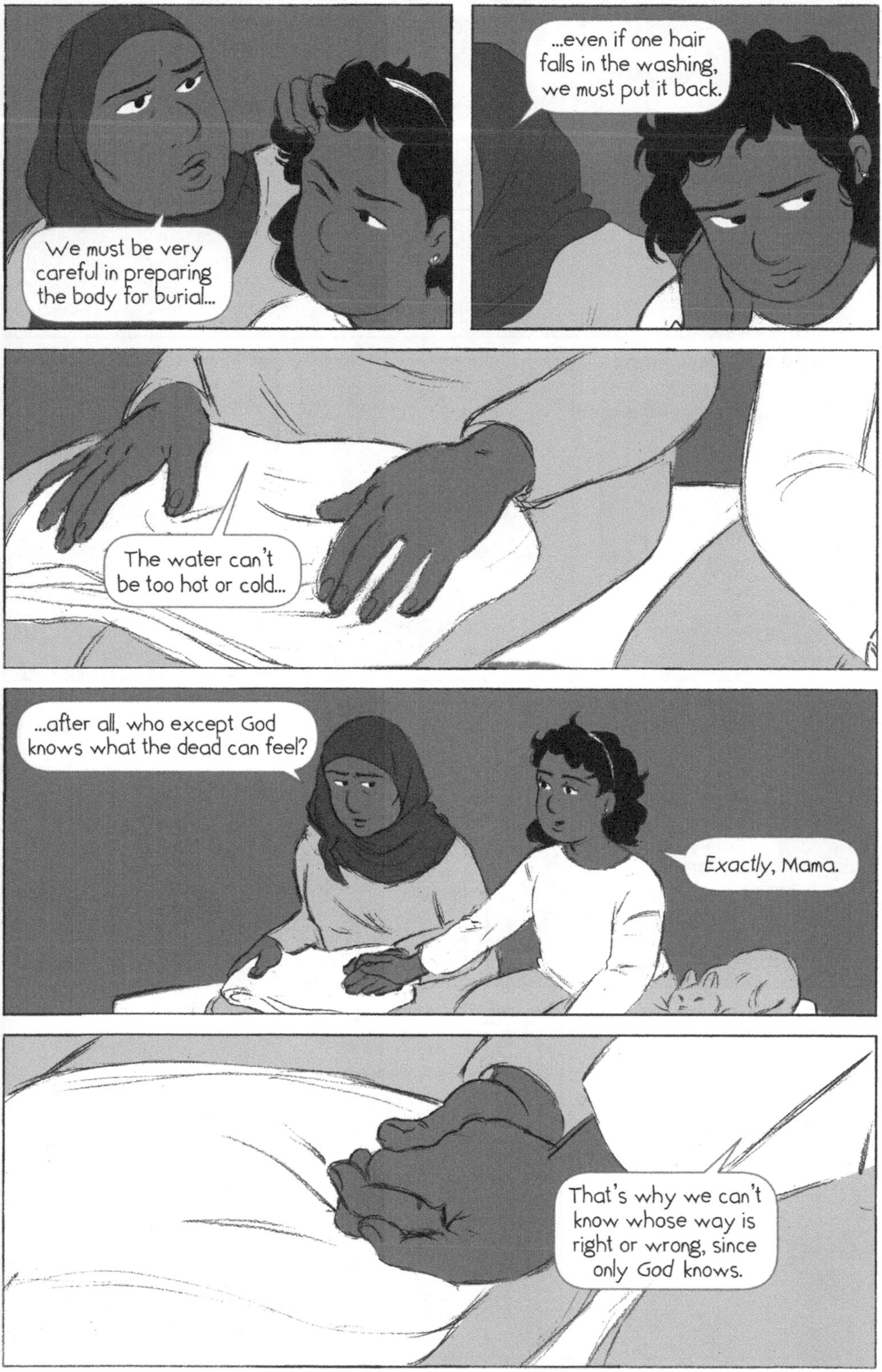
We must be very careful in preparing the body for burial...
...even if one hair falls in the washing, we must put it back.
The water can't be too hot or cold...
...after all, who except God knows what the dead can feel?
Exactly, Mama.
That's why we can't know whose way is right or wrong, since only *God* knows.

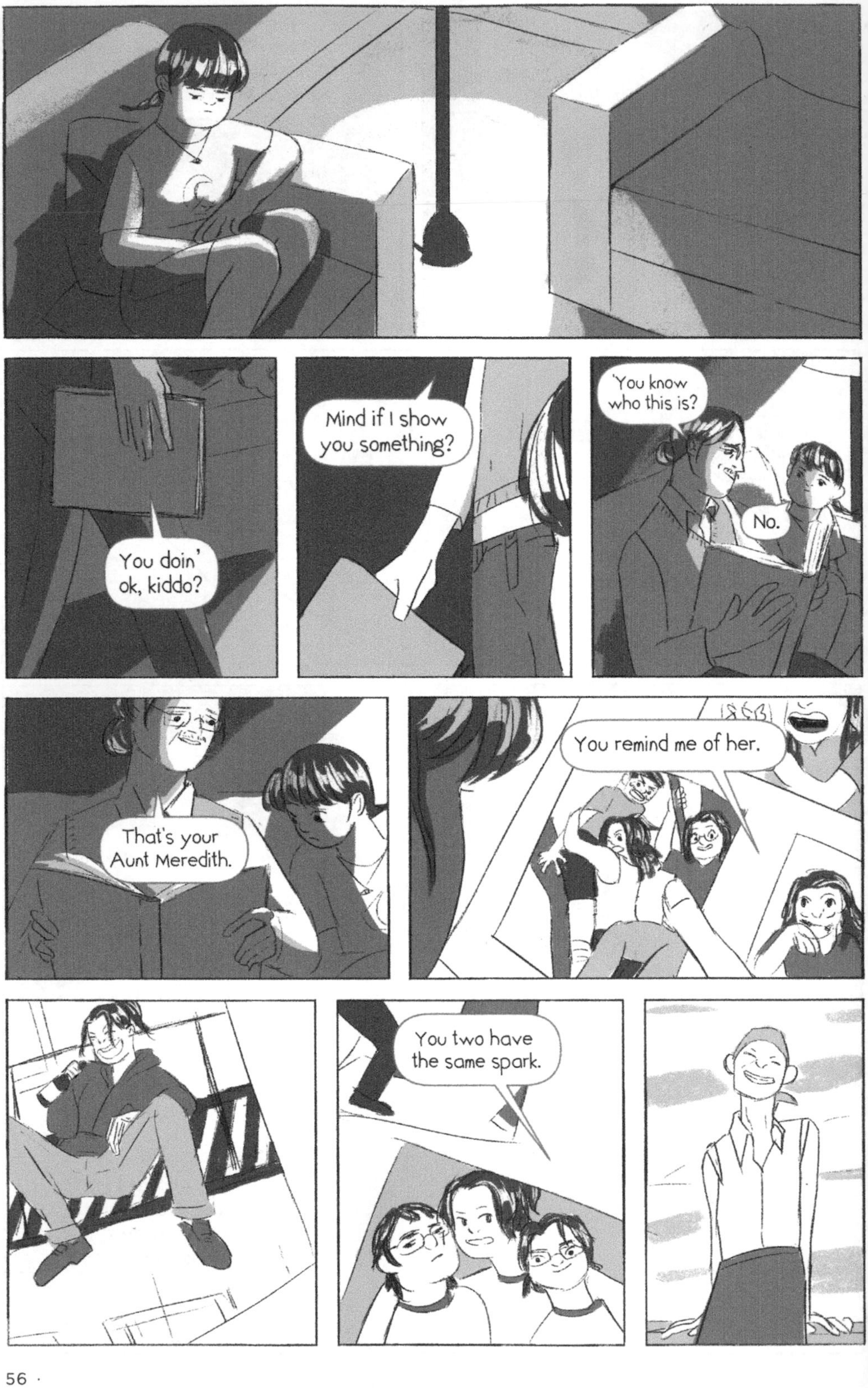
You doin' ok, kiddo?
Mind if I show you something?
'You know who this is?
No.
That's your Aunt Meredith.
You remind me of her.
You two have the same spark.

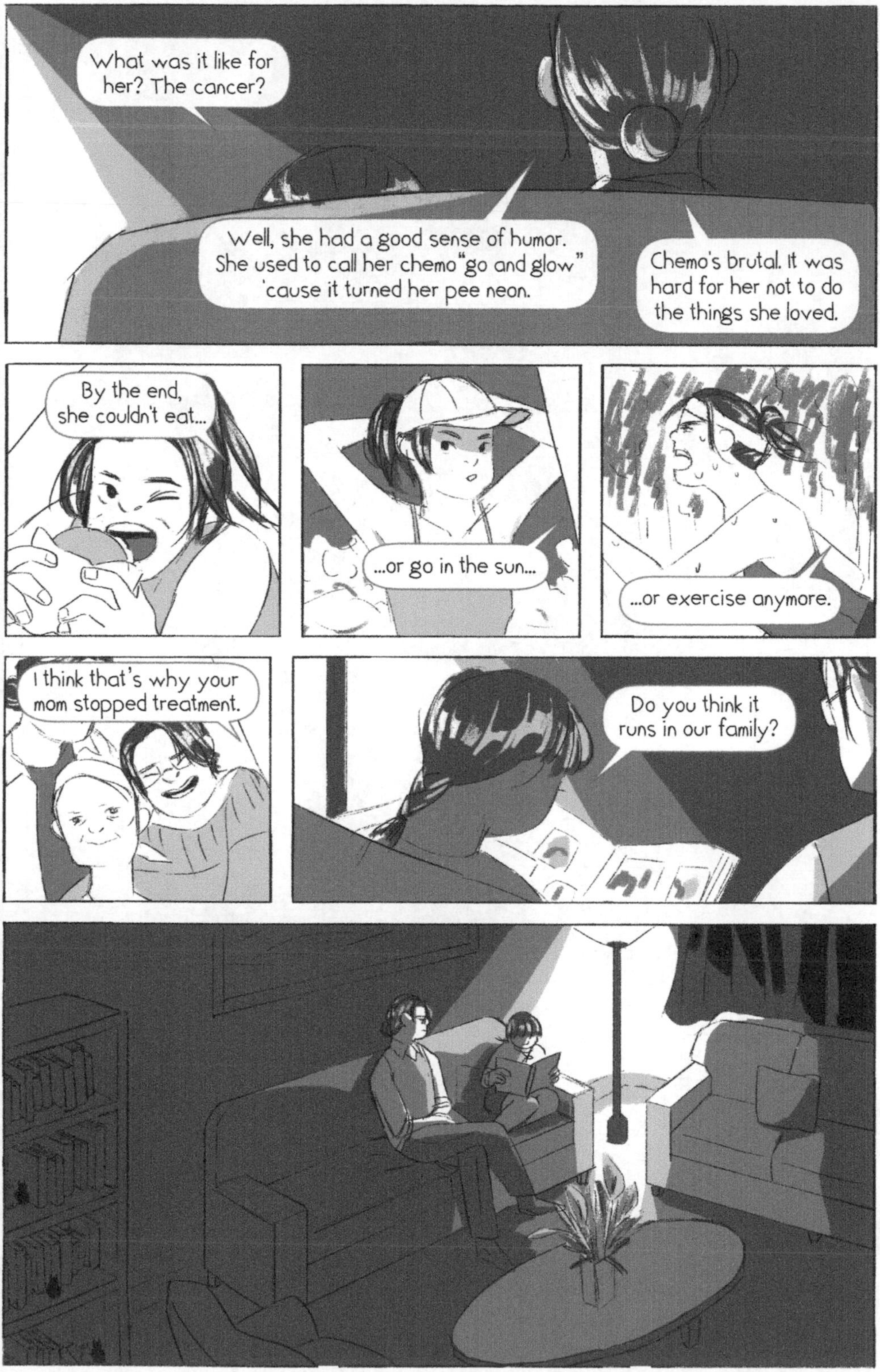
What was it like for her? The cancer?
Well, she had a good sense of humor. She used to call her chemo "go and glow" 'cause it turned her pee neon.
Chemo's brutal. It was hard for her not to do the things she loved.
By the end, she couldn't eat...
...or go in the sun...
...or exercise anymore.
I think that's why your mom stopped treatment.
Do you think it runs in our family?

PART II

FIVE YEARS LATER

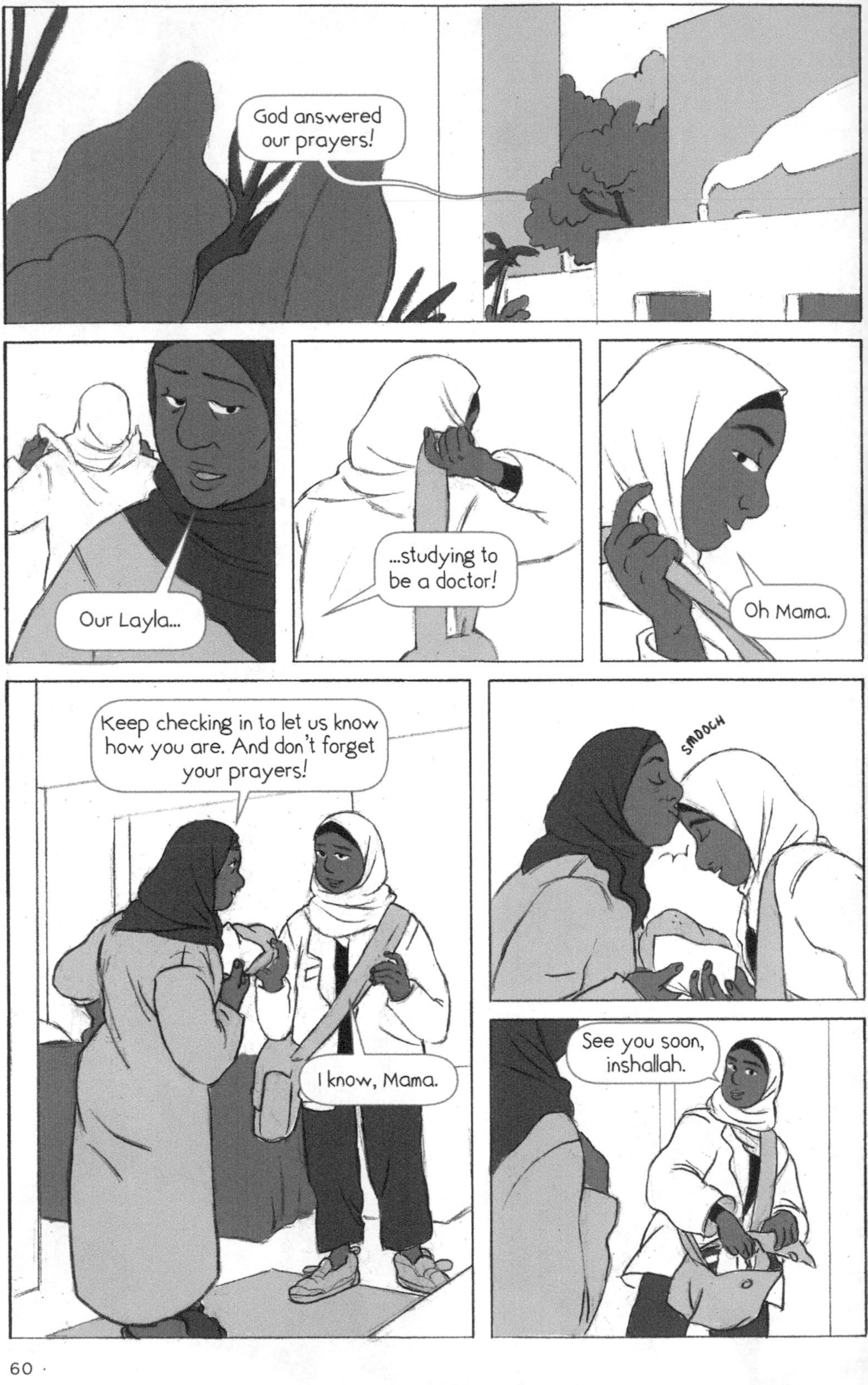
God answered our prayers!
Our Layla...
...studying to be a doctor!
Oh Mama.
Keep checking in to let us know how you are. And don't forget your prayers!
I know, Mama.
SMOOCH
See you soon, inshallah.

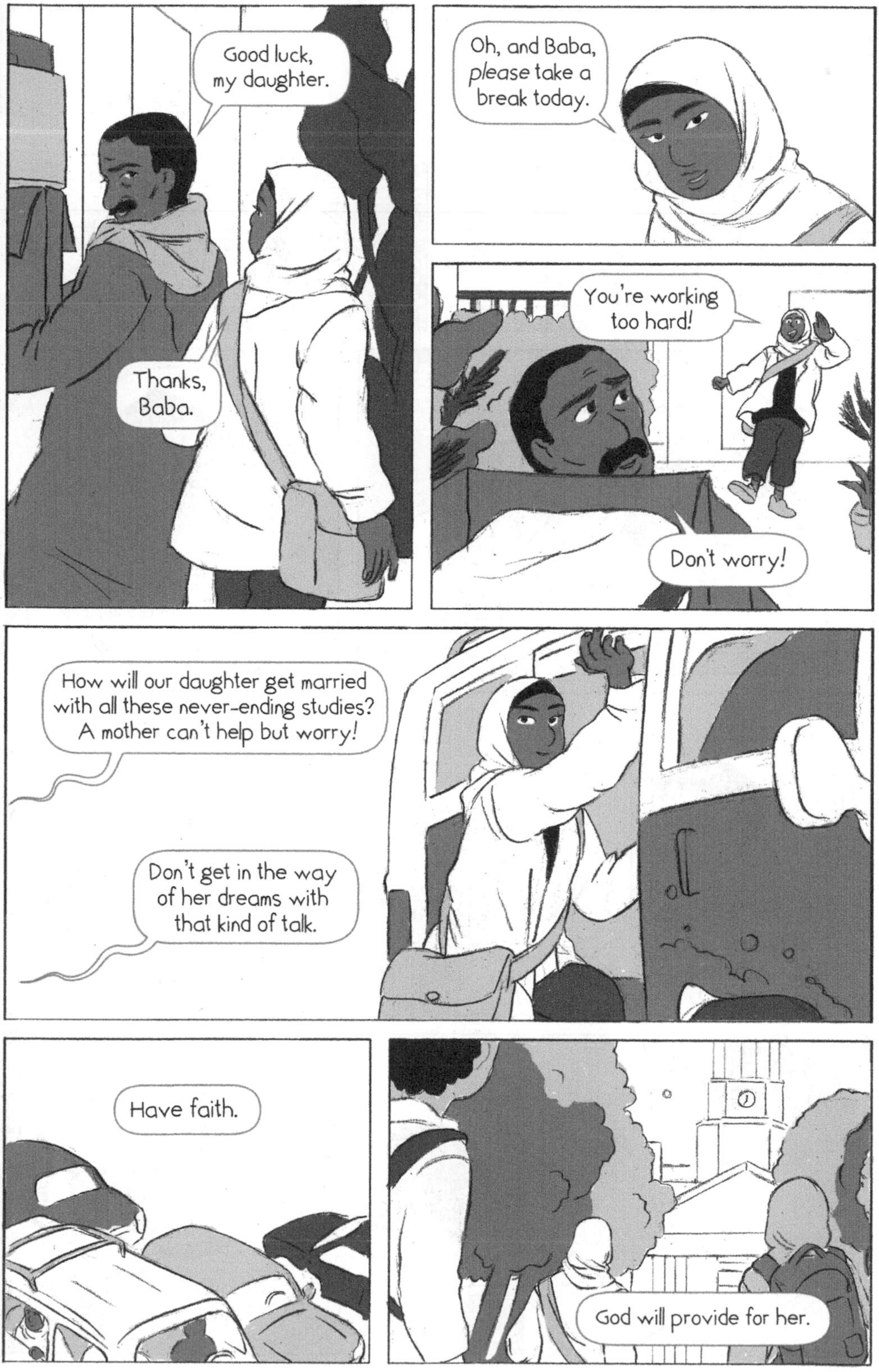
Good luck, my daughter.
Thanks, Baba.
Oh, and Baba, please take a break today.
You're working too hard!
Don't worry!
How will our daughter get married with all these never-ending studies? A mother can't help but worry!
Don't get in the way of her dreams with that kind of talk.
Have faith.
God will provide for her.

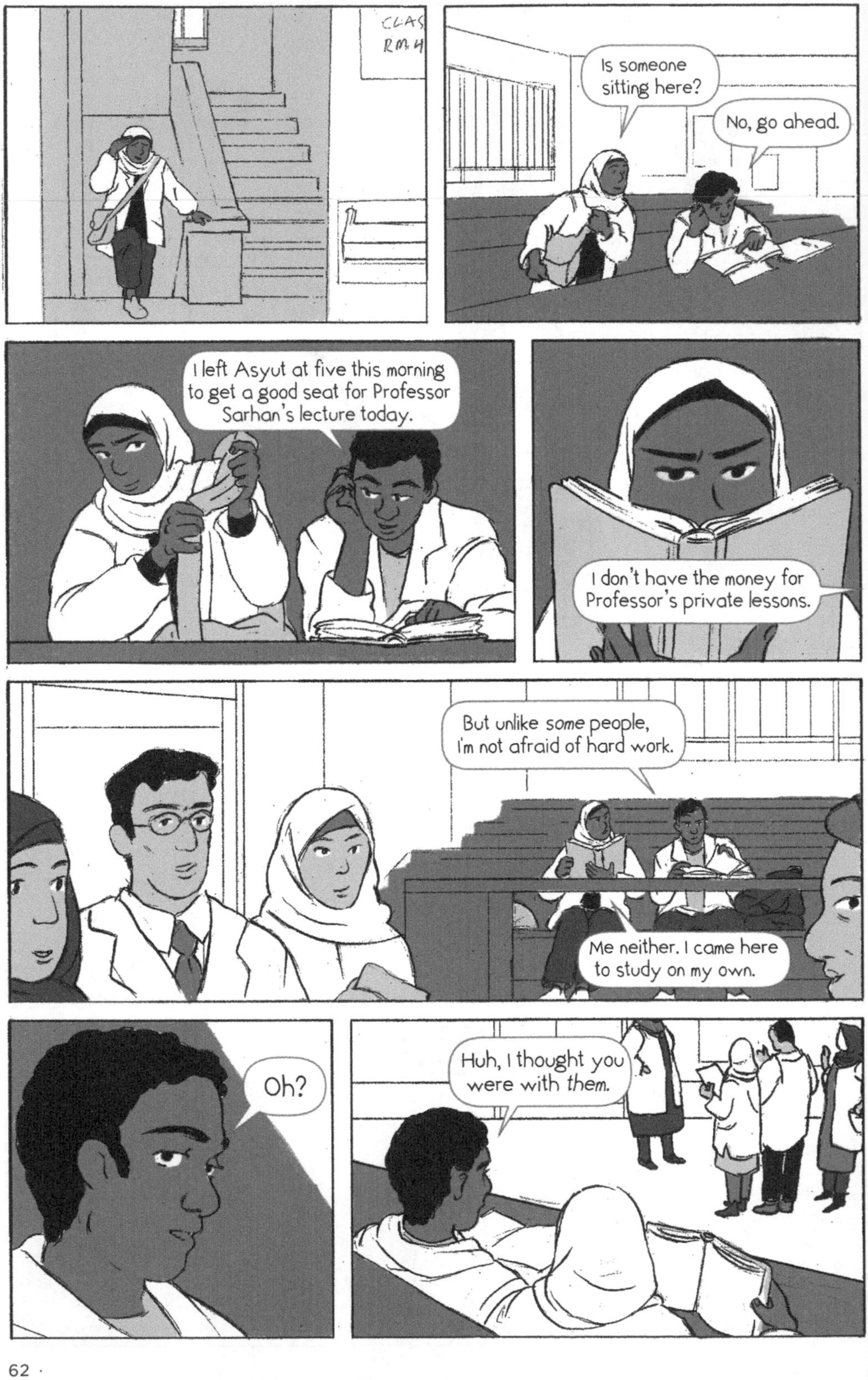
CLAS
RM. 4
Is someone sitting here?
No, go ahead.
I left Asyut at five this morning to get a good seat for Professor Sarhan's lecture today.
I don't have the money for Professor's private lessons.
But unlike *some* people, I'm not afraid of hard work.
Me neither. I came here to study on my own.
Oh?
Huh, I thought you were with *them*.

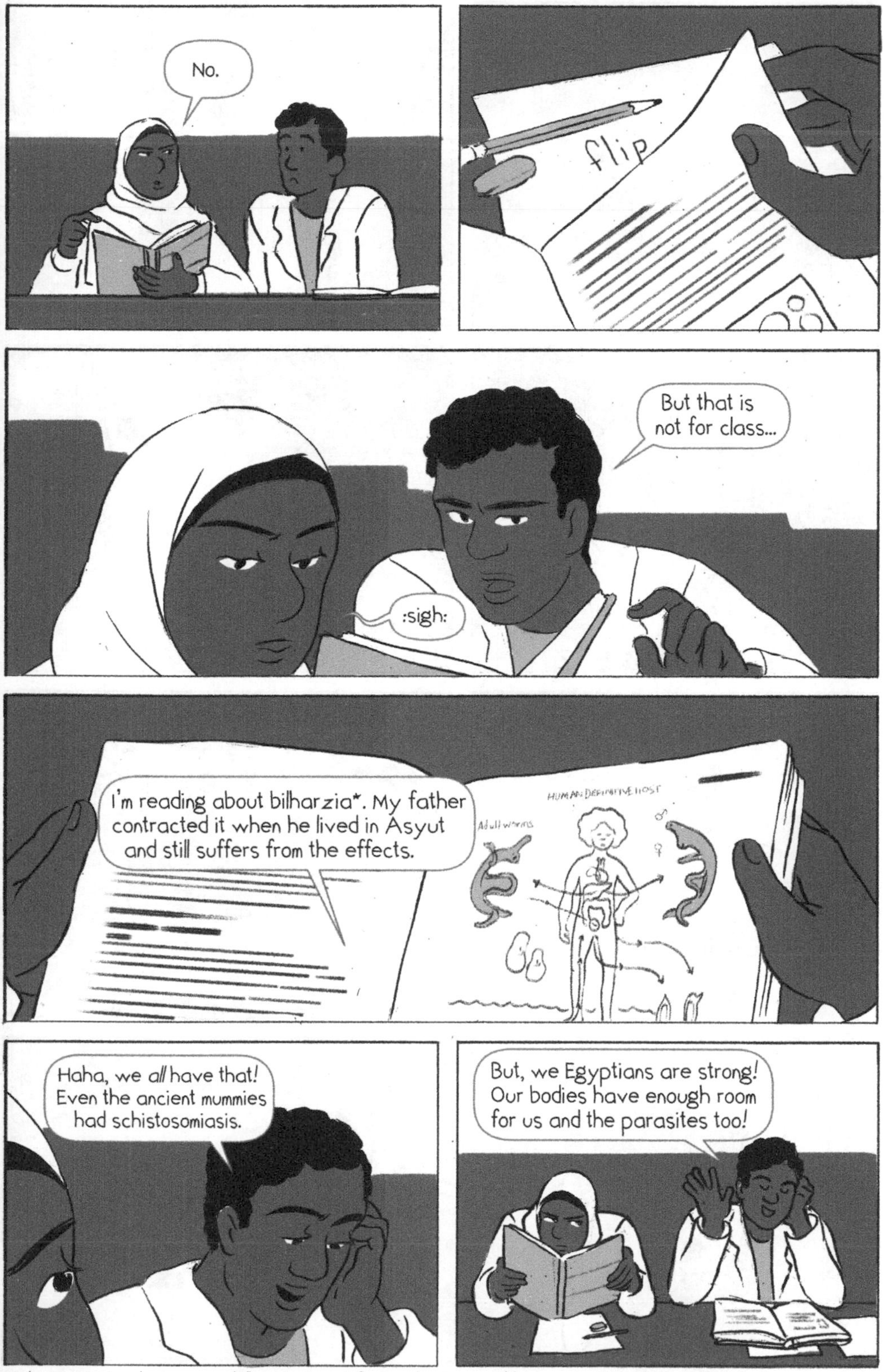
No.
flip
But that is not for class...
:sigh:
I'm reading about bilharzia*. My father contracted it when he lived in Asyut and still suffers from the effects.
HUMAN DEFINITIVE HOST
Adult worms
Haha, we *all* have that! Even the ancient mummies had schistosomiasis.
But, we Egyptians are strong! Our bodies have enough room for us and the parasites too!

*Schistosomiasis, also known as bilharzia, is an infection due to a snail-borne parasite endemic to the Nile; it can damage the bladder, kidneys, and liver.

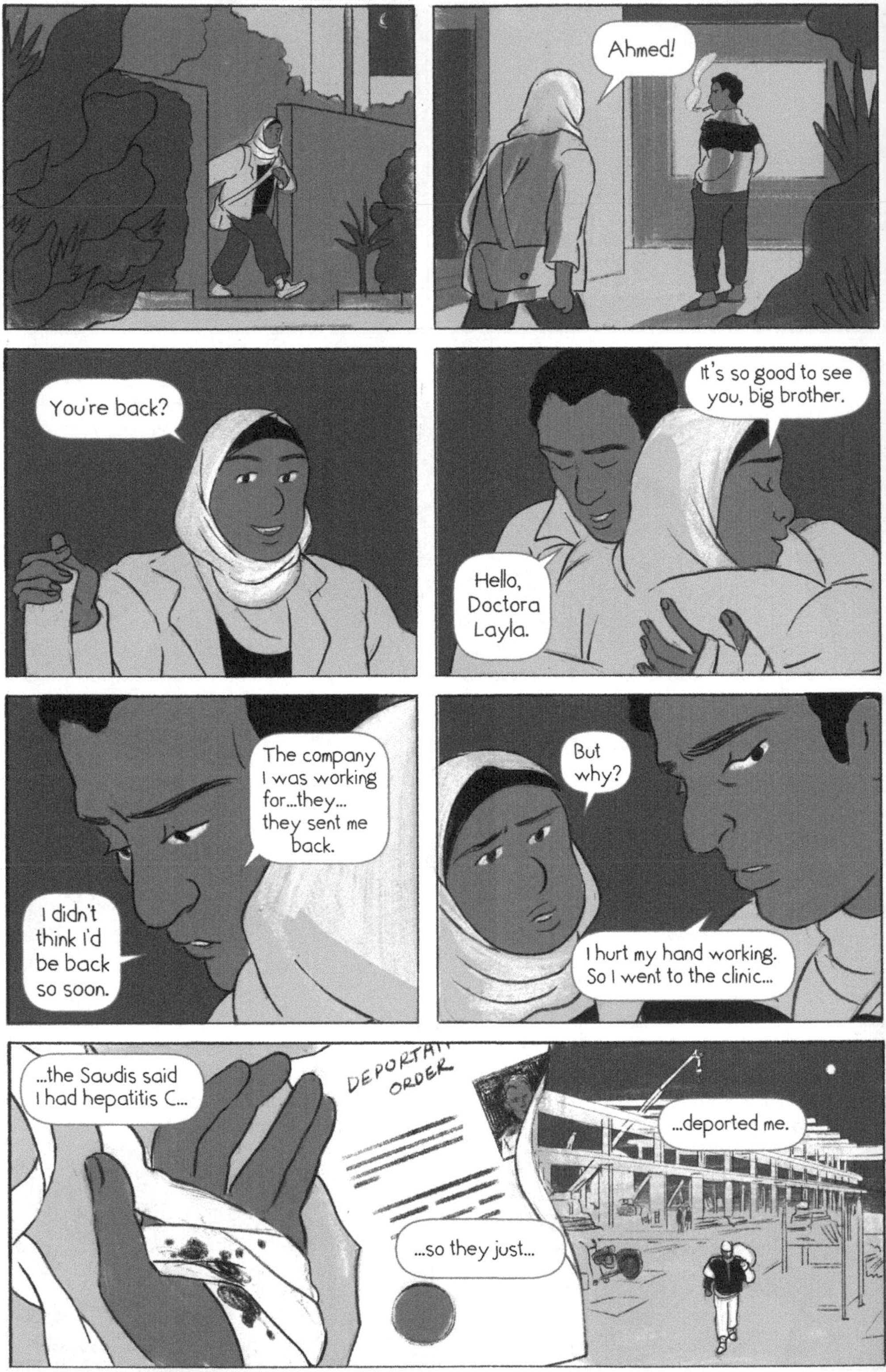
Ahmed!
You're back?
It's so good to see you, big brother.
Hello, Doctora Layla.
The company I was working for...they... they sent me back.
I didn't think I'd be back so soon.
But why?
I hurt my hand working. So I went to the clinic...
...the Saudis said I had hepatitis C...
DEPORTATI ORDER
...so they just...
...deported me.

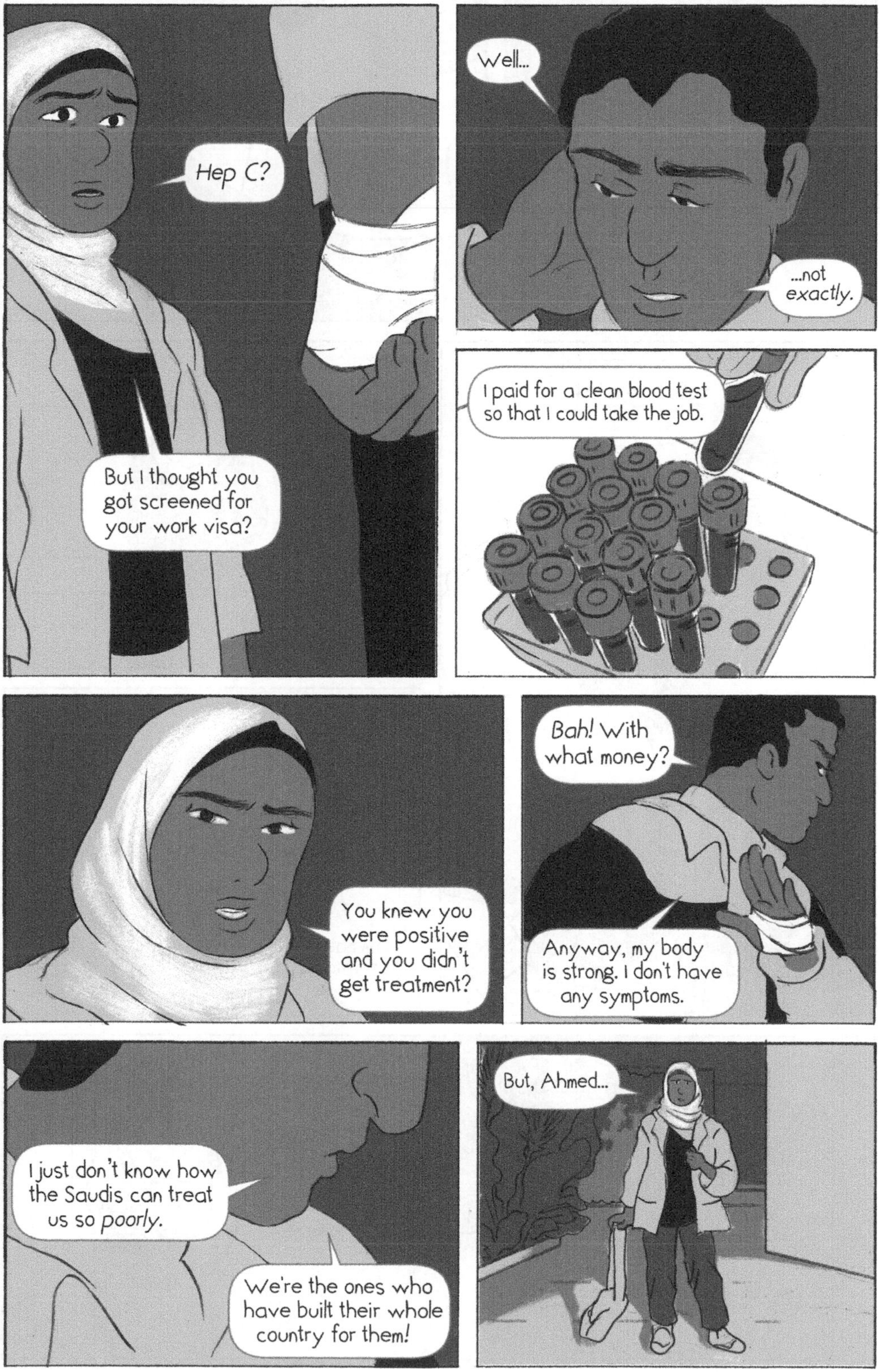
Hep C?
But I thought you got screened for your work visa?
Well...
...not *exactly*.
I paid for a clean blood test so that I could take the job.
You knew you were positive and you didn't get treatment?
Bah! With what money?
Anyway, my body is strong. I don't have any symptoms.
I just don't know how the Saudis can treat us so *poorly*.
We're the ones who have built their whole country for them!
But, Ahmed...

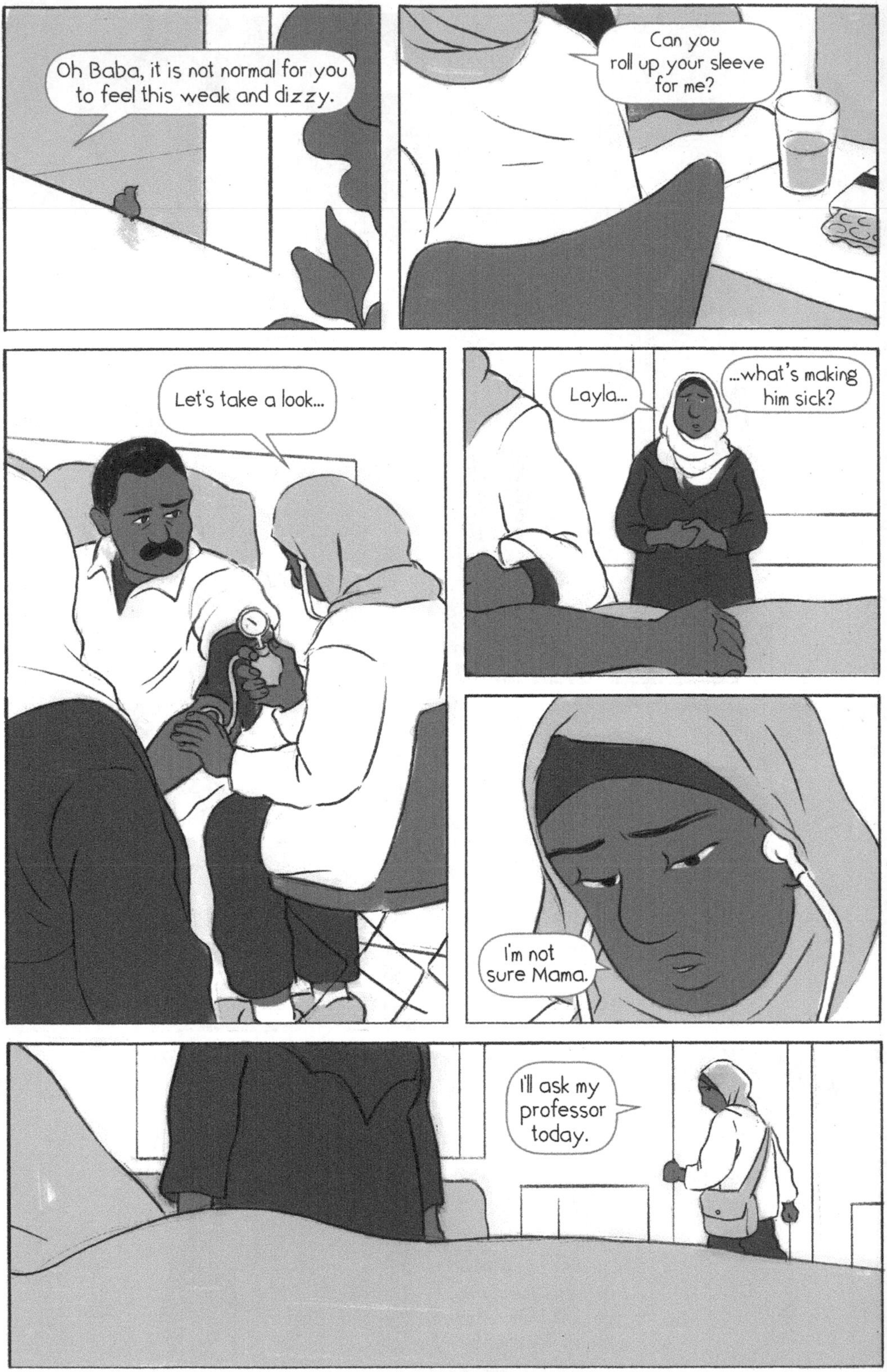
Oh Baba, it is not normal for you to feel this weak and dizzy.
Can you roll up your sleeve for me?
Let's take a look...
Layla...
...what's making him sick?
I'm not sure Mama.
I'll ask my professor today.

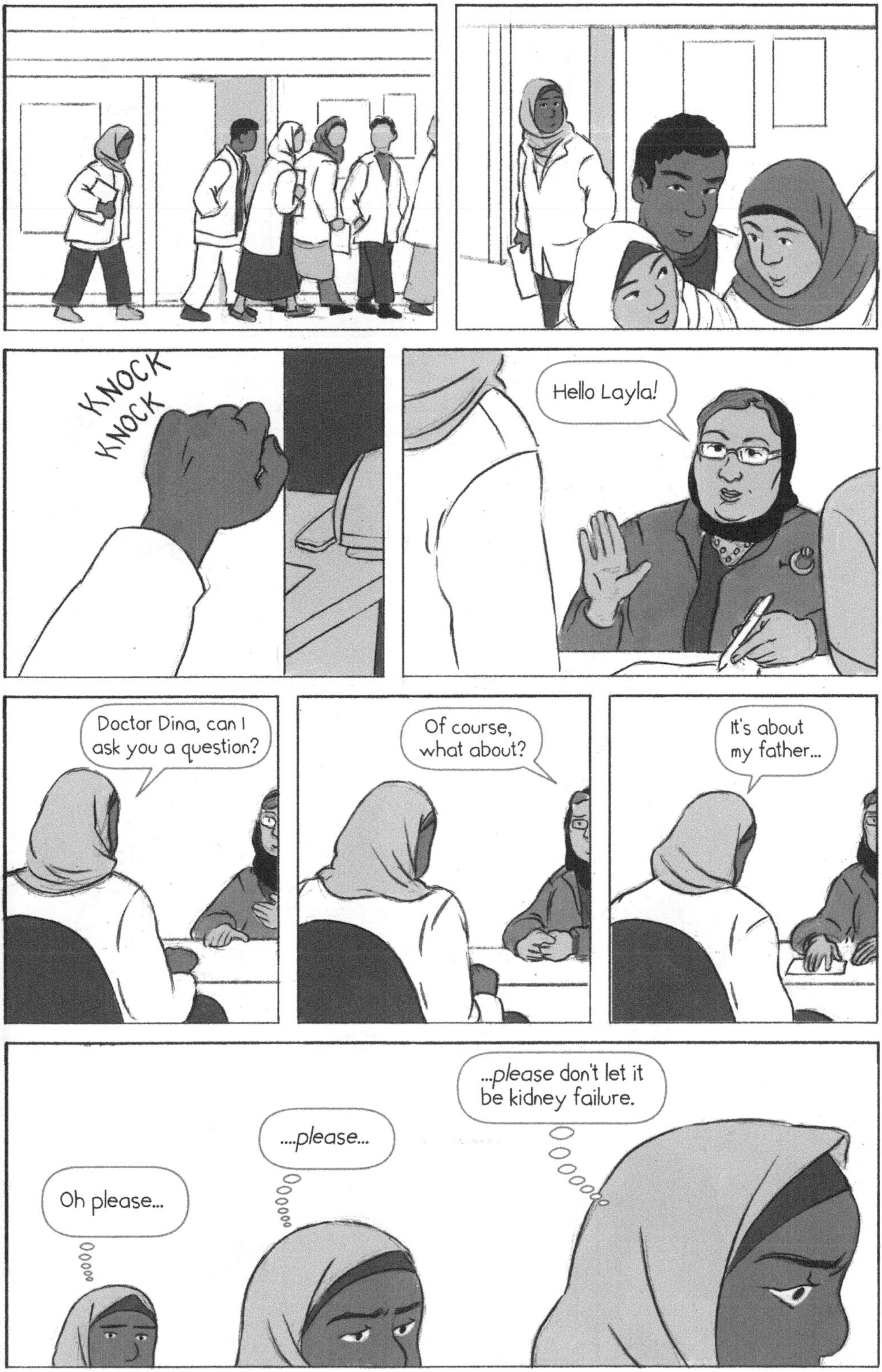
KNOCK
KNOCK
Hello Layla!
Doctor Dina, can I ask you a question?
Of course, what about?
It's about my father...
Oh please...
....*please*...
...*please* don't let it be kidney failure.

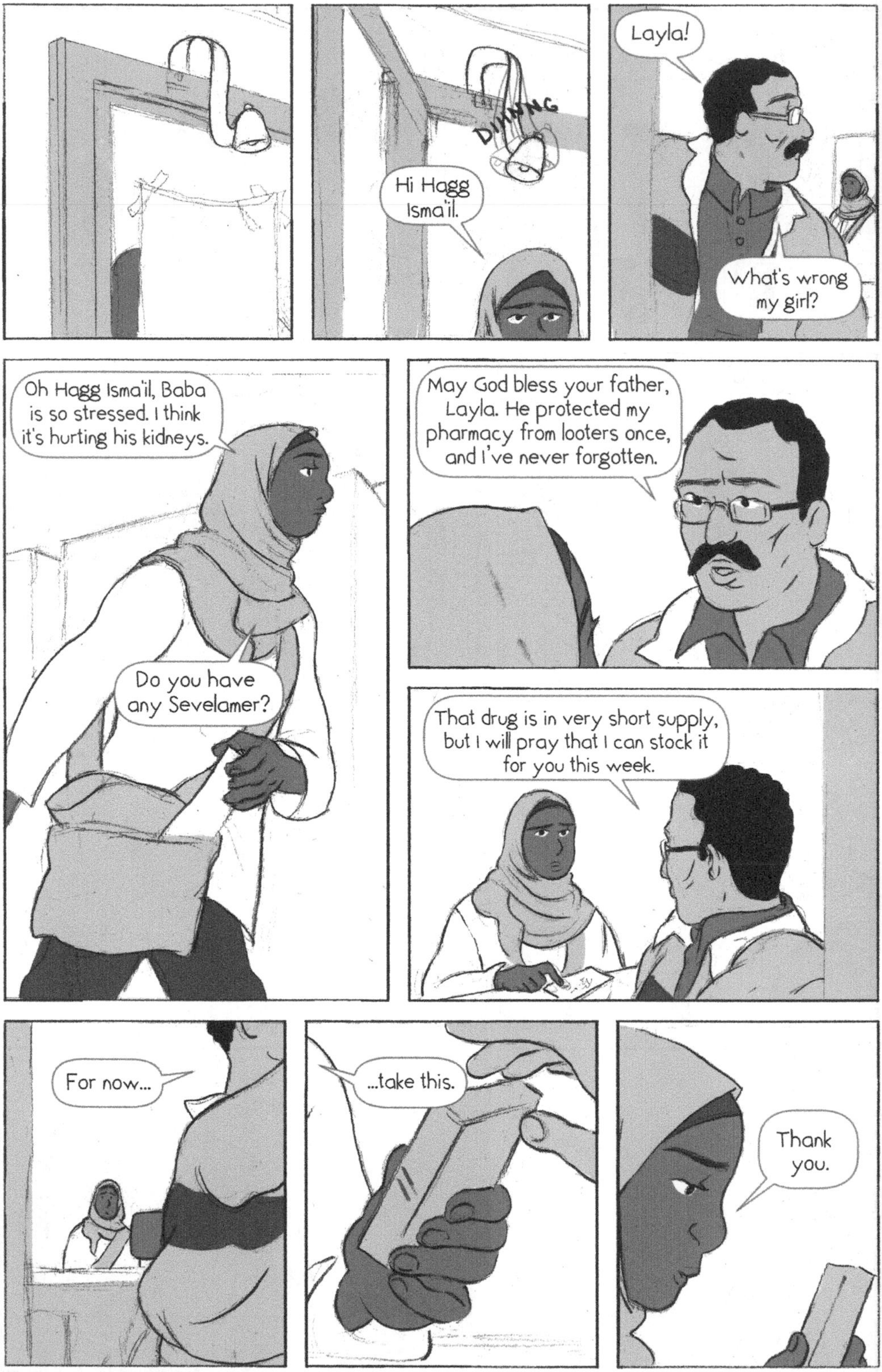
DIIINNG
Hi Hagg Isma'il.
Layla!
What's wrong my girl?
Oh Hagg Isma'il, Baba is so stressed. I think it's hurting his kidneys.
Do you have any Sevelamer?
May God bless your father, Layla. He protected my pharmacy from looters once, and I've never forgotten.
That drug is in very short supply, but I will pray that I can stock it for you this week.
For now...
...take this.
Thank you.

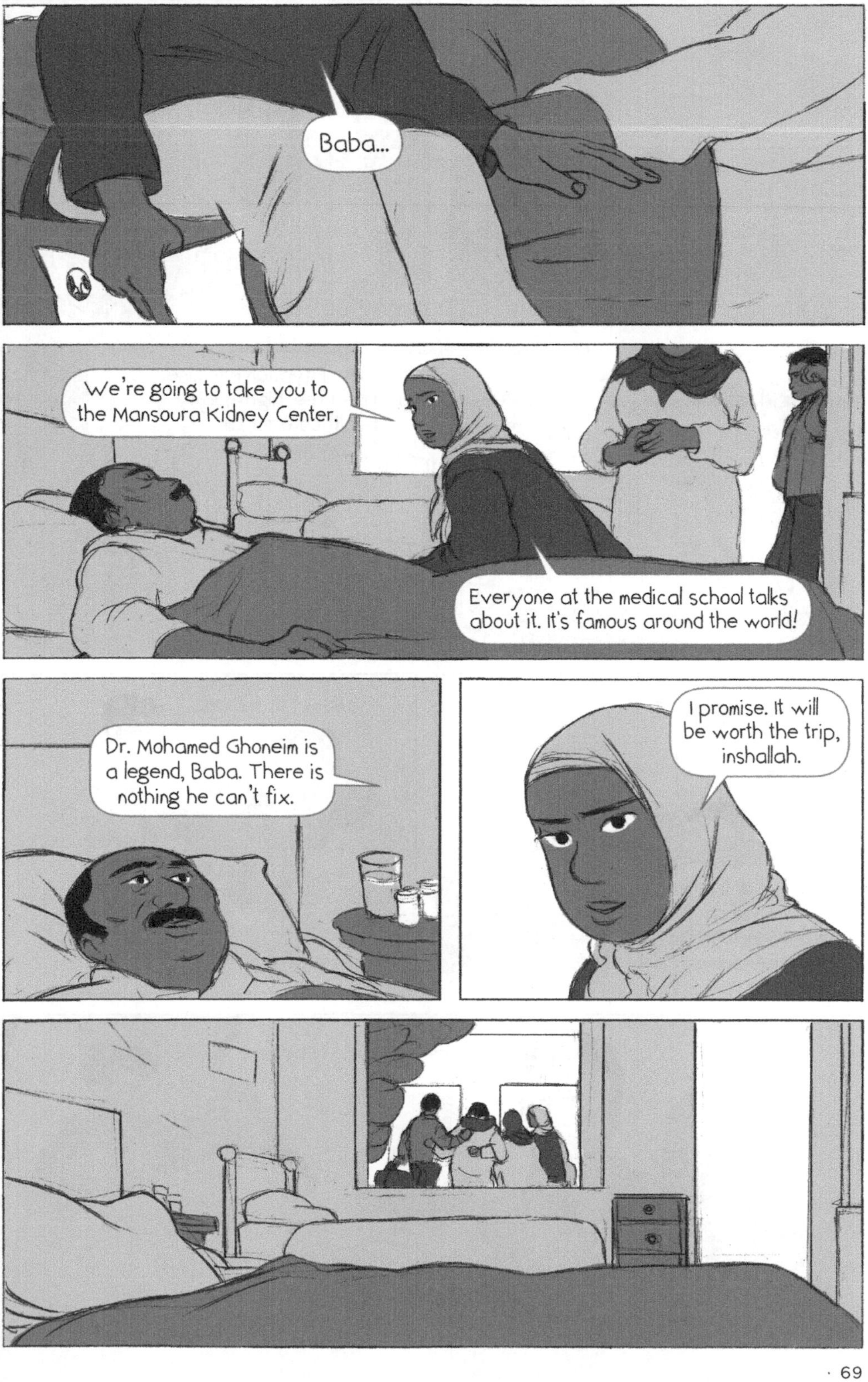
Baba...
We're going to take you to the Mansoura Kidney Center.
Everyone at the medical school talks about it. It's famous around the world!
Dr. Mohamed Ghoneim is a legend, Baba. There is nothing he can't fix.
I promise. It will be worth the trip, inshallah.

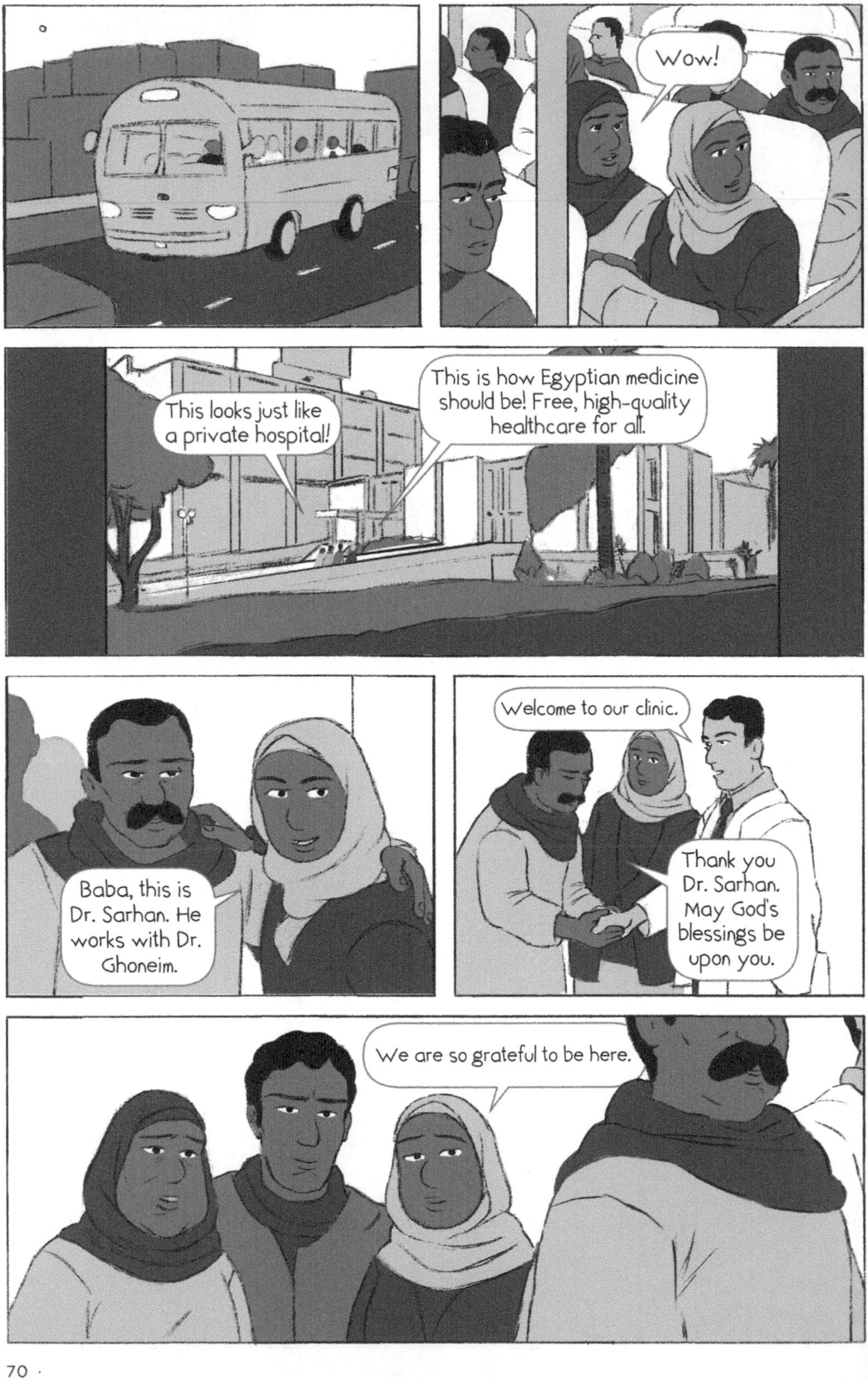
Wow!
This looks just like a private hospital!
This is how Egyptian medicine should be! Free, high-quality healthcare for all.
Baba, this is Dr. Sarhan. He works with Dr. Ghoneim.
Welcome to our clinic.
Thank you Dr. Sarhan. May God's blessings be upon you.
We are so grateful to be here.

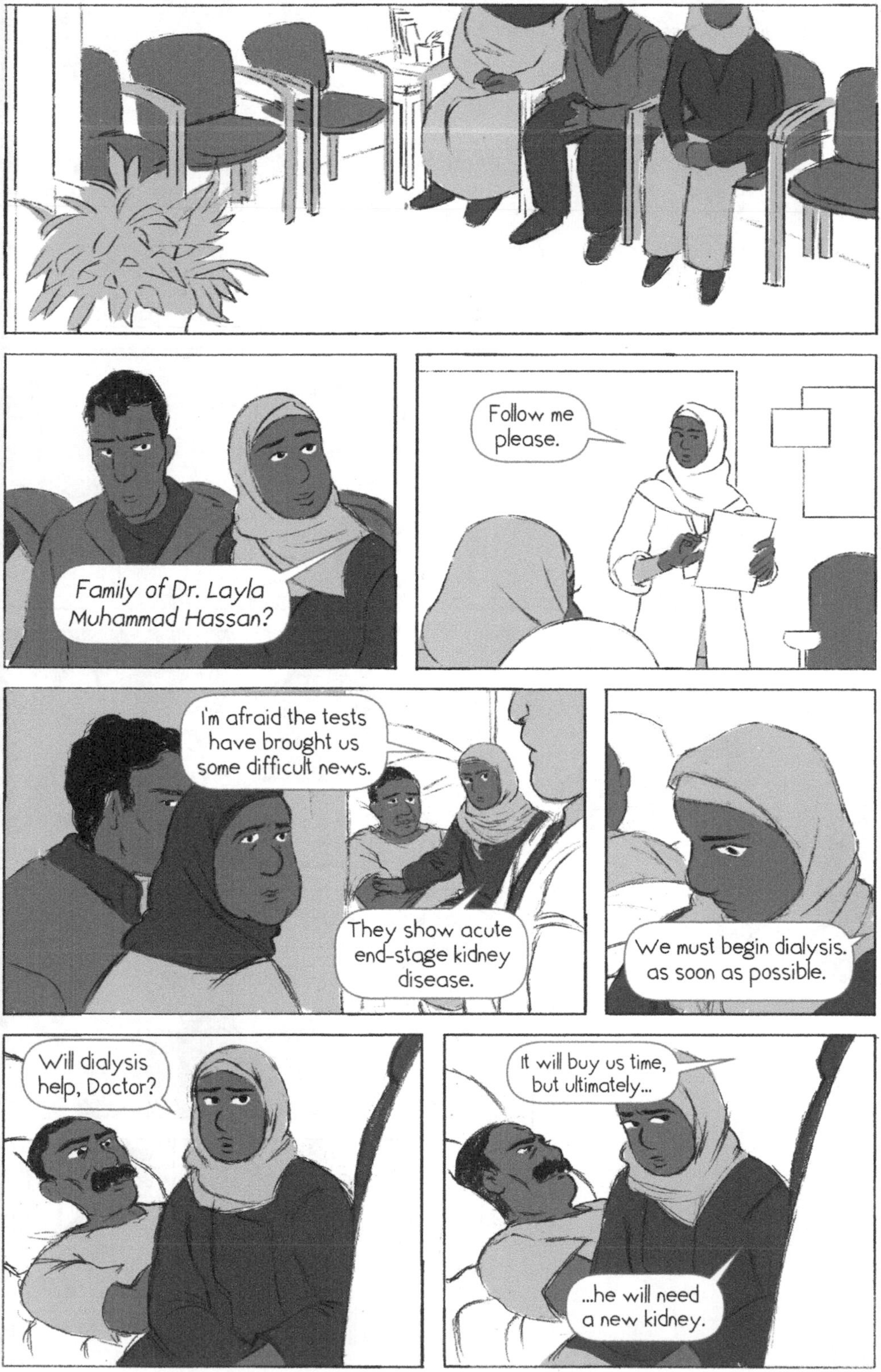
Family of Dr. Layla Muhammad Hassan?
Follow me please.
I'm afraid the tests have brought us some difficult news.
They show acute end-stage kidney disease.
We must begin dialysis. as soon as possible.
Will dialysis help, Doctor?
It will buy us time, but ultimately...
...he will need a new kidney.

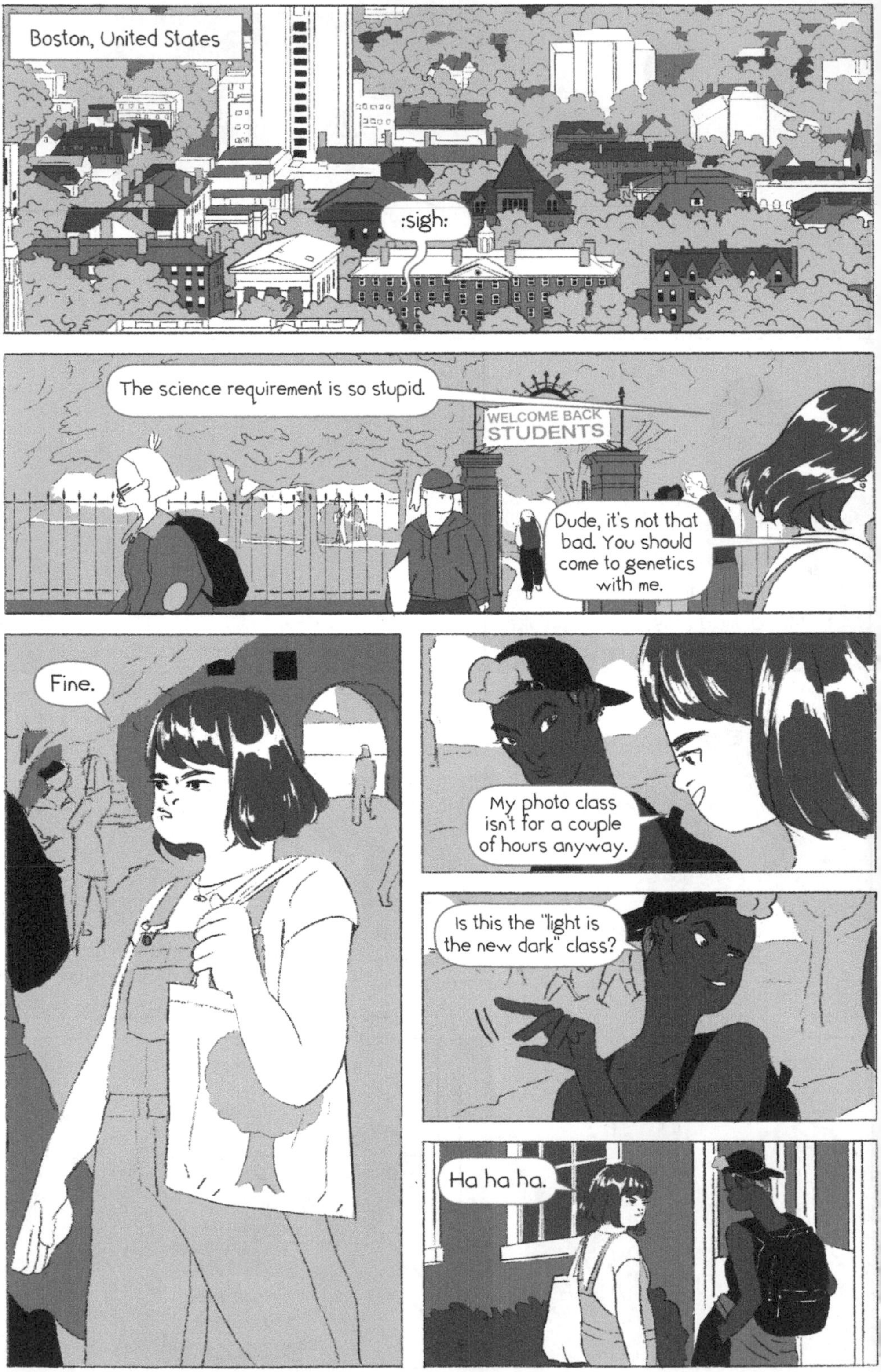
Boston, United States
:sigh:
The science requirement is so stupid.
WELCOME BACK STUDENTS
Dude, it's not that bad. You should come to genetics with me.
Fine.
My photo class isn't for a couple of hours anyway.
Is this the "light is the new dark" class?
Ha ha ha.

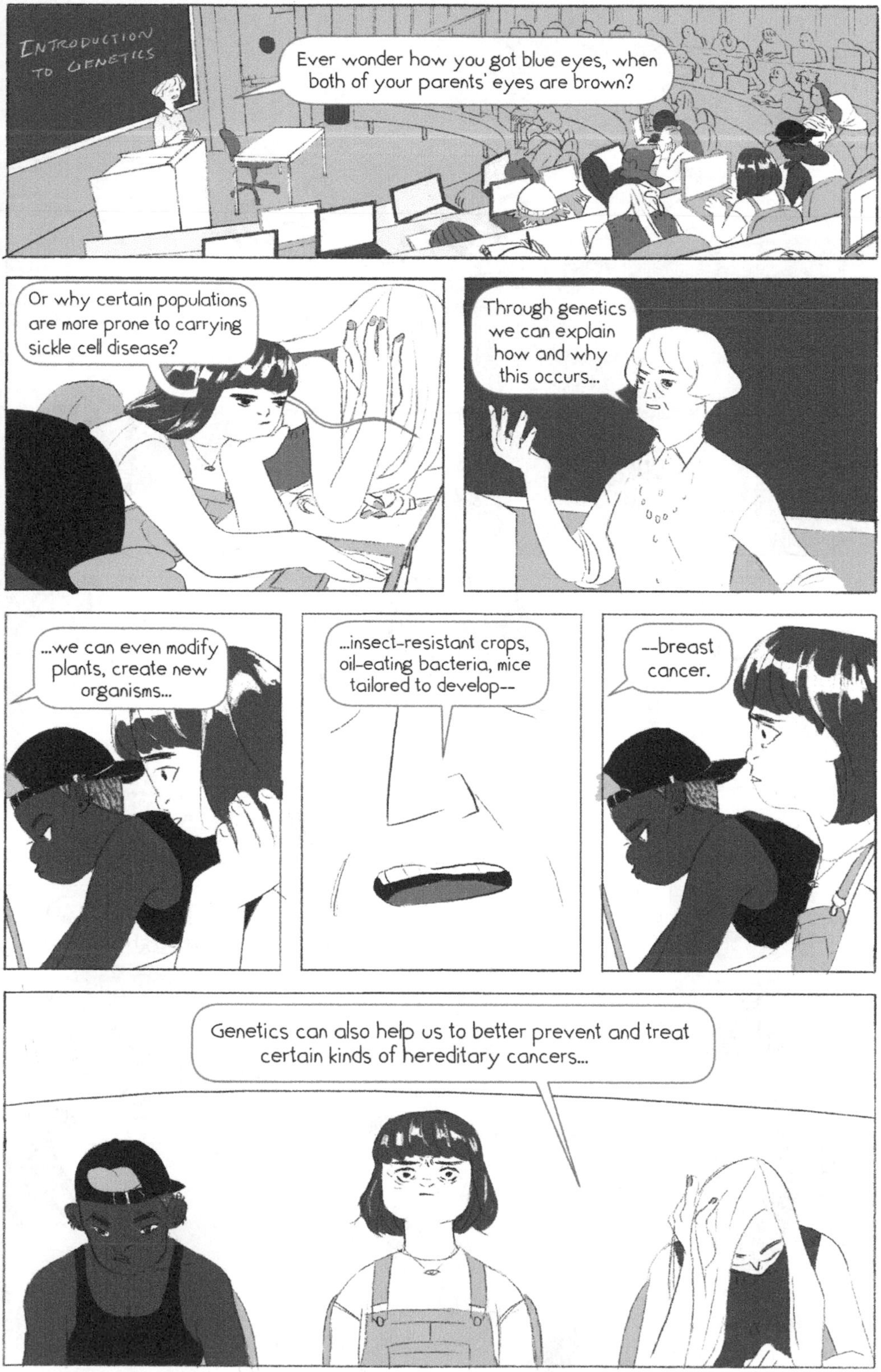
INTRODUCTION TO GENETICS
Ever wonder how you got blue eyes, when both of your parents' eyes are brown?
Or why certain populations are more prone to carrying sickle cell disease?
Through genetics we can explain how and why this occurs...
...we can even modify plants, create new organisms...
...insect-resistant crops, oil-eating bacteria, mice tailored to develop--
--breast cancer.
Genetics can also help us to better prevent and treat certain kinds of hereditary cancers...

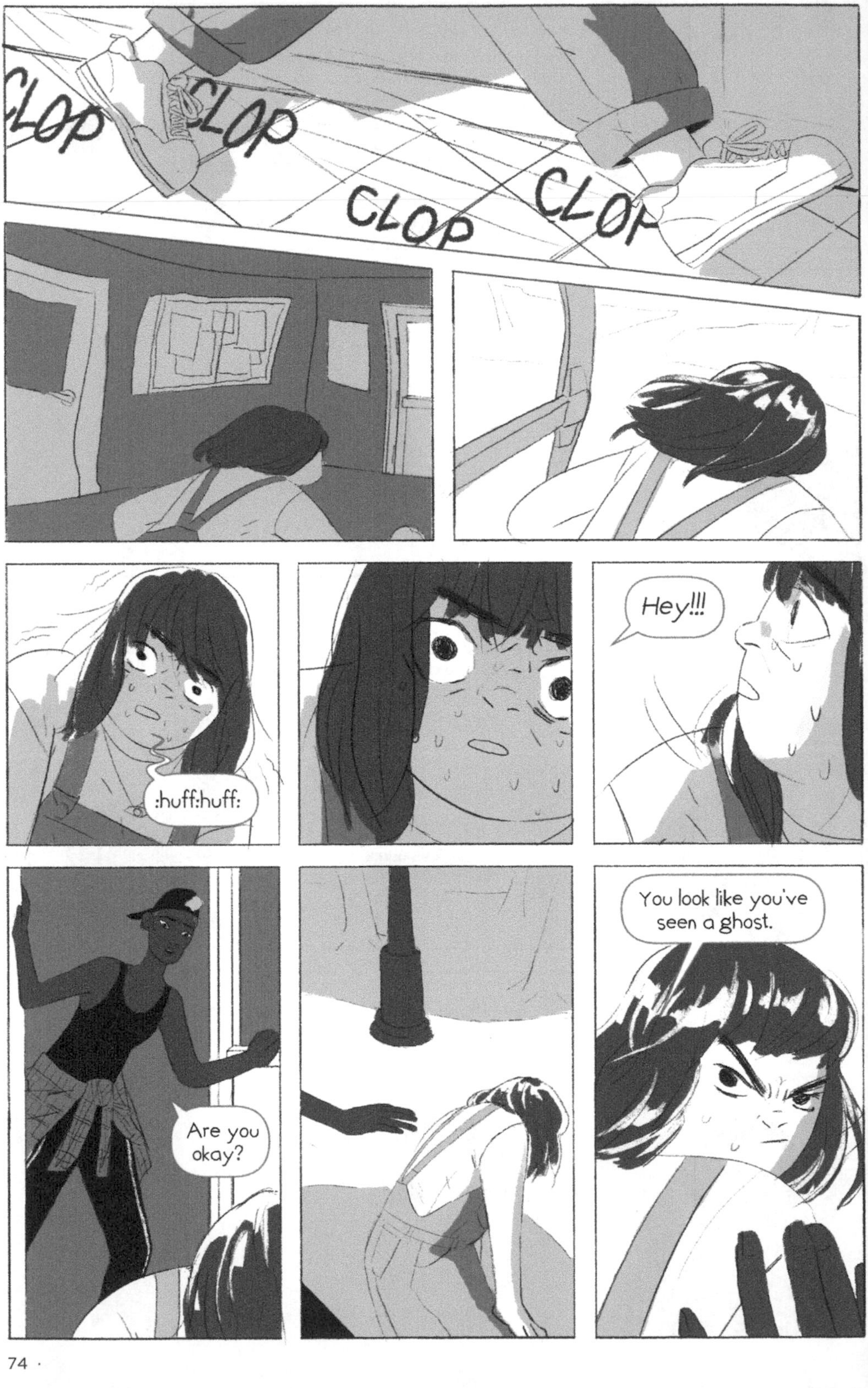
CLOP
CLOP
CLOP
CLOP
:huff:huff:
Hey!!!
Are you okay?
You look like you've seen a ghost.

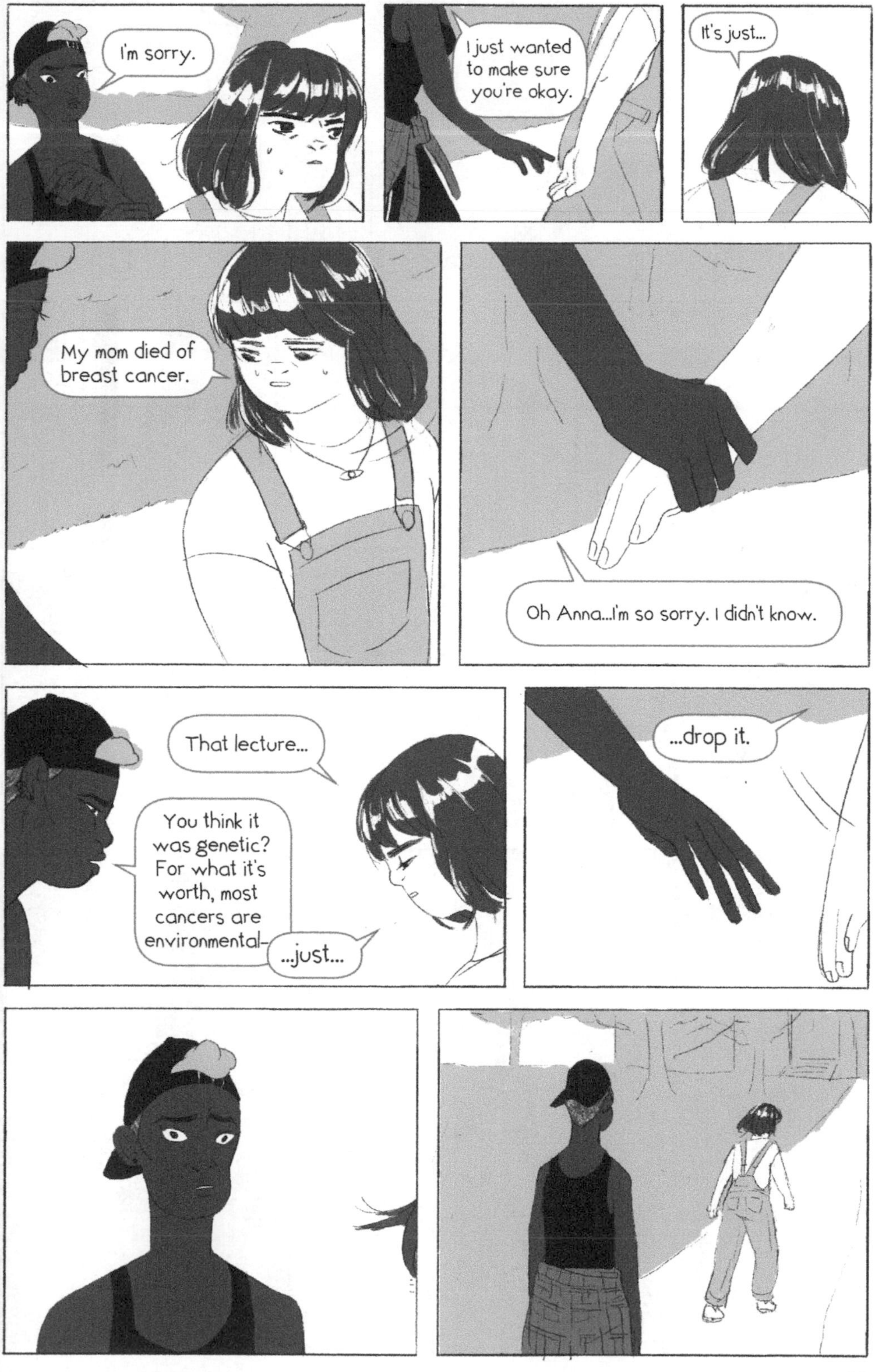
I'm sorry.
I just wanted to make sure you're okay.
It's just...
My mom died of breast cancer.
Oh Anna...I'm so sorry. I didn't know.
That lecture...
You think it was genetic? For what it's worth, most cancers are environmental—
...just...
...drop it.

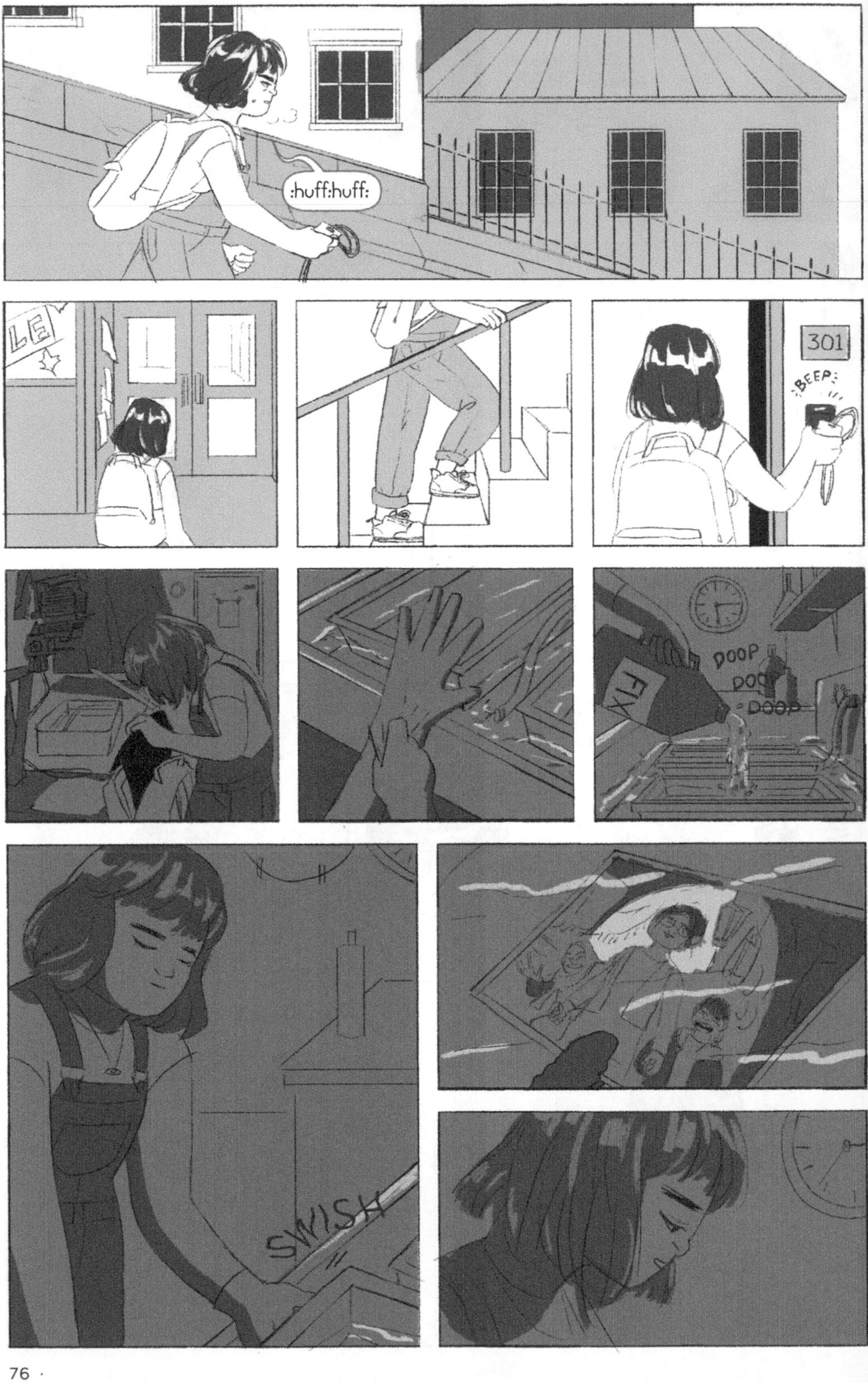
:huff:huff:
LE
301
BEEP
FIX
DOOP
DOOP
DOOP
SWISH

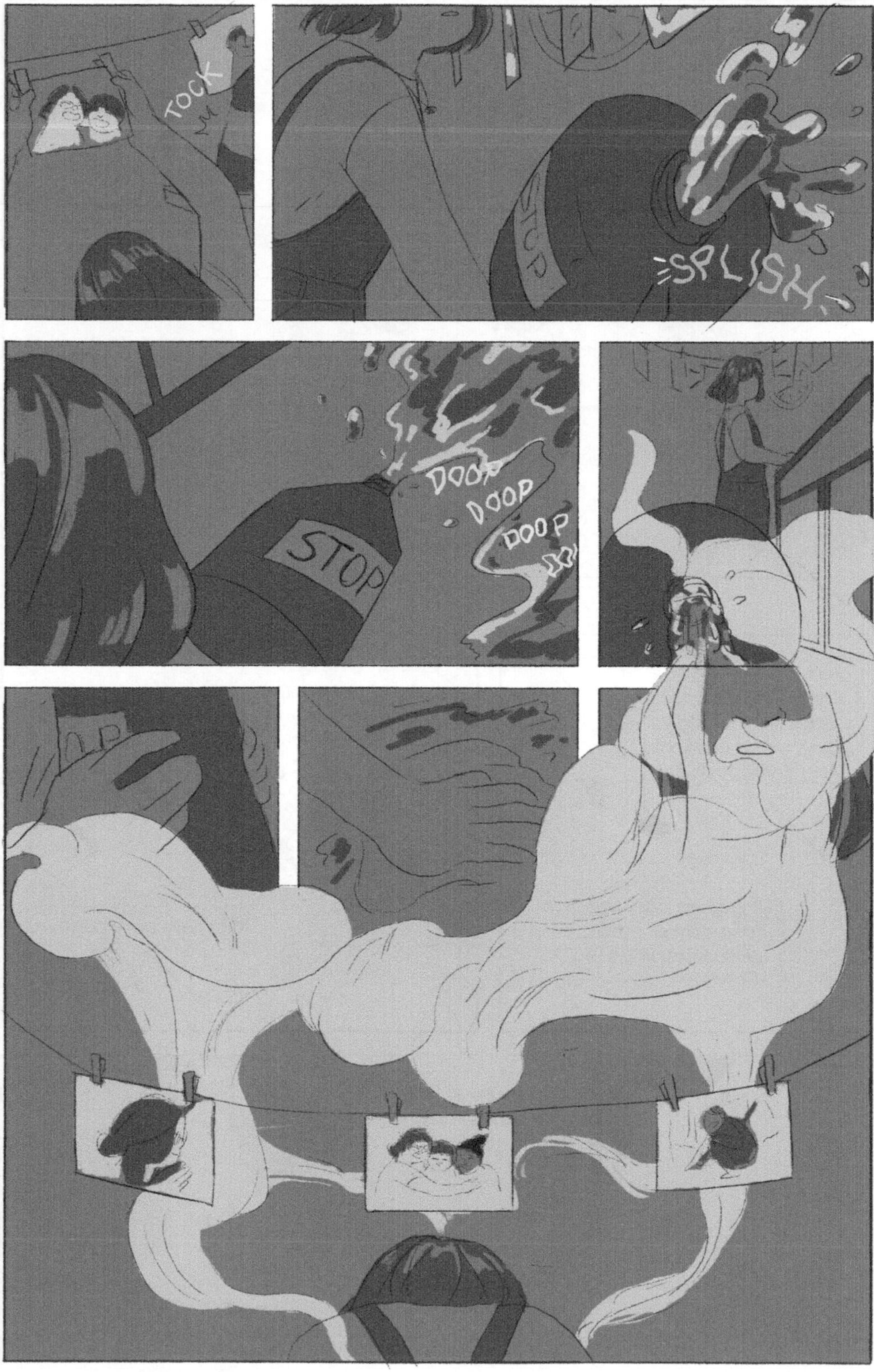
TOCK
STOP
SPLISH
STOP
DOOP
DOOP
DOOP

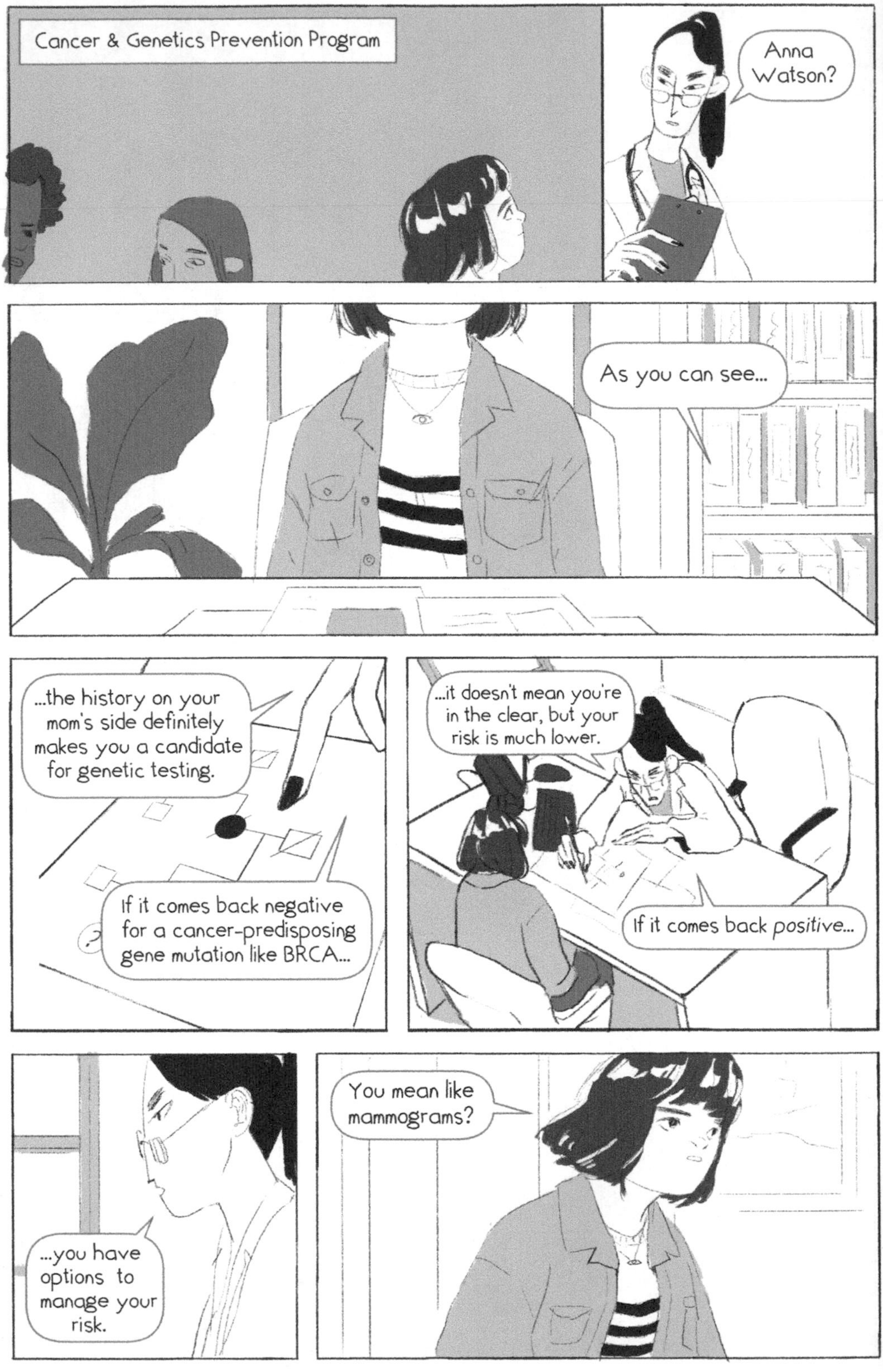
Cancer & Genetics Prevention Program
Anna Watson?
As you can see...
...the history on your mom's side definitely makes you a candidate for genetic testing.
If it comes back negative for a cancer-predisposing gene mutation like BRCA...
...it doesn't mean you're in the clear, but your risk is much lower.
If it comes back *positive*...
...you have options to manage your risk.
You mean like mammograms?

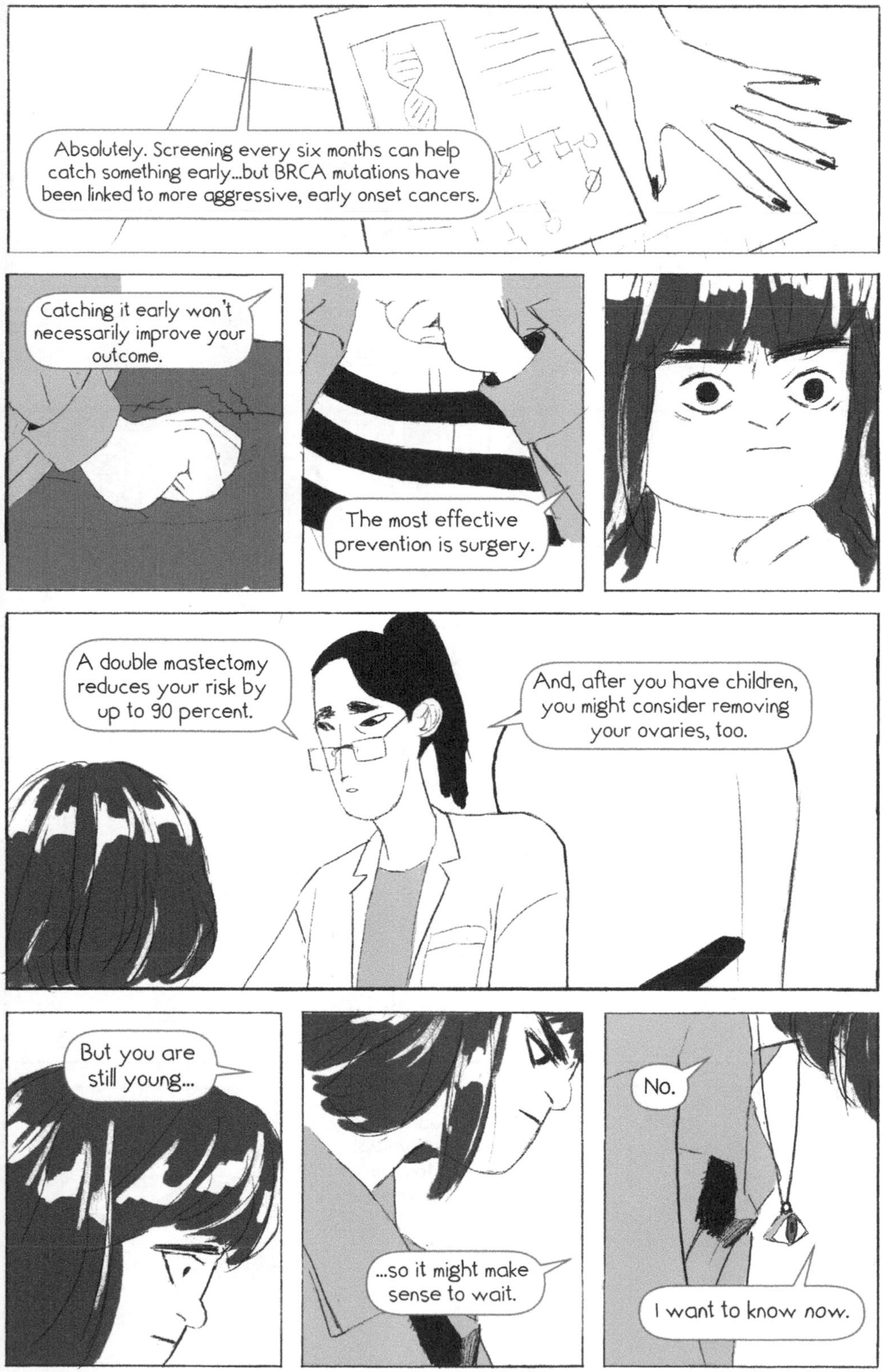
Absolutely. Screening every six months can help catch something early...but BRCA mutations have been linked to more aggressive, early onset cancers.
Catching it early won't necessarily improve your outcome.
The most effective prevention is surgery.
A double mastectomy reduces your risk by up to 90 percent.
And, after you have children, you might consider removing your ovaries, too.
But you are still young...
...so it might make sense to wait.
No.
I want to know *now*.

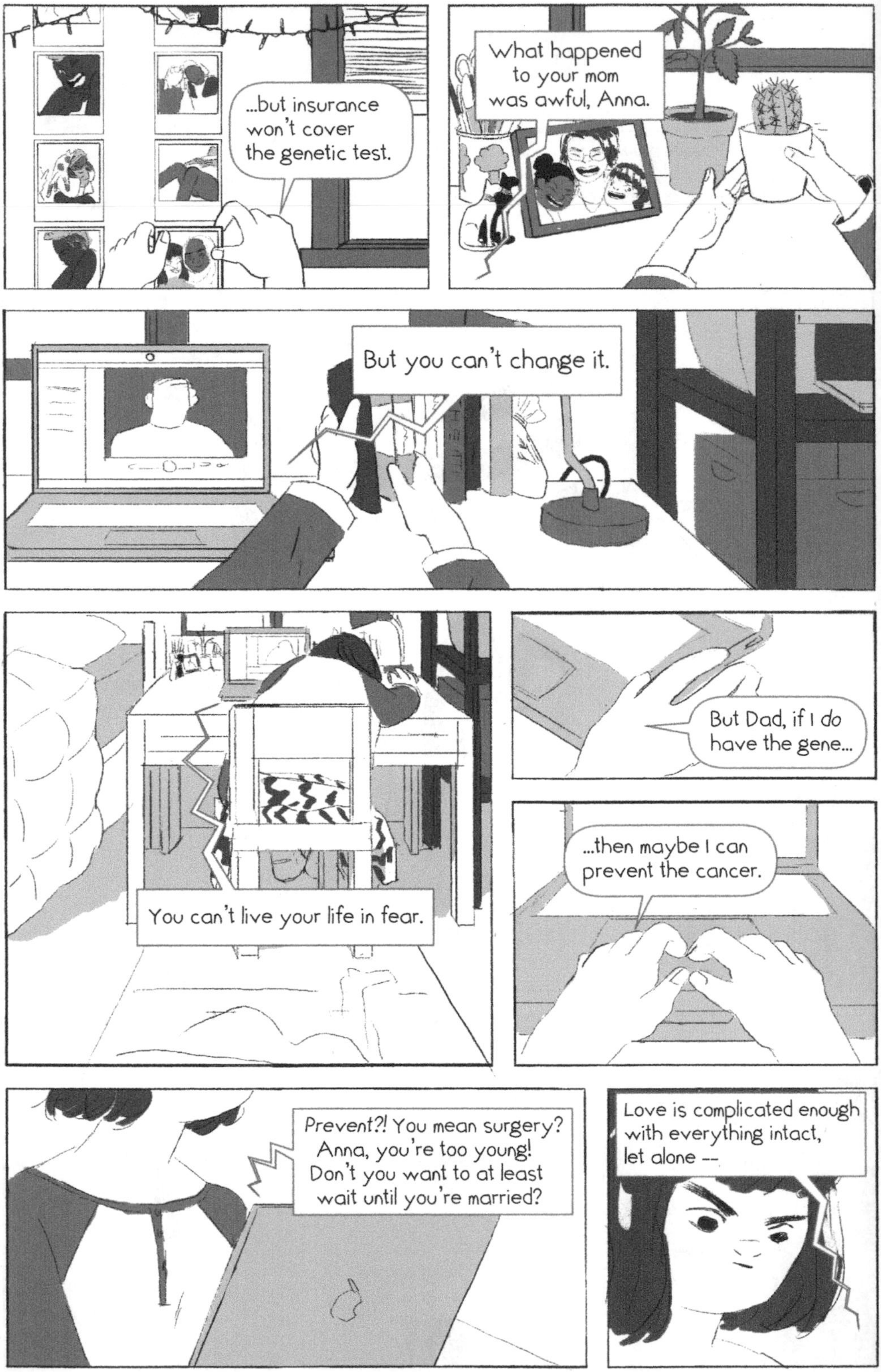
...but insurance won't cover the genetic test.
What happened to your mom was awful, Anna.
But you can't change it.
You can't live your life in fear.
But Dad, if I *do* have the gene...
...then maybe I can prevent the cancer.
Prevent?! You mean surgery? Anna, you're too young! Don't you want to at least wait until you're married?
Love is complicated enough with everything intact, let alone --

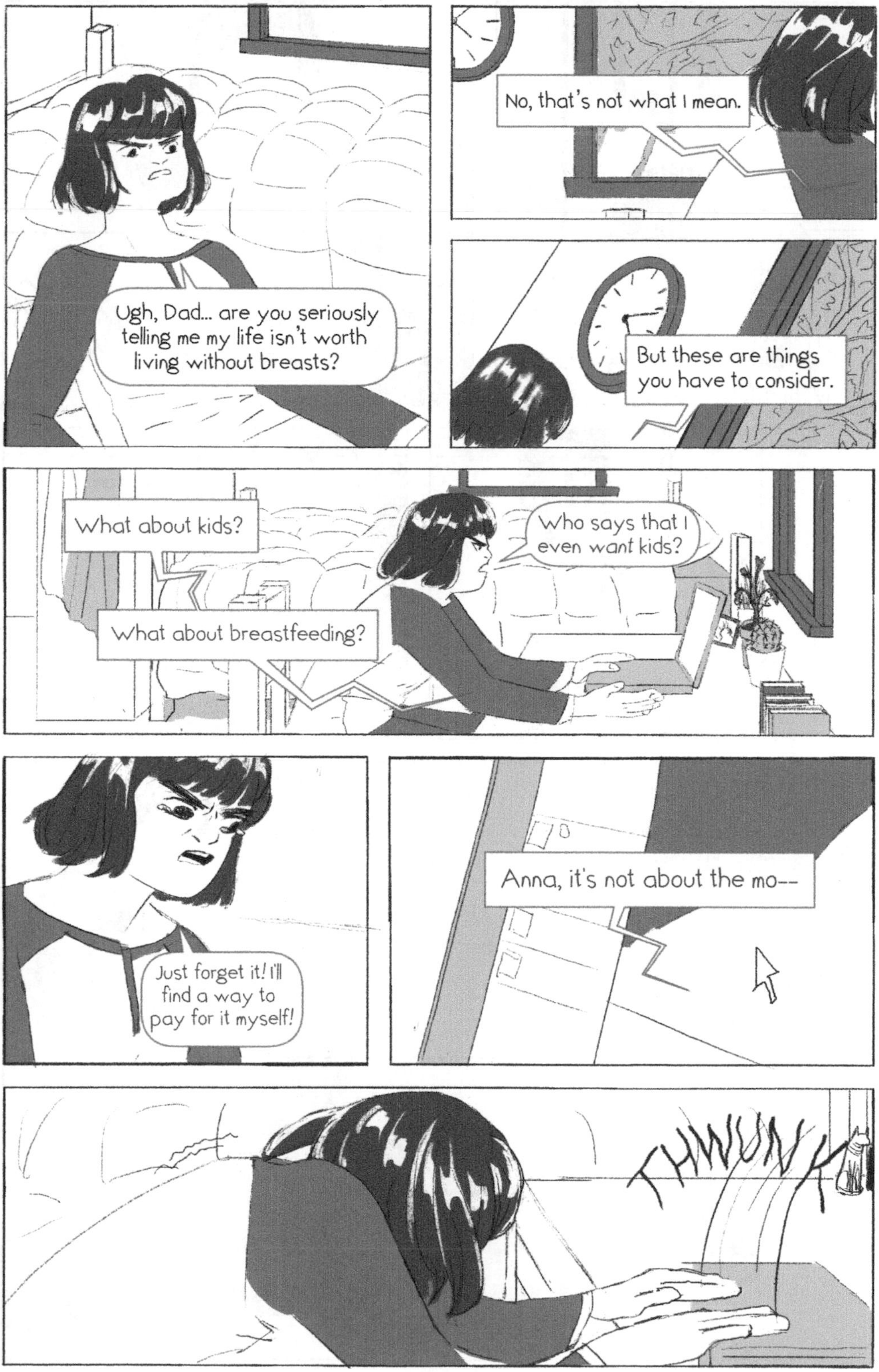
Ugh, Dad... are you seriously telling me my life isn't worth living without breasts?
No, that's not what I mean.
But these are things you have to consider.
What about kids?
What about breastfeeding?
Who says that I even *want* kids?
Just forget it! I'll find a way to pay for it myself!
Anna, it's not about the mo--
THWUNK

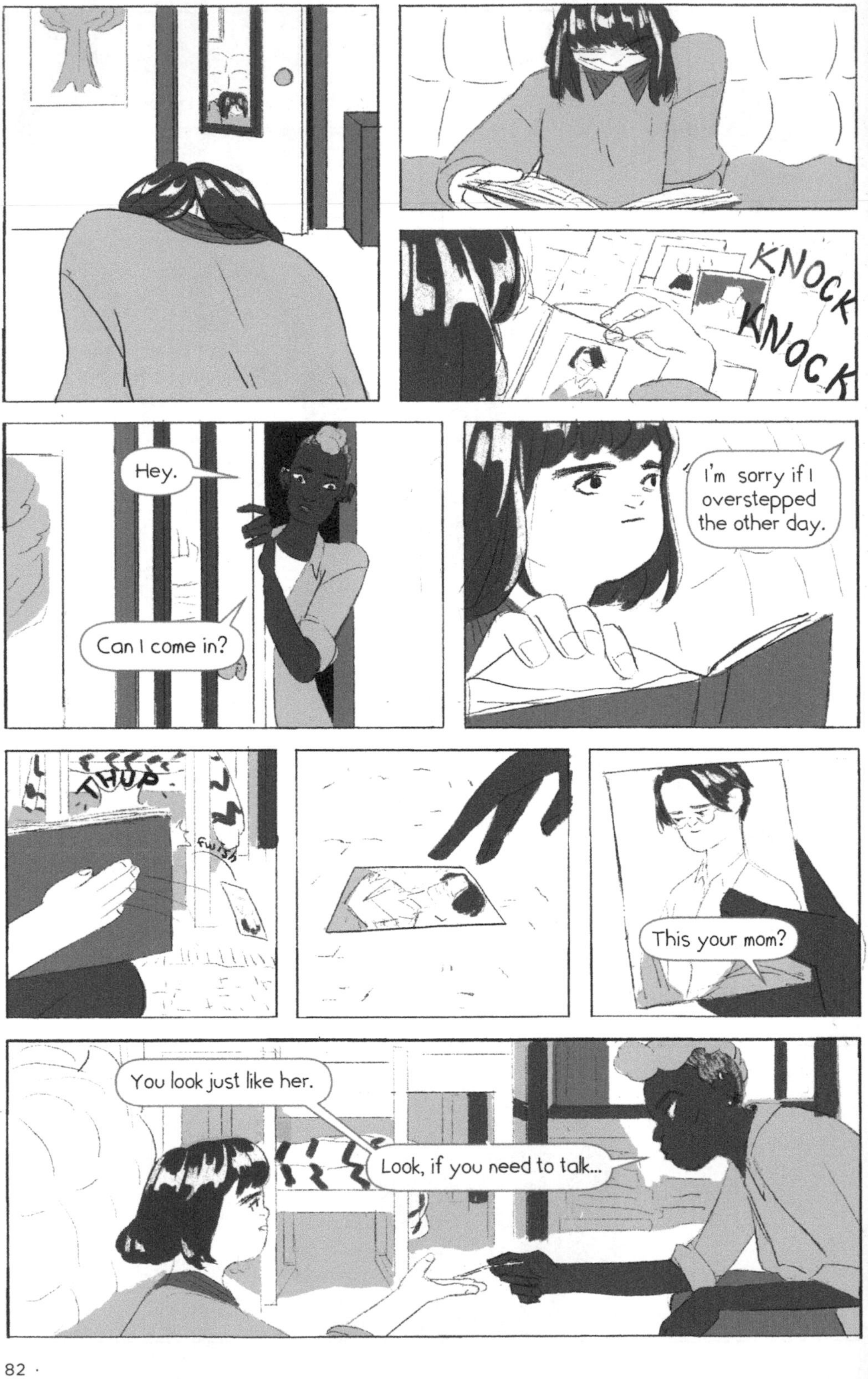
KNOCK
KNOCK
Hey.
Can I come in?
I'm sorry if I overstepped the other day.
THUP
fwish
This your mom?
You look just like her.
Look, if you need to talk...

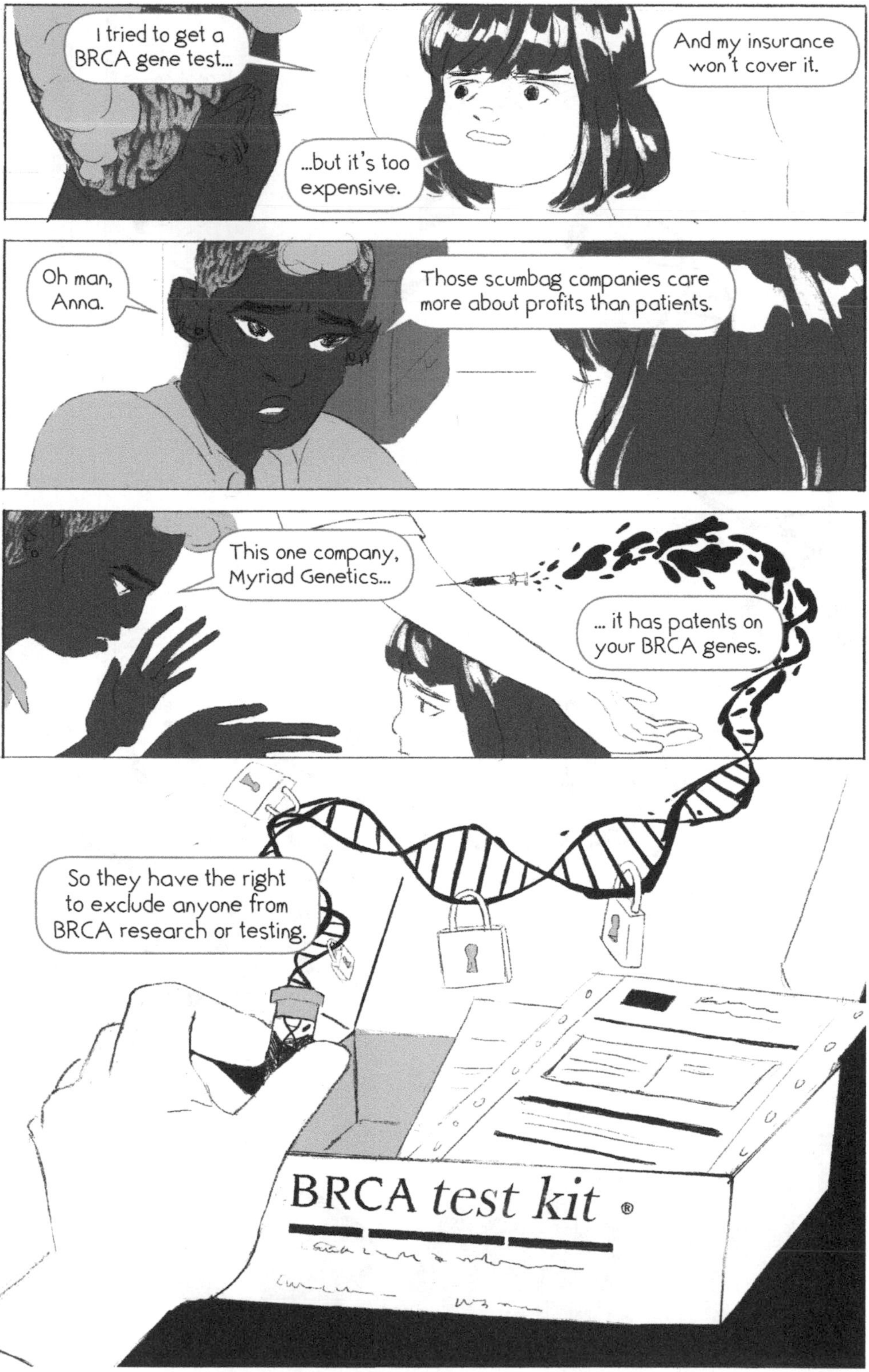

I tried to get a BRCA gene test...
...but it's too expensive.
And my insurance won't cover it.
Oh man, Anna.
Those scumbag companies care more about profits than patients.
This one company, Myriad Genetics...
... it has patents on your BRCA genes.
So they have the right to exclude anyone from BRCA research or testing.
BRCA test kit ®

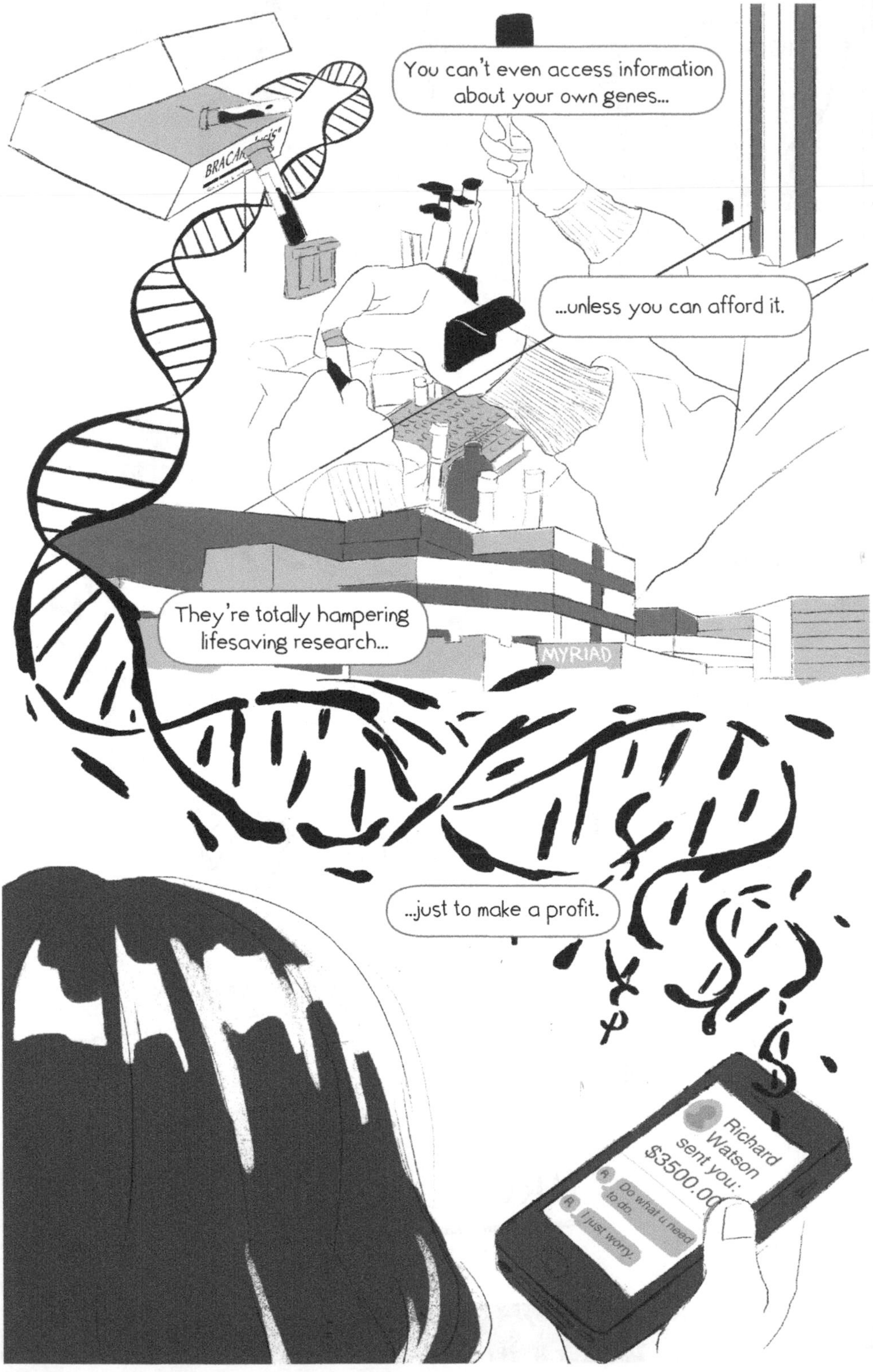
You can't even access information about your own genes...
...unless you can afford it.
They're totally hampering lifesaving research...
MYRIAD
...just to make a profit.
Richard Watson sent you: $3500.0
Do what u need to do.
I just worry.

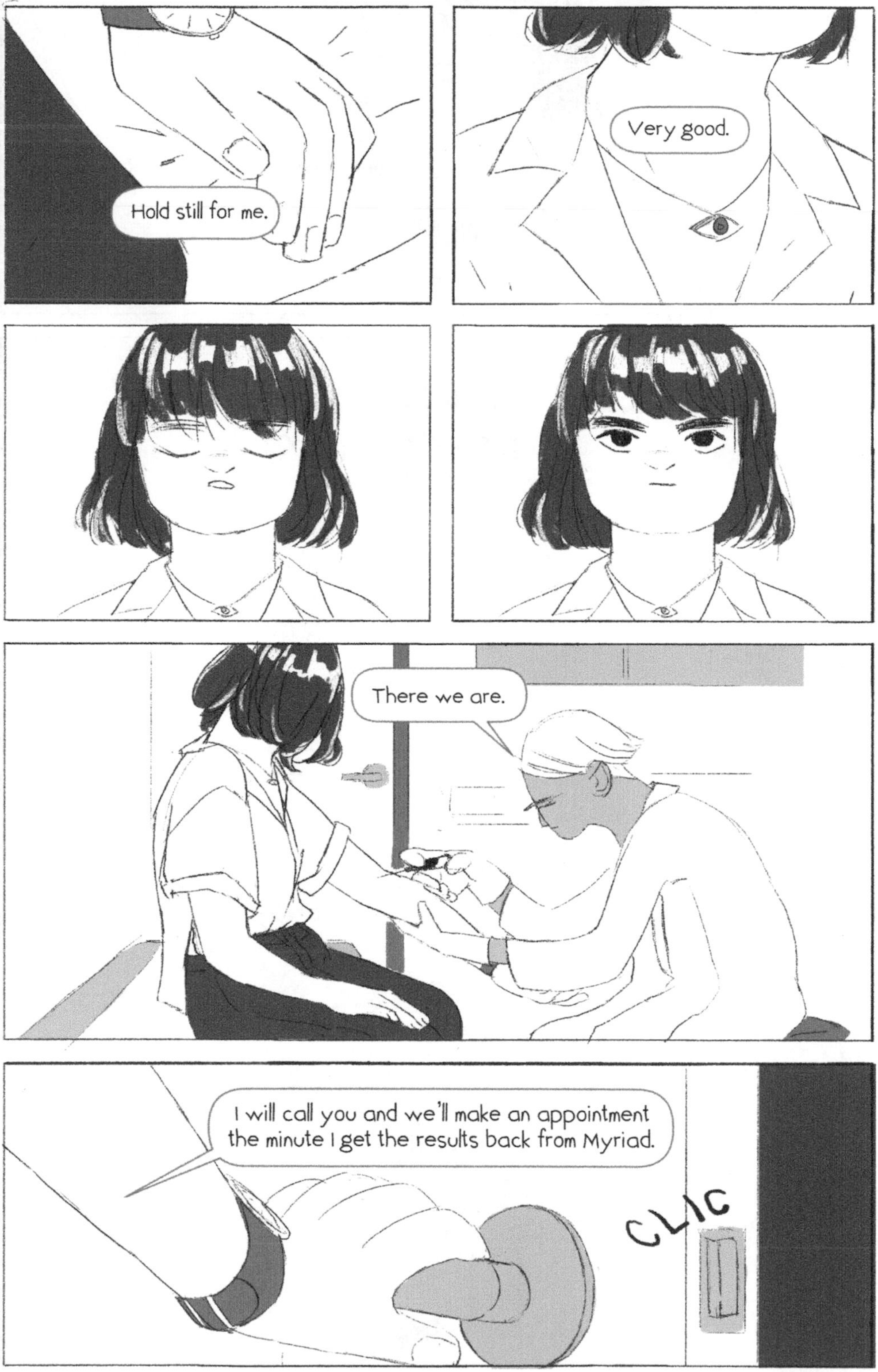
Hold still for me.
Very good.
There we are.
I will call you and we'll make an appointment the minute I get the results back from Myriad.
CLIC

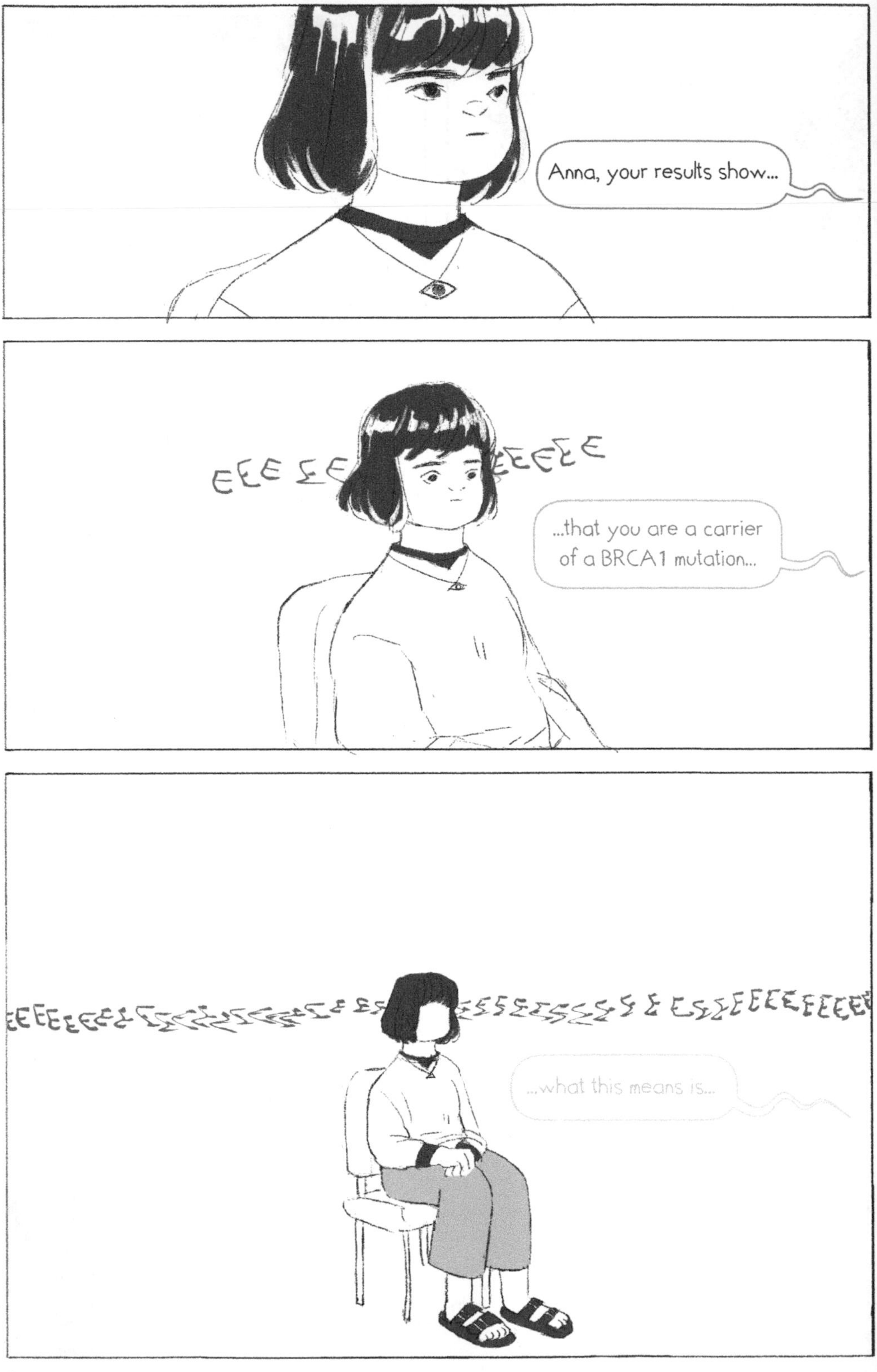
Anna, your results show...
...that you are a carrier of a BRCA1 mutation...
...what this means is...

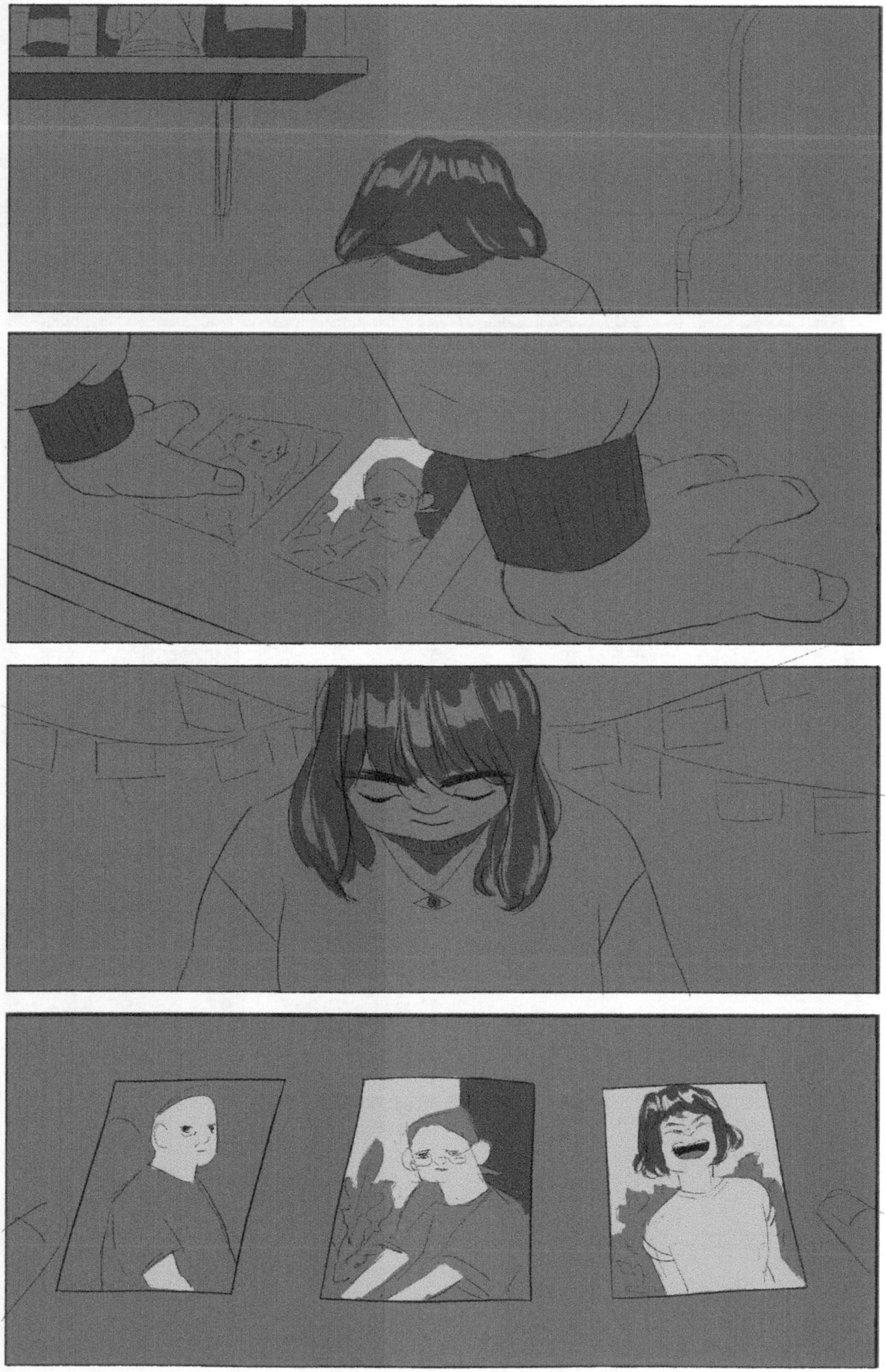

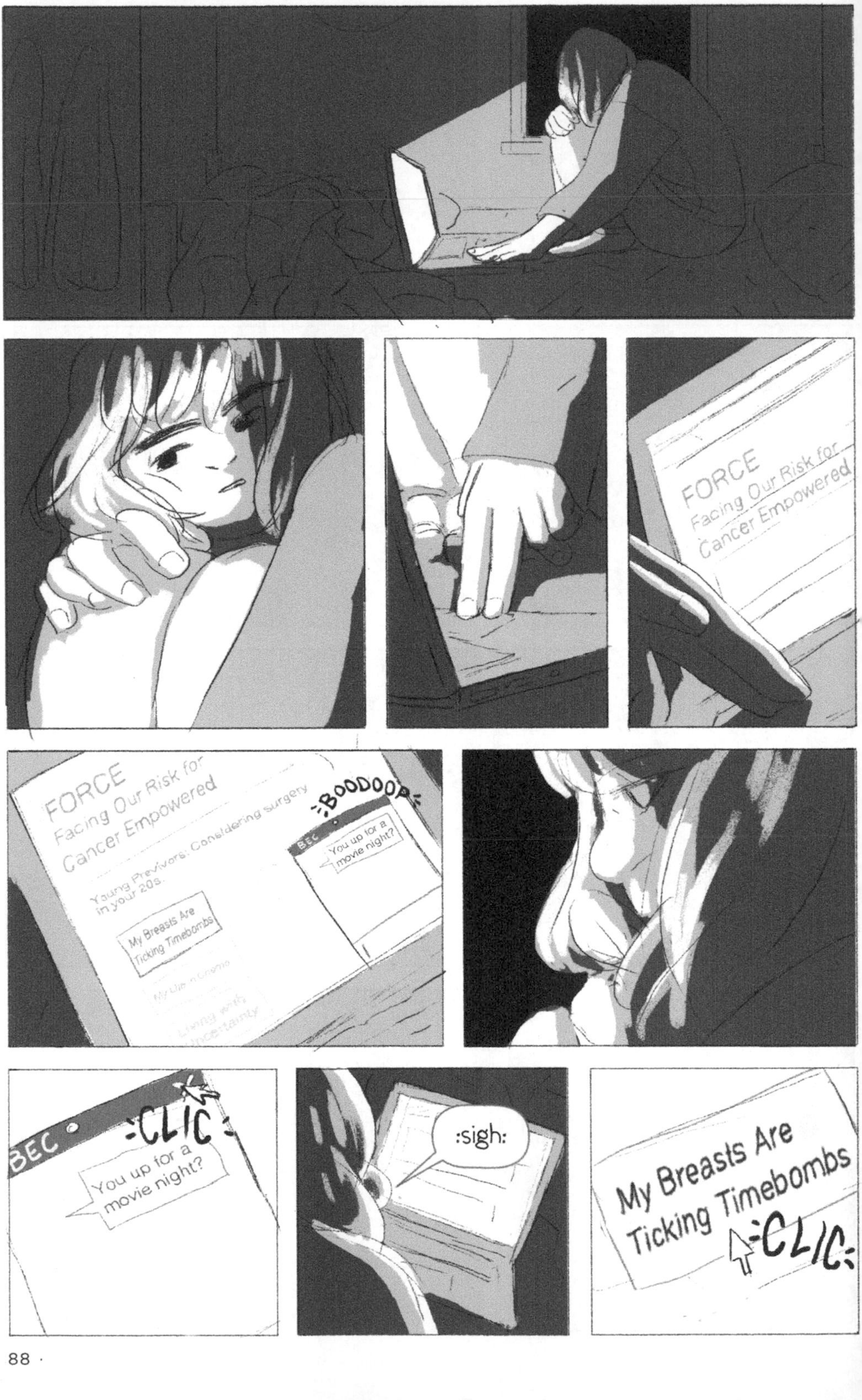
FORCE
Facing Our Risk for
Cancer Empowered
FORCE
Facing Our Risk for
Cancer Empowered
Young Previvors: Considering surgery
in your 20s.
My Breasts Are
Ticking Timebombs
Living with
Uncertainty
BOODOOP
BEC
You up for a
movie night?
BEC
CLIC
You up for a
movie night?
:sigh:
My Breasts Are
Ticking Timebombs
CLIC

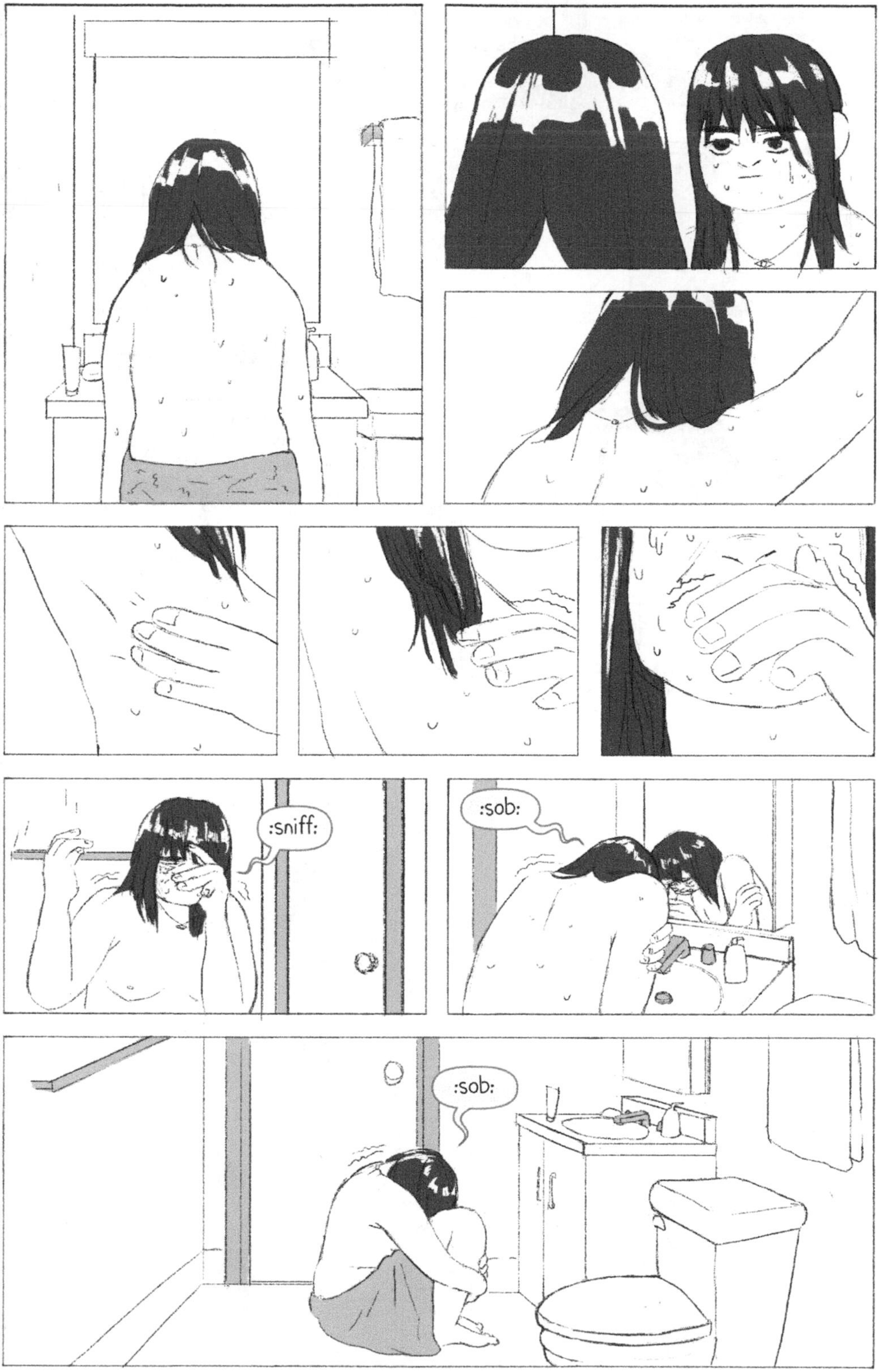
:sniff:
:sob:
:sob:

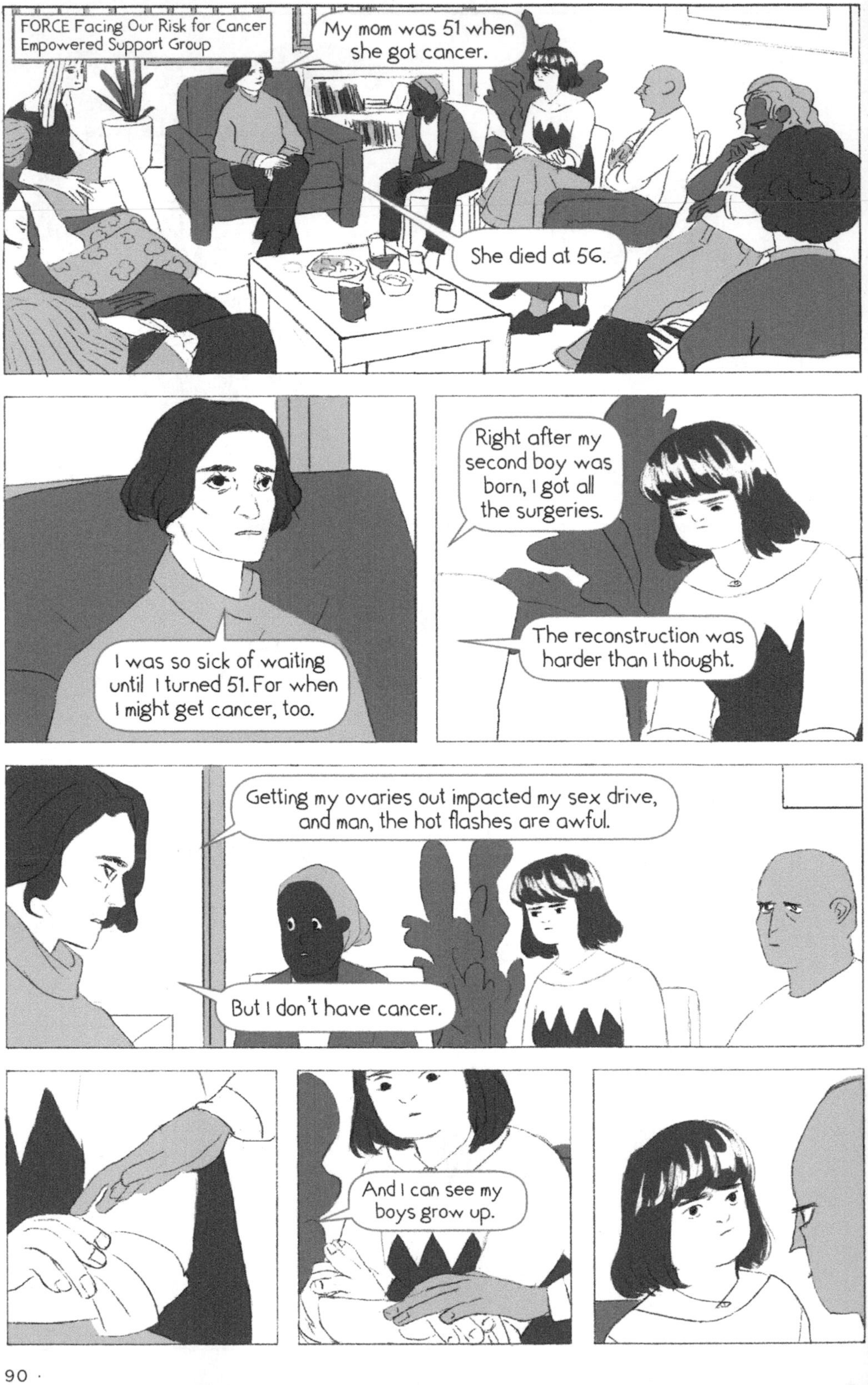

FORCE Facing Our Risk for Cancer Empowered Support Group
My mom was 51 when she got cancer.
She died at 56.
I was so sick of waiting until I turned 51. For when I might get cancer, too.
Right after my second boy was born, I got all the surgeries.
The reconstruction was harder than I thought.
Getting my ovaries out impacted my sex drive, and man, the hot flashes are awful.
But I don't have cancer.
And I can see my boys grow up.

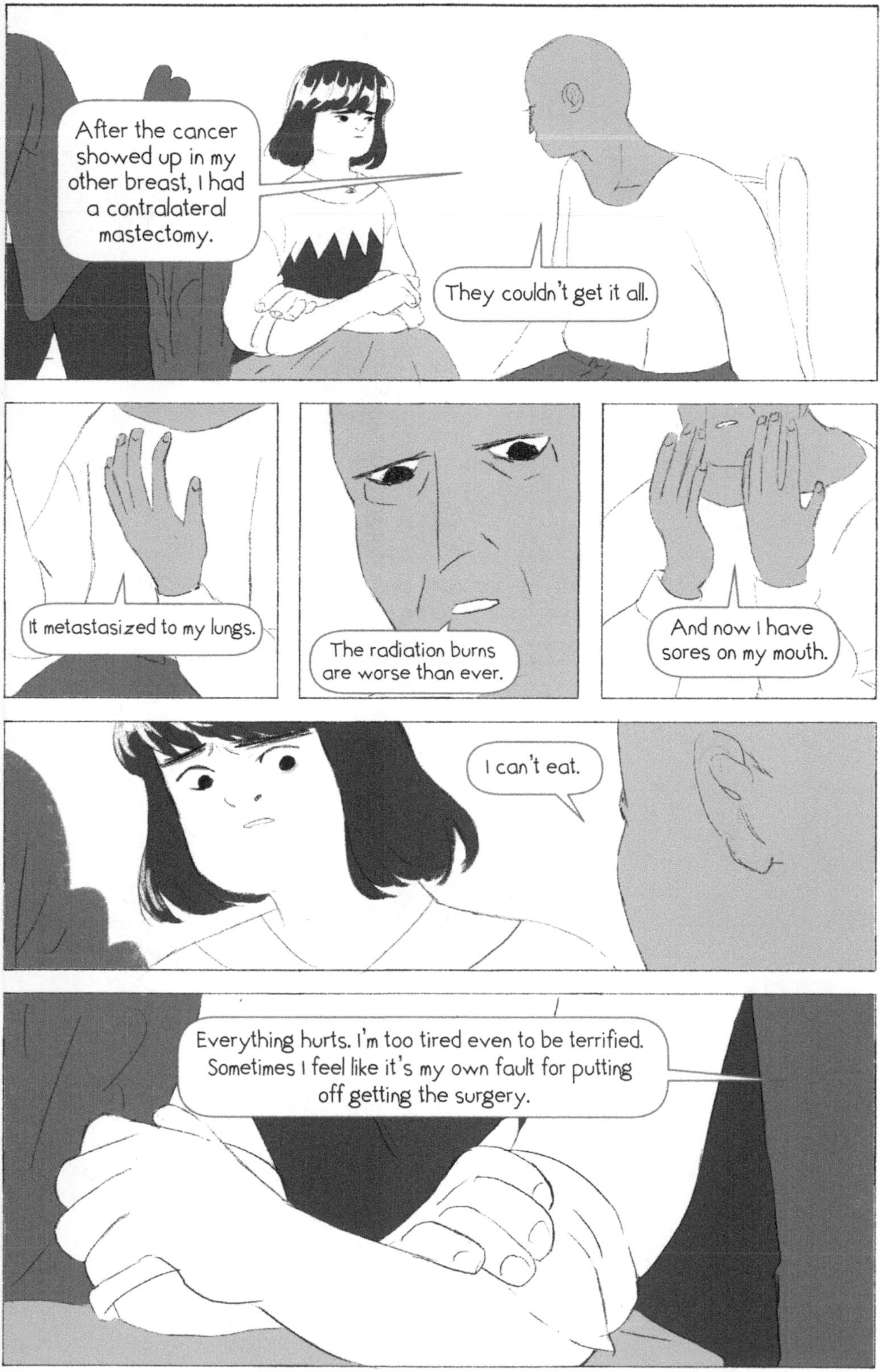
After the cancer showed up in my other breast, I had a contralateral mastectomy.
They couldn't get it all.
It metastasized to my lungs.
The radiation burns are worse than ever.
And now I have sores on my mouth.
I can't eat.
Everything hurts. I'm too tired even to be terrified. Sometimes I feel like it's my own fault for putting off getting the surgery.

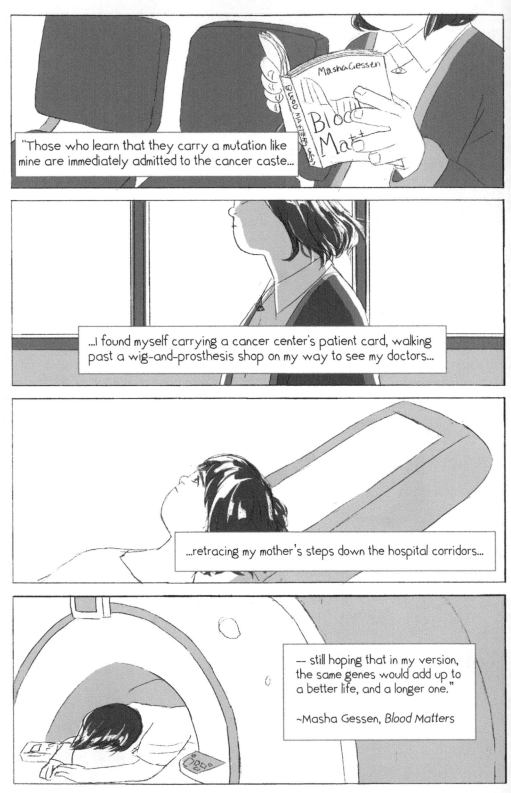

"Those who learn that they carry a mutation like mine are immediately admitted to the cancer caste...

...I found myself carrying a cancer center's patient card, walking past a wig-and-prosthesis shop on my way to see my doctors...

...retracing my mother's steps down the hospital corridors...

-- still hoping that in my version, the same genes would add up to a better life, and a longer one."

~Masha Gessen, *Blood Matters*

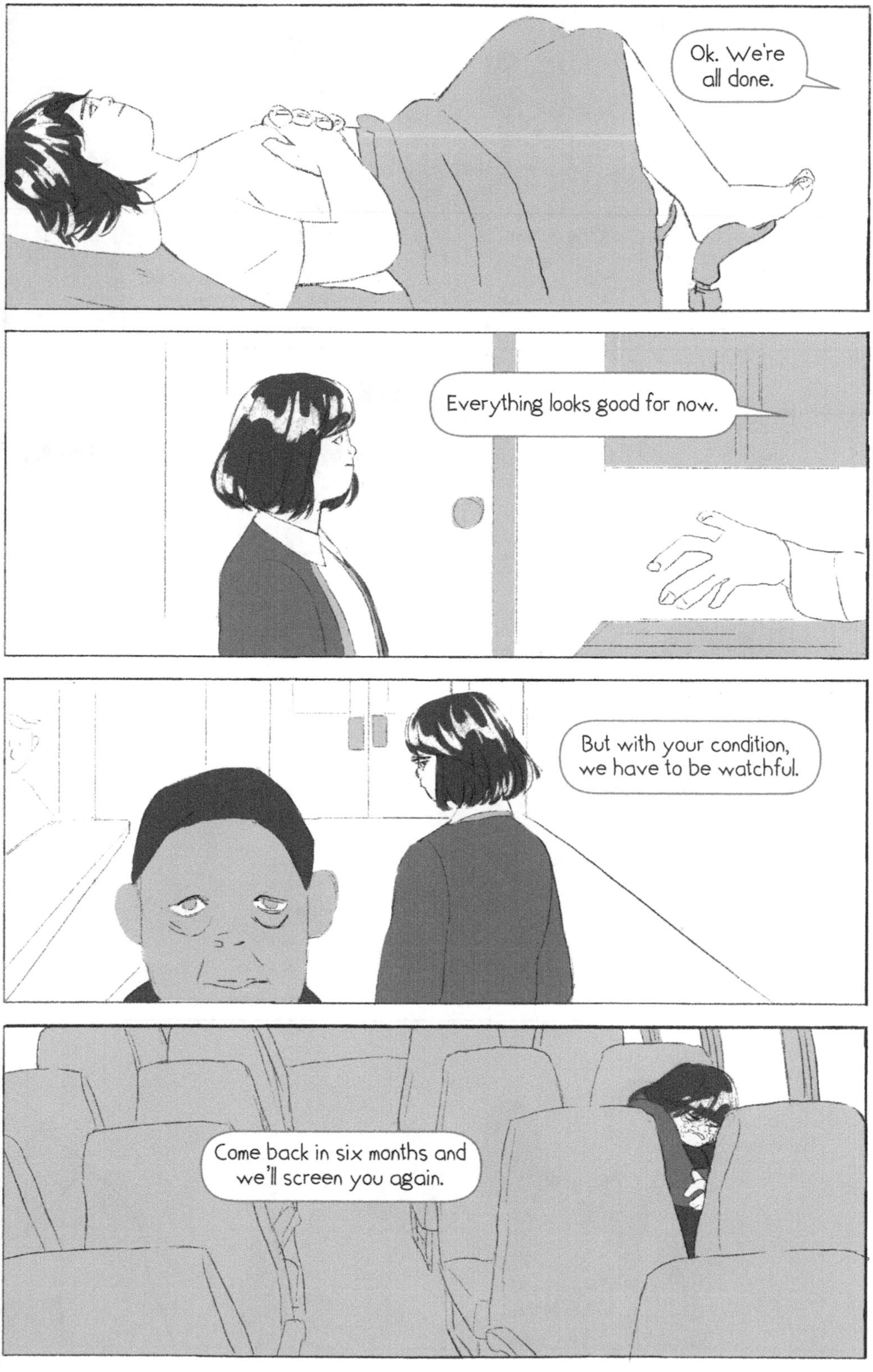
Ok. We're all done.
Everything looks good for now.
But with your condition, we have to be watchful.
Come back in six months and we'll screen you again.

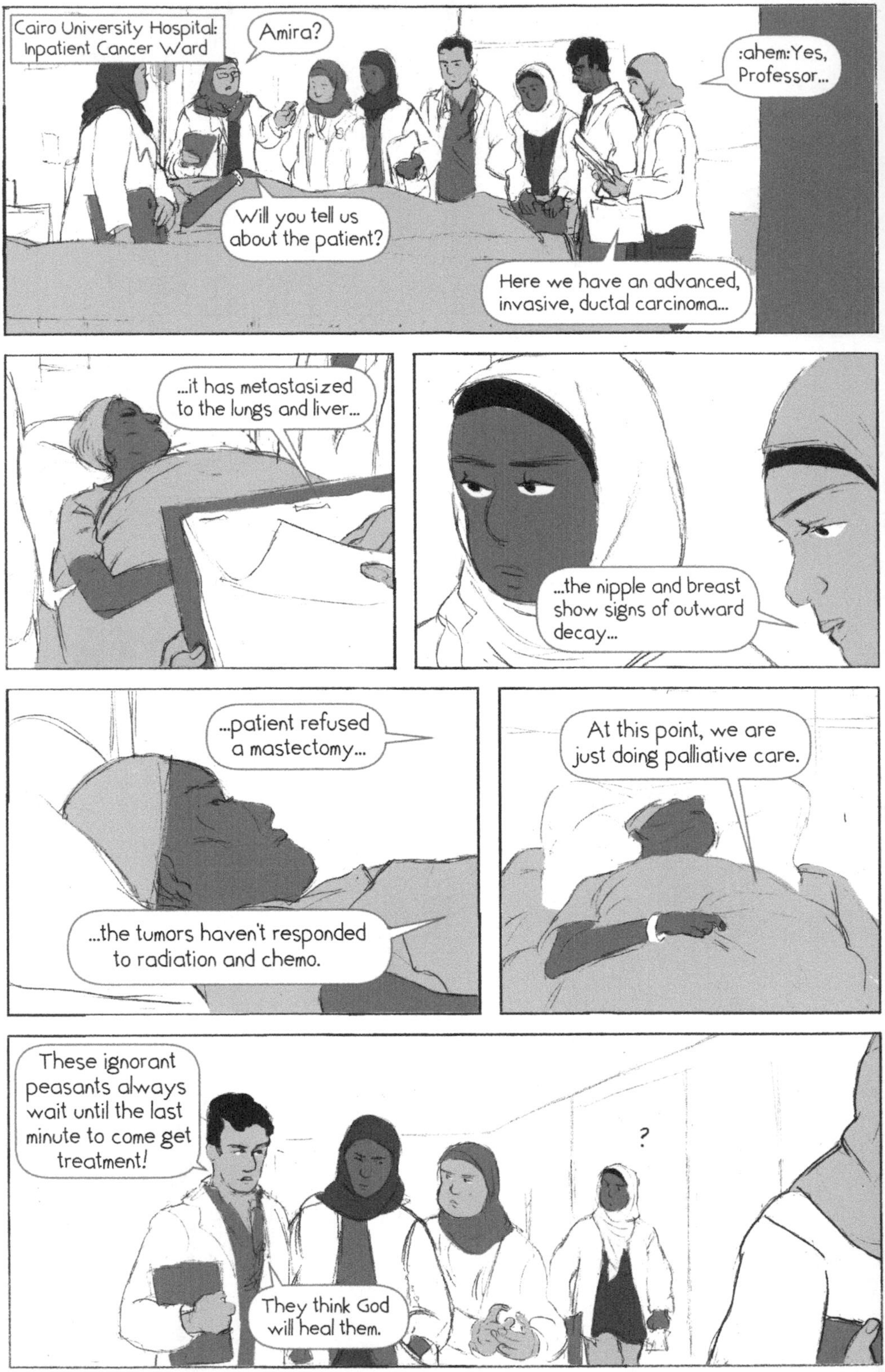

Cairo University Hospital: Inpatient Cancer Ward
Amira?
Will you tell us about the patient?
:ahem:Yes, Professor...
Here we have an advanced, invasive, ductal carcinoma...
...it has metastasized to the lungs and liver...
...the nipple and breast show signs of outward decay...
...patient refused a mastectomy...
...the tumors haven't responded to radiation and chemo.
At this point, we are just doing palliative care.
These ignorant peasants always wait until the last minute to come get treatment!
They think God will heal them.
?

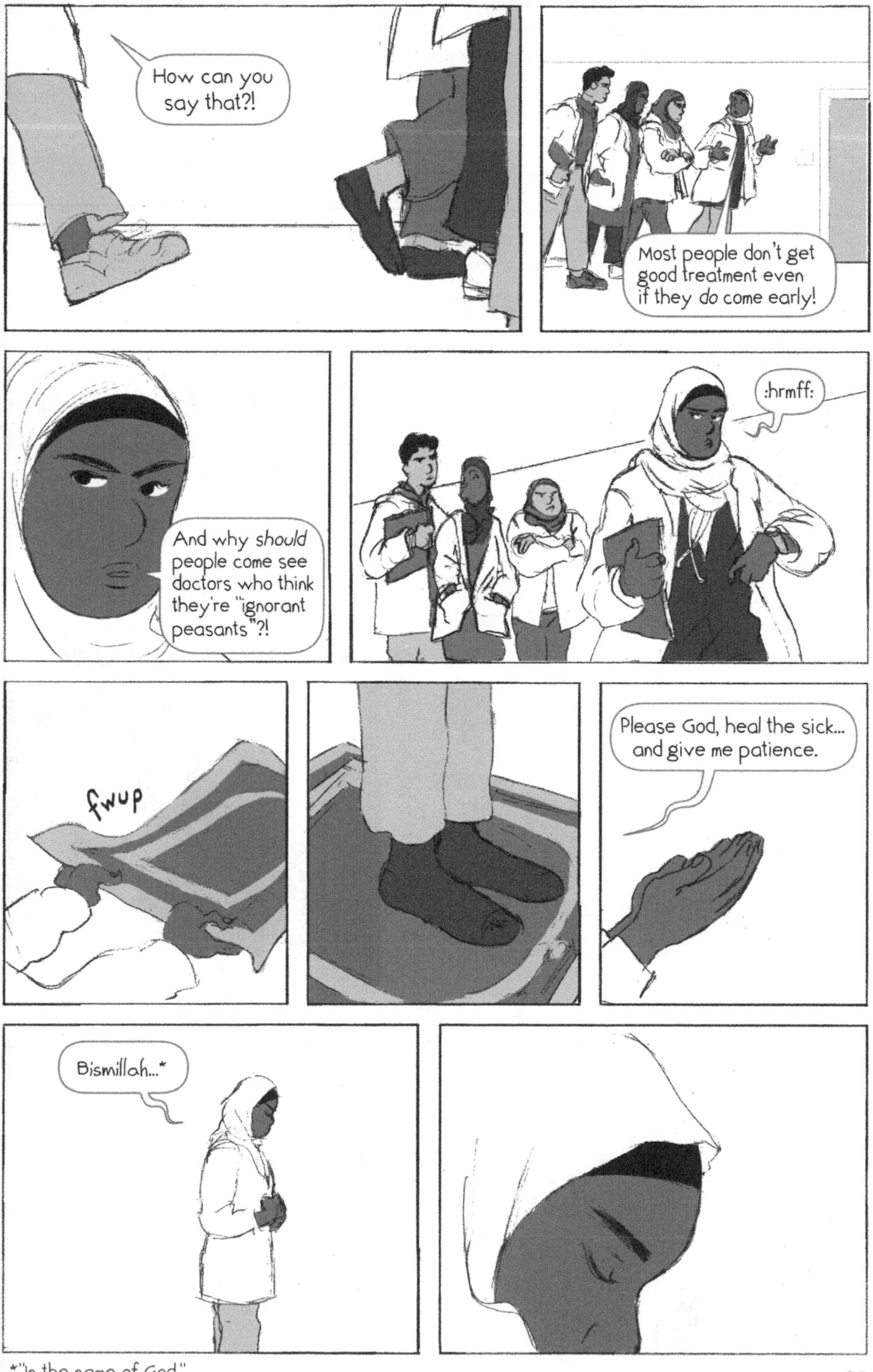
How can you say that?!
Most people don't get good treatment even if they *do* come early!
And why *should* people come see doctors who think they're "ignorant peasants"?!
:hrmff:
fwup
Please God, heal the sick... and give me patience.
Bismillah...*

*"In the name of God."

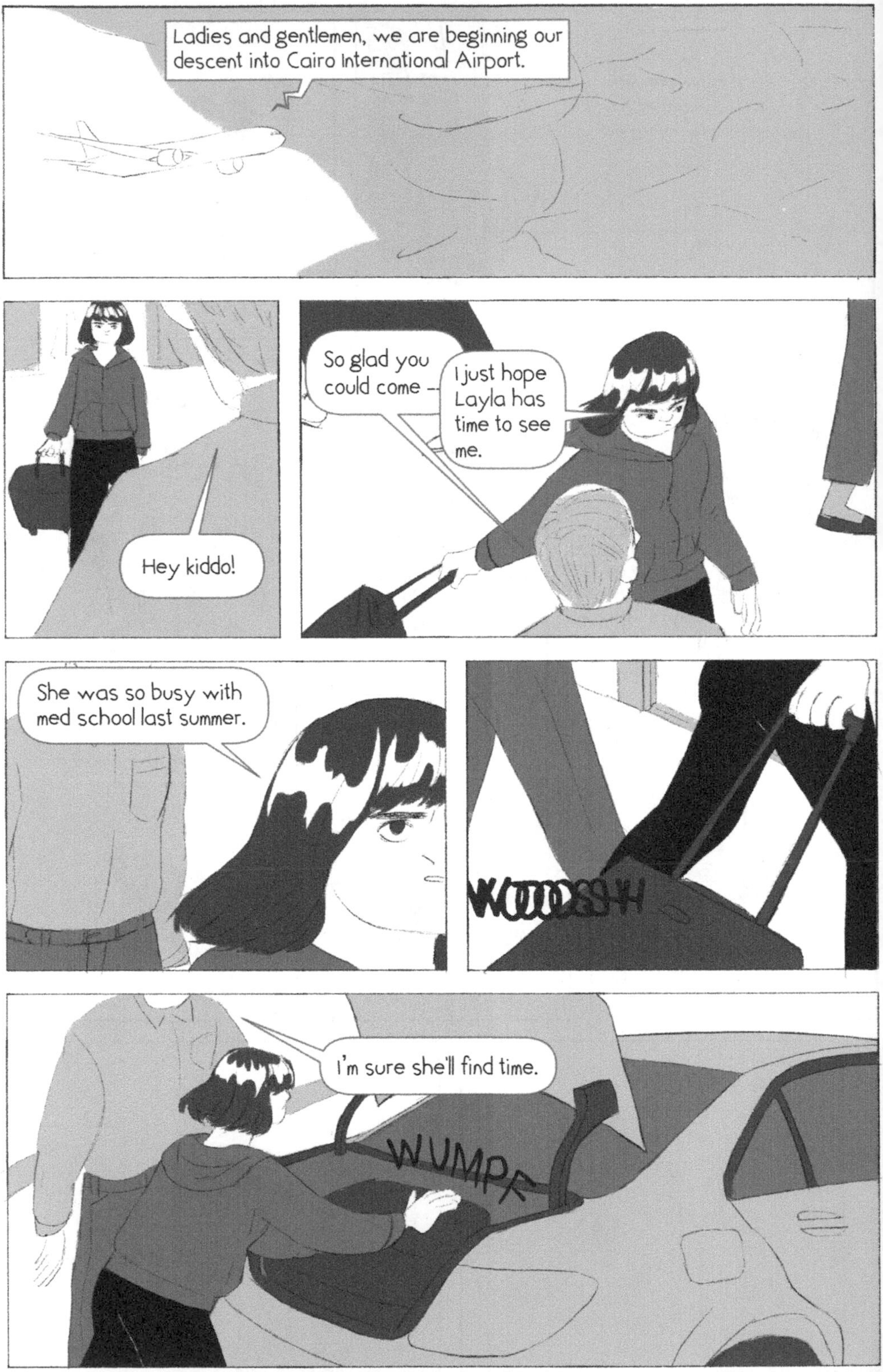
Ladies and gentlemen, we are beginning our descent into Cairo International Airport.
Hey kiddo!
So glad you could come --
I just hope Layla has time to see me.
She was so busy with med school last summer.
WOOOOSSH
I'm sure she'll find time.
WUMPF

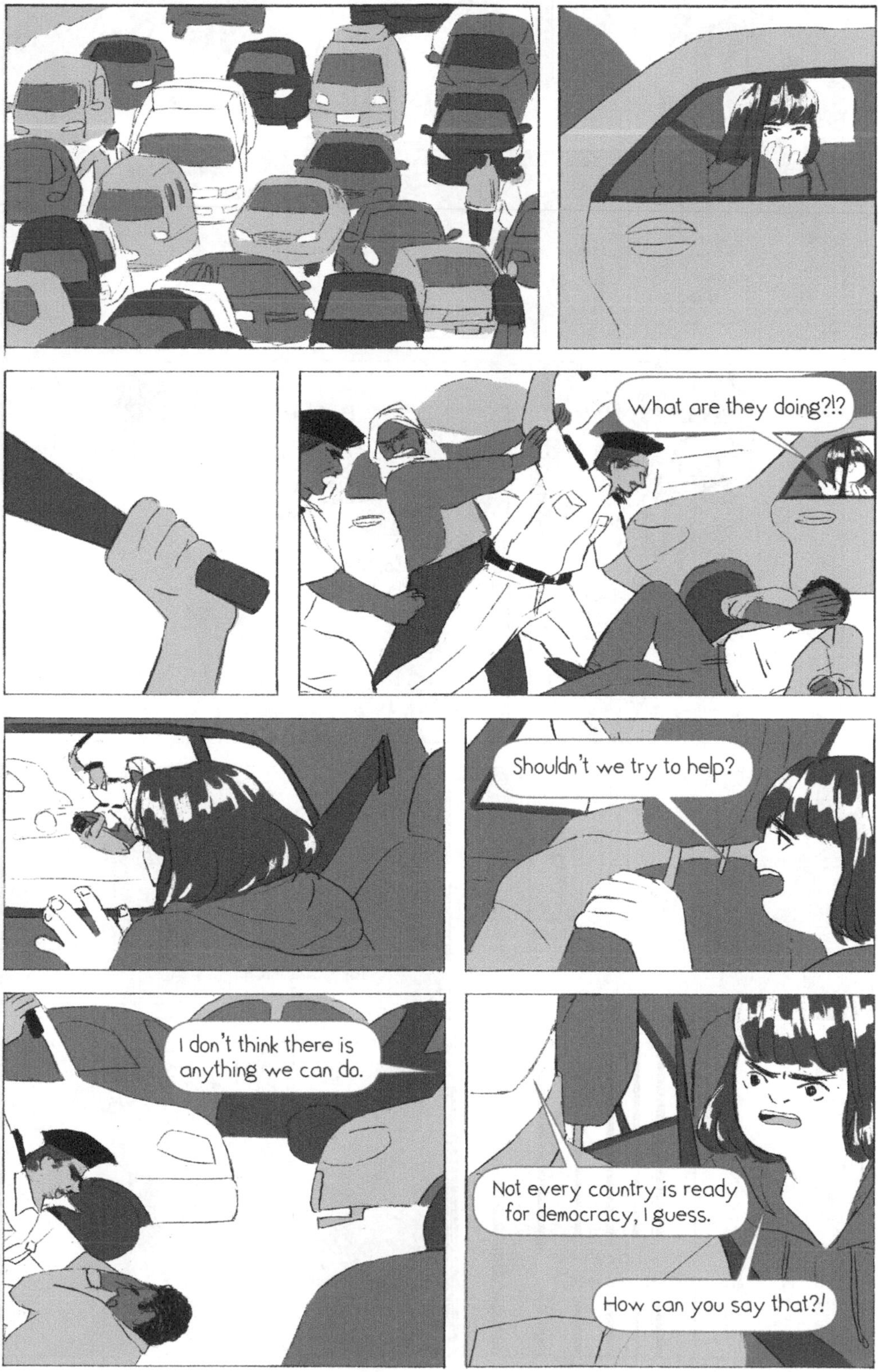
What are they doing?!?
Shouldn't we try to help?
I don't think there is anything we can do.
Not every country is ready for democracy, I guess.
How can you say that?!

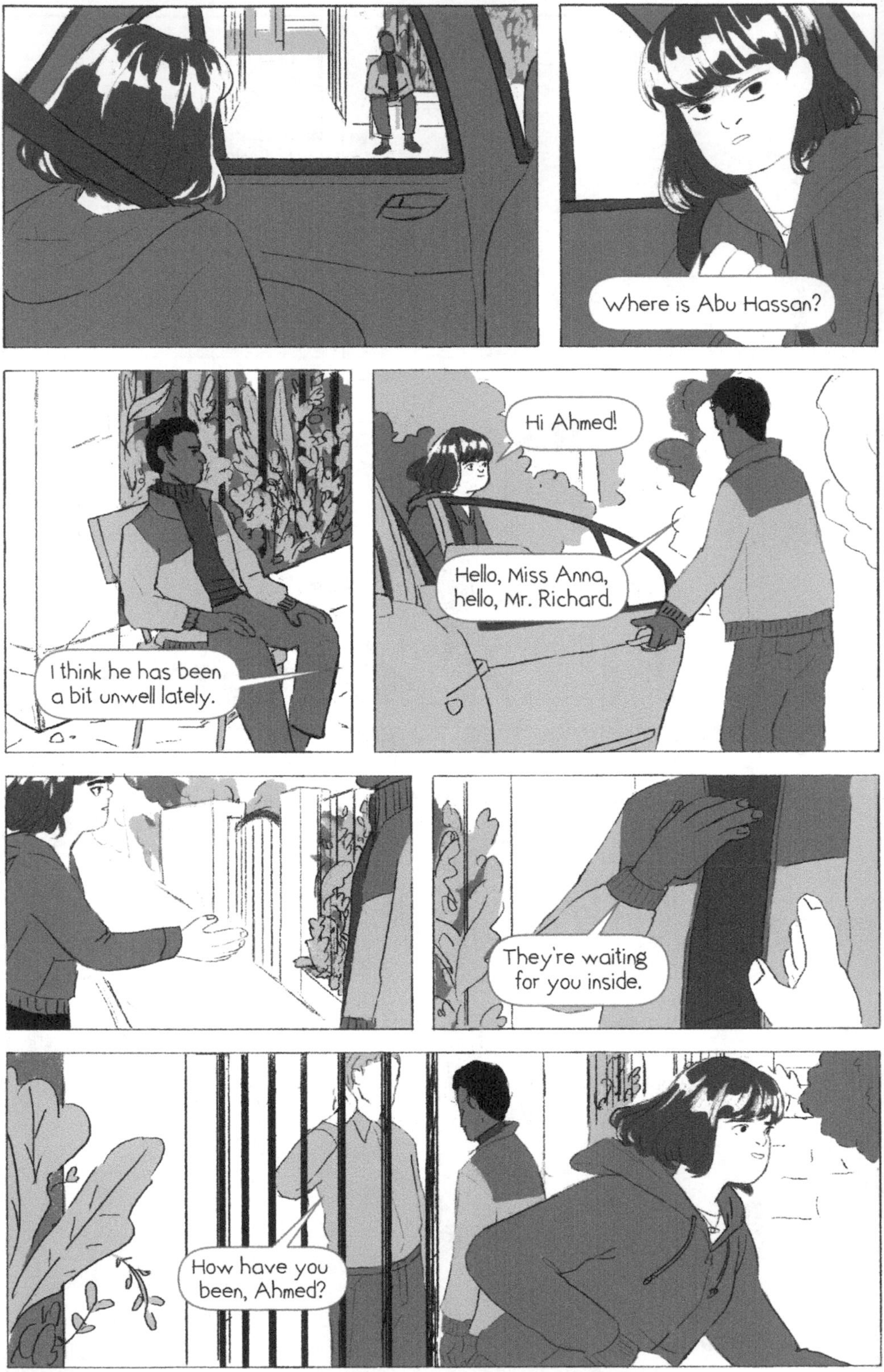
Where is Abu Hassan?
I think he has been a bit unwell lately.
Hi Ahmed!
Hello, Miss Anna, hello, Mr. Richard.
They're waiting for you inside.
How have you been, Ahmed?

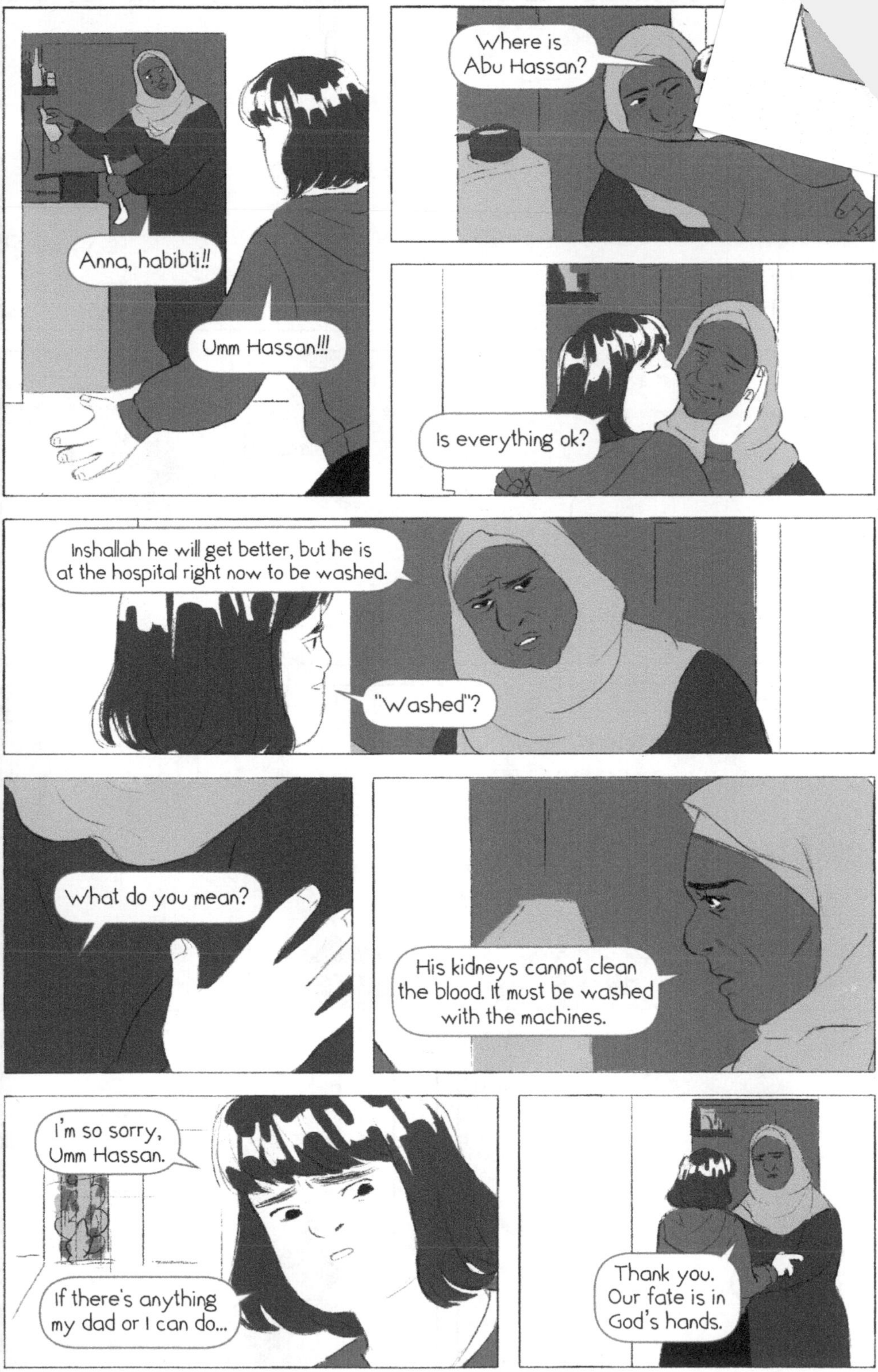
Anna, habibti!!
Umm Hassan!!!
Where is Abu Hassan?
Is everything ok?
Inshallah he will get better, but he is at the hospital right now to be washed.
"Washed"?
What do you mean?
His kidneys cannot clean the blood. It must be washed with the machines.
I'm so sorry, Umm Hassan.
If there's anything my dad or I can do...
Thank you. Our fate is in God's hands.

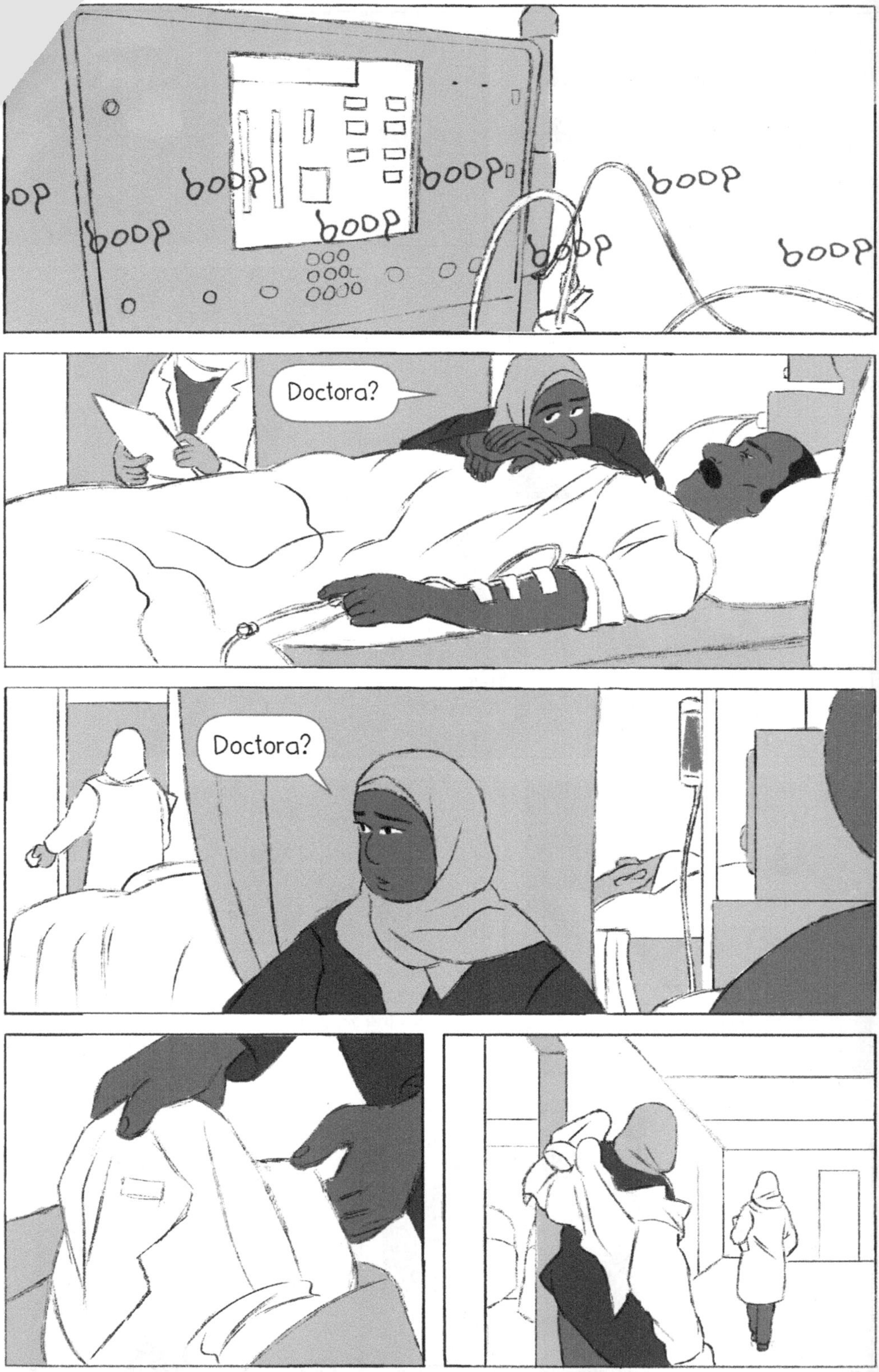

oop
boop
boop
boop
boop
boop
boop
boop
Doctora?
Doctora?

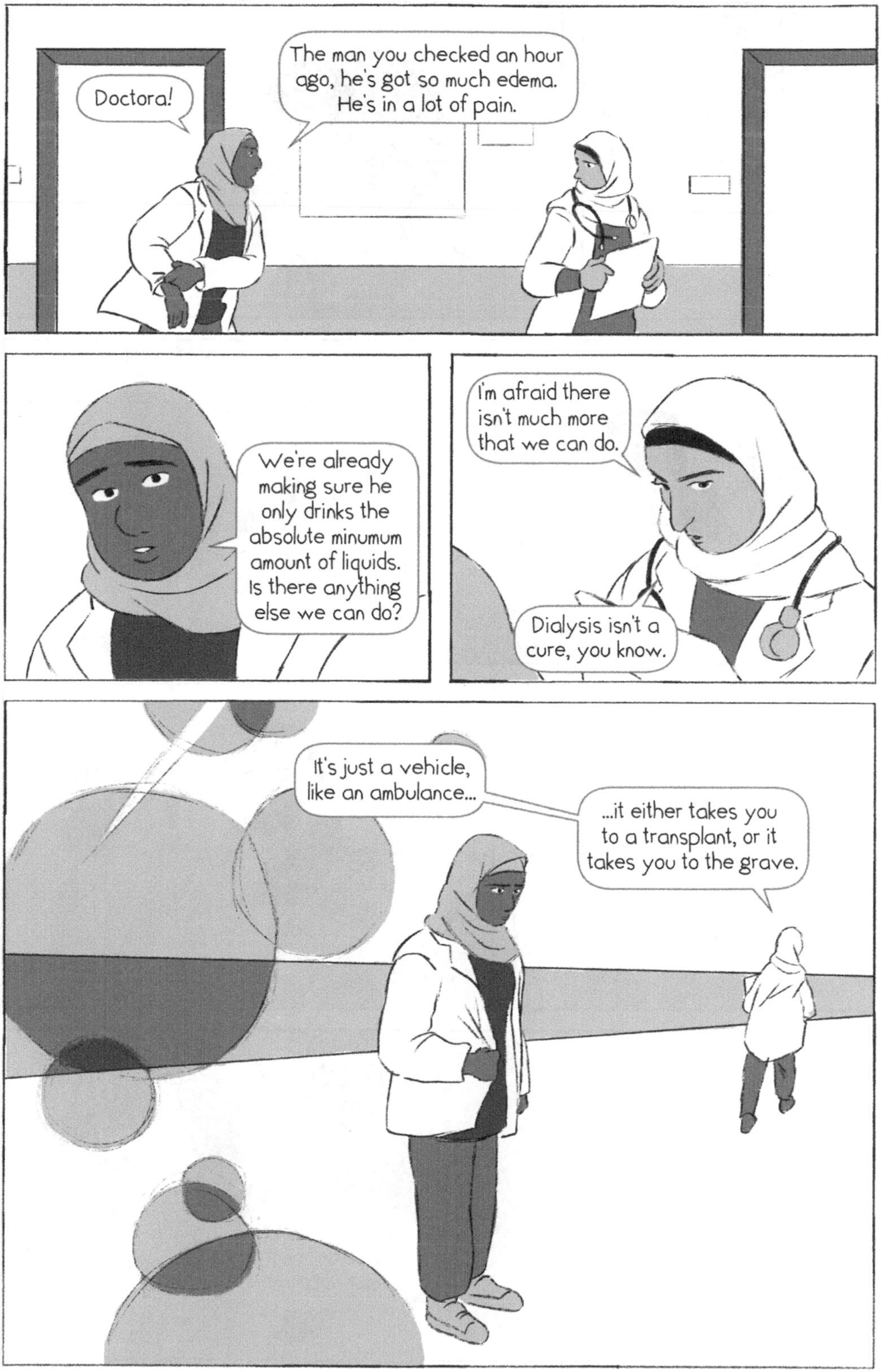
Doctora!
The man you checked an hour ago, he's got so much edema. He's in a lot of pain.
We're already making sure he only drinks the absolute minumum amount of liquids. Is there anything else we can do?
I'm afraid there isn't much more that we can do.
Dialysis isn't a cure, you know.
It's just a vehicle, like an ambulance...
...it either takes you to a transplant, or it takes you to the grave.

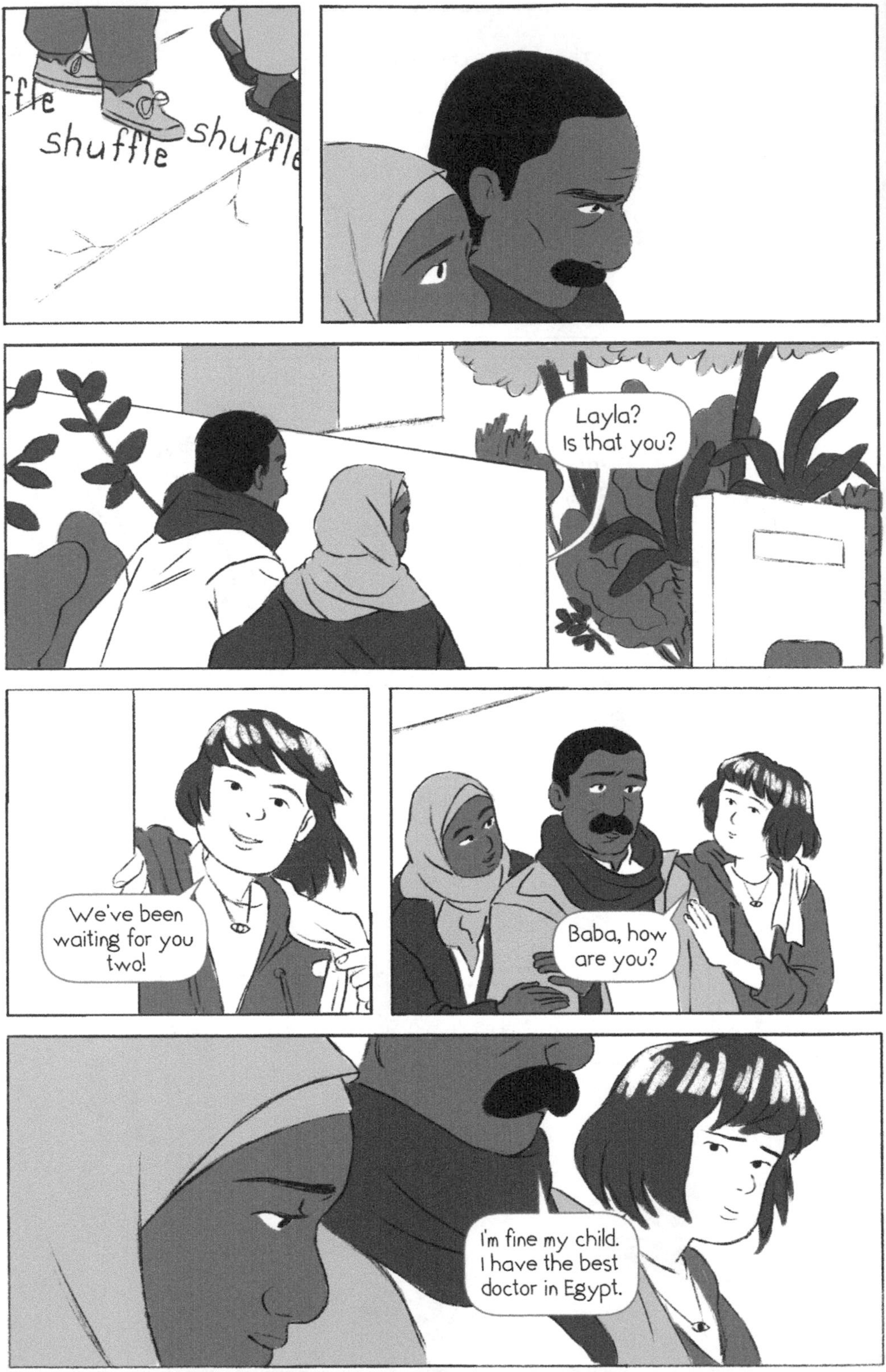
ffle
shuffle
shuffle
Layla? Is that you?
We've been waiting for you two!
Baba, how are you?
I'm fine my child. I have the best doctor in Egypt.

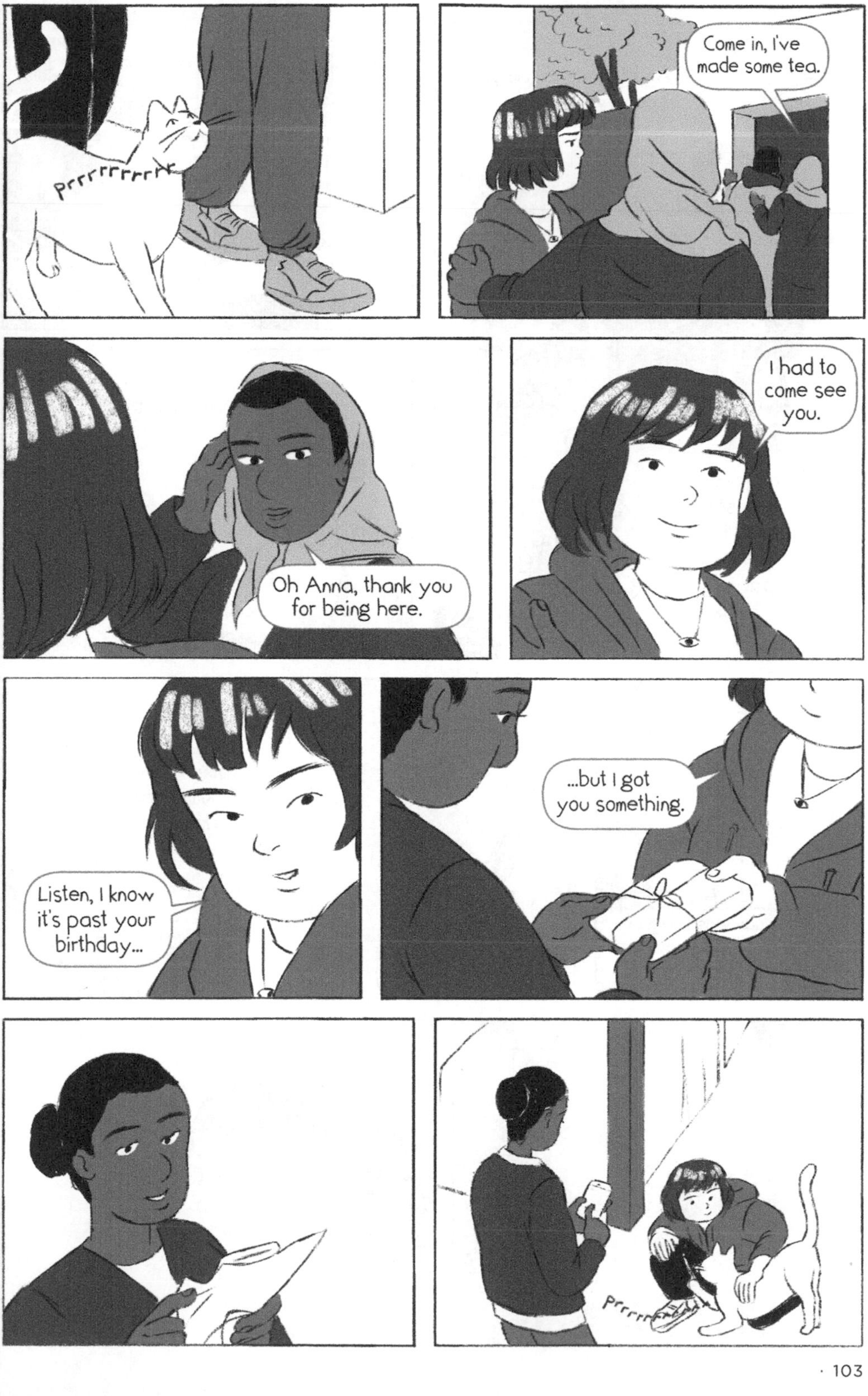

Prrrrrrrrrr
Come in, I've made some tea.
Oh Anna, thank you for being here.
I had to come see you.
Listen, I know it's past your birthday...
...but I got you something.
Prrrrr

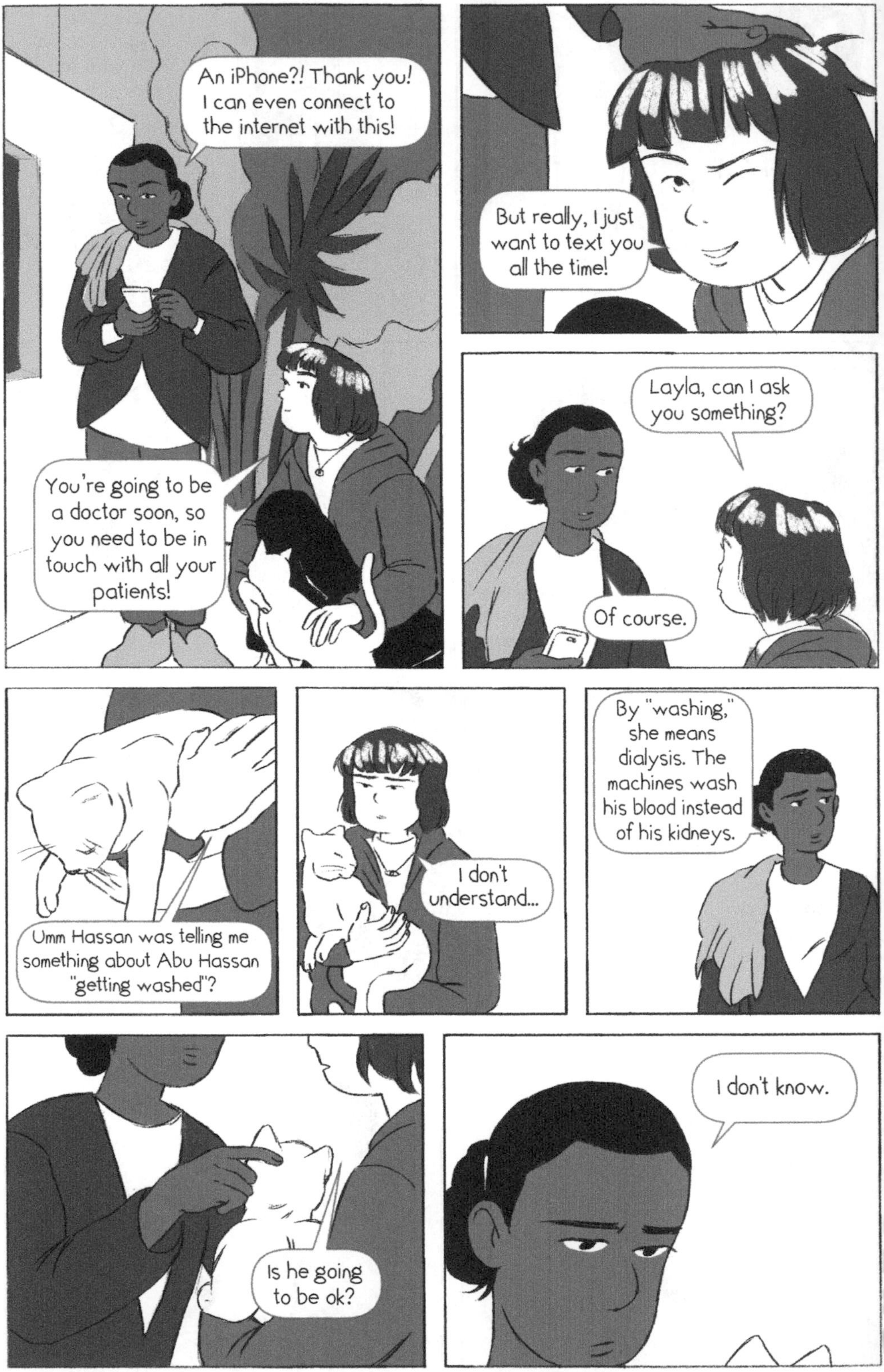
An iPhone?! Thank you! I can even connect to the internet with this!
You're going to be a doctor soon, so you need to be in touch with all your patients!
But really, I just want to text you all the time!
Layla, can I ask you something?
Of course.
Umm Hassan was telling me something about Abu Hassan "getting washed"?
I don't understand...
By "washing," she means dialysis. The machines wash his blood instead of his kidneys.
Is he going to be ok?
I don't know.

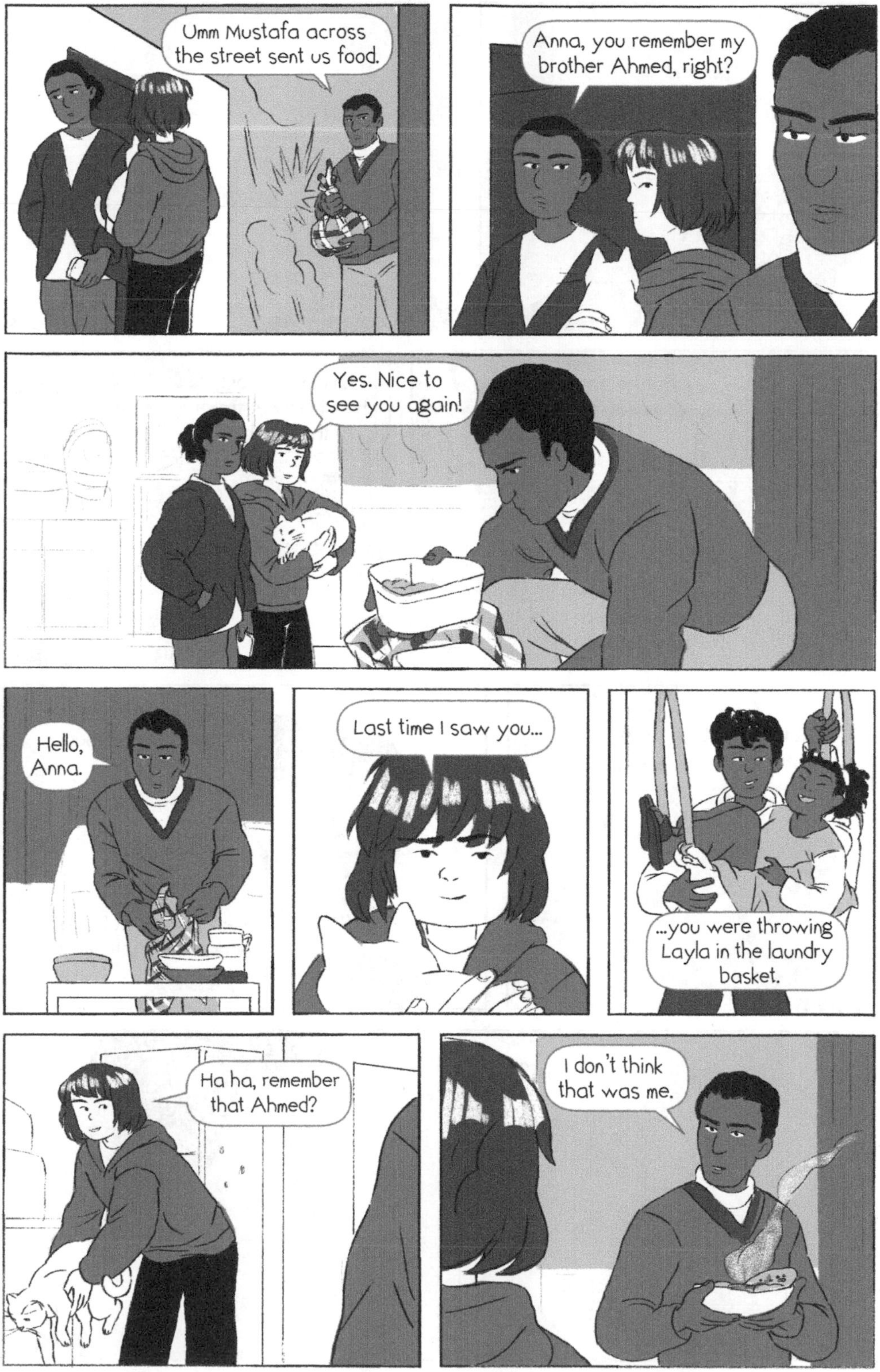
Umm Mustafa across the street sent us food.
Anna, you remember my brother Ahmed, right?
Yes. Nice to see you again!
Hello, Anna.
Last time I saw you...
...you were throwing Layla in the laundry basket.
Ha ha, remember that Ahmed?
I don't think that was me.

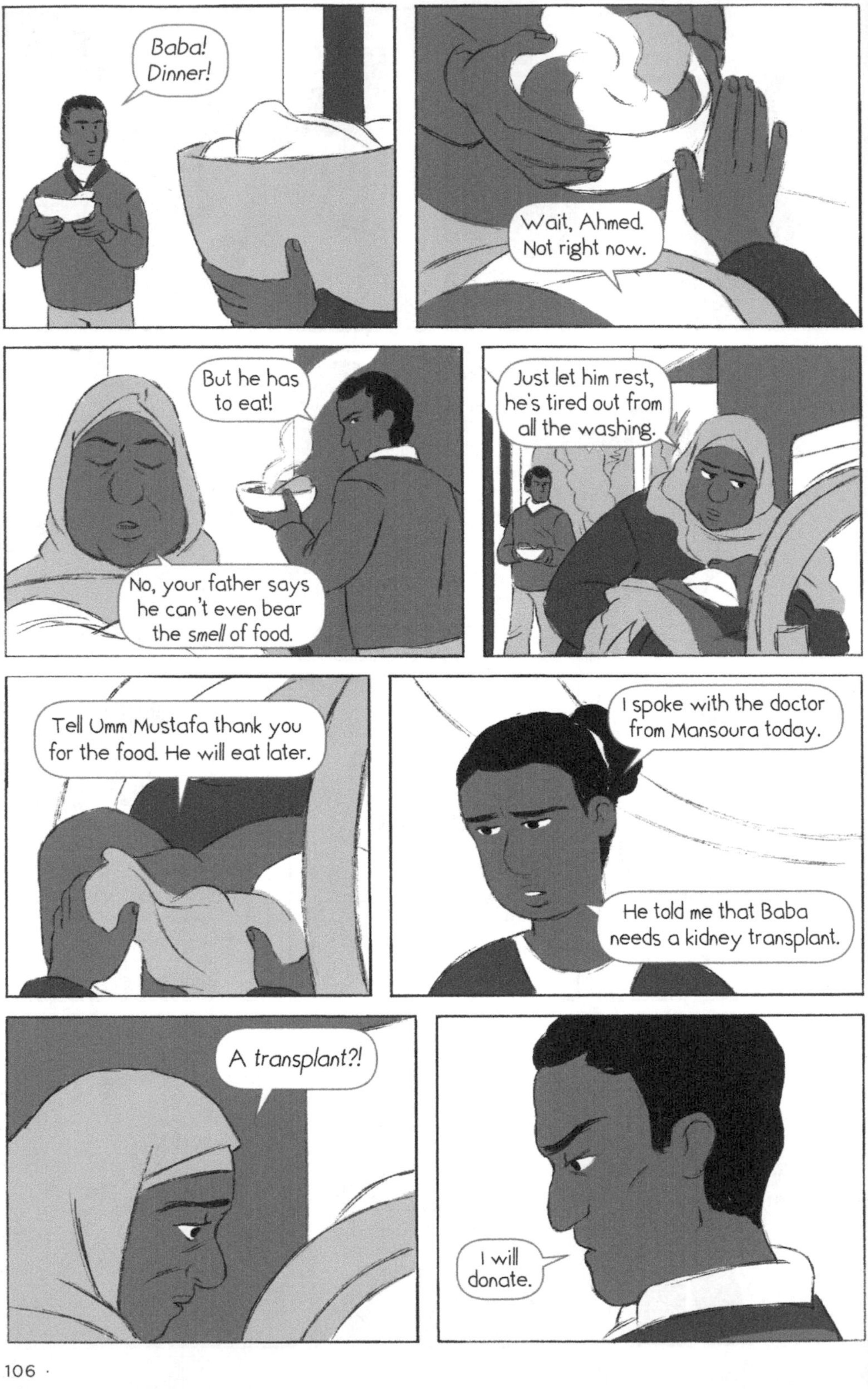
Baba! Dinner!
Wait, Ahmed. Not right now.
But he has to eat!
No, your father says he can't even bear the *smell* of food.
Just let him rest, he's tired out from all the washing.
Tell Umm Mustafa thank you for the food. He will eat later.
I spoke with the doctor from Mansoura today.
He told me that Baba needs a kidney transplant.
A *transplant*?!
I will donate.

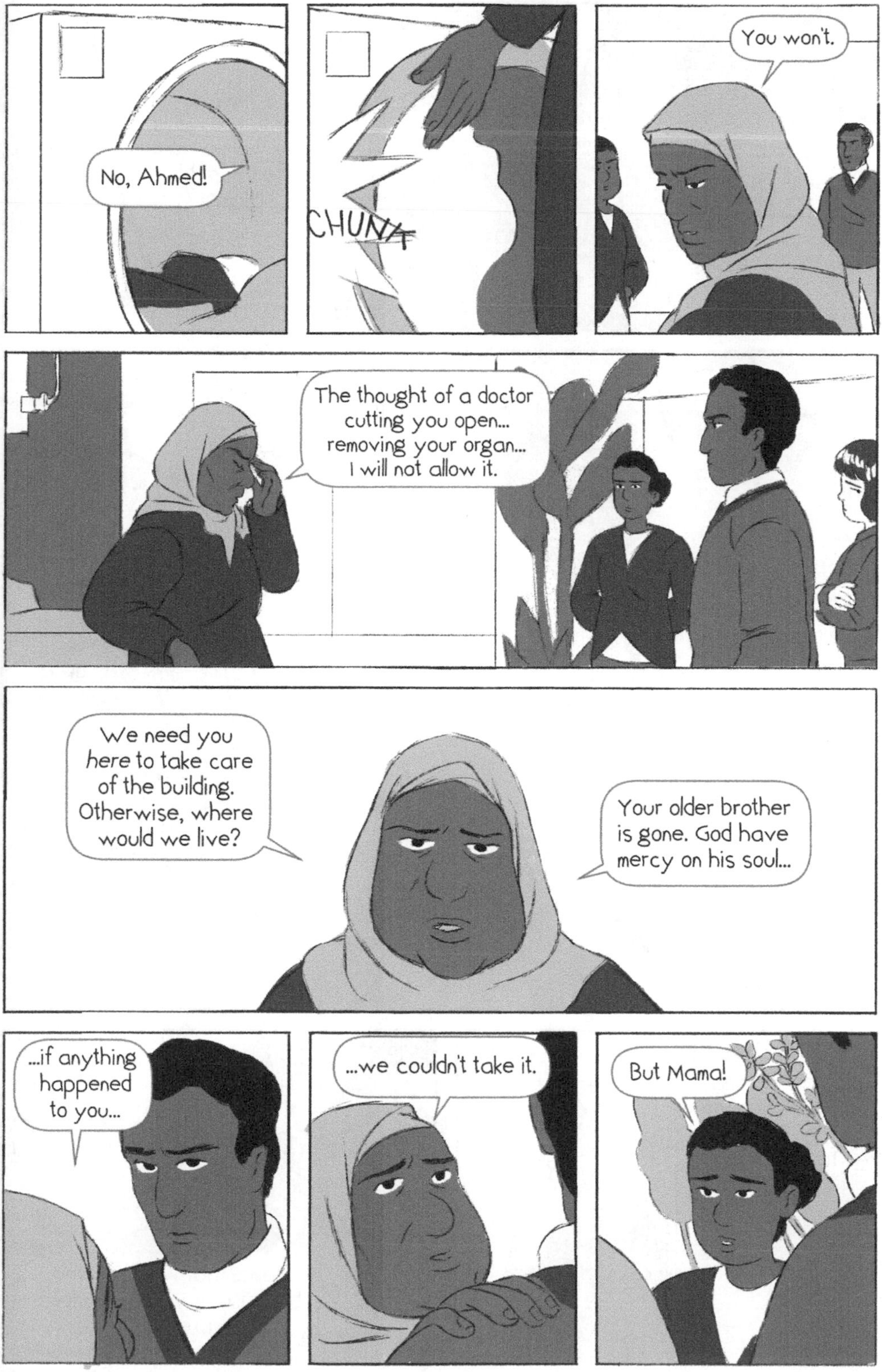
No, Ahmed!
CHUNK
You won't.
The thought of a doctor cutting you open... removing your organ... I will not allow it.
We need you *here* to take care of the building. Otherwise, where would we live?
Your older brother is gone. God have mercy on his soul...
...if anything happened to you...
...we couldn't take it.
But Mama!

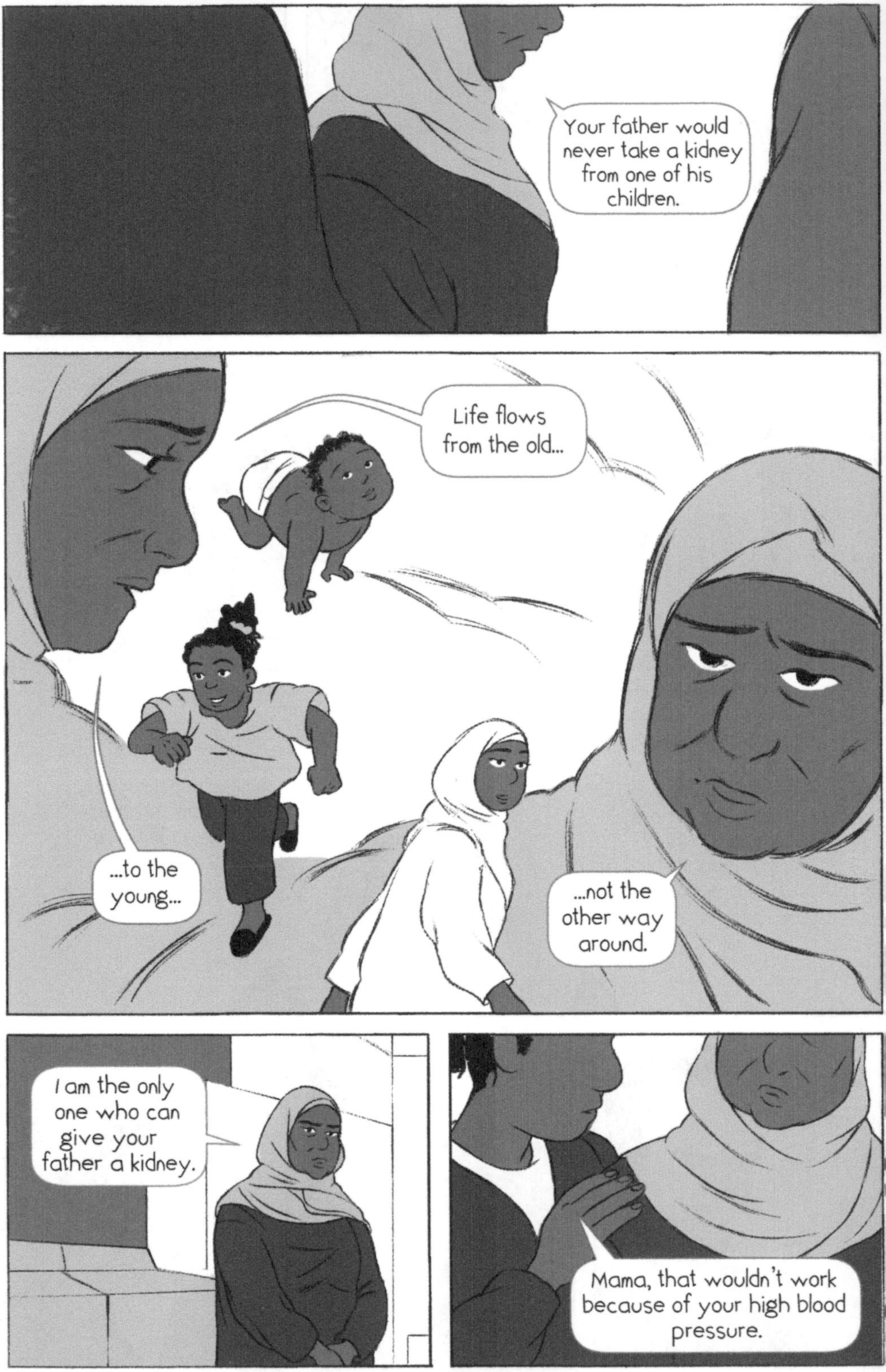
Your father would never take a kidney from one of his children.
Life flows from the old...
...to the young...
...not the other way around.
I am the only one who can give your father a kidney.
Mama, that wouldn't work because of your high blood pressure.

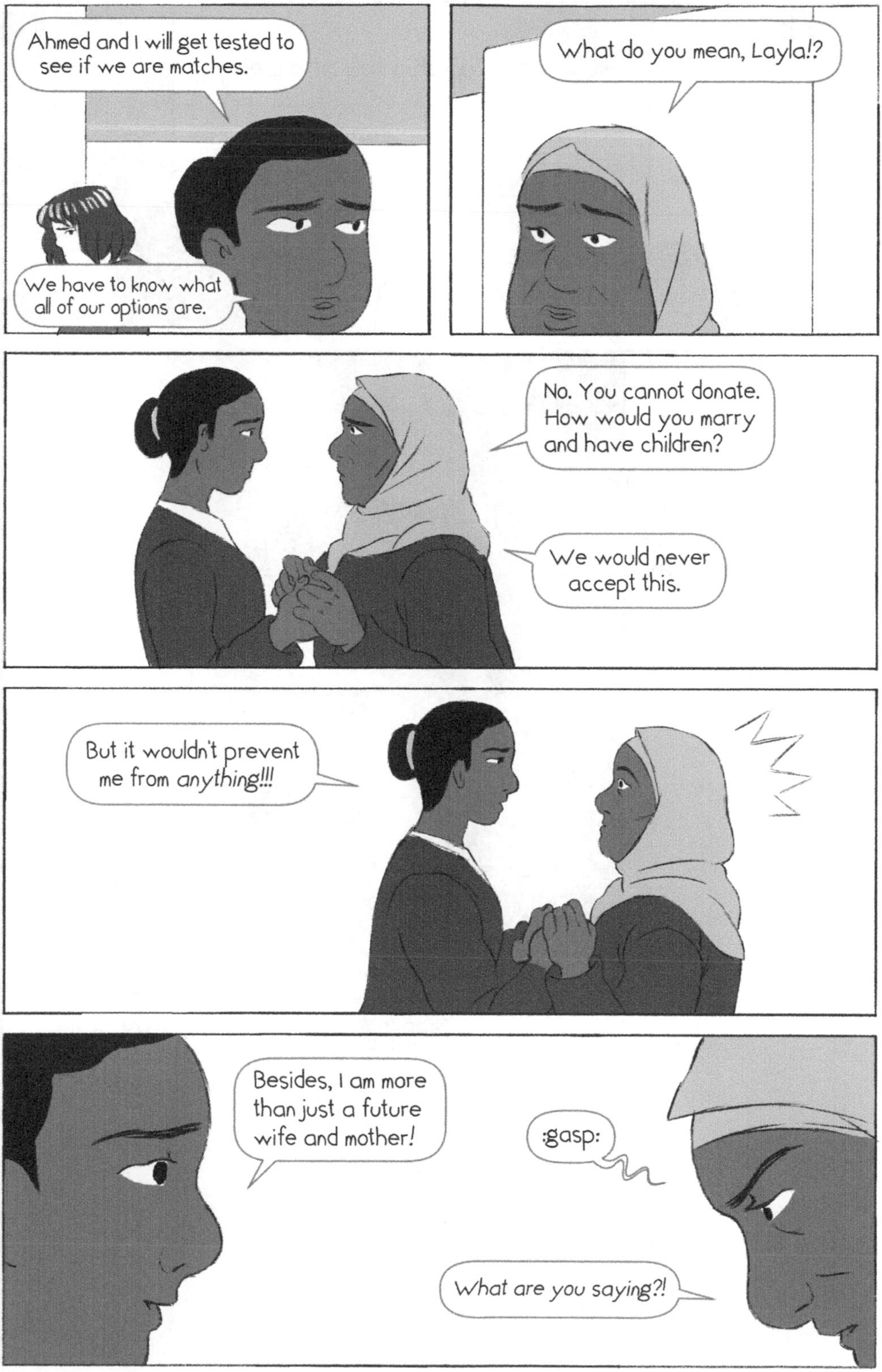
Ahmed and I will get tested to see if we are matches.
We have to know what all of our options are.
What do you mean, Layla!?
No. You cannot donate. How would you marry and have children?
We would never accept this.
But it wouldn't prevent me from *anything*!!!
Besides, I am more than just a future wife and mother!
:gasp:
What are you saying?!

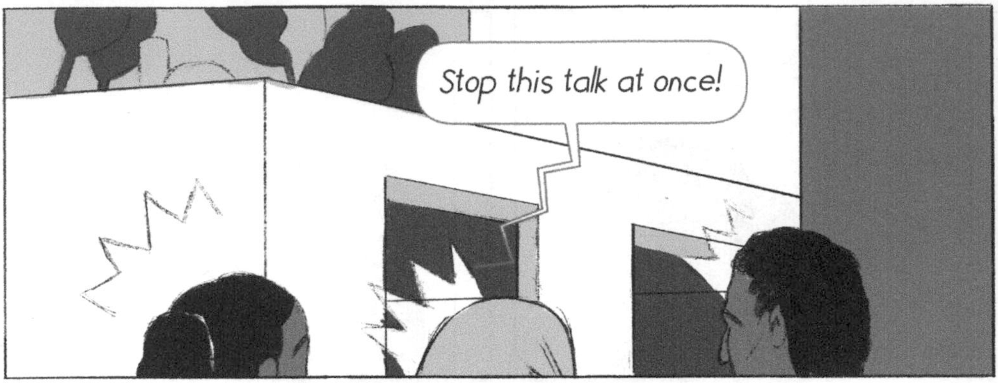
Stop this talk at once!

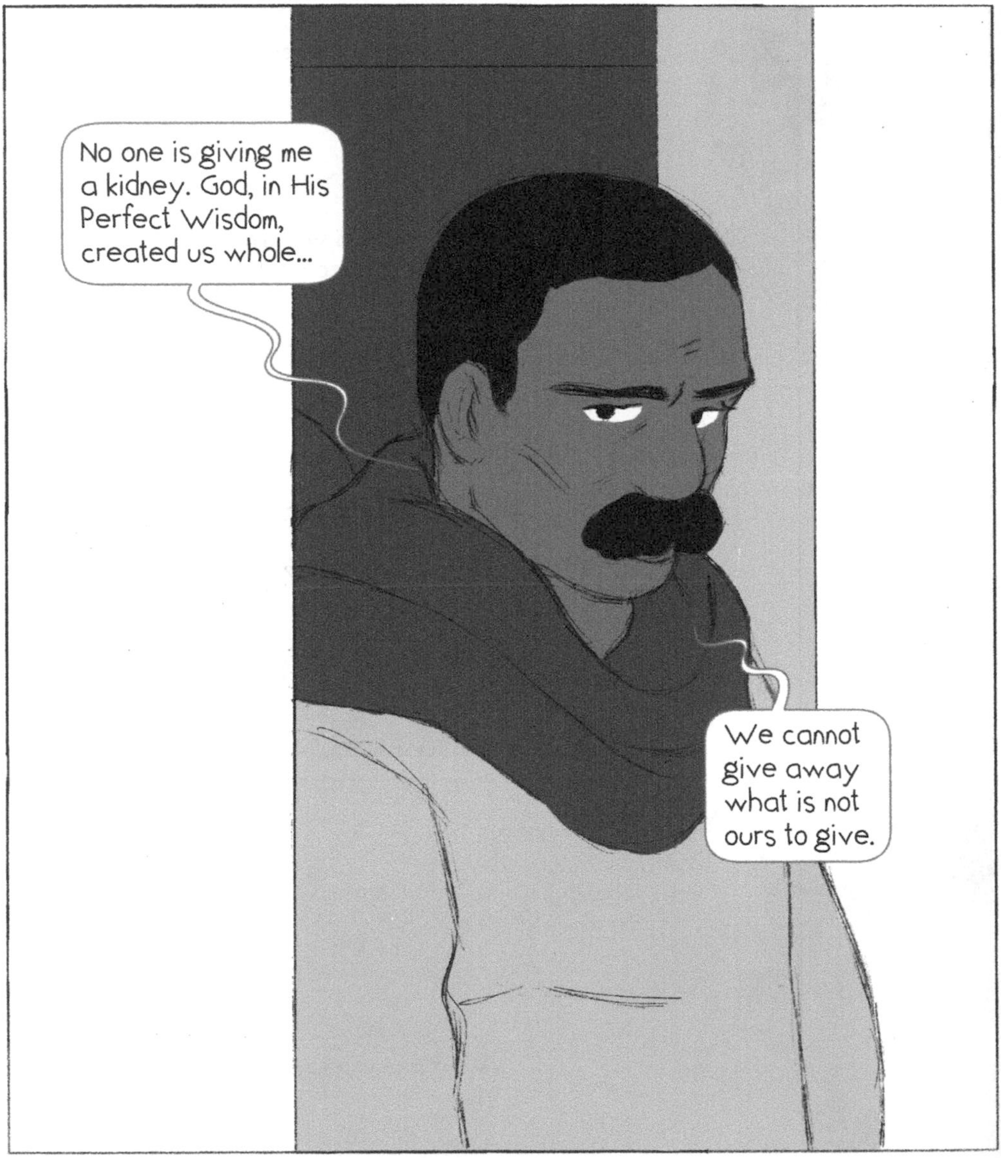
No one is giving me a kidney. God, in His Perfect Wisdom, created us whole...
We cannot give away what is not ours to give.

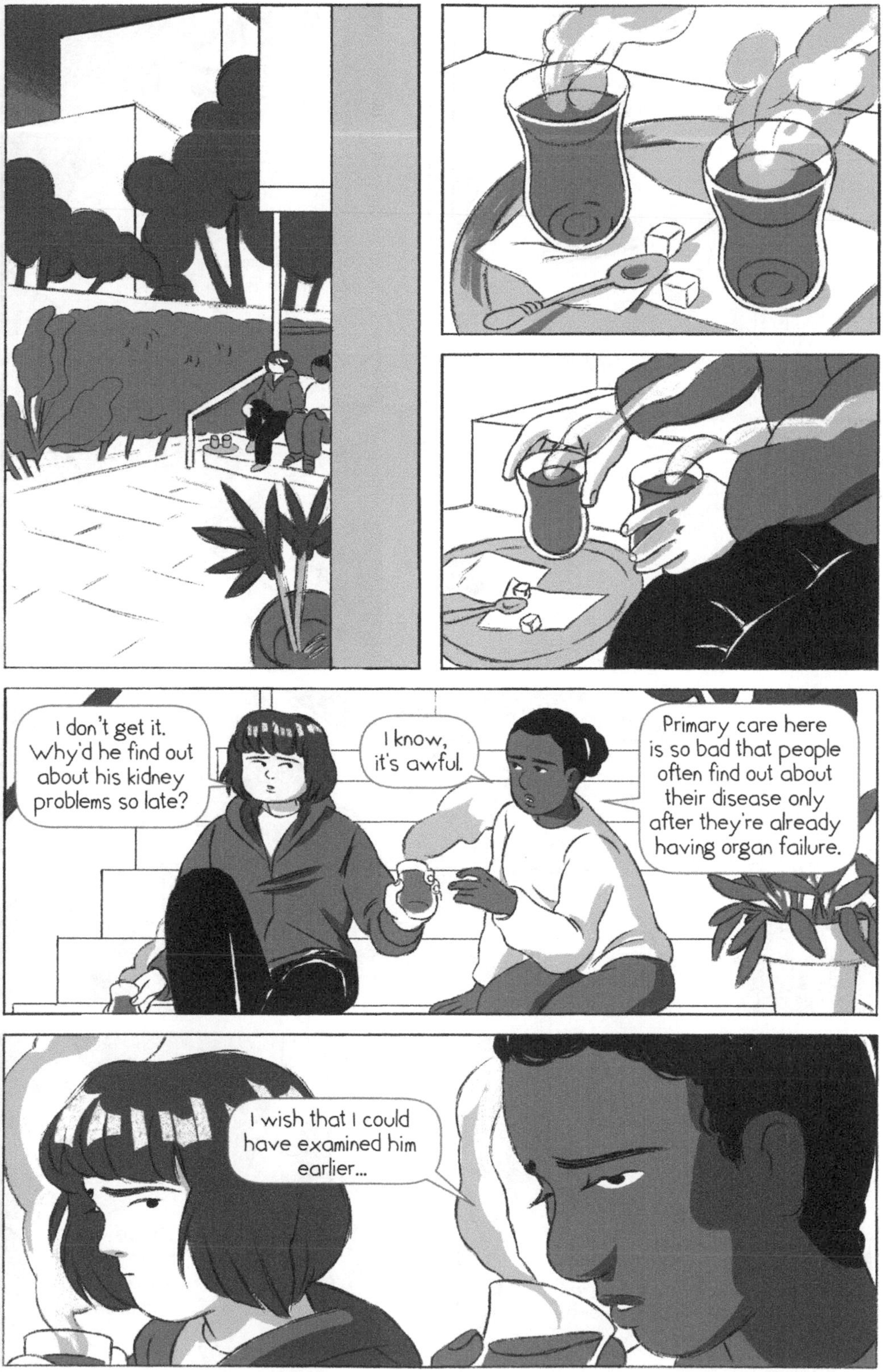
I don't get it. Why'd he find out about his kidney problems so late?
I know, it's awful.
Primary care here is so bad that people often find out about their disease only after they're already having organ failure.
I wish that I could have examined him earlier...

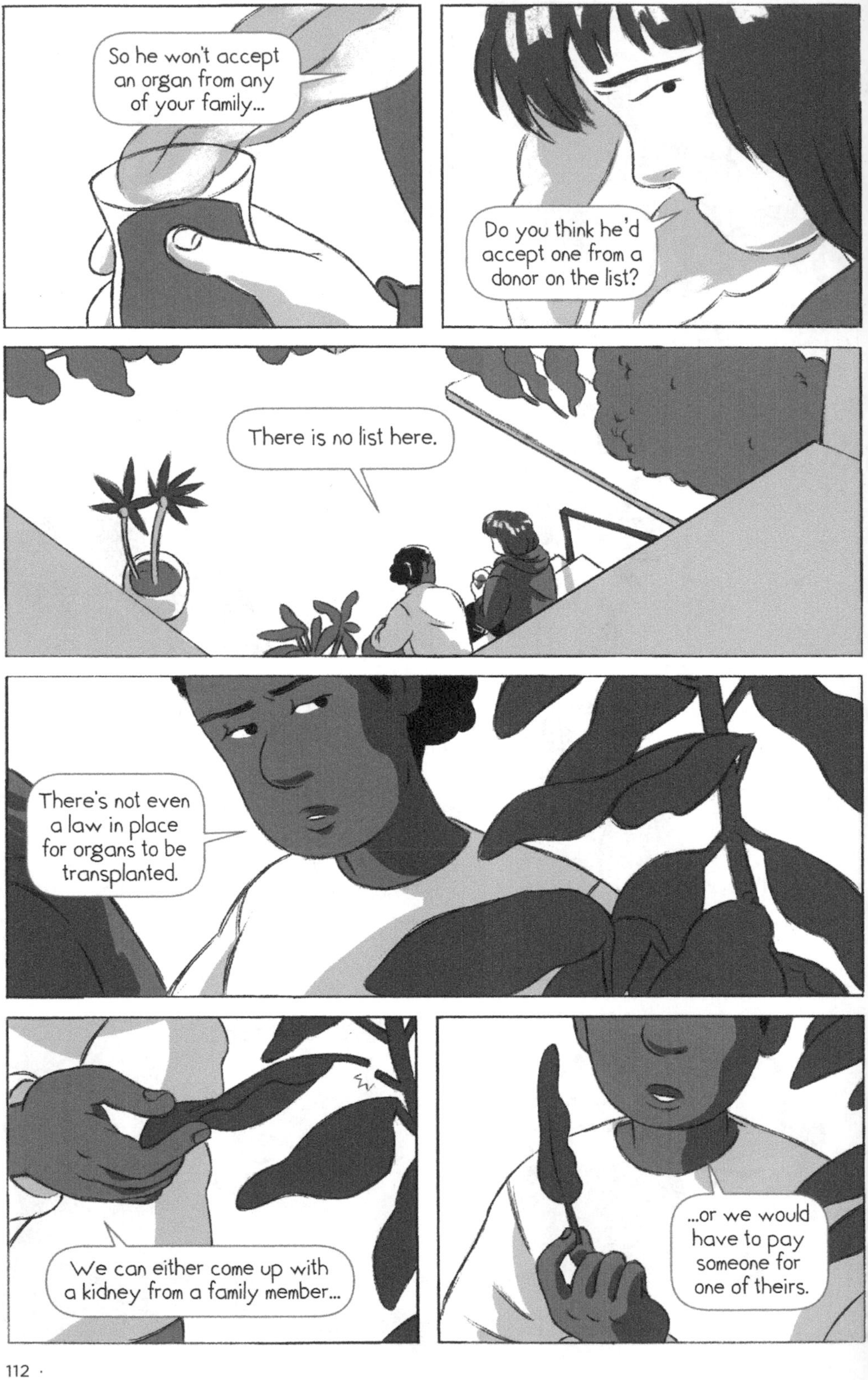
So he won't accept an organ from any of your family...
Do you think he'd accept one from a donor on the list?
There is no list here.
There's not even a law in place for organs to be transplanted.
We can either come up with a kidney from a family member...
...or we would have to pay someone for one of theirs.

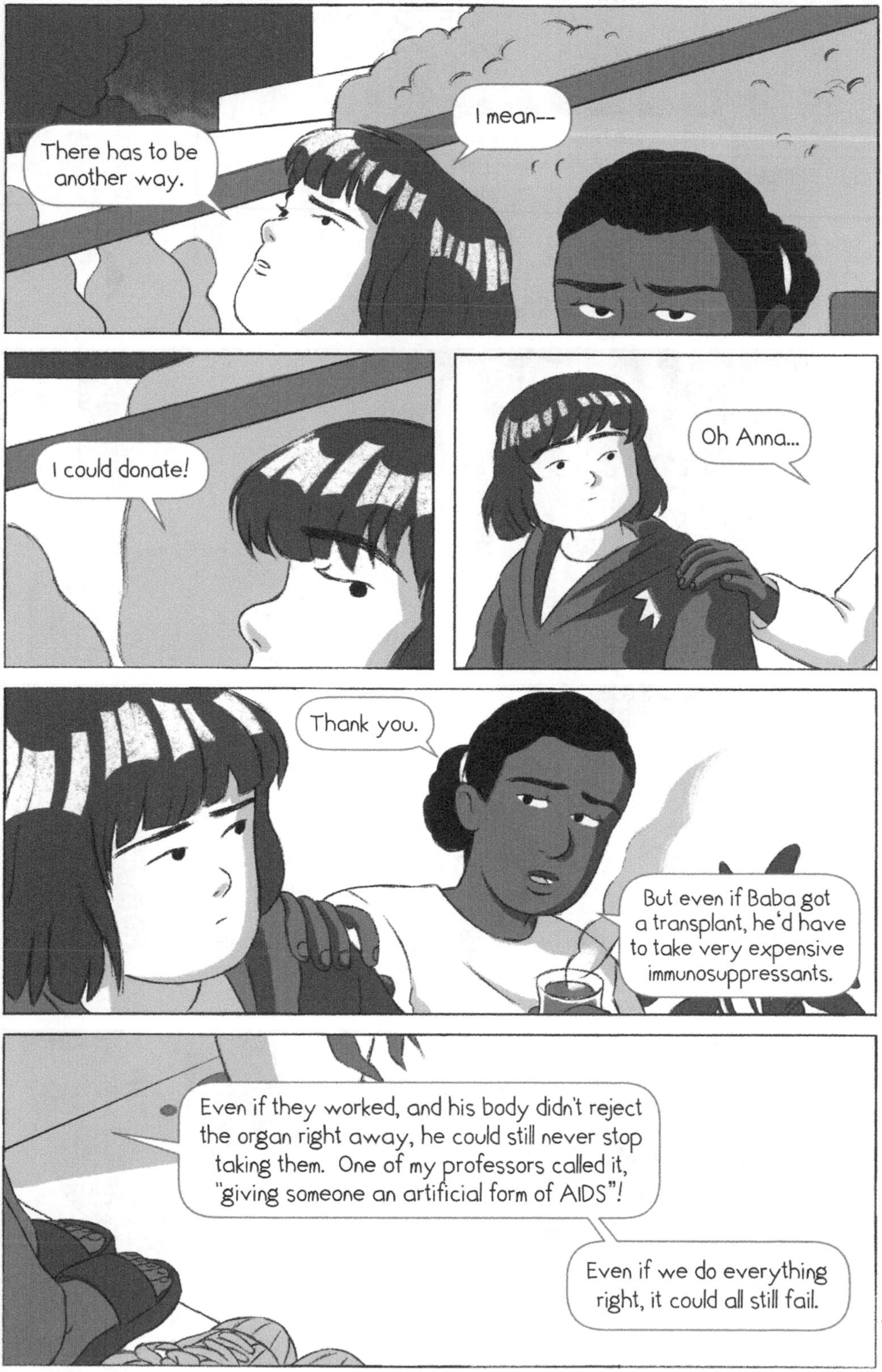
There has to be another way.
I mean--
I could donate!
Oh Anna...
Thank you.
But even if Baba got a transplant, he'd have to take very expensive immunosuppressants.
Even if they worked, and his body didn't reject the organ right away, he could still never stop taking them. One of my professors called it, "giving someone an artificial form of AIDS"!
Even if we do everything right, it could all still fail.

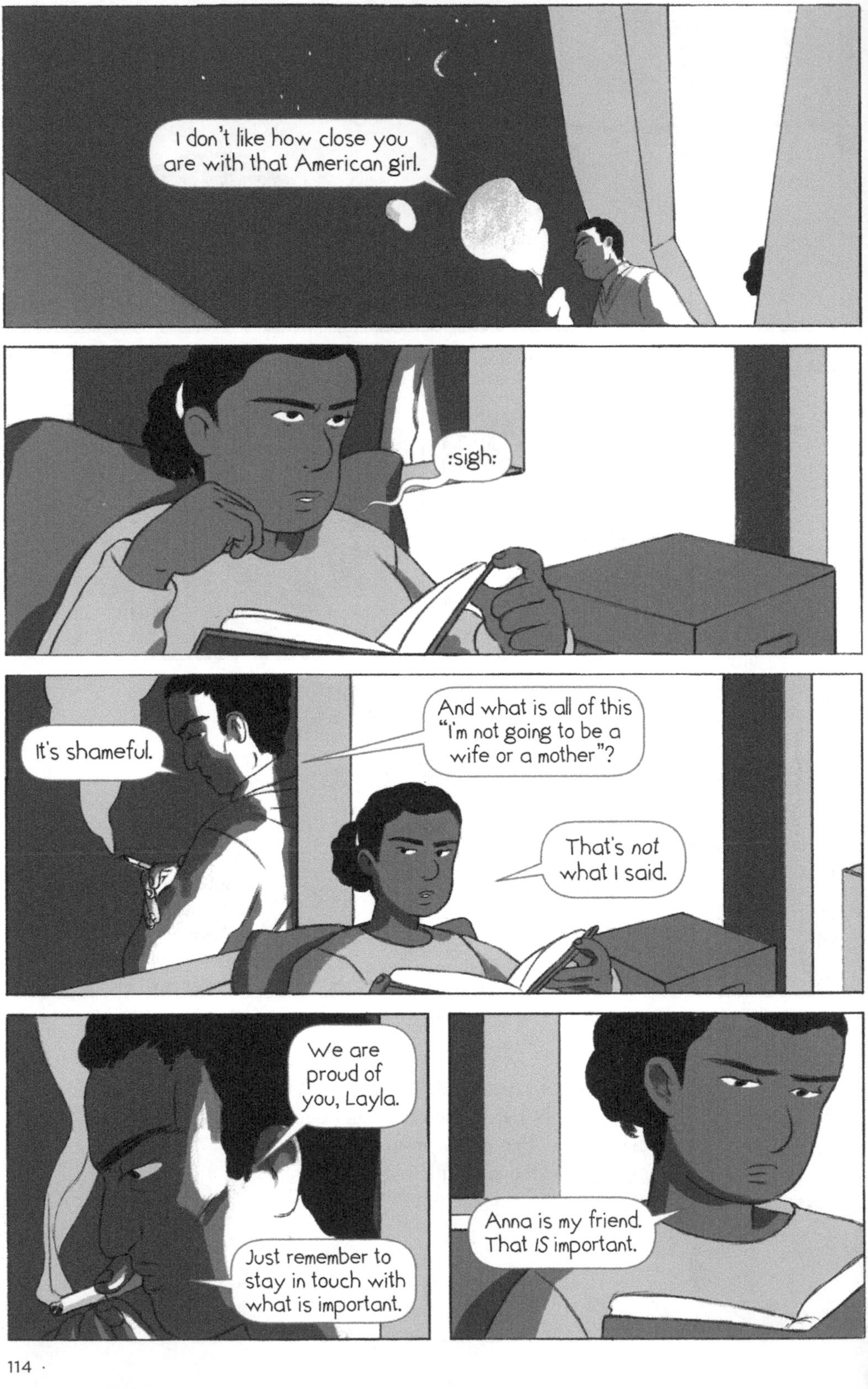
I don't like how close you are with that American girl.
:sigh:
It's shameful.
And what is all of this "I'm not going to be a wife or a mother"?
That's *not* what I said.
We are proud of you, Layla.
Just remember to stay in touch with what is important.
Anna is my friend. That *IS* important.

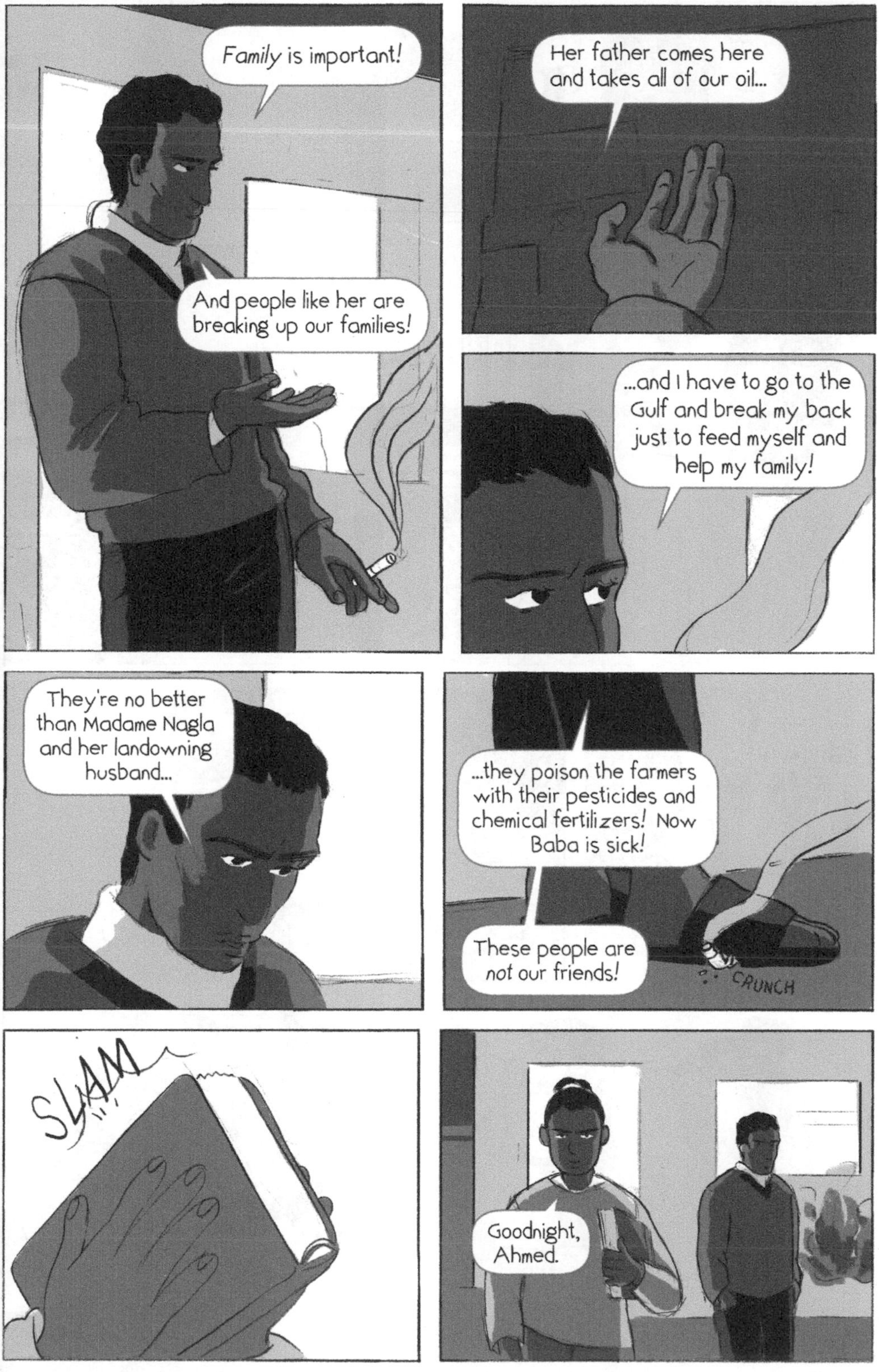
Family is important!
And people like her are breaking up our families!
Her father comes here and takes all of our oil...
...and I have to go to the Gulf and break my back just to feed myself and help my family!
They're no better than Madame Nagla and her landowning husband...
...they poison the farmers with their pesticides and chemical fertilizers! Now Baba is sick!
These people are not our friends!
CRUNCH
SLAM
Goodnight, Ahmed.

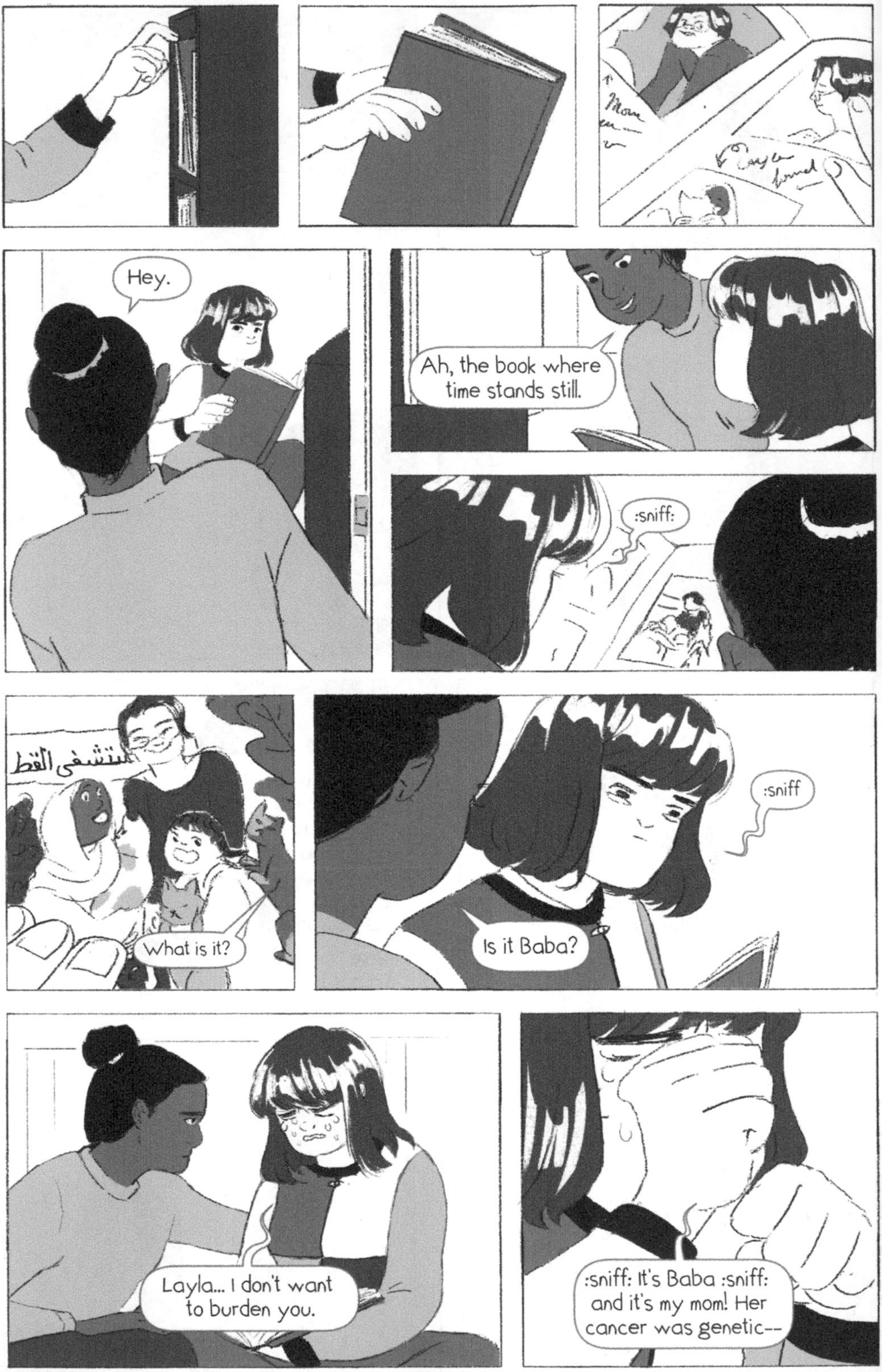

Hey.
Ah, the book where time stands still.
:sniff:
ستشفى القط
What is it?
:sniff
Is it Baba?
Layla... I don't want to burden you.
:sniff: It's Baba :sniff: and it's my mom! Her cancer was genetic--

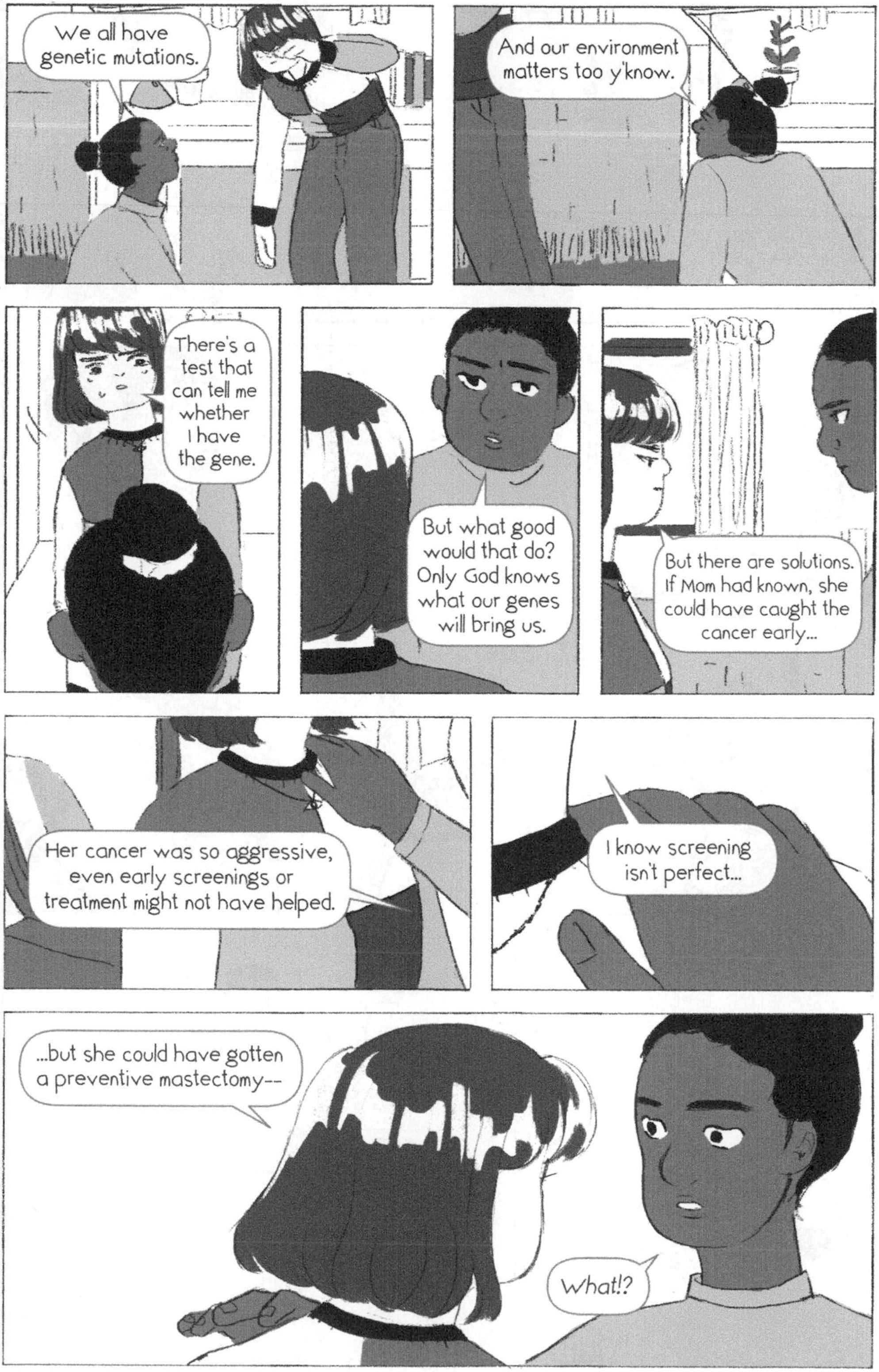
We all have genetic mutations.
And our environment matters too y'know.
There's a test that can tell me whether I have the gene.
But what good would that do? Only God knows what our genes will bring us.
But there are solutions. If Mom had known, she could have caught the cancer early...
Her cancer was so aggressive, even early screenings or treatment might not have helped.
I know screening isn't perfect...
...but she could have gotten a preventive mastectomy--
What!?

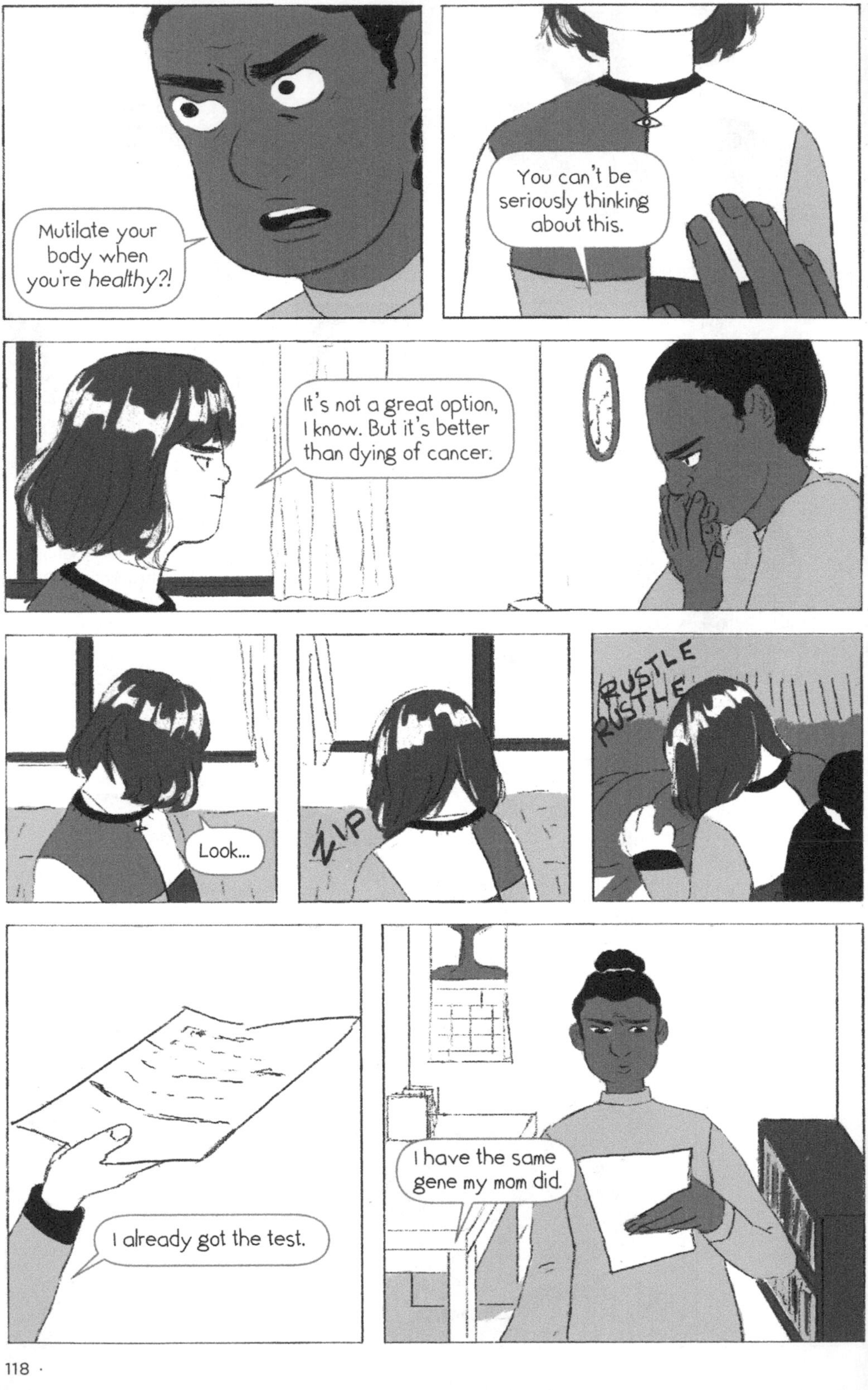

Mutilate your body when you're *healthy?!*
You can't be seriously thinking about this.
It's not a great option, I know. But it's better than dying of cancer.
Look...
ZIP
RUSTLE
RUSTLE
I already got the test.
I have the same gene my mom did.

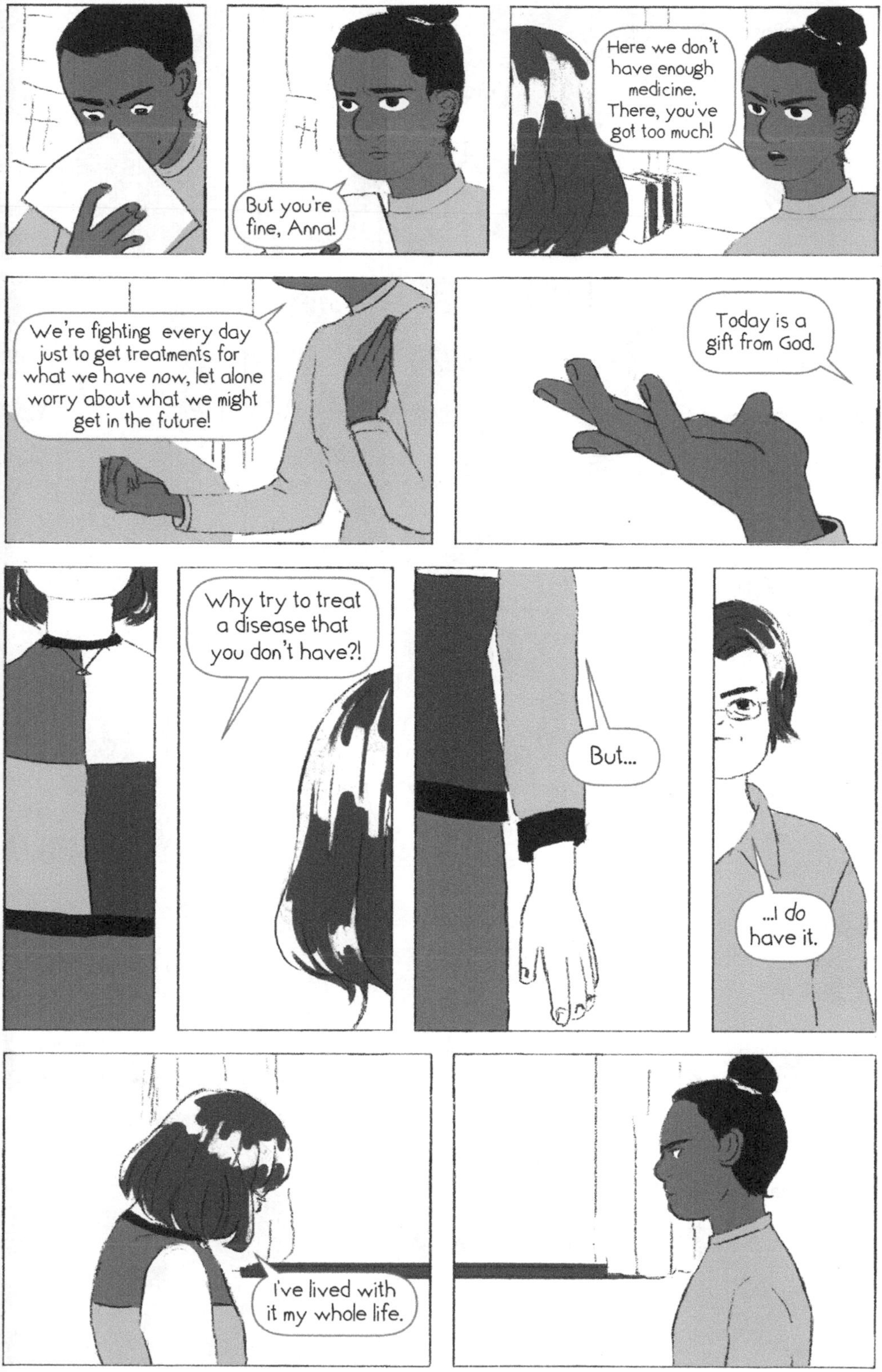
But you're fine, Anna!
Here we don't have enough medicine. There, you've got too much!
We're fighting every day just to get treatments for what we have *now*, let alone worry about what we might get in the future!
Today is a gift from God.
Why try to treat a disease that you don't have?!
But...
...I *do* have it.
I've lived with it my whole life.

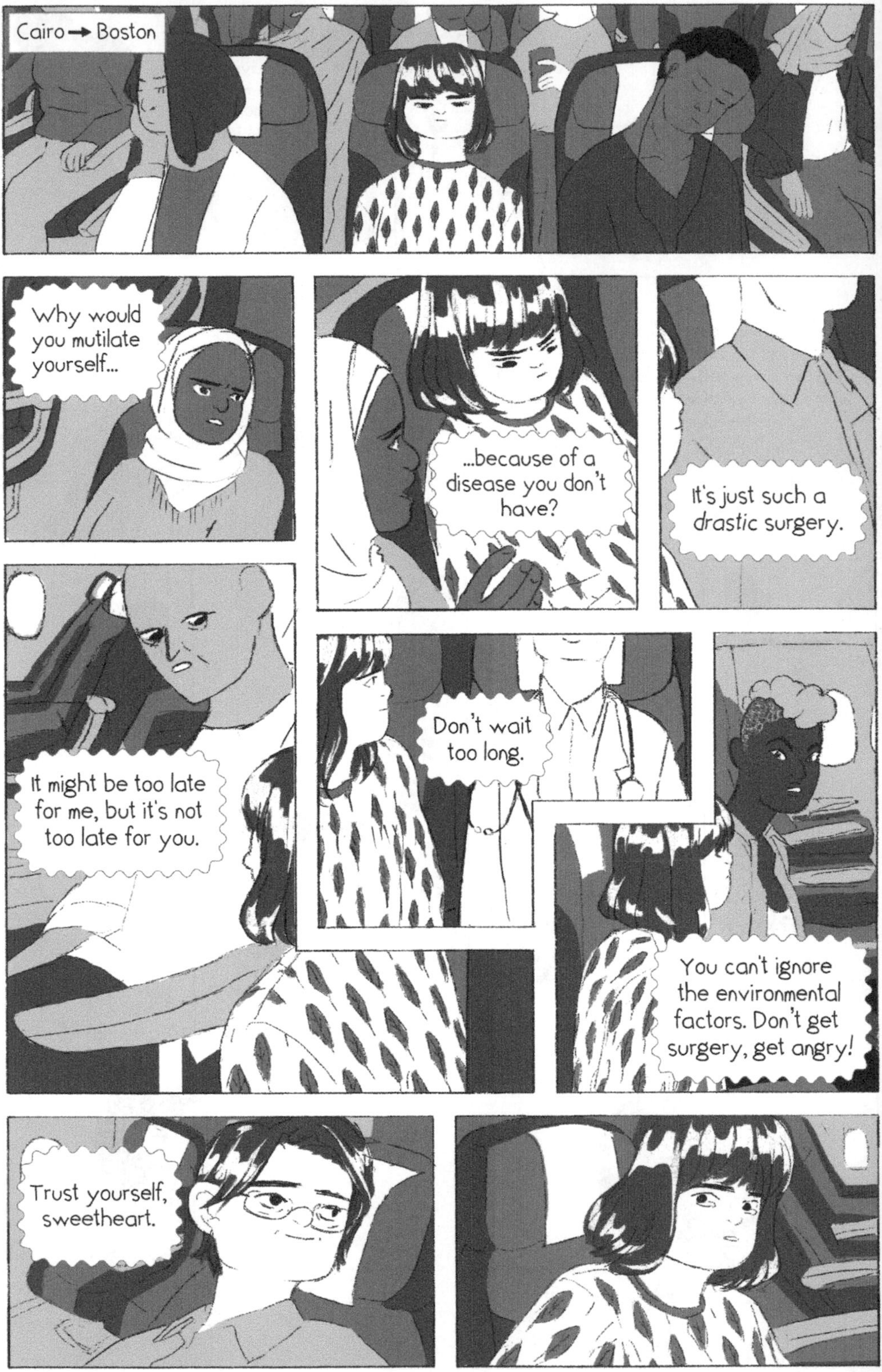
Cairo → Boston
Why would you mutilate yourself...
...because of a disease you don't have?
It's just such a *drastic* surgery.
It might be too late for me, but it's not too late for you.
Don't wait too long.
You can't ignore the environmental factors. Don't get surgery, get angry!
Trust yourself, sweetheart.

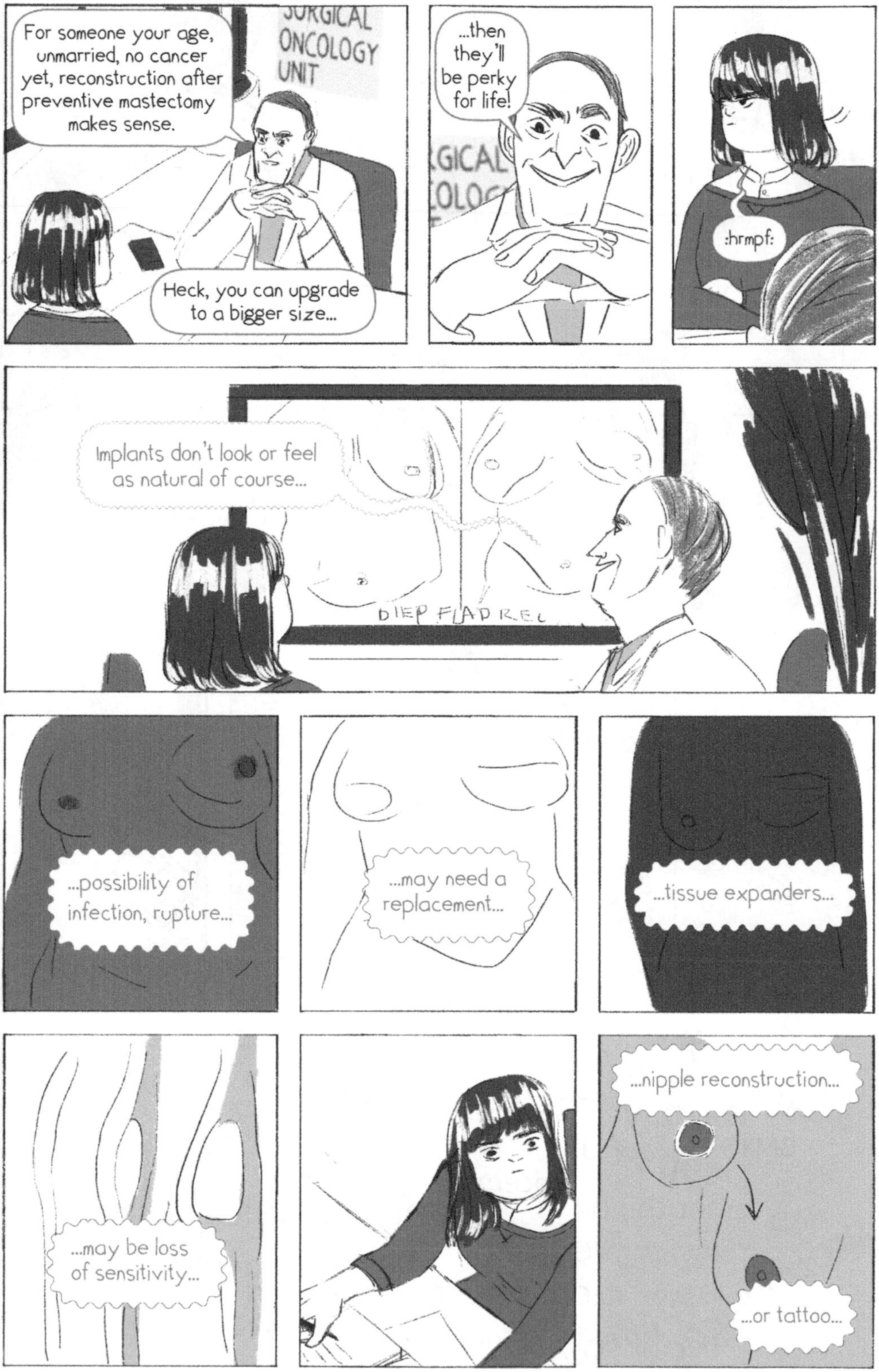
SURGICAL ONCOLOGY UNIT
For someone your age, unmarried, no cancer yet, reconstruction after preventive mastectomy makes sense.
Heck, you can upgrade to a bigger size...
...then they'll be perky for life!
:hrmpf:
Implants don't look or feel as natural of course...
DIEP FLAP REL
...possibility of infection, rupture...
...may need a replacement...
...tissue expanders...
...may be loss of sensitivity...
...nipple reconstruction...
...or tattoo...

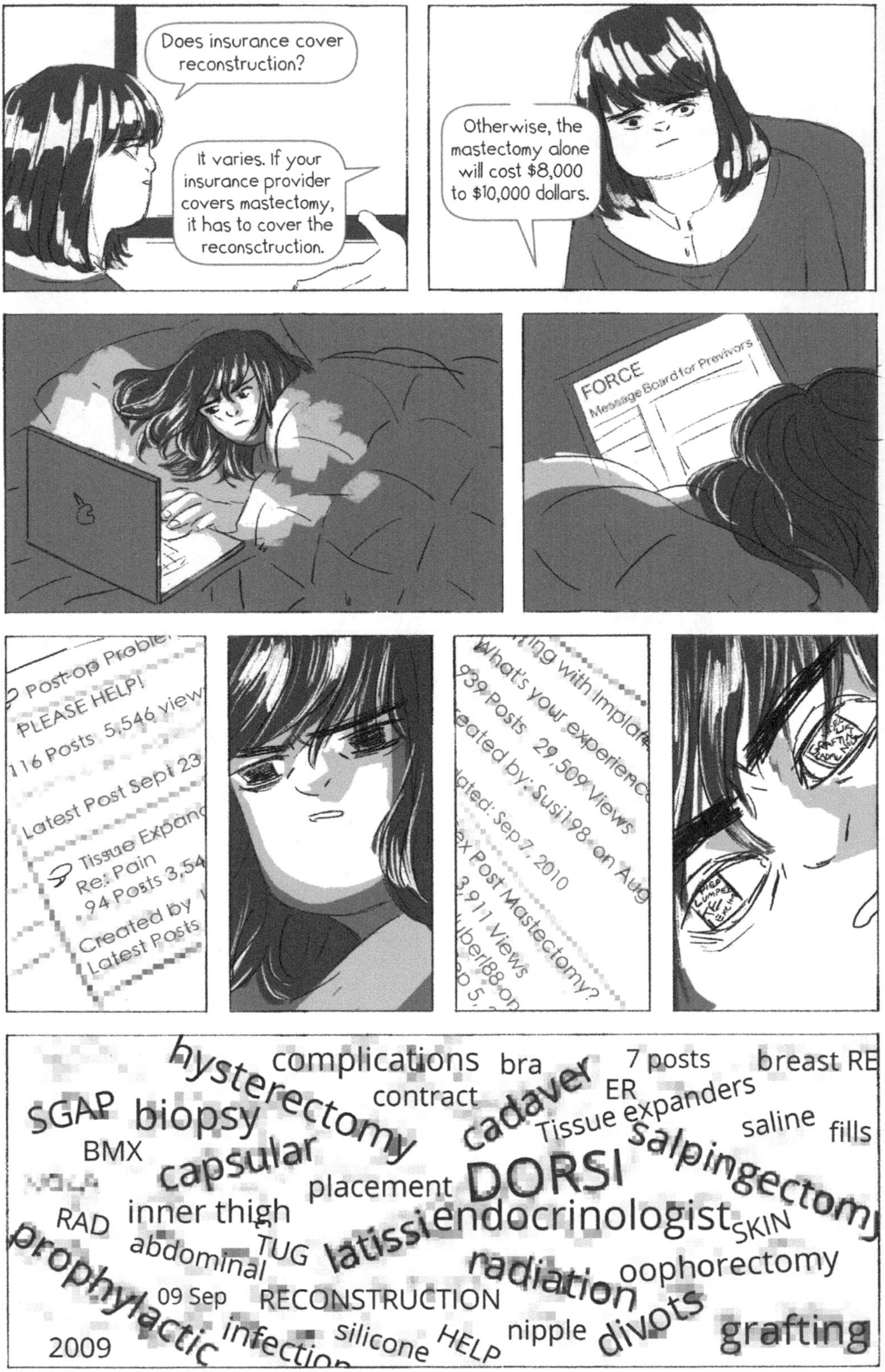
Does insurance cover reconstruction?
It varies. If your insurance provider covers mastectomy, it has to cover the reconsctruction.
Otherwise, the mastectomy alone will cost $8,000 to $10,000 dollars.
FORCE
Message Board for Previvors
Post-op Proble
PLEASE HELP!
116 Posts 5,546 view
Latest Post Sept 23
Tissue Expand
Re: Pain
94 Posts 3,54
Created by
Latest Posts
What's your experienc
939 Posts 29,509 Views
eated by: Susi198 on Aug
ated: Sep 7, 2010
ex Post Mastectomy?
3,911 Views
complications
bra
7 posts
breast RE
hysterectomy
contract
ER
SGAP
biopsy
cadaver
Tissue expanders
saline
fills
BMX
capsular
salpingectomy
placement
DORSI
RAD
inner thigh
endocrinologist
SKIN
latissi
prophylactic
abdominal
TUG
radiation
oophorectomy
09 Sep
RECONSTRUCTION
nipple
divots
grafting
2009
infection
silicone
HELP

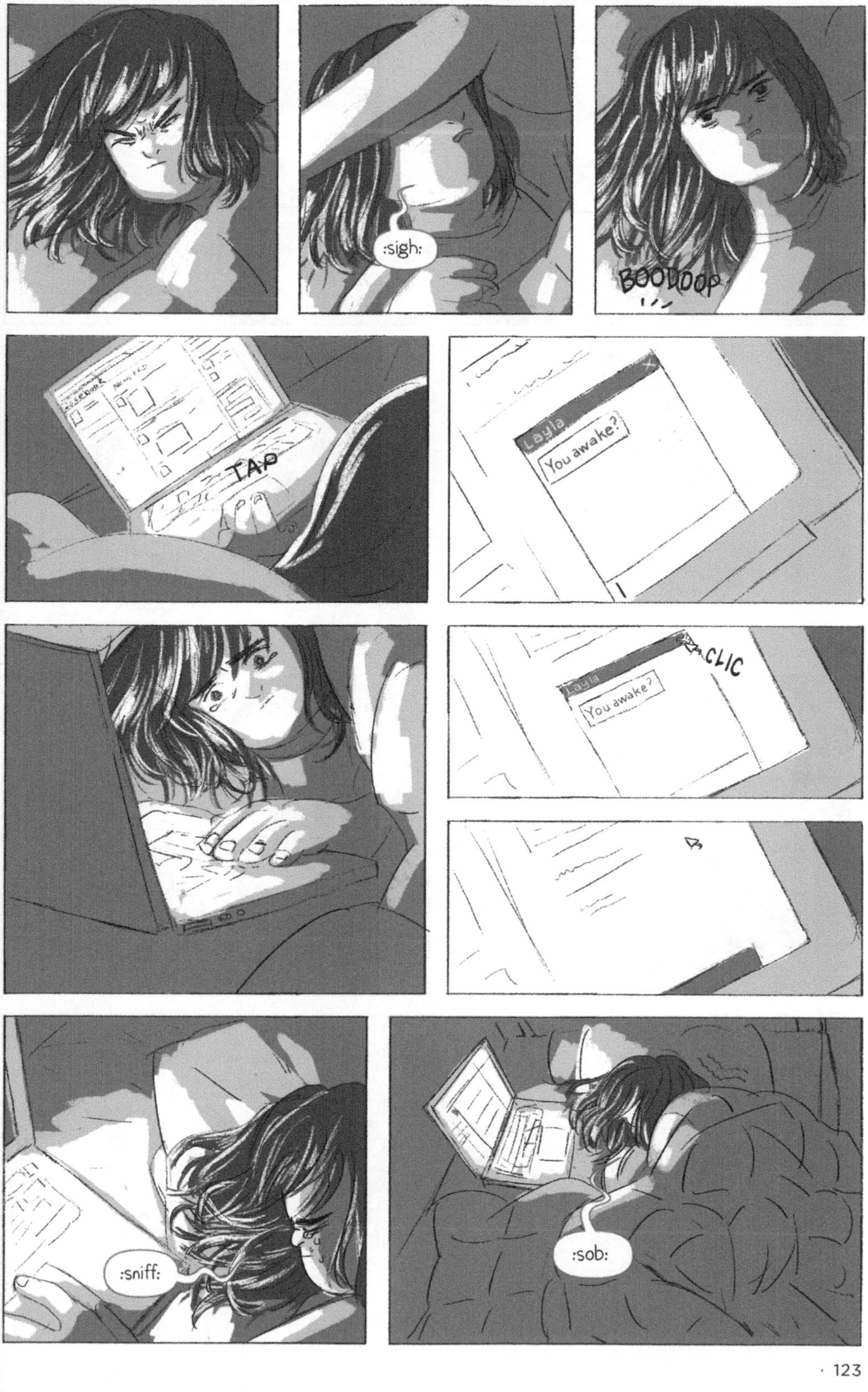
:sigh:
BOODOOP
TAP
Layla
You awake?
Layla
You awake?
CLIC
:sniff:
:sob:

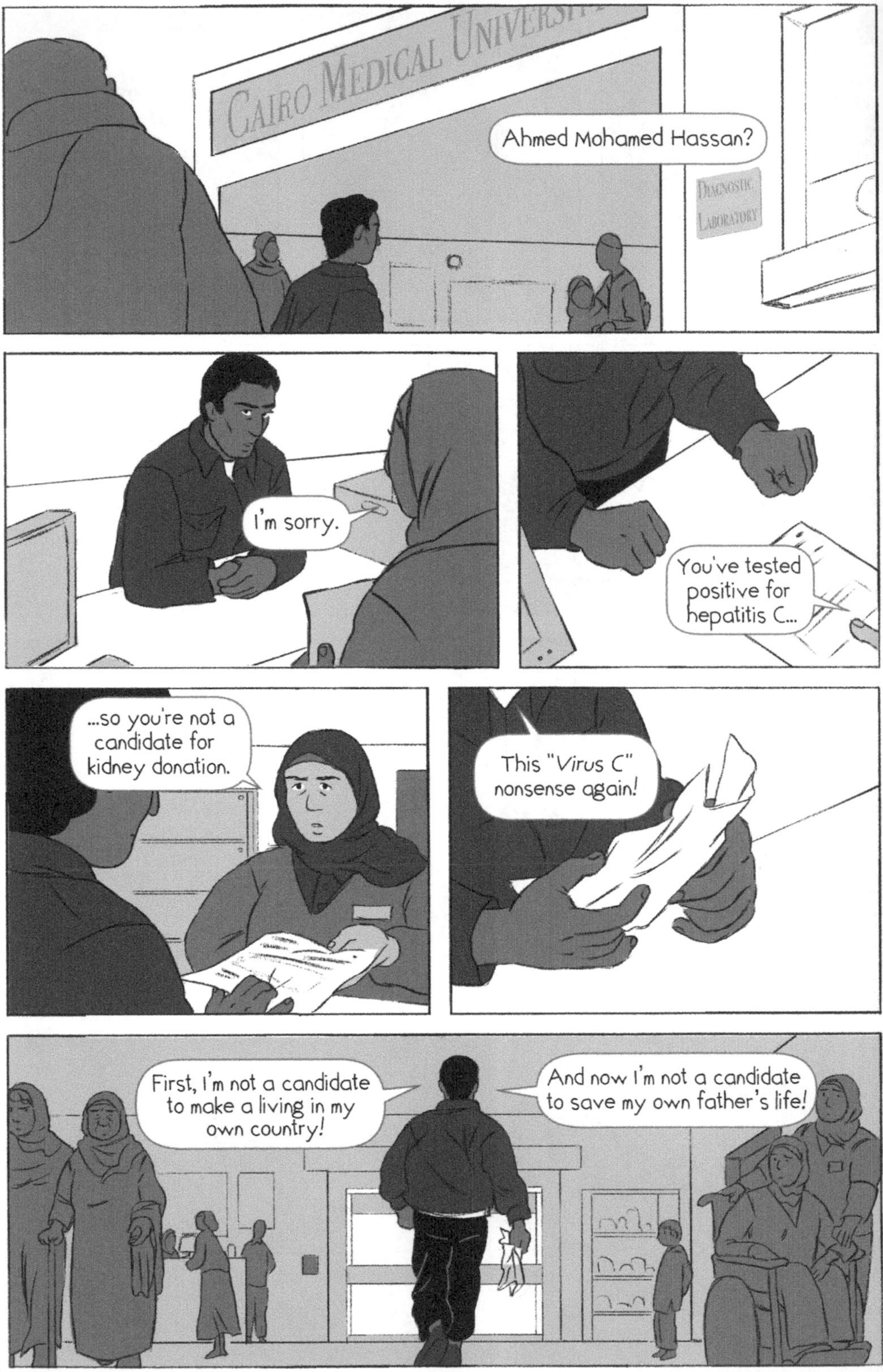
CAIRO MEDICAL UNIVERSIT
Ahmed Mohamed Hassan?
DIAGNOSTIC LABORATORY
I'm sorry.
You've tested positive for hepatitis C...
...so you're not a candidate for kidney donation.
This "*Virus C*" nonsense again!
First, I'm not a candidate to make a living in my own country!
And now I'm not a candidate to save my own father's life!

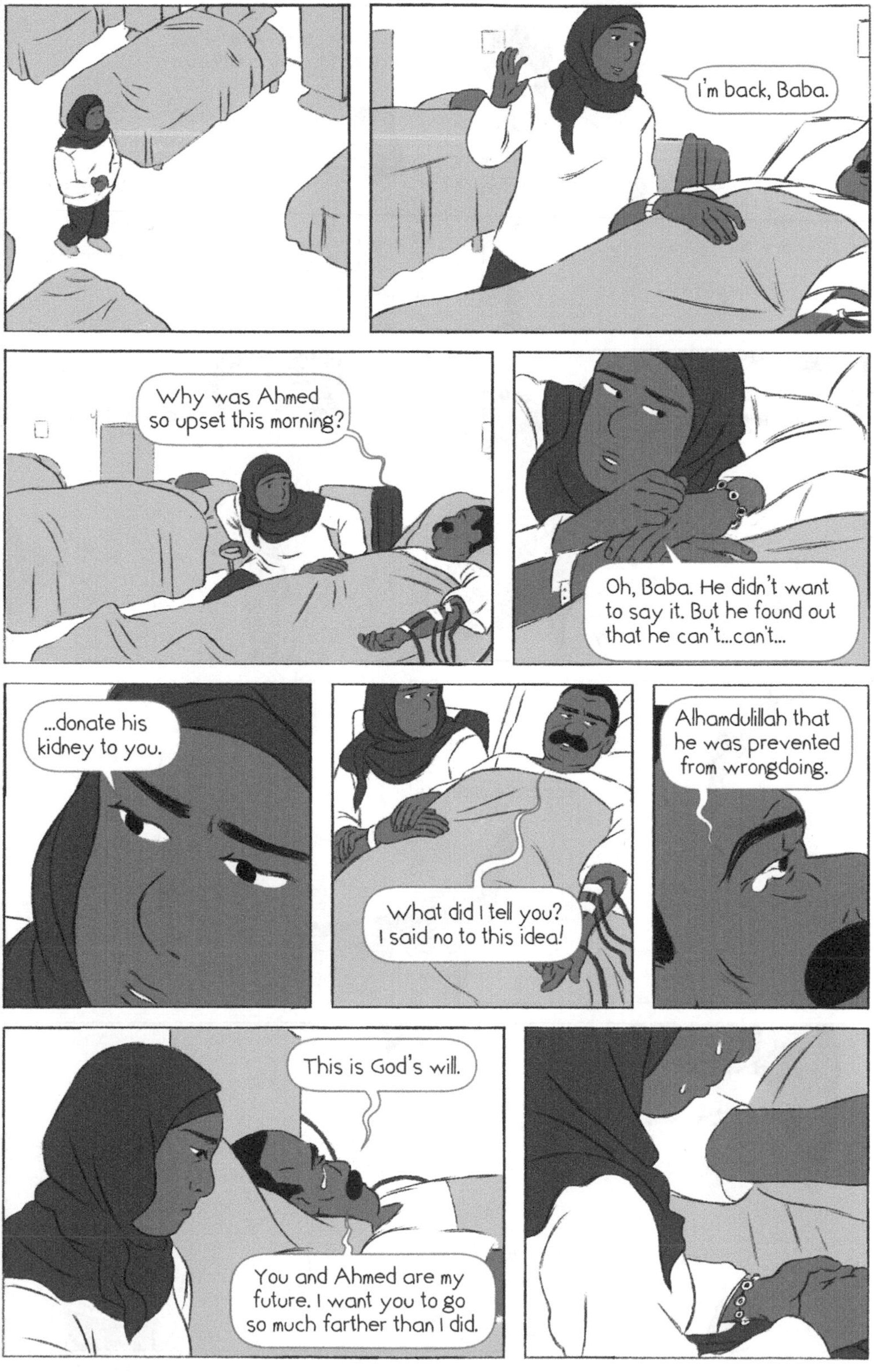
I'm back, Baba.
Why was Ahmed so upset this morning?
Oh, Baba. He didn't want to say it. But he found out that he can't...can't...
...donate his kidney to you.
What did I tell you? I said no to this idea!
Alhamdulillah that he was prevented from wrongdoing.
This is God's will.
You and Ahmed are my future. I want you to go so much farther than I did.

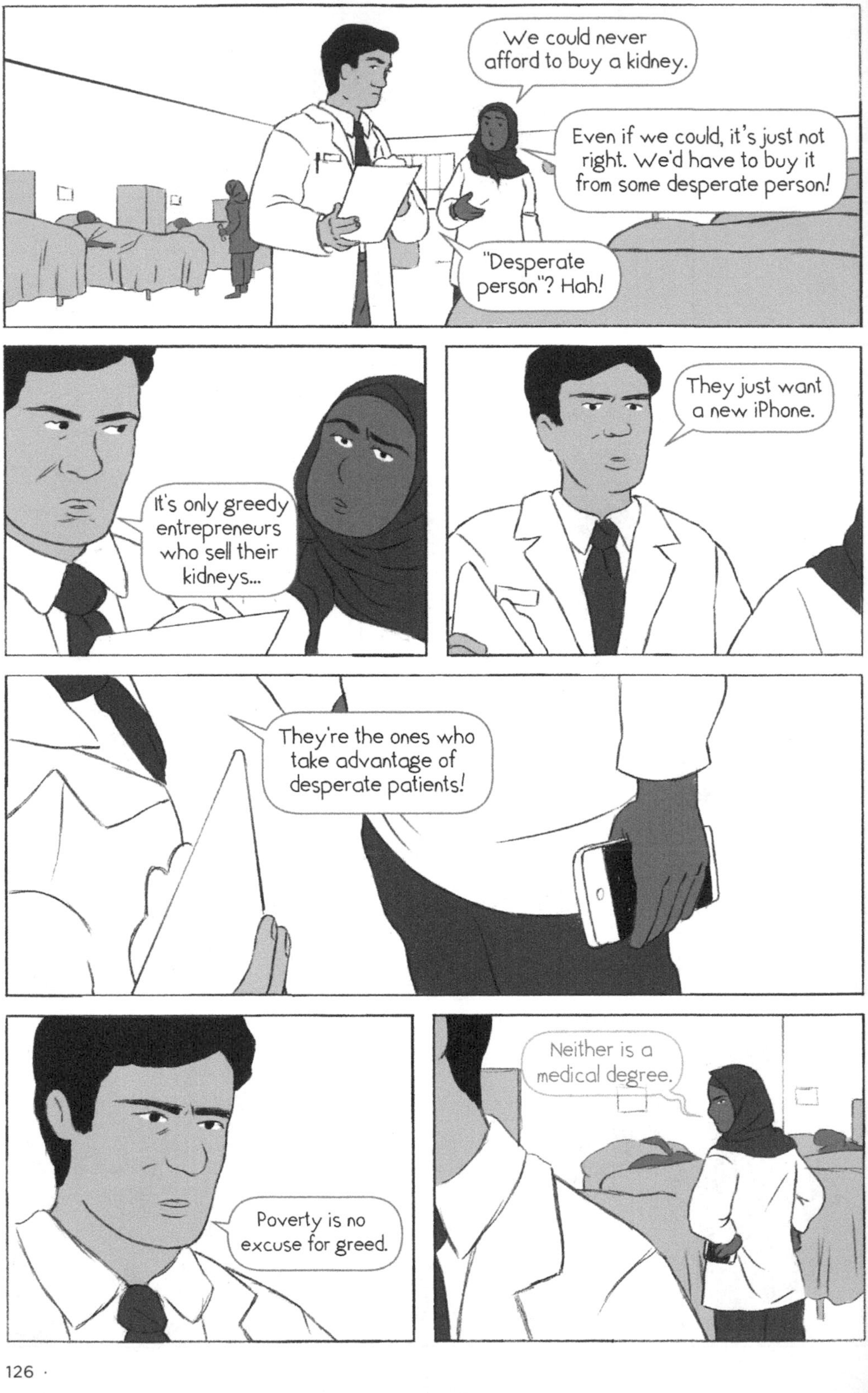
We could never afford to buy a kidney.
Even if we could, it's just not right. We'd have to buy it from some desperate person!
"Desperate person"? Hah!
It's only greedy entrepreneurs who sell their kidneys...
They just want a new iPhone.
They're the ones who take advantage of desperate patients!
Poverty is no excuse for greed.
Neither is a medical degree.

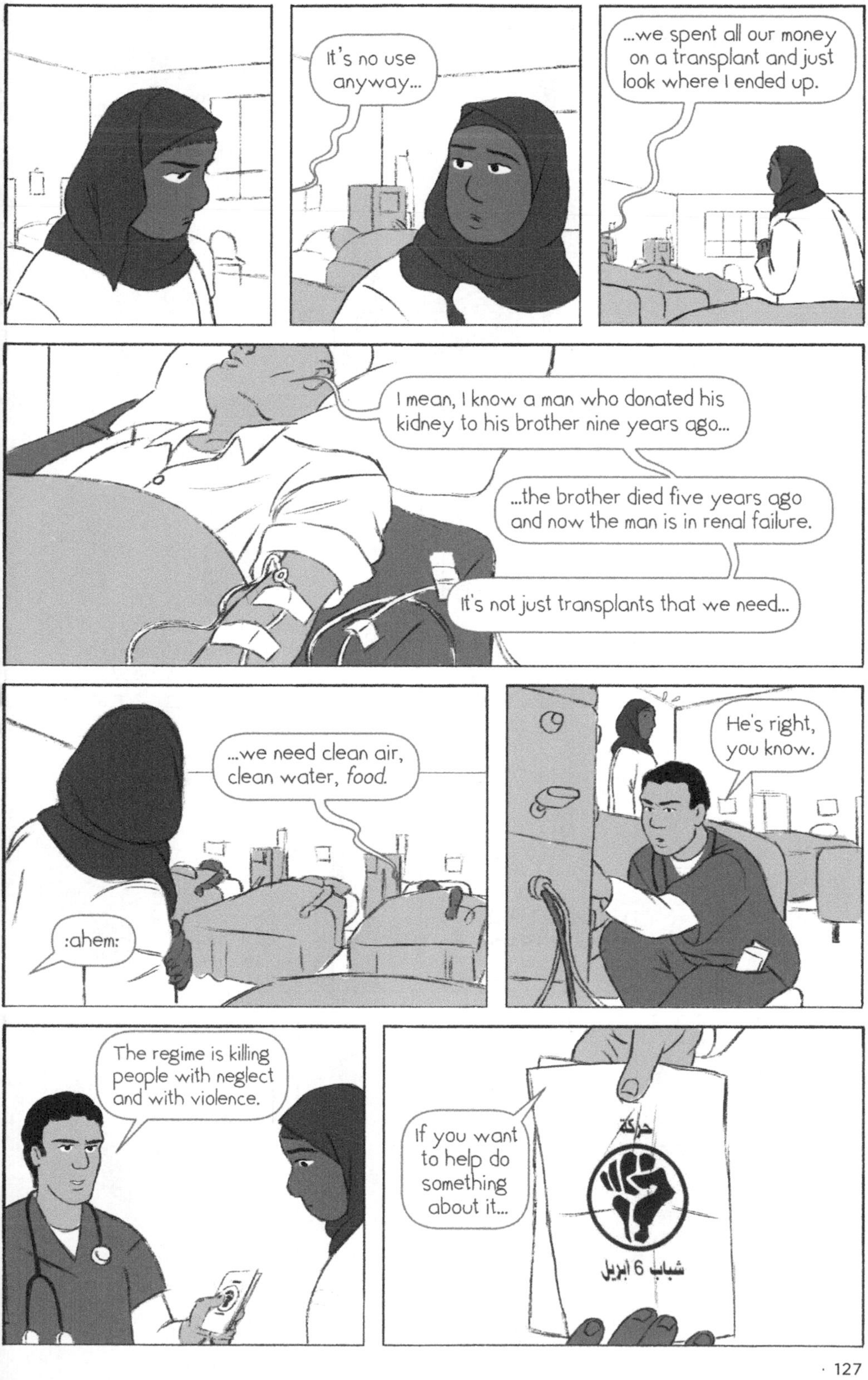
It's no use anyway...
...we spent all our money on a transplant and just look where I ended up.
I mean, I know a man who donated his kidney to his brother nine years ago...
...the brother died five years ago and now the man is in renal failure.
It's not just transplants that we need...
...we need clean air, clean water, *food.*
:ahem:
He's right, you know.
The regime is killing people with neglect and with violence.
If you want to help do something about it...
حركة
شباب 6 ابريل

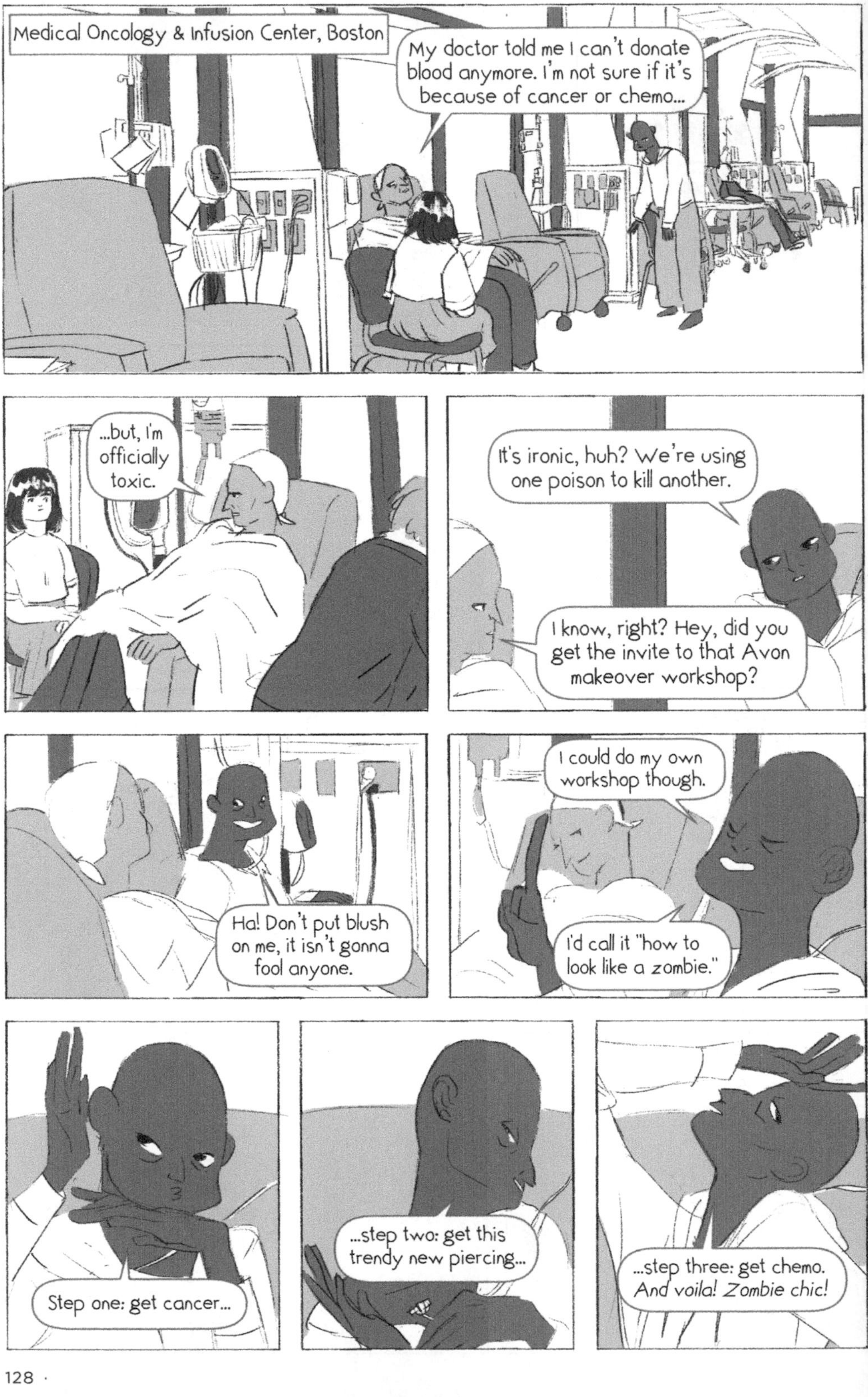
Medical Oncology & Infusion Center, Boston
My doctor told me I can't donate blood anymore. I'm not sure if it's because of cancer or chemo...
...but, I'm officially toxic.
It's ironic, huh? We're using one poison to kill another.
I know, right? Hey, did you get the invite to that Avon makeover workshop?
Ha! Don't put blush on me, it isn't gonna fool anyone.
I could do my own workshop though.
I'd call it "how to look like a *zombie*."
Step one: get cancer...
...step two: get this trendy new piercing...
...step three: get chemo. *And voila! Zombie chic!*

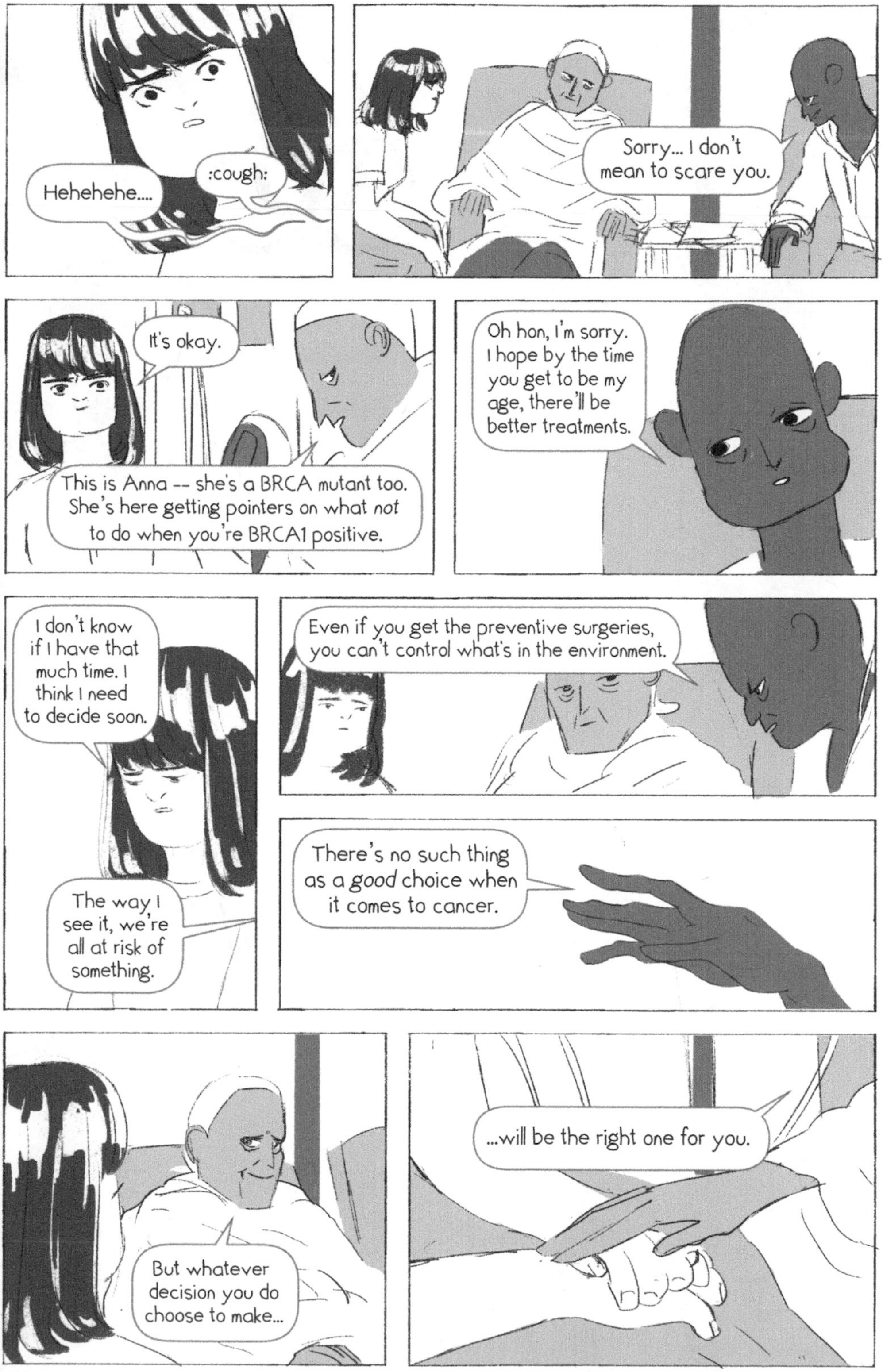
Hehehehe....
:cough:
Sorry... I don't mean to scare you.
It's okay.
This is Anna -- she's a BRCA mutant too. She's here getting pointers on what *not* to do when you're BRCA1 positive.
Oh hon, I'm sorry. I hope by the time you get to be my age, there'll be better treatments.
I don't know if I have that much time. I think I need to decide soon.
The way I see it, we're all at risk of something.
Even if you get the preventive surgeries, you can't control what's in the environment.
There's no such thing as a *good* choice when it comes to cancer.
But whatever decision you do choose to make...
...will be the right one for you.

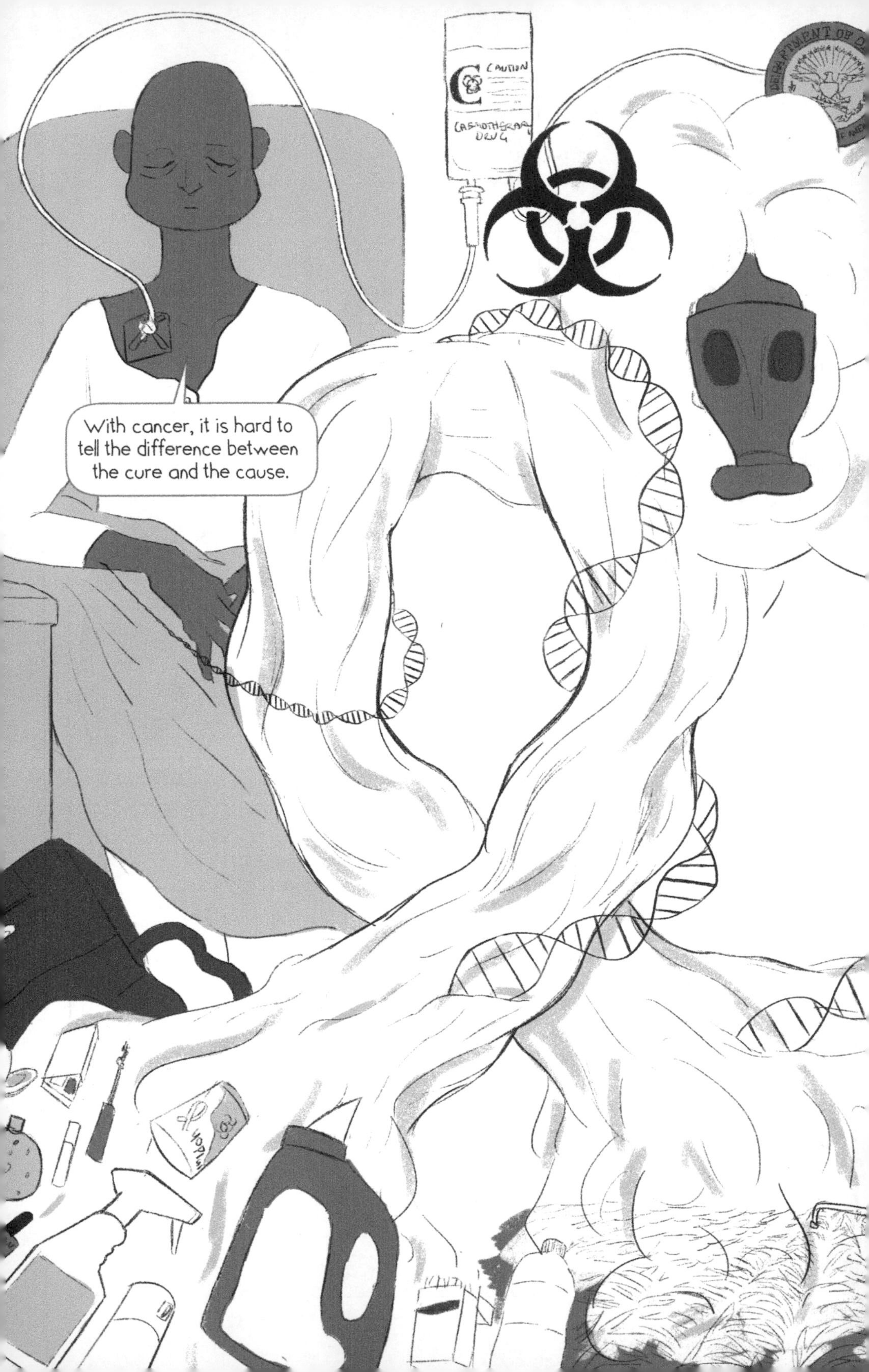
With cancer, it is hard to tell the difference between the cure and the cause.
CAUTION

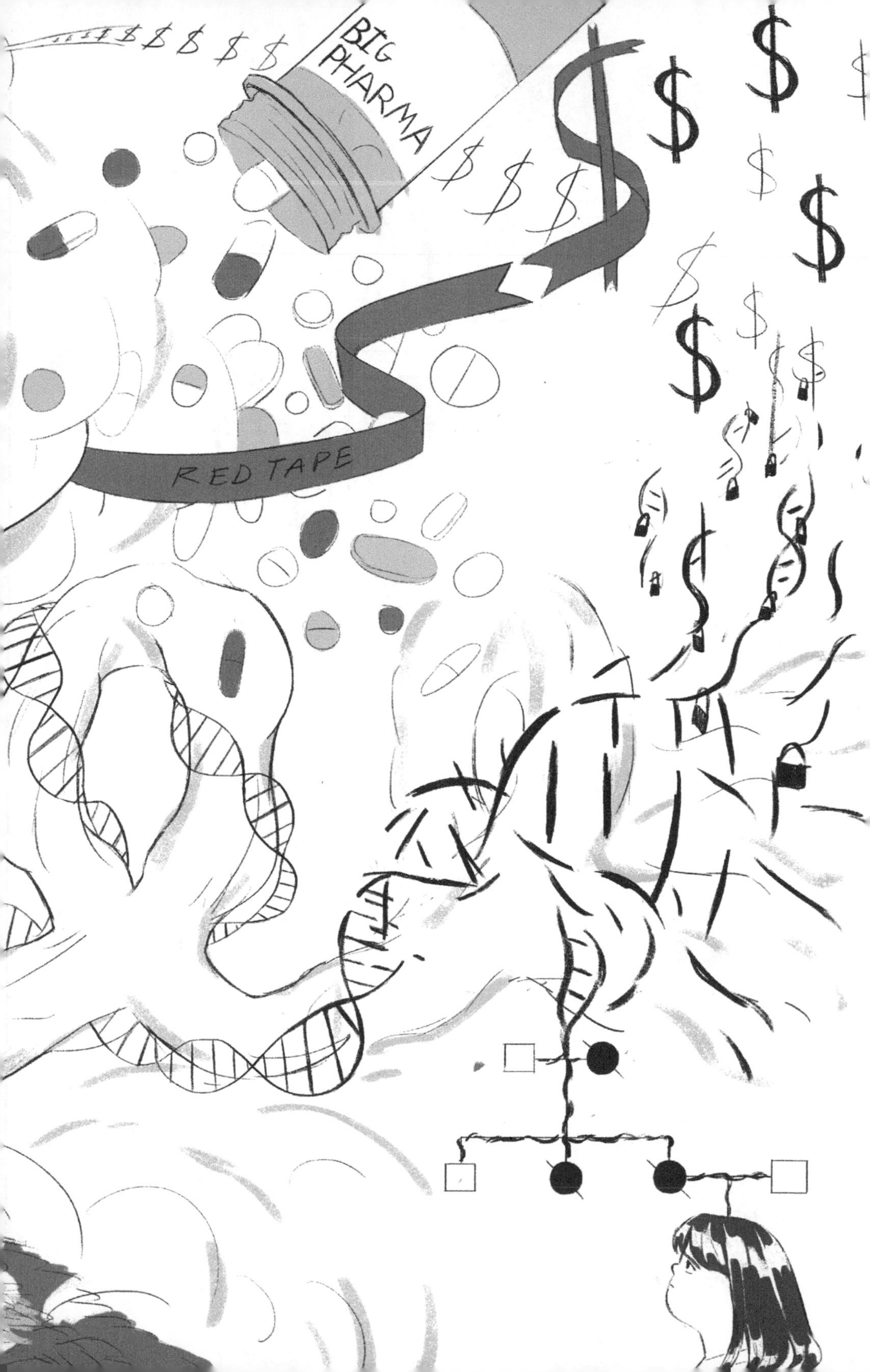
BIG PHARMA
RED TAPE

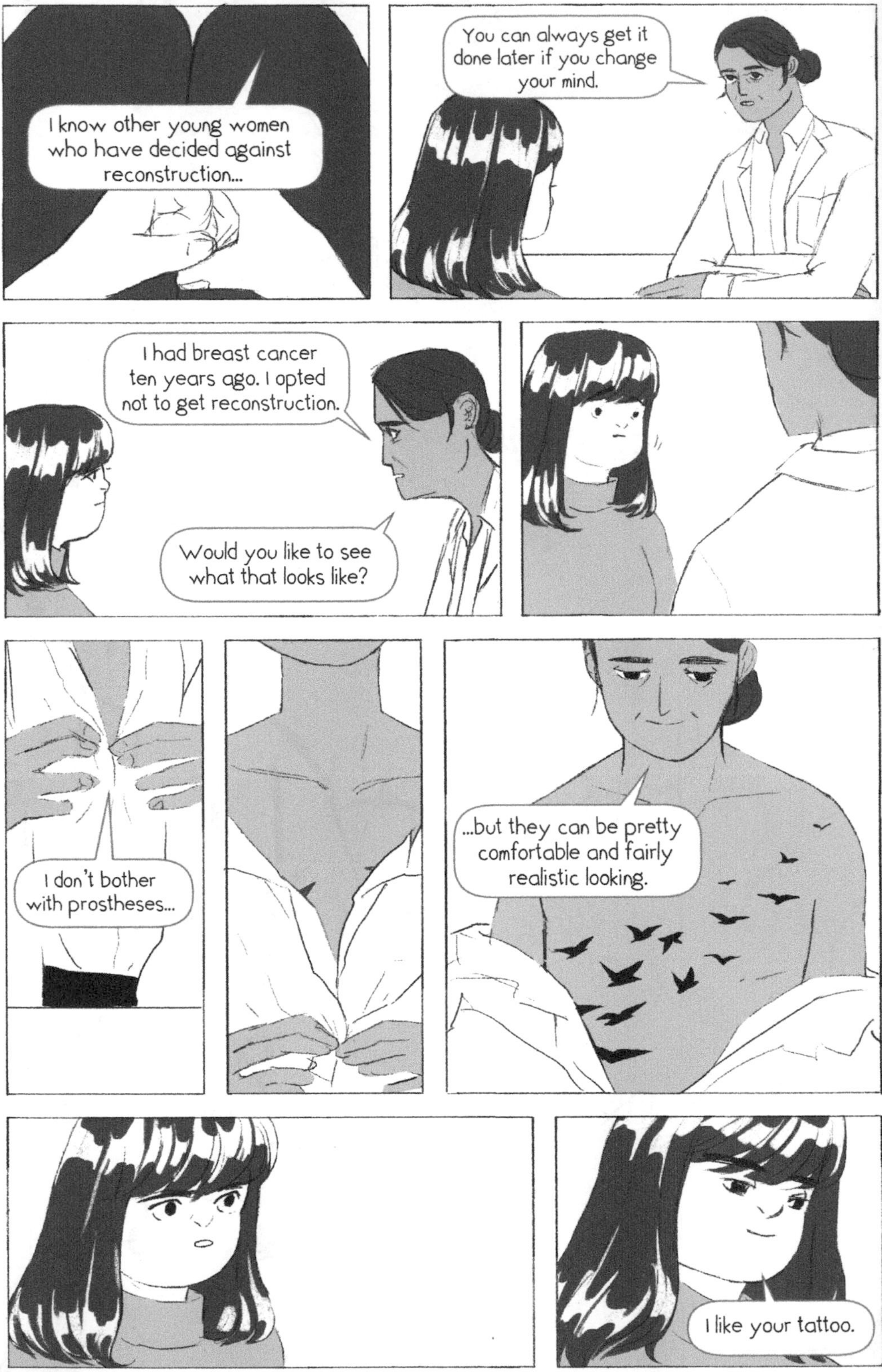
I know other young women who have decided against reconstruction...
You can always get it done later if you change your mind.
I had breast cancer ten years ago. I opted not to get reconstruction.
Would you like to see what that looks like?
I don't bother with prostheses...
...but they can be pretty comfortable and fairly realistic looking.
I like your tattoo.

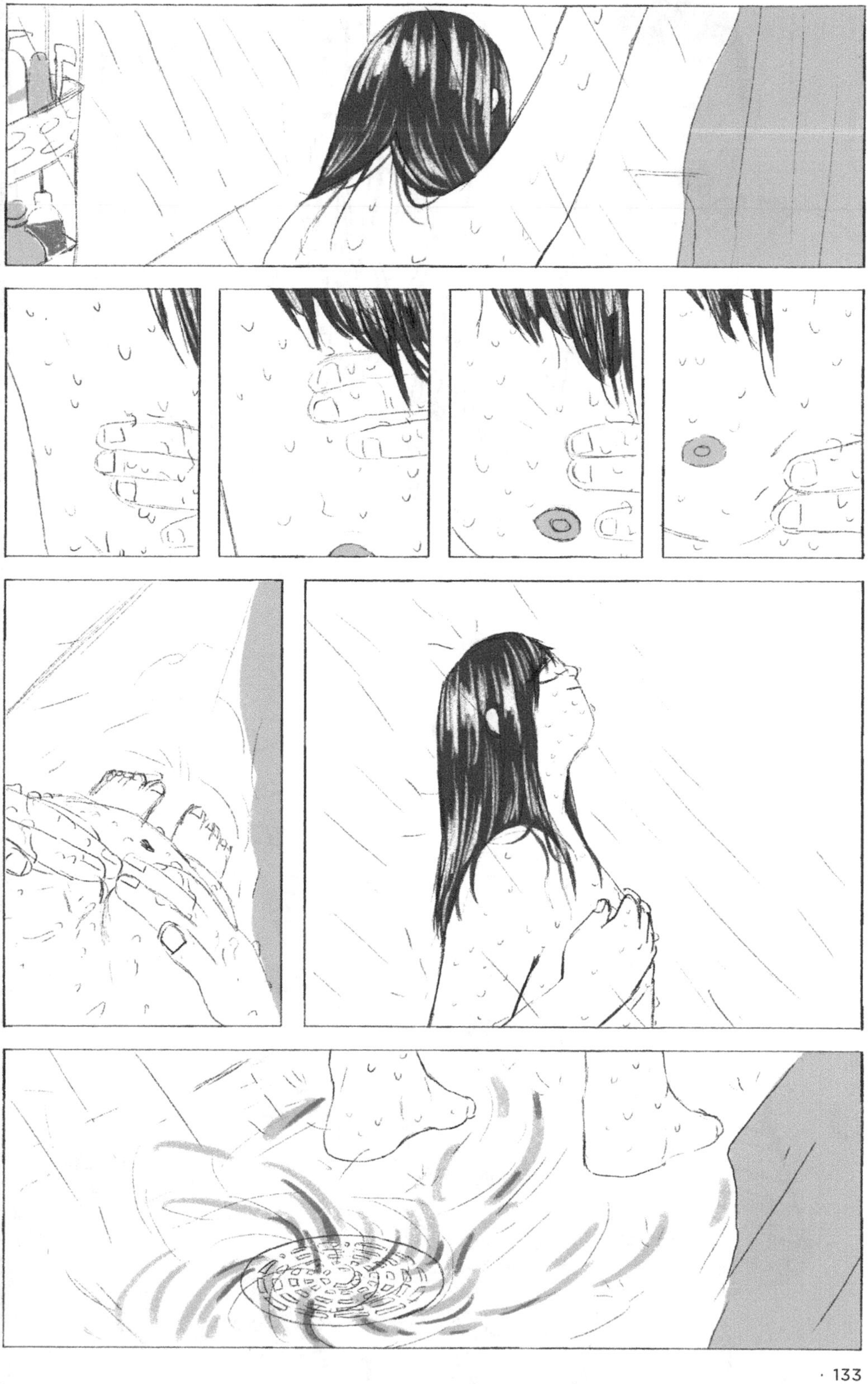

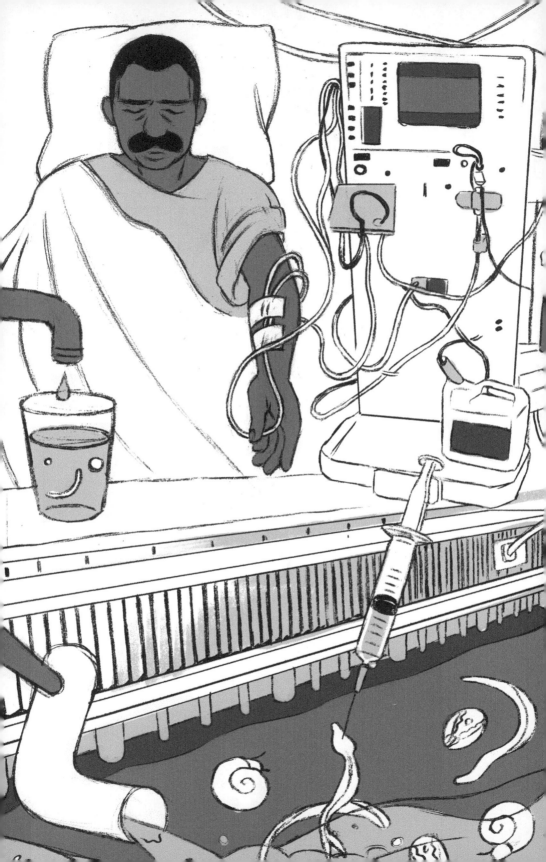

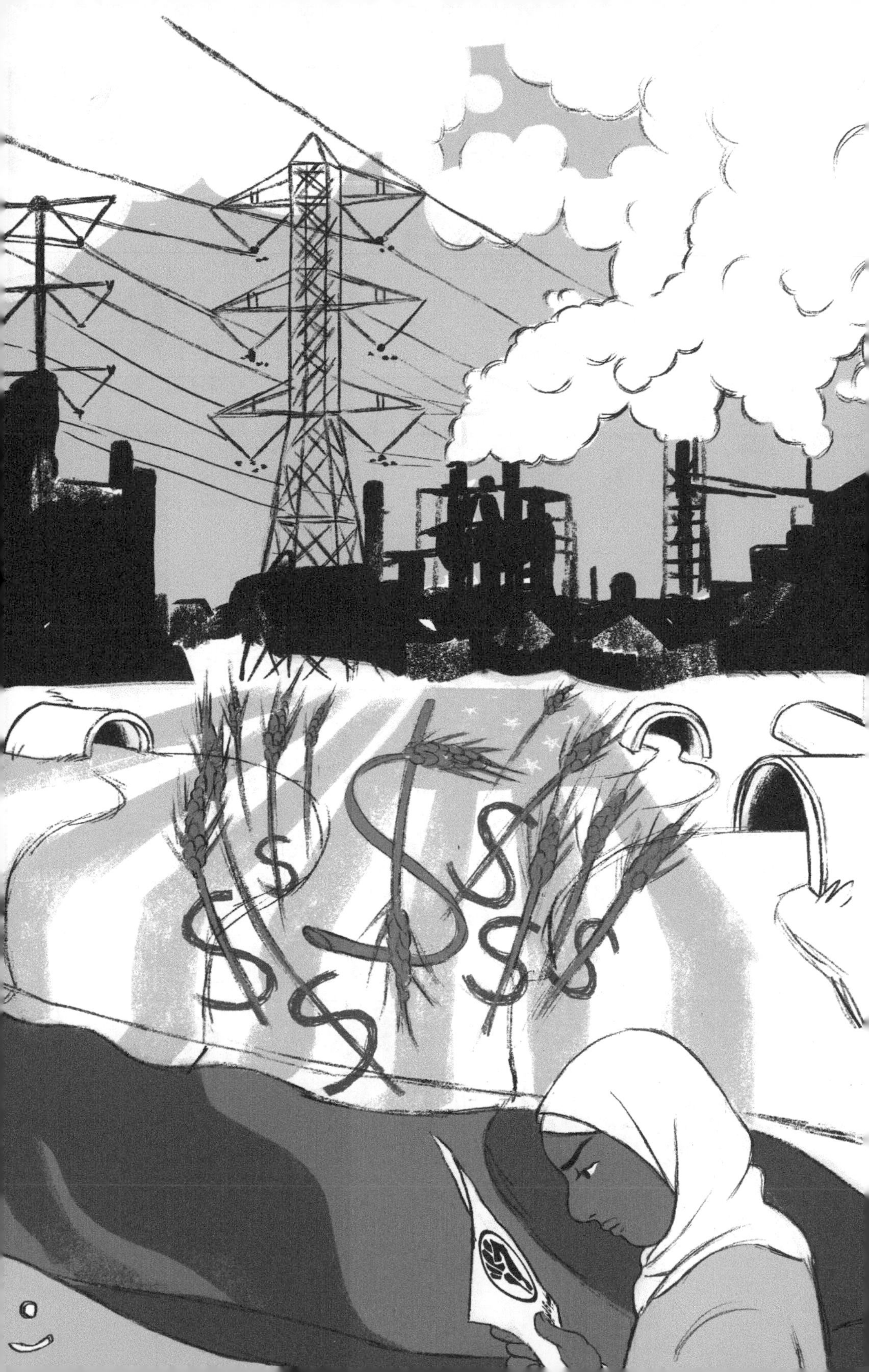

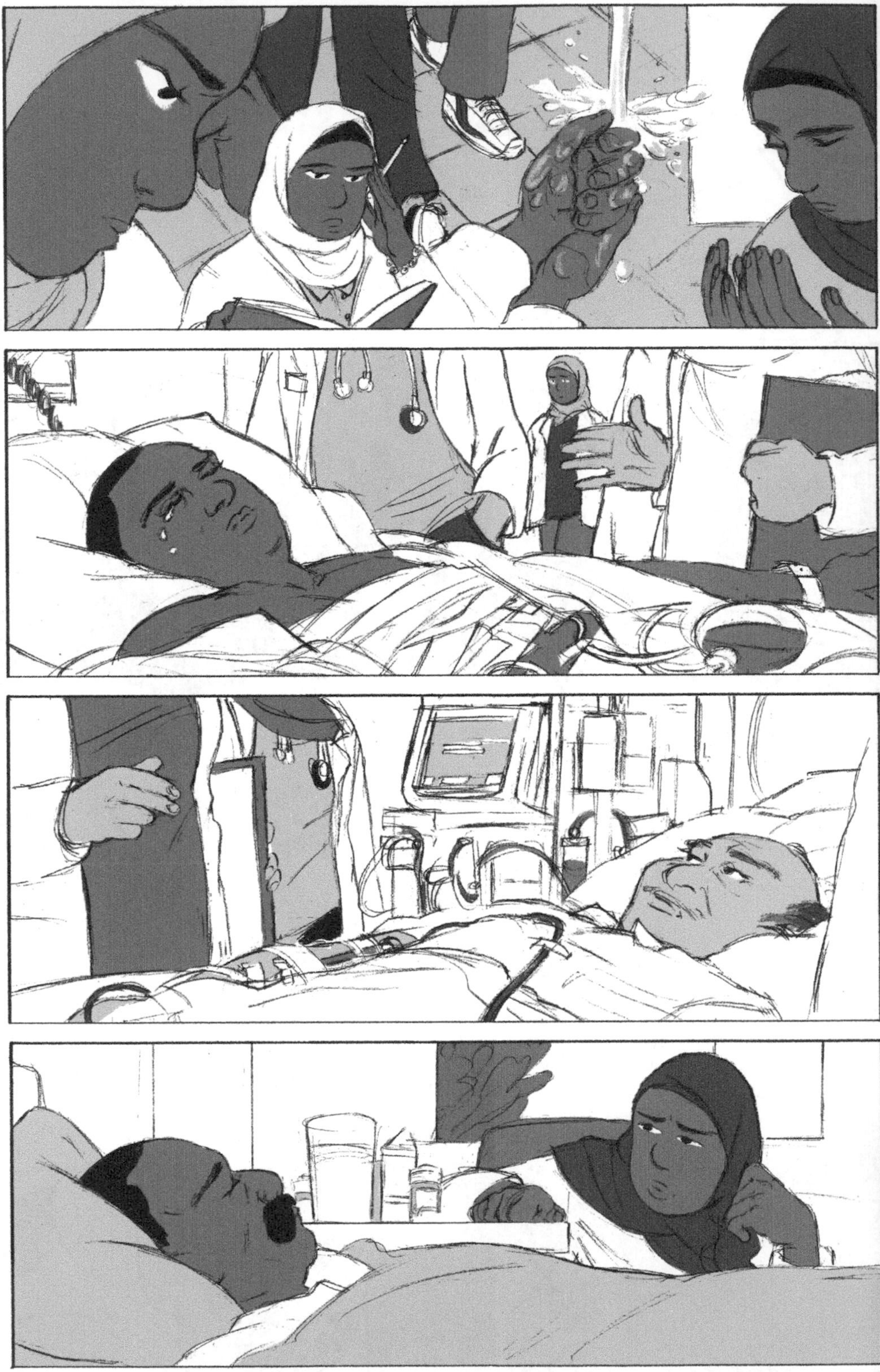

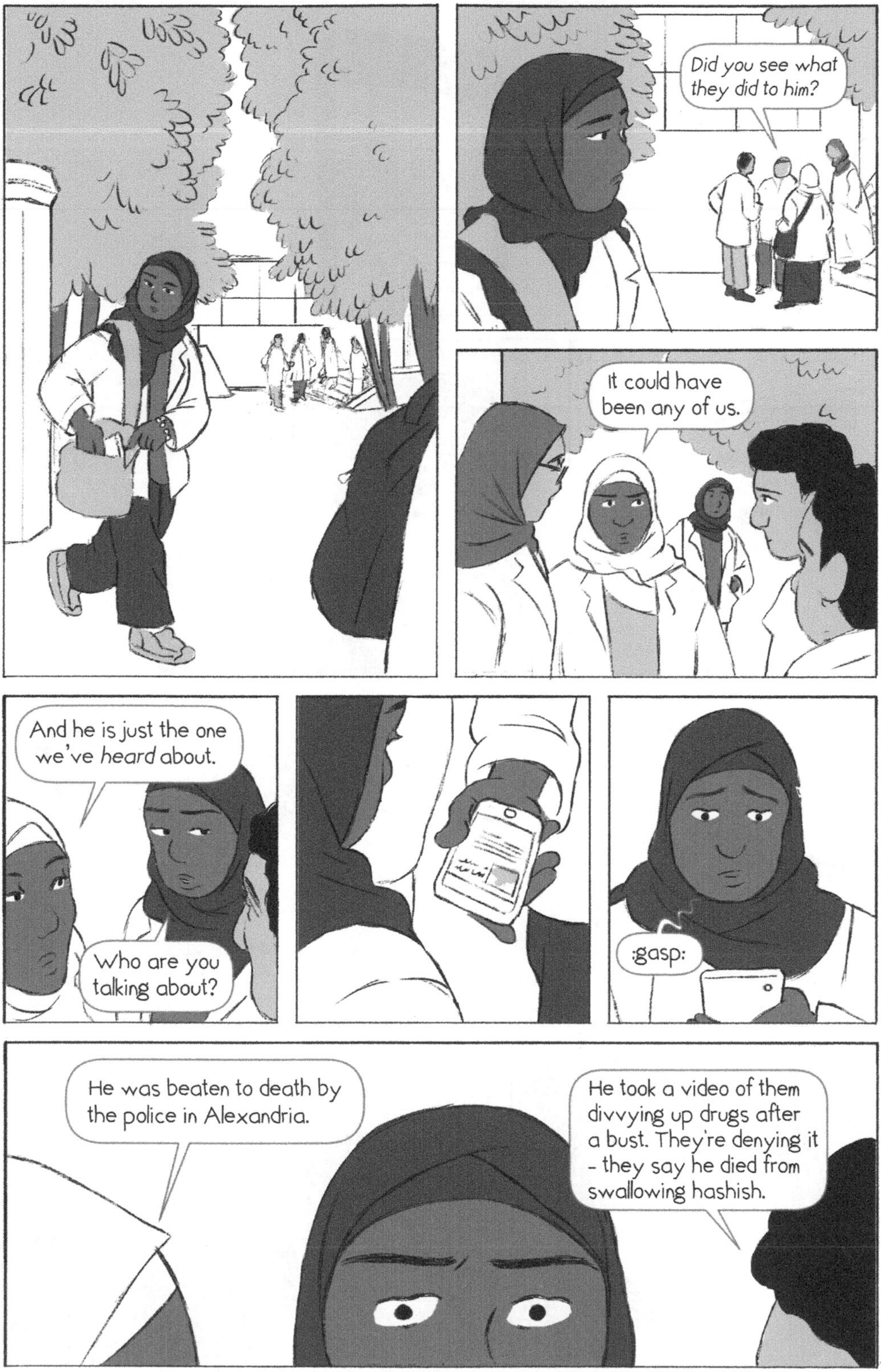

Did you see what they did to him?
It could have been any of us.
And he is just the one we've *heard* about.
Who are you talking about?
:gasp:
He was beaten to death by the police in Alexandria.
He took a video of them divvying up drugs after a bust. They're denying it - they say he died from swallowing hashish.

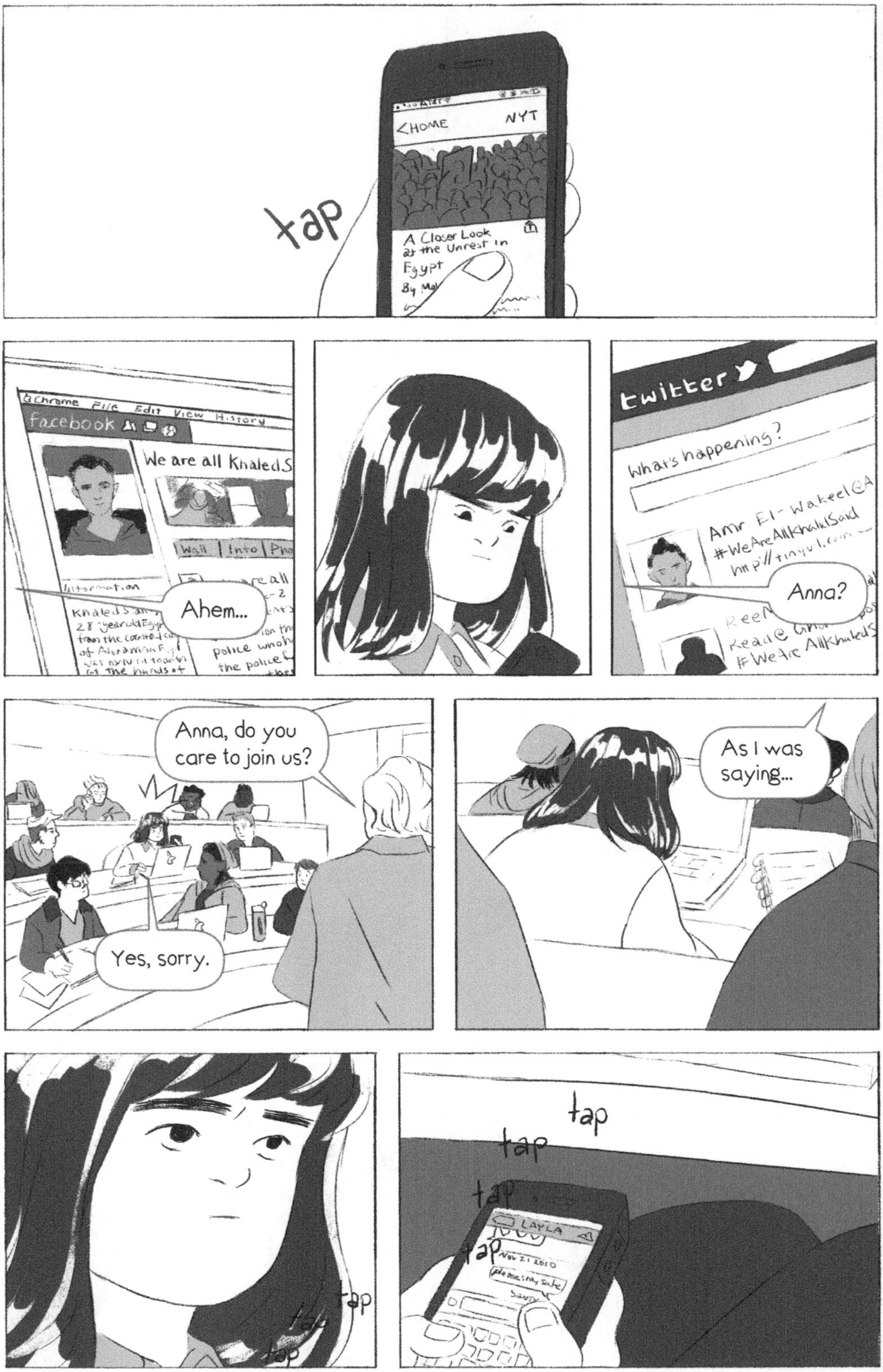
<HOME
NYT
A Closer Look at the Unrest in Egypt
tap
facebook
We are all Khaled S
Ahem...
twitter
What's happening?
Anna?
Anna, do you care to join us?
Yes, sorry.
As I was saying...
tap
tap
tap
tap
LAYLA
Nov 21 2010
please stay safe
tap
tap
tap

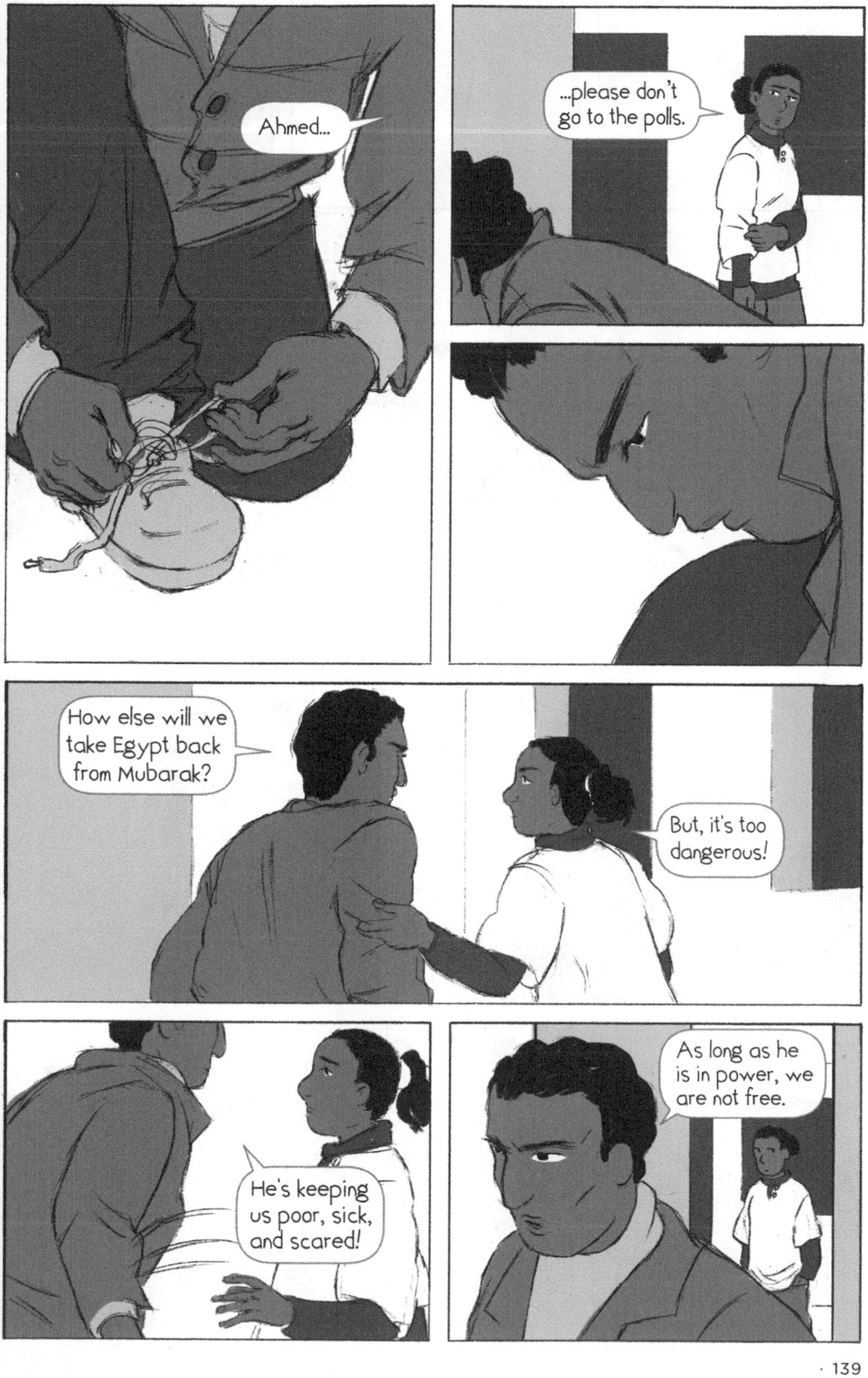
Ahmed...
...please don't go to the polls.
How else will we take Egypt back from Mubarak?
But, it's too dangerous!
He's keeping us poor, sick, and scared!
As long as he is in power, we are not free.

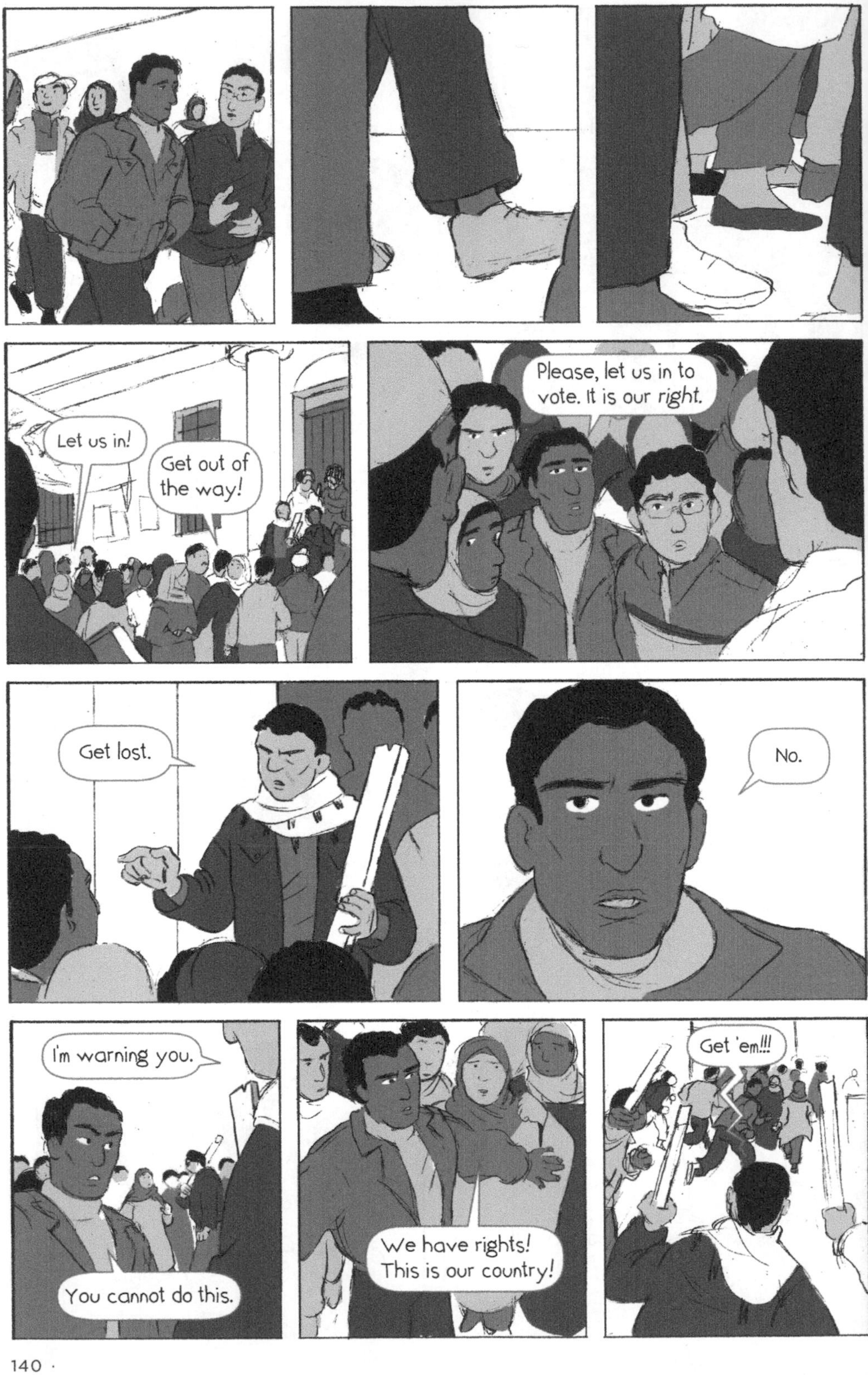
Let us in!
Get out of the way!
Please, let us in to vote. It is our right.
Get lost.
No.
I'm warning you.
You cannot do this.
We have rights! This is our country!
Get 'em!!!

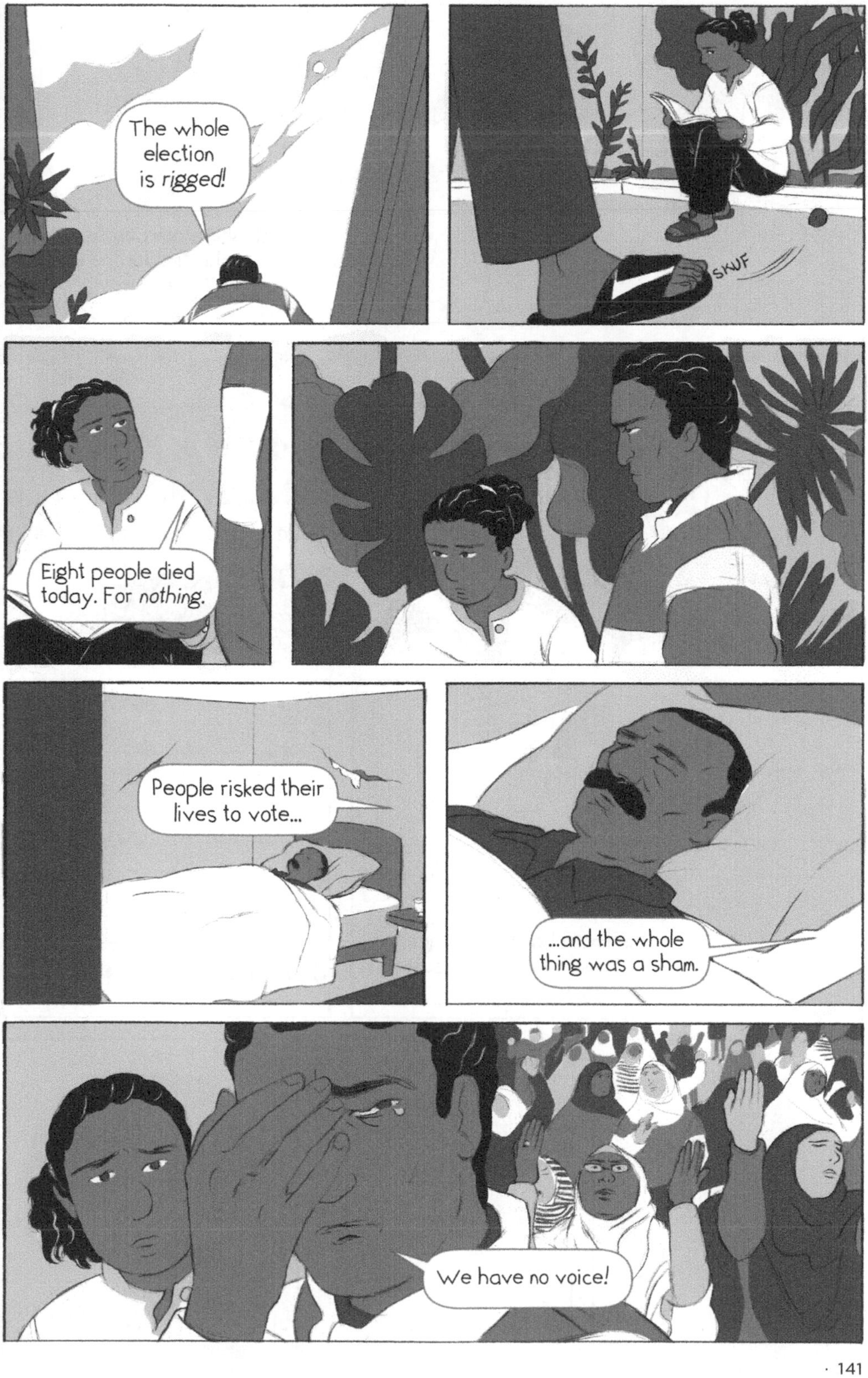
The whole election is *rigged!*
SKUF
Eight people died today. For *nothing.*
People risked their lives to vote...
...and the whole thing was a sham.
We have no voice!

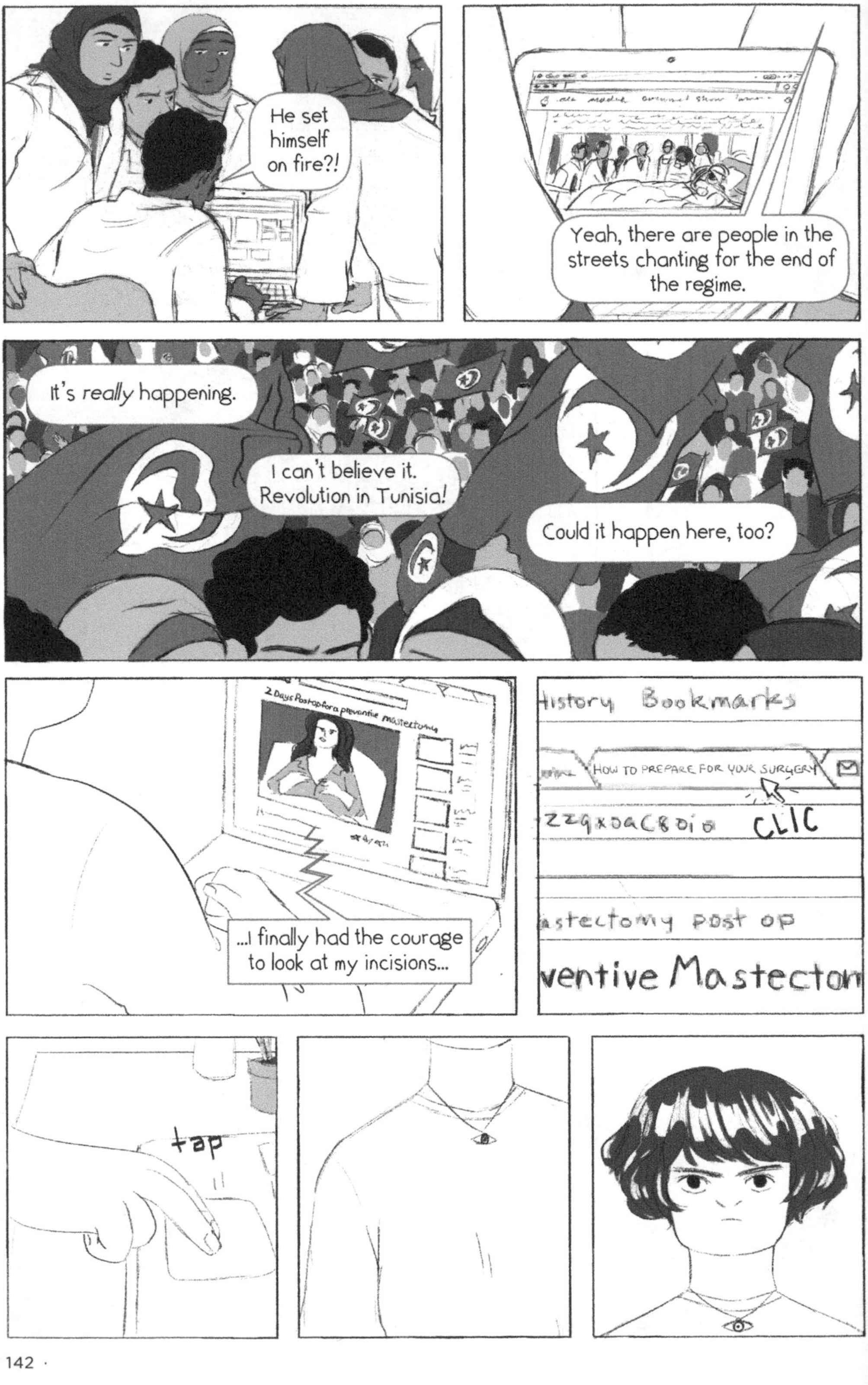
He set himself on fire?!
Yeah, there are people in the streets chanting for the end of the regime.
It's *really* happening.
I can't believe it. Revolution in Tunisia!
Could it happen here, too?
2 Days Postop for a preventie mastectomy
...I finally had the courage to look at my incisions...
History Bookmarks
HOW TO PREPARE FOR YOUR SURGERY
CLIC
astectomy post op
ventive Mastecton
tap

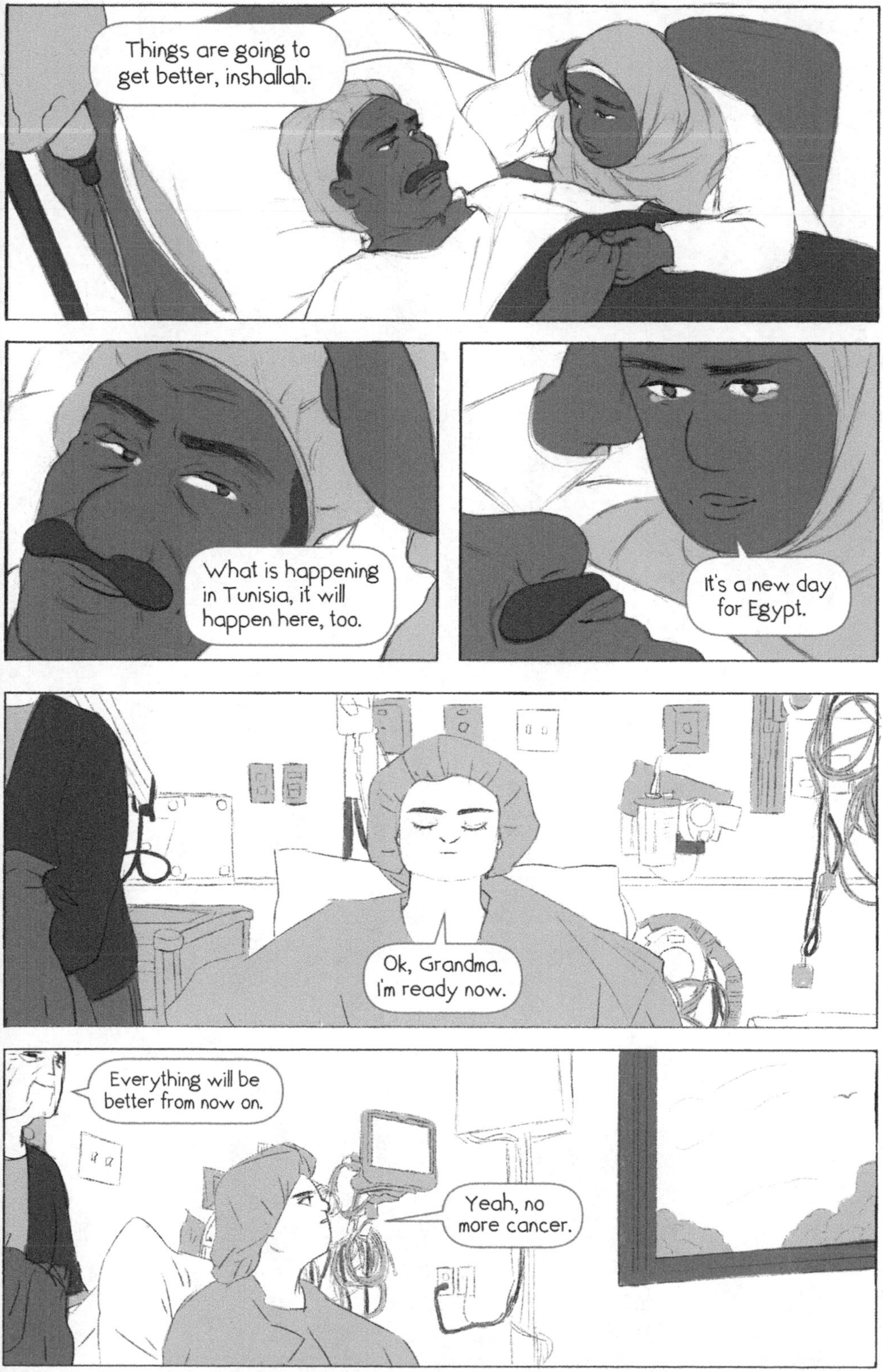
Things are going to get better, inshallah.
What is happening in Tunisia, it will happen here, too.
It's a new day for Egypt.
Ok, Grandma. I'm ready now.
Everything will be better from now on.
Yeah, no more cancer.

PART III

REVOLUTION

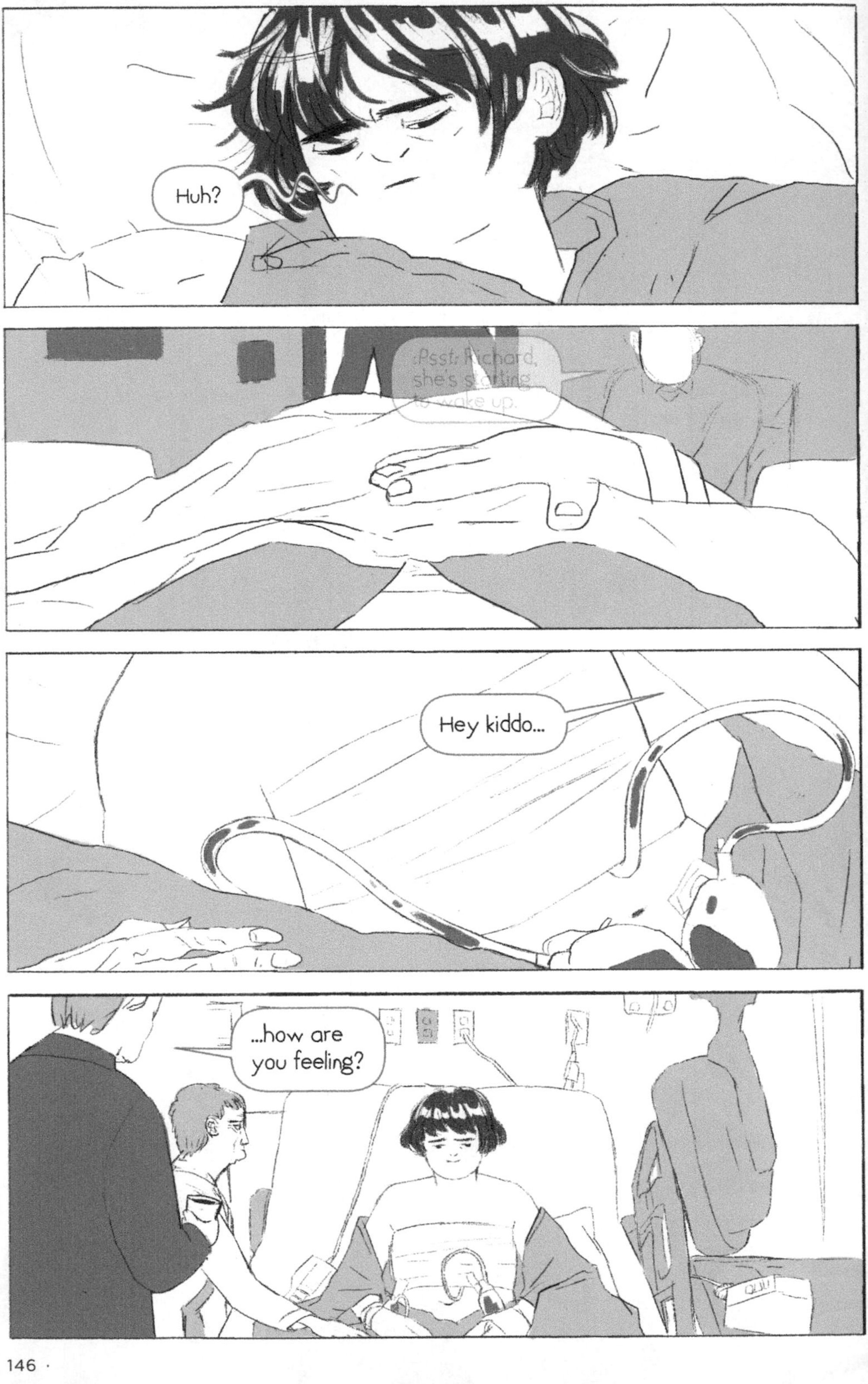
Huh?
:Psst: Richard, she's starting to wake up.
Hey kiddo...
...how are you feeling?

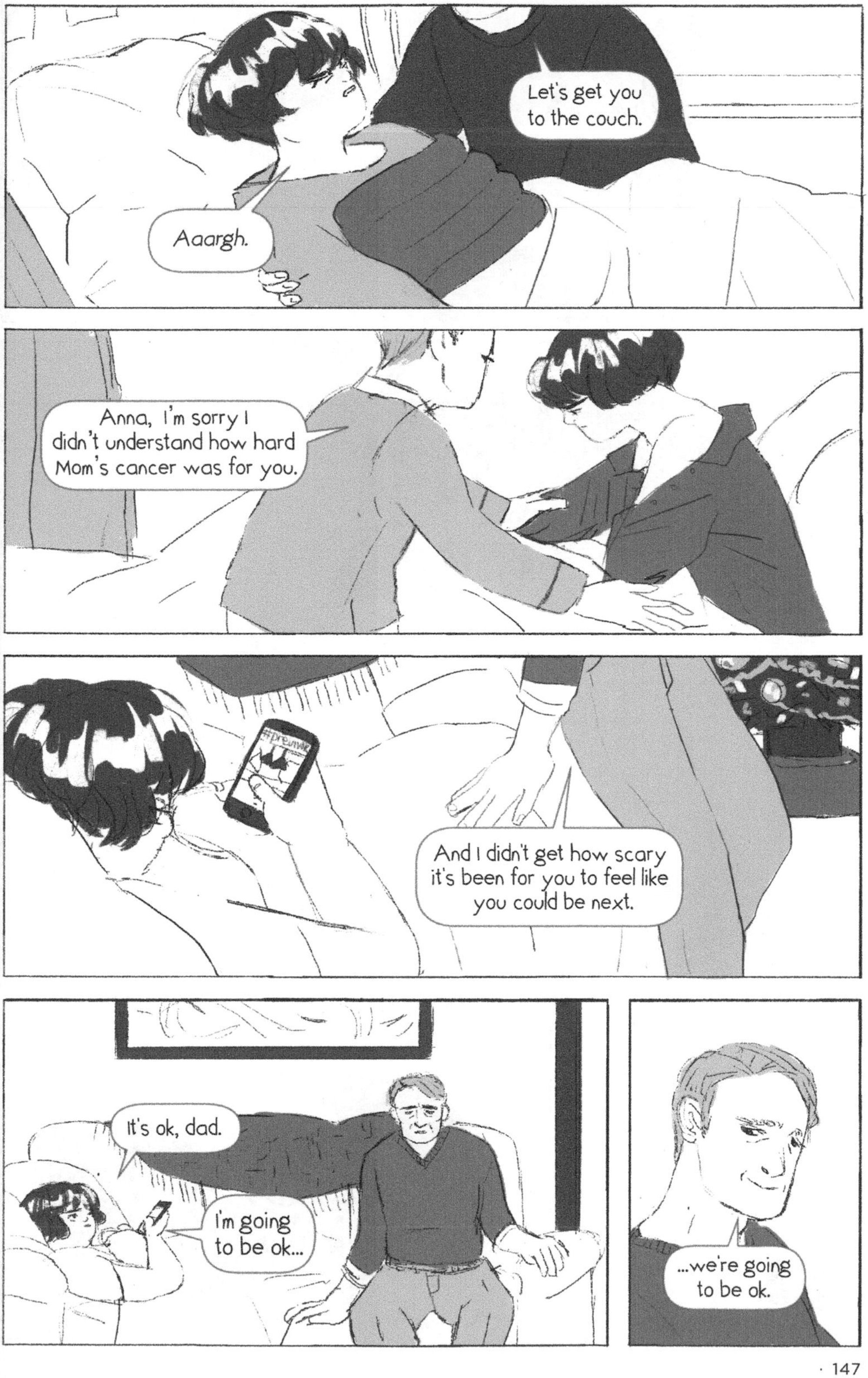
Let's get you to the couch.
Aaargh.
Anna, I'm sorry I didn't understand how hard Mom's cancer was for you.
And I didn't get how scary it's been for you to feel like you could be next.
It's ok, dad.
I'm going to be ok...
...we're going to be ok.

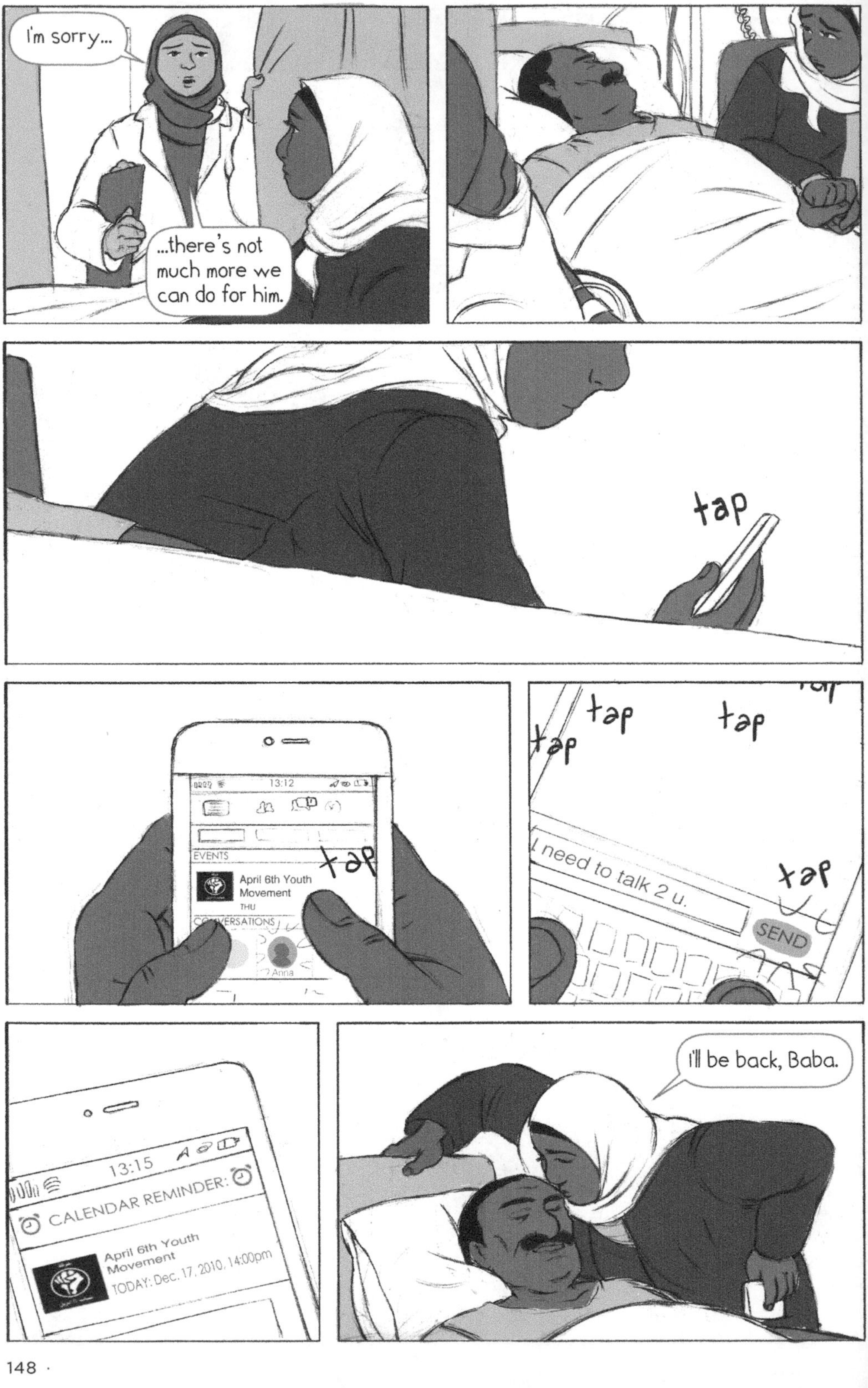
I'm sorry...
...there's not much more we can do for him.
tap
13:12
EVENTS
April 6th Youth Movement
THU
tap
CONVERSATIONS
Anna
tap
tap
tap
tap
I need to talk 2 u.
SEND
13:15
CALENDAR REMINDER:
April 6th Youth Movement
TODAY: Dec. 17, 2010, 14:00pm
I'll be back, Baba.

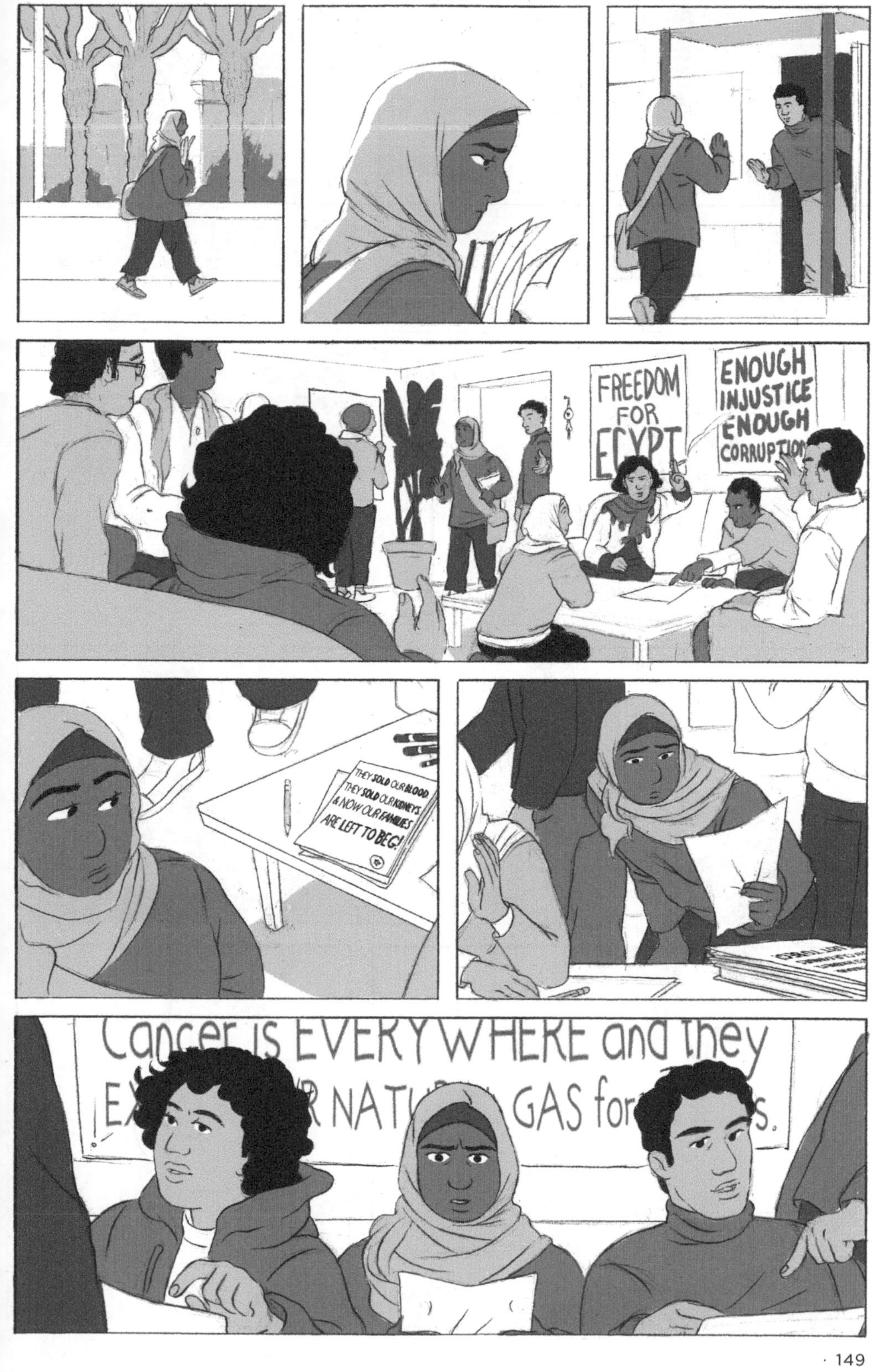
FREEDOM FOR EGYPT
ENOUGH INJUSTICE ENOUGH CORRUPTION
THEY SOLD OUR BLOOD. THEY SOLD OUR KIDNEYS & NOW OUR FAMILIES ARE LEFT TO BEG!
Cancer is EVERYWHERE and they

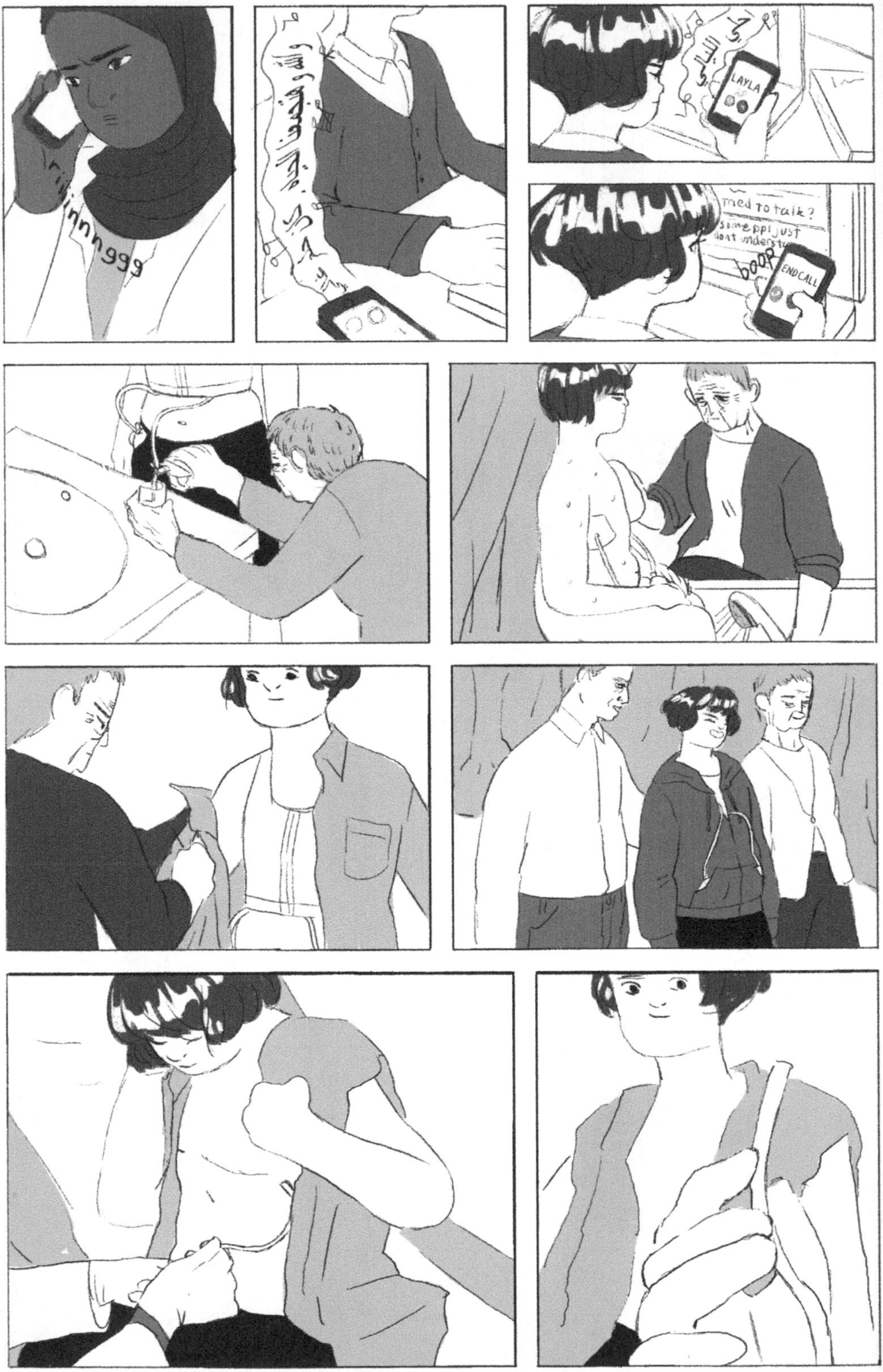
rinnnggg
أحلى الليالي
LAYLA
med to talk?
some ppl just
dont underst
boop
END CALL

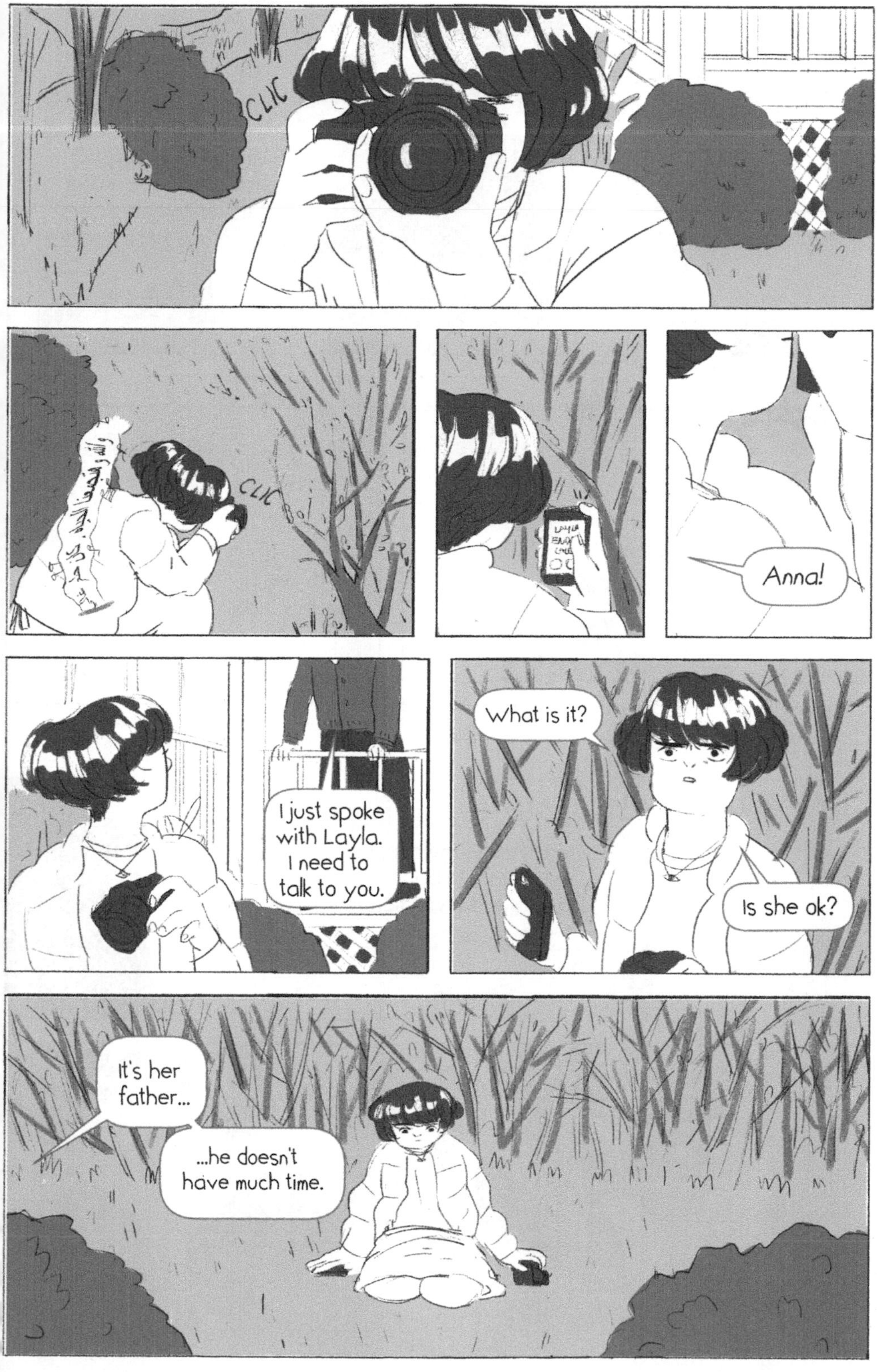
CLIC
CLIC
Anna!
I just spoke with Layla. I need to talk to you.
What is it?
Is she ok?
It's her father...
...he doesn't have much time.

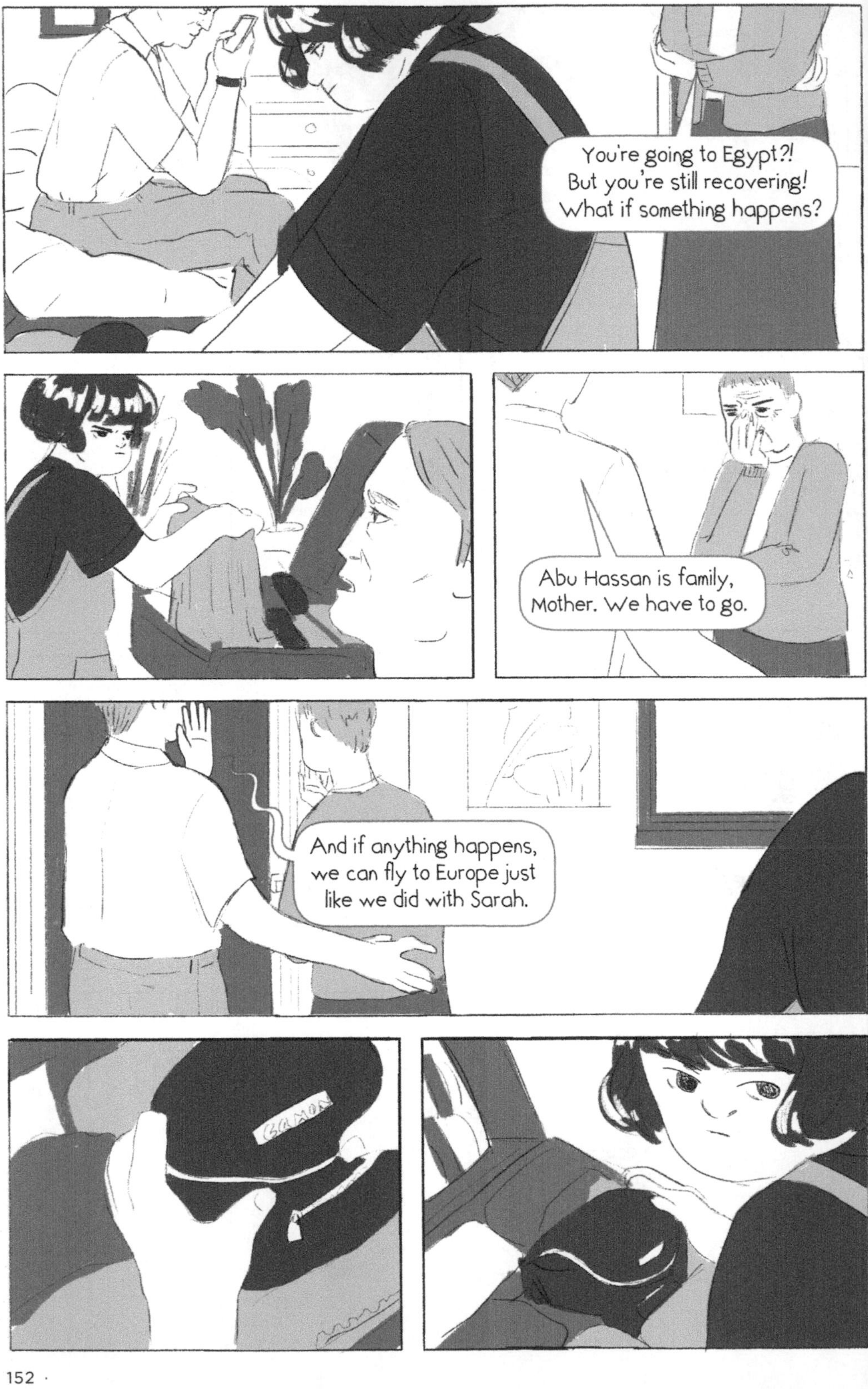
You're going to Egypt?! But you're still recovering! What if something happens?
Abu Hassan is family, Mother. We have to go.
And if anything happens, we can fly to Europe just like we did with Sarah.

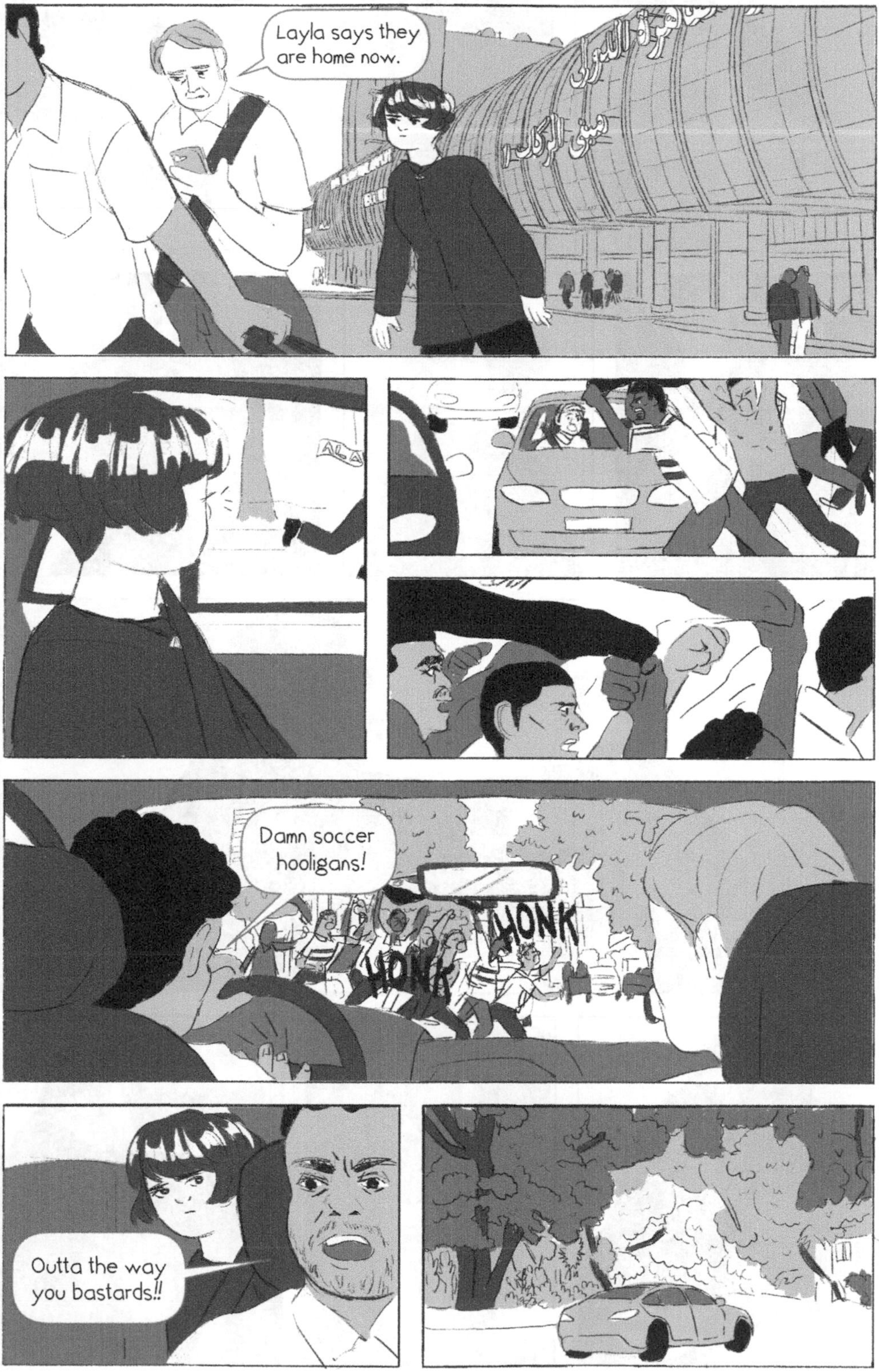
Layla says they are home now.
Damn soccer hooligans!
HONK
HONK
Outta the way you bastards!!

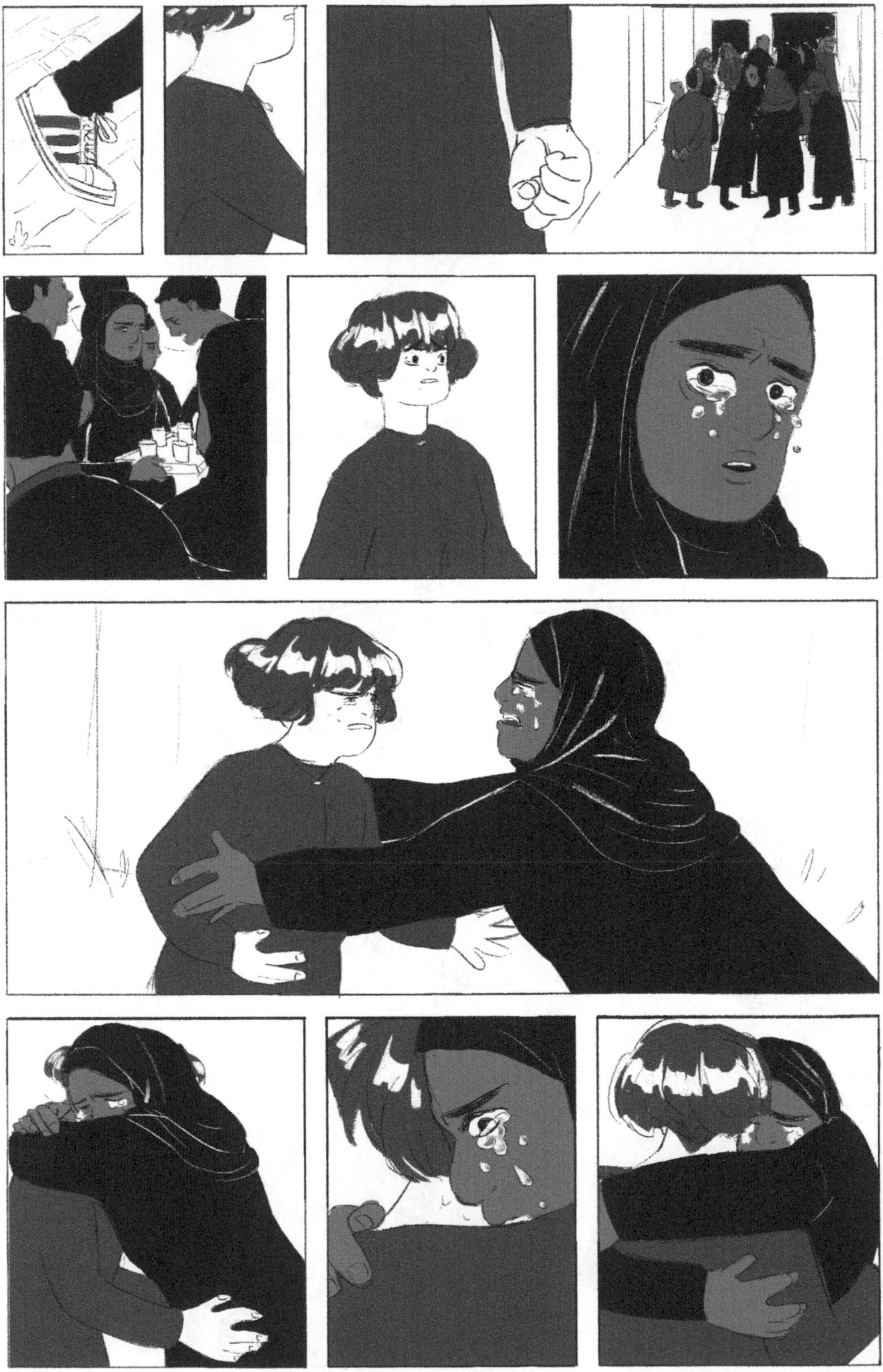

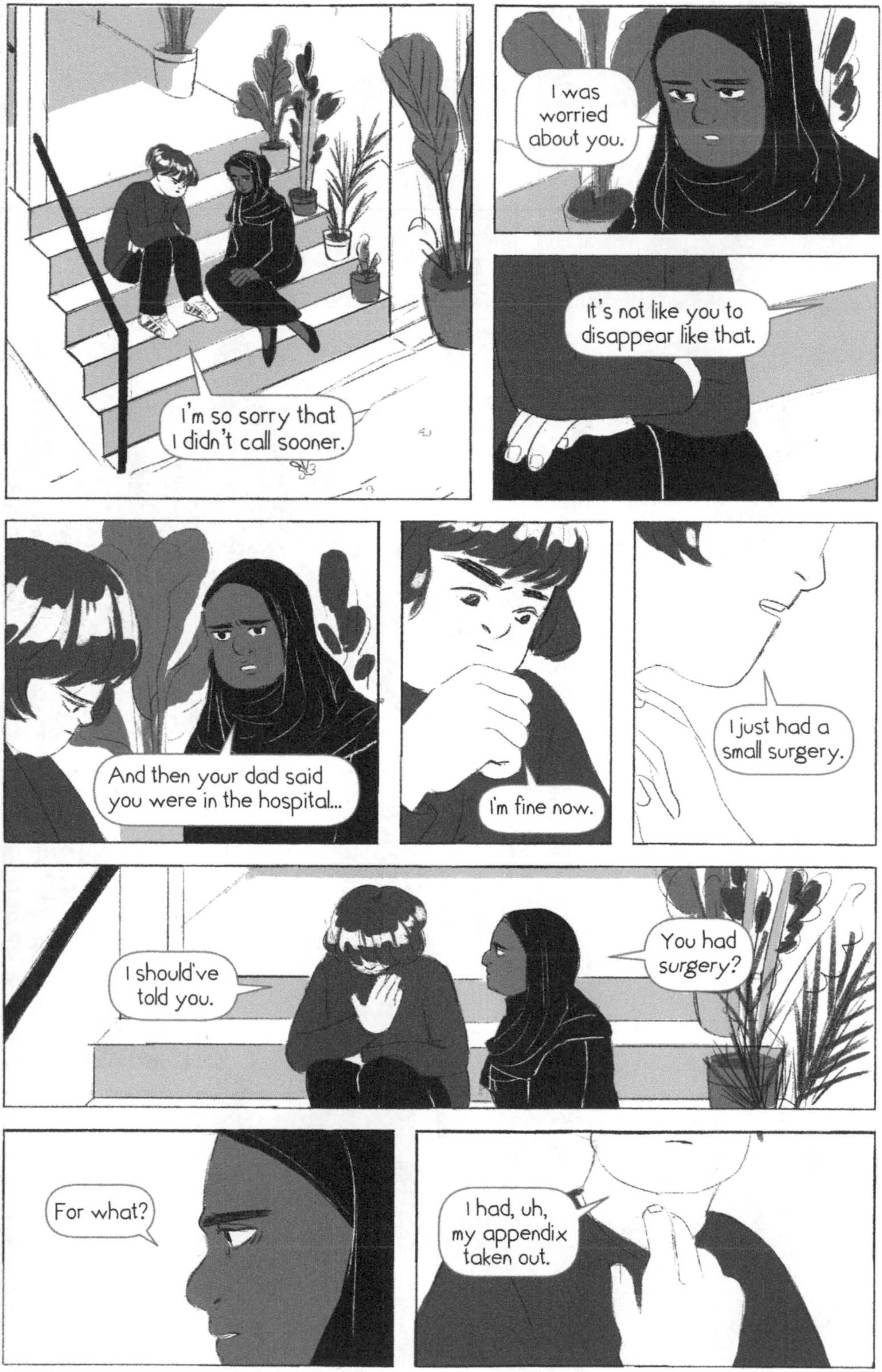
I'm so sorry that I didn't call sooner.
I was worried about you.
It's not like you to disappear like that.
And then your dad said you were in the hospital...
I'm fine now.
I just had a small surgery.
I should've told you.
You had surgery?
For what?
I had, uh, my appendix taken out.

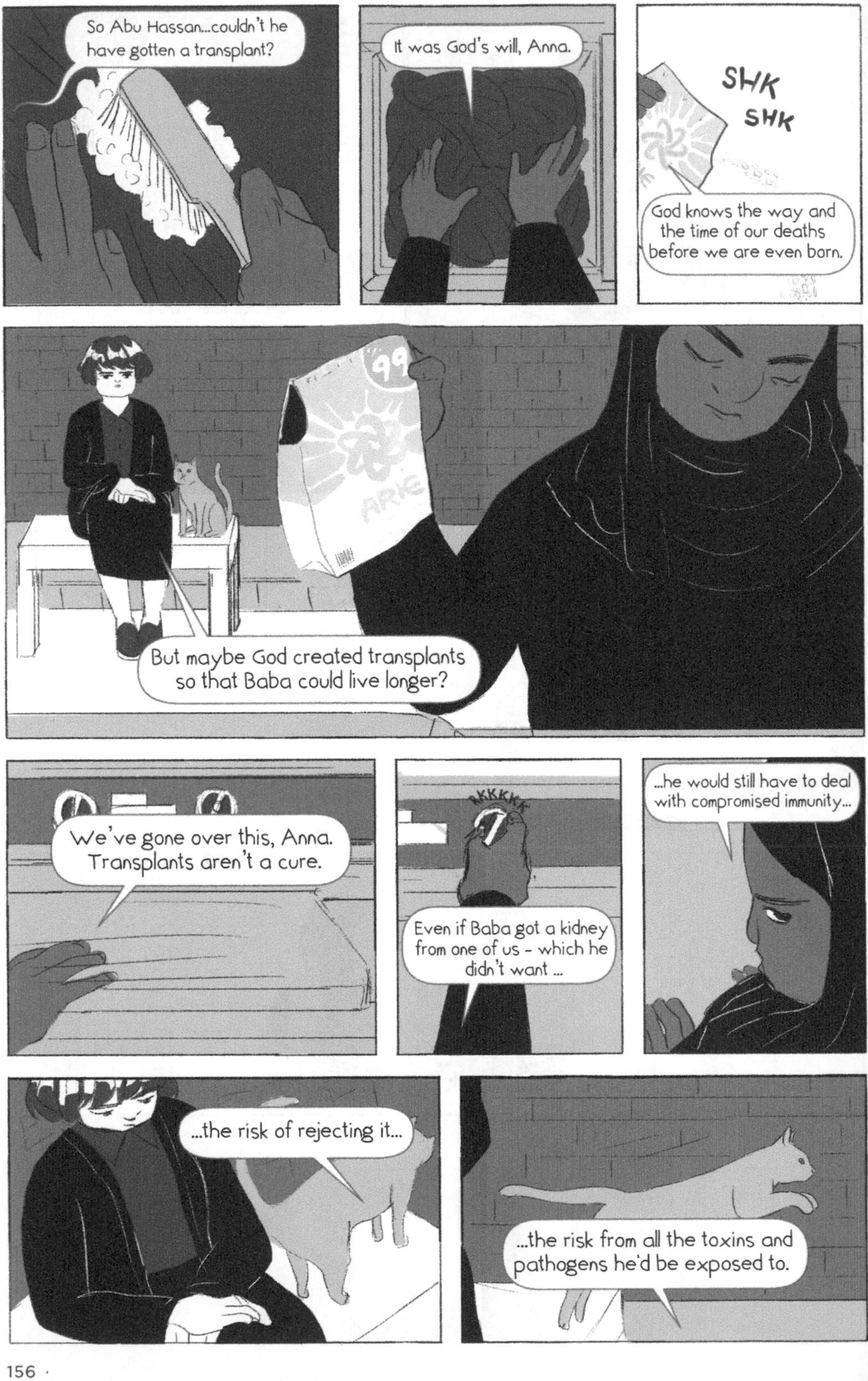
So Abu Hassan...couldn't he have gotten a transplant?
It was God's will, Anna.
SHK SHK
God knows the way and the time of our deaths before we are even born.
'99
ARIE
But maybe God created transplants so that Baba could live longer?
We've gone over this, Anna. Transplants aren't a cure.
RKKKKK
Even if Baba got a kidney from one of us - which he didn't want ...
...he would still have to deal with compromised immunity...
...the risk of rejecting it...
...the risk from all the toxins and pathogens he'd be exposed to.

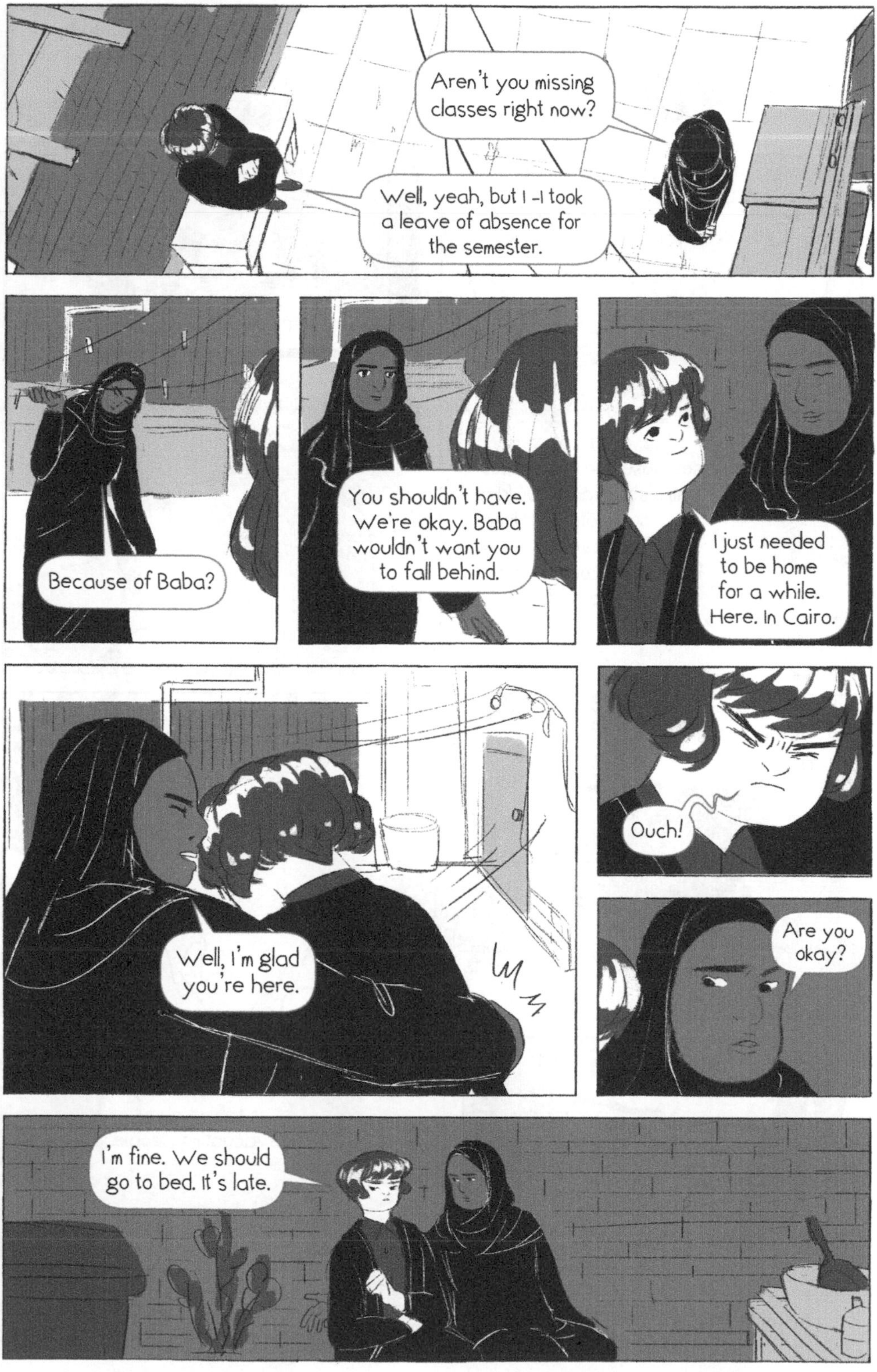
Aren't you missing classes right now?
Well, yeah, but I -I took a leave of absence for the semester.
Because of Baba?
You shouldn't have. We're okay. Baba wouldn't want you to fall behind.
I just needed to be home for a while. Here. In Cairo.
Well, I'm glad you're here.
Ouch!
Are you okay?
I'm fine. We should go to bed. It's late.

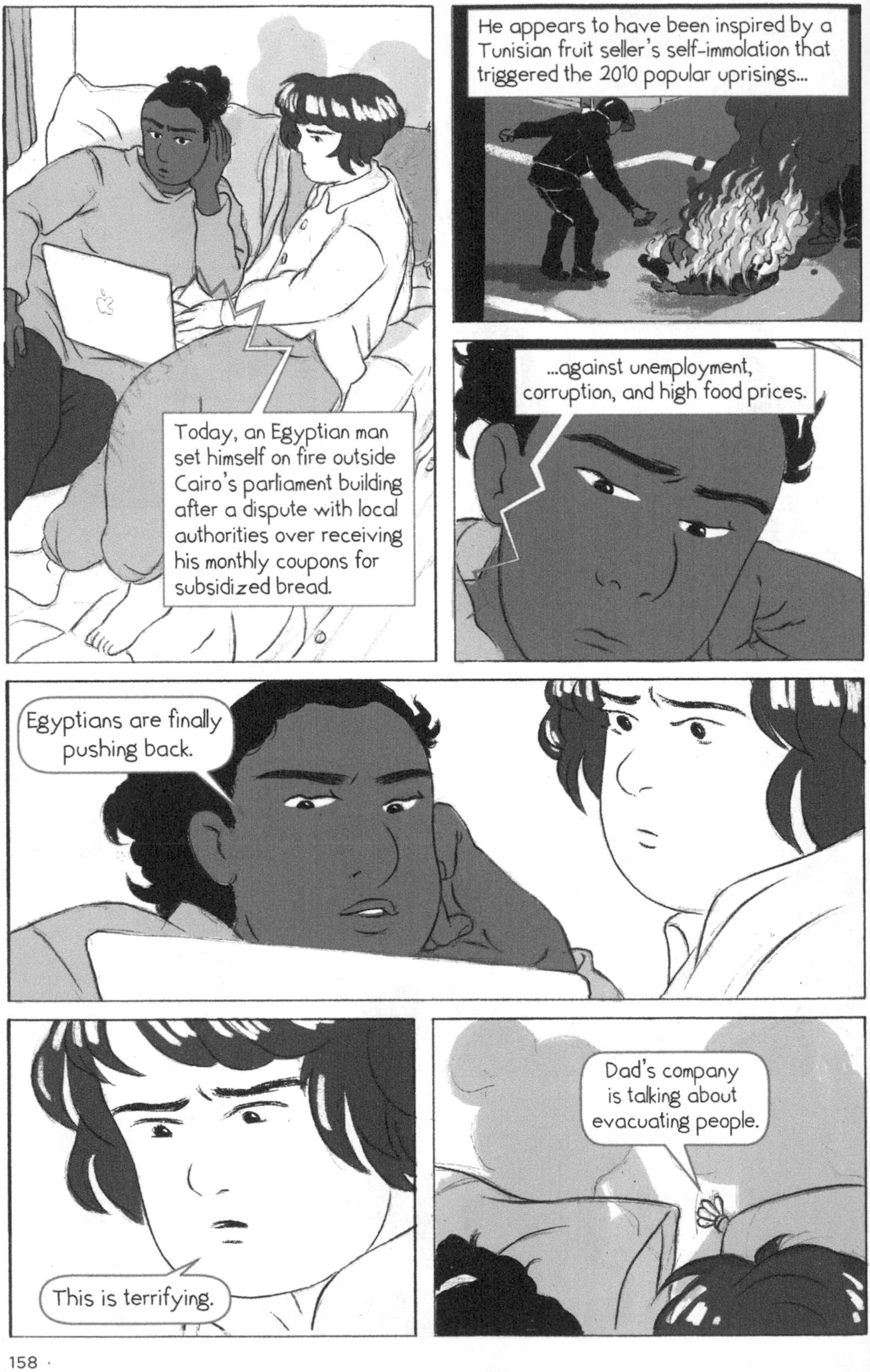
Today, an Egyptian man set himself on fire outside Cairo's parliament building after a dispute with local authorities over receiving his monthly coupons for subsidized bread.
He appears to have been inspired by a Tunisian fruit seller's self-immolation that triggered the 2010 popular uprisings...
...against unemployment, corruption, and high food prices.
Egyptians are finally pushing back.
This is terrifying.
Dad's company is talking about evacuating people.

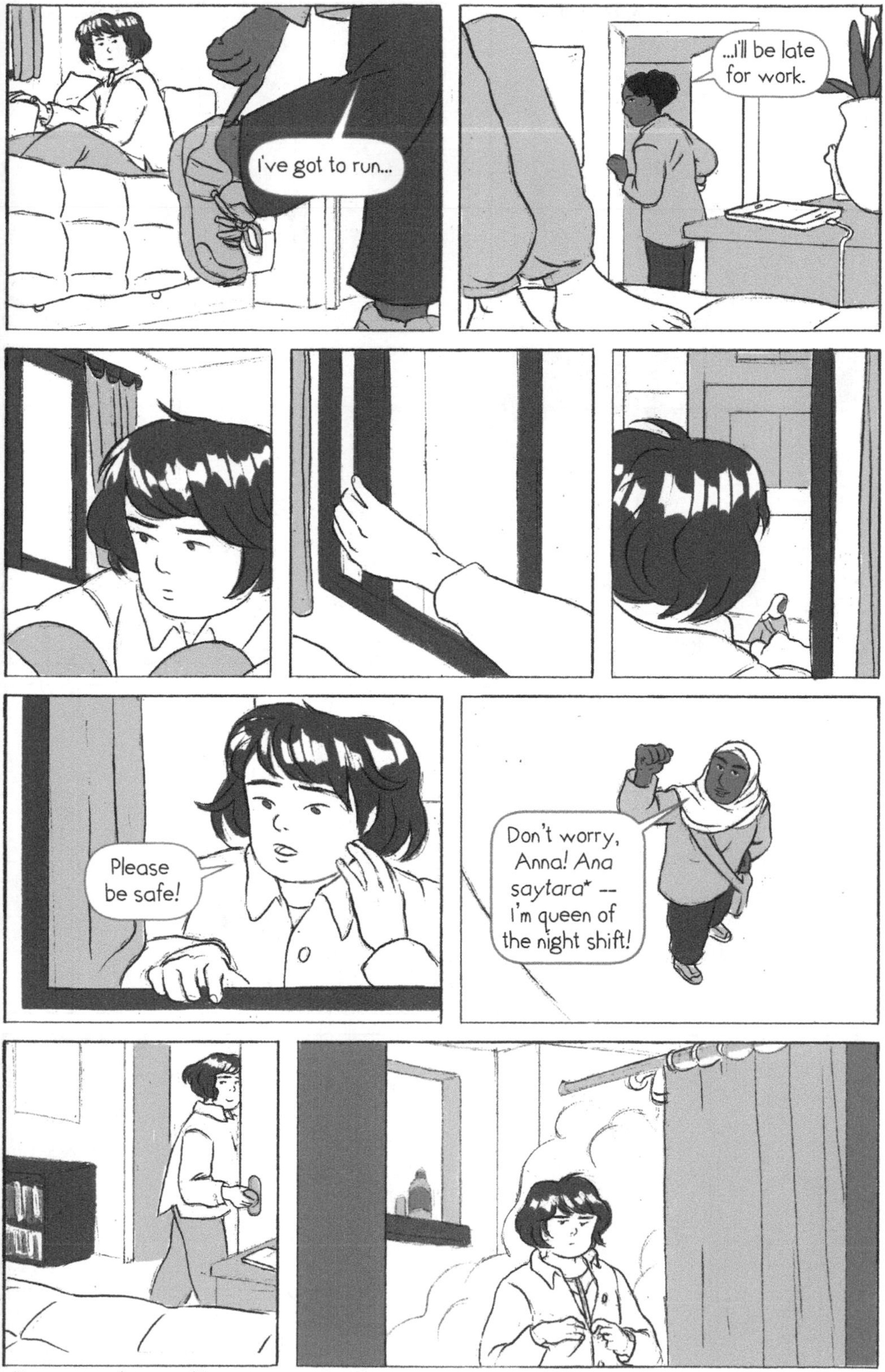
I've got to run...
...I'll be late for work.
Please be safe!
Don't worry, Anna! Ana saytara* -- I'm queen of the night shift!

*"I've got it under control."

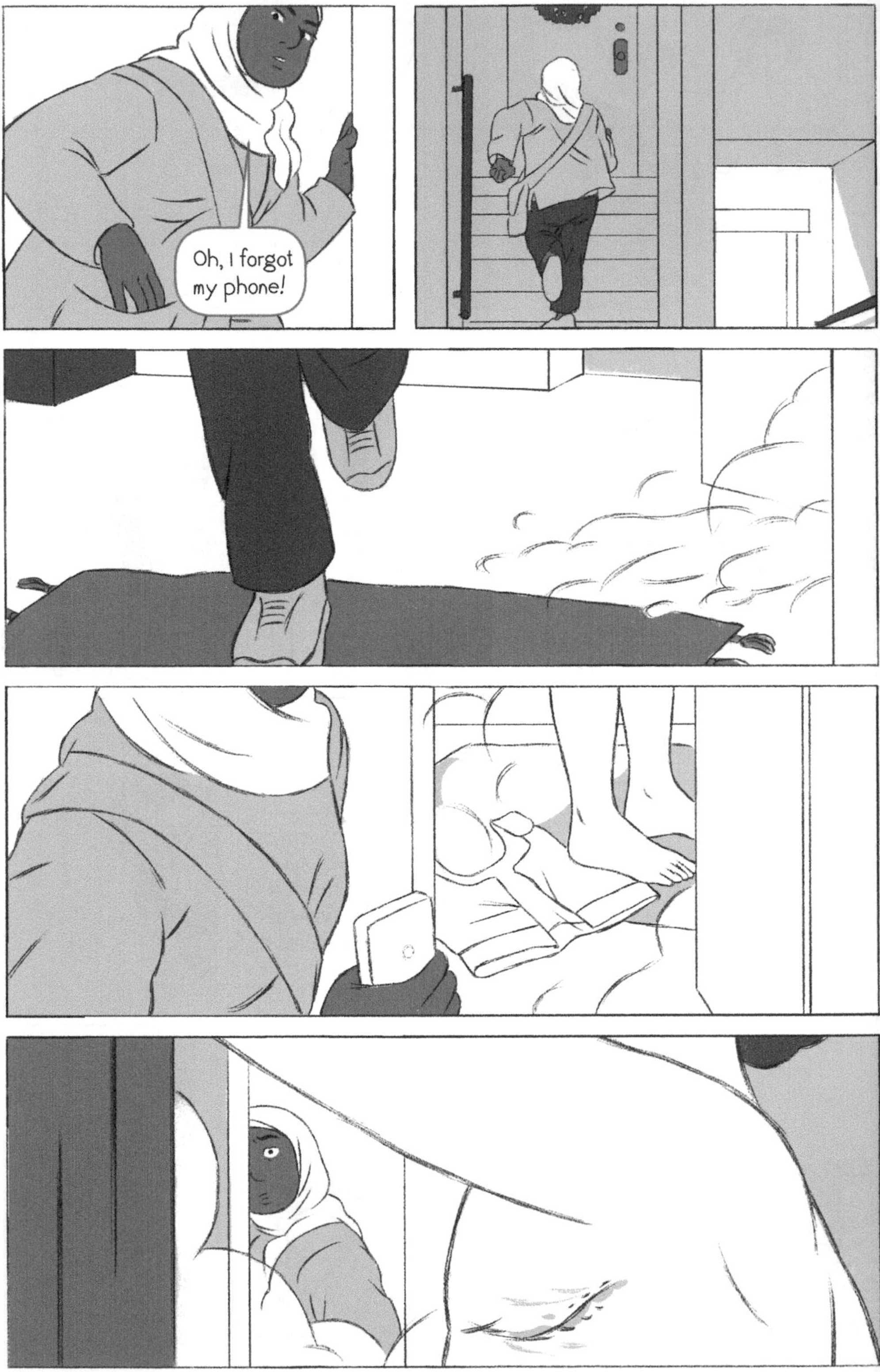
Oh, I forgot my phone!

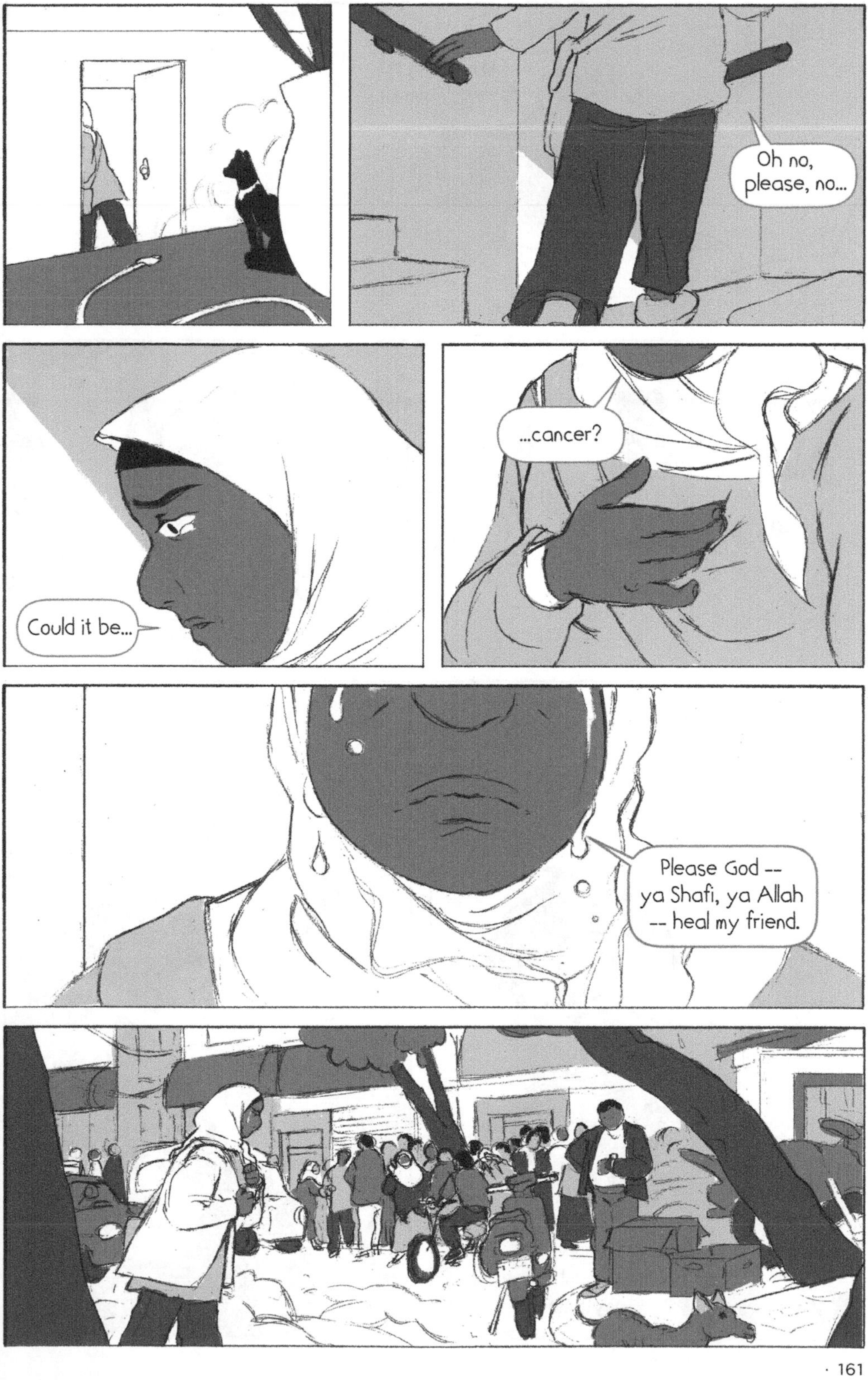
Oh no, please, no...
Could it be...
...cancer?
Please God -- ya Shafi, ya Allah -- heal my friend.

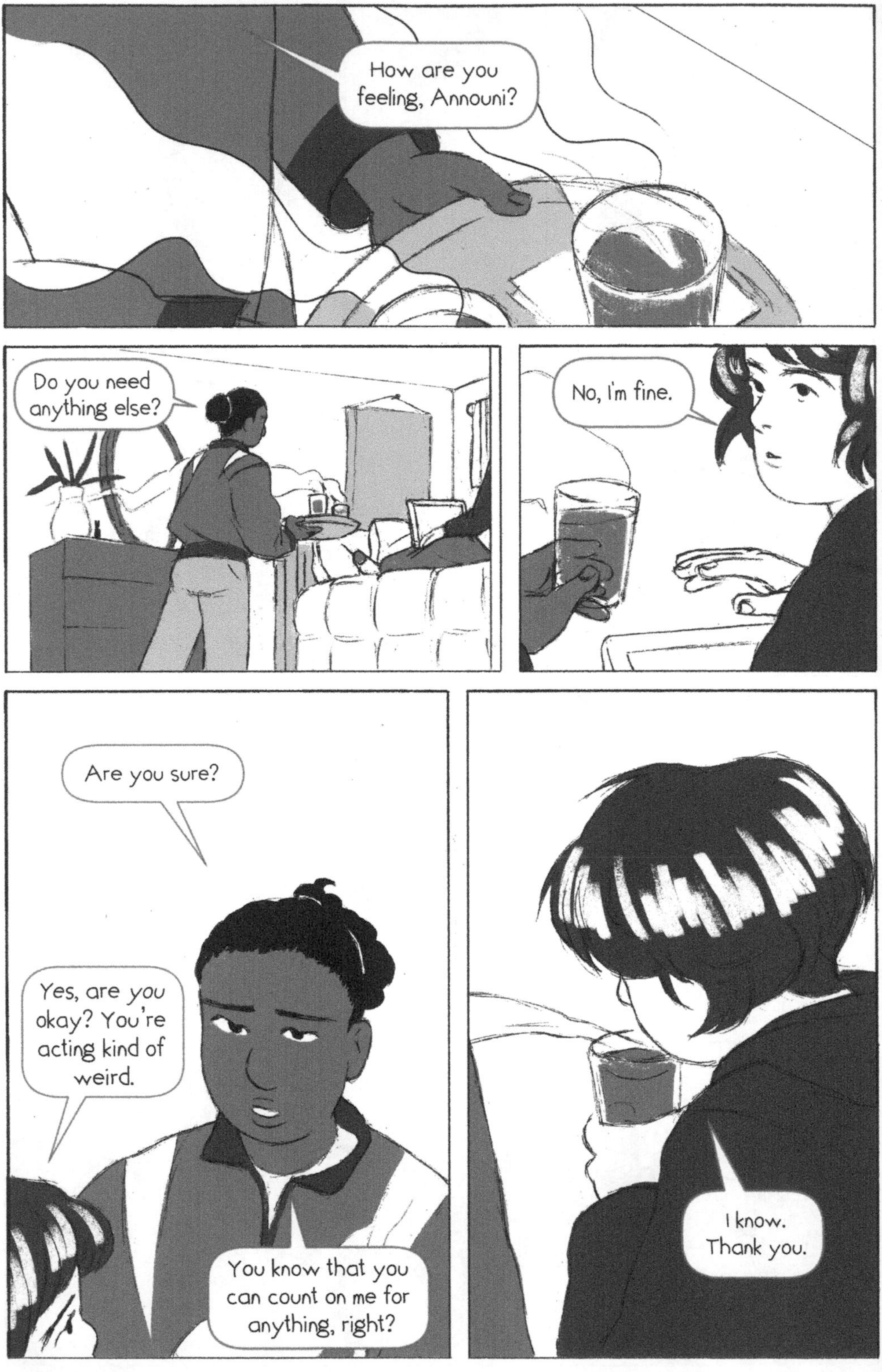
How are you feeling, Announi?
Do you need anything else?
No, I'm fine.
Are you sure?
Yes, are *you* okay? You're acting kind of weird.
You know that you can count on me for anything, right?
I know. Thank you.

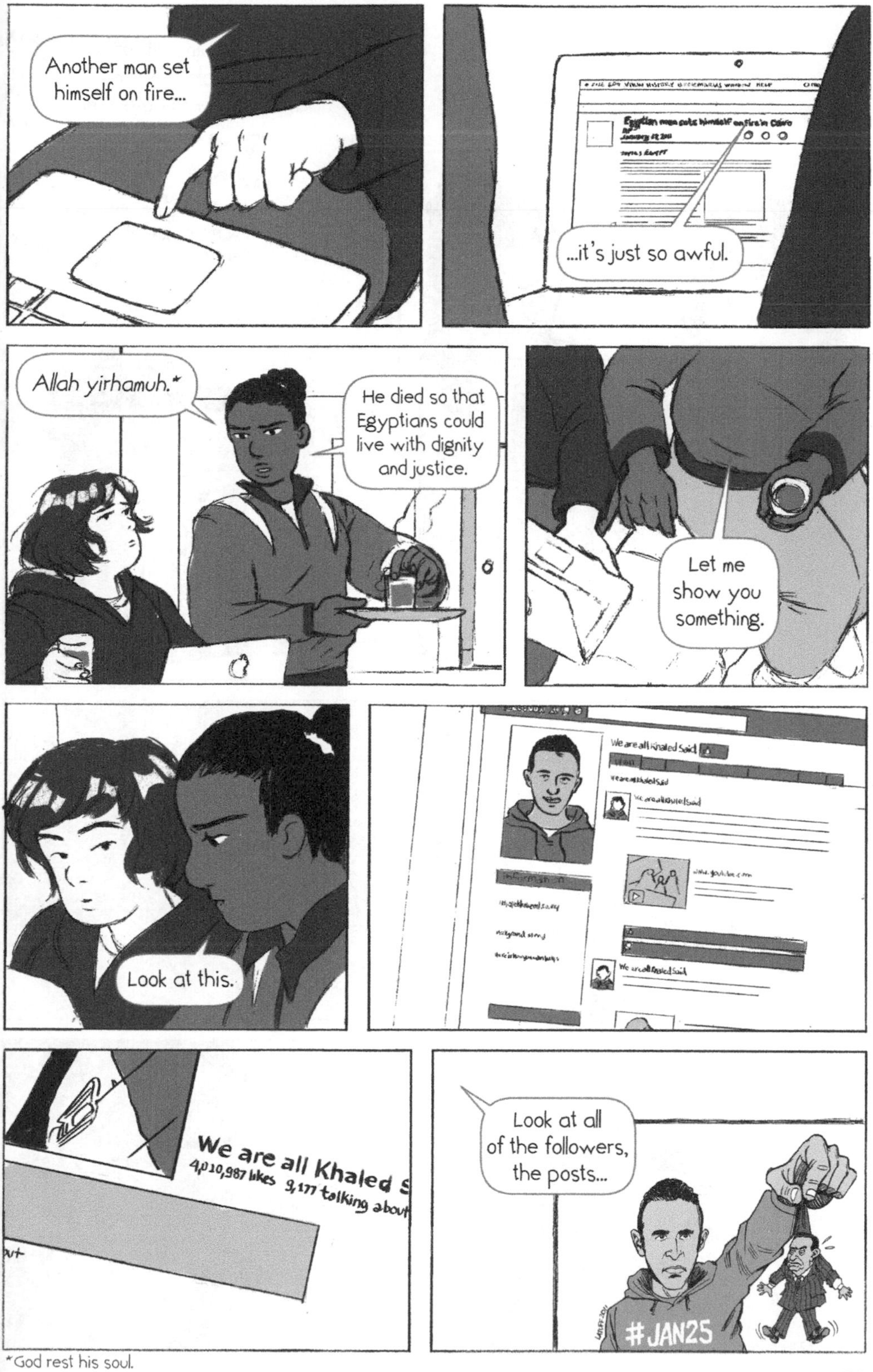
Another man set himself on fire...
...it's just so awful.
Allah yirhamuh.*
He died so that Egyptians could live with dignity and justice.
Let me show you something.
Look at this.
We are all Khaled S
Look at all of the followers, the posts...
#JAN25

*God rest his soul.
**Art (panel 8) by Carlos Latuff

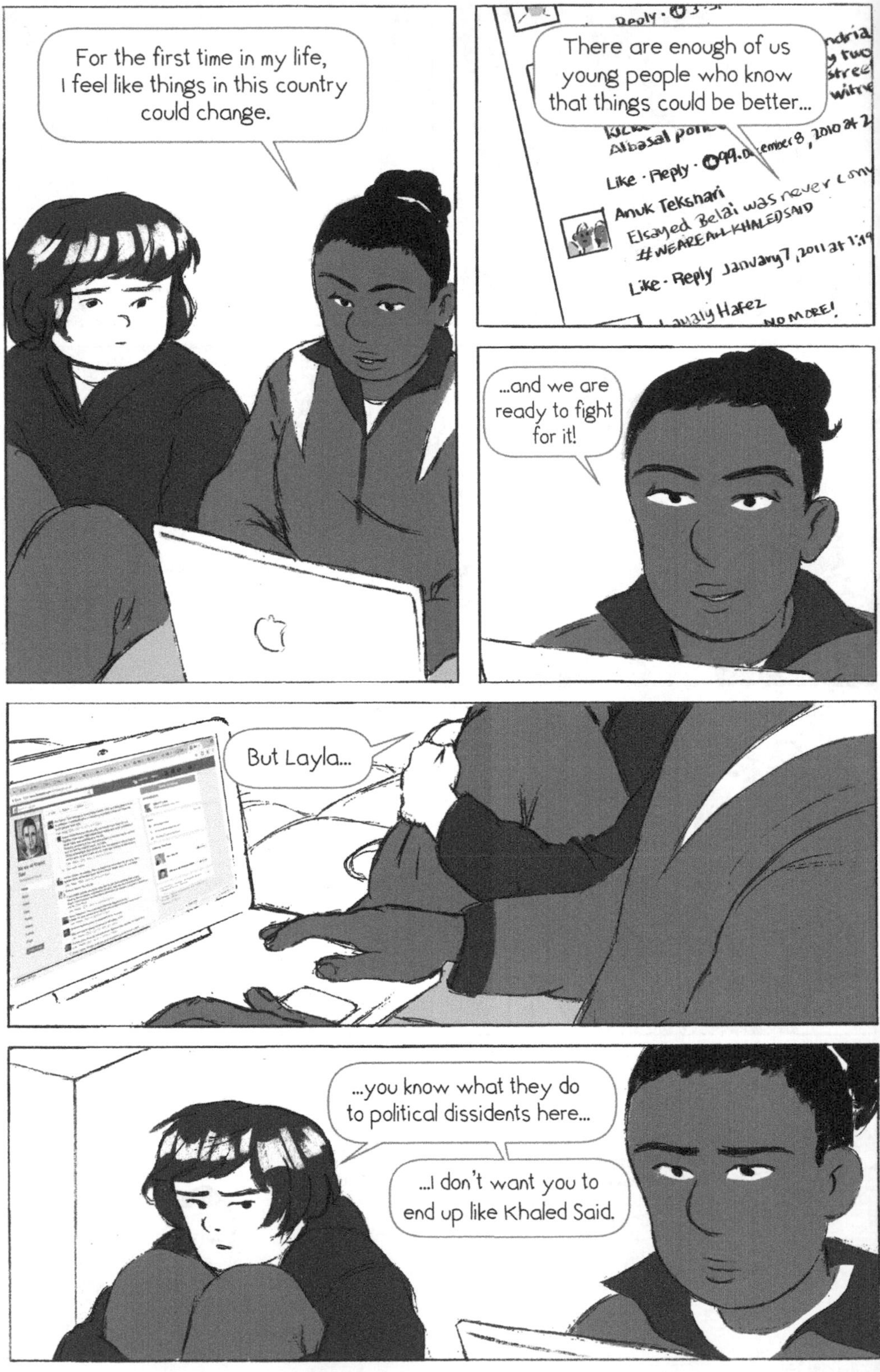
For the first time in my life, I feel like things in this country could change.
There are enough of us young people who know that things could be better...
Like · Reply
Anuk Tekshari
#WEAREALLKHALEDSAID
Like · Reply
NO MORE!
...and we are ready to fight for it!
But Layla...
...you know what they do to political dissidents here...
...I don't want you to end up like Khaled Said.

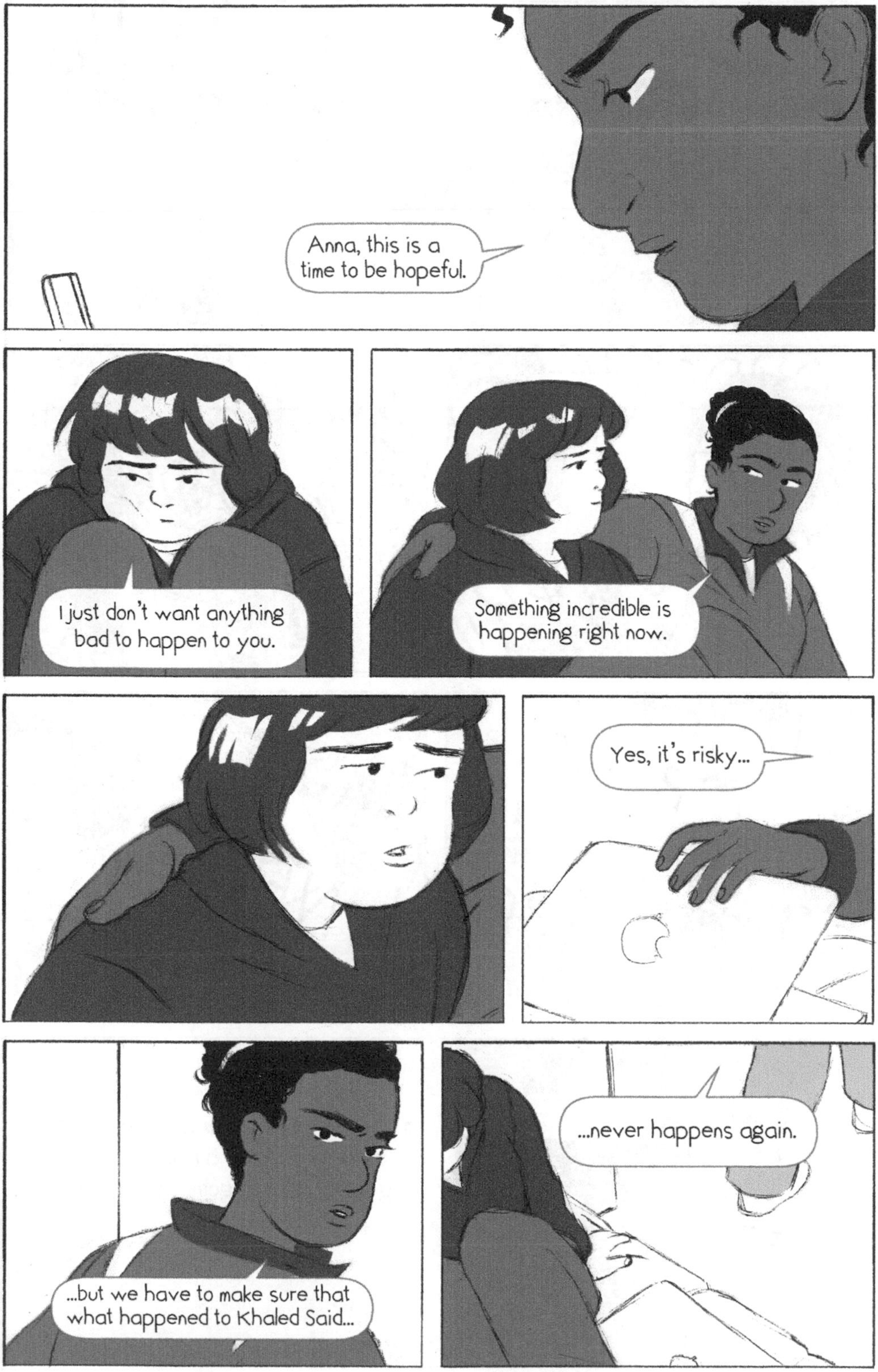
Anna, this is a time to be hopeful.
I just don't want anything bad to happen to you.
Something incredible is happening right now.
Yes, it's risky...
...but we have to make sure that what happened to Khaled Said...
...never happens again.

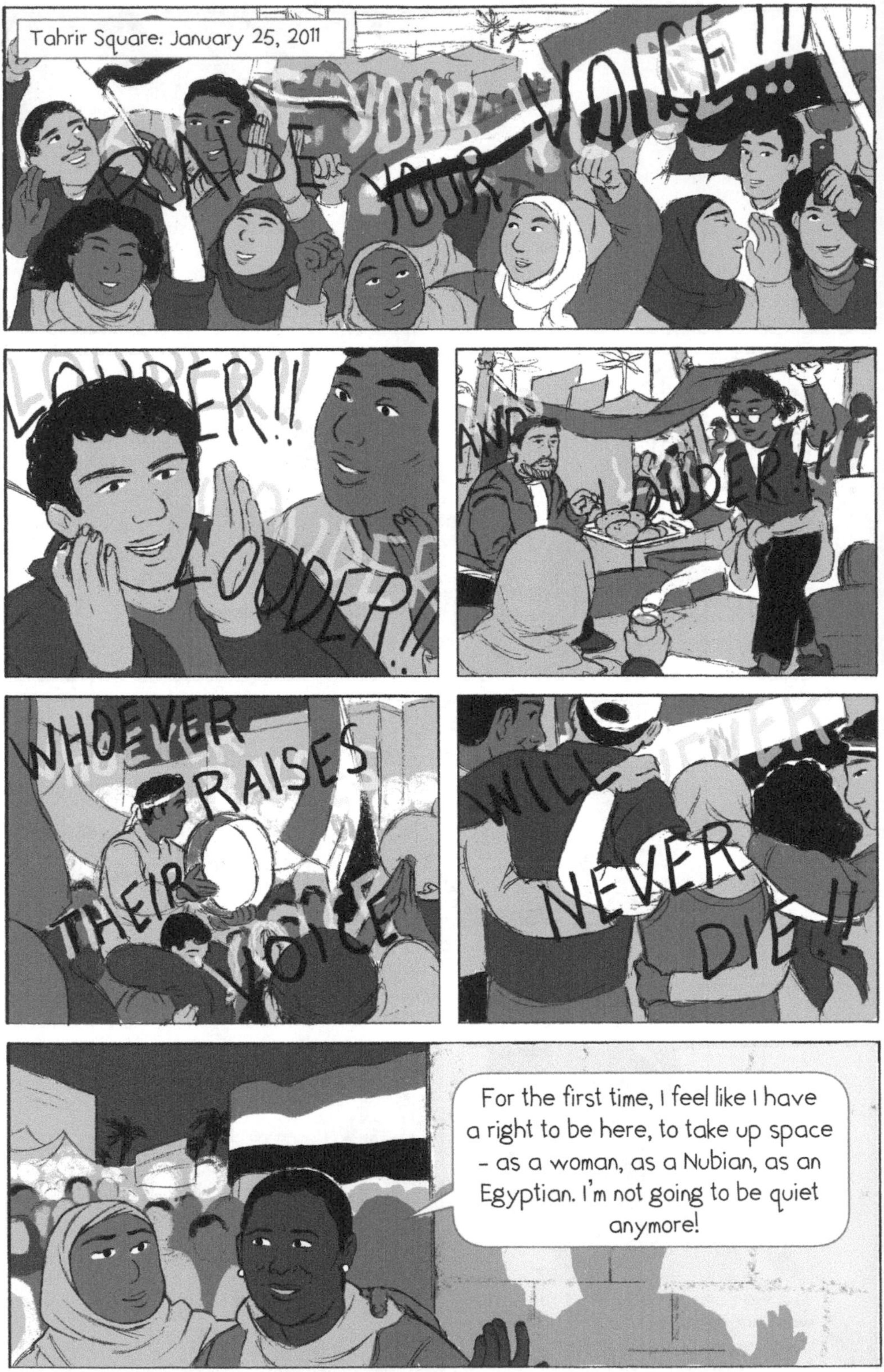
Tahrir Square: January 25, 2011
RAISE YOUR VOICE!!!
LOUDER!!
LOUDER!!
AND LOUDER!!
WHOEVER RAISES THEIR VOICE
WILL NEVER DIE!!
For the first time, I feel like I have a right to be here, to take up space - as a woman, as a Nubian, as an Egyptian. I'm not going to be quiet anymore!

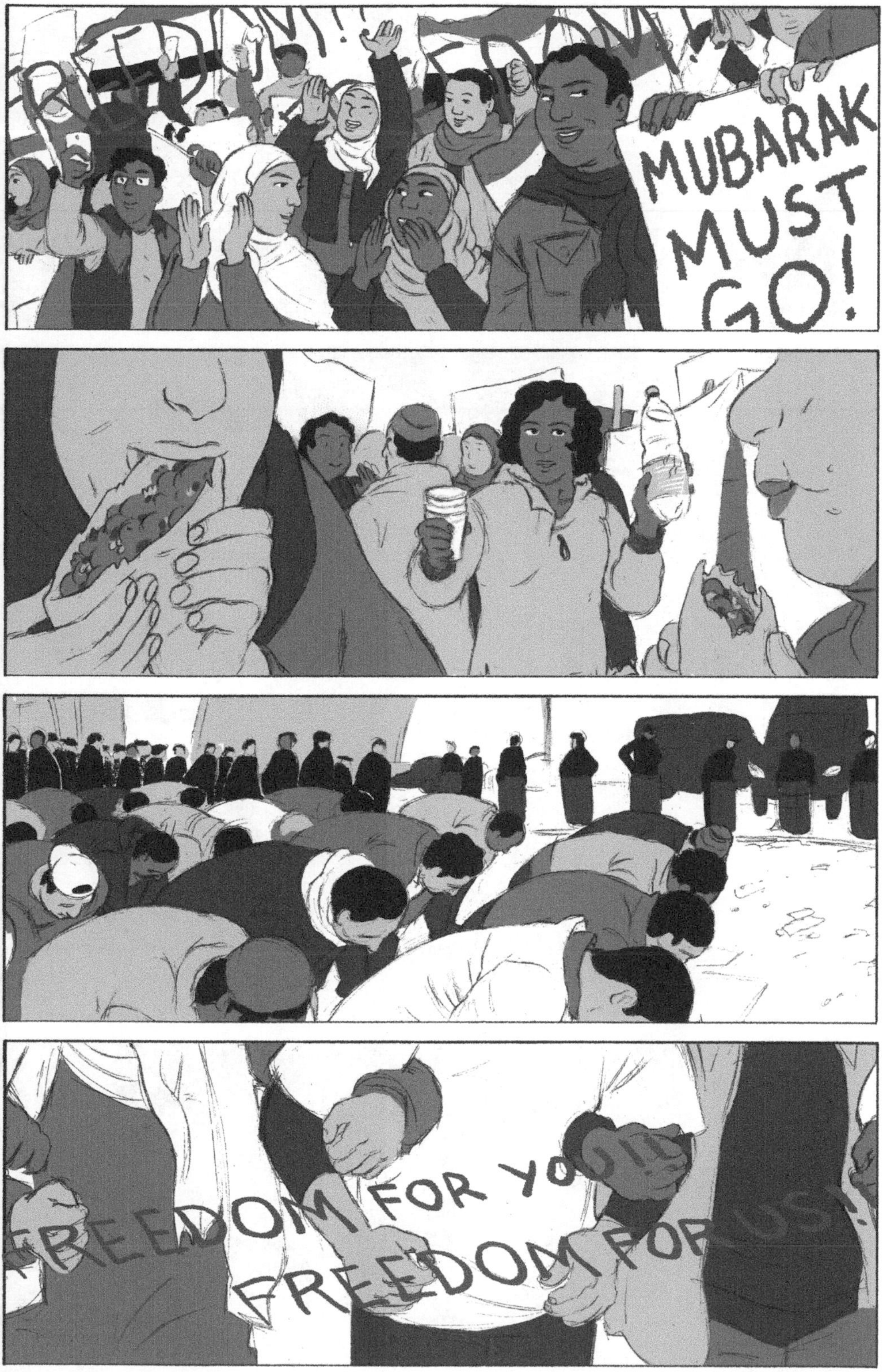
FREEDOM!!
MUBARAK MUST GO!
FREEDOM FOR YOU!!
FREEDOM FOR US!!

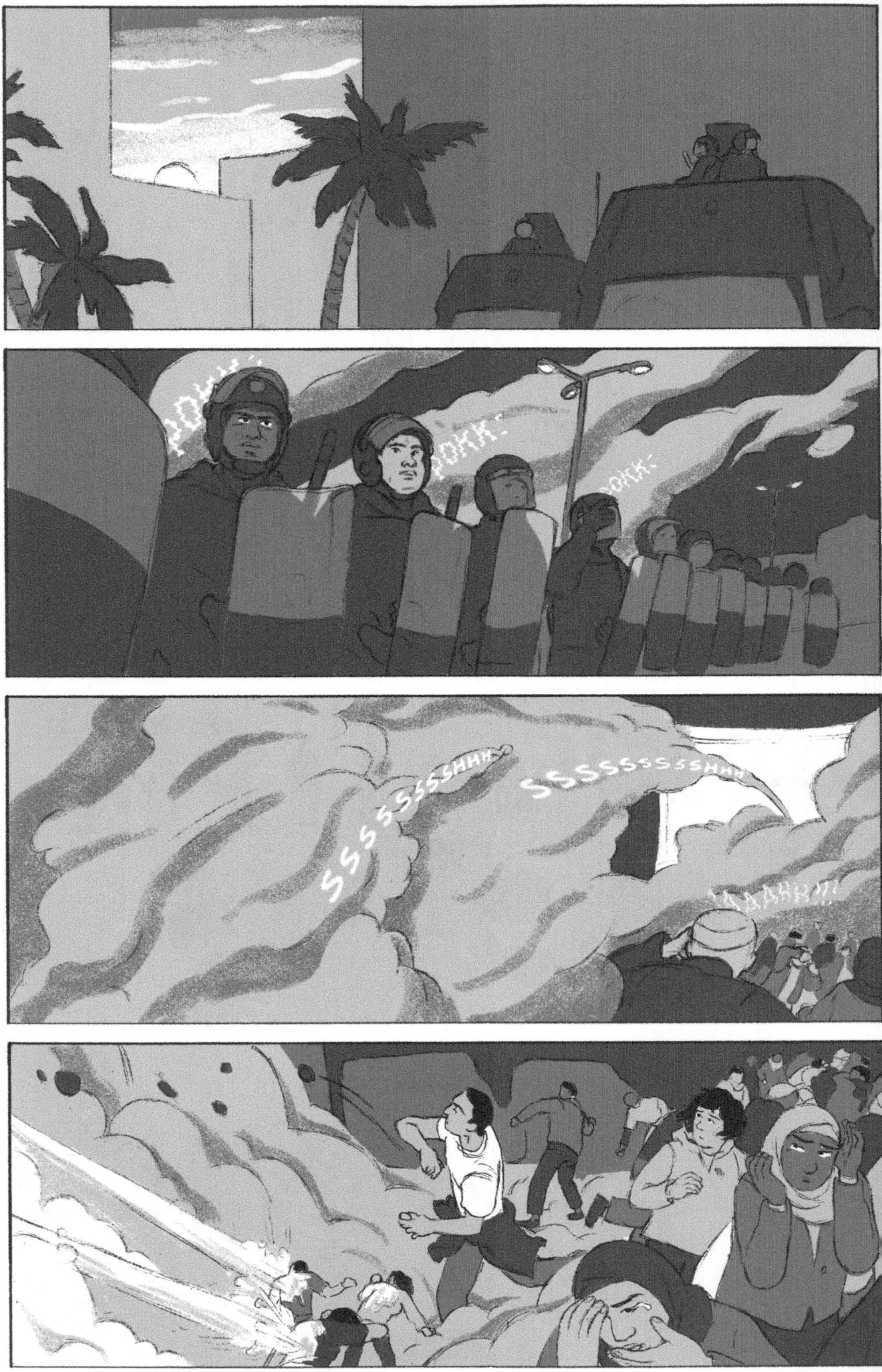
POKK
POKK-
POKK-
SSSSSSSSSSHHH
SSSSSSSSSSSHHH
AAAHH!!

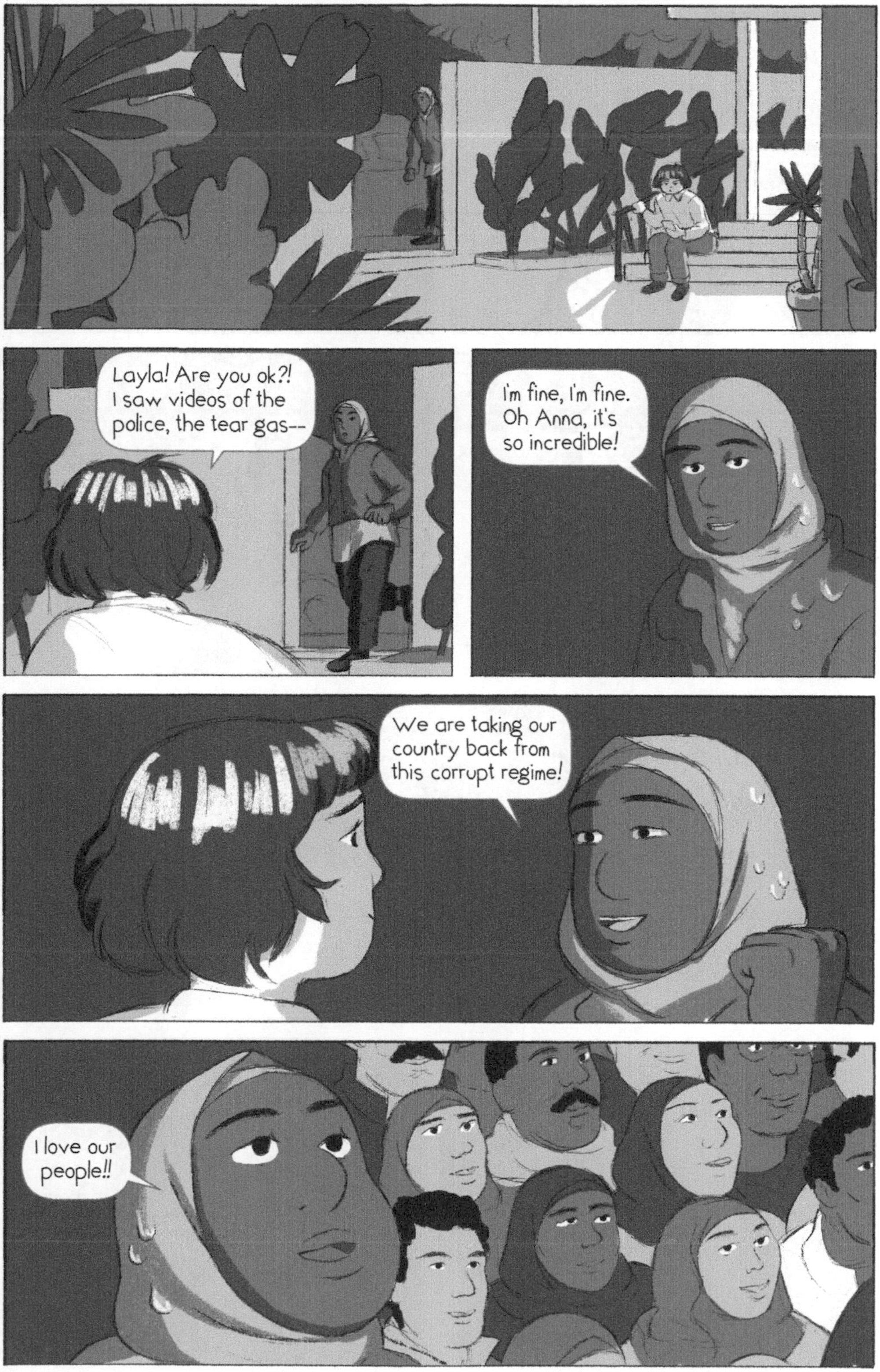
Layla! Are you ok?! I saw videos of the police, the tear gas--
I'm fine, I'm fine. Oh Anna, it's so incredible!
We are taking our country back from this corrupt regime!
I love our people!!

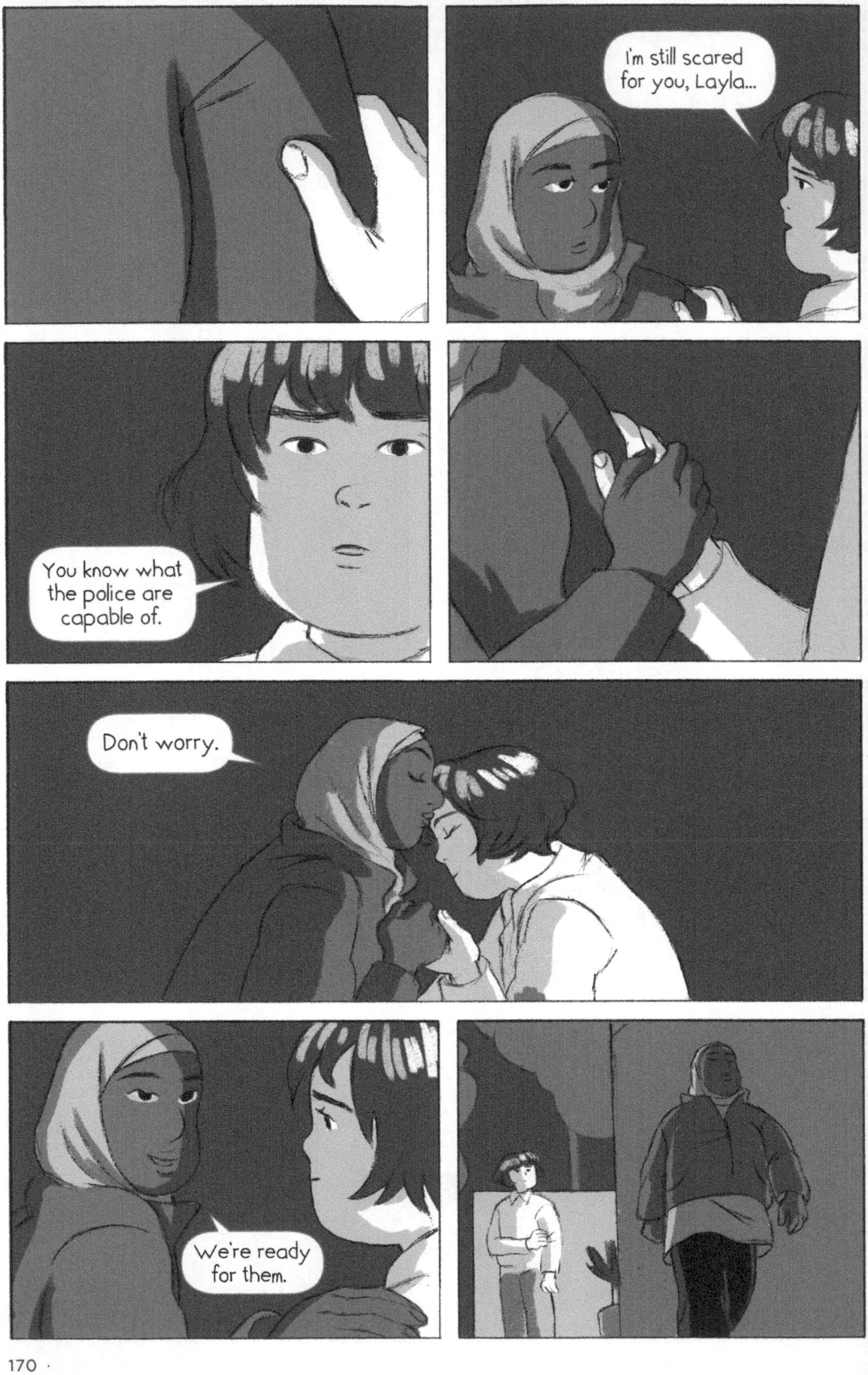
I'm still scared for you, Layla...
You know what the police are capable of.
Don't worry.
We're ready for them.

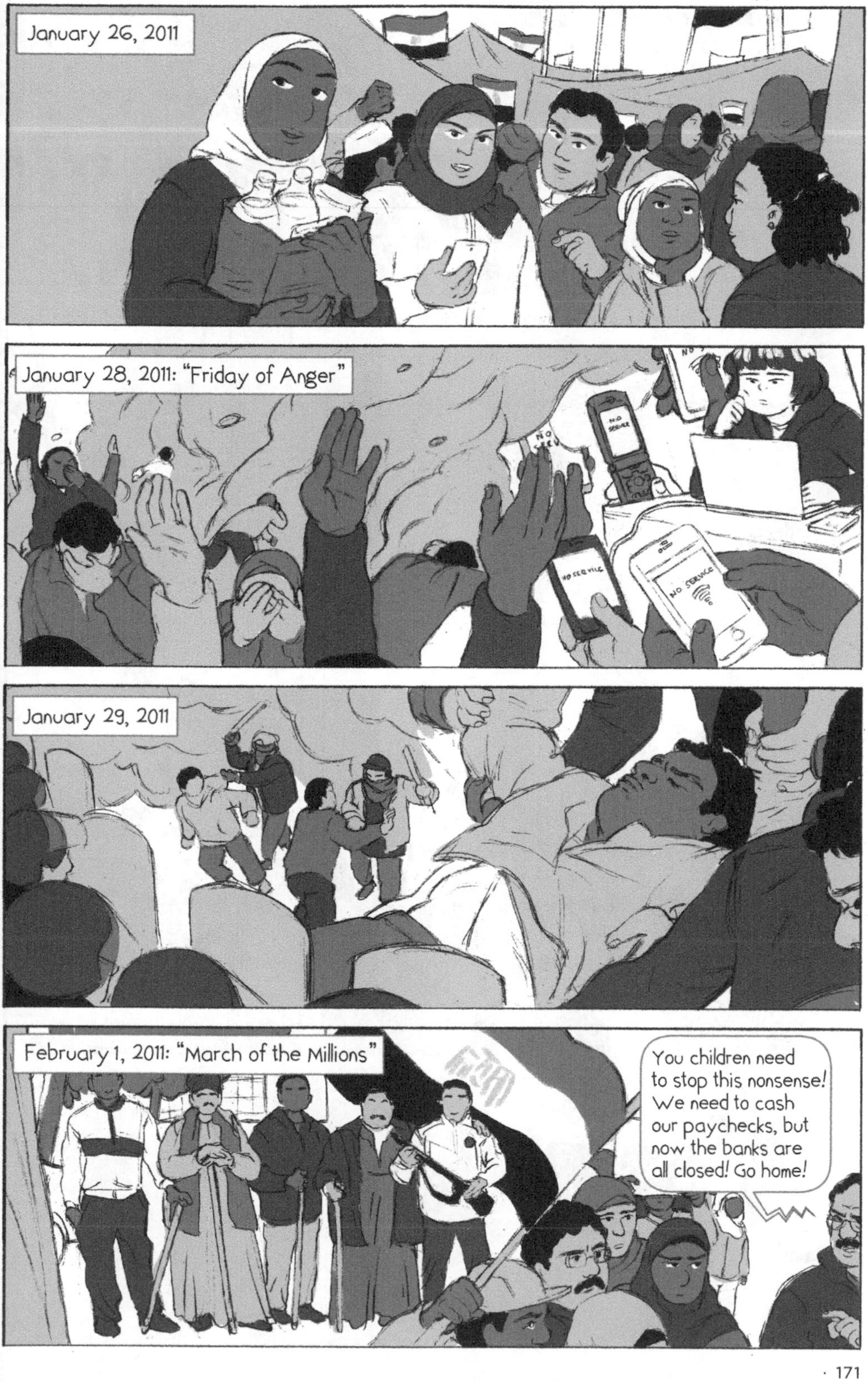

January 26, 2011
January 28, 2011: "Friday of Anger"
NO SERVICE
NO SERVICE
January 29, 2011
February 1, 2011: "March of the Millions"
You children need to stop this nonsense! We need to cash our paychecks, but now the banks are all closed! Go home!

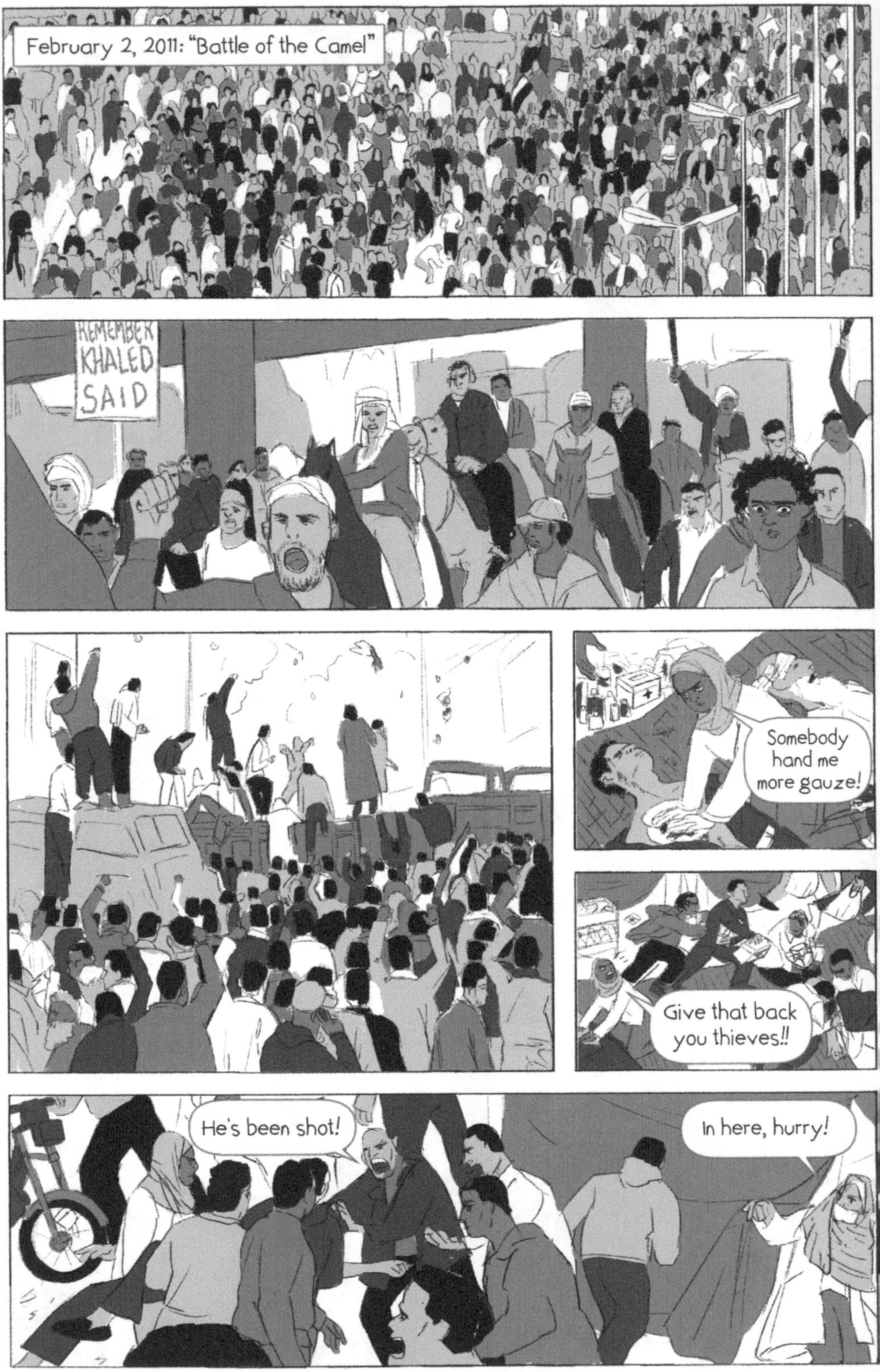
February 2, 2011: "Battle of the Camel"
REMEMBER KHALED SAID
Somebody hand me more gauze!
Give that back you thieves!!
He's been shot!
In here, hurry!

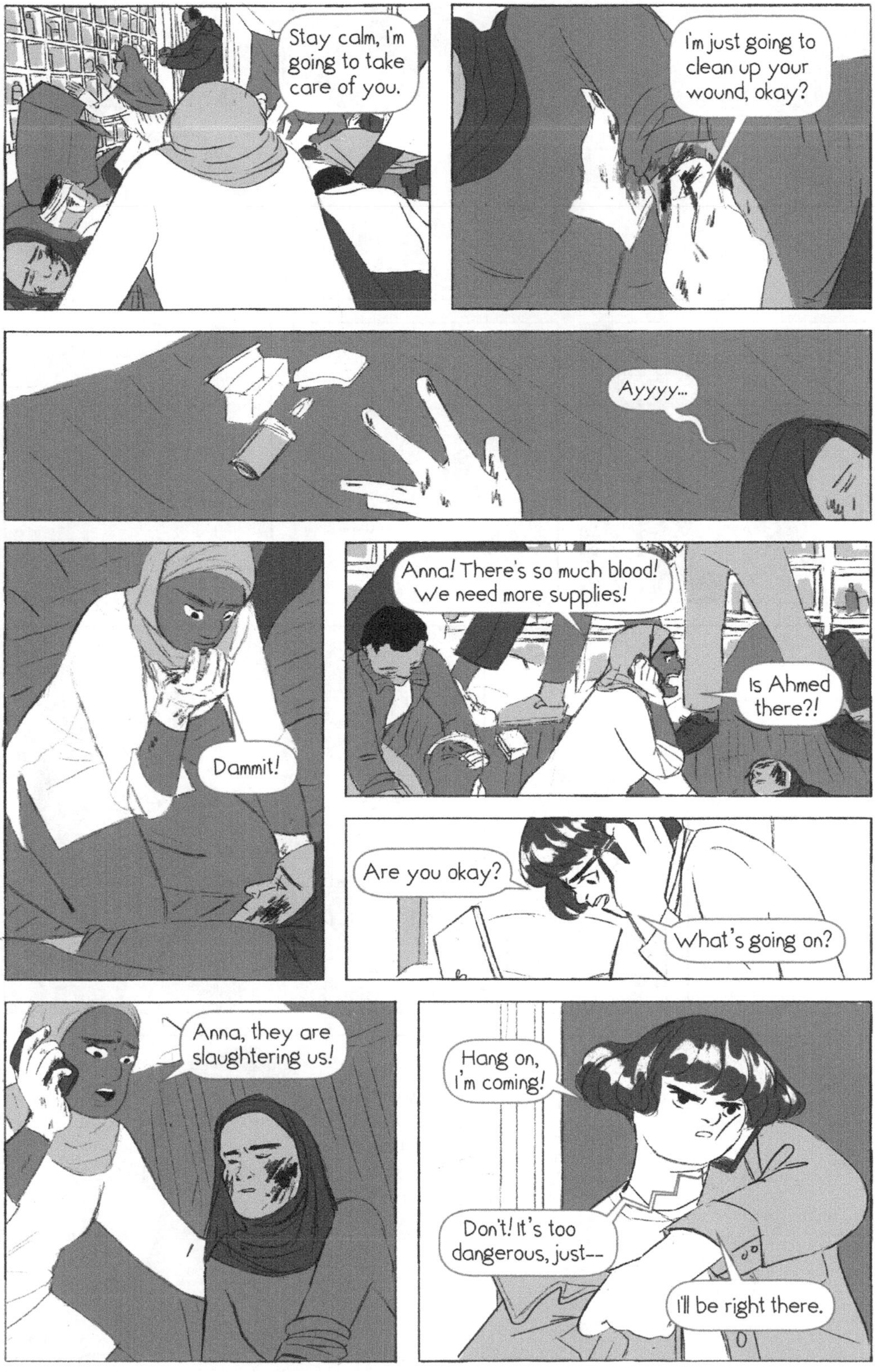
Stay calm, I'm going to take care of you.
I'm just going to clean up your wound, okay?
Ayyyy...
Dammit!
Anna! There's so much blood! We need more supplies!
Is Ahmed there?!
Are you okay?
What's going on?
Anna, they are slaughtering us!
Hang on, I'm coming!
Don't! It's too dangerous, just--
I'll be right there.

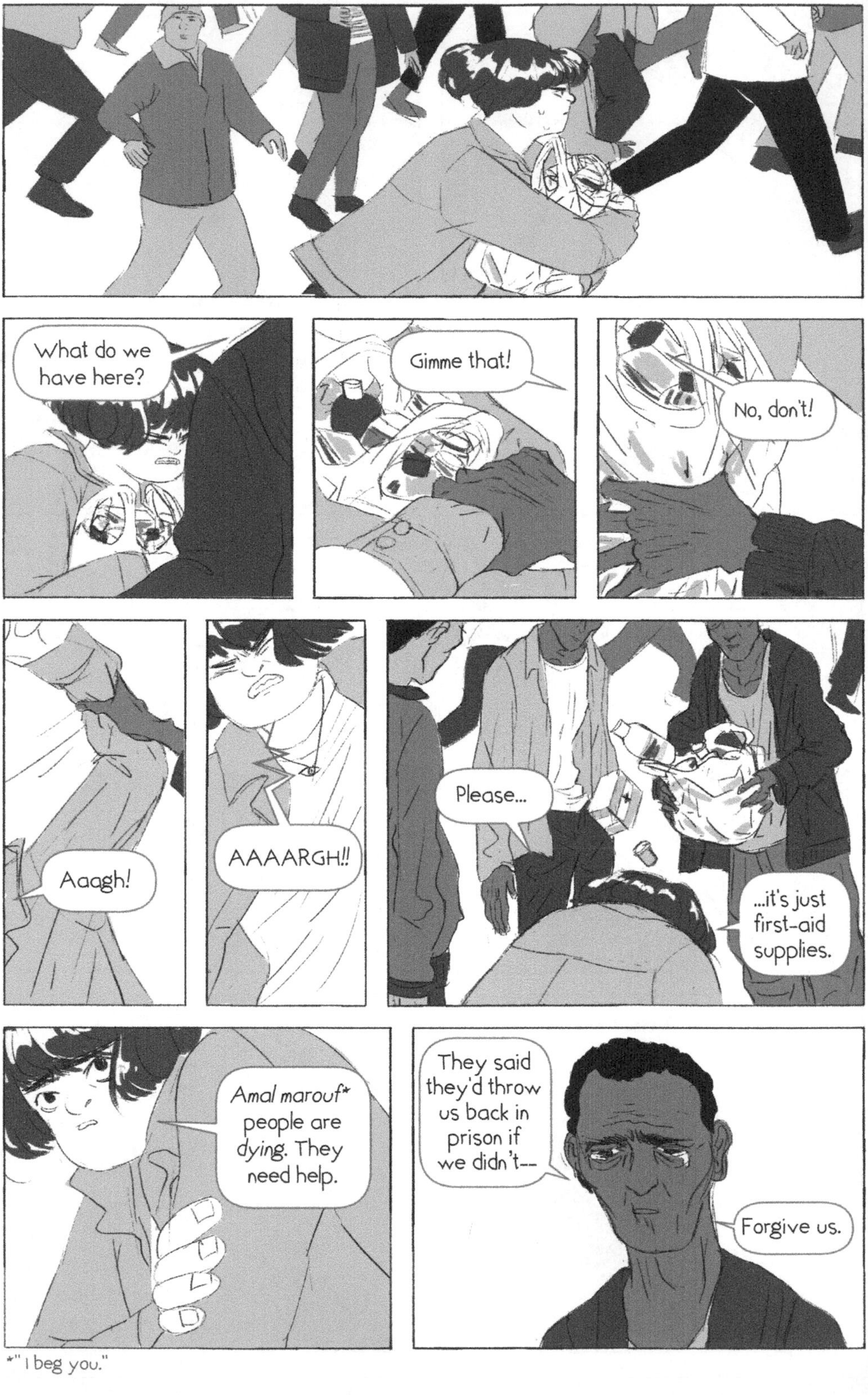
What do we have here?
Gimme that!
No, don't!
Aaagh!
AAAARGH!!
Please...
...it's just first-aid supplies.
*Amal marouf** people are *dying*. They need help.
They said they'd throw us back in prison if we didn't--
Forgive us.

*"I beg you."

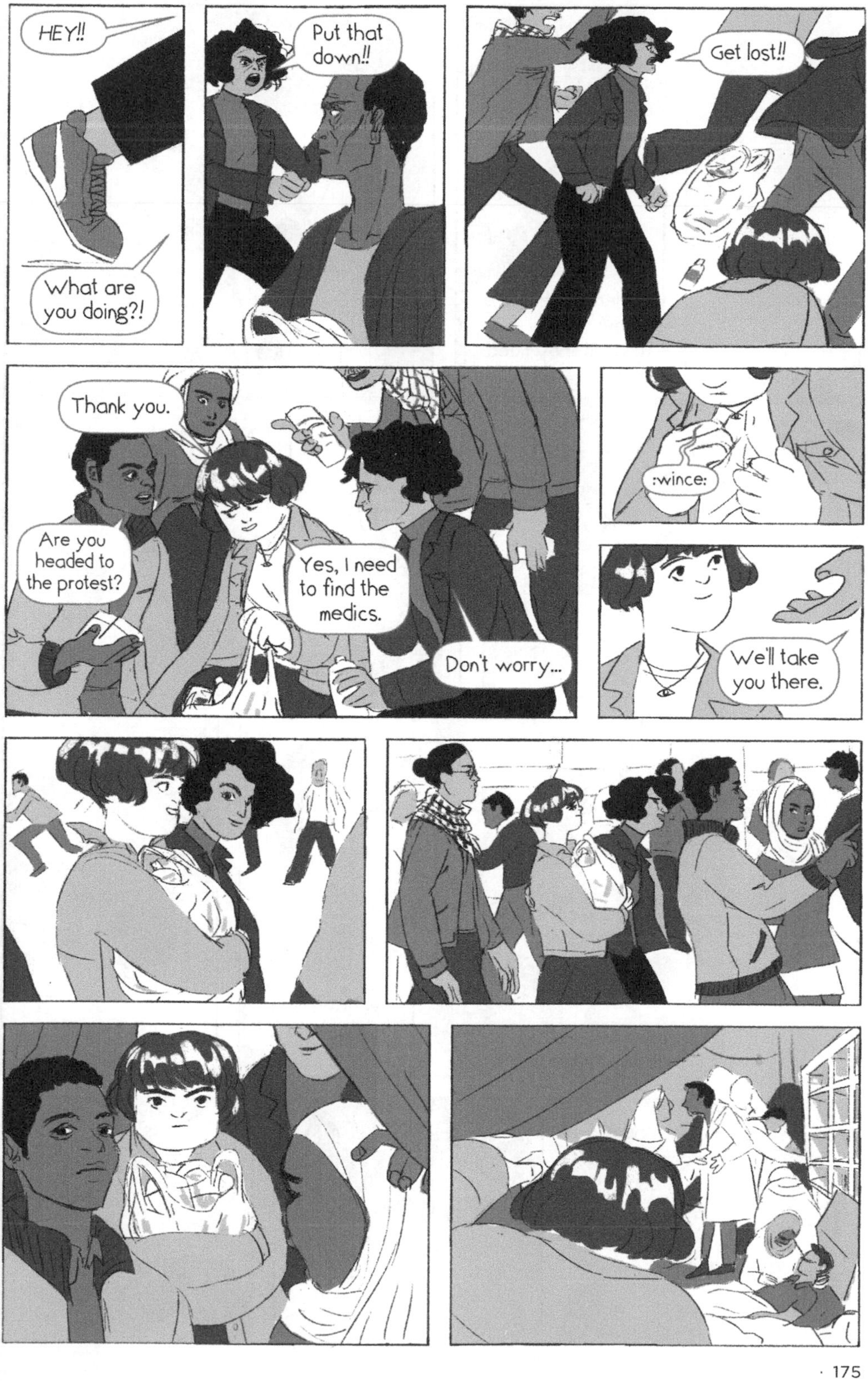
HEY!!
What are you doing?!
Put that down!!
Get lost!!
Thank you.
Are you headed to the protest?
Yes, I need to find the medics.
Don't worry...
:wince:
We'll take you there.

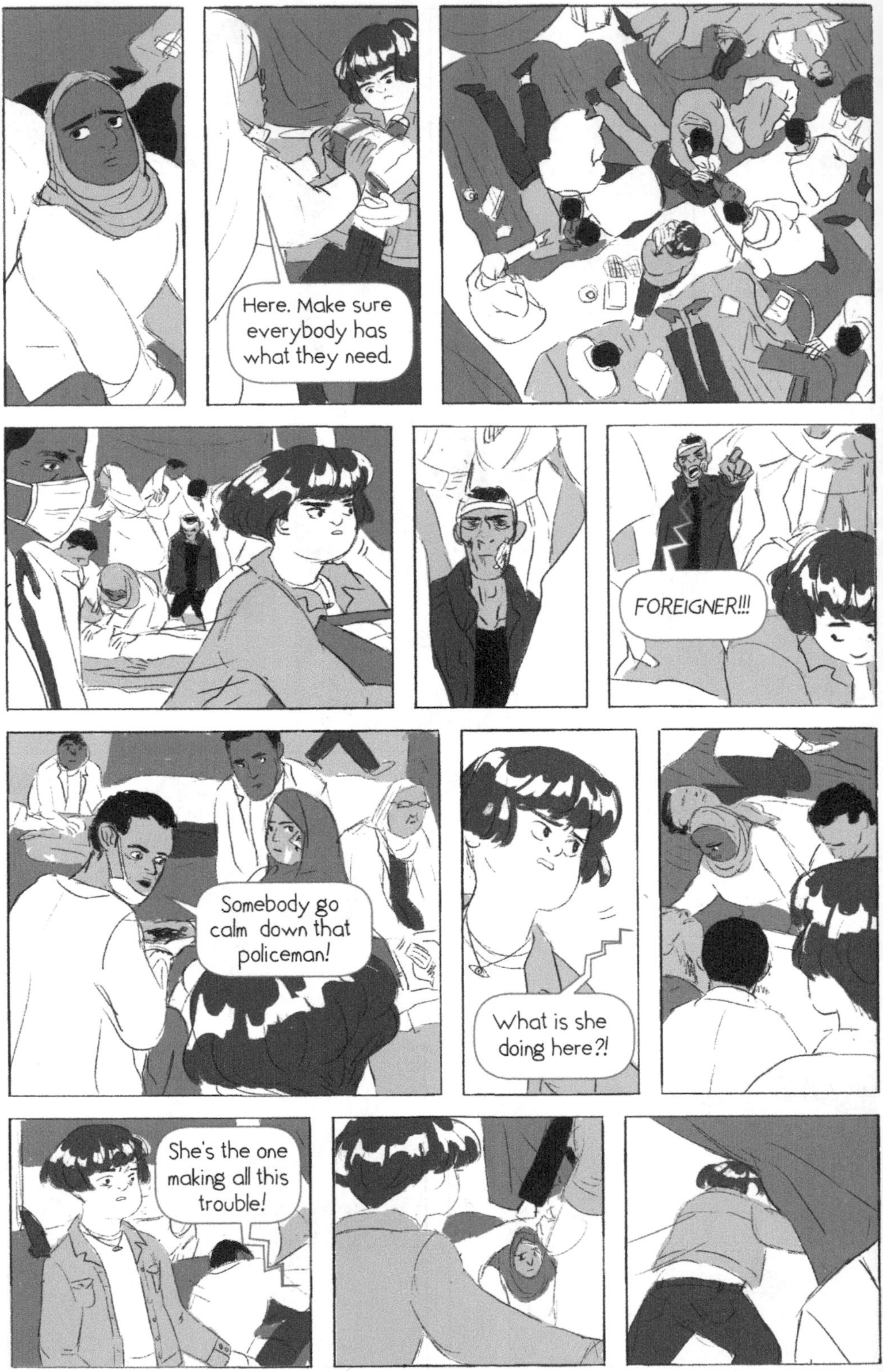
Here. Make sure everybody has what they need.
FOREIGNER!!!
Somebody go calm down that policeman!
What is she doing here?!
She's the one making all this trouble!

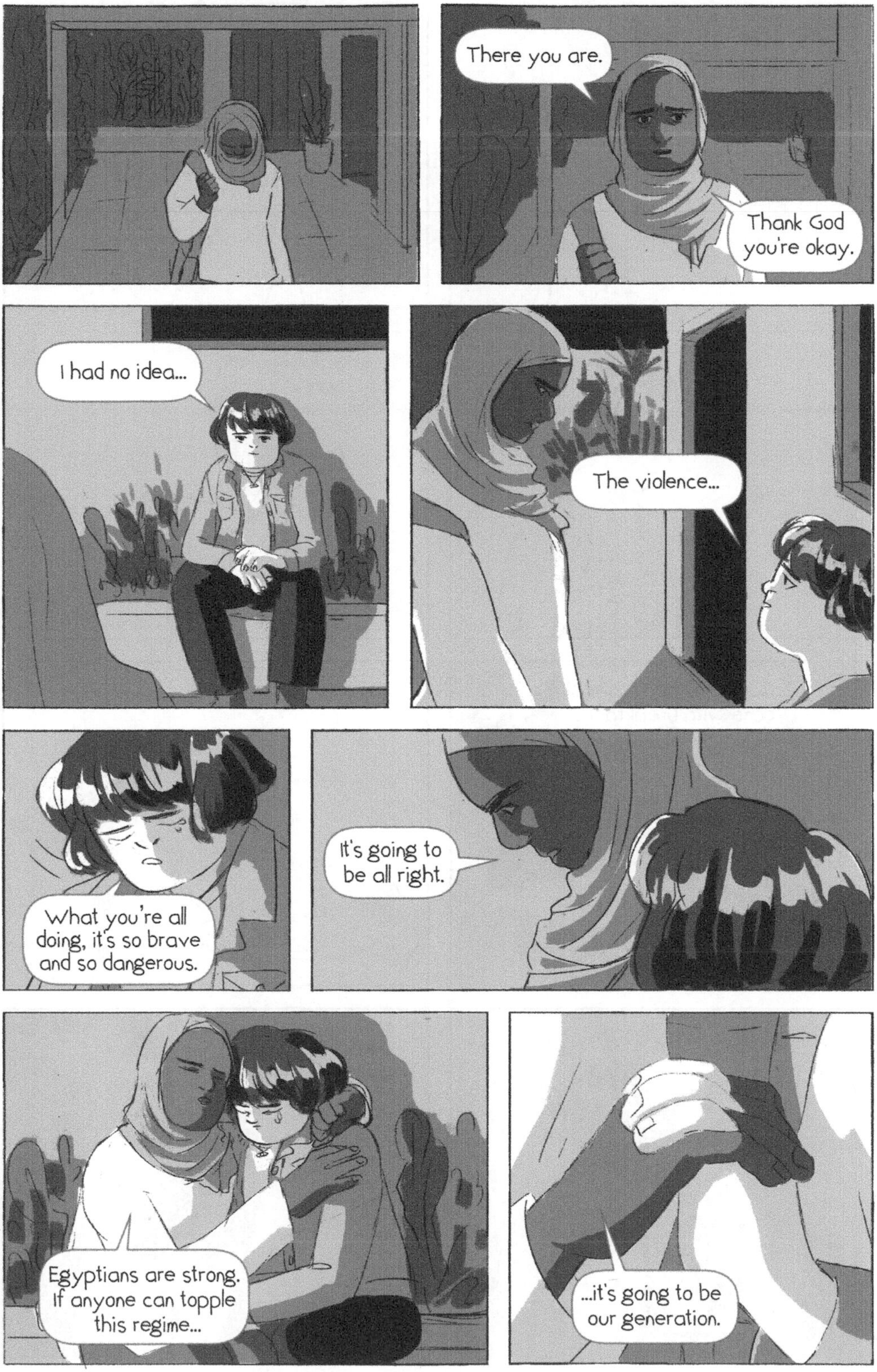
There you are.
Thank God you're okay.
I had no idea...
The violence...
What you're all doing, it's so brave and so dangerous.
It's going to be all right.
Egyptians are strong. If anyone can topple this regime...
...it's going to be our generation.

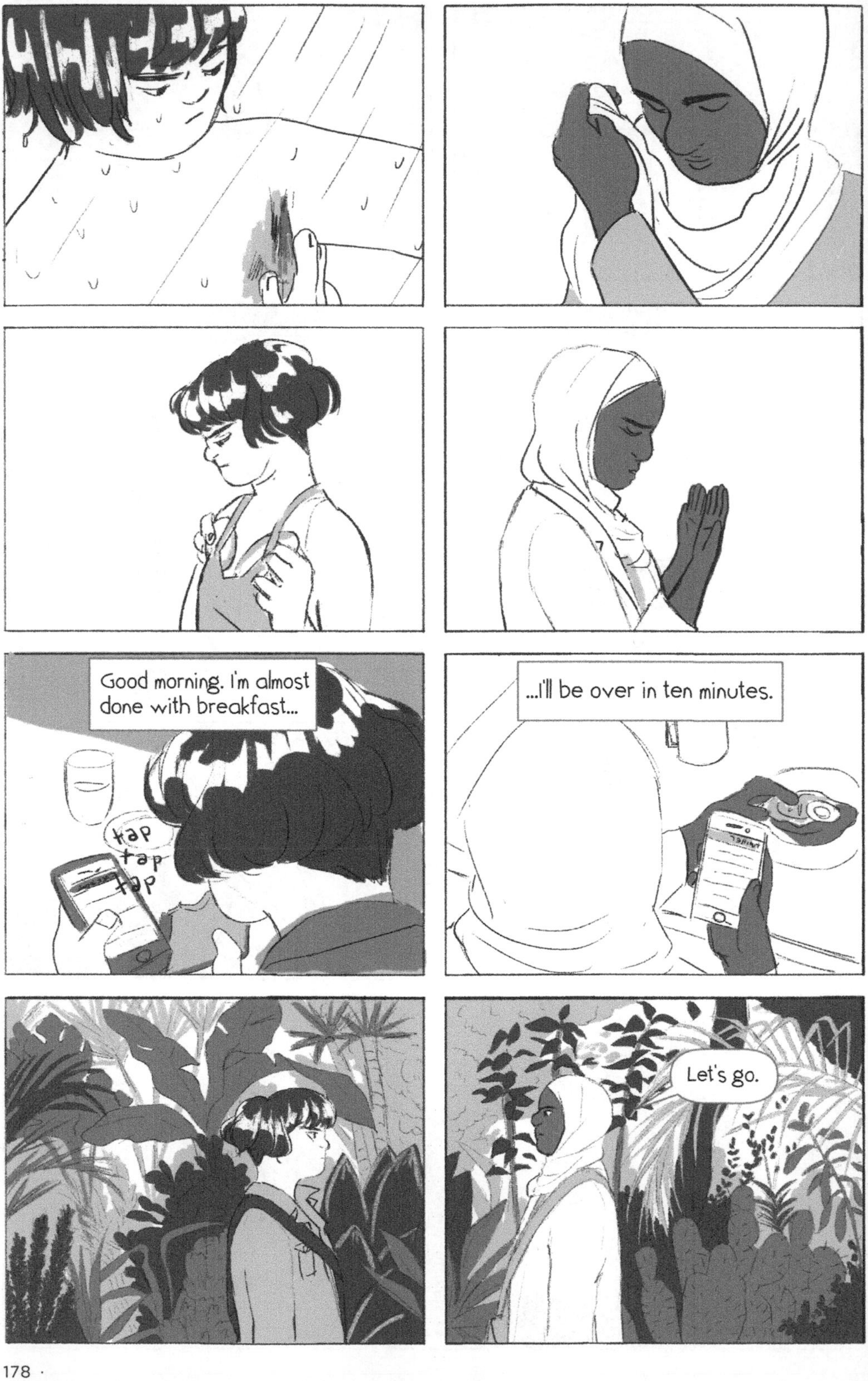
Good morning. I'm almost done with breakfast...
tap
tap
tap
...I'll be over in ten minutes.
Let's go.

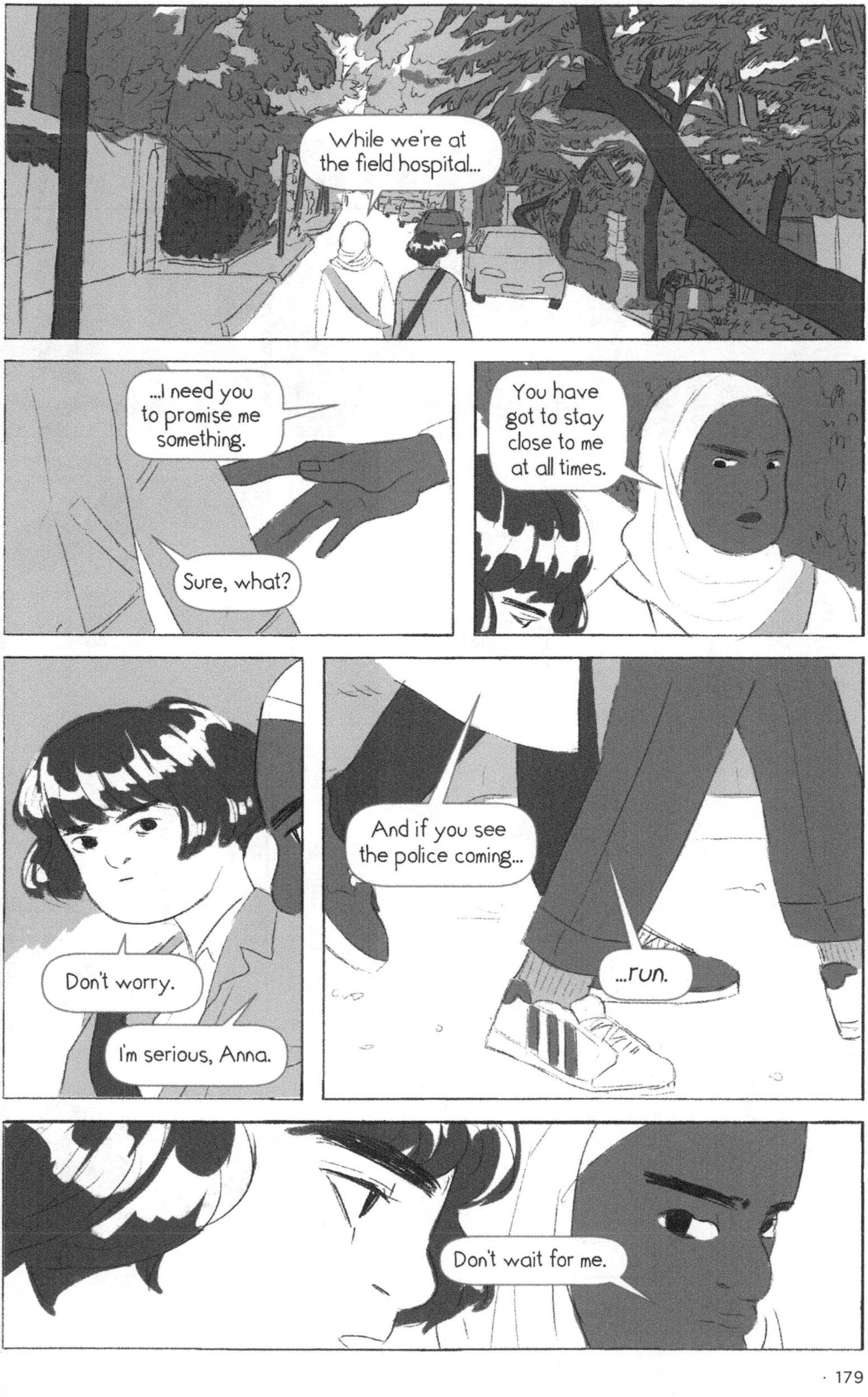

While we're at the field hospital...
...I need you to promise me something.
Sure, what?
You have got to stay close to me at all times.
Don't worry.
I'm serious, Anna.
And if you see the police coming...
...run.
Don't wait for me.

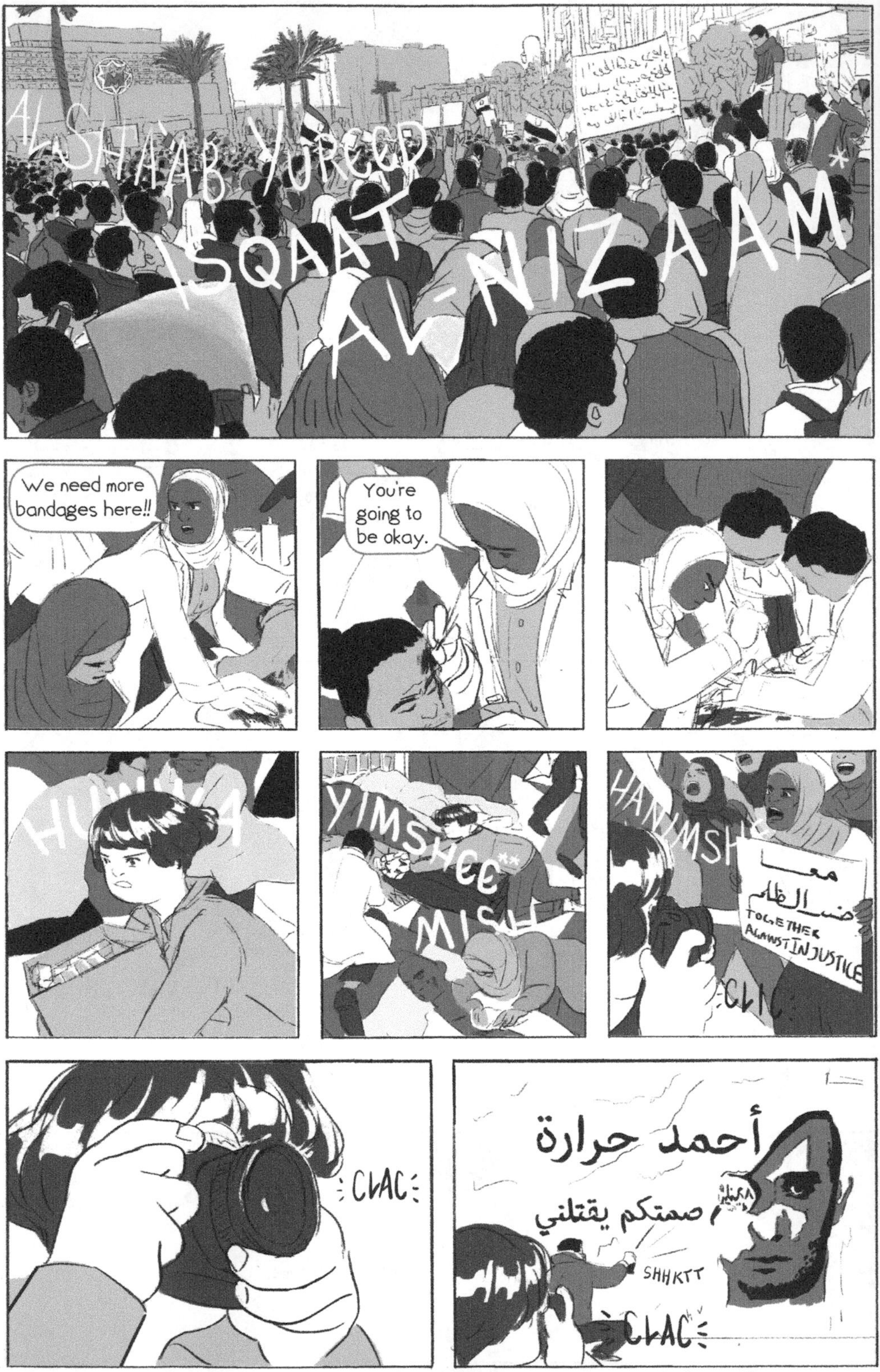

AL-SHA'AB YUREED ISQAAT AL-NIZAAM*
We need more bandages here!!
You're going to be okay.
HUWWA YIMSHEE** MISH HANIMSHEE
معا
ضد الظلم
TOGETHER AGAINST INJUSTICE
CLIC
CLAC
أحمد حرارة
صمتكم يقتلني
SHHKTT
CLAC

*The people demand the downfall of the regime. **Huwwa yimshee mish hanimshee: We're not leaving until he [Mubarak] leaves.
***Graffiti (panel 9) by Amr Nazeer, The mural depicts Ahmed Harara, a dentist who was blinded in one eye by birdshot in January 2011, and in the other by a rubber bullet in November of that year. The graffiti reads: "Your silence is murder."

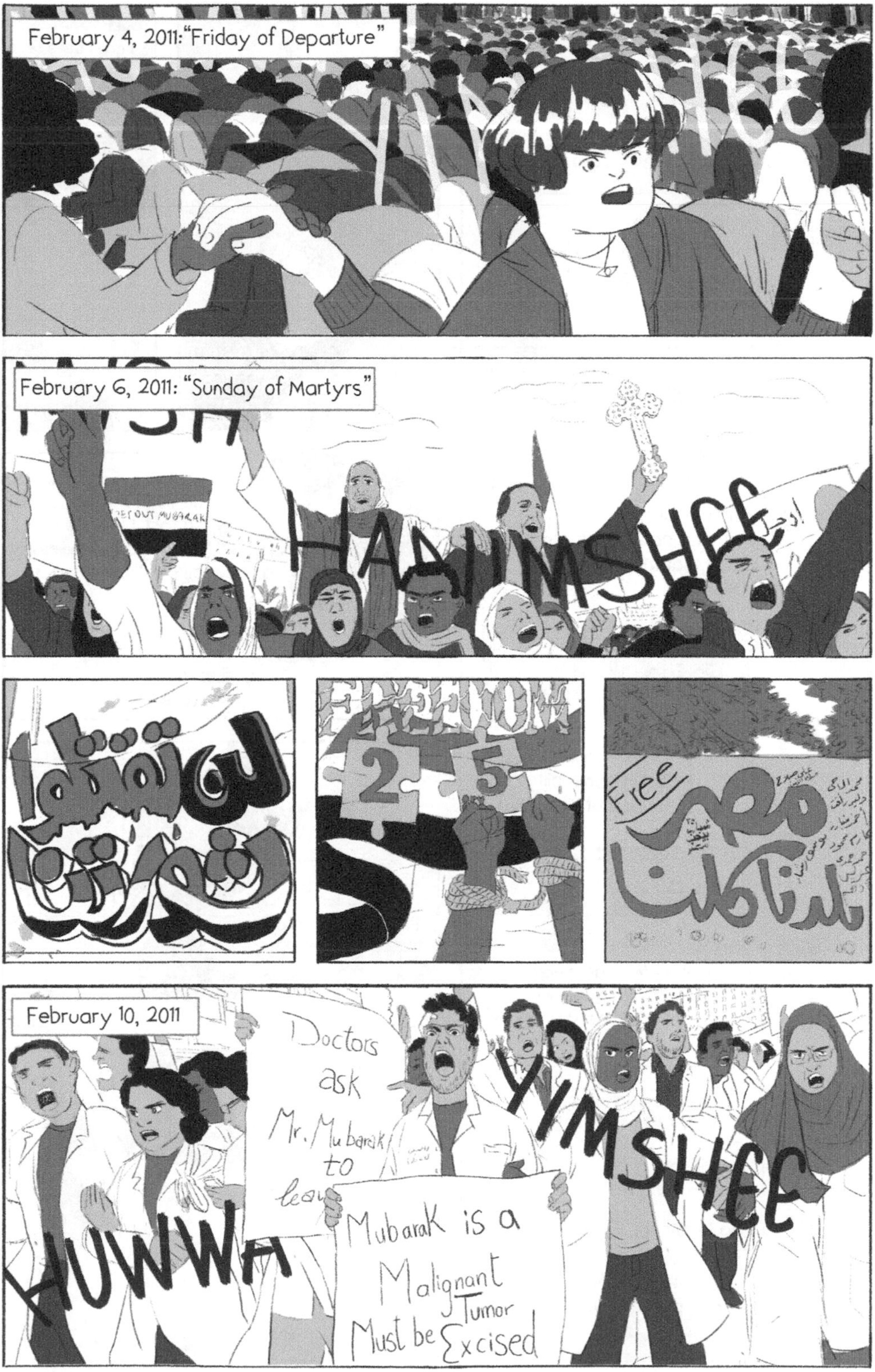
February 4, 2011: "Friday of Departure"
February 6, 2011: "Sunday of Martyrs"
ارحل
لن تقتلوا ثورتنا
FREEDOM
2
5
Free
مصر
بلدنا كلنا
February 10, 2011
Doctors ask Mr. Mubarak to leav
Mubarak is a Malignant Tumor Must be Excised
HUWWA
YIMSHEE

* Graffiti (panel 3) by unknown artist. The graffiti reads, "You will not kill our revolution."

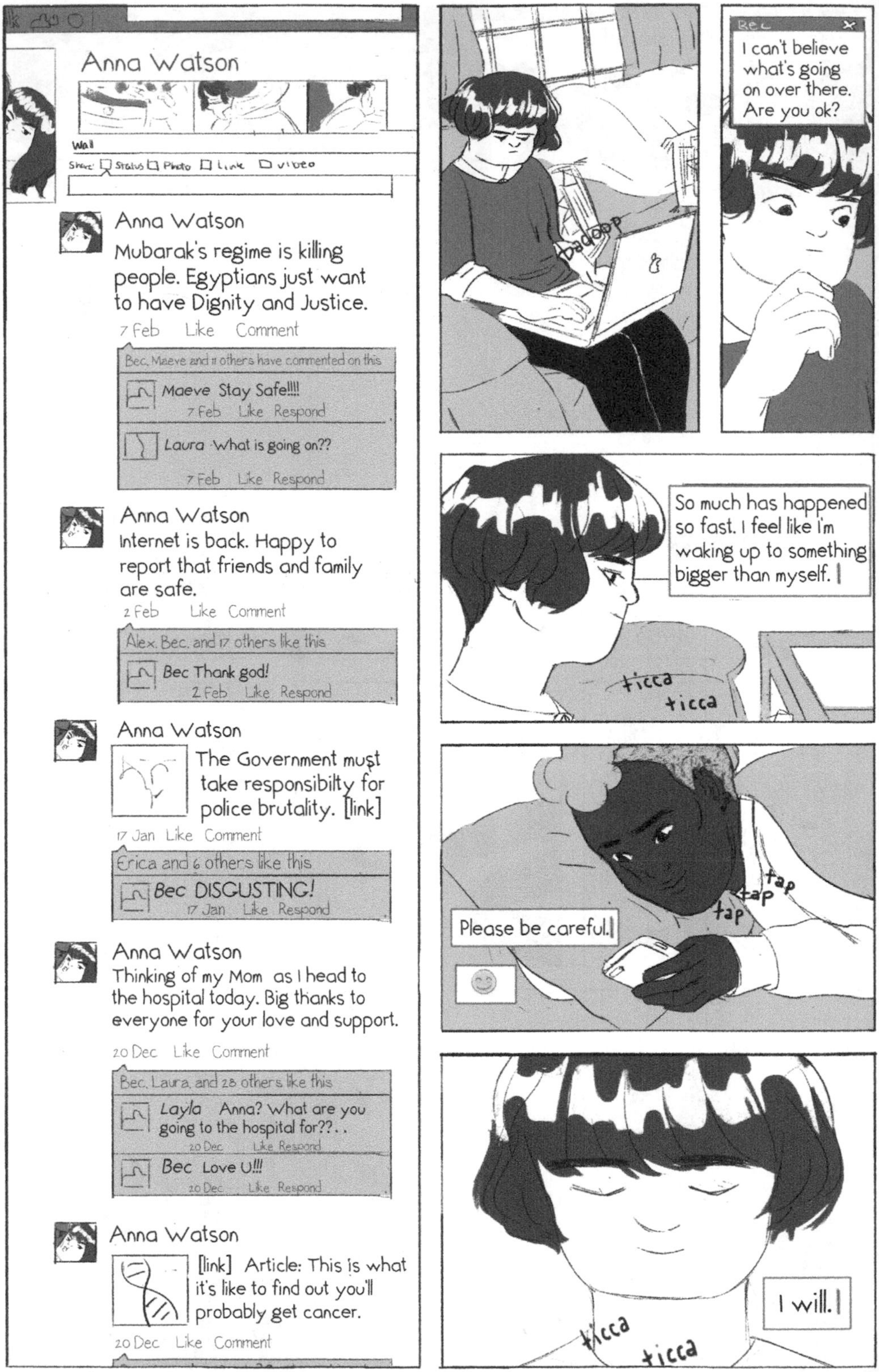
Anna Watson
Wall
Share: Status Photo Link Video
Anna Watson
Mubarak's regime is killing people. Egyptians just want to have Dignity and Justice.
7 Feb Like Comment
Bec, Maeve and 11 others have commented on this
Maeve Stay Safe!!!!
7 Feb Like Respond
Laura What is going on??
7 Feb Like Respond
Anna Watson
Internet is back. Happy to report that friends and family are safe.
2 Feb Like Comment
Alex, Bec, and 17 others like this
Bec Thank god!
2 Feb Like Respond
Anna Watson
The Government must take responsibilty for police brutality. [link]
17 Jan Like Comment
Erica and 6 others like this
Bec DISGUSTING!
17 Jan Like Respond
Anna Watson
Thinking of my Mom as I head to the hospital today. Big thanks to everyone for your love and support.
20 Dec Like Comment
Bec, Laura, and 28 others like this
Layla Anna? What are you going to the hospital for??..
20 Dec Like Respond
Bec Love U!!!
20 Dec Like Respond
Anna Watson
[link] Article: This is what it's like to find out you'll probably get cancer.
20 Dec Like Comment
badoop
Bec
I can't believe what's going on over there. Are you ok?
So much has happened so fast. I feel like I'm waking up to something bigger than myself.
ticca ticca
tap tap tap
Please be careful.
I will.
ticca ticca

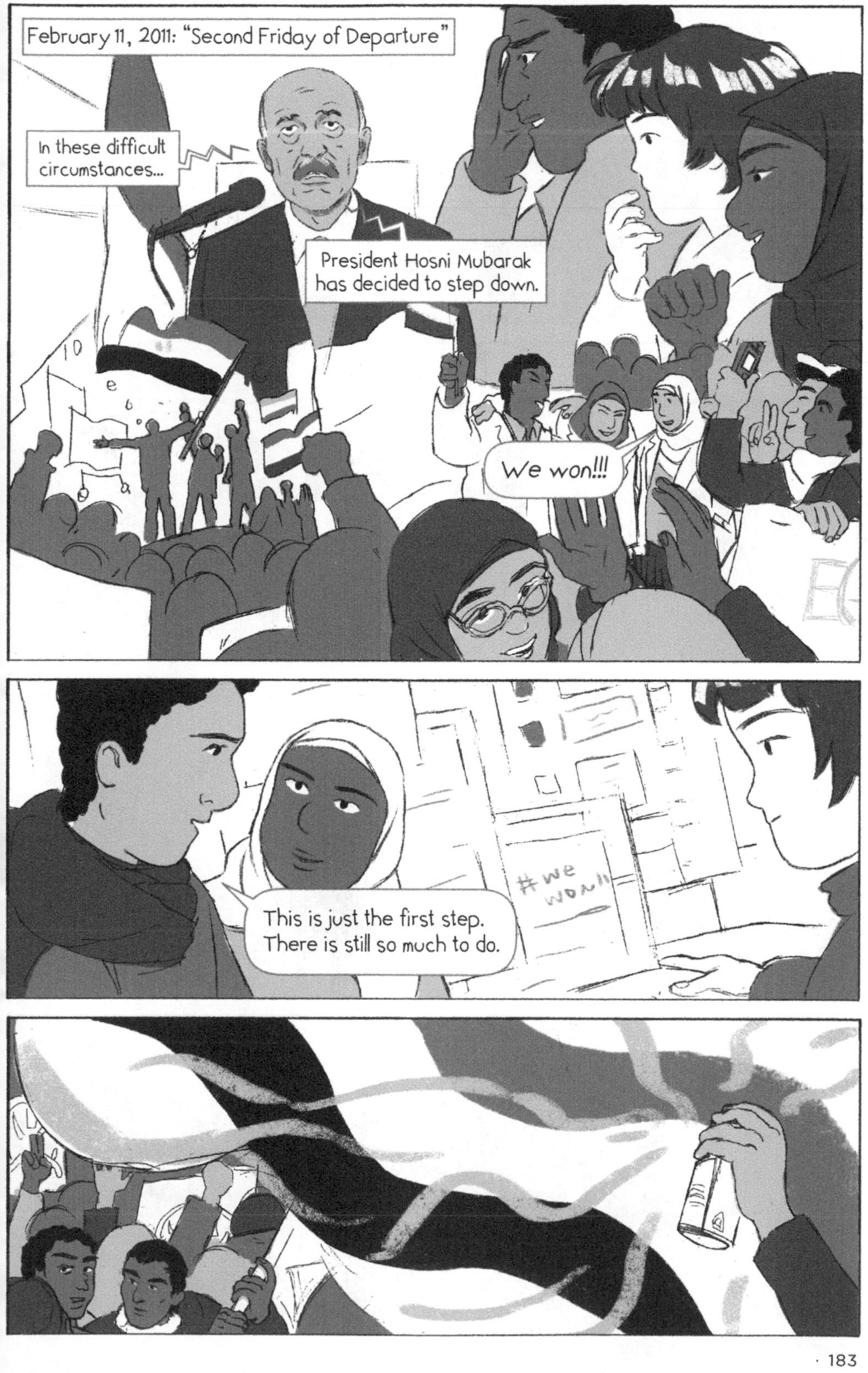
February 11, 2011: “Second Friday of Departure”
In these difficult circumstances...
President Hosni Mubarak has decided to step down.
We won!!!
#we won!!
This is just the first step. There is still so much to do.

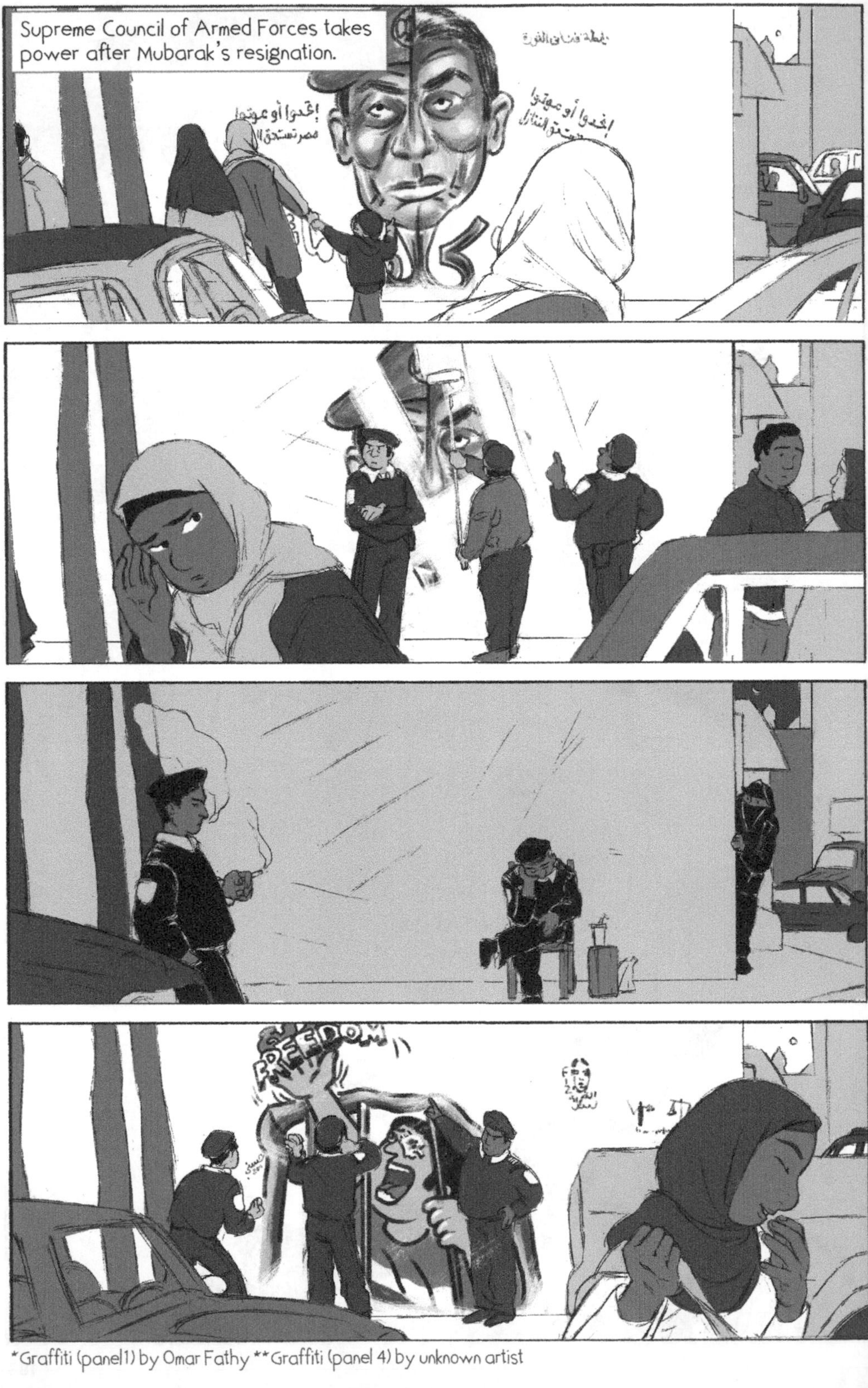
Supreme Council of Armed Forces takes power after Mubarak's resignation.
FREEDOM

*Graffiti (panel1) by Omar Fathy **Graffiti (panel 4) by unknown artist

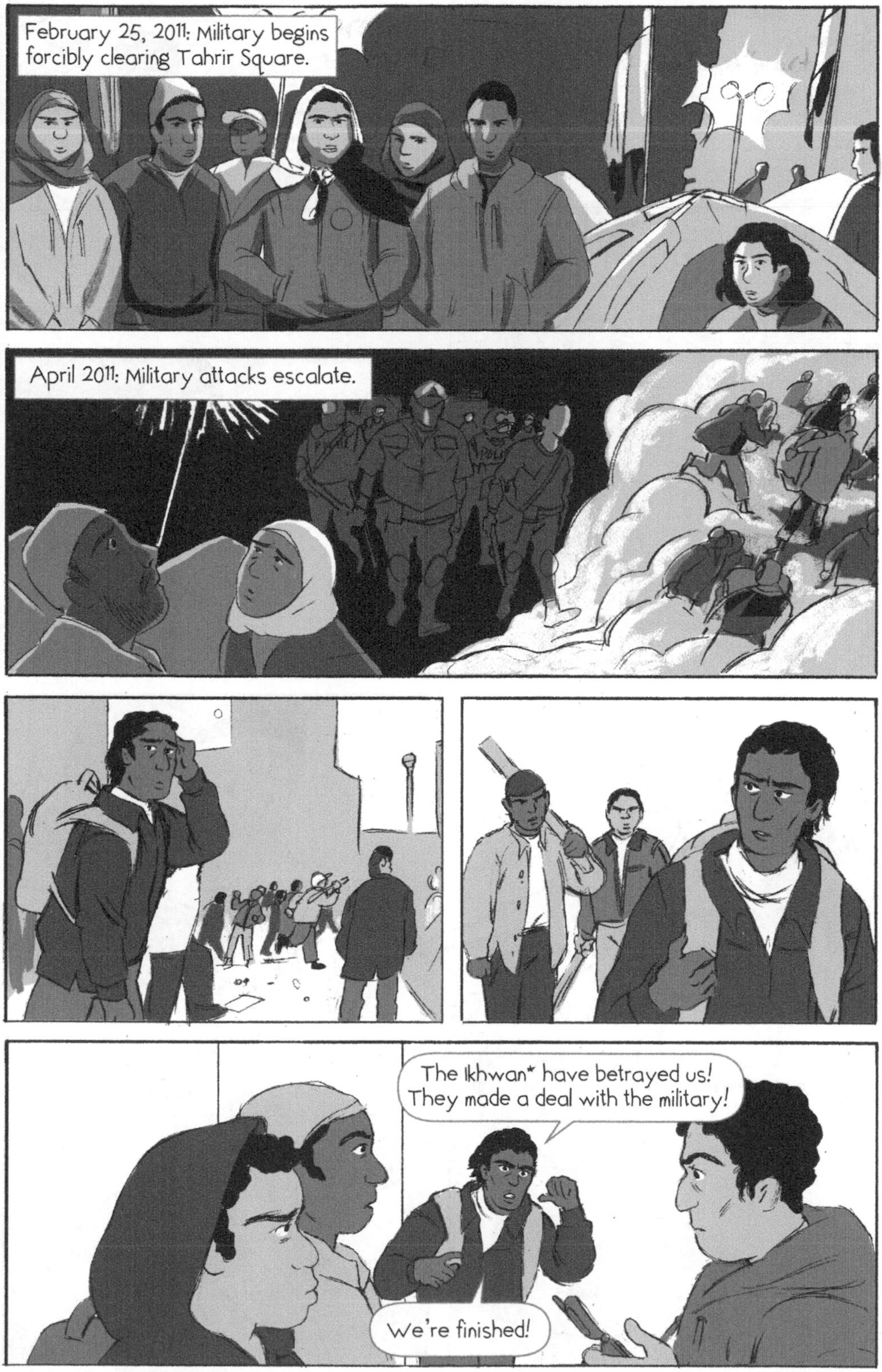
February 25, 2011: Military begins forcibly clearing Tahrir Square.
April 2011: Military attacks escalate.
The Ikhwan* have betrayed us! They made a deal with the military!
We're finished!

*Ikhwan: Muslim Brotherhood

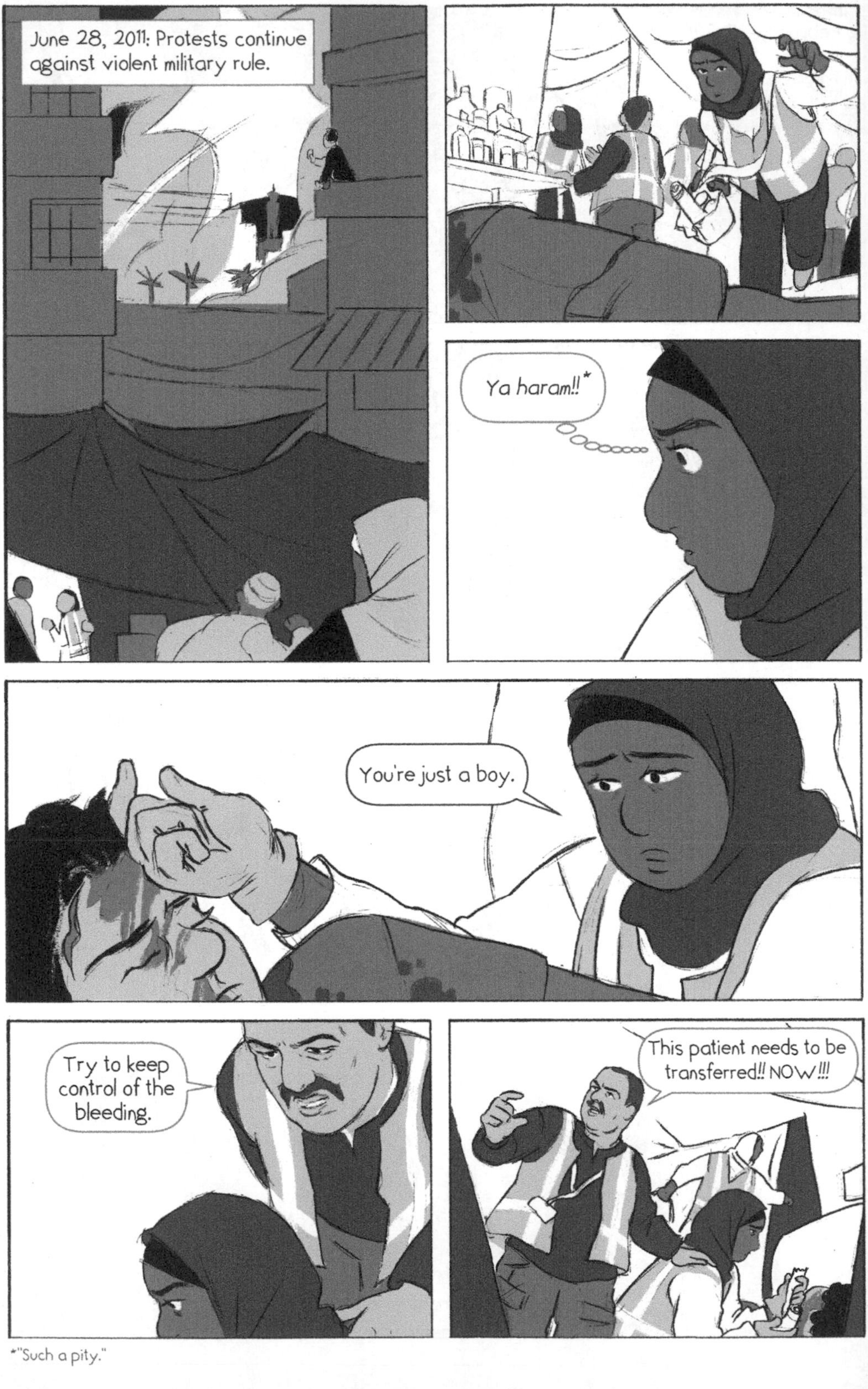
June 28, 2011: Protests continue against violent military rule.
Ya haram!!*
You're just a boy.
Try to keep control of the bleeding.
This patient needs to be transferred!! NOW!!!

*"Such a pity."

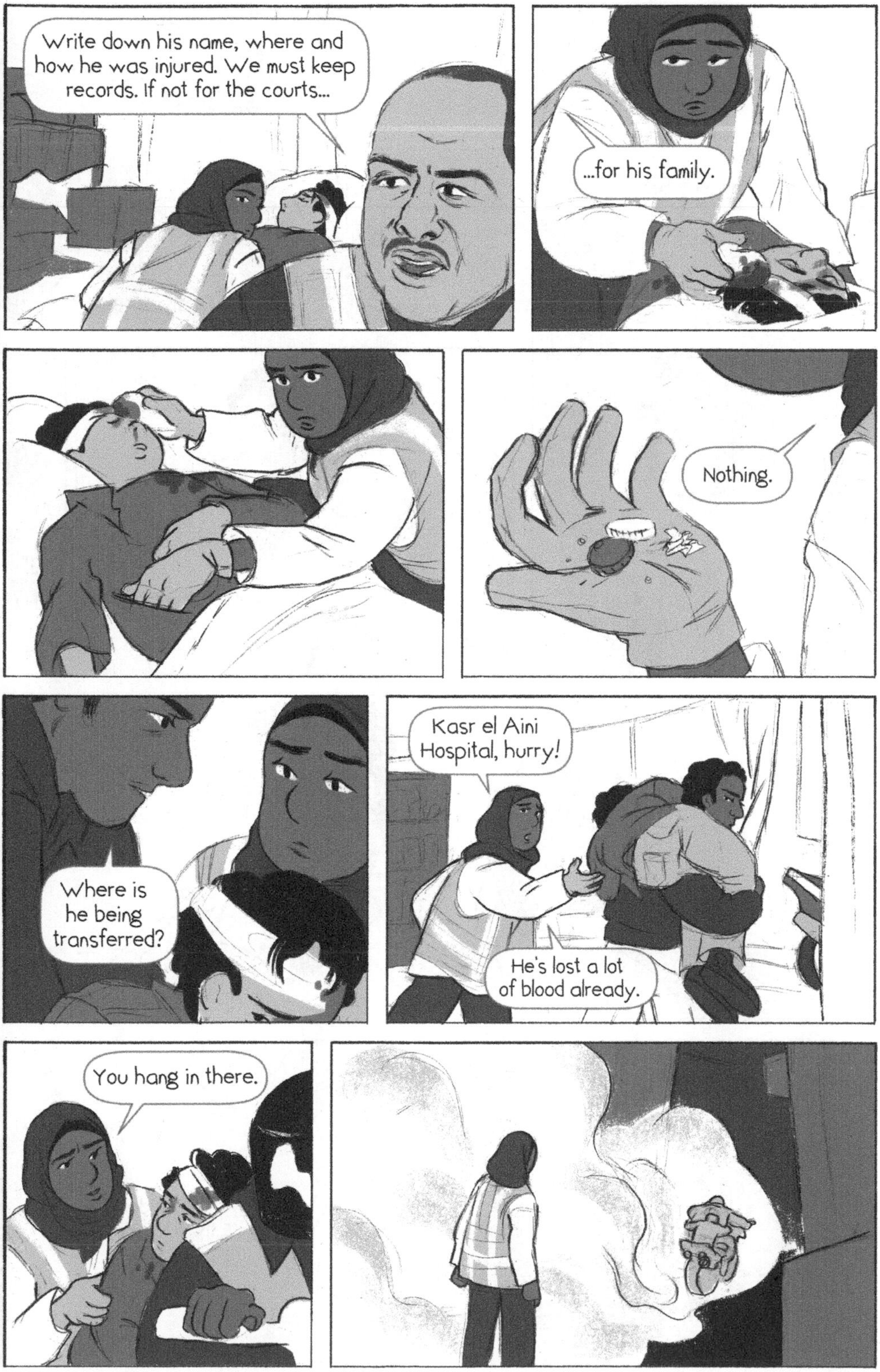
Write down his name, where and how he was injured. We must keep records. If not for the courts...
...for his family.
Nothing.
Where is he being transferred?
Kasr el Aini Hospital, hurry!
He's lost a lot of blood already.
You hang in there.

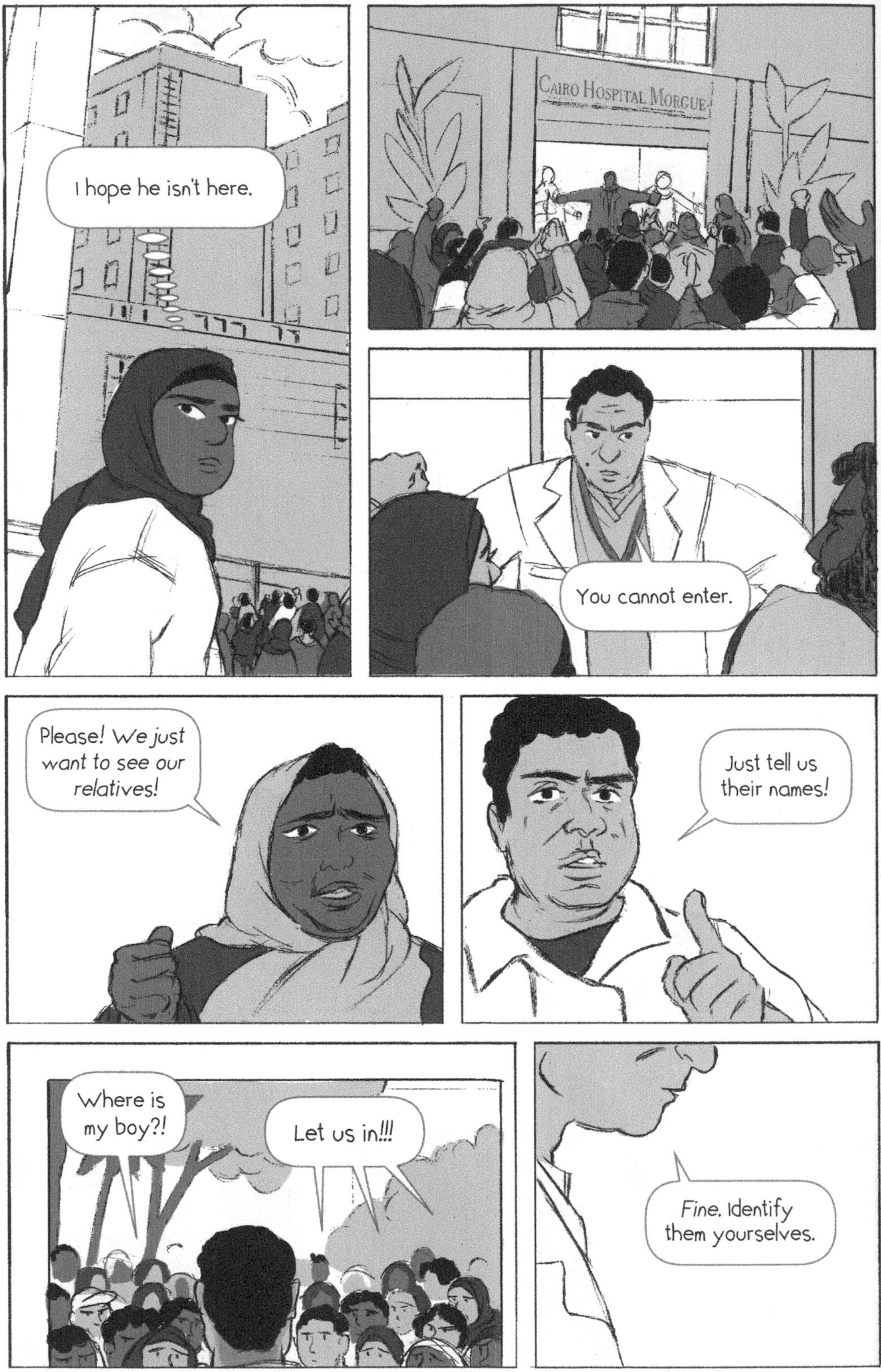
I hope he isn't here.
CAIRO HOSPITAL MORGUE
You cannot enter.
Please! We just want to see our relatives!
Just tell us their names!
Where is my boy?!
Let us in!!!
Fine. Identify them yourselves.

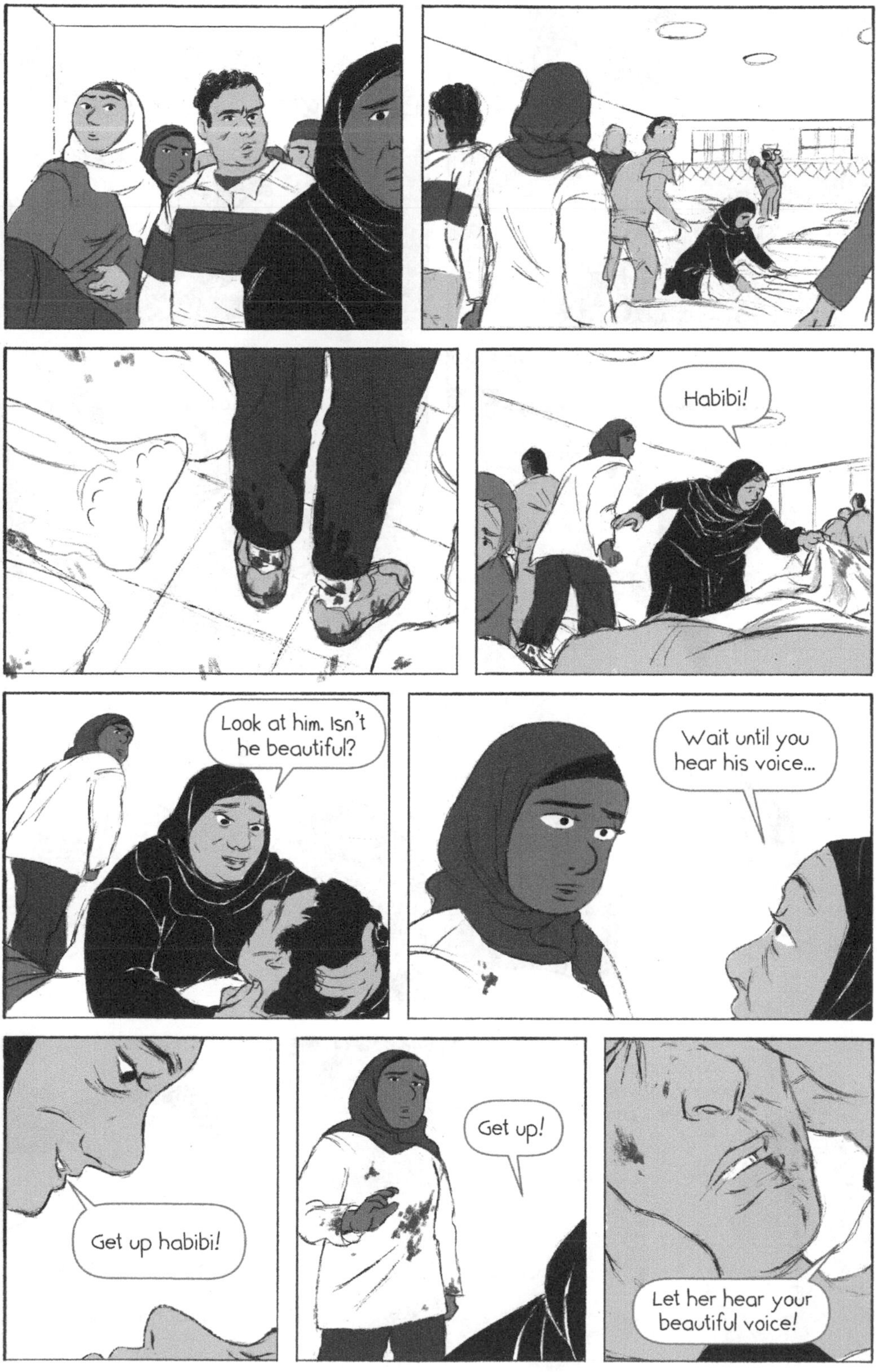
Habibi!
Look at him. Isn't he beautiful?
Wait until you hear his voice...
Get up habibi!
Get up!
Let her hear your beautiful voice!

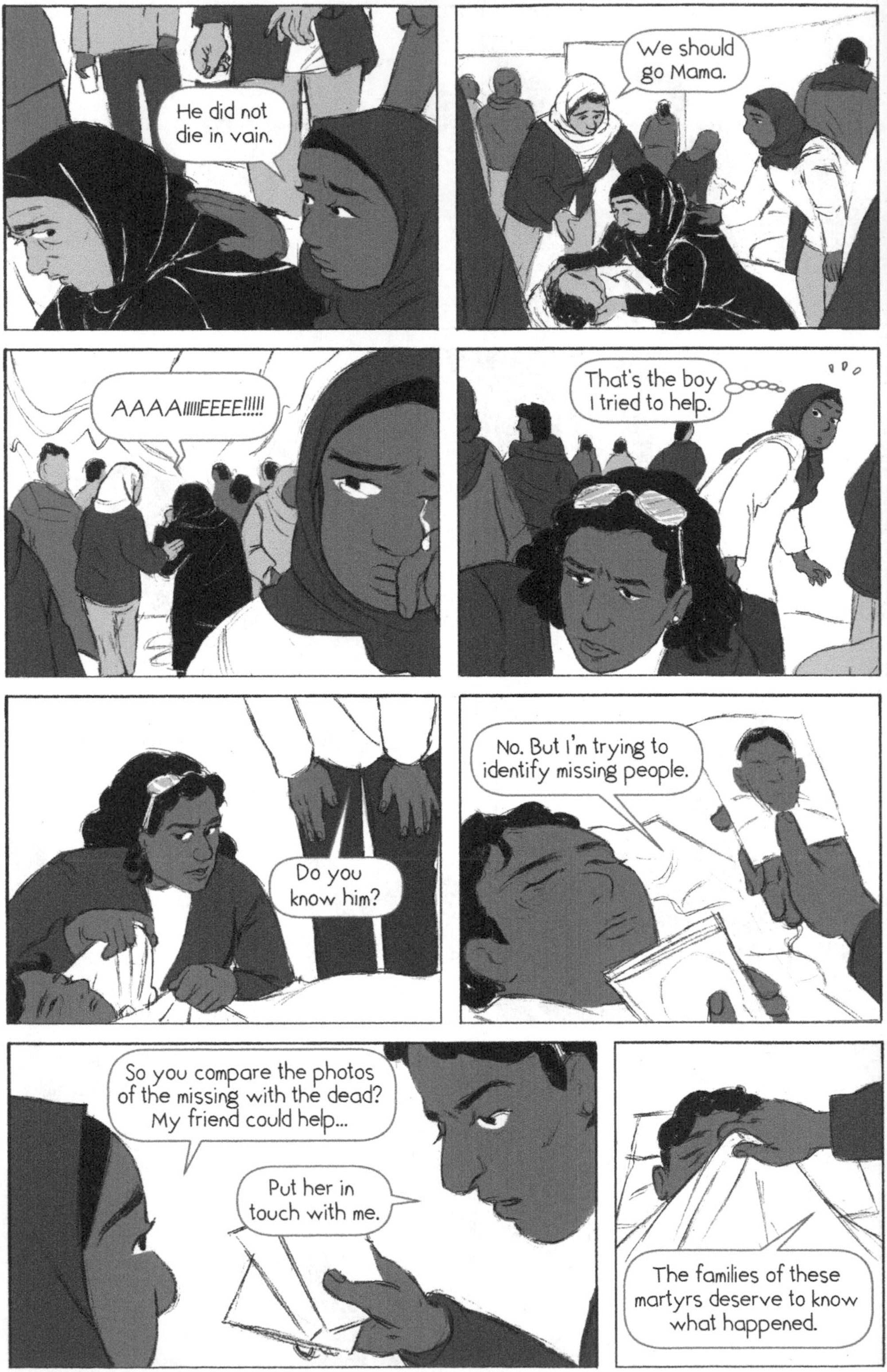
He did not die in vain.
We should go Mama.
AAAAIIIIIEEEE!!!!!
That's the boy I tried to help.
Do you know him?
No. But I'm trying to identify missing people.
So you compare the photos of the missing with the dead? My friend could help...
Put her in touch with me.
The families of these martyrs deserve to know what happened.

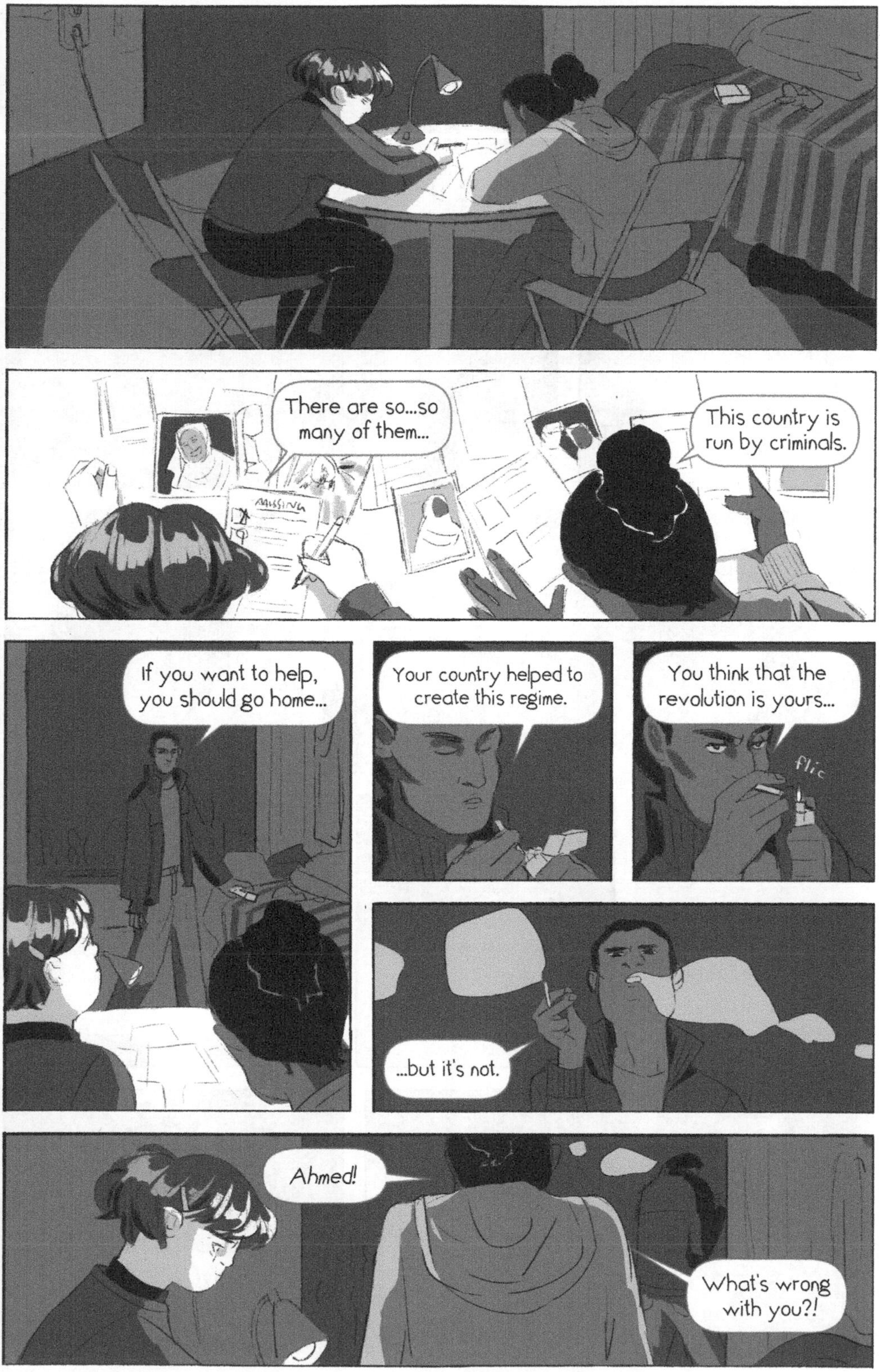
There are so...so many of them...
This country is run by criminals.
If you want to help, you should go home...
Your country helped to create this regime.
You think that the revolution is yours...
flic
...but it's not.
Ahmed!
What's wrong with you?!

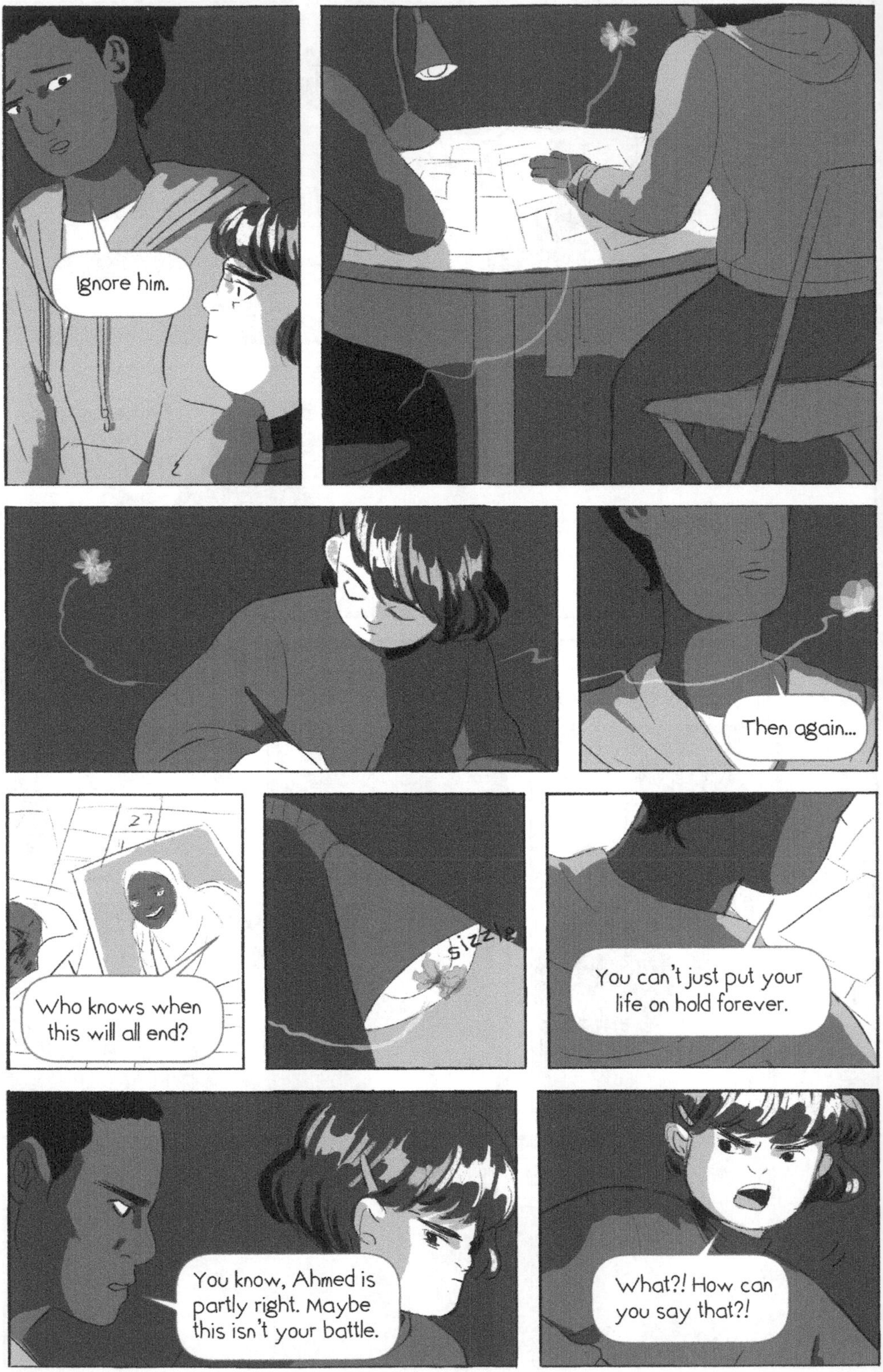
Ignore him.
Then again...
Who knows when this will all end?
sizzle
You can't just put your life on hold forever.
You know, Ahmed is partly right. Maybe this isn't your battle.
What?! How can you say that?!

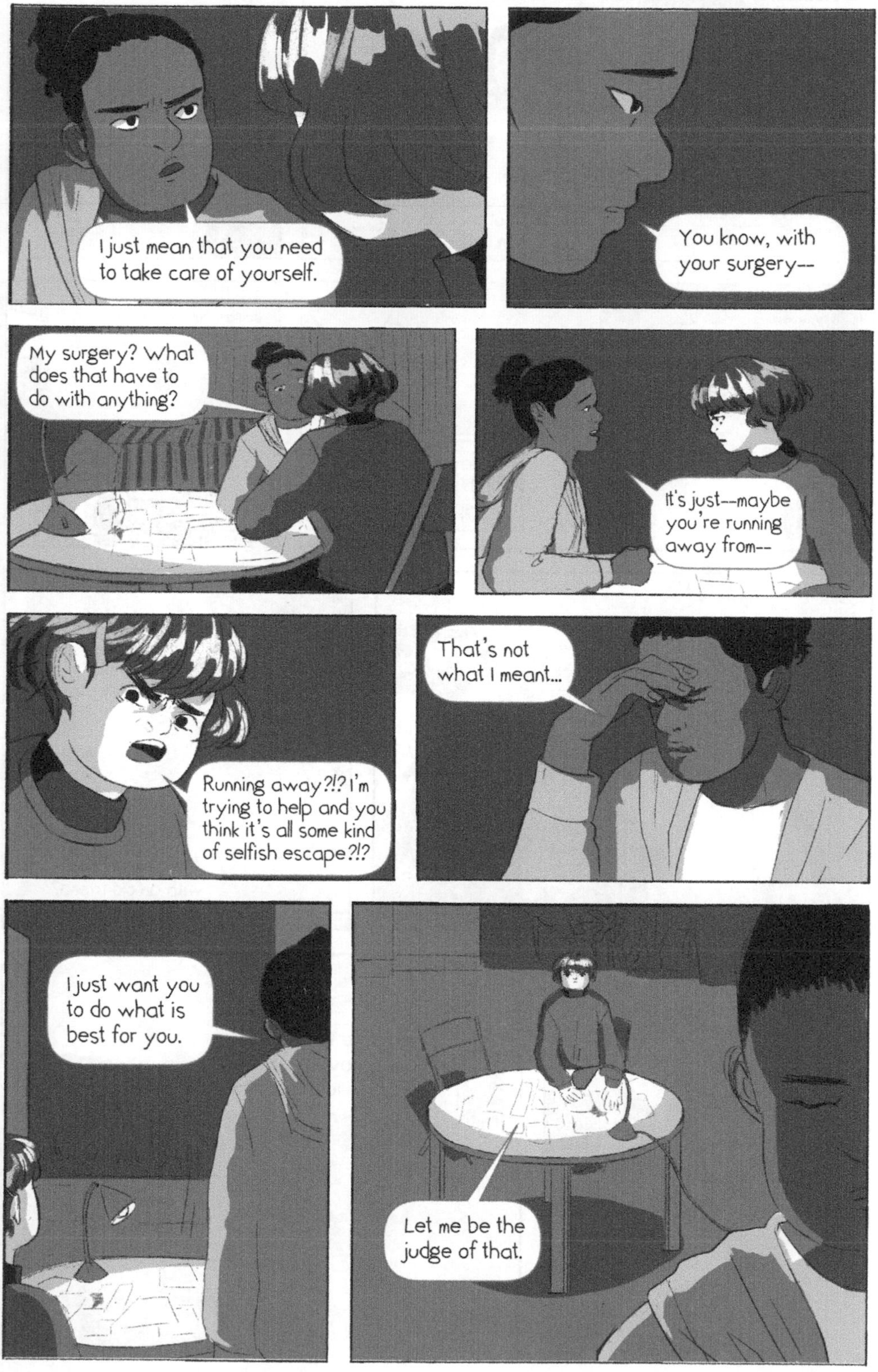
I just mean that you need to take care of yourself.
You know, with your surgery--
My surgery? What does that have to do with anything?
It's just--maybe you're running away from--
Running away?!? I'm trying to help and you think it's all some kind of selfish escape?!?
That's not what I meant...
I just want you to do what is best for you.
Let me be the judge of that.

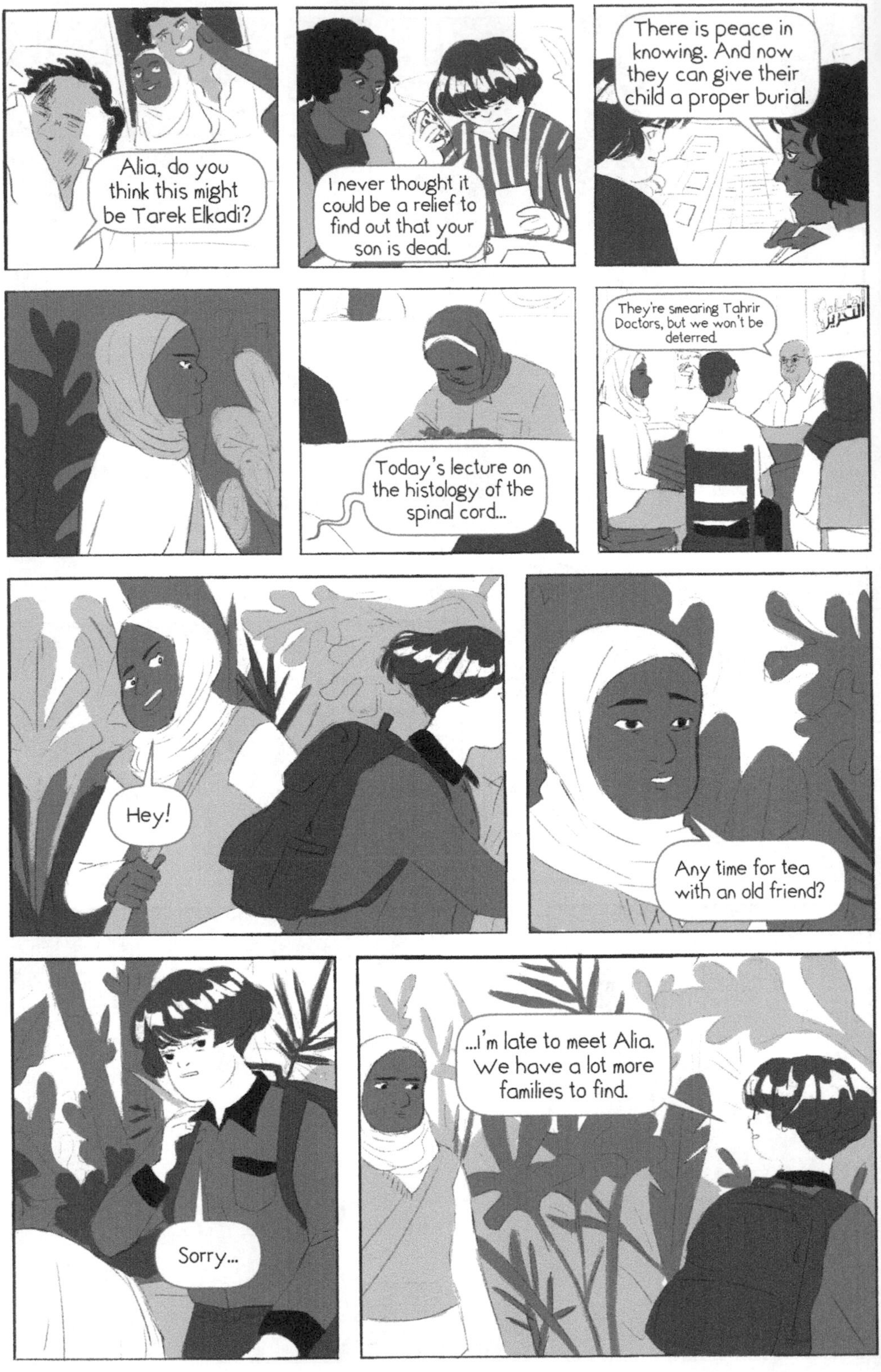
Alia, do you think this might be Tarek Elkadi?
I never thought it could be a relief to find out that your son is dead.
There is peace in knowing. And now they can give their child a proper burial.
Today's lecture on the histology of the spinal cord...
They're smearing Tahrir Doctors, but we won't be deterred.
Hey!
Any time for tea with an old friend?
Sorry...
...I'm late to meet Alia. We have a lot more families to find.

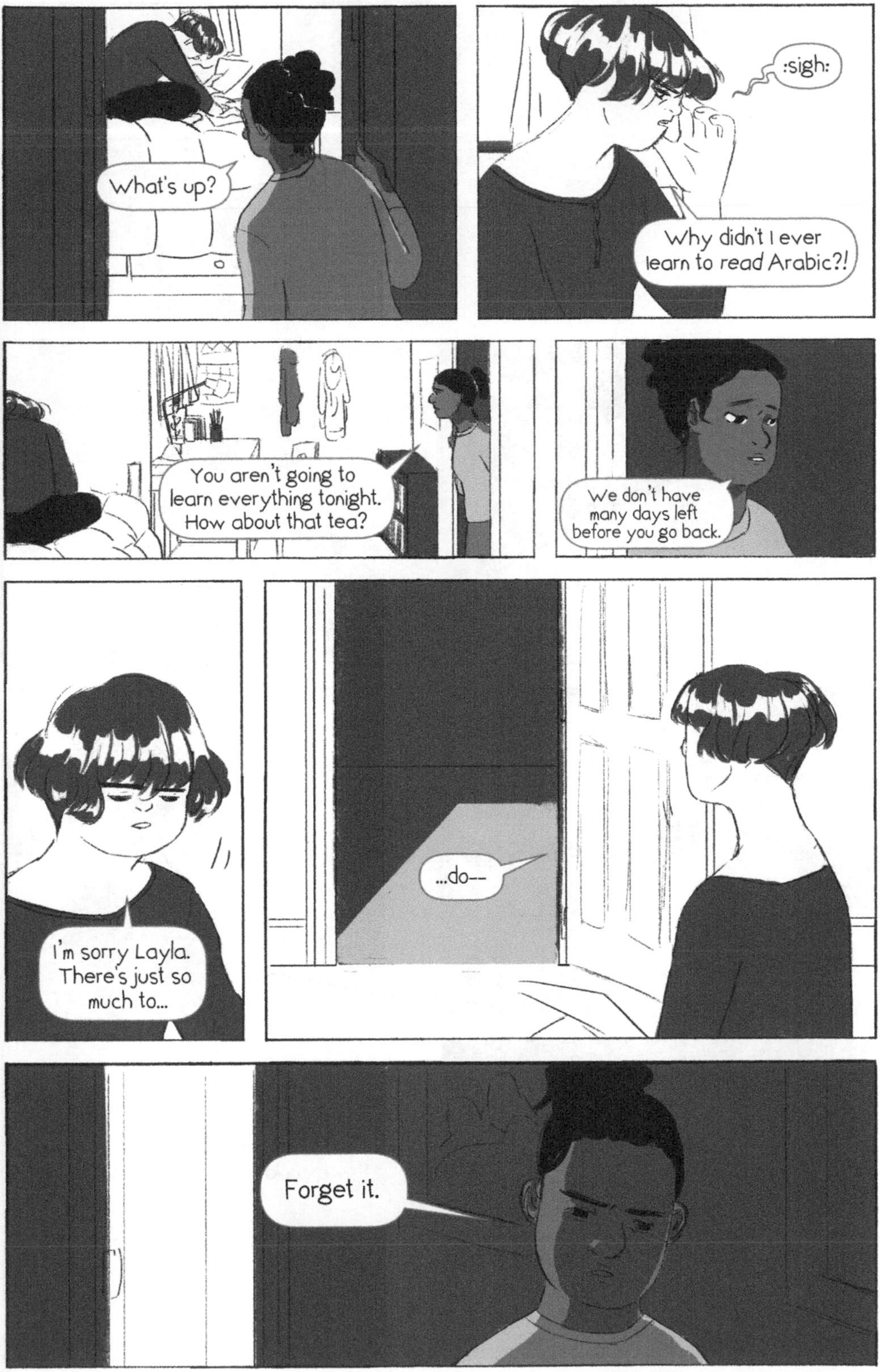
What's up?
:sigh:
Why didn't I ever learn to *read* Arabic?!
You aren't going to learn everything tonight. How about that tea?
We don't have many days left before you go back.
I'm sorry Layla. There's just so much to...
...do--
Forget it.

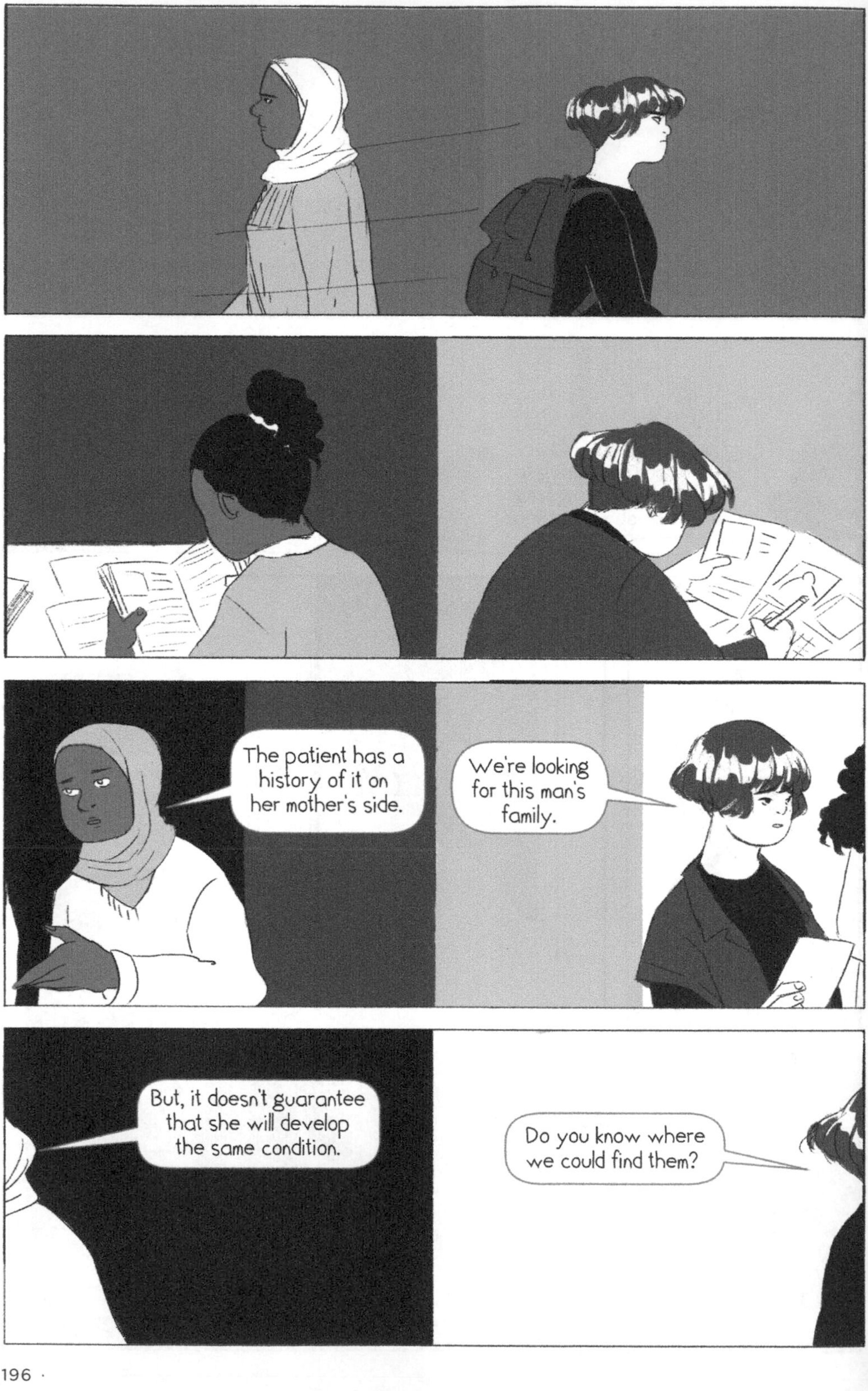
The patient has a history of it on her mother's side.
We're looking for this man's family.
But, it doesn't guarantee that she will develop the same condition.
Do you know where we could find them?

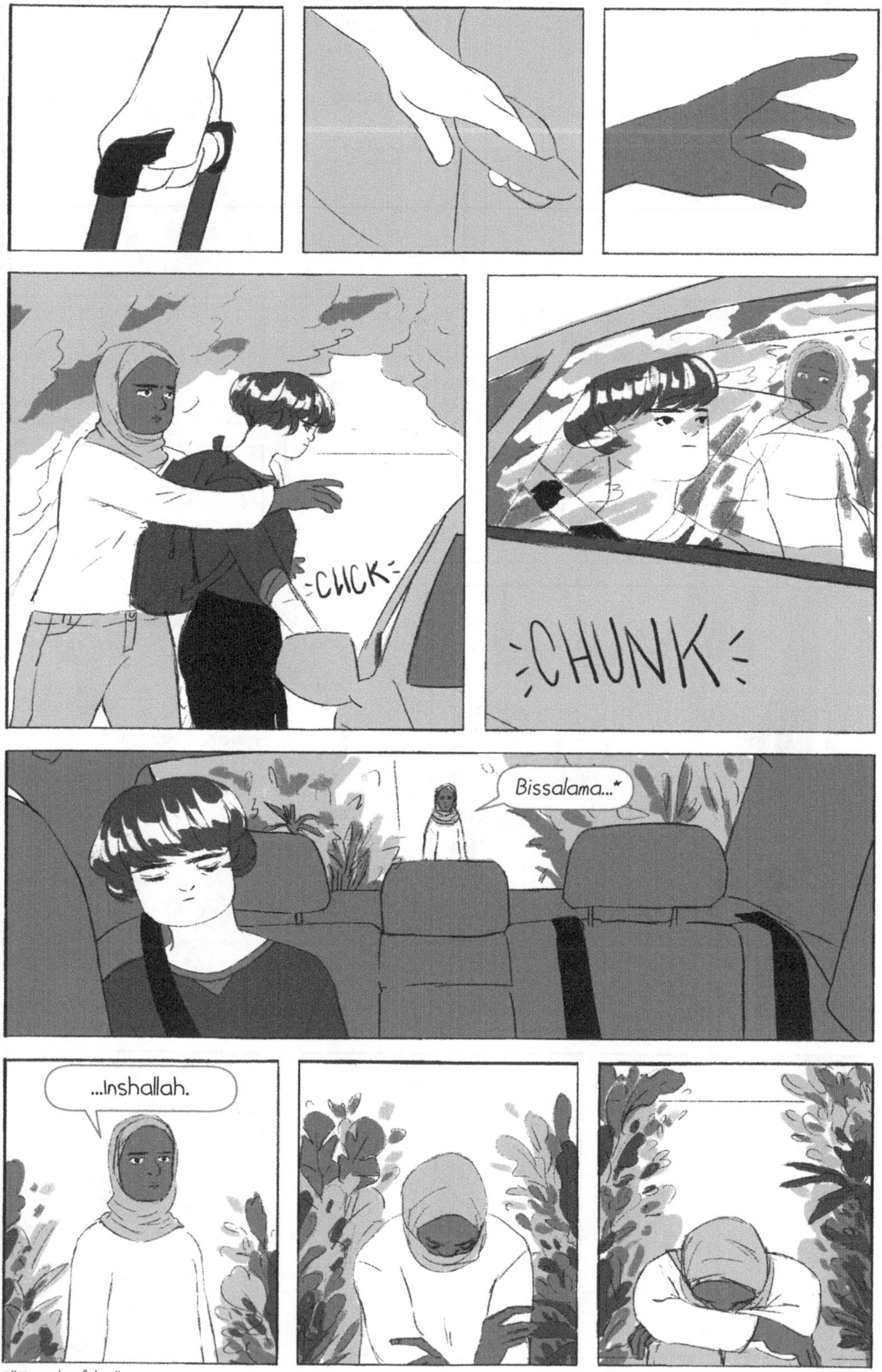
CLICK
CHUNK
Bissalama...*
...Inshallah.

*"Travel safely..."

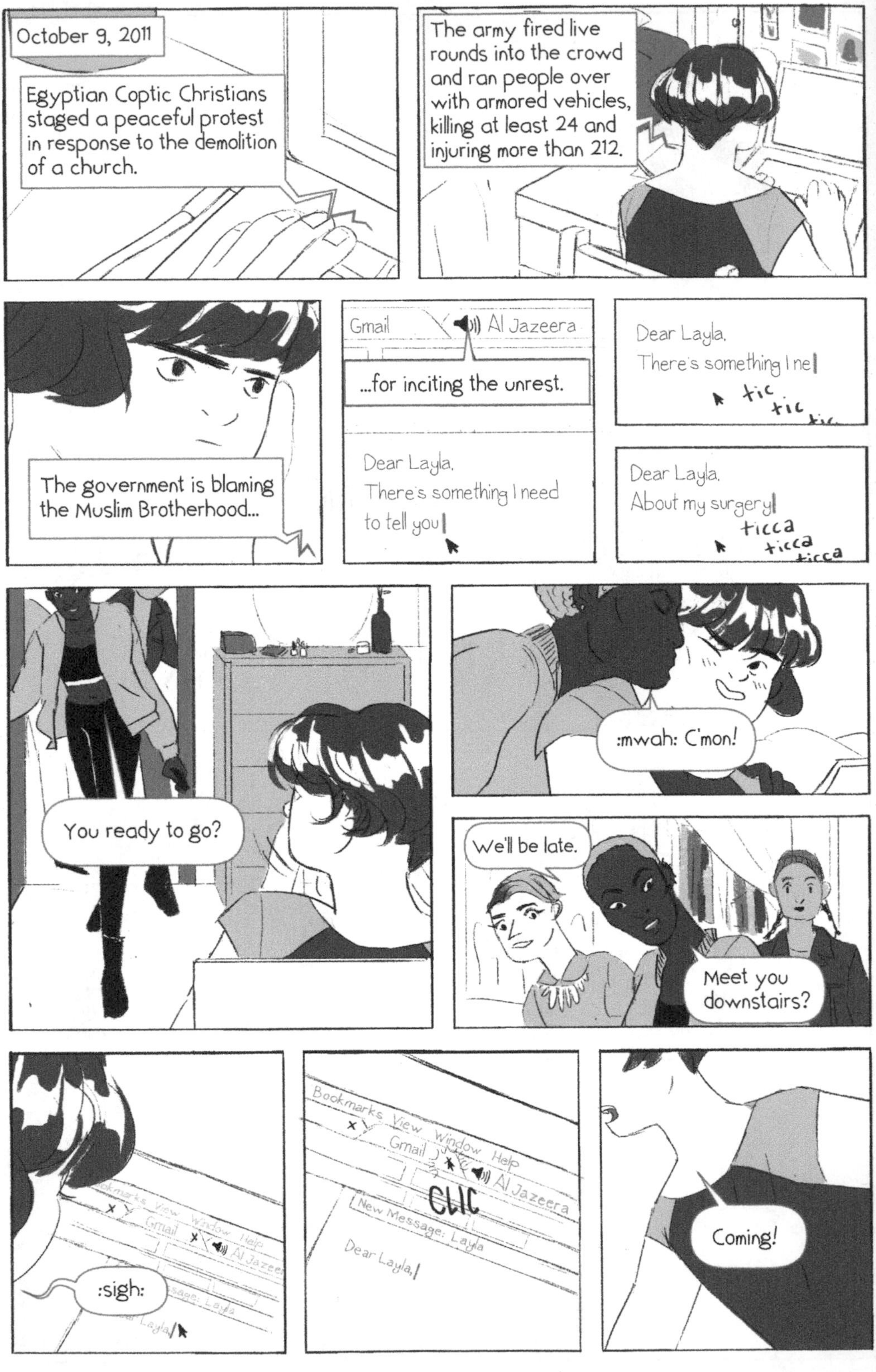

October 9, 2011
Egyptian Coptic Christians staged a peaceful protest in response to the demolition of a church.
The army fired live rounds into the crowd and ran people over with armored vehicles, killing at least 24 and injuring more than 212.
The government is blaming the Muslim Brotherhood...
Gmail
Al Jazeera
...for inciting the unrest.
Dear Layla,
There's something I need to tell you
Dear Layla,
There's something I ne
tic
tic
Dear Layla,
About my surgery
ticca
ticca
ticca
You ready to go?
:mwah: C'mon!
We'll be late.
Meet you downstairs?
:sigh:
Bookmarks View Window Help
Gmail
Al Jazeera
CLIC
New Message: Layla
Dear Layla,
Coming!

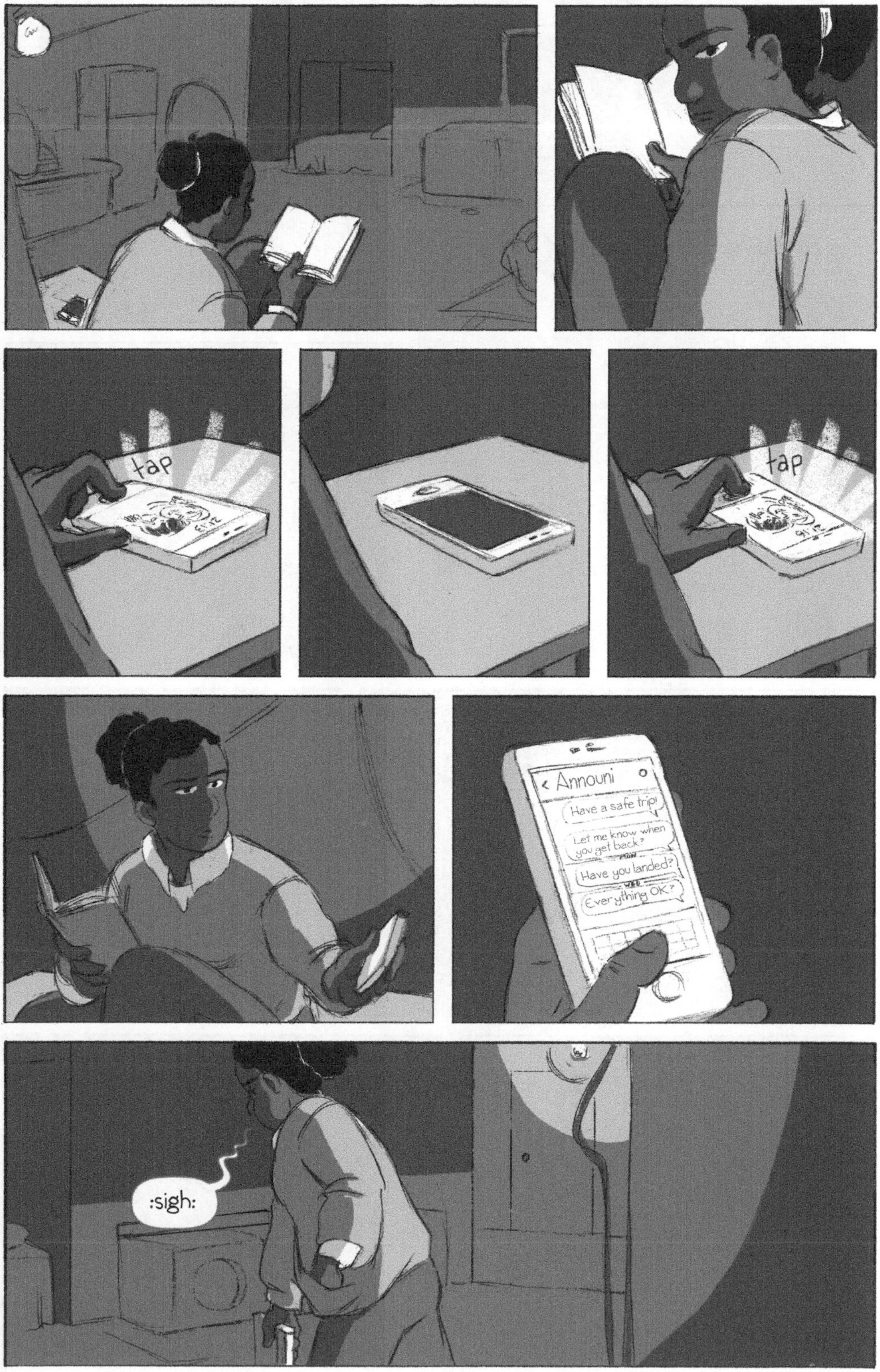
tap
tap
< Announi
Have a safe trip!
Let me know when you get back?
Have you landed?
Everything OK?
:sigh:

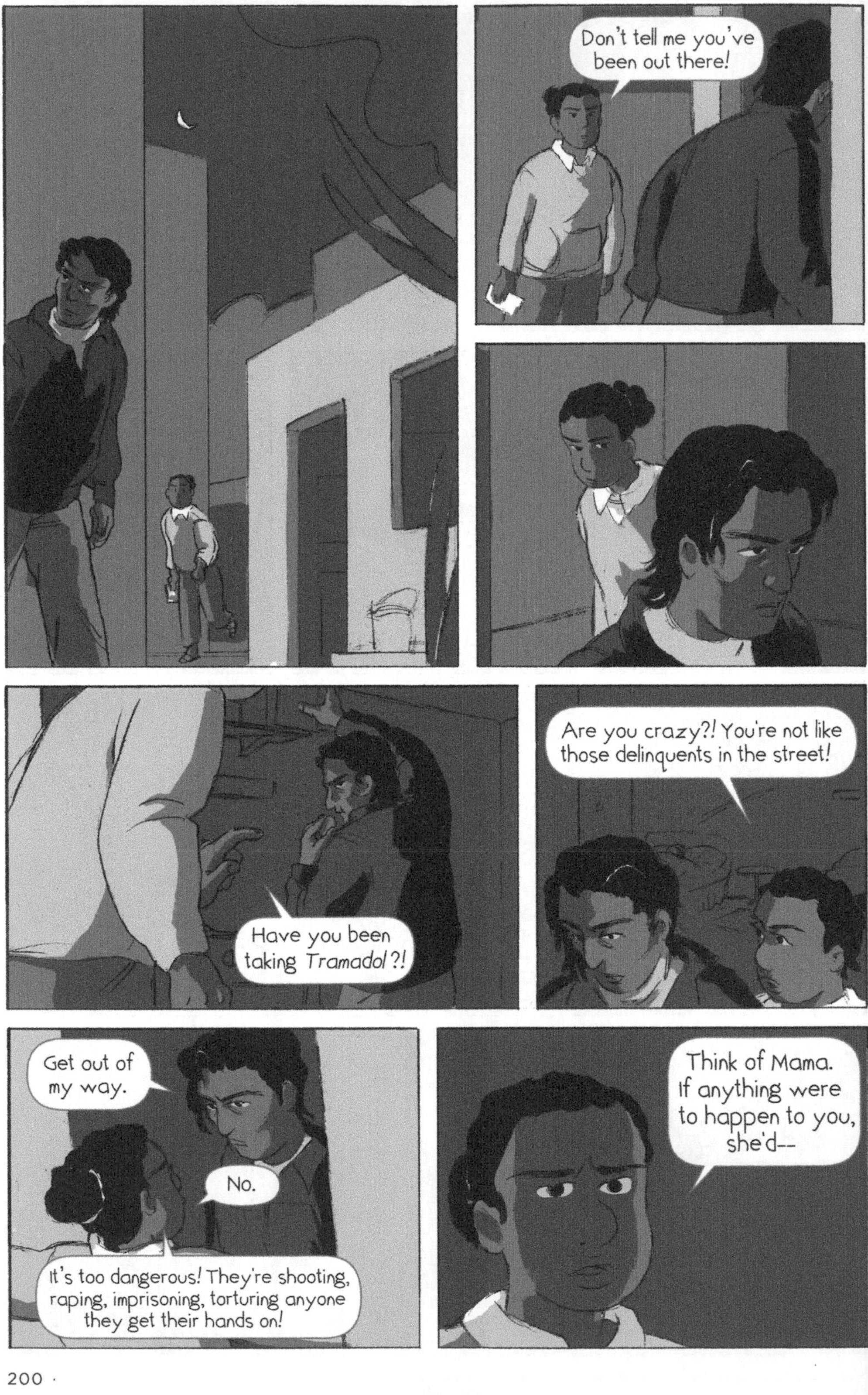
Don't tell me you've been out there!
Have you been taking *Tramadol*?!
Are you crazy?! You're not like those delinquents in the street!
Get out of my way.
No.
It's too dangerous! They're shooting, raping, imprisoning, torturing anyone they get their hands on!
Think of Mama. If anything were to happen to you, she'd--

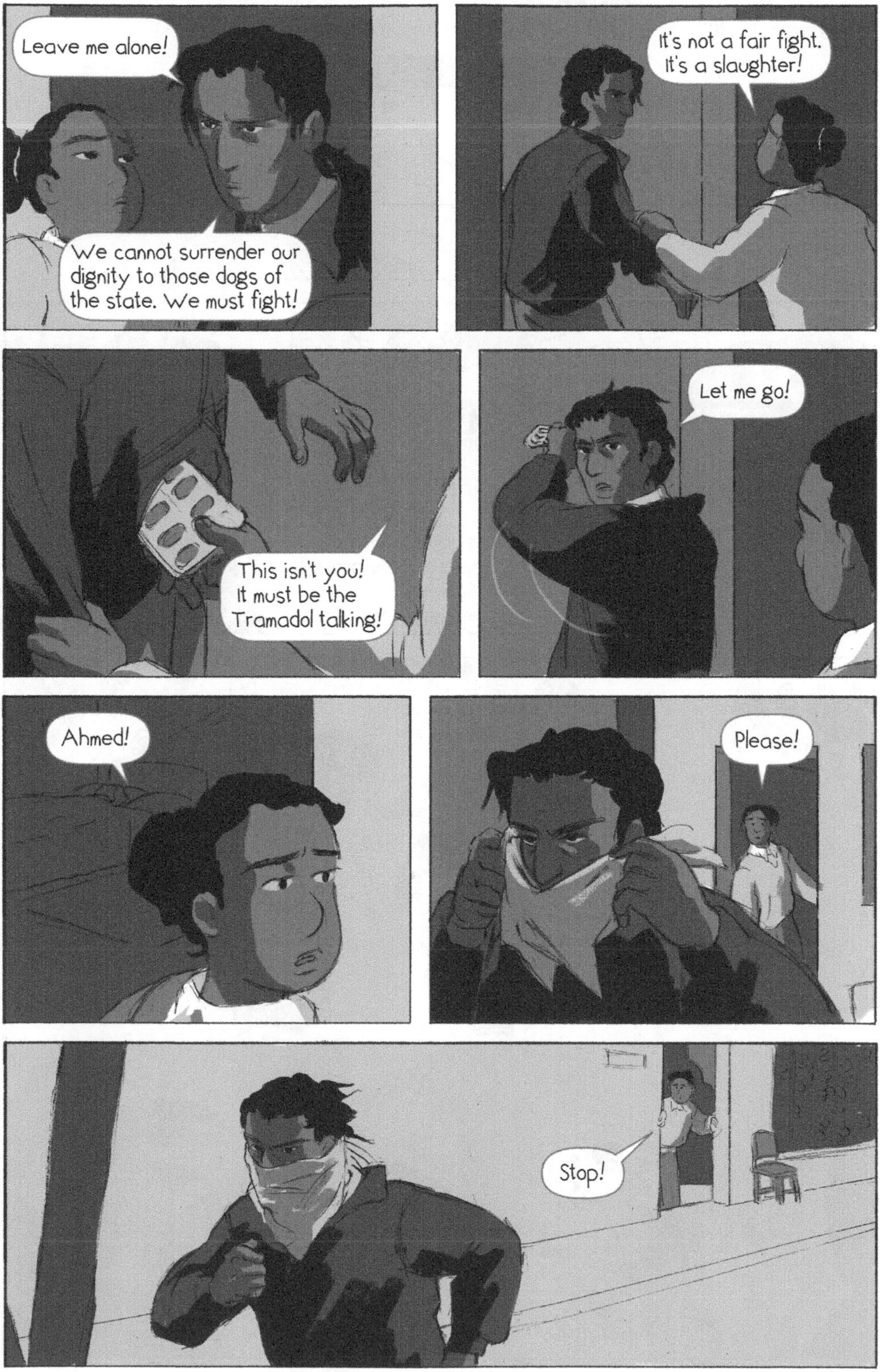
Leave me alone!
We cannot surrender our dignity to those dogs of the state. We must fight!
It's not a fair fight. It's a slaughter!
This isn't you! It must be the Tramadol talking!
Let me go!
Ahmed!
Please!
Stop!

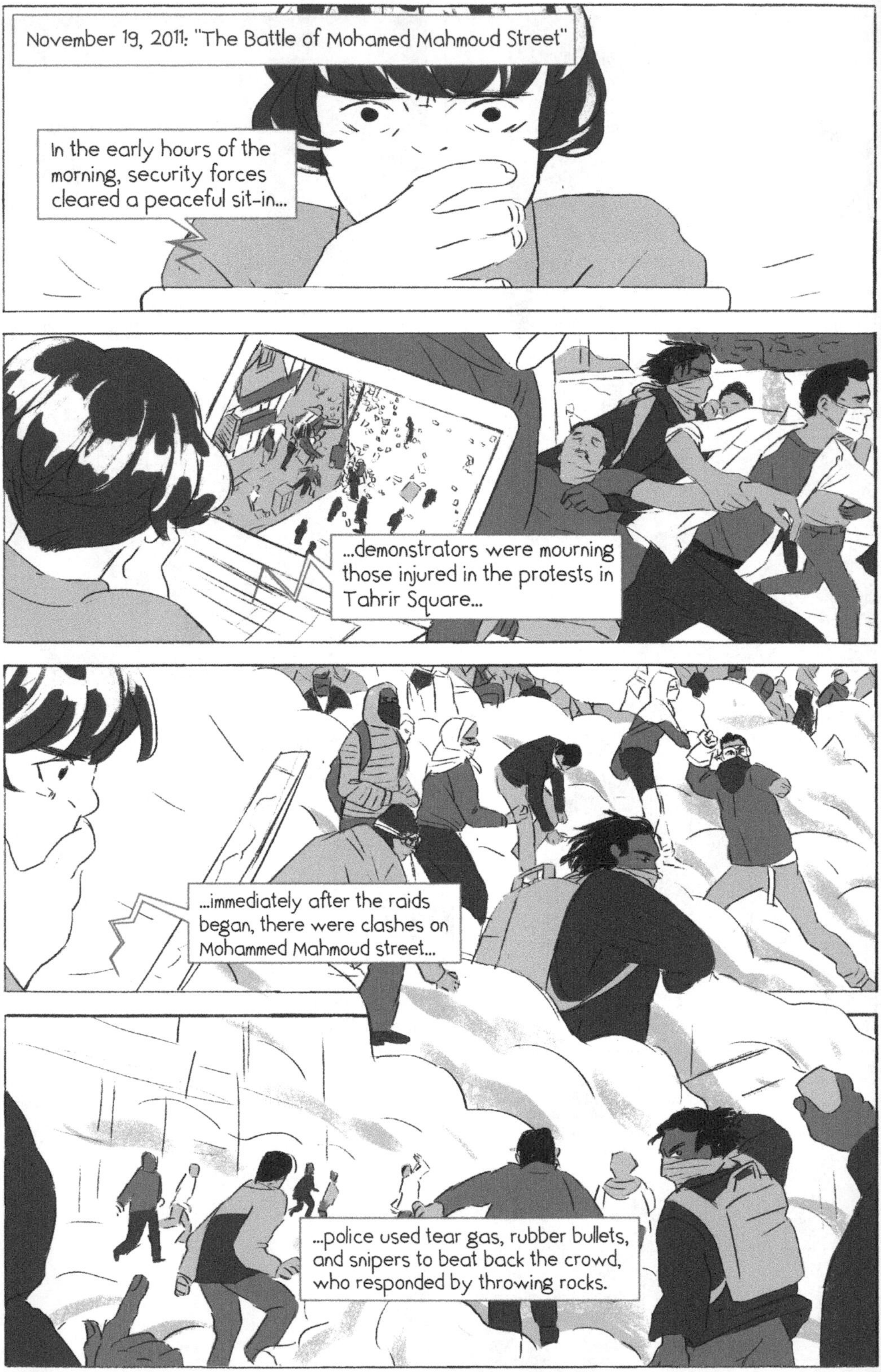
November 19, 2011: "The Battle of Mohamed Mahmoud Street"
In the early hours of the morning, security forces cleared a peaceful sit-in...
...demonstrators were mourning those injured in the protests in Tahrir Square...
...immediately after the raids began, there were clashes on Mohammed Mahmoud street...
...police used tear gas, rubber bullets, and snipers to beat back the crowd, who responded by throwing rocks.

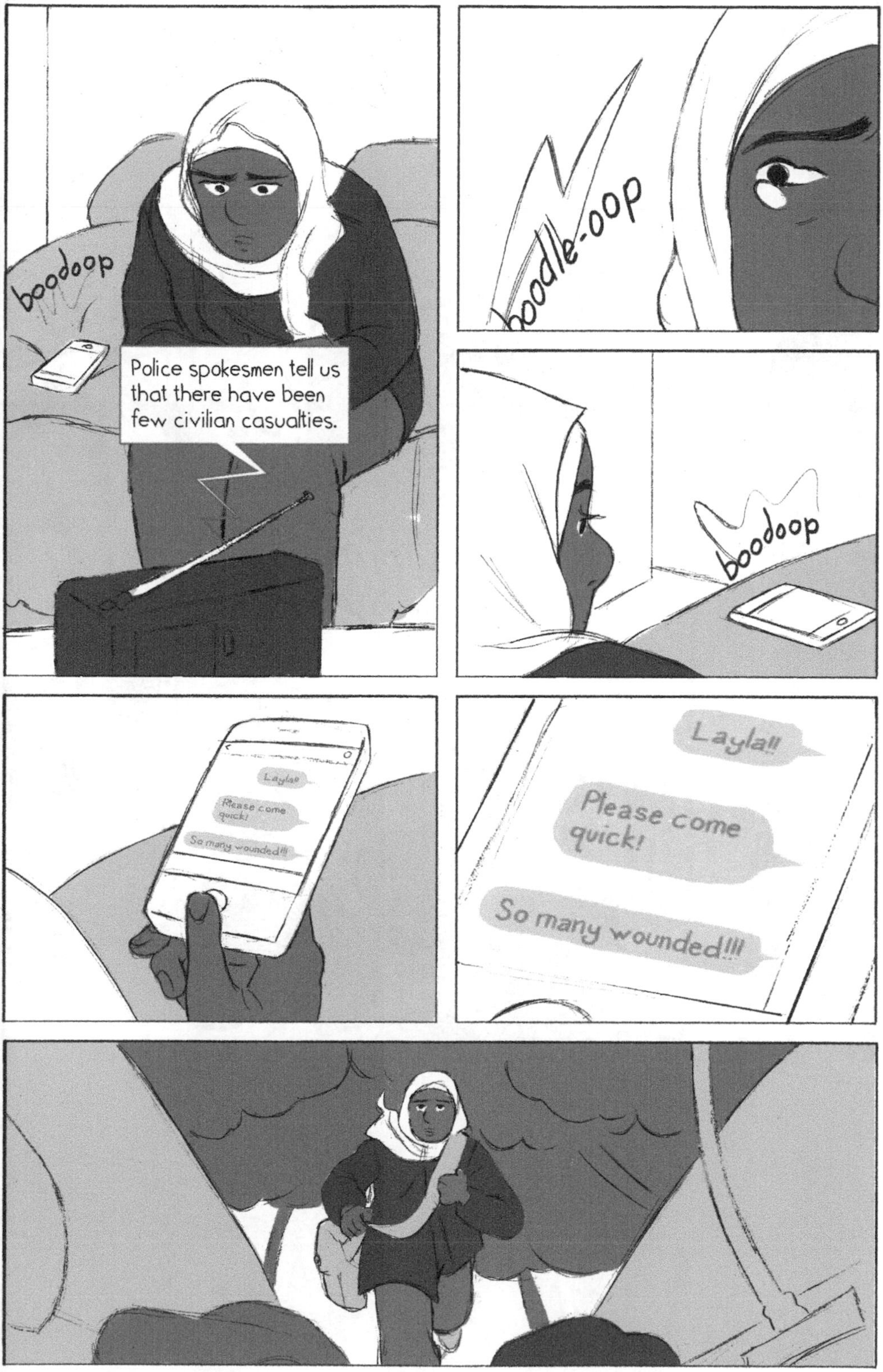
boodoop
Police spokesmen tell us that there have been few civilian casualties.
boodle-oop
boodoop
Layla!!
Please come quick!
So many wounded!!!

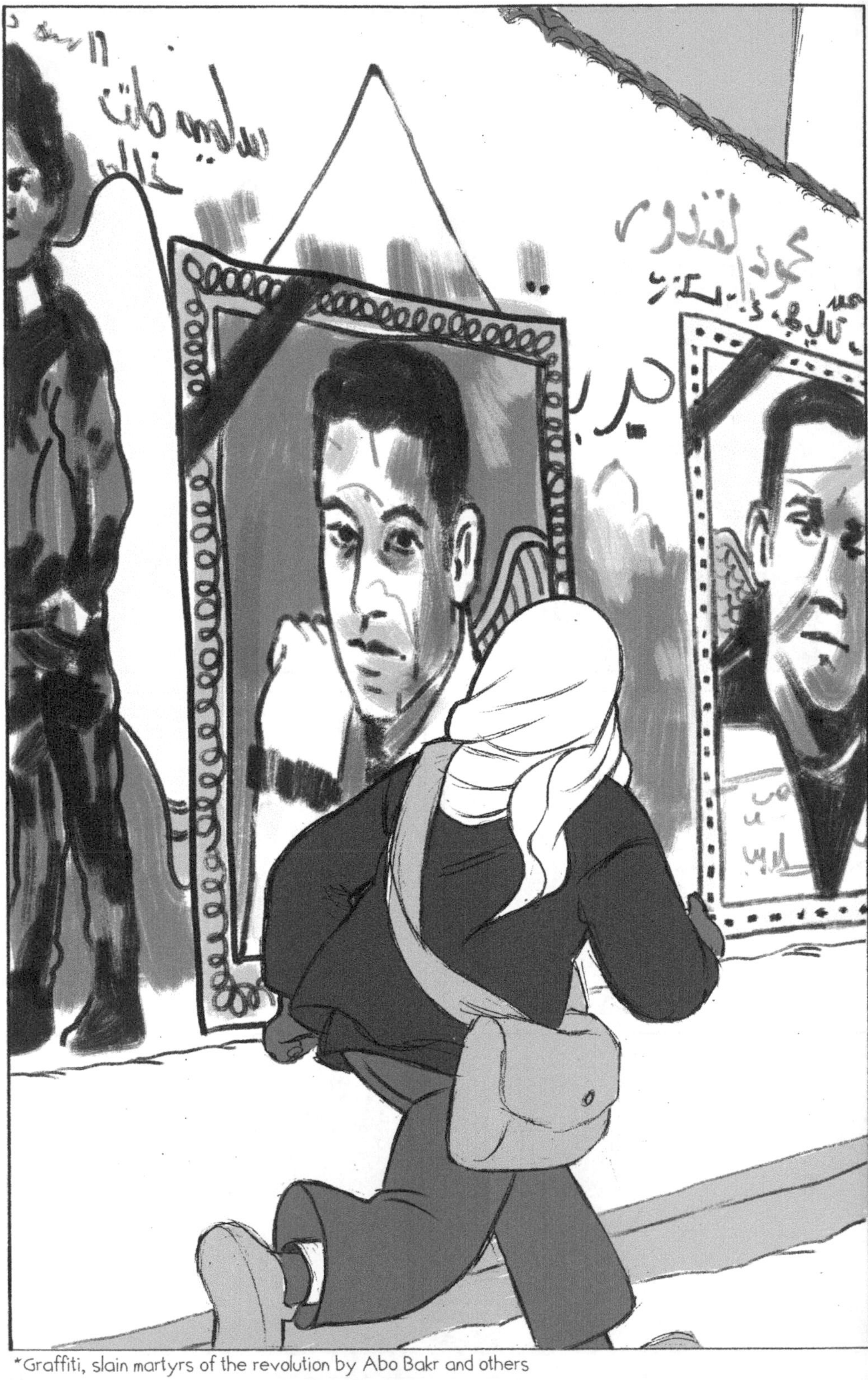

*Graffiti, slain martyrs of the revolution by Abo Bakr and others

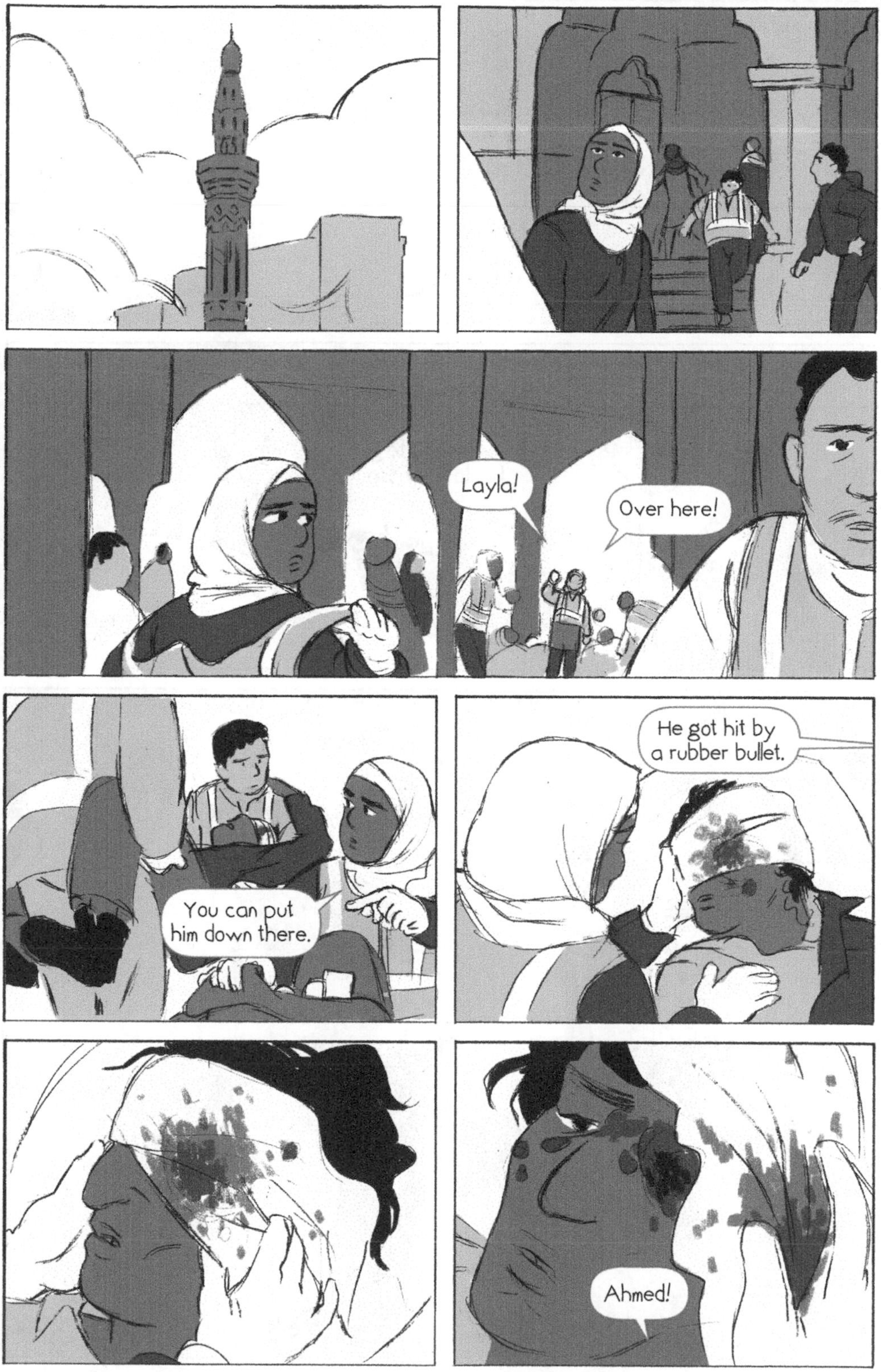
Layla!
Over here!
You can put him down there.
He got hit by a rubber bullet.
Ahmed!

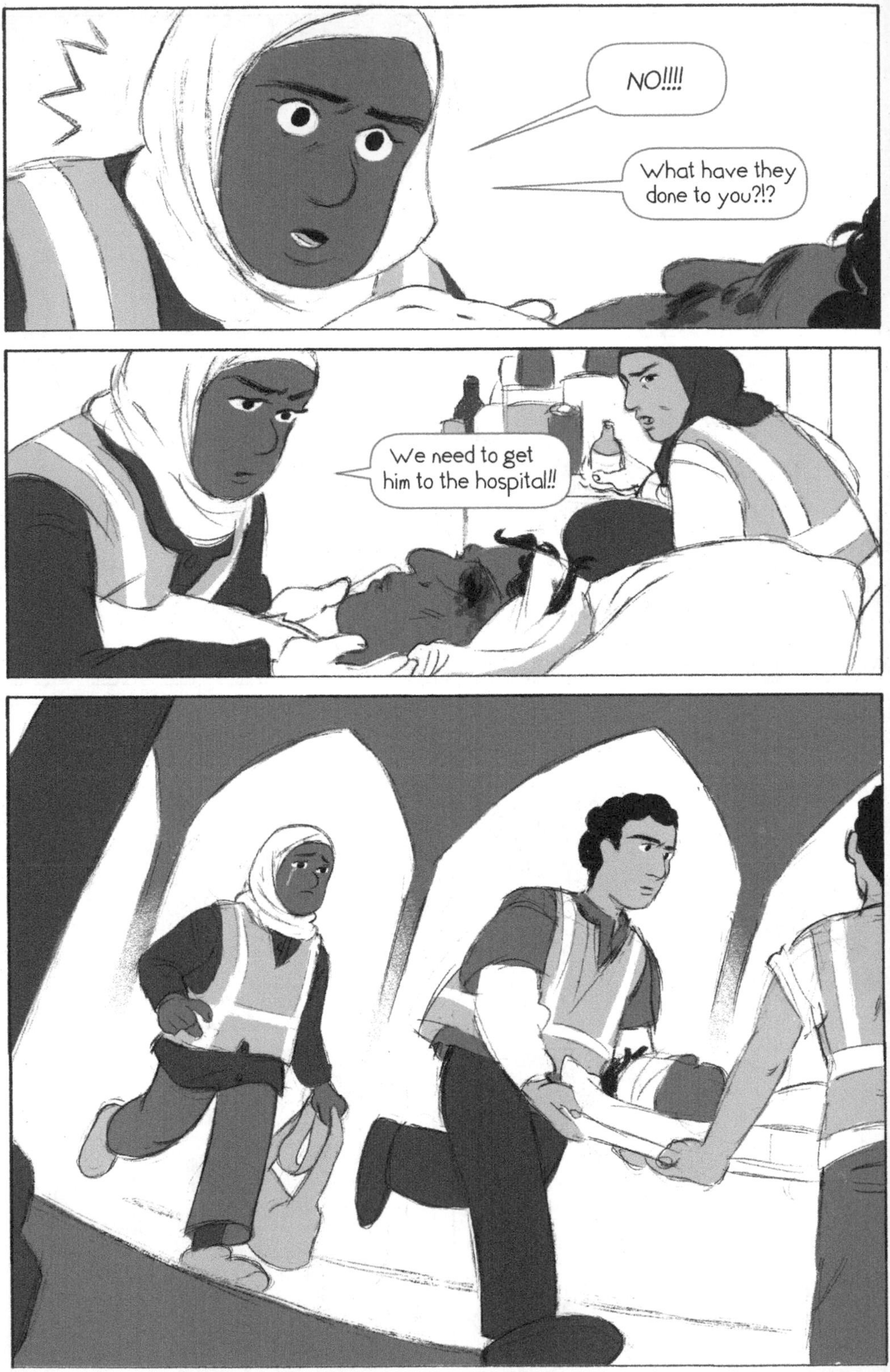
NO!!!!
What have they done to you?!?
We need to get him to the hospital!!

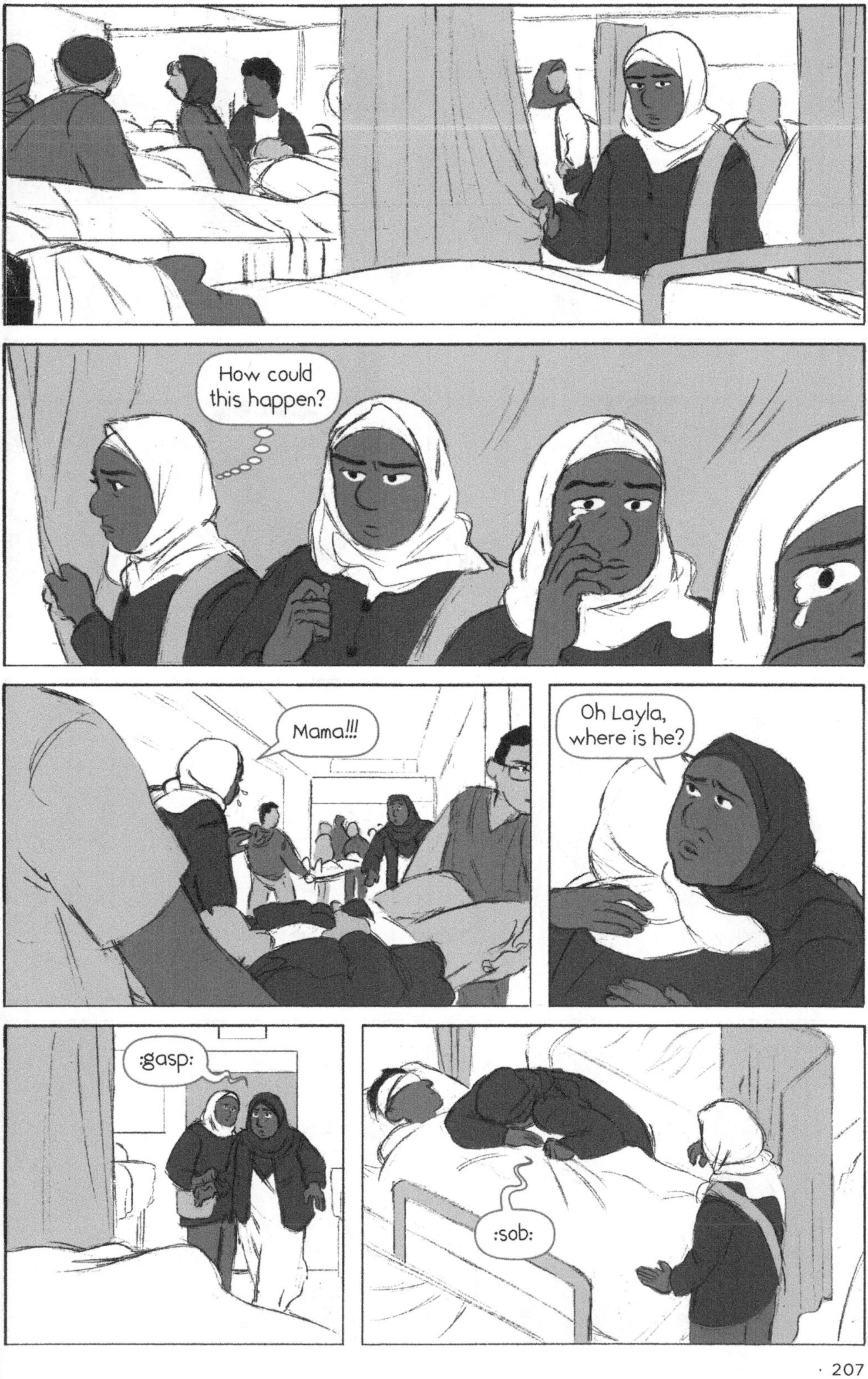
How could this happen?
Mama!!!
Oh Layla, where is he?
:gasp:
:sob:

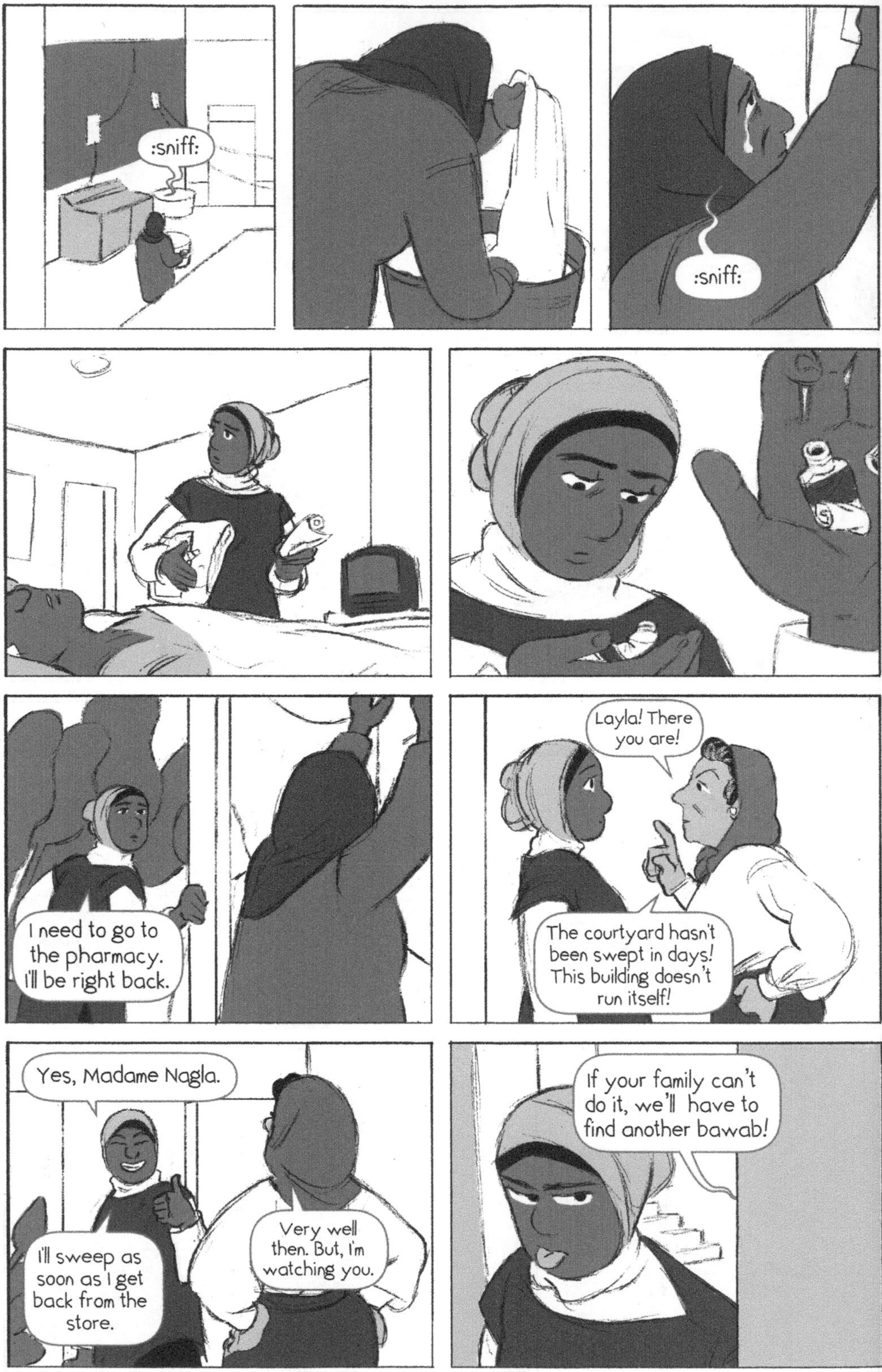

:sniff:
:sniff:
I need to go to the pharmacy. I'll be right back.
Layla! There you are!
The courtyard hasn't been swept in days! This building doesn't run itself!
Yes, Madame Nagla.
I'll sweep as soon as I get back from the store.
Very well then. But, I'm watching you.
If your family can't do it, we'll have to find another bawab!

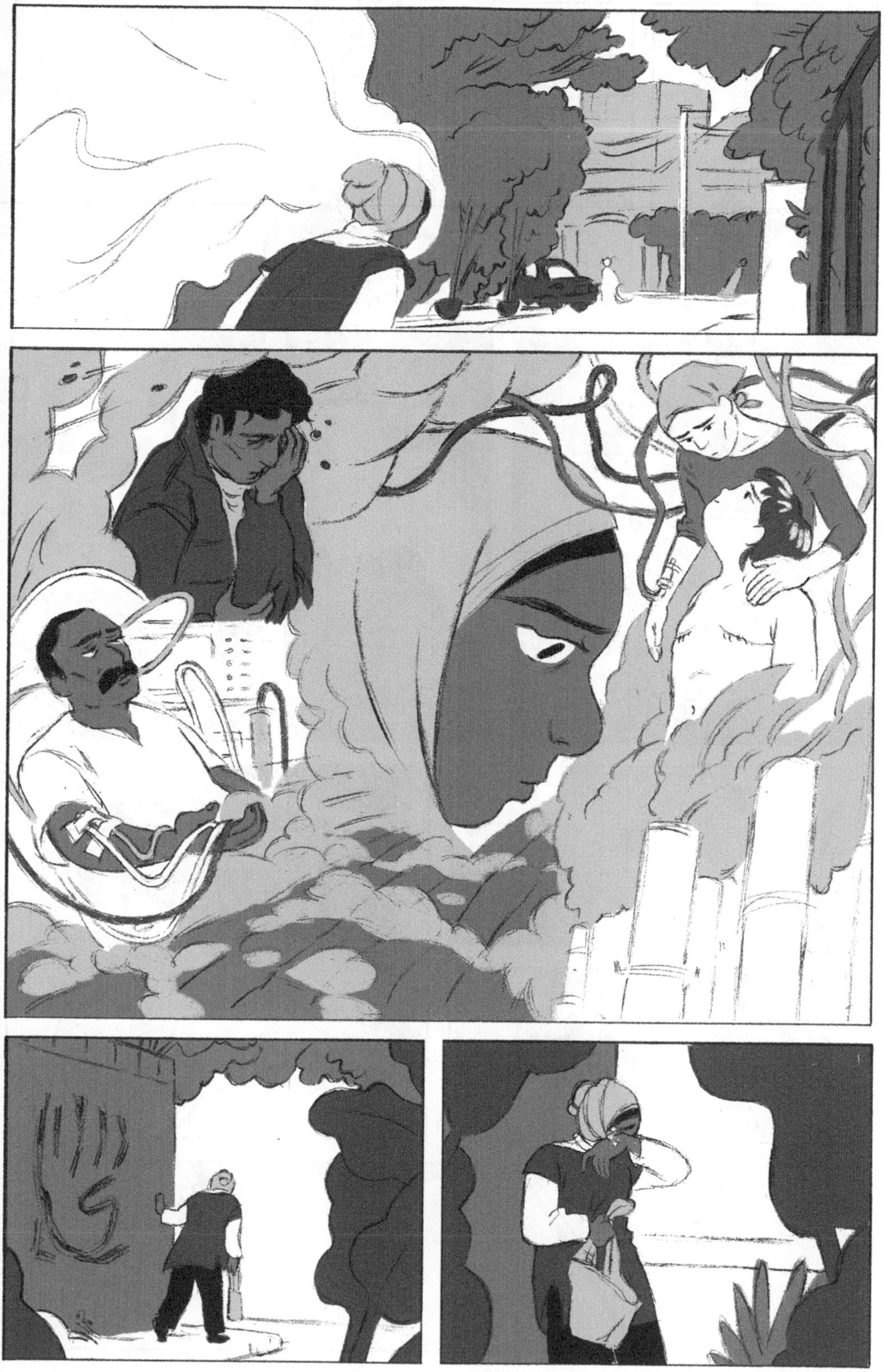

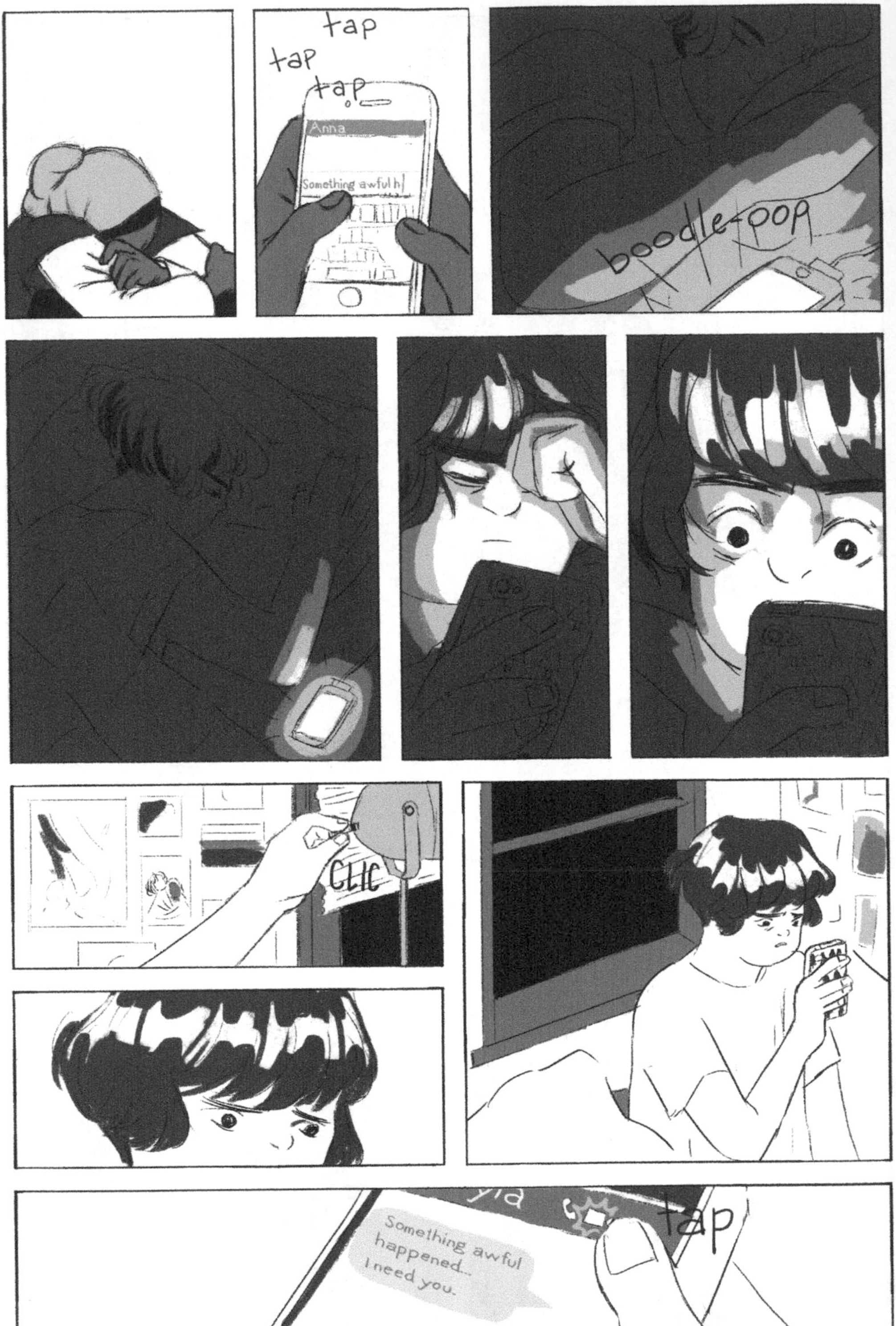
tap
tap
tap
Anna
Something awful h
boodle-pop
CLIC
Something awful happened...
I need you.
tap

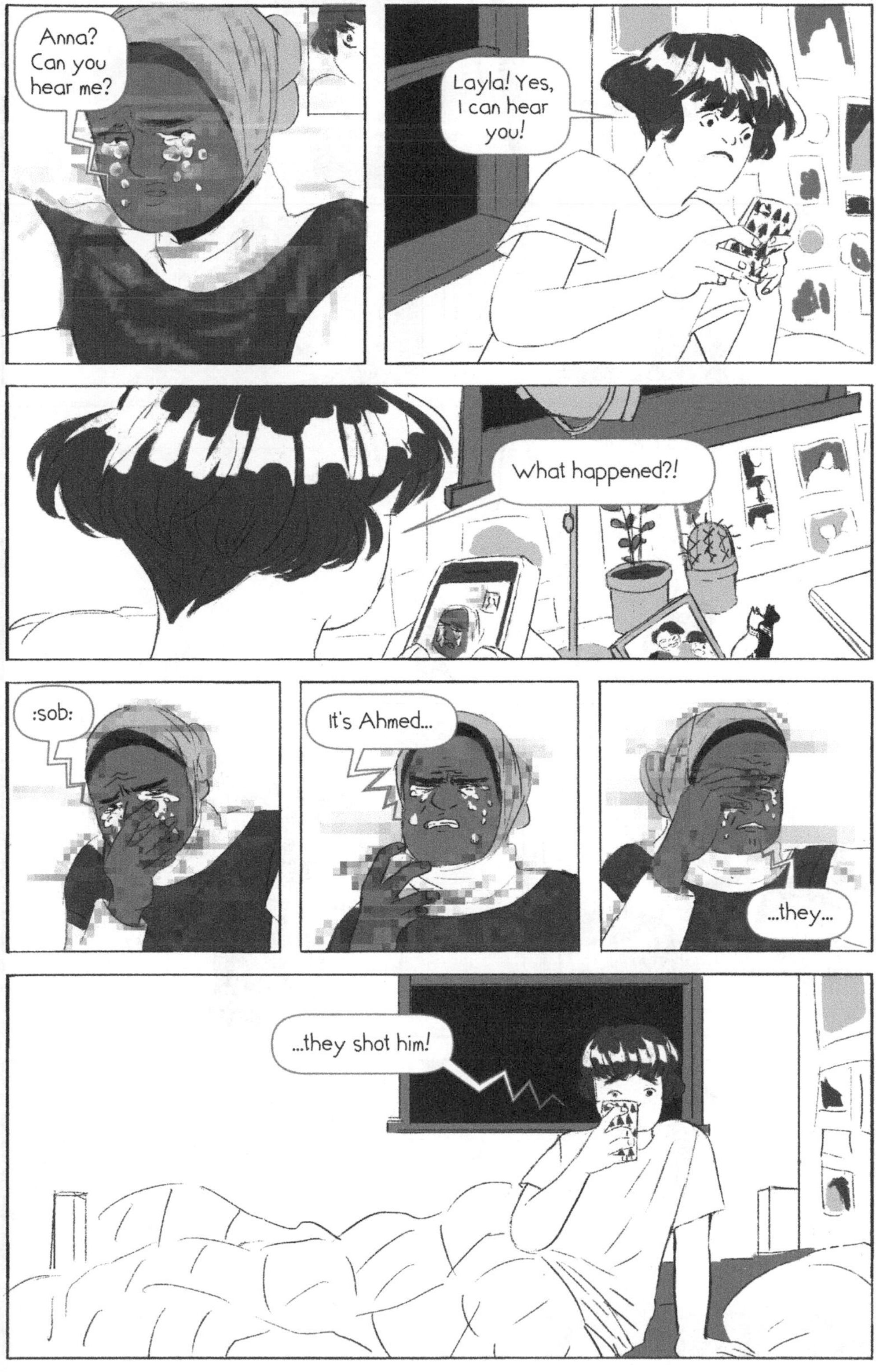
Anna? Can you hear me?
Layla! Yes, I can hear you!
What happened?!
:sob:
It's Ahmed...
...they...
...they shot him!

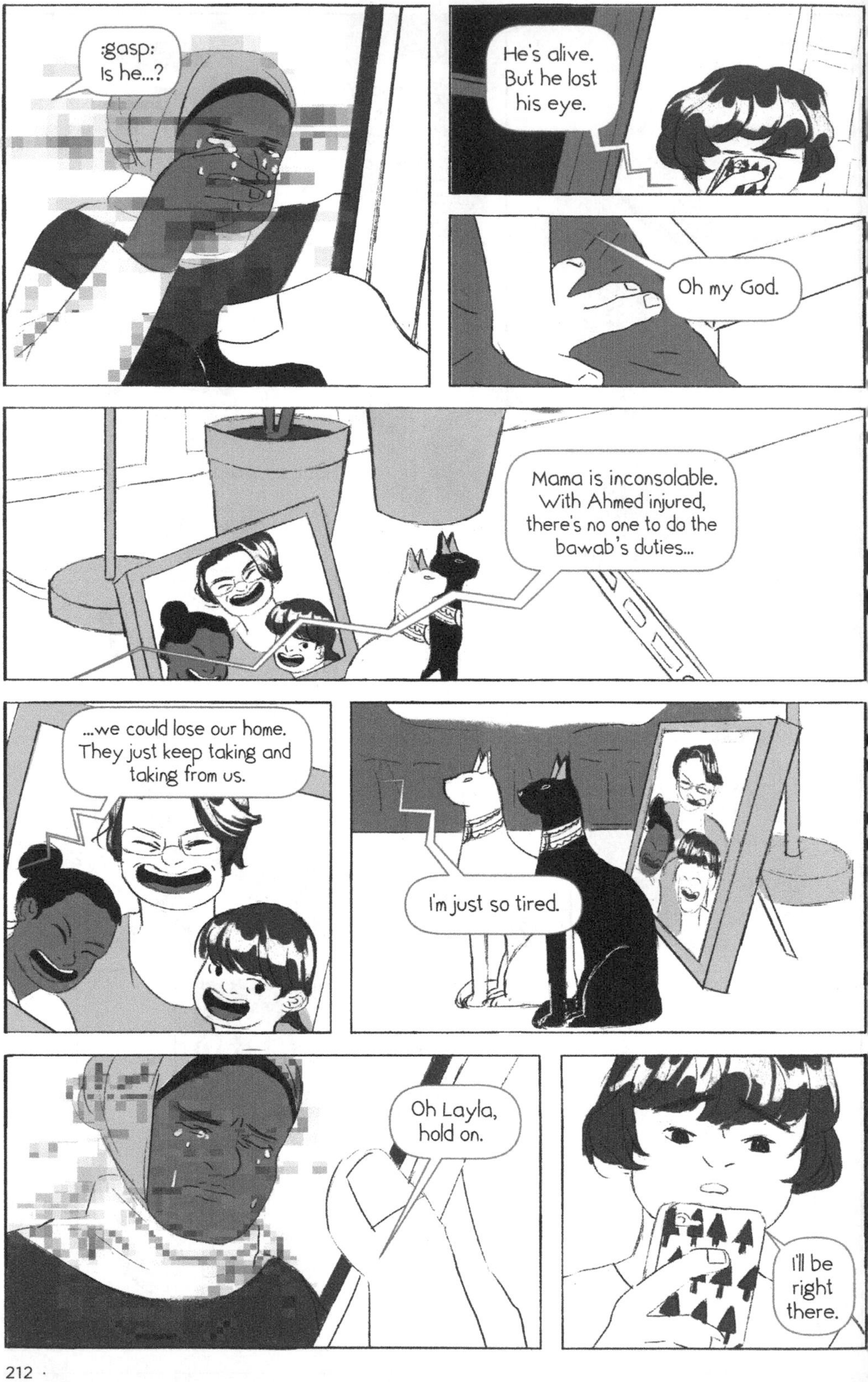
:gasp: Is he...?
He's alive. But he lost his eye.
Oh my God.
Mama is inconsolable. With Ahmed injured, there's no one to do the bawab's duties...
...we could lose our home. They just keep taking and taking from us.
I'm just so tired.
Oh Layla, hold on.
I'll be right there.

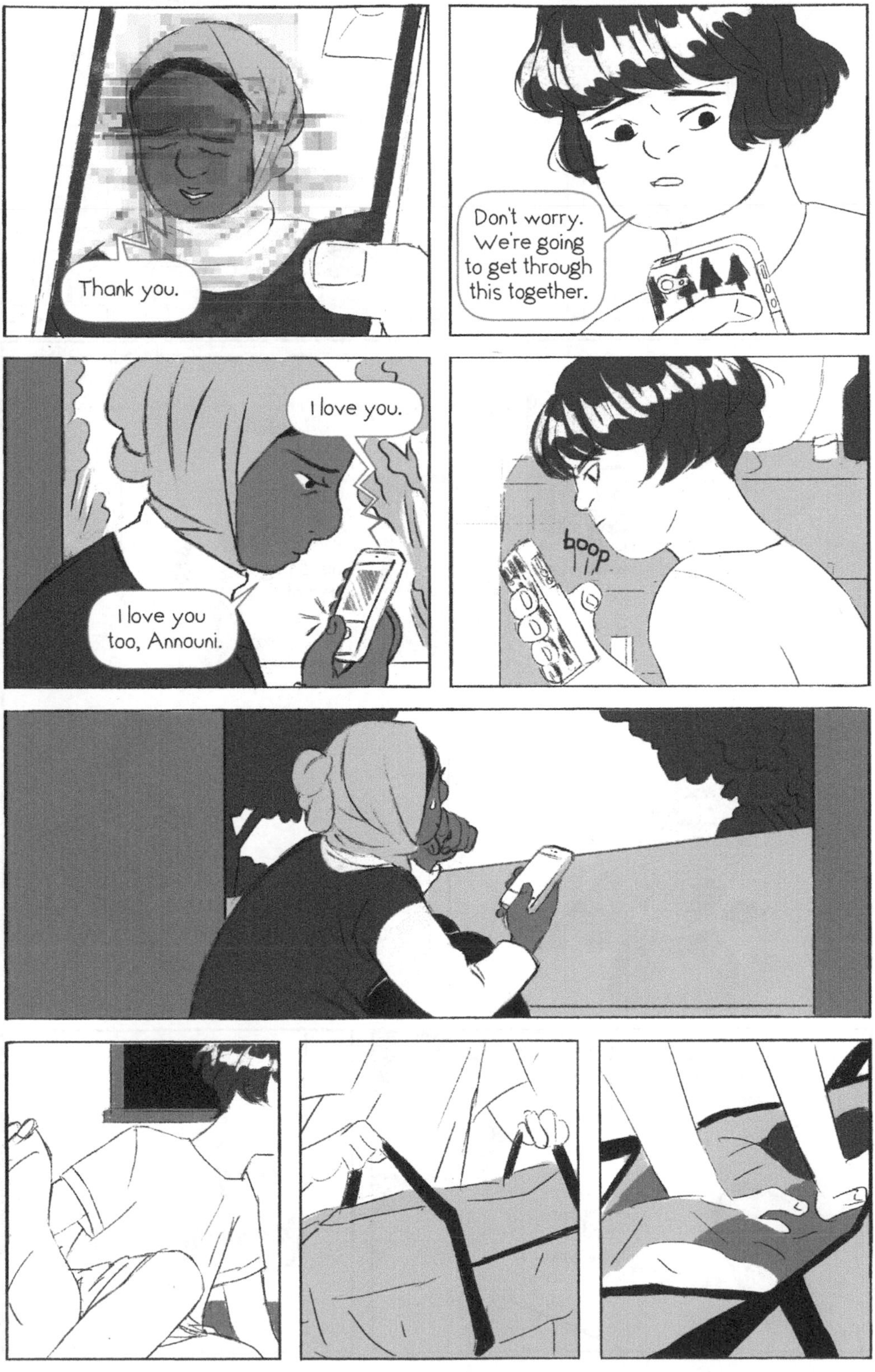

Thank you.
Don't worry. We're going to get through this together.
I love you.
I love you too, Announi.
boop

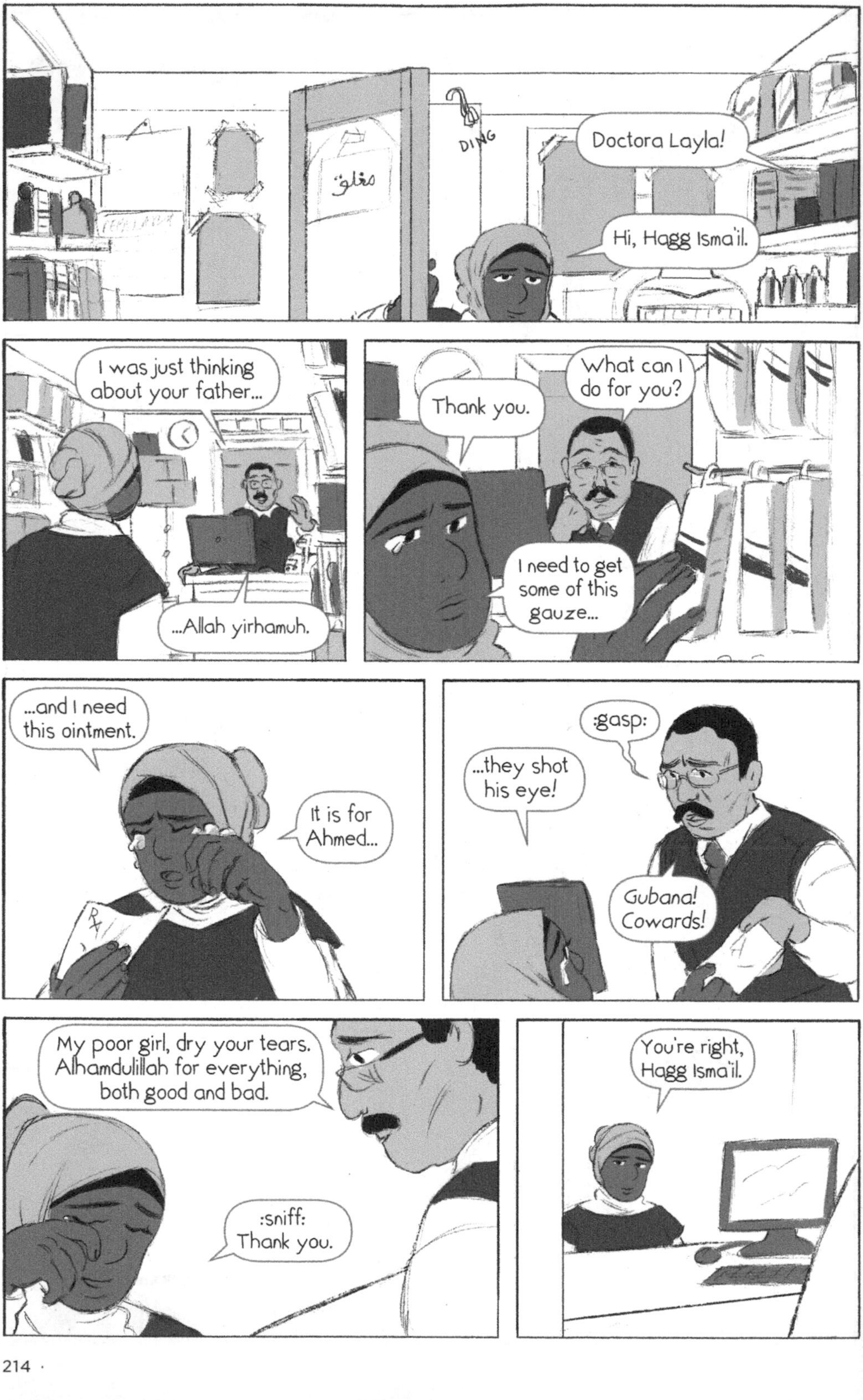
مغلق
DING
Doctora Layla!
Hi, Hagg Isma'il.
I was just thinking about your father...
...Allah yirhamuh.
Thank you.
What can I do for you?
I need to get some of this gauze...
...and I need this ointment.
It is for Ahmed...
:gasp:
...they shot his eye!
Gubana! Cowards!
My poor girl, dry your tears. Alhamdulillah for everything, both good and bad.
:sniff: Thank you.
You're right, Hagg Isma'il.

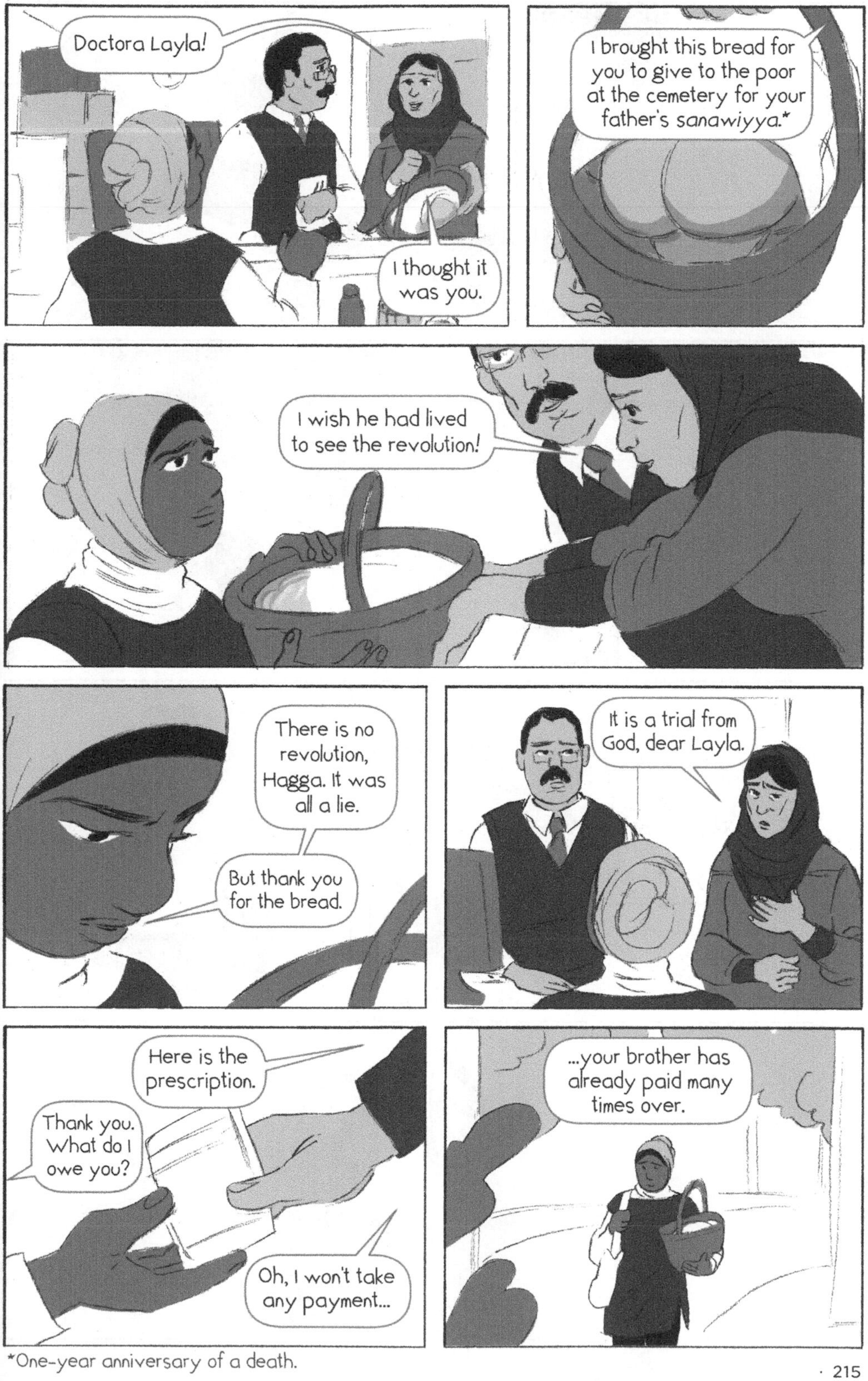
Doctora Layla!
I thought it was you.
I brought this bread for you to give to the poor at the cemetery for your father's sanawiyya.*
I wish he had lived to see the revolution!
There is no revolution, Hagga. It was all a lie.
But thank you for the bread.
It is a trial from God, dear Layla.
Here is the prescription.
Thank you. What do I owe you?
Oh, I won't take any payment...
...your brother has already paid many times over.

*One-year anniversary of a death.

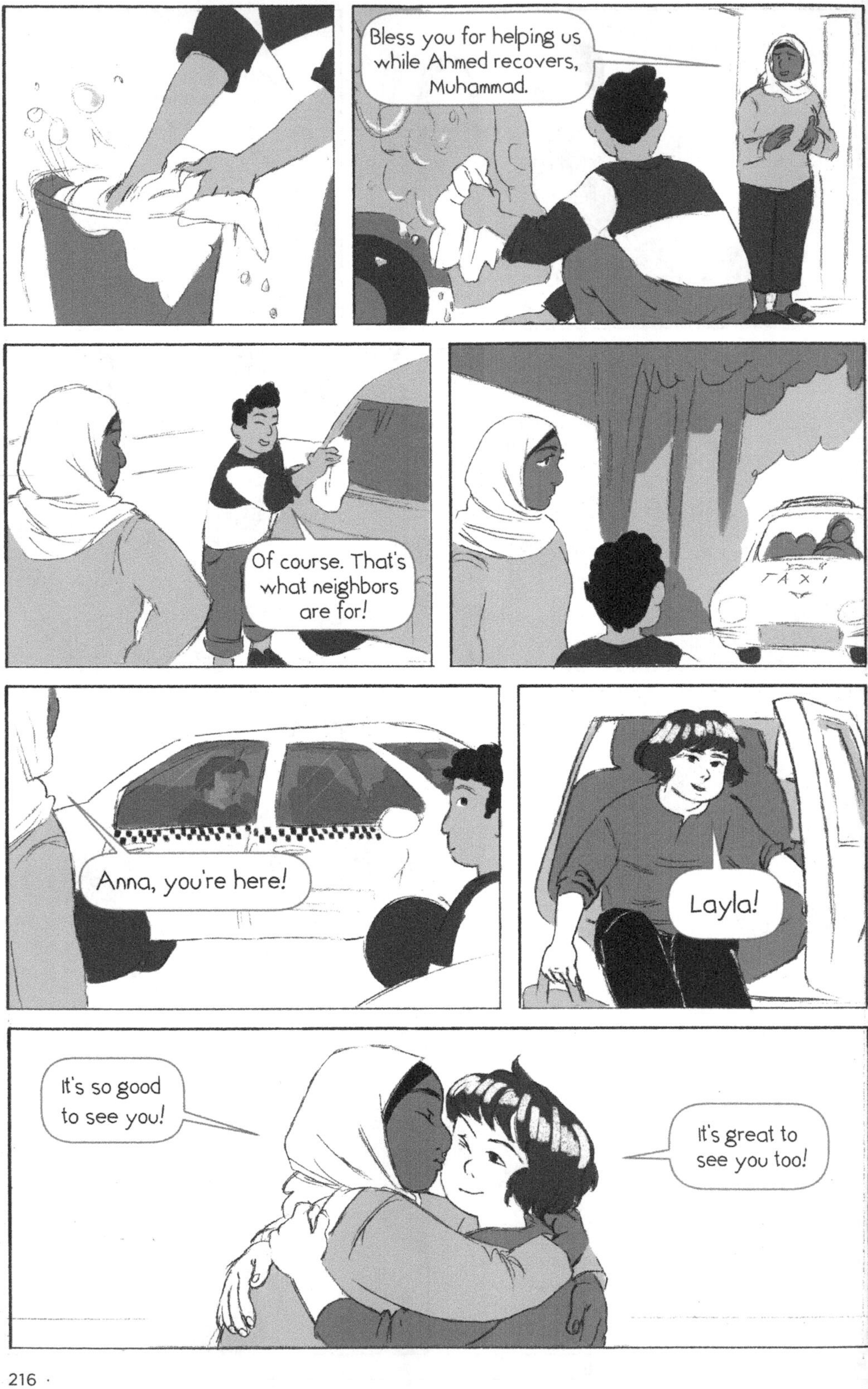
Bless you for helping us while Ahmed recovers, Muhammad.
Of course. That's what neighbors are for!
TAXI
Anna, you're here!
Layla!
It's so good to see you!
It's great to see you too!

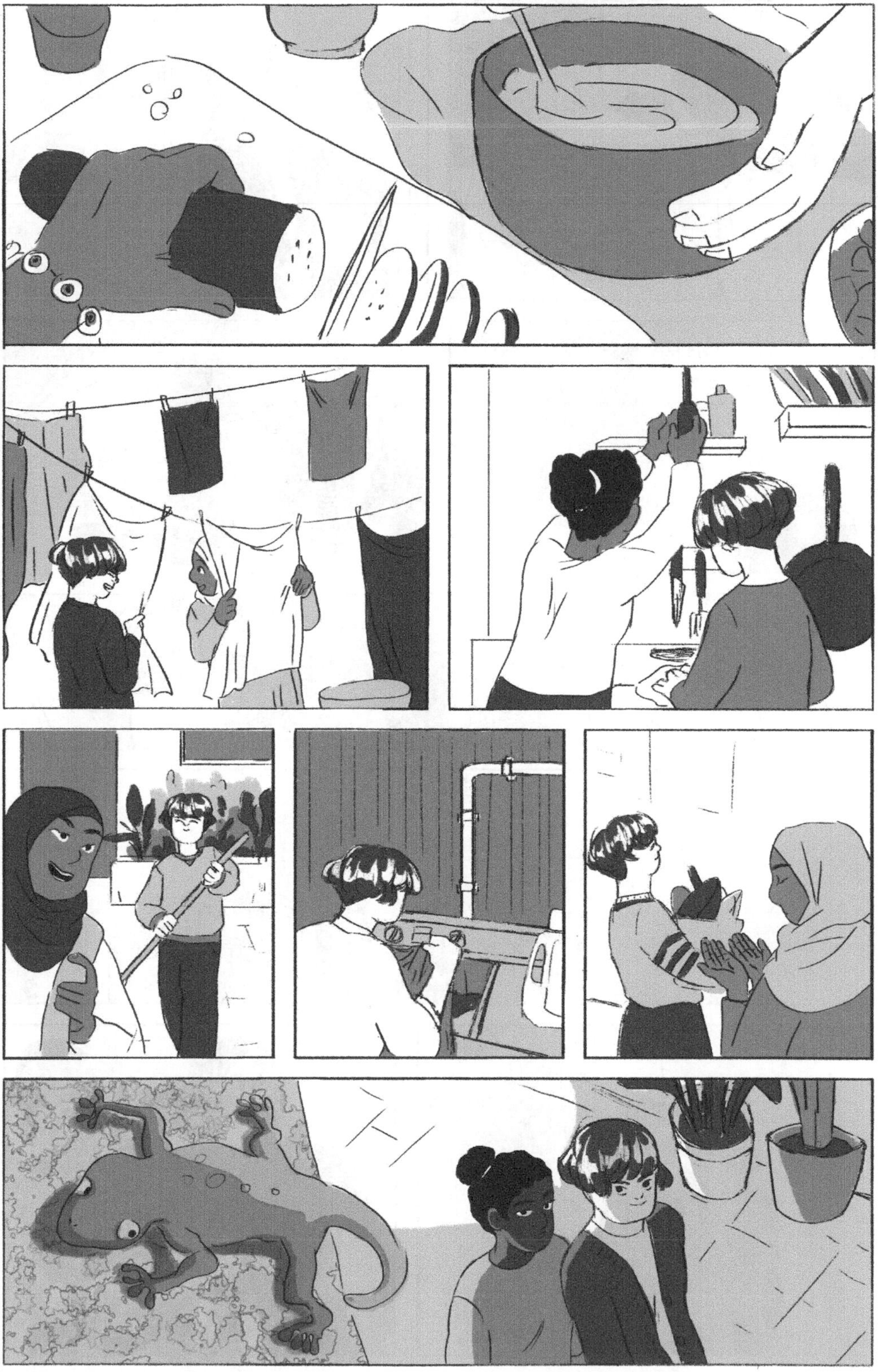

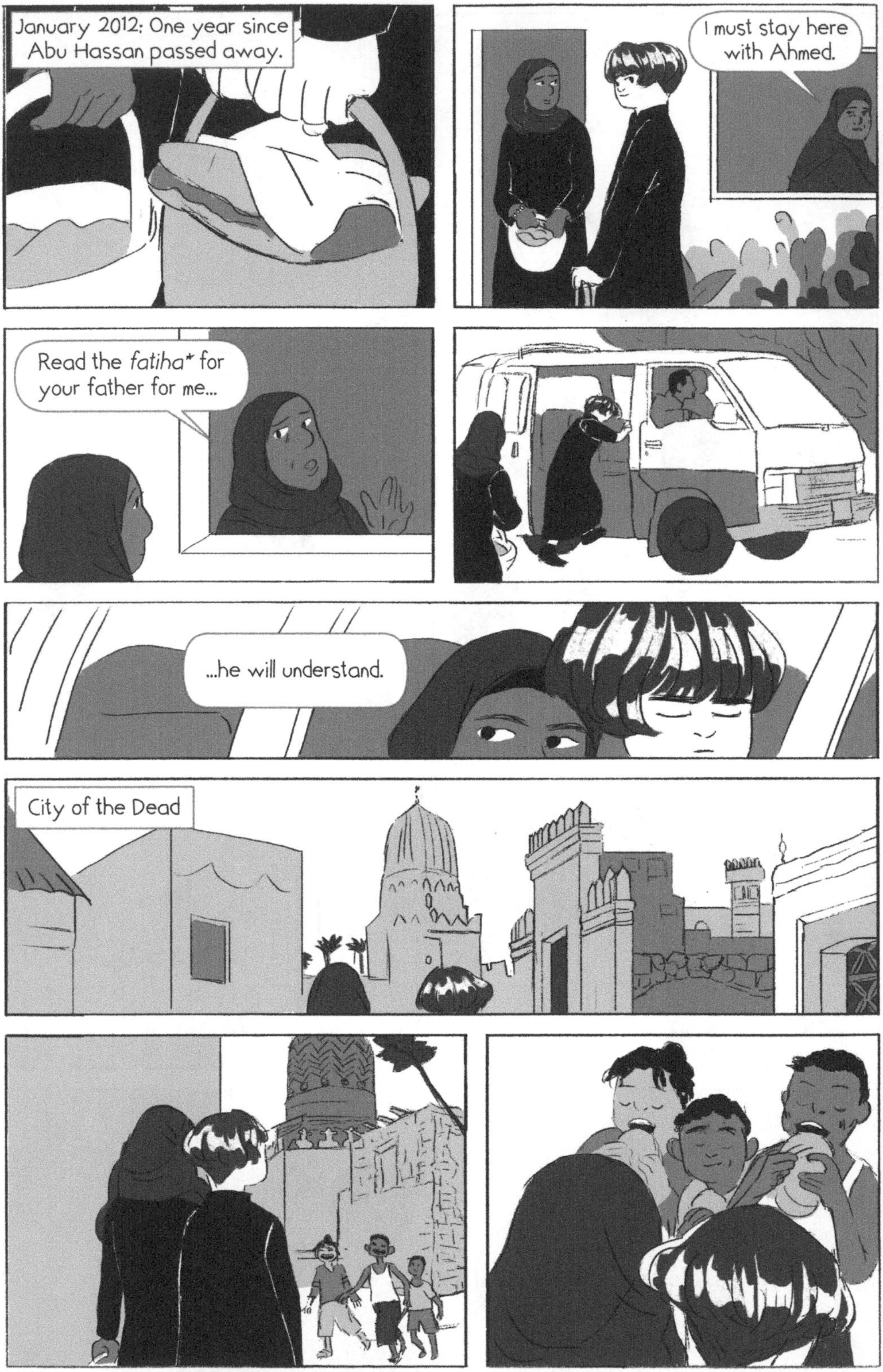
January 2012: One year since Abu Hassan passed away.
I must stay here with Ahmed.
Read the *fatiha** for your father for me...
...he will understand.
City of the Dead

*Opening verses of Qur'an

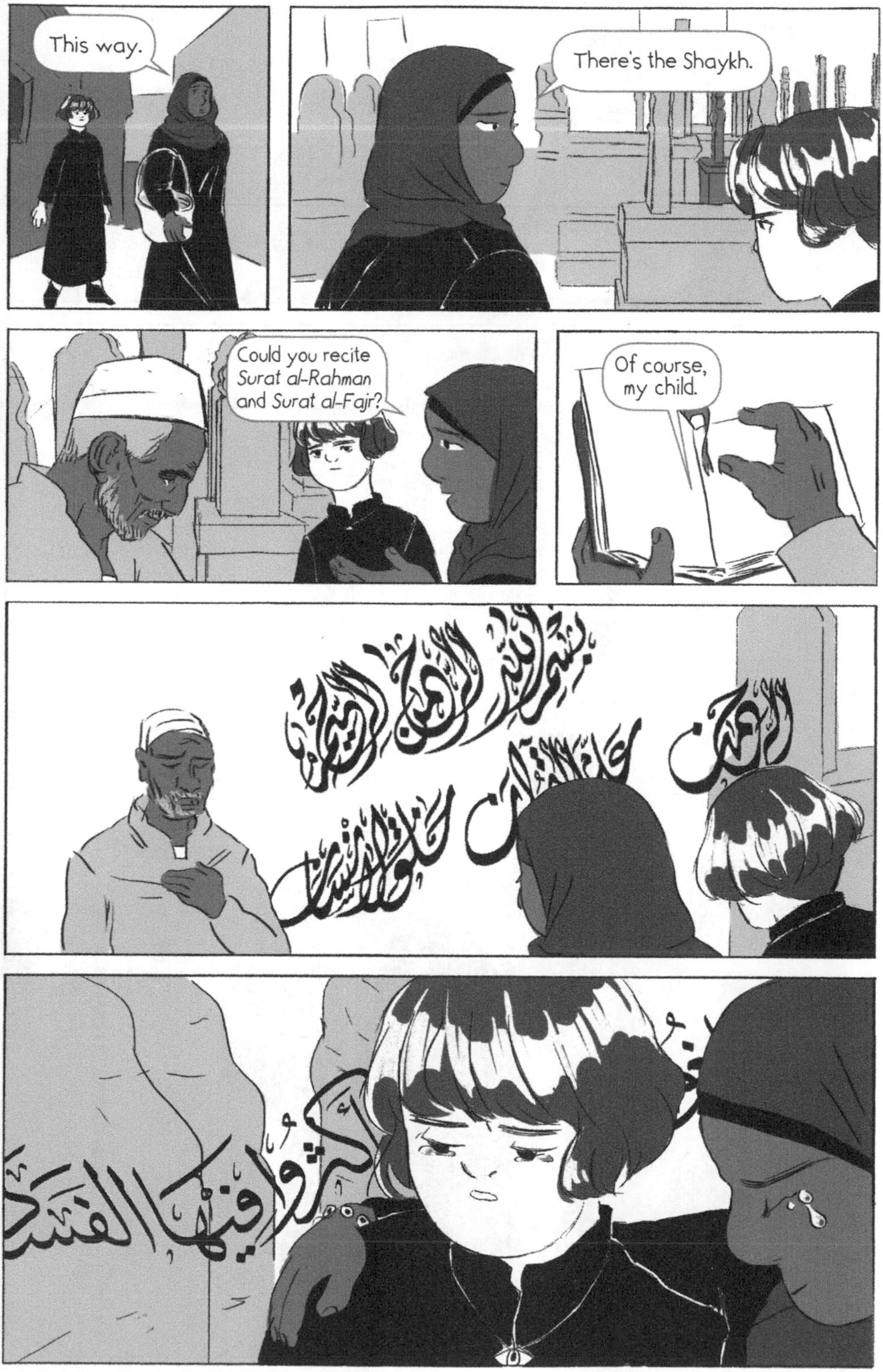
This way.
There's the Shaykh.
Could you recite *Surat al-Rahman* and *Surat al-Fajr*?
Of course, my child.
بسم الله الرحمن الرحيم
الرحمن علم القرآن خلق الإنسان
فأكثروا فيها الفساد

*Calligraphy by Khaled Al-Saai

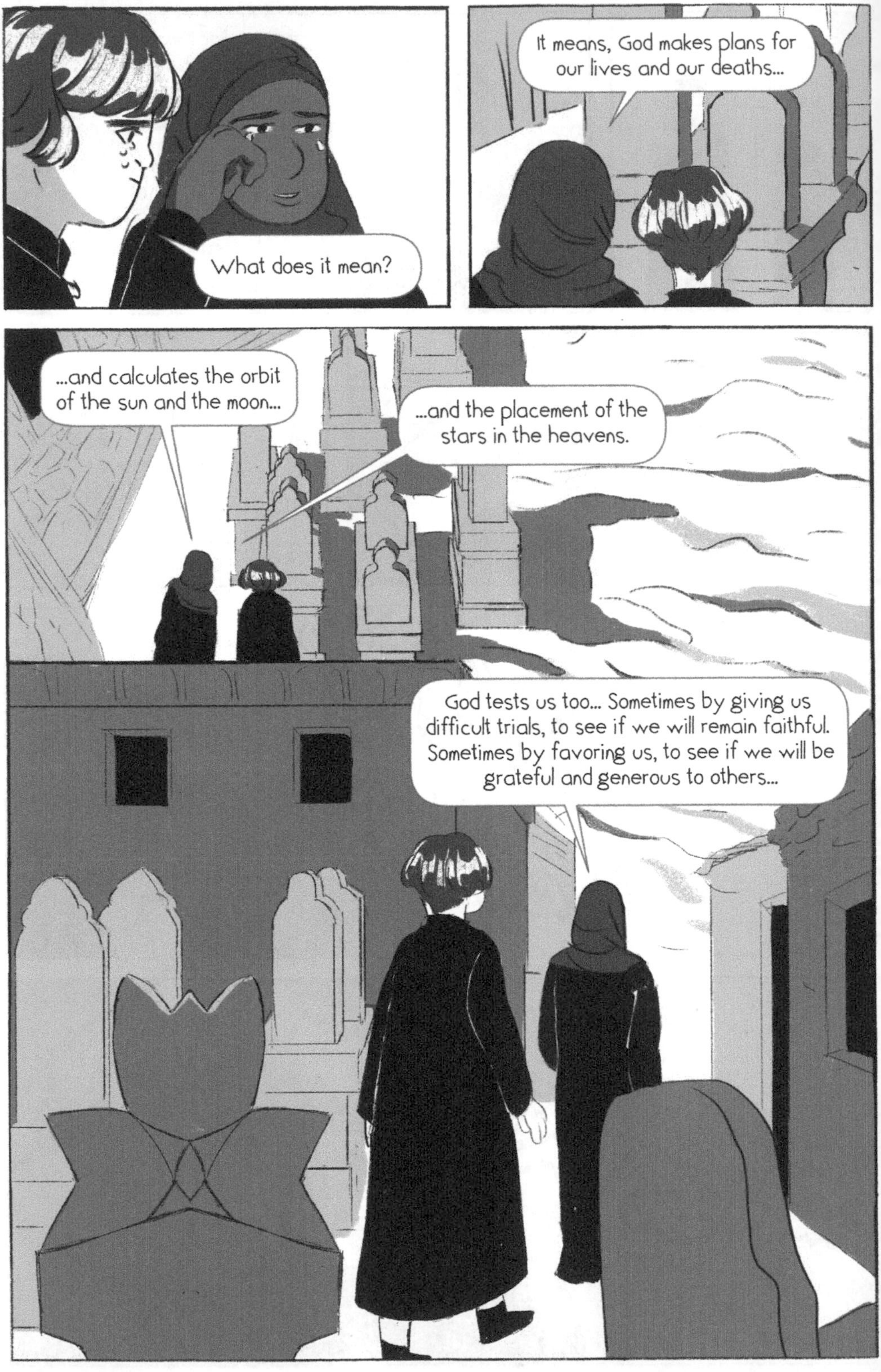
What does it mean?
It means, God makes plans for our lives and our deaths...
...and calculates the orbit of the sun and the moon...
...and the placement of the stars in the heavens.
God tests us too... Sometimes by giving us difficult trials, to see if we will remain faithful. Sometimes by favoring us, to see if we will be grateful and generous to others...

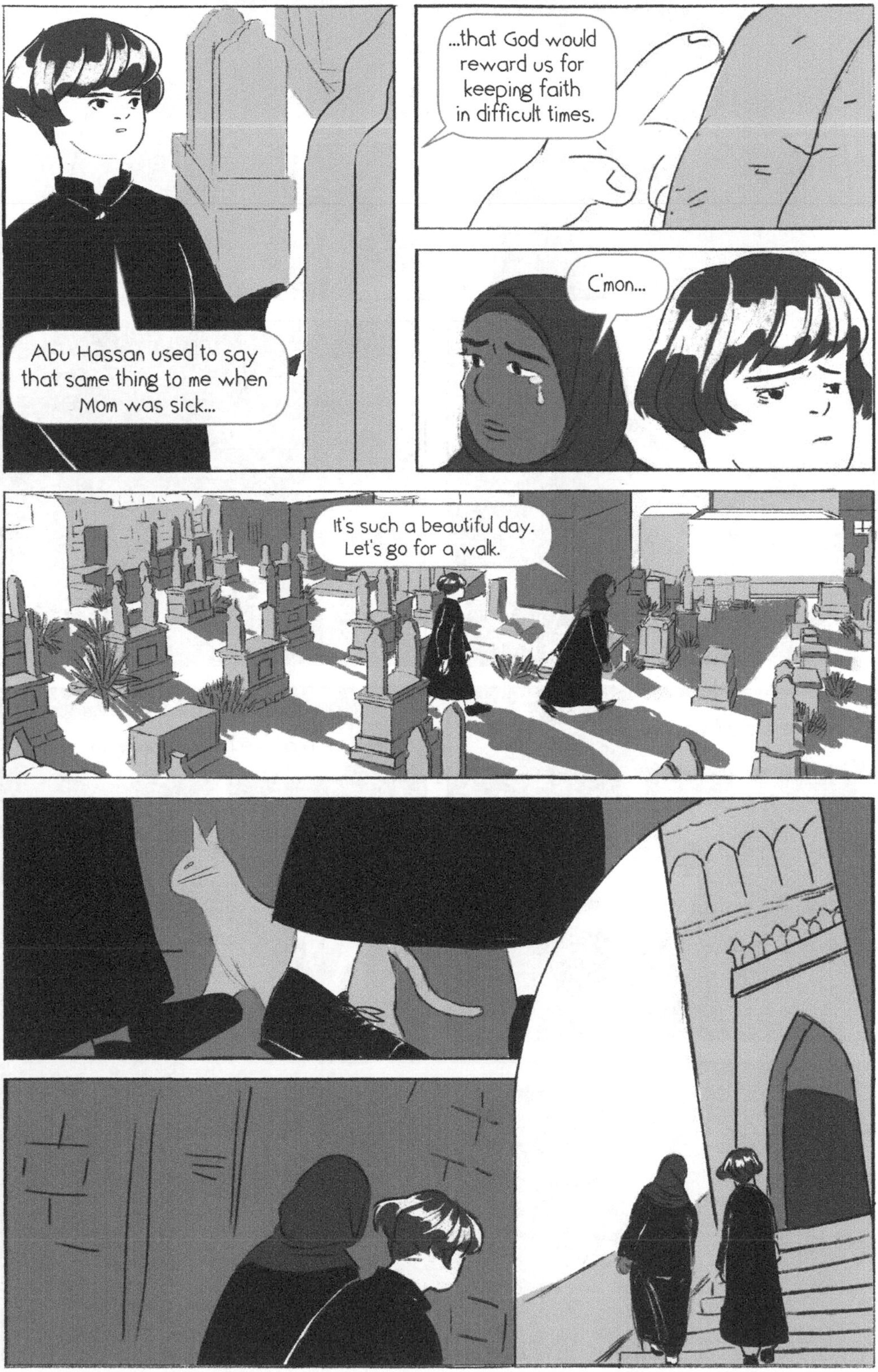

...that God would reward us for keeping faith in difficult times.
Abu Hassan used to say that same thing to me when Mom was sick...
C'mon...
It's such a beautiful day. Let's go for a walk.

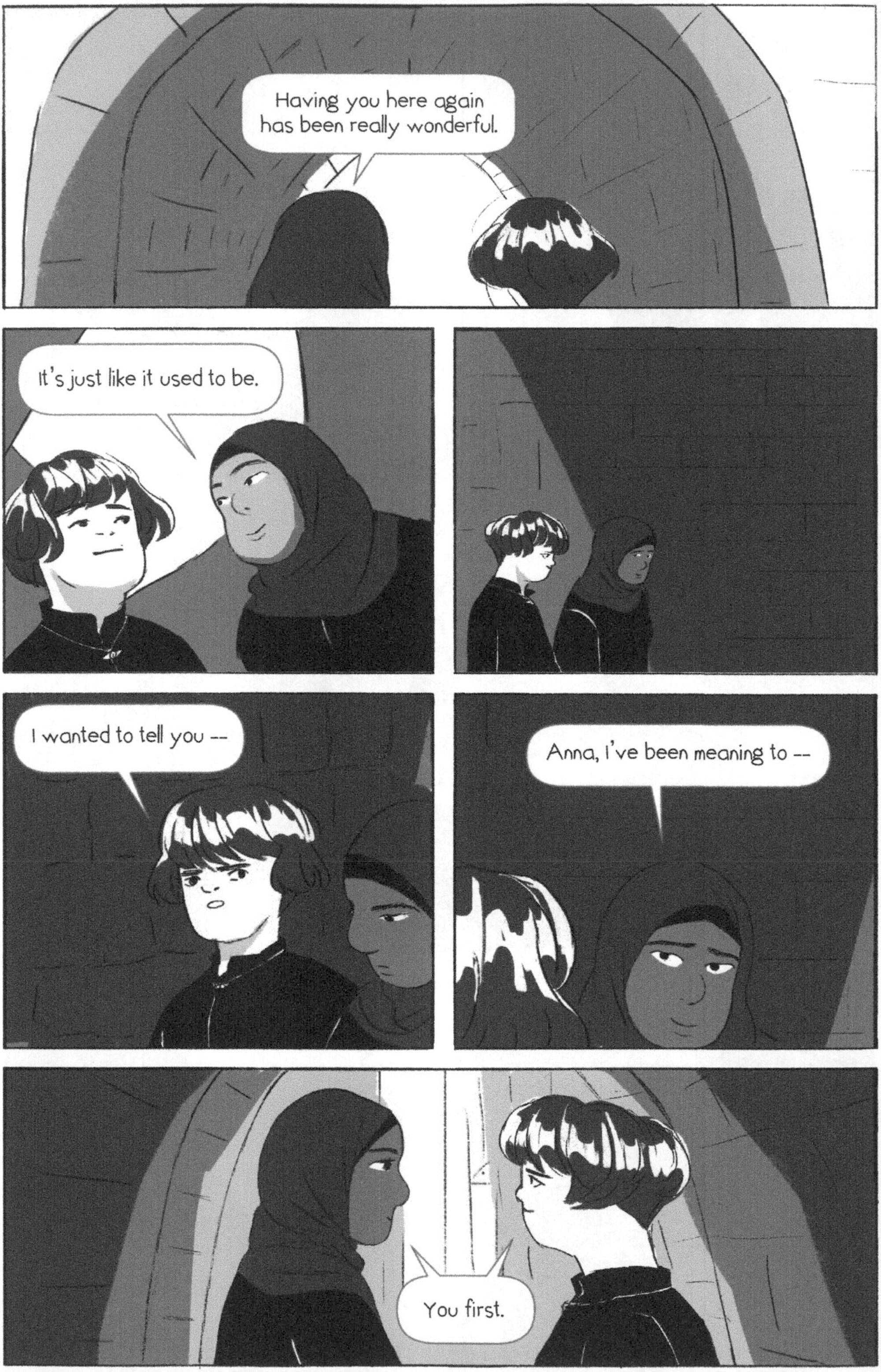
Having you here again has been really wonderful.
It's just like it used to be.
I wanted to tell you --
Anna, I've been meaning to --
You first.

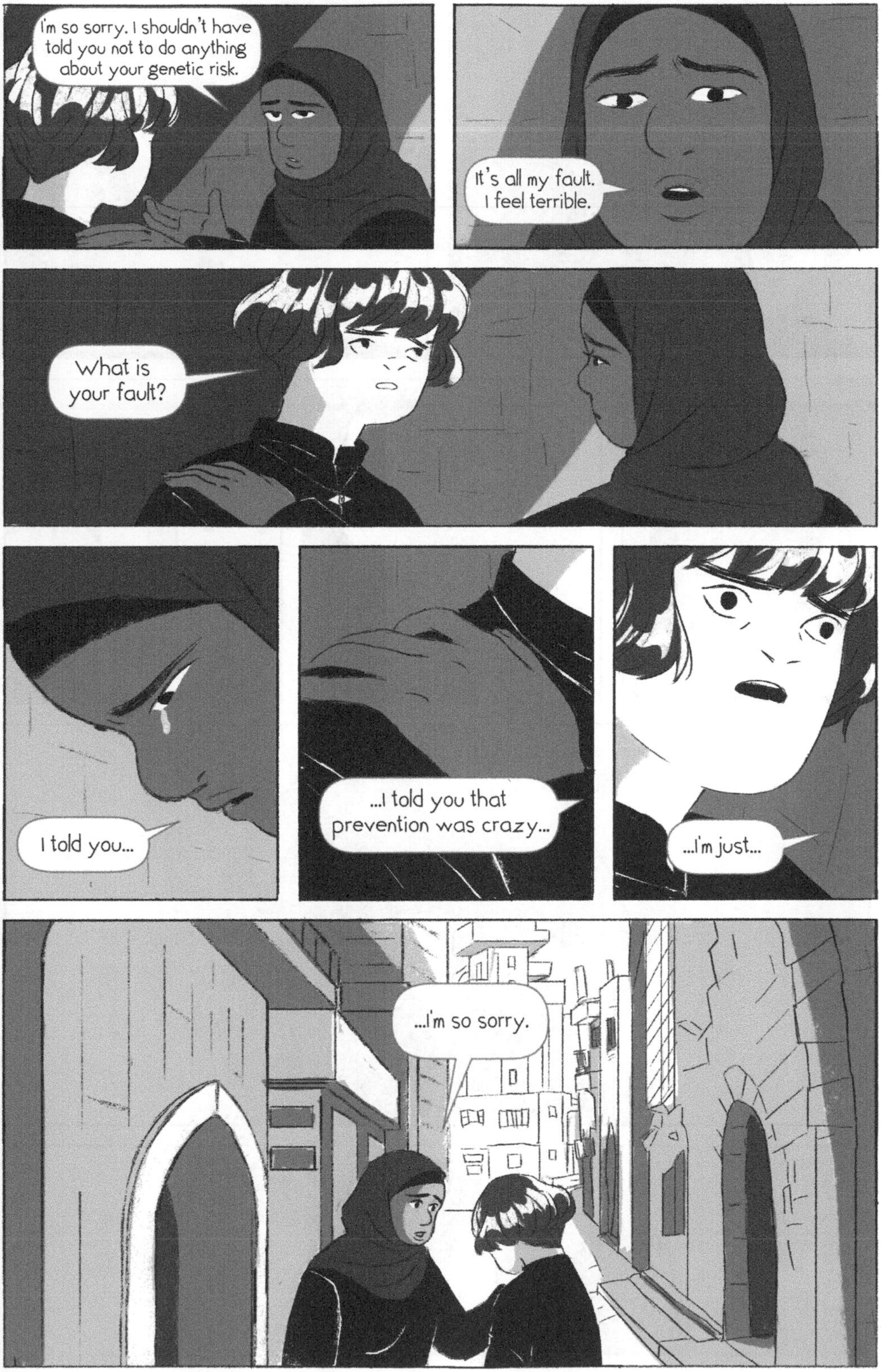
I'm so sorry. I shouldn't have told you not to do anything about your genetic risk.
It's all my fault. I feel terrible.
What is your fault?
I told you...
...I told you that prevention was crazy...
...I'm just...
...I'm so sorry.

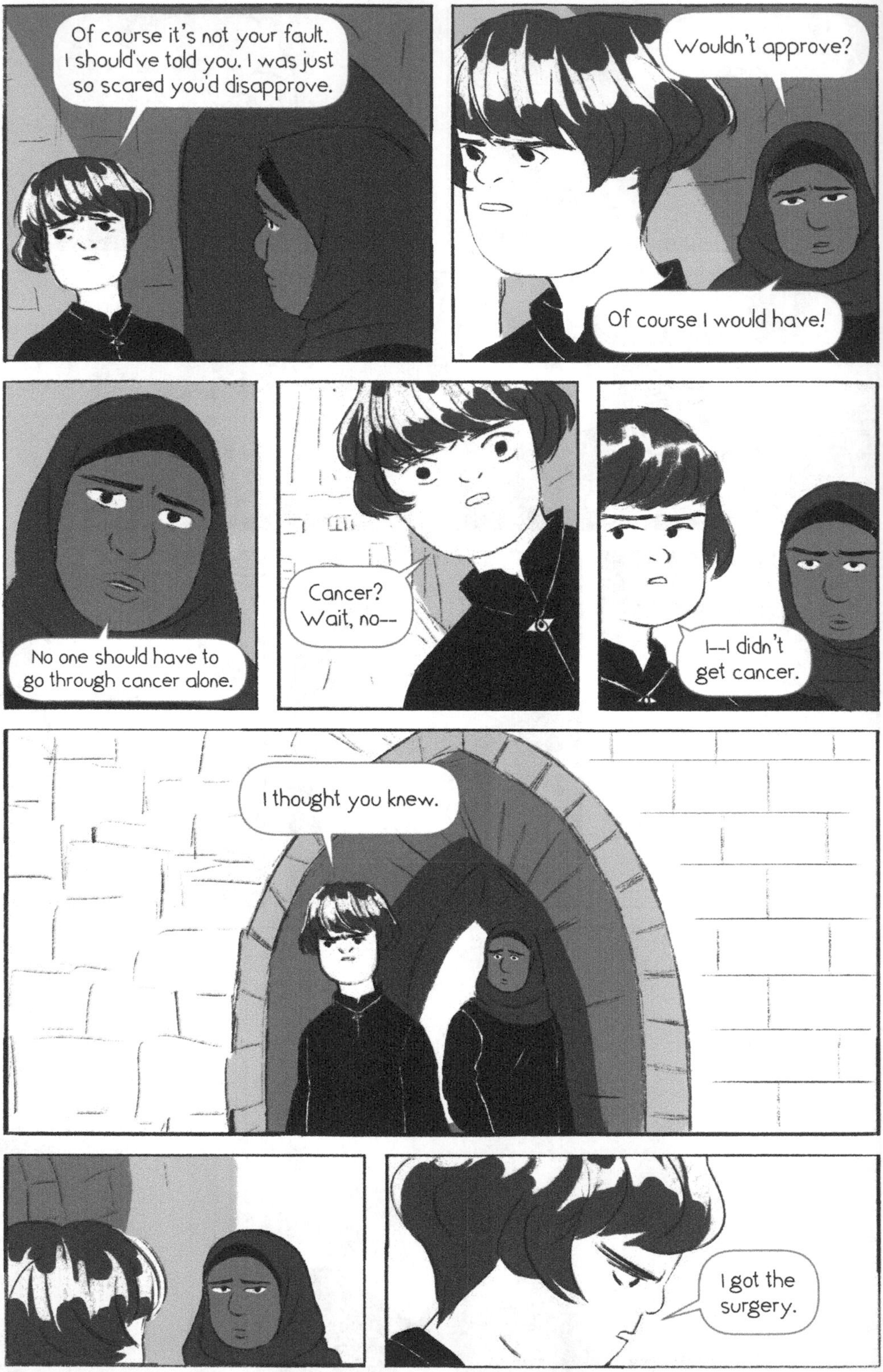
Of course it's not your fault. I should've told you. I was just so scared you'd disapprove.
Wouldn't approve?
Of course I would have!
No one should have to go through cancer alone.
Cancer? Wait, no--
I--I didn't get cancer.
I thought you knew.
I got the surgery.

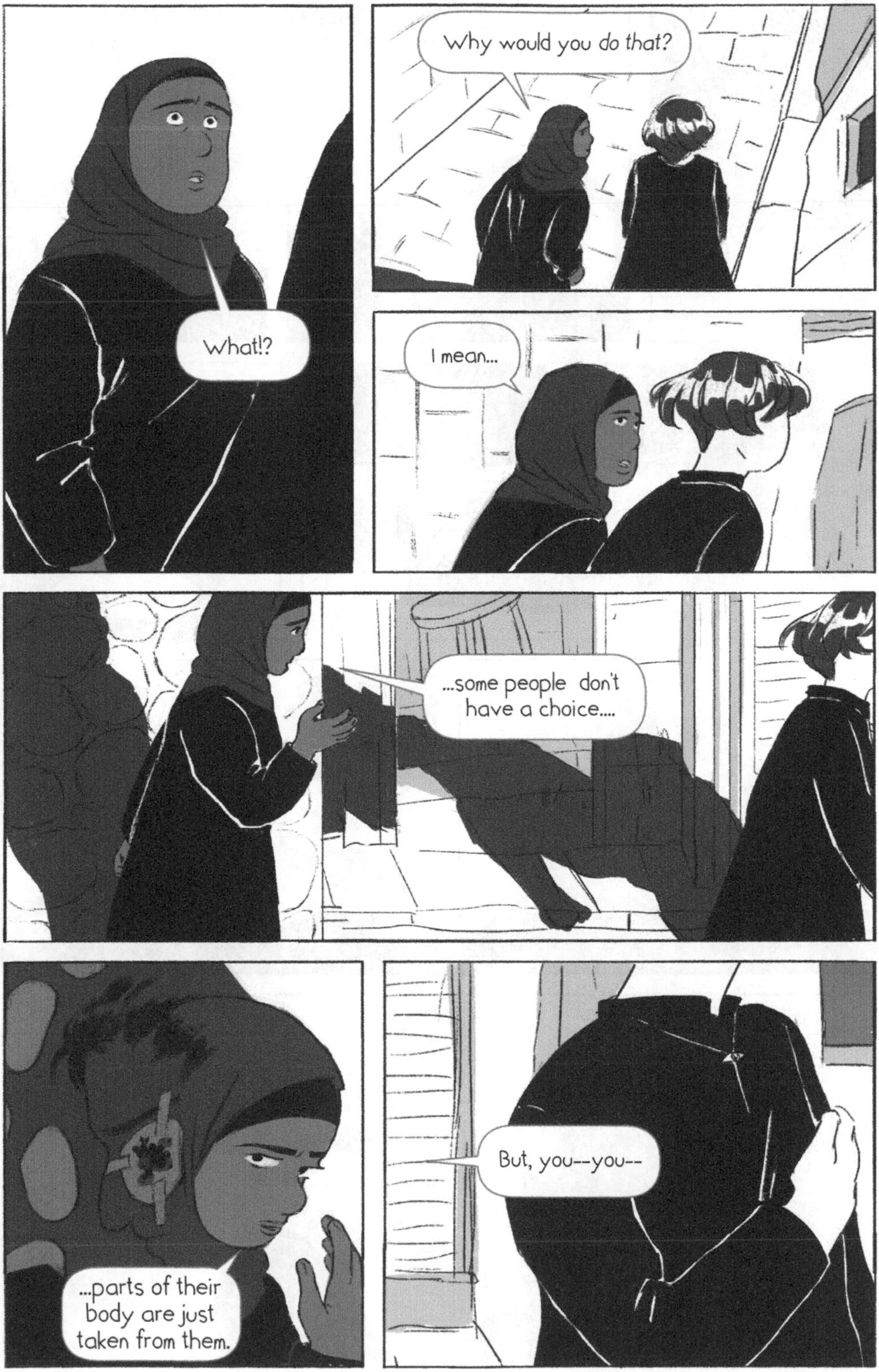
What!?
Why would you do that?
I mean...
...some people don't have a choice....
...parts of their body are just taken from them.
But, you--you--

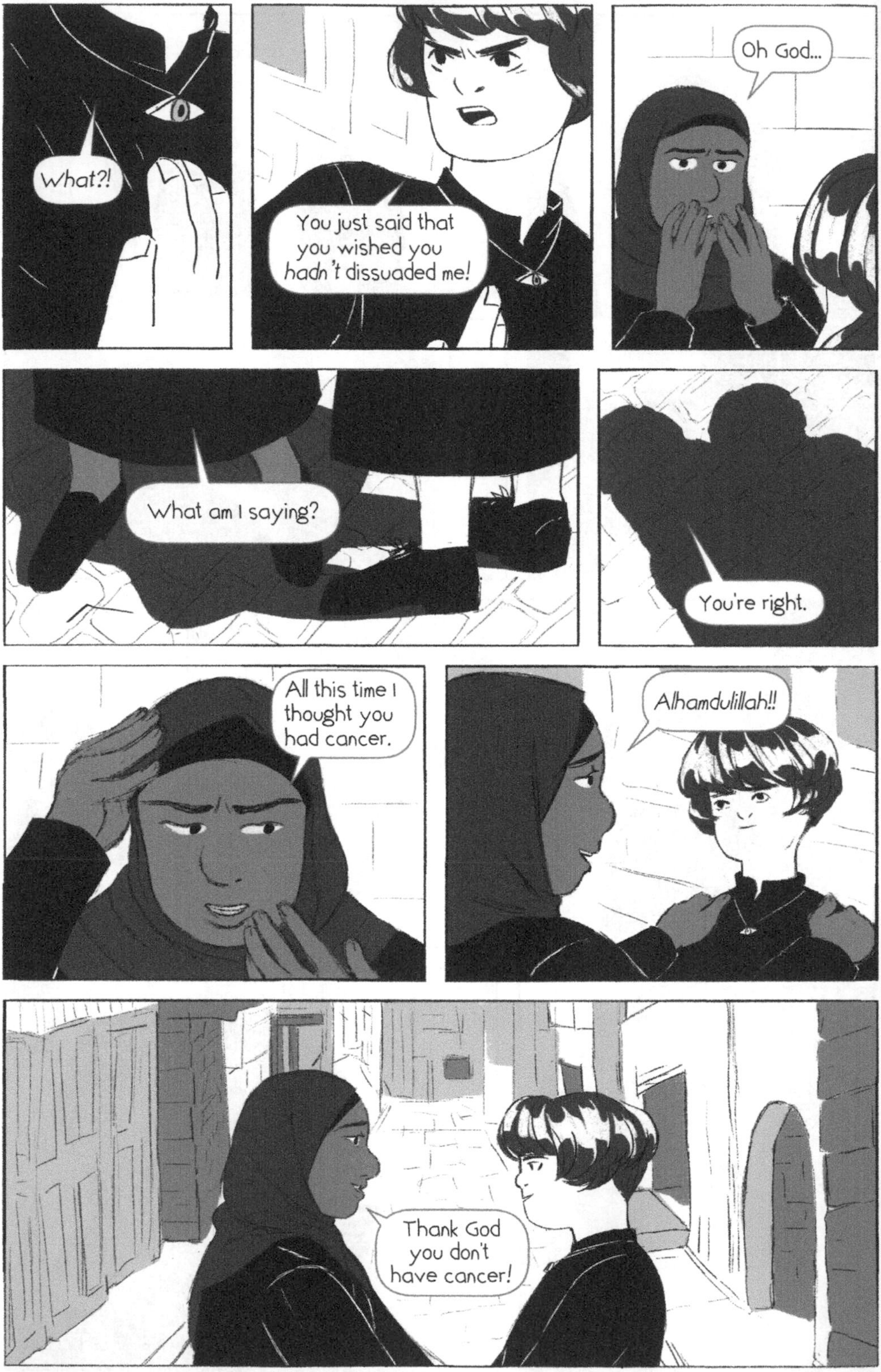
What?!
You just said that you wished you *hadn't* dissuaded me!
Oh God...
What am I saying?
You're right.
All this time I thought you had cancer.
Alhamdulillah!!
Thank God you don't have cancer!

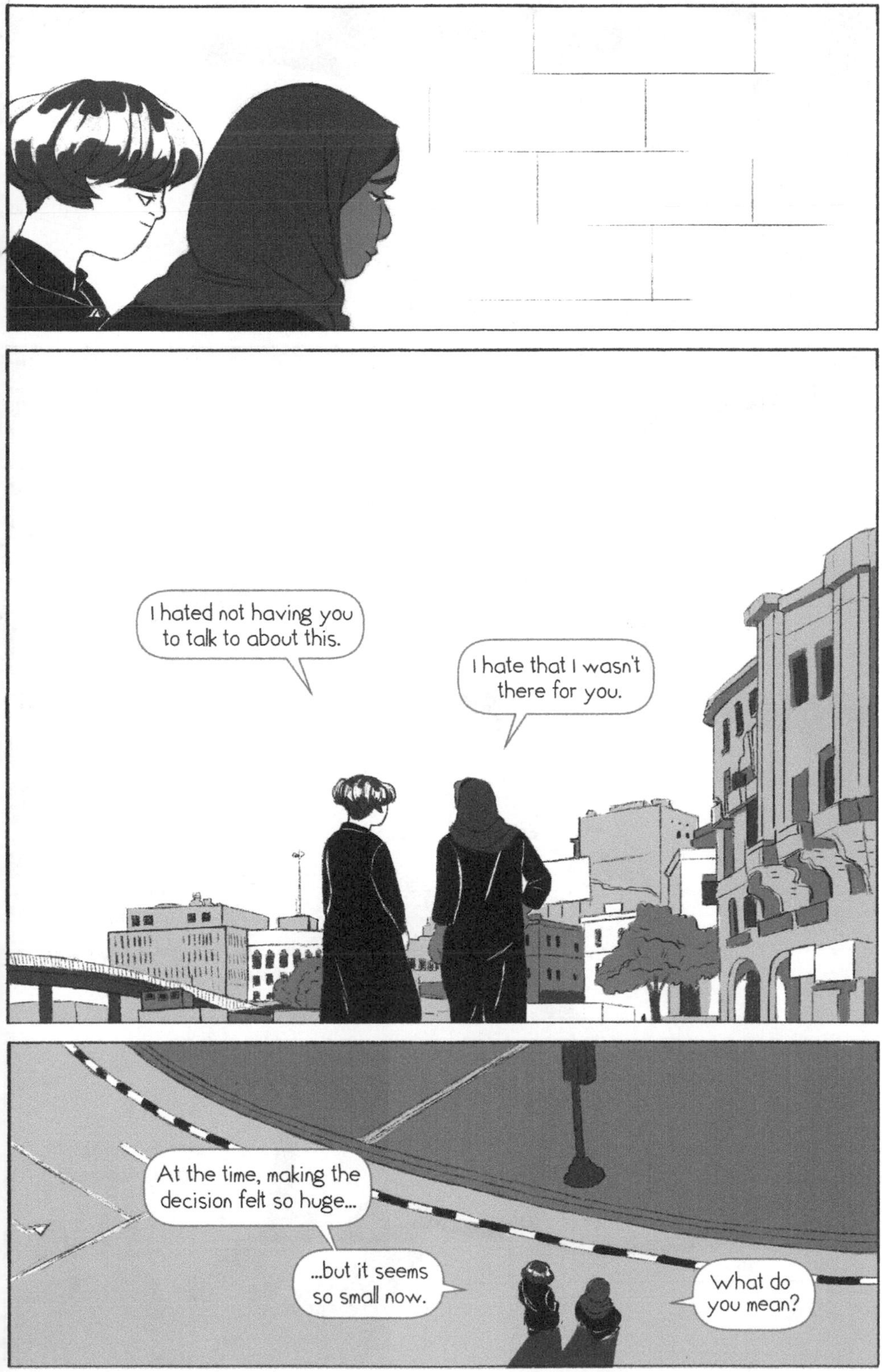
I hated not having you to talk to about this.
I hate that I wasn't there for you.
At the time, making the decision felt so huge...
...but it seems so small now.
What do you mean?

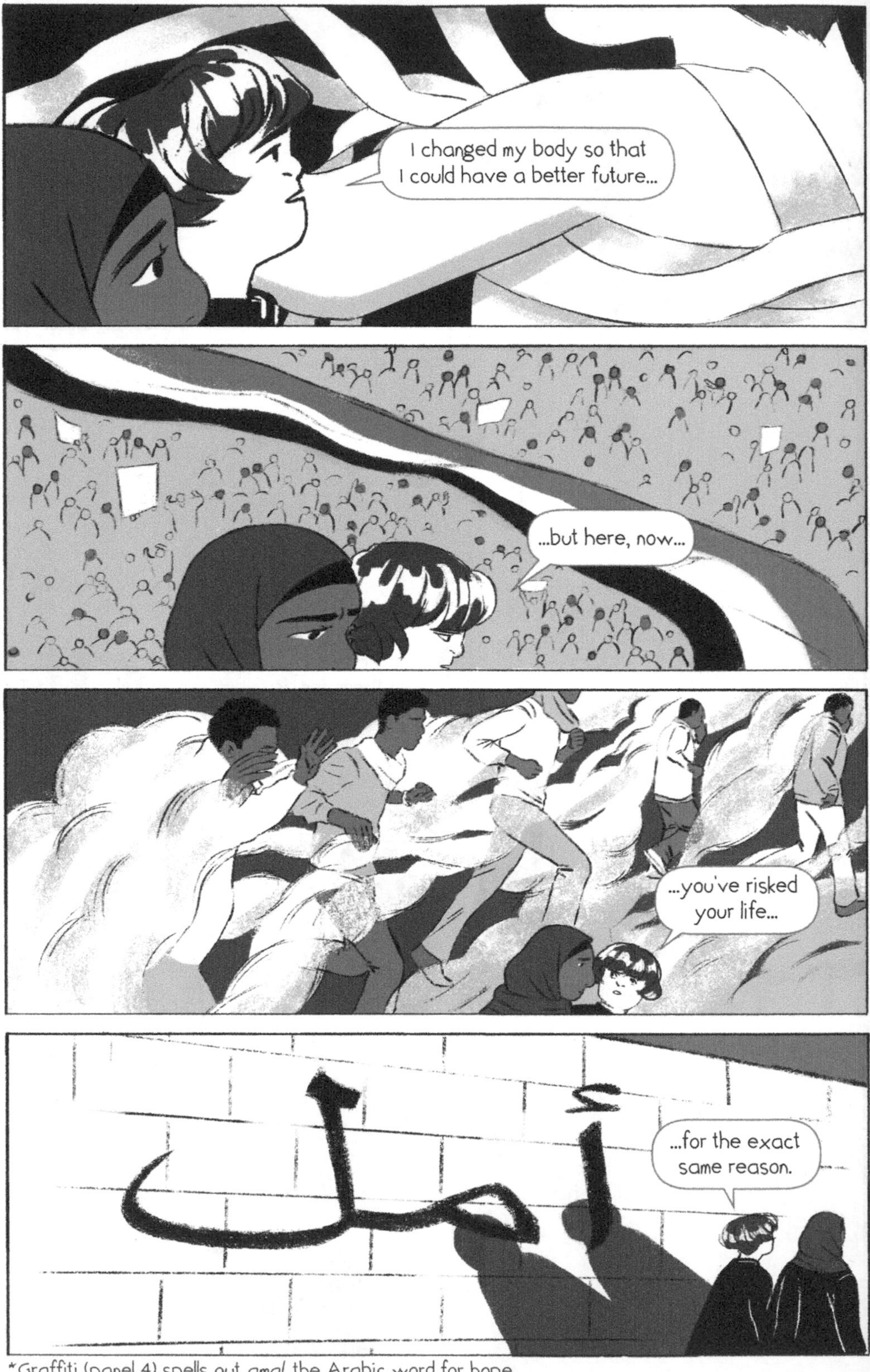
I changed my body so that I could have a better future...
...but here, now...
...you've risked your life...
...for the exact same reason.

*Graffiti (panel 4) spells out *amal*, the Arabic word for hope.

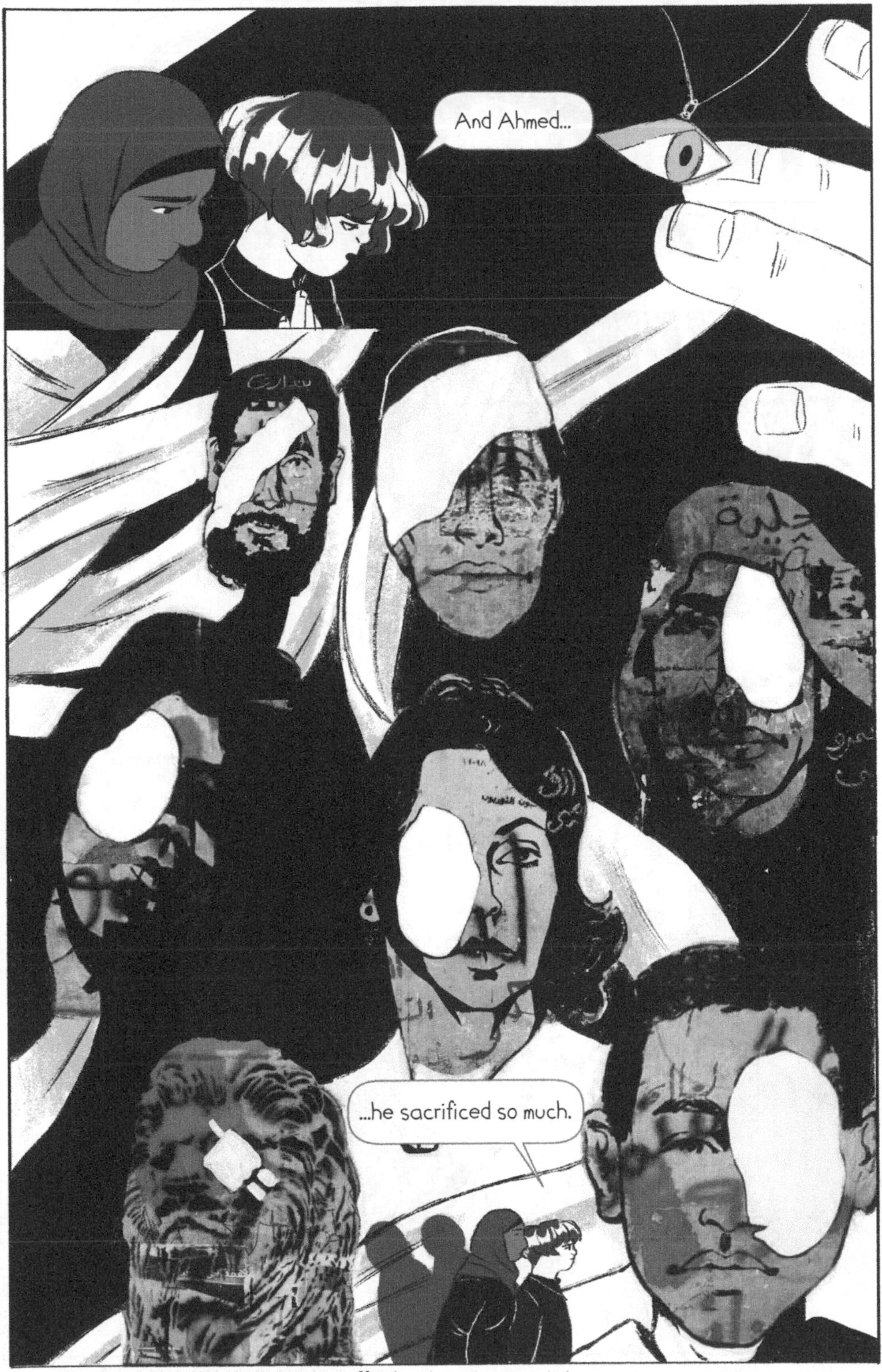
And Ahmed...
...he sacrificed so much.

*Graffiti, "Lost Eyes" by Abo Bakr **Graffiti (lion) by unknown artist

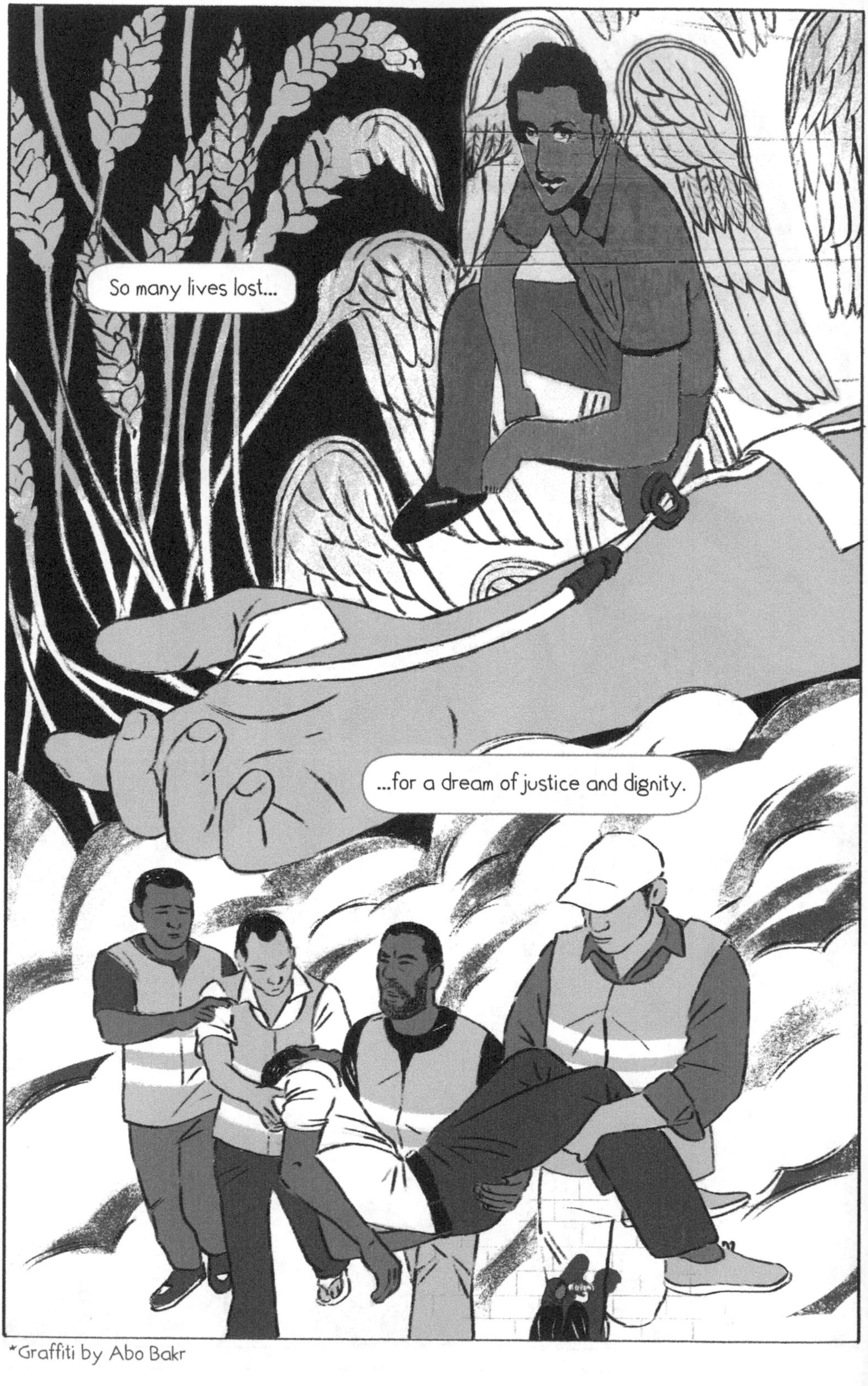
So many lives lost...
...for a dream of justice and dignity.

*Graffiti by Abo Bakr

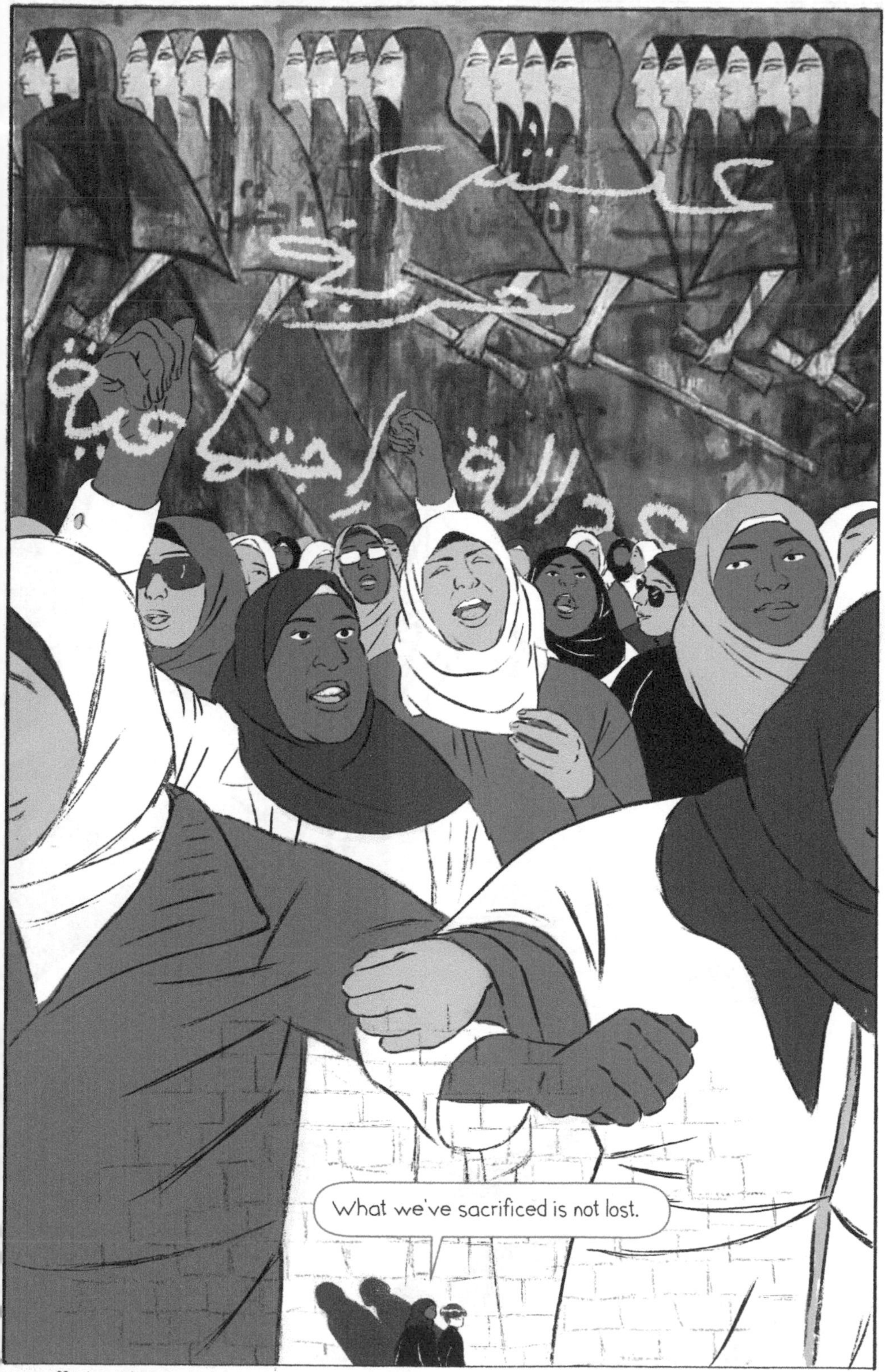
What we've sacrificed is not lost.

* Graffiti by Alaa Awad

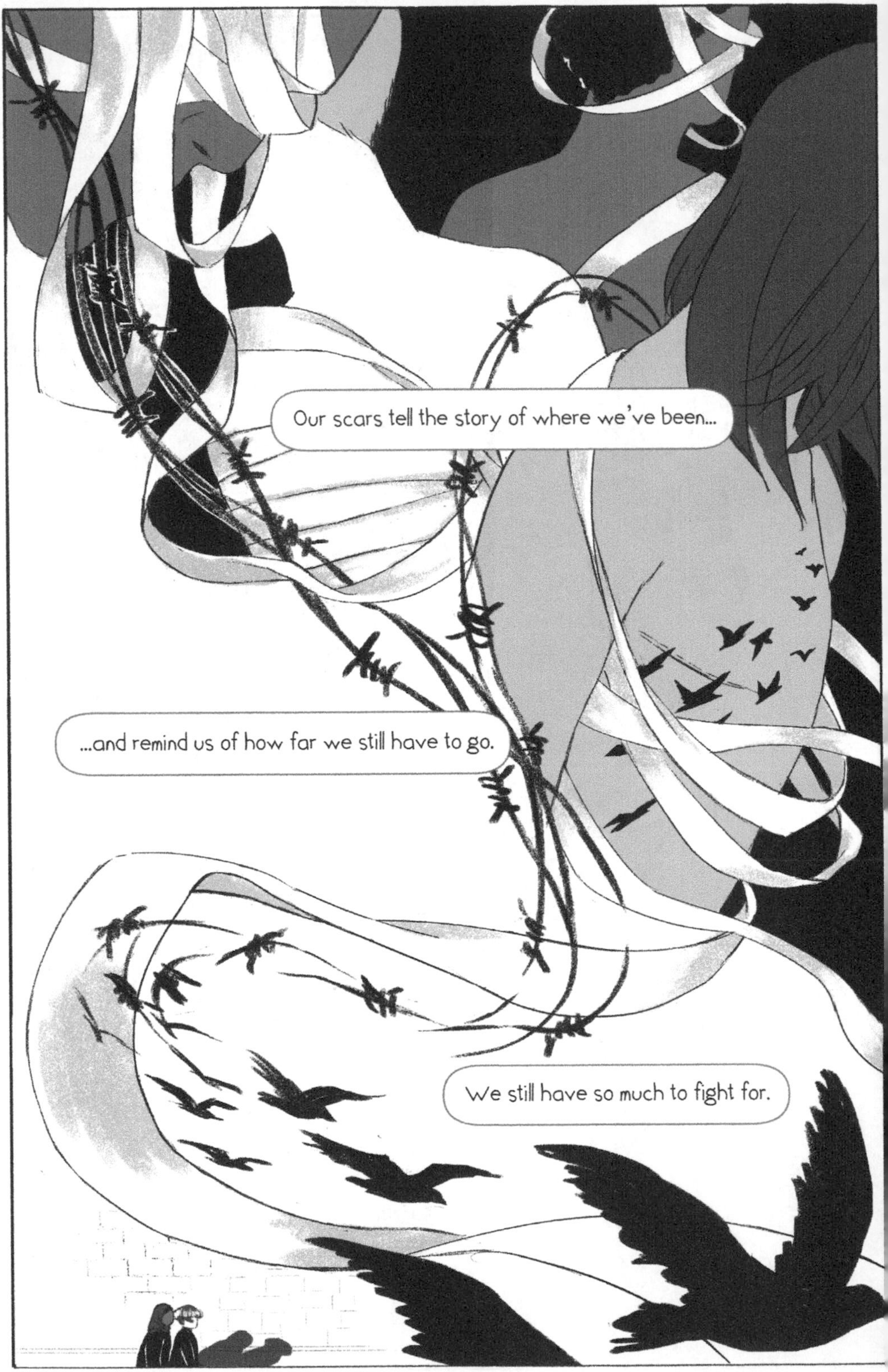
Our scars tell the story of where we've been...
...and remind us of how far we still have to go.
We still have so much to fight for.

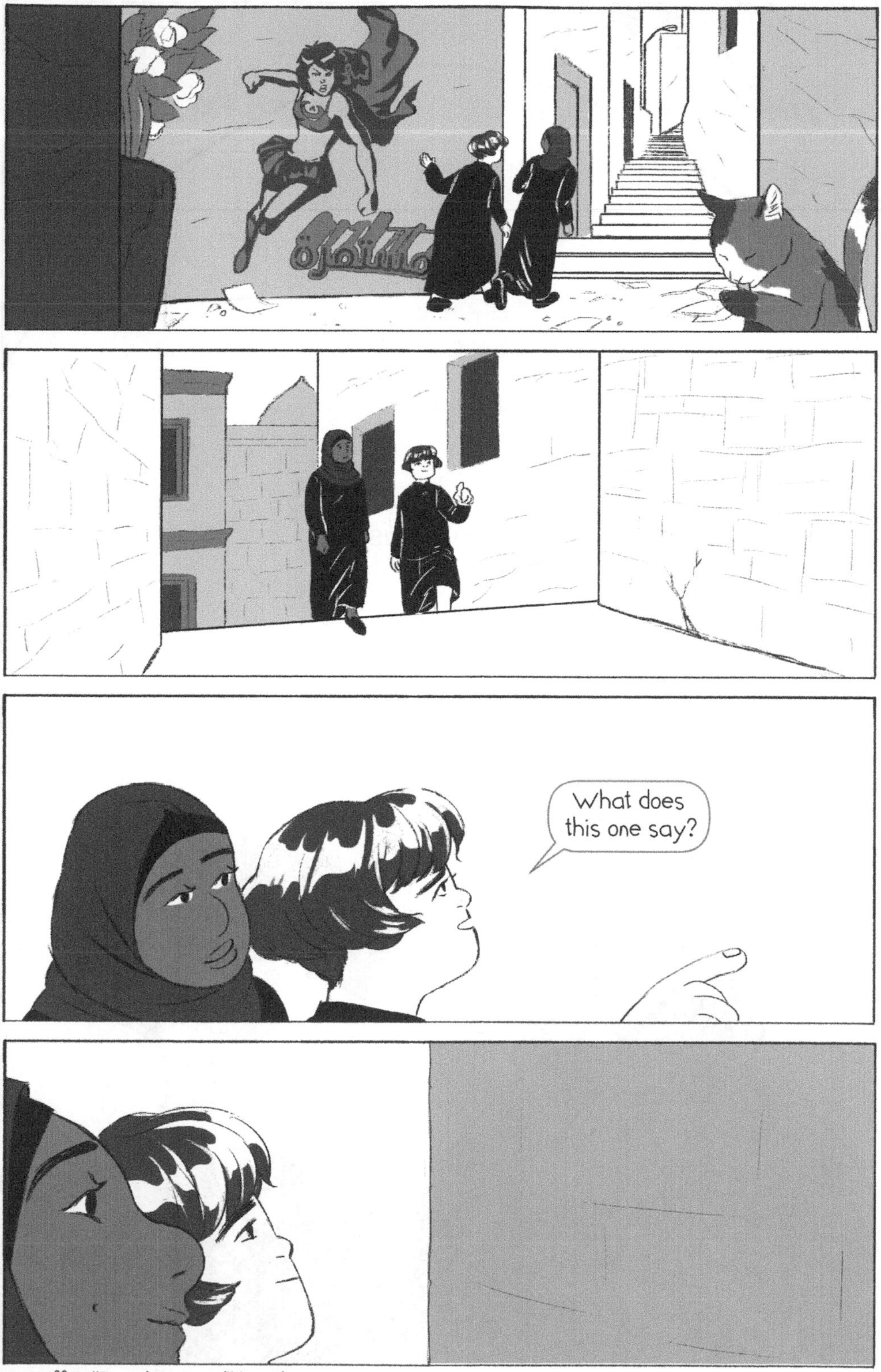
What does this one say?

*Graffiti, "Revolution Girl" by El Teneen

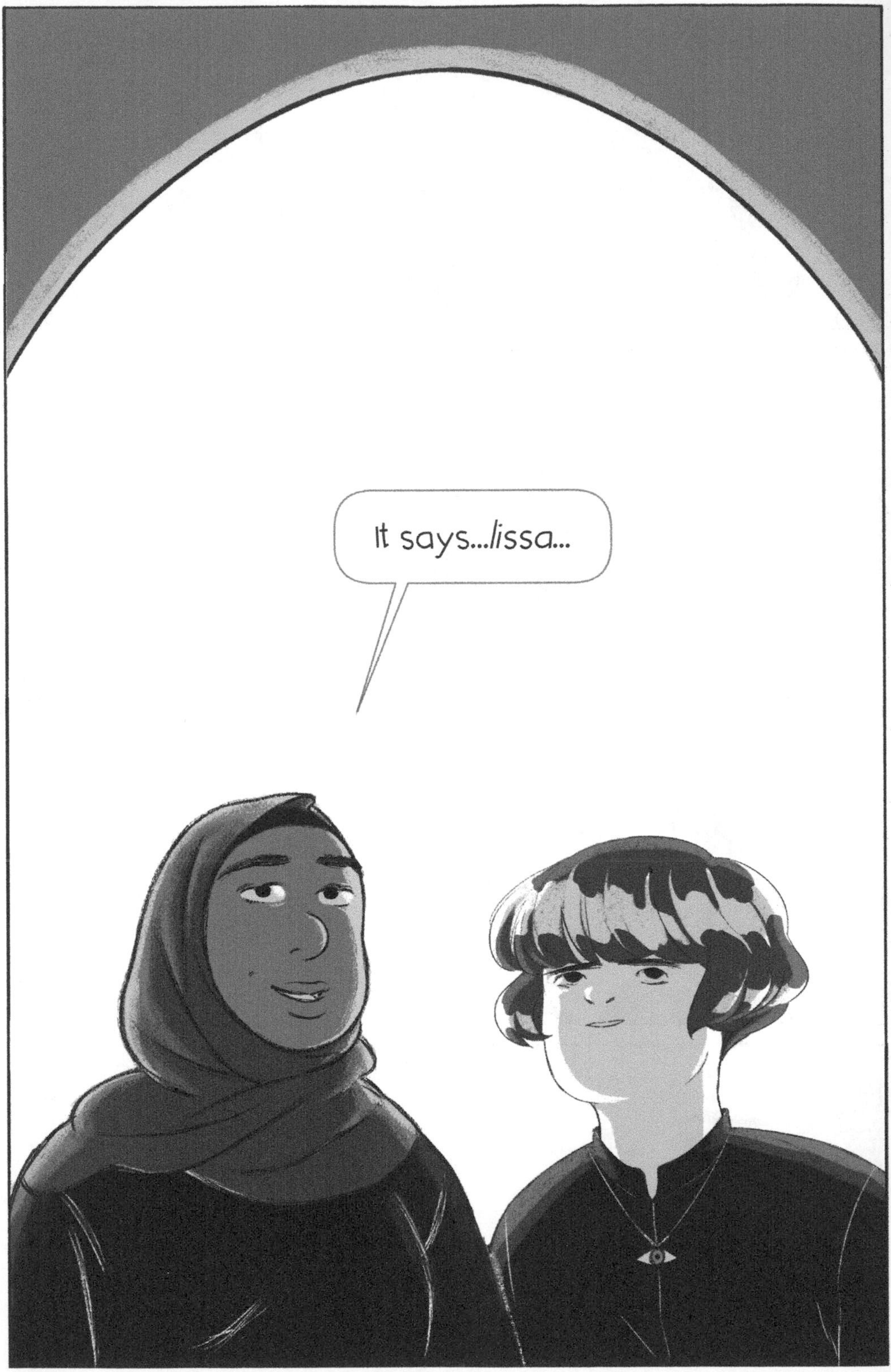
It says...*lissa*...

...there's still time.

*Mural by Ganzeer. See the appendix for more information. **Square-Script Translation (boxed letters in the center upon which the winged cat sits): "The Revolution Will Never Die"

A NOTE ABOUT PAGE 235, FEATURING THE ART OF GANZEER.

In this tremendous composition, Ganzeer integrates the work of his fellow street artists to relay the message to Anna and Layla that *lissa*, still, not all hope is lost.

In following with our hopes to integrate the work of revolutionaries themselves, we were ecstatic that Ganzeer agreed to design the composition of the graffiti on page 235. Ganzeer was a street artist at the time of the Egyptian revolution and is now an author/artist in the us. He is a model of collaboration, often seizing opportunities to showcase the work of his peers. You can learn more about him here: http://www.ganzeer.com/. We provide here short descriptions of the pieces cited in the mural, moving clockwise in numbered order. For more information and for images of the original art works, please visit the official Lissa website at http://www.lissagraphicnovel.com.

1. Ganzeer's "Cat of Defiance" visually echoes the cats who moved through Anna and Layla's lives and friendship. We see the bandages on the cat's injured eye, limb and tail, and the characteristic wings of martyrdom that were used throughout Egypt's revolutionary street art to commemorate those who died for the cause.

2. Directly under the cat's wing is the work of graffiti artist Ammar Abo Bakr, who based this design on a photograph of the activist Sanaa Seif taken on January 25, 2016. On the one-year anniversary of the revolu-

tion, she walked from Mostafa Mahmoud Square to Tahrir Square to commemorate the marches that took place between those spaces from 2011–2014. Seif's jacket was designed by Ammar Abo Bakr and Mohamed El-Moshir with the words "It's still [lissa] the January Revolution."

3. Immediately under the image of Sanaa Seif is an uncredited stencil. It depicts a woman dancing, and is accompanied by the words "Dance to the tunes of the Revolution, not the emergency law."

4. Underneath this is graffiti artist Keizer's stencil of a woman shouting "To the Government—Fear us!"

5. The uncredited calligraphy to the left of Anna and Layla reads, "The Revolution will persist until victory."

6. Just above this on the left hand margin, the iconic calligraphy by Gaber reads "Be with the Revolution." This calligraphic design was ubiquitous throughout the days of protest.

7. To the right of the calligraphy are two hands pressed together in prayer with the sign of the evil eye on them. This piece by El Zeft includes a thread of text along the bottom that reads, "May God let the revolution prevail and never perish.".

8. Just at the tip of the cat's left wing is a stencil by Nooneswa of three women: one bare-headed, one with a head covering, and one with a full face-veil, with the words, "Don't put a label on me."

9. Finally, the blocked letters in the center upon which the winged cat sits, appear as a maze, but when turned clockwise 90 degrees, the Arabic letters—gesturing to the classic Kufic calligraphic style—spell out *al-thawra mustamira*: "The Revolution Will Never Die." This piece was designed by Ganzeer.

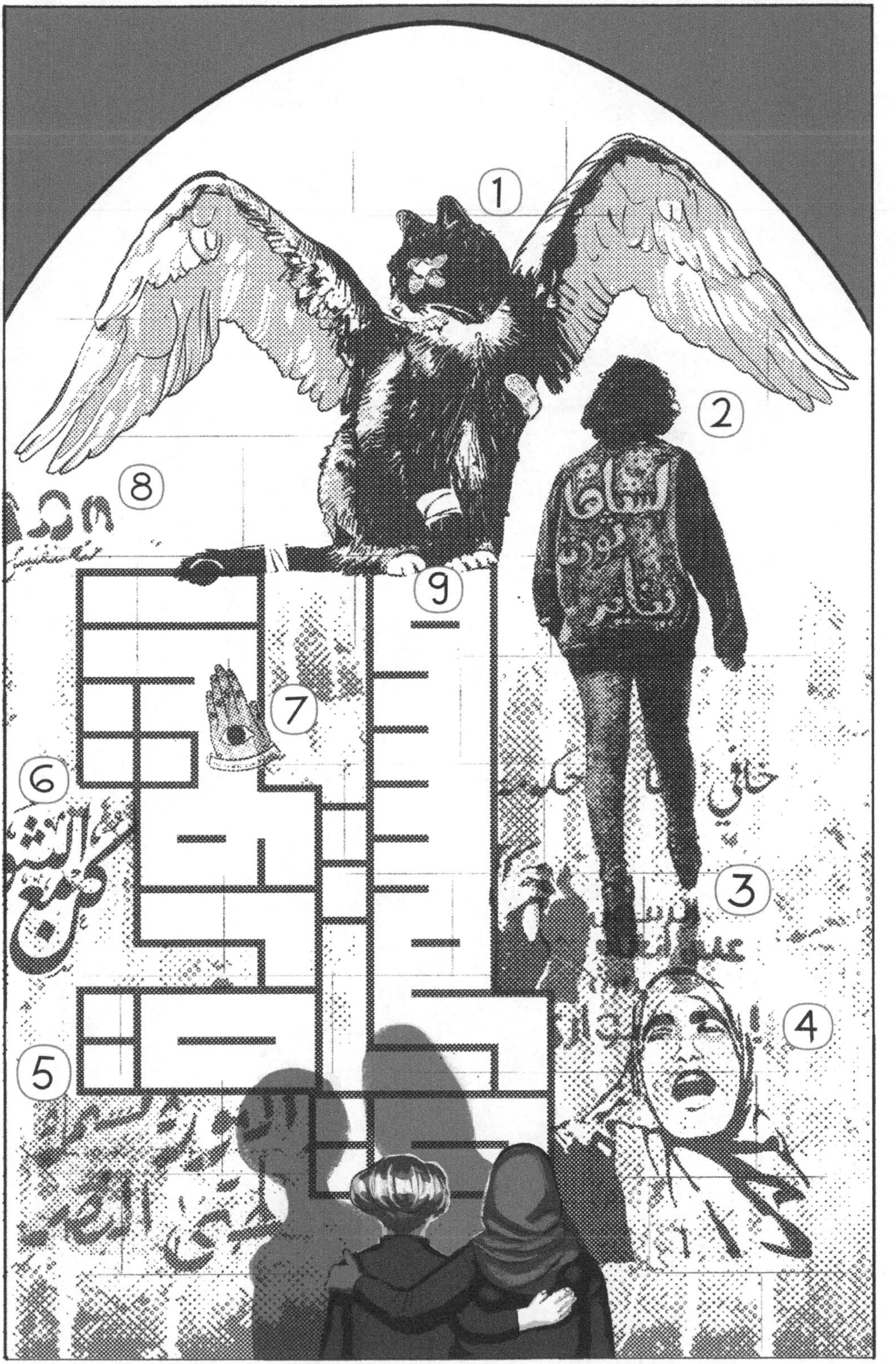
1
2
3
4
5
6
7
8
9

AFTERWORD

READING *LISSA*

PAUL KARASIK*

A friend told me about his recent ride in the Tokyo subway. He sat across from a woman reading one of the ubiquitous monthly manga magazines, not an uncommon sight. Though he tried not to pay attention to her absorbed reading of the digest-sized, square-bound comic book, the sound of her rapidly flipping through the pages was riveting.

They got off at the same stop just as she finished the book.

My friend, a cartoonist, was stunned and shaken. It could take him a week to complete a single page of comics. In the time it took this reader to consume a couple of hundred pages of comics, my friend might have penciled one panel.

There is something so beguiling about the combination of words and pictures in sequence that, once you start, it's hard to stop turning the pages.

Generally, cartoonists structure a page of comics to be easily tracked. If the reader is confused about the order of who is speaking in a panel, for instance, and the reading is detoured, the cartoonist has not done a good job.

But tracking is only one of the tasks. The cartoonist may purposefully use the language of comics to control what the reader knows and, equally important, what the reader *feels* about the information in ways the reader may never notice.

That subway reader sprinted, charging on to find out what was going to happen next, but the cartoonist was no doubt subliminally creating layers of meaning that enhanced the reading, even at that rate of absorption.

---

* Paul Karasik is a cartoonist and comics instructor at RISD. He selected the artists Caroline Brewer and Sarula Bao for *Lissa* and supervised their initial artwork.

Lissa is a complex story spanning two cultures, two families, several medical emergencies, and a sociopolitical revolution, but it never feels confusing. You may not be able to (or *want* to) read it in a single subway ride, as one is intended to read manga, but it flows smoothly.

This is no less an accomplishment given the fact that it was written by two authors—Sherine Hamdy and Coleman Nye—who have expertise in different fields of research, and that it was drawn by two artists—Sarula Bao and Caroline Brewer—who have two distinct drawing styles. All together, they have figured out a unique and clever way of taking ownership of parts of the story while weaving them into a cohesive whole.

This team is more than merely interested in giving you a clear, smooth ride. The authors and illustrators take advantage of their specific knowledge of how comics work to feed the reader more than just the surface story.

Perhaps if I highlight in this introduction a few examples of their control of the medium, the reader can begin to see how intentional cartooning creates layers of meaning and implicit understandings.

* * *

Let's take a look at the depiction of Anna's father. Anna, one of the two main protagonists in *Lissa*, is close to her mother, but her father remains distant. When she needs him, he is not fully there. He is not antagonistic toward his daughter, just unconnected and preoccupied with his work. The artists reinforce this distance by not showing his face, having it obscured, cut off by the panel framing, or, in a scene located at the beach, just barely rendered.

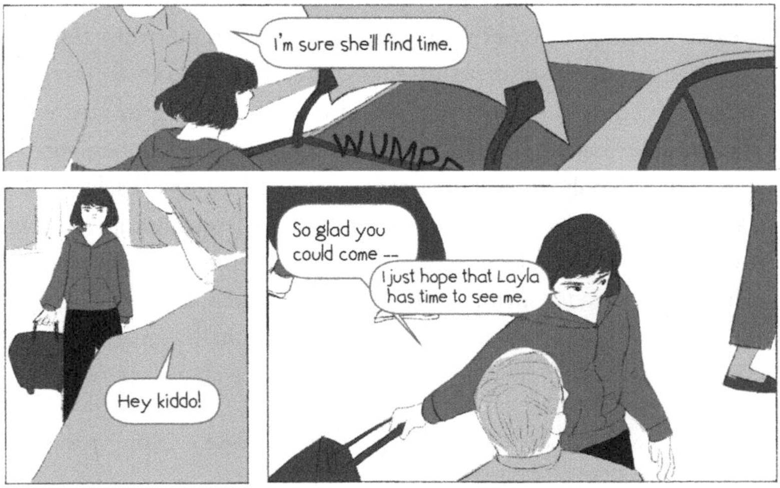
I'm sure she'll find time.
Hey kiddo!
So glad you could come --
I just hope that Layla has time to see me.

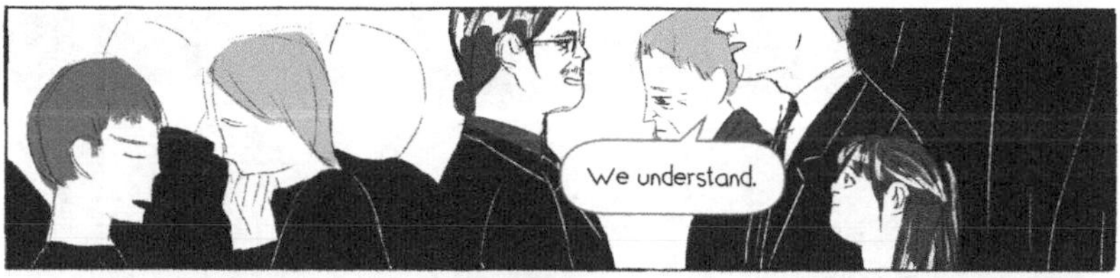
We understand.

It is at the turning point in the father-daughter relationship that his face is suddenly revealed. At that moment, what is also revealed is that it has taken Anna's change of heart to effect the manifestation of her father (and his face) in her life. He has not been the only one keeping them apart; it has been in Anna's power all along to bring him into her heart. The authors make this clear in the dialogue in the panel just before his face is revealed. And when his unexpected face suddenly appears, words collide with pictures and comics magic occurs.

Words and pictures conspiring together to create meaning and understanding in this fashion can only happen in comics.

* * *

Early on, the reader learns that Anna's mother has cancer. A brief scene of the daughter comforting her mother in the bathroom ends with the mother losing clumps of hair, as a consequence of her chemotherapy treatment. Anna pockets those clumps, and the reader forgets that she has held onto them until 9 pages later in the book, when the reader sees Anna putting together her "memory box" and is reminded of the hair in a panel that is located in the same spot on the page as the earlier one: the lower right corner. Another 13 pages after that, the pouch of hair emerges again in Anna's pocket, this time in a panel sequence composed in the same manner as the original.

This is done without any redundant text to underline the obvious because, in comics, there is usually no need to both tell and show. The reader instantly makes the connection to that earlier moment, and a very specific emotional bridge is deftly constructed visually. Again, this is a certain type of visual resonance one can feel only from comics.

* * *

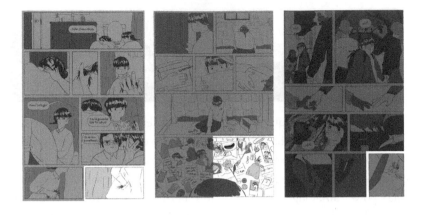

As the end point of a comics page, the bottom right corner is a key location. It can be used to conclude a scene or to pose a question or as a cliffhanger to urge the reader to flip to the next page. Here are a few lower right corner panels lifted out of context. Without knowing what comes before or after, notice how compelling they are. Throughout the book, the creators use this vital location—the lower right corner panel—in intriguing and unexpected ways.

Is it Baba?
:sniff: It's Baba :sniff: and it's my mom! Her cancer was genetic--
Hey!!!
You look like you've seen a ghost.
No, don't!
Please..
..It's just first-aid supplies.
They said they'd throw us back in prison if we didn't--
Forgive us.

* * *

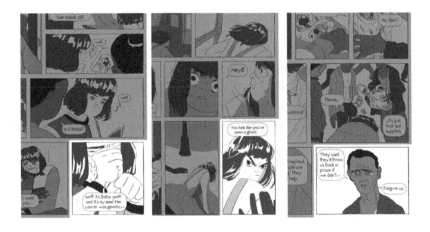

A tier in a comics page is a horizontal row of information that can be used strategically to relate moments in a tight, brief sequence. Throughout *Lissa*, the artists employ the tier to explore the relationship between the two protagonists, Anna and Layla. More than once, the artists use the panel gutters to reinforce the gulf between them.

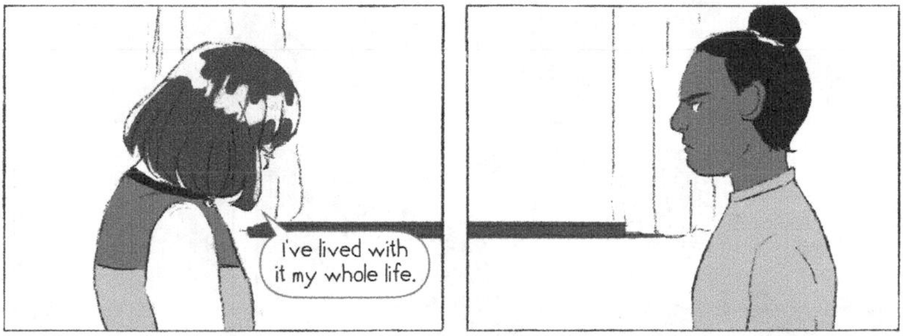
I've lived with it my whole life.

Their friendship ebbs and flows. After a dangerous event separates them, they rush to each other's embrace to reunite in a single panel.

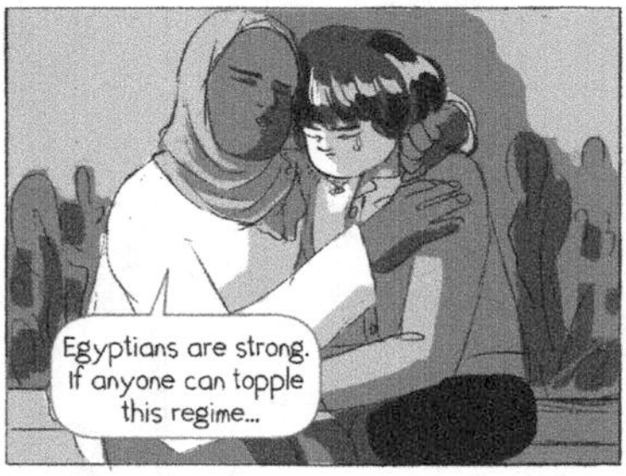
Egyptians are strong. If anyone can topple this regime...

But then personal secrets and misunderstandings pull them apart again on the very next page, with a literal space separating them.

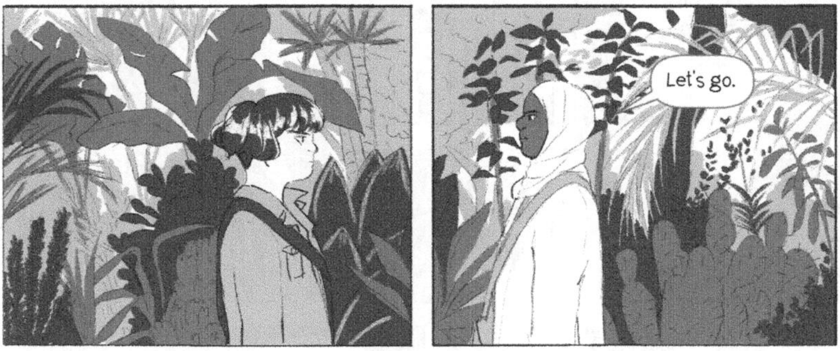
Let's go.

* * *

Moving from an analysis of single panels, through tiers, let's look at the design of an entire page that shows Anna on the cusp of making a life-changing decision.

In this tour de force of whole-page design, the creators show Anna weighing her options on an airplane surrounded by strangers. An establishing shot at the top of the page shows her smack-dab in the center of the panel, the seats of strangers drawn in curved exaggerated perspective stretching away from her. This composition cues the reader as to her self-absorbed mental state.

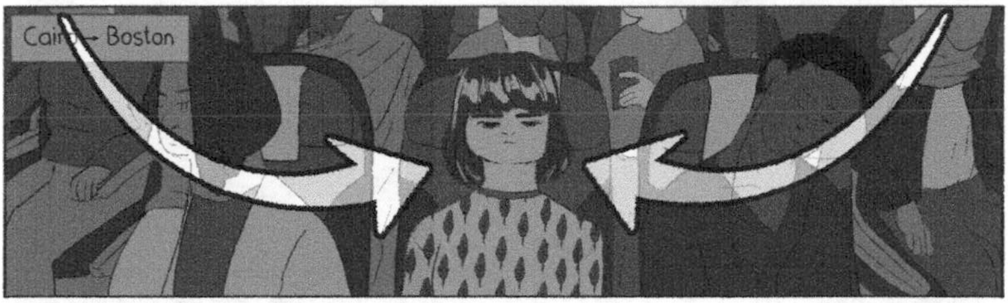

Cai → Boston

It is not a huge leap, then, for the reader to go bouncing from side to side as strangers are replaced by Anna's visions of friends and family giving her advice. It helps that the word balloons are abnormally jagged, tipping the reader off that these are voices of a different sort.

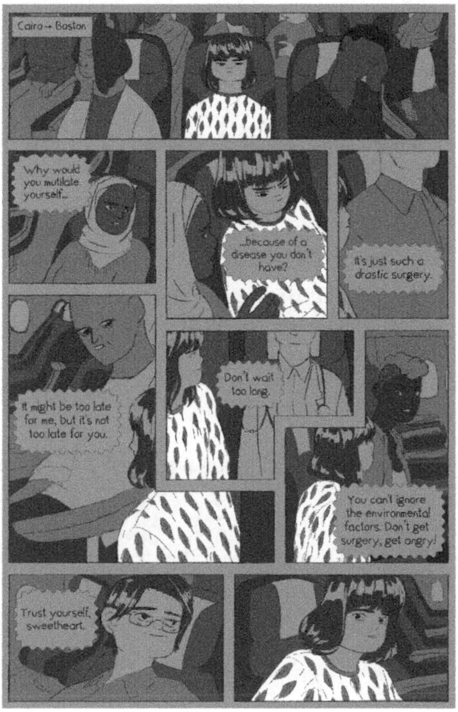

Cairo → Boston
Why would you mutilate yourself...
...because of a disease you don't have?
It's just such a drastic surgery.
It might be too late for me, but it's not too late for you.
Don't wait too long.
You can't ignore the environmental factors. Don't get surgery, get angry!
Trust yourself, sweetheart.

Note how the artists use Anna's shirt to identify her and to anchor the page. Her uniquely patterned top makes Anna instantly recognizable and allows for swift visual tracking as she turns her head back and forth, hearing the voices of imaginary advisors in her head.

The irregular shape and size of the panels help to simulate the herky-jerky rhythm of Anna's head swinging from side to side, yet the page is so thoughtfully composed that we never lose track of the correct sequence of events. Imagine the same page with panels of equal shape and size, which would create a monotonous and calm rhythm, out of step with Anna's turbulent mindset.

Why would you mutilate yourself...
...because of a disease you don't have?
It's just such a *drastic* surgery.
It might be too late for me, but it's not too late for you.
Don't wait too long.
You can't ignore the environmental factors. Don't get surgery, get angry!

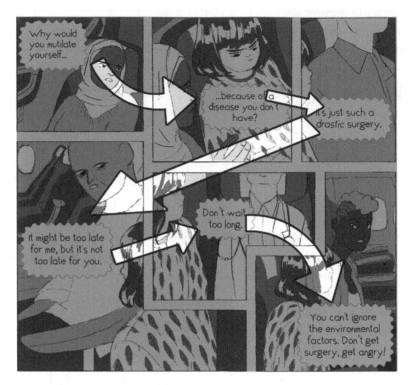

The specter of her mother appears in the penultimate panel with a word of motherly advice. Then, in the final panel, Anna turns toward her phantom mother. Or is it the reader to whom she turns? Because of Anna's direct gaze, we *become* her mother, and there is a look of concern on Anna's mute face, which cannot help but move the reader who has been deftly jockeyed into the place of the mother.

Trust yourself, sweetheart.

A minor but significant detail in that last image is the row of empty seats behind Anna. Over the course of the page, the full plane with flesh and blood passengers has emptied out.

This sneaky detail, overshadowed by Anna's expression, seems subliminally to underline Anna's feeling of isolation as she struggles with her internal conflicts.

* * *

Lissa spans years. As links, visually connecting the friendship of the protagonists, cats prowl throughout this book. They first appear on page 20 when Anna and Layla are young:

flit
flit

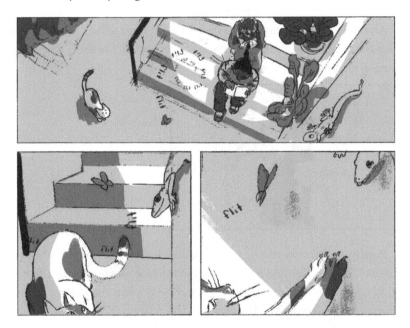

When the girls separate, Layla has a cat to comfort her:

Madame Sarah told me once that we all worship God in different ways. Our religion was revealed in the desert, and we return our bodies to the earth...

When they reunite several years later, a cat is there alongside Anna and Layla.

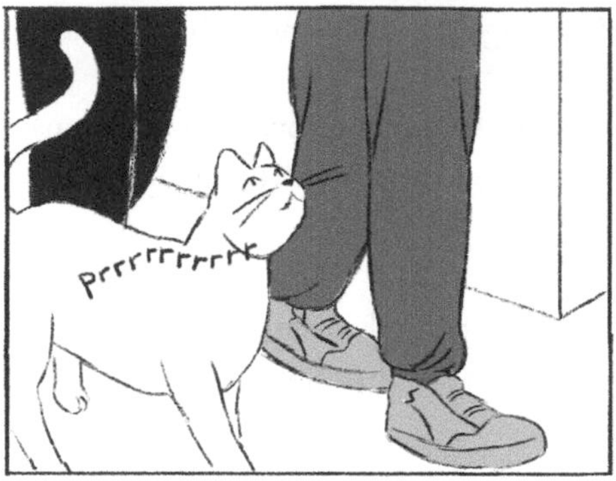
prrrrrrrrrr

And when Anna hears Layla's call for help from across the ocean and makes the difficult decision to overcome bitterness and reunite, a pair of cat statues symbolizes their deep bond.

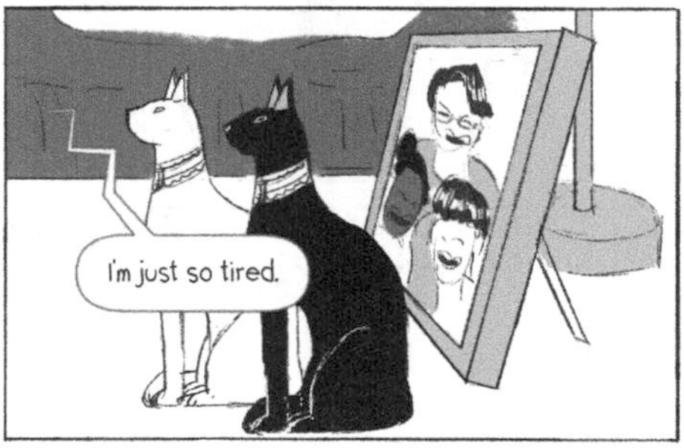
I'm just so tired.

Finally, at the very end of the book, just before the two friends lay all their cards on the table and realize together the true meaning of sacrifice and justice, when they realize that their actions today affect themselves and others tomorrow, when they realize that the dark past could be a stepping stone toward an optimistic future, a cat links their history and leads the way... showing them that there is still time.

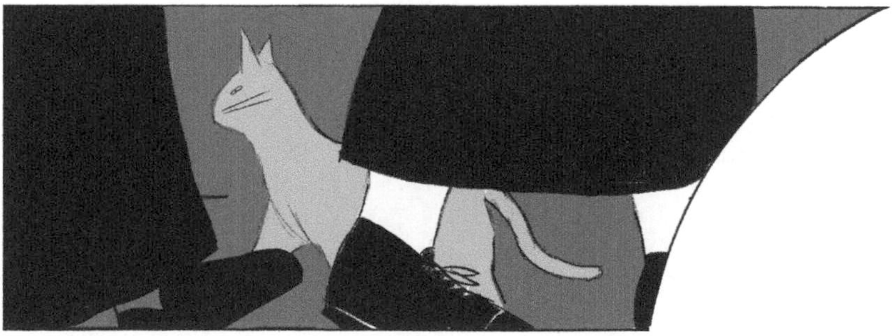

APPENDIX I

TIMELINE OF THE 2011 EGYPTIAN REVOLUTION

A select timeline of events leading up to the revolution or pre-revolution, as depicted in Lissa:

JUNE 6, 2010

Layla and Anna both follow the events around Khaled Said's death. Layla becomes involved with the April 6 Movement, and Anna follows the Facebook posts and international coverage.

→ Twenty-eight-year-old Egyptian Khaled Said is brutally beaten and tortured by two police officers in Alexandria, after reportedly posting a video to the Internet showing several officers sharing the spoils of a drug bust.

→ Images of Said's brutalized face circulate widely, and he becomes a symbol of the corruption and violence of Mubarak's security forces.

→ Five days after Said's death, Wael Ghonim, Google's head of marketing for the Middle East and North Africa, anonymously creates the Arabic-language Facebook page "We Are All Khaled Said" to protest rampant police brutality, torture, and corruption. In January 2011, the page becomes a hotbed of planning and activity for the members of the April 6 Movement and others mobilizing for the Day of Anger on January 25.

Ahmed and others encounter riot police and hired thugs blocking them when they try to vote in the parliamentary elections.

→   Parliamentary elections are held. Many have called this the most fraudulent election in Egyptian history. There is massive, and at times violent, voter suppression, including closed polling stations, armed thugs, and police chasing people away and even tear-gassing observers. Of those who do manage to vote, some report that their ballots were already marked for Mubarak's National Democratic Party (NDP). The results of the election give the overwhelming majority of seats to the NDP.

JANUARY 17, 2011

Layla and Anna watch international news coverage of Abdo Abdel-moneim's self-immolation outside of Cairo's parliament building.

→   Restaurant owner Abdo Abdelmoneim sets himself on fire outside Cairo's parliament building after a dispute with local authorities over receiving his monthly coupons for subsidized bread. One day later, 25-year-old Egyptian Ahmed Hashem el-Sayed in Alexandria is the second Egyptian to set himself ablaze. Both events are apparently inspired by the Tunisian fruit-seller Mohamed Bouazizi, whose self-immolation triggered a popular uprising in December 2010.

THE 2011 REVOLUTION BEGINS
JANUARY 25, 2011—DAY OF ANGER

Layla, Reem, and others take to Tahrir Square to protest corruption and injustice.

→   On National Police Day, over 45,000 protesters take to the streets across Egypt to protest the abuses of the police, as well as to demand the resignation of the minister of the interior, the end of emergency rule, term limits for the president, and the restoration of a fair minimum wage.

JANUARY 27, 2011

→ After internal disagreements, the Muslim Brotherhood declares its support for the protesters.

→ Over 600 people are arrested in Cairo, including 8 Egyptian journalists and Google executive Wael Ghonim (creator of the "We Are All Khaled Said" Facebook page), who was captured early in the morning on January 28.

→ Seven people are reported dead since the revolution started.

JANUARY 28, 2011—FRIDAY OF ANGER/ DAY OF RAGE

→ The government shuts down Internet services to thwart protester communication.

→ Curfew is mandated, but the protesters defy it and set fire to the NDP headquarters.

→ The government deploys the army, although most troops don't want armed confrontation with protesters.

JANUARY 29, 2011

→ Protesters continue to gather in great force in Tahrir Square.

→ At least three people are killed outside the Ministry of the Interior when protestors attempt to storm the building.

→ At least 100 people have been killed in protests so far.

JANUARY 30, 2011

→ Around 5,000 protesters are joined in Tahrir Square by state judges.

→ The army refuses the Mubarak government's order to use live ammunition on the protesters.

→ Mubarak asks Ahmed Shafik, a Mubarak loyalist and aviation minister, to form a new government.

→ *Al Jazeera*'s offices are ordered to be closed and correspondents' credentials are revoked.

FEBRUARY 1, 2011—MARCH OF THE MILLIONS

→ *Al Jazeera* reports over 1 million people gathering in Tahrir Square to march on the Presidential Palace. Hundreds of thousands gather in Alexandria, and 250,000 in Suez.

→ Mubarak announces he won't run in the September 2011 elections

→ The UN reports more than 300 people dead, 3,000 injured since the beginning of the protests

FEBRUARY 2, 2011—BATTLE OF THE CAMEL

Layla frantically attends to wounded protesters in a makeshift field hospital, and Anna brings her supplies but is intercepted by hired thugs.

→ Mubarak supporters storm Tahrir Square on camels and horses and drop Molotov cocktails and firebombs from buildings onto the protesters. At least 11 people are killed and between 600 and 1,000 are injured.

→ Internet services are partially restored after a five-day blackout.

FEBRUARY 3, 2011—CAIRO STANDOFF

→ In front of the Egyptian Museum, the army fires rocks, petrol bombs, and shots at protesters. There is heavy police violence, and hungry protesters are bribed with food, painkillers (Tramadol), and money to support Mubarak.

→ Many international journalists in Egypt are detained, beaten, and threatened by pro-Mubarak protesters.

→ Mubarak and Vice-President Suleiman refuse to step down.

FEBRUARY 4, 2011—FRIDAY OF DEPARTURE

→ The journalist Ahmed Mohamed Mahmoud of Al-Ta'awun dies after sustaining heavy gunshot wounds earlier in the week.

→ Christians form a human chain to protect 2 million Egyptian Muslims who are in Tahrir Square for Friday prayer.

FEBRUARY 5, 2011

→ Pro-Mubarak protesters attempt to assault anti-Mubarak demonstrators in Tahrir Square, but the military fires shots into the air to disperse them.

→ Protestors form a human chain to prevent tanks from entering the square.

FEBRUARY 6, 2011—SUNDAY OF MARTYRS

→ Protests continue and banks open temporarily, generating long queues.

→ Muslim protesters form a ring around Christians as they hold a mass in Tahrir Square in a show of interreligious solidarity (and against state media claims that protesters are violent extremists).

FEBRUARY 7, 2011

→ Wael Ghonim, the Google executive who started the "We Are All Khaled Said" Facebook page, is released from prison. His moving testimony and statement immediately upon his release are broadcast on satellite television.

FEBRUARY 8, 2011—DAY OF EGYPT'S LOVE

→ Approximately 1 million people gather in Tahrir Square to demonstrate and demand Mubarak's resignation.

FEBRUARY 9, 2011

→ There are labor strikes across the country.
→ Demonstrators amass outside of the parliament building, calling for the assembly's dissolution.
→ Egyptians living outside the country return for anti-government protests.
→ The Mubarak government threatens a military crackdown if the protests do not cease.

FEBRUARY 10, 2011

→ Hundreds of lawyers march to the Abdeen Palace, one of Mubarak's residences, calling for his resignation.
→ *Al Jazeera's* blog reports that 1,000 physicians, dressed in their white coats, arrive to join protests in Tahrir Square.
→ Strikes in the tourism and transportation industries continue.
→ Mubarak announces that he will continue as president to the end of his term in September, but will transfer his power to Suleiman.

FEBRUARY 11, 2011—SECOND FRIDAY OF DEPARTURE

Layla, Anna, and Ahmed join others in the street to celebrate Mubarak's resignation.

→ Massive protests continue in Cairo, Alexandria, and other cities.
→ Protesters surround the parliament, presidential palace, and state media building.
→ The army releases a statement saying that it supports Mubarak's choice to stay as *de jure* president.

→ Vice-President Suleiman announces at 7 PM that Mubarak has vacated his position and power has been transferred to the Supreme Council of Armed Forces (SCAF).

THE POST-2011 REVOLUTION

The revolution's second wave (February 2011 to June 2012)

FEBRUARY 12–14, 2011

→ The army suspends the current constitution and announces that the SCAF, along with Mubarak's cabinet, will stay in power until fair parliamentary and presidential elections can be held.

→ A group of activists release a "People's Communiqué No. 1" demanding:

- the dismantling of the interim cabinet Mubarak had formed on January 29, 2011, and the parliament that was elected in 2010;
- a citizen-based transitional government and "transitional presidential council";
- freedom for the media and for syndicates, such as those representing lawyers, doctors, and engineers; and
- freedom to form political parties.

→ Hundreds of police march in Tahrir Square as a show of solidarity with protesters.

→ State employees are still on strike for better pay, and the military threatens to intervene.

FEBRUARY 16, 2011

→ Several former regime ministers are arrested to be put on trial.

FEBRUARY 18, 2011

→ Formerly exiled Muslim cleric Yusuf al-Qaradawi leads a sermon in Tahrir Square that attracts thousands of people.

FEBRUARY 21, 2011

→ The news blackout is lifted as British Prime Minister David Cameron arrives in Egypt for a five-hour visit.

FEBRUARY 22, 2011

→ Yahia El-Gamal is sworn in as the new deputy prime minister.

→ The public is outraged because Mubarak's defense, interior, foreign, finance, and justice ministries are intact.

FEBRUARY 25, 2011

→ Tens of thousands flock to Tahrir Square to continue to show their displeasure at the military's slow rate of progress.

→ The military dispatches several soldiers and security officers disguised as civilians to beat protesters and tear down their tents.

MARCH 3, 2011

→ The military appoints a new civilian prime minister, Essam Sharaf, to replace Ahmed Shafik.

→ The foreign, justice, interior, and oil ministers are all replaced over the next few days.

MARCH 5, 2011

→ Civilians storm Mubarak's Internal Security Agency to seize and protect documents that demonstrate human rights abuses and to demand its closure since it was a site of torture. The Internal Security Agency is finally closed on March 15.

MARCH 9, 2011—FORCED "VIRGINITY" EXAMS

→ Men in civilian clothes storm Tahrir Square, grab roughly 20 women, drag them into the Egyptian Museum, and hand them over to the military. These women are taken to the military prison between March 9 and 13, where they are subjected to "forced virginity tests" and other forms of torture.

MARCH 19, 2011—CONSTITUTIONAL REFERENDUM

→ A vote is held on changes to nine articles in the constitution.

→ Several political parties, including the Alliance of Women's Organizations, pressure the public to vote "no" to the proposed amendments, which do little to limit presidential power. They urge people to call for an entirely new constitution.

→ The Muslim Brotherhood and the remnants (feloul) of the NDP support the amendments as a temporary measure, until redrafting by a newly elected government can be completed.

→ The "Yes" vote is 77.2 per cent, and 22.8 per cent say "No" to the amendments—a stunning defeat for the revolutionaries.

→ Voter turnout for the referendum is 41 per cent: 18,537,954 of 45 million eligible voters.

APRIL 1, 2011—SAVE THE REVOLUTION DAY

→ Protesters fill Tahrir Square to demand that the military move faster to end the Mubarak regime.

APRIL 6, 2011

→ The military arrests Ibrahim Soliman, the former housing minister.

APRIL 8, 2011

→ The Muslim Brotherhood pushes for another demonstration—the "Friday of Prosecution and Purging"—to pressure the government to prosecute high-profile members of the old regime.

→ The National Association for Change holds a mock "people's trial."

APRIL 9, 2011

→ The military rains tear gas and bullets down on the Tahrir camp at night, killing at least two people.

APRIL 16, 2011

→ The NDP is dissolved, and Mubarak's name is ordered removed from all public places on April 21.

APRIL 23, 2011

→ Former energy minister Sameh Fahmy is ordered to stand trial for the secretive deal struck to export Egypt's natural gas to Israel, which critics maintained was below-market price, enriching corrupt Egyptian government officials. Within days, the pipeline in question is attacked.

MAY 7, 2011

→ At least 12 people are killed and 2 Coptic churches are set on fire in the Imbaba district of Cairo during violent clashes between Egypt's Muslim and Coptic Christian populations, which were instigated by a false rumor that a group of Copts had kidnapped a Christian woman who had married a Muslim man and wanted to convert to Islam.

MAY 24, 2011

→ It is officially announced that Mubarak and his two sons will be tried for the deaths of anti-government protesters.

→ Four days later, Mubarak is fined $34 million for the communications blackout.

JUNE 6, 2011

→ Demonstrations are held in honor of Khaled Said, the young man from Alexandria who was beaten to death by the police.

JUNE 12, 2011

→ Egyptian authorities arrest Ilan Grapel, a dual citizen of the United States and Israel, charging he is an Israeli spy attempting to stir up violence during the revolution, even though Israel denies he is a spy. This arrest is used to bolster government claims that the revolution is the plot of "foreign conspirators" rather than the work of Egyptian citizens.

JUNE 28-29, 2011

→ About 5,000 protesters take to the streets to demand more reform; they liken the military to the Mubarak regime.

→ The military responds with brute force and tear gas, injuring at least 1,036 people, 40 police officers included. Many people are arrested and sent to military trials.

JULY 8, 2011—FRIDAY OF DETERMINATION

→ The multi-city demonstration in Suez, Alexandria, and Cairo (also called the "March of Millions") demands immediate reforms be enacted and that Mubarak officials be prosecuted, hoping to start a second revolution.

→ The Muslim Brotherhood is accused of trying to monopolize the protests and undermine the revolutionary demands of those engaged in ongoing sit-ins.

JULY 9, 2011

→ Prime Minister Essam Sharaf says that any person in the security force accused of killing protesters will be fired.

→ For the fourth time, gunmen blow up an Egyptian natural gas pipeline to Israel.

JULY 12, 2011—ELECTION PLANNING
→ The protesters demand a delay of parliamentary elections, arguing that new parties do not have a chance to organize.
→ The military agrees that steps need to be taken to delay the elections.

JULY 17, 2011—"THE REVOLUTION CABINET"
→ Prime Minister Essam Sharaf begins overhauling his cabinet.

JULY 23, 2011—MARCH ON THE DEFENSE MINISTRY
→ Protesters try to march to the defense ministry for the second time. The military claims that the protesters are foreign conspirators attempting to destabilize Egypt and sends in military police with tasers, batons, tear gas, and guns, as well as hired men in street clothes wielding knives, sticks, and stones. According to the health ministry, 231 people are wounded.

AUGUST 1, 2011—CLEARING TAHRIR SQUARE
→ Soldiers and police backed by tanks clear Tahrir Square just two days before Mubarak is to go on trial. The state radio claims 270 people in Cairo were arrested.
→ At this point, most citizens support the military's move, having grown weary of the lack of mobility around the downtown area.

AUGUST 3, 2011—MUBARAK ON TRIAL
→ Mubarak, his two sons, six former police officials, and former interior minister Habib el-Adly are put on trial in a temporary criminal court in the Cairo Police Academy. They plead "not guilty" to charges of corruption and the premeditated murder of peaceful protesters. The judge rules that Mubarak, who is ill, be moved to a military hospital until August 15, when his trial will resume.

SEPTEMBER 9, 2011—"FRIDAY OF CORRECTING PATH"
→ Tens of thousands gather in Suez, Alexandria, and Cairo demanding the resignation of the minister of interior, the independence of the judiciary,

the closure of Israel's embassy, and the end of military trials for ordinary citizens.

→ In response to the August deaths of five Egyptians near the Israel border, at least three of them policemen or border guards, protesters storm the Israeli embassy. Security forces kill 3 protesters and injure more than 1,000.

→ A state of emergency is reimposed.

OCTOBER 9, 2011

→ Egyptian Copts stage a peaceful protest in response to the demolition of a church; they march to the state television building in Maspero Square, where they plan to stage a sit-in. The army fires live ammunition and runs people over with armored vehicles, leaving at least 24 dead and 212 injured.

NOVEMBER 19, 2011—"THE BATTLE OF MOHAMED MAHMOUD STREET"

Ahmed gets hit in the face with a rubber bullet, as military violence escalates.

→ Police, backed by the army, attack a peaceful sit-in to honor *musabi al-thawra*—those wounded and killed during the January and February revolutionary action. A brutal six-day street battle ensues, as police and military fire tear gas (targeting field hospitals), rubber bullets (aimed at people's faces and genitals), and live ammunition. Protesters respond by throwing stones and Molotov cocktails. Close to 50 people are killed and as many as 3,000 are injured during this clash. There were nearly 100 serious eye injuries.

NOVEMBER 28, 2011

→ Parliamentary elections are held. The Islamist party wins the majority of seats.

The timeline of the revolution does not end here. The people of Egypt are still engaged in an ongoing struggle for justice, dignity, and democracy.

THE REIGN OF MORSI AND BEYOND

JUNE 2012–JUNE 2013

→   In June 2012, Mohamed Morsi, the Muslim Brotherhood candidate, wins the presidential elections by a narrow margin. He remains in office for one year, during which he advances a deeply divisive agenda. Morsi works actively to limit freedoms of belief and speech, remove protections of women's rights, and pass legislation to consolidate his power and the power of the Muslim Brotherhood. His regime, as Mubarak's had before, violently suppresses opponents—arresting, assaulting, torturing, and killing protesters, journalists, and residents of neighborhoods in which protests took place.

JULY 3, 2013 TO PRESENT—ABDEL FATTAH EL-SISI
ASSUMES POWER

→   On June 30, 2013, millions of protesters assemble in Tahrir Square, expressing their frustration with Morsi's rule.

→   On July 3, 2013, Army Chief General Abdel Fattah el-Sisi wrests power from Morsi, disbands parliament, and instates Adly Mansour as interim president.

→   On August 14, 2013, security forces brutally clear pro-Morsi protest camps, killing more than 800 people and injuring close to 2,000 in the most gruesome mass killing of protesters since the beginning of the Arab Spring. During the violence of the following eight days, the government reports 900 deaths and more than 4,000 injuries across Egypt.

→   Attacks on Coptic Christian churches follow this unrest.

→   During Mansour's interim presidency, billions of dollars (including stimulus packages from Arab Gulf countries) are issued in building and infrastructure contracts to the military, further consolidating military power over civilian life. In the absence of an elected parliament, Sisi and Mansour issue unilateral decrees that severely limit citizens' freedoms of expression and assembly. They proceed to ban appeals challenging military contracts, remove detention limits for political dissidents, and forbid protests.

→ In March 2014, Sisi resigns from the military in anticipation of his bid for the presidential elections. An Egyptian court issues over 500 death sentences to members of the Muslim Brotherhood and Morsi supporters.

→ After winning the election by a large margin, Sisi is officially sworn in as president on June 8, 2014. Tens of thousands of political dissidents, including journalists, continue to be repressed, assaulted, imprisoned, and tortured under the new laws.

APPENDIX II

CREATING *LISSA*: CONCEPTS, COLLABORATIONS, AND CRAFT

I. Key Concepts in the Story

Q & A WITH SHERINE HAMDY, BY MARC PARENTEAU*

MP: What gave you the idea to tell this story? What did you want your readers to get out of it?

SH: Coleman and I both did anthropological research on how social contexts shape medical decisions in very different sites—Coleman in the US, myself in Egypt—and on very different issues—Coleman on genetic risk for cancer and myself on kidney failure and organ transplantation. We were struck by the similarities and contradictions. During my research in Egypt, I encountered many people with end-stage kidney failure who refused to consider transplantation. This would sometimes frustrate their doctors. In one case I remember vividly, a middle-aged male nephrologist was particularly frustrated with his youngest patient: a woman named Maryam in her early twenties who refused to consider seeking a transplant. The doctor kept telling her, "You are young, and you have your life ahead of you! Don't

---

* Marc Parenteau is a California-based comics journalist. He helped to visually edit the script and artwork for *Lissa* and created the various fonts, word balloons, and sound effects that appear throughout.

you want a life for yourself, a life free of this machine? A transplant could give you that life!" But the patient was despondent and kept repeating quietly that her fate was in God's hands alone.

When I was reading through Coleman's early work on women with BRCA gene mutations in the Netherlands, I was struck by a breast surgeon's frustration with a young woman for the opposite reason. Anita lost her mother to breast cancer at a young age and sought out genetic testing as soon as she turned eighteen. When she found out that she had indeed inherited a BRCA1 mutation, she was adamant about getting a preventive double mastectomy. The doctor was agitated, as he recounted this story to Coleman, saying that "of course" he outright refused to do such a "drastic" and "irreversible" surgery on someone so young. He said that she was wrongly thinking that removing her breasts could somehow fix the grief she felt from her mother's death.

We wanted to think through this seeming paradox. We thought, "What would it be like to bring together two characters with a strong bond of friendship, each of whom has to make a life-and-death medical decision that the other can't understand?"

MP: That's interesting. In the first case the doctor tells the patient that her young age is why she should undergo surgery, and in the second, the doctor tells his patient that she is too young to get the surgery. But these two scenarios are also two totally different cultural contexts...

SH: Yes, well, we knew that because of the very different sites, it would be tempting to turn to cultural explanations. But we did not accept at face value that in Muslim-majority settings, for example, people reference their fate and God's will because they are somehow more "fatalistic" than others. This is a major trope about the Middle East in much Orientalist literature, in which Muslim "fatalism" supposedly contrasts with Euro-American innovation and invention. But this seemed overly simplistic: there were plenty of technology-embracing Muslims in Egypt and plenty of technology-averse (religious or irreligious) folks in Europe and the US.

We wanted to ask, "How do patients and doctors decide whether a medical intervention can really save a life or defy death?" In each of these real cases, the doctors' and patients' views are not aligned. And, in both cases, the patient [Maryam or Anita] is experiencing her illness and treatment as connected to the bodies and lives of other people. In the first instance, a kidney transplant relies on extracting a kidney from a healthy living donor. The physician telling his patient to pursue kidney transplant sees this as an obvious choice because he is thinking on the scale of the patient's individual body.

The patient refuses, knowing all too well that such an intervention requires her enmeshment in, dependency on, and possible endangerment of *another person's body* (the body of the kidney donor). In the second example, on which we based Anna's story, it is an asymptomatic patient anticipating cancer in her own body, as she grieves her mother's death from that same cancer. The physician discouraging the young woman from pursuing a prophylactic mastectomy is horrified (as Layla was) at the thought of removing perfectly healthy body parts. But Anita's social embeddedness in relations of care—with her mother, aunt, maternal grandmother—and her enmeshment in the memories of their bodily suffering and death from breast cancer motivated her to seek medical intervention in the first place.

MP: So are you saying that this is why the doctors and patients aren't agreeing? Because the doctor is just looking at the patient as an individual while the patient is really bound up with the bodies of others?

SH: Yes, we really wanted to highlight what we call the "social embeddedness of the patient." Clinicians are trained to think about interventions with their patients at the scale of the individual patient's bodies, which of course makes sense from the medical perspective. But we see, for example, that often patients' motivations for seeking treatment are to become independent and to free their loved ones from the burdens of care or—in the case of high-cost treatment—to free their loved ones from the burden of the expense. In the case of many "previvors" who test positive for a cancer susceptibility gene, their own histories as caregivers, like Anna's history, make them feel that, in a sense, they have already lived with the disease. Anna's motivation to pursue surgery is partly based on the loss of her own mother to the same disease. For people who are trying to decide how to manage their risk medically, family obligations play an important role, whether it's getting surgery to protect your own children from having their mother die of cancer (Angelina Jolie wrote about this in her op-ed piece in the *New York Times*) or whether parents or siblings pressure a family member to get surgery because they are afraid of losing another loved one to cancer. There's also the broader issue about genetic testing to determine risk of disease—if one family member finds out he or she carries a mutation, the rest of the family is affected by that knowledge.

And in the case of Abu Hassan, the treatment option before him relies on his loved ones making an even greater sacrifice to keep him alive: an operation with a high cost would deplete all their savings and possibly put them in debt, as well as putting them at risk of a major invasive surgery (in donation). The case of organ transplantation brings this discordance to the surface because this particular medical practice relies directly and materially on the bodies of other people. In other medical practices, dependency on others (as in the form of care-taking) is less direct yet is still essential to medical outcome. So by highlighting the problem of focusing on the "individual" and "autonomous" patient, we also wanted to expose what Annemarie Mol has noted about the problem of the tired dichotomy between the "West" and the "Rest."

MP: You mean the ways that "the West" is supposed to be about autonomous individuals and that, in "the Rest" of the world, it's all about traditions and tribes?

SH: Yes, Mol critiques the ways in which we tend to imagine that the autonomous individual is what defines "the West" in contrast to "Others" who are supposedly more embedded in their communities and more bound by tradition. But Mol asks, "Are people in the West indeed autonomous individuals?" She suggests that we contribute to the line of work opened by postcolonial studies not just by countering more tired stereotypes about non-Western "Others" but also by readjusting what it is we assume to be true about the West.

So we took up Mol's challenge, by following a character with an inherited gene mutation that predisposes her to cancer risk, alongside patients in Egypt with end-stage kidney failure. For both cases, the focus on the individual body as the site of intervention places patients in a double bind: to undergo treatment, they must privilege their own bodies over those of their relations, even while their relations are what enable or motivate that very treatment.

MP: I remember you also saying that the focus on the "individual" blinds us to social inequalities.

SH: Right. For example, near where I work, a billboard over the highway features an image of a white girl, maybe four years old, with large blue eyes and a seeming halo of blonde curls. The message reads, "Cancer doesn't care who it picks on." The billboard is meant to draw our attention to this one individual girl, who tells us that even children can get cancer; that it is no one's fault.

But we know from public health research that cancer *does* discriminate: people living in neighborhoods of lower socioeconomic status face higher morbidity and mortality rates in the US; those subject to mismanaged toxic waste face "cancer clusters," and discrepancies in susceptibility and outcome are even more pronounced when we look at it globally, given the widening gap between rich and poor throughout the world. In the discourse on organ donation, the miracles of "saving lives" and "giving the gift of life" through organ donation similarly evoke the notion of individual, neutral, unmarked bodies who are equally susceptible to disease, whose organs, tissues, and blood are interchangeable.

This rhetoric comes up against the dark reality of a shadow market in body parts, in which body matter moves in patterns that Nancy Scheper-Hughes has starkly laid out: from the poor to the rich, from the brown- and black-skinned to the white, from women to men. It also hides the grim actuality that the world's impoverished people who suffer from poor labor conditions, poor nutrition and unclean water, toxic exposure, and medical mismanagement are in fact more susceptible to organ failure in the first place.

Why does the rhetoric of the "individual, equally susceptible body" persist, despite decades of public health research that proves that bodies are *not* equally susceptible? People with less access to resources (such as secure employment, clean air and water, secure housing, education, racial privilege) are at much higher risk of illness. Medical practice is one of the key sites in which the myth of socially equal bodies is enacted through the promises and imperatives of individualized treatment.

MP: Another major theme and, in some ways, a point of conflict has to do with different ideas of what *causes* the disease....Was it the pollution? Bad water? Bad genes? At one point, even Anna, who is focused on her genetic mutation, is freaked out by the toxicity of the chemicals she is using to develop film in the darkroom....

SH: Yes, we wanted to show that, with organ failure and cancer (both of which are illnesses with many complicated interrelated risk factors that can't always be easily parsed or identified), patients have their own ideas of what might have predisposed them to disease. And these ideas about cause of illness would have an effect on their decisions about treatment. In my field research in Egypt, I saw many people with good reason to believe that toxic exposure had predisposed them to kidney failure. These were the patients who were wary to leave their beloved family members bereft of a kidney, to leave them in a sense amputated in the same environment that had made them sick. Maybe if they thought it was their own individual pathology or just bad genetic luck, rather than a shared environmental risk, they'd be more open to the idea of a brother donating a kidney to them.

Anna seems pretty sure that her genetics will predict whether she will get sick or not. The kind of cancer her mother died from is rare in that it can be traced to a specific genetic mutation—whereas the vast majority of cancers have really complicated etiologies. Anna's decision makes sense to her because focusing on her own genetics is something she can better control. But it's also not that simple. A BRCA mutation elevates her risk for getting cancer, but it doesn't cause cancer. And Anna starts to recognize this in that moment in the darkroom, as she sees that her cancer risk is not just in her genes or in her family; it's in her environment, even in the things she holds most dear, like photography. Ultimately, she decides that surgery is the best option in reducing her cancer risk.

So we see that different understandings of the disease (whether one thinks it's caused by individual pathology or bad luck versus a shared environmental risk) shape how people make decisions about medical treatment, and how they view their illness in relation to the bodies of others.

MP: Back to the situation in Egypt. I get that you don't want us to think of the characters as "fatalistic," but why then do you think that they say things like, "The body belongs to God" or "My fate is in God's hands"?

SH: For the young woman I first mentioned, Maryam, to evoke the idea that her fate is in God's hands was a way, I think, for her to come to terms with the pain of knowing that her social relations had failed her—none had come forward with either the bodily or financial sacrifices necessary for a transplant. I often saw devout people going through difficult times evoking God as a way to bring themselves to accept the fact that they could not control or change what terrible thing was happening to them.

The physician expressed frustration at this, I think, because he did not want to accept that his medical skills were not enough to alter the patient's grim prognosis. In other cases involving older patients, such as Abu Hassan, I often heard them say that their "bodies belonged to God" as a protective refusal of any of their children or spouses donating their organs to them. The surgery was seen as both a major bodily sacrifice and a financial cost, and one with an uncertain and complicated outcome.

MP: Even in Anna's case—and she does not have the financial cost of her surgery to worry about—her decisions still aren't easy.

SH: Yes, we wanted to show that the multiplication of patient choices in high-cost, high-technology medicine doesn't always make treatment better. In the case of Anna, in the context of profit-oriented medical tests, she often feels overwhelmed and burdened by her decisions. This is similar to what anthropologist Rayna Rapp demonstrated in her book *Testing Women, Testing the Fetus*, which explored amniocentesis in New York City. Geneticists and clinicians had assumed that screening pregnant women for potential genetic diseases would be a welcome intervention that could potentially reduce incidence of genetic disease in children and the burden of their care (via abortion of affected fetuses). Yet Rapp found that women, in many cases, felt alone and burdened by having to make these moral choices, by having to weigh the value of which form of life should be brought into this world. For many, particularly those with inconclusive results, this added significant stress and anxiety during their pregnancies. This "burden of choice" is also something that Marisa Marchetto captures really well in her comic *Cancer Vixen*.

To be clear, our point is not to criticize the use of high-technology, high-cost options in the space of the clinic but rather their indiscriminate and default use. We want to raise the question of how high-cost medicine can be used prudently to benefit patients' experiences and outcomes. But we don't have the ready answers! We want to open these questions up more to public discussion. Is the emphasis on individual "choice" the best way to go about handling questions like genetic risk? Is Layla right to think Anna's worry about her genetic test is a problem of "too much medicine"? In what ways are medical ethical decisions similar across different settings?

MP: It seems like Abu Hassan and Layla are more realistic about a transplant not "fixing" his situation, whereas Anna is really hoping this surgery will erase cancer from her life. Does it? What was your thinking here?

SH: Well, in Egypt, which doesn't have a well-functioning malpractice system for patient redress and where medical care can be especially uneven, there is certainly a lot of awareness about postsurgical complications, which is why people hope to avoid invasive procedures. In the case of Abu Hassan, we see that he never really believed the promise that a transplant would "fix" his kidney failure. Indeed, throughout the world many who receive transplants do not return to "normal" but rather transition to a post-transplant life that still must be medically regulated and monitored (albeit usually more easily than life on dialysis). After a transplant, patients should get at least six weeks of rest from physical or strenuous labor (which many people cannot afford), and they'll need resources to pay for expensive medications such as immuno-suppressants and for the medical management of opportunistic infections. It doesn't make sense for a patient to liquidate *all* savings and assets for the hope of a "fix" when the result is, in fact, more complicated: a life that will still require bodily and financial resources. Further, it is difficult, if not impossible, to anticipate how a kidney extraction in resource-poor clinical settings would affect the future life of a living donor, upon whom the operation depends.

As for Anna, well, we don't get too much into this in *Lissa* because it would have distracted from the storyline. But Coleman found in her work with cancer "previvors" and survivors that too often this idea of "fixing"—with major surgery or treatment—can turn out to be a false metaphor, obscuring the chronicity of disease and the post-treatment complications patients can undergo. As Annemarie Mol has argued, the rubric of "patient choice" also implies that decisions are transactional, wherein the promise of biomedical intervention is the return to "normalcy." Yet normalcy is forever a moving target in post-transplant life and pre- and post-cancer life.

MP: You're also showing us the different and overlapping senses of time in disease treatment. In Anna's case, she wants to get surgery for the *future* possibility of disease, but also as a form of redress for the *past* loss of her mom.

SH: Exactly. We wanted to ask how decisions about treatment would unfold if we had deeper discussions of the long-term consequences of medical intervention. What would a clinical encounter look like that privileged how patients' lives are enmeshed in the lives of others, and how is their ability to imagine their futures caught up in their experiences of the past? Coleman and I were finding that, in organ transplantation and genetic testing, the biomedical ideal of patient autonomy just doesn't align with the lived reality. The patient's body, health, and choices are shaped by so many other things, such as intimate relationships and family obligations, as well as social context and political environment.

MP: Thanks, Sherine, you've definitely given us a lot to think about!

II. Collaborations: On Comics, Coauthorship, and Ethnofiction

Q & A WITH COLEMAN NYE, BY MARC PARENTEAU

MP: Coleman, you both mention that you had really rich stories from your fieldwork that could easily have made for a compelling narrative. Can you tell us a bit about your decision to fictionalize your ethnographic research?

CN: Yes, the original ideas for this book were informed by our respective fieldwork on ethical dilemmas related to high-cost, highly invasive medical interventions in two very different settings. While we both had rich stories from our own research sites, we didn't have any research bridging the two contexts. So our major dilemma was how to make these two worlds—genetics in the US and transplants in Egypt—converge in a compelling, realistic, and accessible way. We decided to create a fictional narrative in which there were two main characters, each based on our research, whose worlds were deeply intertwined through proximity and friendship, and whose life trajectories reflected the broader medical tensions and affinities we wanted to explore.

So, while Layla and Anna are fictional characters (though they feel so real to us now!), they are not completely fabricated. Instead, they are based on what anthropologists call "composite characters." Composite characters are modeled after real people, but rather than reflecting all of the traits of any one individual, they instead represent select traits, behaviors, or characteristics that are shared by a subset of individuals. So, for Anna, there are things about her character that might be generalizable to many (but certainly not all) other young cancer "previvors" in the US: she has lost several close family members to cancer, and she has to navigate a range of imperfect choices, financial barriers, and social pressures around how to manage her cancer risk. There were also specific choices we made as authors that were based less on data patterns and more on the specific story we wanted to tell. For instance, Anna's decision to forgo reconstruction after her preventive mastectomy is less common for people her age, but we had her story take this direction because of certain plot-based needs. If Anna had opted for reconstruction, it would have made it difficult for her to travel to Egypt so soon after surgery and to remain there for six months.

Beyond bridging our research sites, fiction really gave us the freedom to craft an absorbing, relatable, character-driven narrative—and the flexibility to adapt the narrative in ongoing conversation with our illustrators Caroline and Sarula, as well as with our interlocutors in Egypt who gave us feedback on what worked and what didn't.

MP: Anthropologists often use pseudonyms to protect the confidentiality of the people they are writing about. Were ethical issues, especially with the political turmoil in Egypt and the sensitivity around illness experiences, also part of your decision to fictionalize characters such as Layla?

CN: Well, yes and no. In the case of Anna and Layla, creating composite fictional characters certainly made sense in terms of protecting the identities of people from past research who have trusted us with their personal medical stories. But, interestingly, in the context of the Egyptian Revolution, we have used the names and likenesses of several real people with their consent. You see, revolutionaries wanted to disrupt the brutal suppression of dissent under Mubarak. As part of this effort, they were announcing themselves publicly. The story we tell of the revolution comes in large part from the stories of those who took part in the revolution in Egypt who are named and discussed in their own memoirs, writings, blogs, Facebook posts, artwork, books, articles, and organizations. Their work and actions were in the public sphere, and this is now part of our living memory; we did not want to hide any of these characters or obscure the value of their work in our fiction, even as we recognize that counterrevolutionary forces today continue to punish and repress political actors of all stripes.

MP: Say more about this—actual people who are present as characters in *Lissa*.

CN: Part of this decision to include real people as characters was motivated by our awareness of problematic forms of Western "academic tourism" in the Middle East. We did not want to overshadow or wrongly claim the intellectual production emerging from the revolutionaries themselves and those most immediately affected by the political uprisings. We hoped to make it clear that the critical intellectual work on the revolution belongs to Egyptians, not to us, as outsiders. As part of this effort, we incorporated the work of a range of revolutionaries, intellectuals, and artists.

Two characters that Layla encounters during the Egyptian Revolution— Reem and Alia—are based on Reem Bashery and Alia Mossallam. These women's personal stories of the revolution were recorded by Egyptian feminist researchers from the Women and Memory Forum as part of an oral history project. Many lines of dialogue are taken directly from their narratives, and the work that Anna engages in around trying to locate missing people is based directly on Alia's experiences. For example, Alia Mossallam published an extremely powerful piece on her attempts to locate missing persons—and we used her firsthand account for the scene when Layla meets her in the morgue.

Readers might also recognize Dr. Dina Shokry as Layla's university professor and Dr. Amr Shebaita as her field hospital supervisor. We wanted to capture the actions of Tahrir Doctors [the NGO that Dr. Shebaita co-founded] and acknowledge our own research team's indebtedness in particular to Doctors Shokry and Shebaita, who have made tremendous contributions to health and justice efforts in Egypt, and who very generously gave us feedback on our original script.

We incorporated some remarkable work of graffiti artists, such as Ganzeer, who were already using illustrations in sophisticated and stunning ways to level trenchant political critiques. Through graffiti, we also make reference to Dr. Ahmed Harara—the dentist who lost his eye in the early occupation of Tahrir Square in January 2011. He was then shot by police snipers in his second eye the following November during the unrest in the Muhammad Mahmoud Street protests. And for fictional characters engaging in real events of the revolution, we wanted to highlight the tremendous work that Egyptians themselves were doing in the very acts of fighting off riot police, improvisationally healing the wounded, navigating censorship, and presenting competing counternarratives to state propaganda.

At each of these points of incorporation, collaboration, and citation, we hope to invite readers to challenge their assumptions about authorship and scholarly authority.

MP: Okay, so it's clear why fictionalizing made sense for you. But why comics? Why did you feel that illustration was needed to tell this story?

CN: Like other scholars working in the growing field of what Ian Williams has termed "graphic medicine," we found that the combination of text and image in graphic memoirs such as *Hyperbole and a Half* and *Mom's Cancer* and *Cancer Vixen* powerfully conveys the visceral, temporal, and social dimensions of illness. There's also a levity to the genre that makes it easier to engage with difficult topics such as kidney failure, cancer, or political violence. Ultimately, we are convinced that this form of engaged scholarship opens up possibilities to convey the ethnographic encounter through an accessible, visually rich medium that allows readers to draw their own conclusions about how the material relates to their lives.

MP: It also seems that the illustrations did a great job at introducing readers to otherwise unfamiliar settings—the crowd scenes in Tahrir and the long shots of Cairo are especially powerful.

CN: Yes, definitely. We wanted to exploit the comic medium to bridge audiences in the Arab world with those in the US. We show that layering and juxtaposing multiple perspectives—from people who inhabit distinct worldviews—can only benefit our abilities to examine difficult ethical decisions about life-and-death treatment and the stakes of partaking in political conflict.

One of the most generative aspects of the process has been realizing how much more we can convey through the combination of text and image. Far from "dumbing down" content, comics allow us to convey complex, and often contradictory, anthropological ideas in a highly readable format. For example, the concept of political etiologies that took Sherine roughly 30 pages to describe in an academic article can be graphically illustrated in a two-page spread!

We show Abu Hassan, linked to a dialysis machine, its tubes snaking outward spatially and temporally, connecting the patient's sick body to the parasite-transmitting snails of the Nile, the overproduction of US midwestern wheat upon which the Egyptian population now depends for food, chemical fertilizers, pesticides, failing infrastructure, and the black market in counterfeit medical drugs and equipment. Following connections across scales and times is more fluid in graphic form, facilitating our work between two contrasting global contexts to expose a range of interconnected issues in health, politics, and justice.

MP: What was the actual process like: two authors cowriting the script and then working with illustrators? How did that work?

CN: It has certainly been a learning experience! Years ago, Sherine and I had talked about doing some collaboration based on our two research projects—we had even written an academic article for a workshop (that we never ended up submitting to publication) on some parallels we saw around the limits of the bioethical ideal of patient autonomy. I was still at Brown at the time, and Sherine had this idea to go down the hill to the Rhode Island School of Design (RISD) Illustration Department and propose a collaborative project with them. Luckily, we got funding for this from the Watson Institute at Brown. Rob Brinkerhoff of the RISD Illustration Department put us in touch with Paul Karasik, who teaches comics. Paul selected Sarula and Caroline as students who were ready for a big project like this. They were college seniors at the time, which is doubly impressive when you see the scale and sophistication of their work.

Sherine and I wrote the script together: we brainstormed the initial plot over the summer of 2015 and took turns fleshing it out in a Google doc. Paul gave us feedback on how to make it more visually accessible (the story has changed *a lot* since our first draft!). The following fall, we met Sarula and Caroline for the first time, and their first task was to sketch out the whole script. It was a lot of fun for us to see it all unfold, and it also made each team (the writers and the illustrators) ask hard questions about what each scene was doing, why it was necessary for the plot, etc. It has been a remarkable learning experience, as we have had to translate our anthropological insights and imaginaries for the illustrators, and they have had to teach us about visual language and the technical dimensions of building comics.

And then there was the added issue of how to depict Egypt. Only Sherine had been there before, and we were all relying on her for the visual scenery. Thankfully, Sherine got funding from the Luce Foundation to take the whole team to Cairo. It was an incredible trip, and the story took on new depth and direction as we really began to place the characters in Cairo.

We were lucky to have ethnographic filmmaker Francesco Dragone and medical anthropologist Alice Larotonda to film this whole process in a "behind-the-scenes" documentary. Our aim was to make our methods and process available to other scholars and artists who wish to embark on similar illustrated forms of scholarship and to reflect on the ways in which new forms of visualization allow for communicating academic research—ethnographic, scientific, medical, humanistic—to broader and more diverse audiences.

MP: And how did it work to have two different illustrators?

CN: As for the two artists, each decided to take on a character. Initially, Sarula chose Layla and Caroline chose Anna, but then they switched! Sarula works digitally and Caroline draws traditionally with pen and paper, and they worked really well together to balance their styles. This worked in terms of the plot, because the initial idea was for two characters with different perspectives to slowly come to understand one another. So we see the world through Anna's eyes in Sarula's style and then the world through Layla's eyes in Caroline's style, and then . . . when they come to understand one another toward the end, the two different styles merge.

III. Crafting Comics: Time, Space, Text

Q & A WITH MARC PARENTEAU, BY EDITOR ANNE BRACKENBURY*

AB: Marc, you've had a very interesting role in helping to pull this all together, especially toward the end. Since this is the first book in our *ethnoGRAPHIC* series, we wanted to make the process clear as other ethnographer-illustrator teams embark on their projects.

---

* Anne Brackenbury is the Executive Editor in the Higher Education Division at the University of Toronto Press. The ethnoGRAPHIC series, for which *Lissa* is the debut, is her brainchild.

Could you tell us what your role was in helping the authors and illustrators along?

MP: Sure. First I should say that it's been a pleasure working with the *Lissa* team, and I have learned a lot in the process, which I am very grateful for. That said, I think it's fair to say that most academics aren't overly familiar with the contours of comics as a medium and how they affect the writing of a script. On *Lissa*, I found that the most common difficulties were either rhythm/pacing issues or descriptive/dialogue issues.

The way writing comics—for print anyway—is most affected by rhythm is that, at a minimum, you really have to know if what you are describing occurs on a left-hand or right-hand page, the reason being that, when you open a comic, you can't help but scan the entire two-page spread. So, if Grandma dies on the right-hand page in a comic, the reader knows this before they ever start reading anything on the left. Having reveals of that sort in the wrong place can ruin the "pull" that you want the reader to have throughout the work.

AB: I guess that's what people mean when they refer to the "dual nature" of comics—that you can read it sequentially panel by panel, but you can also get the big picture on a page, or two-page spread, in a way you don't get when you are reading a text-only book. So what does that mean in practice?

MP: Since you have multiple visual elements pushing and pulling with—or against—each other, you have to consider things both in terms of the static composition of the spread and in terms of the flow of the content and composition of image and text within individual panels. There are a million ways to do this in comics, but I think essentially you're aiming for a kind of "readable" circulation of meaning among those multiple elements. It's both challenging and exciting from a creator's point of view, and really unique in terms of what it can provoke in the mind of a comics reader.

AB: OK, that makes sense, but then how do you decide on how many panels are going to go on each individual page?

MP: In terms of an individual page, it depends on a lot things: whether you want things to move quickly or whether you want to draw something out, whether you need the visual emphasis of a full page, etc. But in order to unify a project visually, I think it helps to decide in advance how many panels will be your "basic unit." I liken this to choosing the meter of a piece of music. For *Lissa*, the meter is 8/8. That is, generally speaking, there are two columns and four rows of panels per page. It doesn't mean that you can't deviate from that number; it just means that the deviations from that panel pattern happen in reference to an eight-panel grid. It's kind of like how, in a piece of music that is in 4/4 time, you can still play triplets, have syncopation, counterpoint, etc. So the writer always has to consider whether what's being described will fit in a two- or eight- or however-many-panel sequence.

AB: So who decides this rhythm or meter—the writer or the illustrator?

MP: In terms of the work overall, I would say that the writer needs to figure it out before handing it to an illustrator. It's hugely helpful if the writer develops a script that discretely reflects what is happening on a page-by-page and panel-by-panel basis. So the script looks much more like a screenplay. There are plenty of ways to do this, and whatever works for both the writers and the artists involved is clearly fine. But I tend to format things like this:

Page 22 L

22.1 [i.e., Page 22, Panel 1] Mom is running towards house. Mom: Don't go in there!

22.2 Hansel turns head quickly towards Mom's voice. Hansel: Huh?

22.3 Mom's face close-up. Mom: My pies are still in the oven!

22.4 Hansel's face, downcast. Hansel: You mean me and Gretel have to wait another 20 minutes to cook this old lady who tried to eat us?

Page 23 R

23.1 etc. . . .

I prefer this kind of breakdown when I illustrate for other writers because I can immediately see what action and what dialogue goes with which panel. That way, if I have a question about or a need to change something, I can clearly cite panel and page.

AB: That seems straightforward, but I can imagine all sorts of scenarios where the writer either gives too much information or not enough for the artist to work with.

MP: Definitely. Most problems come out of the fact that words are often more spatially dense than images are. So, for example, it doesn't generally work to have an elaborate sequence of events occurring in a single panel.

"Larry gets up, brushes his teeth, and stares in the mirror thinking about the cruise ship."

This is one sentence, but it's probably at least three panels if you want to actually show those things. And while we're talking about Larry staring in the mirror, a description such as this—

"Larry thinks about the cruise ship, he feels the weight of all the lost souls on his father's ship, which went down in rough seas off the coast of New Jersey while steaming towards a summer in the fjords of Norway."

—is probably not a single panel either, and definitely not a visual direction unless the writer says that we *see* these thoughts in the form of flashbacks or thought bubbles or some other such device.

This means that unless a character or narrator says it, all descriptions of emotional or interior states must be stated in the script in explicitly visual terms or else they are essentially superfluous.

AB: What about dialogue? Are there rules for how much dialogue should be included in any given panel, and do you sometimes have to edit the content of a word balloon to fit it inside a panel?

MP: Copy-fitting of dialogue is a constant concern. Having a single balloon with a 150-word statement in it will slow the readers down to such a degree that you can lose them. My rule of thumb is no more than 30–35 words per balloon, maximum. Fewer is generally better.

AB: So you have to think visually when you are writing the dialogue so you can imagine what the visuals say and what the text says?

MP: Yes, but in my view, dialogue and visuals in comics should pass off the meaning(s) of a work the way that runners pass off a baton in a race. The main difference between my analogy and a real race, though, is that comics should cheat. What I mean is, dialogue should *push the visuals forward* when it hands the baton and the same thing vice versa. So, if you have a panel depicting an angry man, and in that panel the angry man says, "I am an angry man!" Then you could say that rather than passing the baton and giving each teammate a boost, the two runners are battling over the baton, and the reader doesn't know whom to root for and/or thinks the team is very undisciplined. I think these problems happen mostly because, while a writer is in the depths of writing, it can be tough to keep track of where that hand-off is taking place at any given point. I see my role in team *Lissa* as being the person who keeps an eye on all the above. That way, both the writers and artists have maximum latitude to explore the landscape of the medium. I suppose you could say that, if they get stuck or lost, it's my job to go out and find them and get them back on track.

AB: Speaking of keeping things on track, there are around 1,500 individual panels in *Lissa*. How did the artists keep their drawings consistent throughout such a large work? Was there a similar sort of copyediting that took place visually as there was for the text in the comic?

MP: Sarula and Caroline are both very strong artists in their own right, and they did a tremendous job tackling a project like this. They somehow managed to share pages and blend styles in a single, unified way that is extremely difficult to do. As many times as I've been through the book at this point, I am still impressed at what they achieved. But you're right, there are just an awful lot of images to draw in a project like this, and it can be quite difficult after hours of working on a page to remember that, on the previous page, a given character *was* actually wearing a bracelet or *didn't* have her hair tied up or what have you. So throughout the drawing process, I often sent the artists back annotated drawings pointing out, "This character should be looking left" or the like, which must have been supremely annoying for Sarula and Caroline to hear after hours of work. But they were both very gracious and patient with my pestering. So yes, I did keep a close eye on continuity, both in terms of examples like I just mentioned and in terms of consistent facial expression, body language, or other sorts of nitpicky little things that can slide when you're several hours into a page. If you find any fault in the book on that score, by all means you can blame me! Otherwise, the other visual contribution I made was getting to add in sound effects, which I really enjoyed.

APPENDIX III

TEACHING GUIDE

I. Discussion Questions

1. In what way does Anna's family cancer history shape her relationship to her body and her future?

2. Why does Layla think it's crazy for Anna to "treat a disease that she does not have"?

3. Why can't Anna understand the reluctance of Layla's family to consider a transplant for Abu Hassan?

4. In what ways do we see bodies and body parts being commodified (treated as commodities to buy and sell) in both the American and Egyptian medical systems?

5. Layla imagines that there wouldn't be ethical dilemmas in the United States, given how much more resource-rich the medical settings are. Based on Anna's experiences, in what ways do more resources *resolve* certain medical problems and *exacerbate* others?

6. The biomedical approach to illness often conceives of the patient as an autonomous individual whose health, body, and decisions are that patient's

responsibility alone. How do Anna and Layla's experiences of risk and illness in their families challenge or complicate this ideal of patient autonomy?

7. What do the following examples say about the way women's health is often equated with reproductive viability and (hetero)sexual desirability?
   a. Anna gets annoyed that people keep talking about her options for reducing her cancer risk in terms of preserving her reproductive viability or protecting her dating prospects.
   b. Umm Hassan worries that if Layla were to donate a kidney to her father, she would damage her marriage and reproductive prospects.

8. What do the following examples say about the commodification of healthcare and of the body?
   a. Anna has good health insurance coverage via her father's employment, but we still see her stress about certain medical costs that aren't covered under her private plan, such as the Myriad-patented genetic test or reconstructive surgery.
   b. Although poor patients like Abu Hassan can receive government-subsidized treatment at public university centers, such as Cairo University's Kasr el Aini Hospital and the Mansoura Urology and Nephrology Center, these places are under increasing financial strain, have uneven levels of care, and cannot adequately meet the demand in patient care.

9. The timing of medical interventions is also an area of discussion:
   a. What are some examples of characters in Lissa seeming to imagine medical intervention as a single event or transaction that will "fix" the problem?
   b. In what instances is it evident that the medical management of illness is chronic and will require medical tinkering and ongoing care?
   c. How does understanding the temporal nature of the illness (how long it will last, how quickly the treatment will resolve the symptoms) inform medical and ethical decision making?
   d. Medical treatment for organ failure and cancer can be thought of as "life saving" or as "postponing death." How do these different

categorizations of treatment impact how we think about the medical intervention?

    e.   In what ways does the reproductive and sexual viability of women inform medical decision making?

10. Why do you think Abu Hassan insists that "the body belongs to God"? What does this have to do with the medical treatment decisions he is facing?

11. Online and through social media, Layla learns about revolutionary movements in Egypt, and Anna finds a community of "previvors" in the United States. How did the use of the Internet shape their experiences and life choices? In what ways does their sense of belonging to online communities mark a generational shift from their parents?

12. Do you think Anna is right that Egypt is in a sense her country too? Do you think Ahmed has reason to resent her presence there and her participation in the revolution?

13. During the postrevolutionary protests against the military government, police snipers began targeting people's eyes. What is the symbolic weight of deliberately blinding protesters like Ahmed?

14. How does Layla use humor as a coping mechanism as she faces challenges in her family life and everyday routines?

15. How does Anna's relationship to photography change over the course of the story? What is the import of this change?

16. How does the impact of the political uprisings affect Anna's and Layla's understanding of one another?

17. What does the title *Lissa* (colloquial Arabic meaning "not yet, still time") capture about the story?

II. Elaborating on Images, Mapping Connections
MAP 1
Toxic Ecologies of Cancer

On a two-page spread on pages 130–131, we see Anna's friend getting chemotherapy, as she says, "With cancer, it's hard to tell the difference between the cure and the cause." Cancer is a complex disease in which mutations in DNA lead to uncontrolled cell growth. On the left page, we see this woman's DNA interacting with chemicals in everyday household and personal care products, "pink ribbon" food items, pesticides and chemical fertilizers, and cytotoxic drug infusions (chemotherapy) developed from military weapons (mustard gas) funded by the US Department of Defense. On the right page, we see her DNA interact with pharmaceutical companies' drugs, insurance companies' "red tape," biotech companies' gene patents, "pink ribbon" corporate charity campaigns, and family cancer histories. By the time the DNA has interacted with all of these factors, it has started to break apart and mutate. What might have contributed to these mutations? How many of the same things that might have caused these cancerous mutations are part of the cure?

Group Exercise: Cause or Cure?
In small groups, create two columns on a page. Label one column "cause" and label the other column "cure." Now go through each of the following components and, based on preliminary research and discussion, determine whether they go in "cure," "cause," or both.

- Cytotoxins
- Chemical weapons
- US Department of Defense
- Dairy products (such as yogurt)
- Cosmetics
- Household cleaners
- Cigarettes
- Plastics
- Pesticides
- Chemical fertilizers
- Inherited gene mutations

- Patented genetic tests
- Pharmaceutical drugs
- "Pink ribbon" campaign products
- Insurance coverage

Compare and discuss your finalized columns with another small group.

MAP 2

Toxic Ecologies of Kidney Disease

A patient on page 127 tells Layla that a kidney transplant doesn't necessarily work when there are so many elements of the food, water, and air that will continue to make a person sick. This critique highlights how biomedical interventions into the individual's body are insufficient if there aren't also interventions into the broader social, political, and environmental determinants of illness.

On the two-page spread on pages 134–135, we see a partial mapping of the connections between Abu Hassan's kidney disease and the larger political context of Egypt that has contributed to his illness.

Step 1: Labeling the Map

In small groups, work to label the following dimensions:

- Aswan High Dam
- Schistosomes
- Antischistosomal injections
- Hepatitis C virus (through tainted injections and dialysis machines)
- Hydroelectric power grid
- High salinity water
- Chemical fertilizers and pesticides
- Industrial waste
- American wheat
- Air pollution

Step 2: Drawing Connections

Based on Sherine Hamdy's 2008 article "When the State and Your Kidneys Fail" and her 2013 article "Political Challenges to Biomedical Universalism," work to establish the connections (a) among the different dimensions listed above and (b) between each dimension and kidney disease. For example, how does the Aswan High Dam connect to water salinity, chemical fertilizers, and antischistosomal injections? What do they have to do with Abu Hassan's failing kidneys?

Using different colored pencils or string for each component, draw these connections on the page. Then, create a key for the map that briefly explains (a) each different component and (b) their connections to each other and to kidney disease.

MAP 3

Toxic Connections between the United States and Egypt

Do some of your own research on the connections between the United States and Egypt (we recommend starting with our annotated bibliography!). How is "big pharma" in the United States connected to medicine in Egypt? What place do American pesticides, toxic waste, and wheat have in Egypt? What role does the US military play in Egypt? How do these connections challenge your understanding of national boundaries or of bodily boundaries?

After examining these connections between the United States and Egypt, work to draw your own map of "toxic connections" across the borders and bodies of these two nation-states.

III. Translating from Words to Image and Vice Versa

1. Translate from image to text (in written prose).
   a. The role of certain visual motifs or symbols in the story (e.g., the cats, the washing machine, or the darkroom development).
   b. Visually complex scenes, such as Anna making her decision on the airplane.

2. Find a written news article or patient story about a medical decision or bioethical dilemma, and try to visually depict this in comic form.

IV. Drawing the Revolution

EXERCISE 1: SYMBOLISM

(a) On page 235, Layla and Anna face a wall with a number of different pieces of graffiti art that together convey the message that "lissa – there is still time." At the top center of page 235 is a piece by Egyptian graffiti artist Ganzeer entitled "The Cat of Defiance." In small groups, discuss the symbolic meanings of (1) the cat (2) the wings, and (3) the bandages. Think about the story that this imagery tells in relation to the characters' lives, the lives of those who took part in the street protests, and the graffiti art of the revolution.

(b) Looking again at Page 235, discuss the significance of Ganzeer's inclusion of each piece in relation to the story.

(c) On pages 229, 230, 231, and 233, illustrators Sarula Bao and Caroline Brewer blend original pieces of revolutionary street graffiti with their own art. In small groups, consider how this strategy of layering imagery visually advances the plot and places the individual characters within their broader social and political worlds.

EXERCISE 2: AUTHORSHIP

Much graffiti art is uncredited, and the artist remains unknown. Graffiti is generally understood to be a subversive and radical art form that runs counter to dominant institutional modes of recognition and authority. Each of the graffiti artists featured in Lissa goes by a pseudonym and has a unique and identifiable style. In the context of Egypt's political repression, graffiti artists can be subject to arrest, detention, and/or state-sanctioned violence. Yet in the immediate aftermath of the revolution, many of Cairo's street artists gained international acclaim for their work and their real identities have become public knowledge. Some of these artists whose status is public now live in exile. In small groups, discuss the politics of authorship, ownership, and citation in graffiti. How is it different from other forms of art? How is it similar?

KEY REFERENCES
AND FURTHER READING

I. THE EGYPTIAN REVOLUTION

FILM AND VIDEO

Noujaim, Jehane (director). 2013. *The Square.* **Cairo: Noujaim Films.**
This documentary follows three Egyptian revolutionaries from the beginning of the protests in 2011 through to the rise and fall of Morsi in the following years. The film depicts the remarkable intellectual, activist, and artistic work being undertaken by Egyptians to challenge a corrupt regime, and it brings the viewer into Tahrir alongside protesters to see the joy, solidarity, and violence they experienced during and after the revolution.

Women and Memory Forum: Archive of Women's Voices
Two of the characters that Layla encounters during the Egyptian Revolution—Reem and Alia—are based on real women with the same names. Reem Bashery's and Alia Mossallam's personal stories of the revolution were recorded by researchers from the Women and Memory Forum as part of an Egyptian women's oral history project. The Women and Memory Forum is an organization of researchers, activists, and academics that focuses on the critical social and intellectual role women play in the Arab world. When we visited the Women and Memory Forum during our trip to Cairo in January 2016, Dr. Hoda Elsadda and Dr. Amina Elbendary met

with us and showed us the video testimonies of Reem and Alia (weblinks included below). We incorporated Reem and Alia into our story as part of our commitment to not only citing, but centering the critical political and intellectual work undertaken by Egyptian women in the revolution. Many lines of dialogue are taken from these women's narratives, and the work that Anna engages in around trying to locate missing people is based directly on Alia's experiences.

LINKS

→ Women and Memory Forum website: http://www.wmf.org.eg/en/
→ Archive of Women's Voices (oral history) website:
  http://oralhistoryarchive.wmf.org.eg/
→ Alia Mossallam's oral narrative video on YouTube (in Arabic with English subtitles): https://www.youtube.com/watch?time_continue =2&v=sHoRB6dpxgw
→ Reem Bashery's oral narrative video on YouTube (in Arabic with English subtitles): https://www.youtube.com/watch?v=yvBD_07Uchw

BOOKS AND ARTICLES

Mossallam, Alia. 2011. "Remembering the Martyrs."
Egypt Independent, **June 29.**

As stated above, our character Alia Mossallam, whom Layla meets in the morgue, is based on an actual person with the same name. Mossallam is an assistant professor in political science and history at the American University in Cairo, and she is the founder of "Ihky ya Tarikh," a series of workshops on the social and political histories of marginalized communities in Egypt. During the revolution, Mossallam engaged in the important and difficult work of trying to locate missing persons. In 2011, she wrote a poignant article in the *Egypt Independent* about her experience in a morgue in Alexandria. Mosallam's powerful narrative is the basis for the scenes in the morgue (pages 188–190) in which Layla locates the boy she had been treating in Tahrir and meets a bereaved mother lovingly speaking to her dead son. It is also worth quoting a passage from the article that beautifully aligns with the sentiments about risk and hope voiced by Anna and Layla in the final pages of the graphic novel: "People died because they believed something in their society was changing. Hope was so imminent that they risked not seeing the future. Our martyrs left us with that hope and it's up to us to realize it."

LINKS
→   The full article is available at the *Egypt Independent* website: http://www.egyptindependent.com/opinion/remembering-martyrs

Colla, Elliott. 2011. "The Poetry of Revolt." *Jadaliyya*, **January 31.**
In this piece, literary scholar Elliott Colla places the catchy rhythms of the slogans that formed the revolutionary soundscape in the context of a rich tradition of Arabic poetry and rhyming couplets. When Layla goes to her first April 6 Movement meeting, she is struck by what is written in a flyer and also on a sign on the wall, which feature two particularly salient slogans that were used during the revolution:

(*al-saratan fi kulli makan/ wal-ghaz mitba` bil-magan*)
"Cancer is everywhere, and they export our
natural gas for peanuts"

(*ba`u damana wa ba`u kilawina/ wa binishhat ihna wa ahalina*)
"They sold our blood, they sold our kidneys, and left us to beg
with our families"

LINKS
→   The full article is available at the *Jadaliyya* website: http://www.jadaliyya .com/pages/index/506/the-poetry-of-revolt

Shenker, Jack. 2016. *The Egyptians: A Radical History of Egypt's Unfinished Revolution.* **New York: New Press.**
In this highly readable text, journalist Jack Shenker expands the concept of "revolution" beyond the 2011–12 timeline and places Egyptians' struggle against oppression within the context of the country's deeper history, beginning with agrarian reform against feudal tyranny, movements against colonial rule, and everyday struggles for environmental and social justice. He also extends the revolution beyond the space of Tahrir Square, traveling throughout Egypt's countryside and reporting from cities and rural villages. Most

important, Shenker places Egyptians' struggle for social justice within the context of our interconnected global political economy—and makes a compelling case that Egyptians are on the frontlines of a larger conflict of popular resistance against the concentration of wealth and power, a conflict that is far from over and one that affects us all.

Abaza, Mona. 2011. "Academic Tourists Sight-Seeing the Arab Spring." *Jadaliyya*, September 27. (Reprinted from *Ahram Online*, September 26, 2011.)

As academics from Western institutions writing about the Egyptian Revolution, we find it important to acknowledge and address our role in a troubling international intellectual trend. In this short online piece, Mona Abaza, a sociology professor from the American University in Cairo, points to the enduring inequalities that inhere in international scholarship on revolutionary action, in which Western researchers rely on "local" academics and revolutionaries in the Middle East as "service providers" and then benefit disproportionately from these exchanges through access to funding, visibility, and publications. Abaza argues this trend reinforces an Orientalist worldview, in which "European thinkers remain pervasively as the 'knowing subjects' whereas non-Europeans continue to be the 'objects of observations and analyses of European theorists.'" Not only does this reproduce a damaging and ill-founded division of labor and authority in global knowledge production, it also obscures and undervalues (intellectually and financially) the important theoretical, artistic, and activist work being done by local scholars and revolutionaries. In this project, we have attempted to foreground this work being done in Egypt by Egyptians through forms of citation, collaboration, and incorporation. That said, we as authors recognize that we still benefit disproportionately from this scholarship on a revolution and on revolutionary thinking that is not our own.

LINKS

→   The full article is available at the *Jadaliyya* website: http://www.jadaliyya
     .com/pages/index/2767/academic-tourists-sight-seeing-the-arab-spring

→   The original is available at the *Ahram Online* website: http://english.ahram
     .org.eg/News/22373.aspx

IMAGE-RICH SOURCES ABOUT THE EGYPTIAN REVOLUTION, WHICH *LISSA*'S ARTISTS DREW ON FOR VISUAL REFERENCES

Attia, Omar. 2011. *The Road to Tahrir : Front Line Images by Six Young Egyptian Photographers*. Photographs by Sherif Assaf, Omar Attia, Rehab K. El Dalil, Timothy Kaldas, Zee Mo, and Monir El Shazly and additional text by Timothy Kaldas. Cairo: American University in Cairo Press.

Beugnies, Pauline. 2016. *Génération Tahrir*. Edited by Ammar Abo Bakr and Ahmed Nagy. Marseille: Le Bec en l'air.

Hamdy, Basma, Don Stone Karl, and Stone (graffiti writer). 2014. *Walls of Freedom: Street Art of the Egyptian Revolution*. Berlin: From Here to Fame GmbH.

Heide, Florence Parry, and Judith Heide Gilliland. 1995. *The Day of Ahmed's Secret*. Illustrated by Ted Lewin. New York: Mulberry Books.

Khalil, Karima. 2011. *Messages from Tahrir: Signs from Egypt's Revolution*. Cairo: American University in Cairo Press.

Hamdy, Sherine F. 2016. "All Eyes on Egypt: Islam and the Medical Use of Dead Bodies amidst Cairo's Political Unrest." *Medical Anthropology* 35 (3): 220–35.

Ahmed's eye trauma was not an isolated occurrence. Protestors' eyes were intentionally targeted during the popular uprisings in Egypt. One of the most publicized instances of this was when Ahmed Harara, a young dentist living in Cairo, sustained a serious injury to his right eye on January 28, 2011, when riot police violently attacked protestors in and around Tahrir Square. After Mubarak resigned following the demonstrators' 18-day occupation of public spaces, Dr. Harara was celebrated in state media and through official award ceremonies; he often deflected the attention aimed at him to recall the slain protesters and their families who had suffered much greater losses than he had. In doing so, Dr. Harara voiced the revolutionary cry that the lives lost would not be in vain; he even vowed that he would sacrifice his second eye if it meant securing freedom and justice for Egypt. During the interim military rule in November 2011, a fresh wave of protests broke out, and Dr. Harara again took to the streets. In a perverse act of spite, a police sniper shot a rubber bullet at his remaining seeing eye, leaving Dr. Harara completely blind. He became known as "the living martyr."

In January 2012, the April 6 Youth Movement galvanized an online response to the mass eye trauma incurred by political protesters: they called for a cornea donation campaign. Galal Amer, a satirist in Cairo, along with a group of eye doctors, began similar endeavors, asking people to consent to giving up their own eyes upon death so that the corneas could be used for transplants for blinded protesters. The article details what happened to this revolutionary cornea donation campaign, in the context of Egypt's larger experiences with organ donation.

LINKS

→   See Agence France-Presse, "Ahmed Harara, the Blind Hero of Egypt's Revolution," *The National*, November 28, 2011: http://www.thenational.ae/news/world/middle-east/ahmed-harara-the-blind-hero-of-egypts-revolution

Hamdy, Sherine F., and Soha Bayoumi. 2016. "Egypt's Popular Uprising and the Stakes of Medical Neutrality." *Culture, Medicine, and Psychiatry* 40 (2): 223–41.
Sherine Hamdy and Soha Bayoumi interviewed doctors and medical students who took part in assembling makeshift field hospitals during the popular uprisings in order to understand how doctors made sense of being attacked for aiding the injured protesters.

II. CANCER AND GENETICS

There have been two important developments in BRCA genetics that are not captured in Anna's narrative. First, in the United States, the federal Genetic Information Nondiscrimination Act (GINA) was passed in 2008, which makes it unlawful to discriminate against a person for insurance or employment. However, more recent legislation may undermine these protections by making employment "wellness tests" compulsory, thereby opening people up to forced disclosure of genetic status and to penalties for noncompliance. Second, in a 2013 landmark decision in the *Association for Molecular Pathology v. Myriad Genetics, Inc.*, the US Supreme Court ruled that unmodified DNA is not patentable subject matter, but upheld patents on cDNA. This decision loosened corporate strangleholds on genetic research such as Myriad's.

FILM AND VIDEO

Rudnik, Joanna (director). 2008. *In the Family: How Much Do You Sacrifice to Survive?* Chicago: Kartemquin Films.

In this compelling documentary, Joanna Rudnick explores the social, political, and personal landscape of BRCA genetics in the United States. After finding out that she has inherited a BRCA1 mutation from her mother, 31-year-old Joanna is faced with the same difficult decisions as Anna: vigilant screening to detect cancer early or invasive surgeries to remove her breasts and ovaries to prevent a cancer that she may never develop. In this moving and informative film, Joanna brings the reader into her decision-making process. Like Anna, she develops new relationships with other BRCA mutation carriers who help her to understand how it has impacted them, while also navigating competing pressures from her family, friends, partner, and doctors. Joanna also delves into the larger social and political dimensions of BRCA testing. She interviews major researchers in the field of cancer genetics; explores the racial and economic disparities that inhere in BRCA research, testing, and treatment; and takes the reader inside Myriad Genetics—the for-profit company that had exclusive patents on the BRCA genes until a 2013 Supreme Court case (*Association for Molecular Pathology v. Myriad Genetics, Inc.*) loosened the company's monopoly on BRCA research and testing.

LINKS

→   The *In the Family* film website includes film clips, discussion forums, updates on Joanna's life, and educational resources: http://inthefamily.kartemquin .com/film

Pool, Léa (director). 2011. *Pink Ribbons, Inc*. Ottawa: National Film Board of Canada.

On pages 130–131 of *Lissa*, we see how the cancerous body of Anna's friend is connected to toxic treatments (chemotherapy), toxic environments (pesticides), toxic "self-care" products (perfume, lotion, cleaning supplies), and toxic economies (for-profit health systems and companies such as insurance and pharmaceuticals, as well as "pink ribbon" campaigns). This feature documentary based on the book of the same name by Queen's University professor Samantha King (2006) traces some of these toxic routes as it examines the collaborations between the federal government, charities, and corporations in the United States that have turned breast cancer into a highly profitable cause in a global marketplace. Though pink ribbon products and "runs for the cure" claim to generate funds for breast cancer research, they also generate profits for corporations and governments that benefit from the manufacture of carcinogenic products, the production of toxic chemicals, and the commodification of health. This film and book show how breast cancer became a commodity and how global economies of "pinkwashing" continue to contribute to health inequalities on the basis of class, race, and gender.

→   See also Samantha King. 2006. *Pink Ribbons, Inc.: Breast Cancer and the Politics of Philanthropy*. Minnesota: University of Minnesota Press.

Habash, Ahmad (director). 2009. *Fatenah*. Ramallah: Dar Films Productions.

This 30-minute animated film is based on the true story of a 28-year-old Palestinian woman's struggle to access medical treatment for her breast cancer under Israeli military occupation. This stunning, simple, and deeply moving film shows how sociopolitical forces dramatically affect a person's health. Fatenah faces barrier after barrier—from lack of resources in Gaza to an ambulance under fire to aggressive Israeli guards at checkpoints—that conspire against her continual efforts to access cancer treatment.

LINKS

→   The full film can be screened for free on director Ahmad Habash's website: http://www.ahmadhabash.com/fatenah/ or at https://vimeo.com/19811163

WEBSITES

FORCE (Facing Our Risk of Cancer Empowered)

As Anna is trying to decide what to do about her hereditary cancer risk, she starts spending time on discussion boards on the FORCE website and attending support group meetings for other BRCA mutation carriers. FORCE is a nonprofit, patient-run organization dedicated to providing support and information for people living with hereditary cancer risk. This organization was also vocally opposed to gene patenting, and it joined forces with the American

Civil Liberties Union and others to oppose Myriad Genetics, Inc.'s patents on the BRCA genes in the 2013 Supreme Court case.

LINKS
→   FORCE website: http://www.facingourrisk.org/index.php

Breast Cancer Action®
Much of Bec's stance on health justice, as it pertains to problems of environmental toxicity, gene patenting, and the commodification of health, reflects the position of the independent patient-run cancer watchdog organization Breast Cancer Action® (BCA). This organization is committed to addressing systemic issues that affect breast cancer risk rather than focusing solely on individual and medical interventions that treat women's bodies while leaving intact the larger problems of toxicity, profit, and inequality, all of which negatively impact women's health. BCA has launched successful campaigns against "pinkwashing" and fracking, among other practices. Like FORCE, this organization was vocally opposed to gene patenting and joined forces with the American Civil Liberties Union and others to oppose Myriad Genetics, Inc.'s patents on the BRCA genes.

LINKS
→   BCA website: http://www.bcaction.org

BOOKS AND ARTICLES
Gessen, Masha. 2008. *Blood Matters: From Inherited Illness to Designer Babies, How the World and I Found Ourselves in the Future of the Gene*. Orlando: Harcourt.
A quotation from this memoir by Russian-born American journalist Masha Gessen follows Anna through the hospital as she undergoes screening tests for breast and ovarian cancer. Gessen wrote this memoir after she discovered that she had inherited a deleterious mutation in her BRCA1 gene from her mother, who died of breast cancer. Gessen's memoir chronicles her experience of managing her genetic cancer risk, and it also includes research-based chapters in which she interviews doctors, examines the surgical options in detail, and charts the medical histories of locating and preventing hereditary cancers.

Gibbon, Sahra, Galen Joseph, Jessica Mozersky, Andrea zur Nieden, and Sonja Palfner (editors). 2014. *Breast Cancer Gene Research and Medical Practices: Transnational Perspectives in the Time of BRCA*. New York: Routledge.

This edited volume of social scientific research situates BRCA research and practice in a global context. This book draws together the perspectives of patients, researchers, clinicians, and policymakers from around the world on such issues as global variations in medical approaches to BRCA testing and prevention, international BRCA gene patent controversies, challenges to normative gender expectations around embodiment and reproduction, and racial and economic disparities in cancer risk and public health genomics.

Nye, Coleman. 2012. "Cancer Previval and the Theatrical Fact." *TDR: The Drama Review* 56 (4): 104–20.

When Anna tells Layla about her BRCA mutation, Layla admonishes her: "But you are fine, Anna! Here we don't have enough medicine. There, you have too much! We're fighting to survive every day and can't even get treatment for our diseases, let alone worry about what we might get in the future [. . .] Why would you try to treat a disease that you don't have?!" Anna shoots back, "But I do have it—I've been living with cancer my whole life . . . ."

This article provides the context to understand both women's perspectives. Anna lives in a privatized, for-profit health care system in which risk is increasingly being treated like a disease. This medical culture of risk places the responsibility on the individual and fails to address adequately the broader risks that impact health, such as environmental toxicity or social inequality. In this context, Anna is faced with the medical and moral responsibility to manage her cancer risk once she accesses the expensive test. In some ways, Anna is grateful to have this knowledge, as it confirms what she already knew about her cancerous inheritance and gives her an opportunity to intervene in it. In other ways, she is overwhelmed with the responsibility and the array of choices she must make among imperfect options. Further, Anna is part of a population that has the "privilege of futurity": she is socially, medically, and financially secure enough to protect her future health by "previving." For marginalized populations in the United States and globally, the stakes and temporalities of survival are very different.

Jain, S. Lochlann. 2013. *Malignant: How Cancer Becomes Us.* Berkeley: University of California Press.

After surviving breast cancer, American anthropologist S. Lochlann Jain created this intimate and expansive portrait of cancer in the United States. Though the book does not focus on the BRCA genes specifically, Jain examines the uncertainties that underpin cancer risk and diagnosis and challenges dominant depictions of gender and sexuality in breast cancer through her reading of "cancer butch." Jain also explores cancer pasts and futures in "the time-arresting medium of photography" (41) through a close-reading of artist Hannah Wilke's photo-documentation of her mother's cancer and then her own. This section is particularly interesting to read in relation to Anna's uses of photography.

III. ORGAN TRANSPLANTATION IN EGYPT AND BEYOND

FILMS

Fathy, Safaa (director). 2012. *Mohammed Saved from the Waters.* Paris: TS Production.

This 93-minute documentary features the filmmaker's brother, Mohammed, and his experience with kidney failure in Upper Egypt. The film documents the family's concerns with toxicity and water quality connected to industrial waste in the Nile, and it also shows the family's debates about whether or not to pursue a kidney donation. Mohammed, like Abu Hassan, reiterates that he refuses to take a kidney from anyone because "the body belongs to God." The film also explores the lucrative black market in kidneys in Cairo.

BOOKS AND ARTICLES

Hamdy, Sherine F. 2012. *Our Bodies Belong to God: Organ Transplants, Islam, and the Struggle for Human Dignity in Egypt.* Berkeley: University of California Press,

The stories of Abu Hassan and Layla are based on the experiences of people whom Sherine Hamdy interviewed during two years of field research in the Egyptian cities of Cairo, Tanta, and Mansoura. In this book, Hamdy analyzes the national debate over organ transplantation in Egypt as it unfolded during a time of major social and political transformation—including mounting dissent against a brutal regime, the privatization of healthcare, advances in science, the growing gap between rich and poor, and the Islamic revival. The study delves into topics including current definitions of brain death, the authority of Islamic fatwas, reports about the mismanagement of toxic waste predisposing the poor to organ failure, and the Egyptian black market in organs.

Hamdy, Sherine F. 2008. "When the State and Your Kidneys Fail: Political Etiologies in an Egyptian Dialysis Ward." *American Ethnologist* **35 (4): 553–69.**

In *Lissa*, we see patients in the ward link their illness to larger social and political ills, including to a corrupt regime that does not protect its citizens from environmental toxins, dangerous labor conditions, and medical mismanagement. This article draws out these narratives and argues that patients are pointing to the "political etiologies" of their kidney failure. Such political etiologies capture why patients like Abu Hassan fear the consequences of leaving their potential donors to fend in an unhealthy environment with only one kidney. It also shows why doctors like Layla become invested in revolutionary calls for justice, as they so clearly draw connections between the state and the suffering of their patients.

Crowley-Matoka, Megan. 2005. "Desperately Seeking 'Normal': The Promise and Perils of Living with Kidney Transplantation." *Social Science and Medicine* **61 (4): 821–31.**

Throughout *Lissa*, Anna struggles to understand why Layla and her family don't see a kidney transplant as a "magic bullet," a solution that will permanently fix Abu Hassan. At one point, Layla tries to explain this to Anna, describing how he would have to go on immunosuppressants for the rest of his life and would always risk rejecting the organ. In this article, based on research in Guadalajara, Mexico, Crowley-Matoka demonstrates the great promises held out for kidney transplantation to "cure" people with a terminal disease and give them a "normal" life—and how these promises come up against the grimmer reality of post-transplant life in which people have yet another form of chronic illness to manage and are left in a state between "healthy" and "ill."

Scheper-Hughes, Nancy. 2000. "The Global Traffic in Human Organs." *Current Anthropology* **41 (2): 191–224.**

One of Abu Hassan's doctors derisively describes "greedy entrepreneurs who sell their kidneys because they want a new iPhone." Here, he is mischaracterizing the plight of poor people in places such as Cairo, who sell their kidneys on the black market in order to make ends meet. This influential article brought the phenomenon of black markets in human organs to scholarly attention. In it, Scheper-Hughes famously wrote, "In general, the flow of organs follows the modern routes of capital: from South to North, from Third to First World, from poor to rich, from black and brown to white, and from female to male" (193).

Crowley-Matoka, Megan, and Sherine F. Hamdy. 2016. "Gendering the Gift of Life: Family Politics and Kidney Donation in Egypt and Mexico." *Medical Anthropology* **35 (1): 31–44.**

Umm Hassan chastises Layla for considering donating her kidney to her father, as it would impede her opportunities for marriage and motherhood. Layla is frustrated that her mother reduces her to her reproductive potential. In this collaborative article, Megan Crowley-Matoka, who researched kidney transplantation in Mexico, and Sherine Hamdy, who researched this same topic in Egypt, examine the gendered dimensions of giving and receiving organs. The ways that people justify their decisions around kidney giving and receiving are highly gendered, in some cases reflecting a disproportionate flow of organs from women to men and, in other contexts, from men to women. People's decisions around kidney transplantation rely on social ideas of women's domesticity, the protection of women's fertility and sexuality, and heteronormative ideas of wives and mothers' "natural" capacity for sacrifice.

IV. Conceptual Framework

Mol, Annemarie. 2008. *The Logic of Care: Health and the Problem of Patient Choice.* **New York: Routledge.**

For our framework, we have drawn on Annemarie Mol's eloquent problematization of the notion of "choice" in biomedical practice (2008). She argues that, of course, autonomy and choice are preferable to coercion, but the logic of *choice* comes from realms that might not be best applied to the medical encounter and patient care—namely from the realms of the market (consumer choice) and of civics (democracy). What if we were to come up with a different logic? Mol gives it a name: the logic of *care*. While "choice" presumes that the patient acts as an individual, "care" recognizes a patient's embeddedness in social relations. While "choice" presumes a single transaction, "care" affirms the necessary ongoing tinkering, doctoring, adjusting, and negotiation of patienthood. Perhaps most important, the concepts of "freedom" and "choice" are logically inconsistent because, to make a proper choice, one has to understand social norms, and once indoctrinated in social norms, one is no longer a "free" autonomous individual. Further, these notions are not always appropriate to patienthood and illness because freedom is a fictitious and unattainable promise to someone with a chronic disease. For the patients we came to know, there was always the risk of cancer's return, always the threat of a transplanted organ being rejected. The burden of making the right choices can add to the stress people live with under the shadow of illness. What, then, might their treatment and illness experiences look like under a framework of practicing long-term care?

V. Comics and Medicine

WEBSITES
Graphic Medicine: The Interaction of Comics & Healthcare: graphicmedicine.org

BOOKS ABOUT COMICS
Czerwiec, M. K., Ian Williams, Susan Merrill Squier, Michael J. Green, Kimberly R. Myers, and Scott T. Smith. 2015. *Graphic Medicine Manifesto*. University Park: Pennsylvania State University Press.

McCloud, Scott. 1993. *Understanding Comics: The Invisible Art*. New York: HarperPerennial.

GRAPHIC MEMOIRS ABOUT ILLNESS
Ian Williams refers to the use of comics or graphic novels in illness as "graphic medicine." Susan Squier refers to illustrated illness memoirs as "pathographics." This list is in no way comprehensive. For more options, please see the graphic medicine website listed above.

Marchetto, Marisa Acocella. 2009. *Cancer Vixen: A True Story*. New York: Pantheon.

Brosh, Allie. 2013. *Hyperbole and a Half: Unfortunate Situations, Flawed Coping Mechanisms and Other Things That Happened*. New York: Touchstone.

David, B. 2005. *Epileptic*. New York: Pantheon.

Fies, Brian. 2006. *Mom's Cancer*. New York: Harry N. Abrams

Small, David. 2010. *Stitches: A Memoir*. New York: W.W. Norton & Co.